Jan Sudeikat

Engineering Self-Organizing Dynamics in Distributed Systems:

Jan Sudeikat

Engineering Self-Organizing Dynamics in Distributed Systems:

A Systemic Approach

Südwestdeutscher Verlag für Hochschulschriften

Imprint

Any brand names and product names mentioned in this book are subject to trademark, brand or patent protection and are trademarks or registered trademarks of their respective holders. The use of brand names, product names, common names, trade names, product descriptions etc. even without a particular marking in this work is in no way to be construed to mean that such names may be regarded as unrestricted in respect of trademark and brand protection legislation and could thus be used by anyone.

Publisher:
Südwestdeutscher Verlag für Hochschulschriften
is a trademark of
Dodo Books Indian Ocean Ltd., member of the OmniScriptum S.R.L Publishing group
str. A.Russo 15, of. 61, Chisinau-2068, Republic of Moldova Europe
Printed at: see last page
ISBN: 978-3-8381-2390-5

Zugl. / Approved by: Hamburg, U, Diss., 2010

Copyright © Jan Sudeikat
Copyright © 2011 Dodo Books Indian Ocean Ltd., member of the OmniScriptum S.R.L Publishing group

Abstract

This dissertation addresses the utilization of self-organization principles in the development of distributed software systems. In *self-organizing* processes, the coaction of multitudes of system elements, which are by themselves autonomous, leads to the formation of global structures that are continuously and independently adapted to a changeable environment. The use of these phenomena in the development of distributed software systems is particularly attractive as it allows distributing flexible problem solving abilities for complex global problems among the basic system elements. Hence, these processes can be used as powerful means for the decentralized coordination of distributed systems.

In general, self-organization is applicable when large scale systems have to be coordinated in decentralized ways. When software systems have to operate in a dynamic execution context, their autonomous operation is desirable. Forward-looking next-generation distributed systems, in consequence of the support for non-functional properties, e.g. the scalability, the physical distribution, the complicatedness of the constituent system elements, or the volatile dynamics of the execution context, often prohibit manual system administrations. In contrast, the decentralized automation of run-time adjustments intently supports scalability and robustness as the failures of single system elements have limited effects on the system-wide adaptivity.

This dissertation proposes a construction framework for self-organizing distributed systems — whereas self-organization is understood as the participation of system elements in decentralized, adaptive processes, as a supplement to the functional software system. This approach allows equipping applications with self-organizing features. A systematic development approach is enabled by the elevation of the adaptive, decentralized inter-agent process, which governs the self-organized structure formation, to an independent design element. Explicit models allow planning for the intended system dynamics. At first, an established modeling technique is adapted to describe the coaction of agents by expressing the distributed feedbacks among system agents. This modeling approach is used to analyze application dynamics and describe recurring template processes. The construction of self-organizing applications is supported by a corresponding programming model. It is based on a reference-architecture for the integration of self-organizing processes that encapsulates and automates coordination-related activities. A configuration language allows process models to be annotated with implementation-specific details that are required for the automated execution of processes. Based on these tools, the systematic conception and integration of processes is supported by: (a) a novel development procedure that describes the conception of processes and their tailoring for a specific software system, (b) a description concept for modeling the application behavior as is and the intended system behavior, and (c) the identification and refinement of process fragments that are appropriate to bring about the intended system behavior and can be integrated using the programming model. Based on these three aspects, this dissertation proposes a comprehensive construction approach to the use of self-organizing processes.

Preface

This dissertation is a result of my work in the *Multimedia Systems Lab* (MMLab) at the Hamburg University of Applied Sciences (HAW Hamburg) and I am particularly indebted to my supervisors whose cooperation enabled me to conduct research. They complemented each other splendidly, while facing an interdisciplinary research topic. Prof. Dr. Wolfgang Renz from the HAW, as an expert in self-organizing and stochastic processes, guided my research work with great effort plus personal dedication. My research perspective benefited a lot from our lively and serious discussions. On the other hand, Prof. Dr. Lamersdorf from the University of Hamburg, as an expert in distributed systems, was always available for active support, well-considered advice, and encouragement when necessary. Based on their joint efforts, I found guidance and the freedom to explore novel ideas/approaches.

Two workgroups provided me a friendly and creative atmosphere. In the MMLab, I found an active research environment. The HAW supported my research by funding a position and a subsequent scholarship for initiating and continuing my studies. I especially appreciate that the HAW supports its graduates in obtaining doctoral degrees. Besides, I want to thank Gregor Balthasar, Thomas Preisler, and Peter Salchow for their friendly collaboration. In addition, the *Distributed Systems and Information Systems* (VSIS) workgroup at the *Department of Informatics* of the *University of Hamburg* provided an open environment for discussing and experimenting agent-oriented software engineering approaches. In particular, I would like to thank Dr. Lars Braubach, Dr. Alexander Pokahr, and Ante Vilenica for inspiring discussions and open cooperation. The final stages of the dissertation were funded by the *German Research Foundation* (DFG) in the project *Selbstorganisation durch Dezentrale Koordination in Verteilten Systemen*[1] (SodekoVS). This project is a joint effort of the MMLab and the VSIS group.

This dissertation also benefited from national and international collaboration. The members of the DFG-funded project *Formal Modeling, Safety Analysis, and Verification of Organic Computing Applications* (SAVE ORCA), namely Prof. Dr. Wolfgang Reif, Hella Seebach, Florian Nafz and Jan-Philipp Steghöfer, introduced me to resource-flow-systems and helped, with their insights in this application domain, to revise a decentralized reconfiguration approach. Prof. A. Taleb-Bendiab and Dr. Martin Randles were valuable partners for discussion and they shared their expertise in formal modeling and engineering techniques for self-organizing systems. I cordially thank Dr. Rafael H. Bordini for discussing and reviewing the formalization of the operation principle of activated agent modules. Finally, I would like to thank Prof. Huaglory Tianfield for allowing me to be a Program Chair for the *1st International Conference on Swarm Intelligence and Emergent Computing* (SIEC 2010) and Professor Yu Wu for chairing this event cooperatively.

At the end, I want to sincerely thank my family for their never-ending support and encouragement, in particular, my wife Jie, my daughter Jonah, my parents Ulrike and Bernd † as well as my parents-in-law Yundong Cai and Caiying Li.

---

[1] Self-Organisation by Decentralized Coordination in Distributed Systems

Contents

1 Introduction   **1**
1.1 Motivation: Building Next-Generation Distributed Systems 1
1.2 Focus of this Dissertation 3
1.3 Contributions 5
1.4 Outline of the Thesis 7

I   Technical Foundations   **9**

2 Agent-Oriented Software Engineering   **11**
2.1 Multi-Agent Systems 11
2.2 Software Agents 13
     2.2.1 Agent Architectures 14
     2.2.2 Programming Agents 16
2.3 Environments 18
     2.3.1 Infrastructures 20
     2.3.2 Multiple Environments 21
2.4 A Conceptual Model of Multi-Agent Systems 22
2.5 The Coordination Concept: A Pragmatic Perspective 24
2.6 Engineering Agent-based Software Systems 26
     2.6.1 Designing Agent-Based Applications 26
     2.6.2 Validating Agent-Based Applications 27
     2.6.3 Development Methodologies 30
2.7 Effects on the Structure of Software Implementations 36
2.8 Application Areas 41
2.9 Conclusions 42

3 Self-Organization: A Software Perspective   **43**
3.1 Self-Organization in Software 43
     3.1.1 Self-Organization 43
     3.1.2 Self-Managing & Self-Adaptive Software Architectures 46
     3.1.3 Manifestations of Self-organization in Software Systems 48
     3.1.4 The Fundamental Design Element: *Distributed* Feedback 51
     3.1.5 The Relevance of Self-Organization for Multi-Agent Systems 53
     3.1.6 The Relevance of Self-Organization for Self-Adaptive Systems 54
3.2 The Construction of Self-Organizing Systems 55
     3.2.1 Decentralized Coordination Mechanisms 58
     3.2.2 Self-Regulatory Coordinating Processes 62
     3.2.3 Development Principles 63
     3.2.4 Development Methodologies 65
3.3 Conceptual Model of a Self-Organizing MAS 67
3.4 Intermediate Behavior Classification 69

	3.4.1	Redesigning Multi-Agent Systems	70
	3.4.2	Example: Collaborative Sorting / Clustering	71
	3.4.3	Example: The Minority Game	74
3.5	Application Areas		80
3.6	Conclusions		83

II A Systemic Development Approach   85

4 Systemic Modeling of Collective Phenomena in MASs   87
- 4.1 Motivation 87
  - 4.1.1 Challenges 88
  - 4.1.2 Related Work 89
- 4.2 Systemic Modeling Approach 90
  - 4.2.1 System Dynamics 91
  - 4.2.2 Applications in Software-Engineering 97
  - 4.2.3 Agent Causal Behavior Graph 100
- 4.3 Systemic Analysis of MAS Behavior 104
  - 4.3.1 Processing Agent-Oriented Application Designs 106
  - 4.3.2 Constructing the Systemic Abstraction 109
  - 4.3.3 Analyzing the System Behavior 110
  - 4.3.4 Example: Marsworld Dynamics 111
- 4.4 Systemic Design of Decentralized MAS Coordination 118
  - 4.4.1 Structural Classification of Coordination Strategies 119
  - 4.4.2 Example: A Simplified Computer Immune System 127
- 4.5 Conclusions 131

5 A Systemic Programming Model   135
- 5.1 Motivation 135
  - 5.1.1 Challenges 136
  - 5.1.2 Related Work 137
- 5.2 Architecture: Decentralized Coordination Enactment 140
  - 5.2.1 Reference Architecture for Embedding Self-Organization 141
  - 5.2.2 Conceptual Model 145
  - 5.2.3 Coordination Endpoints 147
  - 5.2.4 Activated Agent Modules 148
  - 5.2.5 Formalization of Activated Agent Modules within BDI Agents 150
  - 5.2.6 Application Examples of Activated Modules 153
  - 5.2.7 Event-based Configuration Interface 155
  - 5.2.8 Extending Agent-Interfaces by Adaptivity Components 158
  - 5.2.9 Agent-State Interpreter 160
  - 5.2.10 Coordination Media 161
  - 5.2.11 Coordination Information Interpreter 164
- 5.3 MASDynamics: Coordination Configuration 165
  - 5.3.1 Language Structure 166
  - 5.3.2 Coordination Language Model 167
  - 5.3.3 Notation(s) 175
  - 5.3.4 Automated Agent Preparation 180
  - 5.3.5 Prototype Realization: DeCoMAS on Jadex 182
- 5.4 Case Studies 183
  - 5.4.1 Case Study I: Bee-Inspired Adaptive Server Allocation 183
  - 5.4.2 Case Study II: Integration of Convention Emergence 187
- 5.5 Conclusions 192

CONTENTS

6 Systematic Integration of Decentralized Coordination — 195
  6.1 Motivation — 195
    6.1.1 Challenges — 196
    6.1.2 Related Work — 197
  6.2 Designing Decentralized Self-Organization — 198
    6.2.1 Partial Resolution of the Contradiction — 199
    6.2.2 Principled Development Strategies — 199
  6.3 Process-Integration: Coordination Development — 201
    6.3.1 Process Life-Cycle and Modified Work Products Overview — 204
  6.4 Adaptivity Requirements — 206
    6.4.1 Domain Analysis — 207
    6.4.2 Adaptivity Description — 208
    6.4.3 System Animation — 208
  6.5 Coordinating Process Definition — 209
    6.5.1 Map Feedback-Structure to Application-Model — 209
    6.5.2 Systemic Coordination Refinement — 210
    6.5.3 Identify Interaction Type — 210
  6.6 Coordinating Process Integration — 211
    6.6.1 Coordination Alignment — 212
    6.6.2 Interaction Configuration — 213
    6.6.3 Agent Model Preparation — 214
  6.7 Coordination Validation — 214
    6.7.1 The distinction between Qualitative and Quantitative Validations — 214
    6.7.2 Fundamental Structure — 215
    6.7.3 Coordination Validation (Qualitative) — 217
    6.7.4 Prototype: Automating Coordination Validations — 221
  6.8 Case Studies — 222
    6.8.1 Decentralized Reconfiguration of Resource-Flow Systems — 223
    6.8.2 Shoaling Glassfishes: Decentralized (Web) Service Management — 233
    6.8.3 Patching Dynamics in Agent Societies — 239
  6.9 Conclusions — 245

III Conclusions and Appendixes — 249

7 Conclusions — 251
  7.1 Summary — 251
  7.2 Discussion of Contributions and Outlook — 253
    7.2.1 Outlook — 257

Appendices — 263

A The Stochastic π-Calculus — 263

B Coordination Medium Implementations — 267
  B.1 Routing-based Media — 268
    B.1.1 Random Routing — 268
    B.1.2 Network Routing — 268
    B.1.3 Input/Output-Graph-based Routing — 269

C Publications — 271

List of Figures

1.1 The essential aspects in the development of self-organizing processes 3
1.2 The dissertation structure 7

2.1 Illustration of an MAS, following [Jennings, 2001] 12
2.2 Basic agent model, following [Russell and Norvig, 1995] 13
2.3 Taxonomy of agents, following [Franklin and Graesser, 1997] 14
2.4 The range of agent architectures, following [Ferber, 1999] 15
2.5 Languages for the MAS development, following [Ferber, 1999] 17
2.6 A canonical model of a Jadex-based MAS [Sudeikat et al., 2006] 18
2.7 Layered MAS architecture, following [Viroli et al., 2007] 21
2.8 Conceptual structure of an MAS 23
2.9 A generic goal-plan tree. 24
2.10 Testing stages for MASs [Sudeikat et al., 2006] 29
2.11 Elements of a Development Methodology, following [Sturm and Shehory, 2003] . . 31
2.12 The platform-dependent evaluation of methodologies [Sudeikat et al., 2004] 33
2.13 Graph-based representation of object- and agent-oriented software systems, following [Sudeikat and Renz, 2007b] 38
2.14 The commutative distributions of the degree of incoming edges (dependents, I) and the affected nodes (II) [Sudeikat and Renz, 2007b] 40
2.15 Application design aspects for agent-oriented applications; Self-Organizing application designs, discussed in Chapter 3, address system level aspects that are based on and extend these characteristics (see Figure 3.17). 41

3.1 The phenomenological properties of self-organizing software systems 45
3.2 A hierarchy of adaptive system properties (self-*), adapted from [Salehie and Tahvildari, 2009] 49
3.3 Illustrations of a generic autonomic control loop (I), adapted from [Dobson et al., 2006], and a distributed feedback among autonomous system elements (II) 53
3.4 Self-organization within a managed, distributed system 55
3.5 The basic elements for the establishment of distributed feedback are *external* self-adaptive software components (I), following [Salehie and Tahvildari, 2009], and the propagation of influences (II). 56
3.6 The relationships between the software Application, the observable Dynamics, the Coordinating Process and the Coordination Mechanisms, following [Sudeikat and Renz, 2010c] 57
3.7 Decentralized Coordination Mechanisms as patterns for establishing mutual agent interdependencies, adapted from [Sudeikat and Renz, 2008b,a] 59
3.8 Aspects of the methodology support 65
3.9 The conceptual structure of a self-organizing software application, adapted from [Sudeikat and Renz, 2009c] 68
3.10 Micro-, Meso- and Macroscopic modeling of self-organizing system phenomena, adapted from [Sudeikat and Renz, 2008a] 70

3.11 Micro-, meso- and macroscopic models [Renz and Sudeikat, 2006] 71
3.12 Transportation behaviors (I, II; following [Sudeikat and Renz, 2008a]), and simulation screen-shots (III, IV) 73
3.13 Collective clustering simulation results [Sudeikat and Renz, 2006] 74
3.14 The stochastic selection process inside agents (I) and a sample simulation run that exemplifies the rotation of the *Schwarzer Peter* behavior (II). 76
3.15 The transitions between the implemented agent behaviors [Renz and Sudeikat, 2006] 78
3.16 The squared global loss of the microscopic and mesoscopic implementations models, plotted as a function of the scaled numbers of agents [Renz and Sudeikat, 2006, 2005a] 79
3.17 Design concerns that motivate the adoption of self-organizing solutions 81

4.1 Modeling techniques for self-organizing MASs 90
4.2 Fundamental modes of behaviors, following [Sterman, 2000] 95
4.3 Examples of combined behavior modes: S-shaped growth, growth with overshoot and growth with collapse, following [Sterman, 2000] 95
4.4 A characterization of the relation between *individual* system elements and system *observables*, following [Parunak et al., 1998] 98
4.5 Systemic feedback models describe types of Coordinating Processes [Sudeikat and Renz, 2010c]. 99
4.6 Projection of software designs to systemic models 101
4.7 ACBG notation, adapted from [Sudeikat and Renz, 2010a, 2008b; Renz and Sudeikat, 2009] 102
4.8 ACBG example, following [Sudeikat and Renz, 2009c] 103
4.9 ACBG refinement / abstraction operations, adapted from [Sudeikat et al., 2009b] . 104
4.10 Qualitative examination of the dynamics of MAS designs 105
4.11 The qualitative analysis process [Sudeikat and Renz, 2011] 106
4.12 Conceptual models of intermediate data structures that prepare for ACBG construction, following [Sudeikat and Renz, 2011] 107
4.13 The Interaction Extraction, represented by a stereotyped UML Activity Diagram . 108
4.14 The Agent Behavior Extraction, represented by a stereotyped UML Activity Diagram.109
4.15 ACBG construction, following [Sudeikat and Renz, 2011] 110
4.16 Application design, following [Sudeikat and Renz, 2011]. I: Tropos Actor / Goal Diagram, II: (A)UML Sequence Diagrams. 112
4.17 ACBG representation of the Marsworld dynamics, following [Sudeikat and Renz, 2011] 114
4.18 Simulation model of the Marsworld ACBG: Stock-and-Flow model 115
4.19 Simulation results for the Marsworld dynamics, from [Sudeikat and Renz, 2011] . . 117
4.20 A visualization of the stochastic process that governs the initialization of the Marsworld scenario (I), following [Sudeikat and Renz, 2007a], and the averaged activations of the specialized agent behaviors (II) [Sudeikat and Renz, 2007a] 119
4.21 Systemic models of amplifying coordination strategies 122
4.22 Systemic models of the compensating coordination strategies 125
4.23 Systemic models of selective coordination strategies 126
4.24 ACBG refinement example (1), II adapted from [Sudeikat and Renz, 2008c] 128
4.25 ACBG refinement example (2), adapted from [Sudeikat and Renz, 2008c] 129
4.26 Simulation results of the intrusion detection system 131

5.1 Orthogonal aspects of the integration of inter-agent coordination; cut surfaces describe an overlap in the characteristics and the support for a specific aspect is approximately reflected by edge length of cuboids 138
5.2 The layered structure of the coordination enactment architecture, following [Sudeikat et al., 2009a] 142
5.3 The operating principle of the coordination enactment, adapted from [Sudeikat and Renz, 2008b] 143

LIST OF FIGURES

5.4 Conceptual model of the realization of the reference architecture, following [Sudeikat and Renz, 2009b] ... 146
5.5 Conceptual Structure of coefficient capabilities [Sudeikat and Renz, 2010b] ... 149
5.6 Operating principle of activated modules, following [Sudeikat and Renz, 2010b] ... 150
5.7 The reasoning cycle of Agentspeak-based BDI agents, following [Vieira et al., 2007] ... 151
5.8 Monitoring of agent execution, following [Sudeikat and Renz, 2007a] ... 154
5.9 Adaptivity components are an optional means for defining events for the observation/manipulation of agents ... 159
5.10 Alternatives for the realization of Coordination Media [Sudeikat and Renz, 2008b] ... 163
5.11 An overview of the systemic coordination language ... 166
5.12 The detailed structure of the systemic coordination language, adapted from [Sudeikat and Renz, 2009c]; The layout relates to the three principal partitions of the language model (I,II,III; see Figure 5.11) ... 168
5.13 The structure of the specification of a decentralized inter-agent process and the Definitions section ... 169
5.14 The structure of the specification of system variables ... 170
5.15 The structure of the specification of system relations ... 173
5.16 DSL editor screenshot ... 180
5.17 The processing of an MASDynamics-based model to configure agent instances, represented by a UML Activity Diagram ... 181
5.18 Honey-Bee inspired (web) server management ... 184
5.19 Excerpts from the process definition in abridged notation, adapted from [Sudeikat and Renz, 2009c] ... 186
5.20 Convention Emergence process model ... 187
5.21 Convention Emergence simulation results ... 190
5.22 The relations between the concepts and tools introduced in this chapter ... 192

6.1 Coordination Development ... 202
6.2 Self-contained Activities supplement development disciplines, adapted from [Sudeikat and Renz, 2009e] ... 204
6.3 Systematic integration of coordination, adapted from [Sudeikat and Renz, 2009e] ... 206
6.4 Task: Adaptivity Requirements ... 207
6.5 The conceptual model of Adaptation Requirements (I) [Sudeikat and Renz, 2007c] and example (IIa,IIb) ... 208
6.6 Activity: Coordinating Process Definition, adapted from [Sudeikat et al., 2009b] ... 209
6.7 The Coordination Refinement ... 211
6.8 Activity: Coordinating Process Integration ... 212
6.9 The Tasks within the *Coordinating Process Integration* Activity, adapted from [Sudeikat and Renz, 2009e] ... 213
6.10 The distinction between qualitative and quantitative validations [Sudeikat and Renz, 2007c] ... 215
6.11 The generic structure of simulation-based validations of Coordinating Processes ... 216
6.12 Activity: Coordination Validation (Qualitative), adapted from [Sudeikat et al., 2009b] 218
6.13 Conceptual model of hypotheses specifications (I) and the schematic illustration of simulation preparations (II) [Sudeikat and Renz, 2009h] ... 220
6.14 A sample correlation measurement ... 221
6.15 Conceptual Testbed architecture, adapted from [Sudeikat and Renz, 2009h] ... 222
6.16 A flexible production line [Sudeikat et al., 2010a] ... 223
6.17 The static structure of the Organic Design Pattern, following [Sudeikat et al., 2010a] 224
6.18 The Problem and Solution Dynamic of the ODP [Sudeikat et al., 2010a] ... 225
6.19 The ACBG of the wave-like, decentralized reconfiguration algorithm, following [Sudeikat et al., 2010a] ... 226
6.20 Simulation Model of the Solution Dynamic in Stochastic π-Calculus [Sudeikat et al., 2010a] ... 227

6.21 Simulation time series 228
6.22 Exemplification of the decentralized reconfiguration, following [Sudeikat et al., 2010a] 229
6.23 Measurements of a single reconfiguration 230
6.24 Simulation results 231
6.25 Decentralized, agent-based service management architecture 235
6.26 Balancing service deployments 236
6.27 The configuration of the service deployment process 237
6.28 Server utilization management 238
6.29 Patching dynamics: Problem Dynamic, Solution Dynamic and the embedded Coordinating Process 240
6.30 Patching dynamics: Animation of the Problem Dynamic 241
6.31 Patching dynamics: Animation of the Solution Dynamic(s) 243
6.32 Patching dynamics: Sample simulation run 244
6.33 Patching dynamics: Simulation results [Sudeikat and Renz, 2010a] . 245
6.34 Combining top-down and bottom-up development practices 247

7.1 An integrated development approach for self-organization processes . 254
7.2 Characterization of the programming model (I) and development procedure (II) . 257

A.1 Example π-calculus models, adapted from [Blossey et al., 2006] 264

B.1 Illustrations of routing-based Coordination Media 269

Chapter 1

Introduction

The means of constructing large-scale, highly distributed software systems are in a state of continuous development. Modern software systems are characterized by increasing demands for spatial distributions and increasing abilities of the interconnected system elements. Advancements in this field, as to enable next-generation distributed systems, carry with them the challenge of enabling software systems to be managed effectively. Sources of the ever increasing complications in application management originate in both the system elements, e.g. their spatial distribution and heterogeneity, as well as in the dynamics of application contexts, e.g. the volatility communication-relationships and (remote) resources. In addition to ensuring error less operation, application management must also satisfy increasing demands on the dynamics and flexibility of software systems. Under these conditions, manual management becomes prohibitive, thus making and the *autonomous* operation of software systems indispensable. The software must be designed to manage itself, i.e. to adjust itself at run-time.

One attractive as well as challenging approach to equipping software systems with adaptive features is enabling their *self-organization*. In self-organizing systems, system elements can adjust themselves according to their mutual interactions and interdependencies. This approach allows for system level adaptiveness to be embedded among the system elements. The advantage of this *decentralized* approach is that the adaptiveness does not depend on particular system entities, a situation which can lead to bottle necks or single points of failure. Making use of self-organization is, however, a challenge for traditional software engineering techniques. The development of these kinds of systems requires the consideration of system-level dynamics, i.e. the activities and interactions of traditionally designed system elements must be revised to achieve the intended system-level adjustments. Bringing the gap between these design-levels is a fundamental research topic.

This dissertation discusses a novel development framework for the utilization of self-organization principles in distributed systems. Enabling a software system for self-organization requires a set of enhancements that address the purposeful coaction of system elements. The self-organizing inter-agent process, distributed among system elements, is elevated to an independent software development concept. A conceptual framework is given for the systematic conception of these processes and their integration into distributed software systems.

1.1 Motivation: Building Next-Generation Distributed Systems

The continuous development of concepts and tools for the development of distributed software systems enables advanced applications with enhanced potentials, e.g. concerning the growing numbers of contained elements, increasing individual capabilities, and advanced interactions among them. Innovative application scenarios for *distributed* systems demand the combination of *self-adaptivity* with *decentralized* application architectures. Both aspects, seen individually, are actively-researched areas and the research has resulted in sophisticated development concepts and tool sets. However, their combination is a serious challenge in computer science and has led researchers to consider novel concepts which originate outside the field of informatics. Accepting this challenge is of general concern to support next-level distributed applications. Examples of areas in which the described combination would be of great benefit are space missions by collectives of low-cost satellites [Truszkowski et al., 2004], the automatic reconfiguration of server farms [Jeffrey et al., 2008; Nakrani and Tovey, 2004], and the adaptive control of production lines [Jennings and Bussmann, 2003; Seebach et al., 2007], just to name a few. When applications demand both for a high number of autonomous system entities and their decentralized management, novel software concepts are necessary.

To an increasing degree, today's software applications are built as distributed systems, in which a network of computational software elements that communicate with each other achieve the intended functionality [van Steen and Tanenbaum, 2002]. When the context in which these elements are deployed changes, e.g. when the number of connected components or the individually available resources change, the functioning of the elements needs to be adjusted to continue to provide system functionality. Modern application architectures and software frameworks support the configurability of applications. Service-oriented architectures are a prominent example, where the functional aspects, for example *work flows* and their *orchestration*, can be controlled by externalized models that are interpreted at run-time (e.g. see Singh and Huhns [2005]).

However, the run-time adjustment of applications is a research challenge. One successful strategy is to use control-oriented approaches that equip software systems with managing entities. These entities contain and execute the adjustment algorithms. These adaptations range from parameter adjustments to structural changes, e.g. the inclusion, removal, or exchange of system elements. The consolidation in distinguished system elements of information and control needed to manage a system has advantages and drawbacks. The development of control algorithms using aggregated information is simpler then the conception of decentralized techniques. However, the outsourcing of management is associated with additional overhead, due to the necessary aggregation of information, the reasoning on appropriate adjustments, and the distribution of the management decisions. Following this approach, the range of unintended system configurations must be anticipated and appropriate countermeasures for resolving these configurations must be conceptualized.

In complex, highly dynamic environments, this is problematic and alternative techniques that construct software systems of autonomous, pro-active entities, i.e. software agents (e.g. discussed in relation to service-oriented software systems in [Singh and Huhns, 2005]) are studied. The system functionality results from the interplay of agents in a *Multi-Agent System* (MAS). Each agent can serve as the local manager of system components or serve as service providers for other system elements. These are equipped with local reasoning techniques, and thus can impose a local management of resources and computational entities. Agent-orientation is an intuitive development approach for complex distributed [Jennings, 2001] and socio-technical [Sterling and Taveter, 2009] systems.

In decentralized settings, the adjustments must be initiated by the interplay of software entities. System level adaptivity has to result from the concurrent local activities and interactions of system elements. These operations form a background process that operates alongside the actual system functionality. The development of this process is particularly intricate but yields inherently scalable and robust controls for adaptiveness. The absence of centralized control entities is relevant for industrial applications as it obviates bottlenecks and single points of failures. Instead the management is evenly distributed among the system elements. Since autonomous software entities are already equipped with computational abilities, using them can be economic, also for the purpose of coordination and managed adaptation. The necessity for additional entities, such as managing components and the related computational overhead (see above), are eliminated.

A central issue in the conception of these processes is the use of self-organization principles. Self-organization describes system level phenomena that occur in biological, physical, and social systems, which establish and maintain structures in decentralized ways. These system-wide structures arise from the low-level, localized (inter-)actions of elements, e.g. insects, molecules, or individuals. The application of these phenomena to software engineering allows self-adaptive fea-

1.2. FOCUS OF THIS DISSERTATION

tures to be embedded in the interplay of the system elements. The control of the system adaptivity and the required information are equally shared among elements. The use of self-organization challenges conventional engineering techniques but results, when appropriately applied, in scalable and robust solutions to challenging coordination problems.

1.2 Focus of this Dissertation

The adoption of self-organization principles is an unusual endeavor in software engineering contexts. Applications are based on the mapping of structure formation processes to computational problems. Structures can be imposed on system environments, for example to cluster data (see Section 3.4.2, page 71), or to configure the system itself, e.g. in response to a changeable environment (see Section 5.4.1, page 183). The creation of structures, e.g. system configurations, is handed over to the interactive functioning of the system elements, and detailed properties of the resulting effects are governed by stochastics. This transfer of control can lead to powerful mechanisms, but is a challenge for traditional software engineering practices. The systematic treatment of these effects demands tools and concepts to plan for the dynamics of collectives of software entities.

This dissertation addresses the systematic development of self-organizing, distributed software systems. It elaborates a coherent development conception that concerns three essential aspects of the process development (see Figure 1.1). *Modeling* describes the conception of self-organizing inter-agent processes. A fundamental complication for the utilization of self-organization in software is the fundamental gap between individual, low-level agent interactions and the arising collective, system-wide structures. *Programming* concerns the integration of self-organizing features, i.e. their participation in the conceived processes, into agent-based software systems. Typically, the development of self-organizing applications is approached by designing specialized algorithms tailored toward specific application scenarios. These algorithms are integrated by blending the control flow inside agents with the business and the process-logic. A conceptual and technological separation of the self-organizing process and the application logic is of conceptual and practical interest, i.e. to support the reuse and exchangeability of process types. The *Development Process* denotes the alignment of the construction of the self-organizing process with the overall application development. Sophisticated development methodologies are available for the construction of agent-based software systems. Research on self-organizing applications typically concerns the building from scratch of an application that shows self-organizing features. Here, how features are integrated into a conventionally developed application is also of interest.

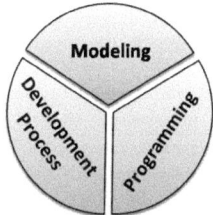

Figure 1.1: The essential aspects in the development of self-organizing processes

This dissertation approaches these problems by a novel development approach. The self-organizing process, distributed among system elements, is elevated to a discrete development artifact. A modeling approach allows to express the underlying causal structure of self-organized inter-agent processes. The programming of these processes is supported by a distributed middleware layer. It provides a reference architecture for the integration of processes and a tailored configuration language allows to prescribe the process execution. Based on these concepts, the systematic development of processes in parallel to the application development is discussed.

A set of hypotheses grounds the work that is described in this dissertation. These characterize development aspects that are fitted in order to support the construction of self-organizing applications (see Table 1.1). The major development activities are the *modeling* and *programming* of self-organization. In this context, modeling refers to the expression of decentralized coordination and programming refers to the embedding of the modeled processes into application (see Figure 1.1). These are construction-related activities that crosscut the software development. The hypotheses are related to the requirements, analysis, design and implementation disciplines of software development [Jacobson et al., 1999]. The supportive validation that the developed product shows the intended behavior is also part of the development process and makes use of system simulations (see Section 6.7). Modeling-related activities support requirements and analysis disciplines. They enable the description of inter-agent processes to conceptualize the present and/or the intended system dynamics. The related hypotheses (1.1, 1.2) describe necessary aspects for a modeling technique that is appropriate for the description of self-organizing processes in engineering contexts. These hypotheses apply to both requirements and analysis disciplines in the application development. Design and implementation disciplines in the process development deal with the detailing and mapping of processes to an actual software system. The related two hypotheses (1.3, 1.4) describe support for the construction of self-organizing systems. A clear separation of the system functionality and the system coordination is a consequent step towards the enforcement of systematic development principles.

Modeling	Programming	Development Process
1.2		Requirements
1.1		Analysis
	1.3	Design
	1.4	Implementation

Table 1.1: The underlying hypotheses

Hypothesis 1.1 *(Modeling of MAS Dynamics) The adequate modeling of distributed feedbacks among system agents, as an auxiliary description-level for MAS-based development efforts, allows to analyze and design collective phenomena in MASs that result from the coaction of agents.*

Starting from the observation that the ability to show self-organizing and emergent behaviors is an inevitable property of agent-oriented software systems, as argued in Chapter 3, the analysis and planning for these properties, to ensure their presence or absence, is discussed. Self-organizing phenomena result from distributed feedbacks (see Section 3.1.4). System elements react on each other and the cyclic propagation of interdependencies and influences among system elements can control structure formations. In Chapter 4, a corresponding modeling level is introduced as a supportive modeling approach that supplements established design techniques with an additional description level. Collective phenomena, which result from concerted coaction of autonomous agents, due to Inter-agent processes, are addressed. These purposeful design of these processes allows for the decentralized coordination of agent activities.

Hypothesis 1.2 *(Multi-Level Modeling of MAS Dynamics) Multi-level modeling techniques that support the transition between, microscopic, mesoscopic, and macroscopic description levels enable the incremental refinement as well as abstraction which are necessary during the analysis and design of distributed feedbacks.*

A fundamental property of self-organization is that macroscopic system-level effects result from the low-level, microscopic inter-action of system elements (see Section 3.1). Thus transitions between these description levels, enabled by intermediate *mesoscopic* description levels, should be prepared to support analysis and design techniques. The use of intermediate modeling levels is discussed in Section 3.4.

Hypothesis 1.3 *(Separate configuration of Coordinating Processes) The separation of inter-agent coordinating processes, as stand-alone design elements, is necessary as it allows for the experimentation with process configurations to tune the application behavior.*

The development of self-organizing applications is intrinsically related to bottom-up development practices (discussed throughout Section 3.2). While this dissertation discusses design stances that enable a degree of top-down refinements, the processes and mechanisms that govern the self-organization of an application are subjects to incremental revisions and iterative fine-tuning efforts, e.g. to finalize microscopic model parameters. The externalization of process models, within a self-contained development artifact, supports experimental setups, e.g. prototyping-based developments, where process details are frequently adjusted (development alternatives are discussed in Section 6.2.2).

Hypothesis 1.4 *(Separate conception of Coordinating Processes) The externalization of inter-agent coordinating processes, as stand-alone design elements, allows for the supplementation of inter-agent coordination to stand-alone, functional software systems.*

A considerable research area in distributed systems development is the enabling of self-adaptive software systems that configure autonomously in order to respond to external influences and perturbations [Salehie and Tahvildari, 2009]. A goal is that software engineers are able to integrate adaptivity into existing software systems, e.g. as discussed in [Cheng et al., 2005]. Thus the adaptivity is not necessarily built-in during the systems development, but can be provided as a supplement. The consolidation of the otherwise scattered adaptation logic is identified as key criterion for the realization of this goal, e.g. see [Cheng et al., 2005] (page 162).

In this respect, self-organization is one alternative design principle that can be applied to realize self-adaptivity (e.g. see [Salehie and Tahvildari, 2009], pages 5, 23). The externalization of the process models that steer self-organizing dynamics allows the comparative supplementation of adaptive dynamics. The collective behavior of agent-based applications are analyzed. Based on an understanding of the possible dynamics and the conception of the intended dynamics, a delta can be defined that, if supplemented, enables the system to exhibit the intended dynamics (discussed throughout Chapter 6). Externalized coordination processes provide the means for the explicit definition of these supplements. The supplements can be separated from the agents, since they only involve inter-agent coordination.

1.3 Contributions

In the following section, the major contributions of this thesis are summarized. Previous works concerning the analysis, validation and design of agent-based software systems, as well as supporting case studies, are omitted here. A complete list of references is given in Appendix C.

Conceptualization of Self-Organizing Software Systems

The fundamental operating principle of a self-organizing software system is the presence of feedbacks among distributed system elements. Based on this notion, conceptual models of (1) the generic structure of a self-organizing MAS as well as (2) the cooperative processes that steer the formation and maintenance of structures are derived. These models unify design concepts and serve as a foundational basis for the development approach that is devised in this thesis. Due to the diversity of development concepts, modeling techniques, and design principles for self-organizing applications, the conceptual model is a valuable basis for systematic development techniques [Sudeikat and Renz, 2008a, 2010c].

Systemic Modeling Technique

The modeling of self-organizing applications requires the microscopic activities of individual system elements, mostly agents, to be related to the macroscopic observable system behavior. In agreement with mathematical modeling techniques, a modeling technique is transferred to MASs that allows the collective dynamics of agents to be described. This modeling technique is based on established models for complex systems, and it highlights the structure of feedbacks among system elements that affect the collective processes among agents. Emphasis is given to the transfer between different modeling levels, which facilitates analysis as well as design efforts. Different aspects of this modeling approach are the description of the requirements on the system behavior [Sudeikat and Renz, 2009d], the conception of the intended system behavior by feedback refinement [Sudeikat and Renz, 2008c], and the analysis of the space of potential system behaviors [Sudeikat and Renz, 2009g]. The practicability of this modeling stance is demonstrated by the analysis of MAS dynamics [Sudeikat and Renz, 2009h], the cataloging of nature-inspired (template) self-organization processes [Sudeikat and Renz, 2010c], and the combination of these templates [Sudeikat and Renz, 2008c].

Systemic Programming Model

A novel programming model for decentralized coordination is proposed. It enables developers to configure, embed and enact process models with minimal intervention in the agent models. The principal parts of this programming model are: a reference architecture for the integration of self-organizing features in software systems, and a tailored configuration language that allows partitions of generic process models to be detailed to application dependent specifications. Using this tool set, process partitions can be supplemented to conventionally developed MASs by automating the participation in decentralized, collaborative processes. The practicability of the proposed separation and integration is demonstrated in two case studies (see Section 5.4). The proposed middleware layer is an architectonic conception [Sudeikat and Renz, 2009b] for the encapsulation and reuse of interaction mechanisms [Sudeikat and Renz, 2008b], as well as the automation of the participation of agents in collaborative processes [Sudeikat and Renz, 2010b]. The configuration of these aspects is addressed by a tailored configuration language [Sudeikat and Renz, 2009c]. The separation and integration of inter-agent processes is demonstrated in two simulation models [Sudeikat and Renz, 2009c, 2010a].

Systematic Supplementation of Decentralized Coordination

The fundamental tasks for the construction of a decentralized, adaptive software system are identified and discussed with respect to the novel programming model. A corresponding set of development activities and the control flow among them is defined using a standardized notation. A detailed development process for the conception and integration of self-organizing processes is proposed. Besides documenting the use of the programming model presented here, the described process defines the fundamental development steps and guides their realization. The conceived process [Sudeikat et al., 2009b], contains the requirements analysis [Sudeikat and Renz, 2007c,e], the conception of processes by refining distributed feedback structures [Sudeikat and Renz, 2010a], the detailed configuration of process partitions and their integration in MASs [Sudeikat and Renz, 2009e], and the validation of the system behavior [Sudeikat and Renz, 2009h]. The conception of processes and their integration in MASs are exemplified in [Sudeikat and Renz, 2010a; Sudeikat et al., 2010b; Sudeikat and Renz, 2010b, 2009f]. The usability of the programming model is demonstrated. The intended system level dynamics, appropriate for a specific development context, are modeled and the programming model is used to effect the intended dynamical properties.

1.4 Outline of the Thesis

The structure of this dissertation is illustrated in Figure 1.2. In the following two chapters (2, 3) fundamental concepts are discussed which will be referred to throughout the rest of the thesis. The subsequent chapters (4 to 7) address particular development aspects. Each chapter is organized as a self-contained discussion. These contain an individual motivation, a review of the related work, and case study applications. The dissertation ends with a critical discussion of the provided tools and concepts, as well as an outlook for future work.

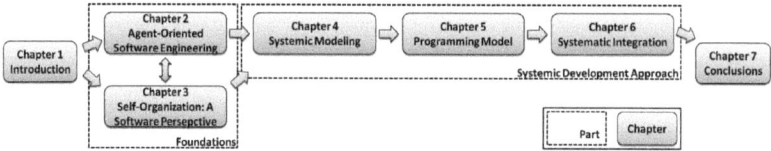

Figure 1.2: The dissertation structure

Chapter 1: Introduction

In this chapter, the goals and objectives of the thesis are given. The motivation for scientific interest and applicability of engineering approaches for self-organizing software systems are explained and the elaborated contributions are outlined.

Chapter 2: Agent-Oriented Software Engineering

Agent-oriented software engineering is a major technological foundation for the construction of self-organizing distributed software systems. In the second chapter, this paradigm is introduced. The relevant concepts and construction techniques are discussed.

Chapter 3: Self-Organization: A Software Perspective

The self-organization phenomenon, as studied in complex adaptive systems research, is a crucial concern for the development of distributed systems that are composed of autonomous software entities. These phenomena are introduced and their relevance in software engineering contexts is discussed. The state-of-the-art practices for analyzing and purposefully creating these phenomena in software systems are outlined.

Chapter 4: Systemic Modeling of Collective Phenomena in MAS

A major challenge is the conception of the coaction of system elements to cause intended levels of collective dynamics, i.e. self-organization. In this chapter, a systemic modeling approach to the dynamics of MASs is presented. This modeling level supplements established design models with a phenomenological abstraction of system behavior. The systematic derivation of these abstractions from MAS designs is discussed and demonstrated. In addition, an example for the design of application dynamics using this modeling technique is given. The modeling approach is also used to describe prominent, nature-inspired templates for inter-agent coordination. The behavioral properties of the structure formation within these templates are discussed and their combination, by connecting underlying feedback structures, is shown.

Chapter 5: A Systemic Programming Model

The previously described modeling techniques are the basis for a corresponding programming model that is introduced in this chapter. The model is based on two major contributions that enable the treatment of coordinating processes as executable MAS design elements. First, a reference architecture is presented that guides the integration of self-organizing processes in software systems. This architecture is discussed and the prototypic realization, on top of an established agent platform, is discussed. Secondly, a configuration language is presented that provides a detailed description level for systemic models of coordinating processes. This language allows annotating the application specific information that is needed to automate the enactment of a process. The practicability of this programming approach is exemplified in two case studies.

Chapter 6: Systematic Integration of Decentralized Coordination

The systematic conception of self-organizing processes and their integration into agent-based applications is discussed in this chapter. The fundamental design approaches to self-organizing systems are discussed and the principal development objectives are divided into a set of generic development activities. These outline the design of a self-organizing software system and are refined to guide the use of the previously-described programming model. In three application scenarios, the conception of the intended application dynamics, the derivation of the required process configuration, as a supplement to the already present application dynamics, and the integration of the supplement in MASs is demonstrated.

Chapter 7: Conclusions

Finally, the contents of this dissertation are summarized and discussed in Chapter 7. The contributions are critically reviewed and prospects for future work, particularly in an associated research project, are given.

Part I

Technical Foundations

Chapter 2

Agent-Oriented Software Engineering

In this chapter, a technological foundation for the development of self-organizing systems is discussed. Self-organizing applications are composed of locally adaptive software entities and agent-technology is a means for building these entities. *Agent-Oriented Software Engineering* (AOSE) is a relatively young development paradigm for distributed software systems [Jennings, 2001; Wooldridge, 2002] that provides practical design concepts and development tools, for example by middleware frameworks and programming languages, that can be used to conceive and synthesize distributed software systems as ensembles of *autonomous* actors. This is an intuitive design approach but the composition of systems as a compound of interacting, self-determined entities has implications for engineering practices. This development approach is relevant for the construction of self-organizing systems, since software systems are designed as sets of autonomous system entities. This constructive viewpoint can be exploited to give rise to dynamics that correspond to natural self-organizing systems. These dynamics and their embedding in software systems are discussed in Chapter 3.

In this chapter, the agent-oriented design and construction of distributed software systems is introduced. The review focuses on practical development approaches and technologies. In the remainder of this dissertation, these means for constructing software are adopted as a technological foundation for the development of self-organizing systems. The basic concepts, in particular Agents and Environments, are discussed and the application development — the construction and assembly of these elements into Multi-Agent Systems — is characterized by an outline of available development infrastructures and design support. Here, a practical viewpoint towards the construction of agent-based software systems is adopted and the subset of tools and concepts that are relevant for the remainder of this thesis are introduced.

2.1 Multi-Agent Systems

Agent-orientation is a novel approach to the analysis, design and implementation of distributed software systems [Jennings et al., 1998]. As a relatively young research field in computer science, it address the construction of collectives of autonomous software components that interact to bring about the intended system functionalities. These collectives are called *Multi-Agent Systems* (MASs)[1], e.g. in [Wooldridge, 2002] (page 3):

> ... A multiagent system is one that consists of a number of agents, which *interact* with one another, typically by exchanging messages through some computer network infrastructure. ...

---

[1] An alternative spelling is: *Multiagent Systems*

A central element of the agent-oriented development paradigm is the collaboration of actors based on purposeful interactions. The functional software systems are conceived as ensembles of *agents* and the *environment*(s) in which these agents operate. These fundamental building blocks are discussed in the following Sections 2.2 and 2.3.

In [Jennings, 2001], the principal structure of MASs is discussed (see Figure 2.1). This discussion also stresses the importance of the influences among agents. Agents are understood as problem-solvers that operate in an environment. Their partial ability to observe and modify this environment is described by *spheres of visibility and influence*. These problem-solvers are also expected to serve as actors that work on behalf of system stakeholders. Thus agents are embedded in organizational contexts which partition the application design (cf. Section 2.6.1). A set of fundamental characteristics of MASs are given in [Jennings et al., 1998]:

1. the limited view-points of agents about the whole system

2. the absence of a global system control

3. the decentralization of data

4. the asynchronous execution of computations

Due to limitations in their individual capabilities or the locally available information, single agents are not able to achieve the system's objective by themselves (1). Thus the interaction and collaboration of agents is needed and the adoption of an MAS-based design approach is justified. The MAS as a whole is not explicitly controlled (2), therefore the function of the system arises from the coaction of agents. The data within agents and the environment elements are distributed among the system elements (3) and the activities of agents are not synchronized but rather their individual execution is independent from another (4).

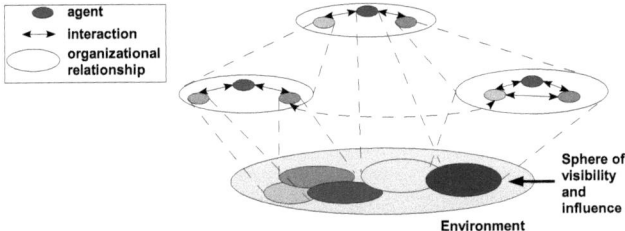

Figure 2.1: Illustration of an MAS, following [Jennings, 2001]

Agent technology originated in research on distributed problem solving and artificial intelligence. Based on these foundations a distinct research area emerged [Kirn et al., 2006]. Five fundamental research perspectives have been identified [Kirn et al., 2006]. One aspect is the arrangement of agent collectives in organizational structures that result partially from social relationships and behaviors (*social perspective*). Additional issues are the problem solving abilities of individual agents as well as collectives of agents (*AI perspective*). These issues deal with the reasoning techniques for individual agents and mechanisms of the cooperation of agents, e.g. via planning algorithms or negotiations. From an *economic perspective* agents are understood as computational elements that behave rationally, despite their individual limitations, e.g. bounded rationality and knowledge. The appropriateness of agent-oriented design and development approaches is addressed by the *application perspective*. The *engineering perspective* concerns the use of agents as practical elements of software system development. In the remainder of this chapter the (software) engineering aspects are especially stressed.

2.2 Software Agents

The concept of (software) agents is subject to a range of definitions that focus on different properties of these system elements. A unifying viewpoint that expresses the minimal properties of agency in software is given in [Wooldridge, 2002] (page 15):

> An *agent* is a computer system that is *situated* in some *environment*, and that is capable of *autonomous action* in this environment in order to meet its design objectives.

This definition focuses on the autonomy of agents and their ability to modify their context, i.e. an environment. Another fundamental and commonly agreed property of agents is their *pro-activity*, i.e. the ability to initiate modification of the environment. This viewpoint on agency is stressed in [van Steen and Tanenbaum, 2002] (page 173):

> ... we define a **software agent** as an autonomous process capable of reacting to, and initiating changes in, its environment possibly in collaboration with users and other agents. The feature that makes an agent more then just a process is its capability to act on its own, and, in particular, to take initiative where appropriate.

The inherent autonomy of agents is emphasized in [Odell et al., 2000], where agents are understood as extensions to objects. The autonomy is distinguished between pro-activity, i.e. the ability to initiate actions by themselves (here called dynamic autonomy) and the control of the agent activities, which allows them to refuse or modify requests for the execution of activities (deterministic autonomy, page 3):

> ... our basic definition of an agent is "an object that can say 'go' (dynamic autonomy) and 'no' (deterministic autonomy)". ...

In [Russell and Norvig, 1995] (chapter 2) a comparable viewpoint is adopted and the abstract operation of agents is illustrated (cf. Figure 2.2). An element that senses its environment through *sensors* and modifies its surrounding through *effectors* is understood as an agent. This viewpoint particularly allows agents to be regarded as encapsulations of reasoning techniques that decide upon the appropriate actions according to the perceived state of the environment.

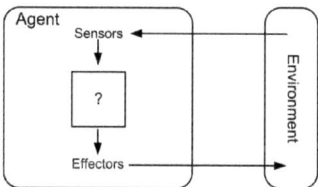

Figure 2.2: Basic agent model, following [Russell and Norvig, 1995]

The definitions do not exactly distinguish agents from other software components and different types of computational and natural systems can satisfy the given criteria. In [Franklin and Graesser, 1997] software agents are distinguished from other types of agents in a taxonomy (see Figure 2.3). *Autonomous Agents*, are distinguished between living entities (*Biological Agents*), robots (*Robotic Agents*), and from software entities (*Computational Agents*). Computational agents are further subdivided into Software components and entities in artificial life simulations (*Artificial Life Agents*). Artificial life pertains to simulations for analyzing of the structures and principles of living systems [Langton, 1989]. *Software Agents* are used for constructing software applications and are categorized into three principal types according to their designated tasks. Agents that address application-specific tasks are called *Task-specific Agents*, and are distinguished from agents that are constructed for malicious (*Viruses*) or for entertaining purposes (*Entertainment Agents*).

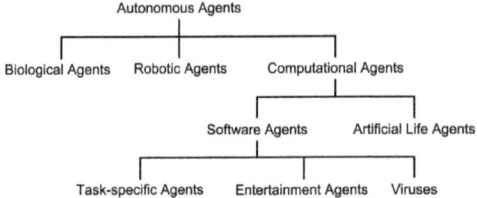

Figure 2.3: Taxonomy of agents, following [Franklin and Graesser, 1997]

Agents can be understood on different abstraction levels. First, agents can be treated as a design abstraction. This viewpoint is argued in [Russell and Norvig, 1995] (page 33):

> The notion of an agent is meant to be a tool for analyzing systems, not an absolute characterization that divides the world into agents and non-agents.

Agents are used to conceptualize the application domain and the software system. Alternatively, tools and frameworks are available for directly implementing the conceived agent models. These tools range from architectures, that guide the realization of an agent, to design methodologies that systematize the application development.

2.2.1 Agent Architectures

Agent architectures guide the realization of agents by prescribing their internal structure. A range of architectures has been proposed for the development of agents and the selection of an architecture that is appropriate for the realization of a specific software system is a non-trivial task [Müller, 1999]. The proposed architectures range between two extremes [Ferber, 1999] (Chapter 1). At one end of the spectrum, *cognitive* architectures address the construction of MAS that are composed of "intelligent" agents. These agents contain a knowledge base and an inference mechanism that enables individual reasoning, based on symbolic representations, about the actions to take. A common feature is that this type of architecture allows the *intentions* of an individual to be expressed, e.g. by explicit representations of goals and plans that enable agents to pursue desirable states of affairs. At the other extreme, the internal control of an agent is compacted to a mechanism that describes how agents respond to perceived events, e.g. in [Brooks, 1986]. These *reactive* agents map events to activities or behaviors. It has been shown that this design stance can be used to bring about interesting collective behaviors, e.g. [Deneubourg et al., 1990].

This range of agent architectures is illustrated in Figure 2.4. In [Ferber, 1999], the containment of symbolic representations is used as a criterion for evaluating the abilities of individual agents, i.e. their competence in accomplishing complicated tasks on their own. A consensus was reached that agents, as autonomous software components, require both the ability to work towards desirable goals, e.g. states in their environment, as well as the ability to quickly respond to immediate changes in their environment. Thus, the dichotomy of agent architectures is not strictly enforced but a range of *hybrid* agent architectures is available. The ability to prescribe both reactivity and individual deliberation in agent models is a practical development concern. The development concepts that are presented in this thesis are generally applicable but a specific agent model has to be adopted for the practical realization of tools and case studies. A hybrid agent model is used in order to account for the range of architectural styles. Therefore, agents are enabled to exhibit both purely reactive behaviors and individual deliberation. An additional criterion is the widespread adoption of the example agent architecture in the research community. In the following, the selected architectural style is discussed. It will be used for the implementation of MASs in the remainder of this dissertation.

2.2. SOFTWARE AGENTS

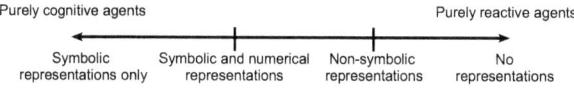

Figure 2.4: The range of agent architectures, following [Ferber, 1999]

Example: The Belief-Desire-Intention Agent Architecture

A widespread architectural style for constructing agents is the *Belief-Desire-Intention* (BDI) model. This agent design stance is originally based on a theory of practical reasoning [Bratman, 1987] that describes rational behaviors by *Belief*, *Desire* and *Intention* concepts. The transfer of this model to a formal theory and an executable model is facilitated by supplementing it with the concrete *goal* and *plan* concepts [Rao and Georgeff, 1995; Rao, 1996].

Beliefs represent the information that is available to agents. This knowledge describes both the agent environment and the internal agent state. The structure of the beliefs defines how the agent perceives itself and its context. Goals represent the desires of an agent. These are typically expressed as specific target states of belief values. This general conception can be used to express pro-activity, as agents decide their commitments and achieve goals on their own. Different versions of BDI systems provide varying types of goals [Braubach et al., 2005c]. Most goal types describe the state of affairs that agents attempt to bring about, e.g. the achievement or the maintenance of system states. Finally, agents are provided with a set of executable plans. Plans are associated to goals to denote that a plan is a means for achieving a particular goal, i.e. bringing about the desired state of affairs. Single plans are not only sequences of atomic actions, but may also induce the adoption of sub-goals. Consequently, the successful execution of a plan depends on the successful satisfaction of the associated sub-goals. This leads to a tree structure that is discussed in Section 2.4.

The execution of BDI agents is controlled by an *interpreter*. The control is event-based, i.e. the interpreter identifies the events that are to be processed, such as incoming messages, and then controls the activation of agent elements, e.g. plans, to handle these events. An abstract model of the event-based reasoning cycle is given in [Rao and Georgeff, 1995]. Realizations of agent platforms have led to refinements, for example the identification of the basic steps of reasoning and the description of the transitions between these steps in operational semantics [Vieira et al., 2007]. This formalization is described and extended in Section 5.2.5. Alternatively, so called *meta-actions*, to structure BDI-based reasoning, were identified in [Pokahr et al., 2005b] and integrated in a flexible execution architecture that particularly allows for extensibility.

The BDI architecture applies *reactive planning* [Georgeff and Lansky, 1987]. Contrary to the generation of executable plans at run-time, as discussed in [Russell and Norvig, 1995] (Chapter 11), agents are equipped with a set of precomputed plans [Bordini et al., 2004]. These plans are realized at design-time and the agent reasoning controls the activation of these plans in order to achieve the agent's goals. Two processes control how an individual agent decides about the activation of plans [Wooldridge, 2002] (page 66). First, it determines what objectives, i.e. goals, it is committed to achieve. This is known as (goal) *deliberation* [Pokahr et al., 2005a]. For a particular goal, several plans can be applicable at a given time-point. The agent reasoning must select one of them, using *means-end reasoning* [Wooldridge, 2002]. These reasoning processes made possible by annotating goals and plans with *conditions* that describe constraints on their applicability.

A crucial development concept is support for the modularization of individual agents. For BDI agents, *Capabilities*, i.e. accumulations of agent concepts, have been proposed to structure agent implementations [Busetta et al., 2000]. Originally, Capabilities contain beliefs, plans, and events. Rules describe the visibility of events that are (1) generated outside the capability and (2) that are generated inside the Capability. Two possible extensions are a generic import/export mechanism to control the visibility of the contained elements and the preparation of run-time modifications of agent models by adding/removing capabilities [Braubach et al., 2006a]. Further extensions address the control of the functionalities contained in agent modules, for example the provision of operations for the explicit control of modules at run-time [Dastani and Steunebrink, 2009] and the activation of modules in specific situations in the agent execution [Hindriks, 2008]. In Section 5.2.4, an enhancement is discussed, based on [Sudeikat et al., 2006; Sudeikat and Renz, 2007a, 2010b], that automates the activation of activities which are contained in modules. These modules deliberately observe and influence their immediate context, i.e. the host agent.

The BDI model is not a strictly defined implementation architecture. A set of programming languages and programming frameworks concretize this model and provide practical development tools. Example realizations include the *Procedural Reasoning System* (PRS) [Georgeff and Lansky, 1987], the *Agentspeak* language [Rao, 1996] and its realization in the *Jason* framework [Bordini et al., 2007], and the *Jadex* system [Braubach et al., 2005b]. In this dissertation, the example MASs are realized with the Jadex system. It is presented in Section 2.2.2.

2.2.2 Programming Agents

Specialized programming environments facilitate the construction of agents. The diversity of agent architectures is reflected by the large number of agent-oriented programming languages and development tools, e.g. as surveyed in [Bordini et al., 2006]. The major tools are dedicated programming languages and execution platforms/frameworks.

Agent Programming Languages

On a conceptual level, five categories of languages for the description of MASs can be distinguished [Ferber, 1999]. This categorization refers to the different semantics that are necessary to specify and implement the structures and computations that constitute the individual agents. In Figure 2.5, these languages are arranged according to their level of abstraction. *Implementation languages* (L1) are used to realize the executables. These languages can be used to realize low-level functionality, such as the computing structures for agents, the sending and receiving of messages, and the parallelism within agents. This language level deals with the technical realization of the executable agents.

Communication languages (L2) are used to prescribe the message-based interactions between agents. In heterogeneous MASs, where agents are realized by different architectures and/or programming languages, a common communication language enables interoperability.

Behavior Description languages (L3) allow the operations inside agents and environments to be prescribed, while abstracting the details of the implementation language used. These prescriptions can be given in various formalisms, e.g. productions rules, automata, or petri-nets [Ferber, 1999] and provide a means for efficiently describing behaviors of system elements that are independent from the actual implementation of the agents.

Knowledge representation languages (L4) are used to describe the knowledge that is available to agents. The knowledge about the environment and the agent itself is described. For cognitive agents, the description formalisms enable the reasoning and prediction techniques. For reactive agents this language may not be required, but for most agents types the description of the internal information is mandatory.

Specification languages (L5) refer to high-level abstractions that can be used to formally specify the operations of agents. These *meta* languages are used to describe abstract concepts of the MAS design, e.g. interactions or intentions, or aspects and conditions that system realizations have to consider and adhere to.

For the development of an MAS, these language levels are connected to describe the application. In [Ferber, 1999], the example of a negotiation protocol is given. The prescription of such a protocol uses an L2-level language to describe the conversations and an L3-level language to describe how messages are processed. In principle, different languages can be used for each language type. A common design objective for development environments is the provision a consistent programming model for the development of agents. Thus the conceptual distinction between the language models is not made explicit but is concealed by a specific language model. However the conceptual

2.2. SOFTWARE AGENTS

distinction between the language models is inherent in the programming of MASs, as argued in [Ferber, 1999] (pages 23,24). Programming environments typically allow developers to equip agents with artifacts in this programming language, e.g. to enable the implementation of basic agent activities or to override default implementations in the provided execution infrastructure (see Section 2.2.2).

The outlined language types structure the prescription of agent functionalities. In addition, auxiliary language models are provided by individual programming environments. These address recurring aspects of the development of ensembles of agents. Examples are the *Agent-Society Configuration Manager and Launcher* (ASCML) [Bellifemine et al., 2007] (Chapter 11), which provides a language for describing distributed deployments of agents, and languages for prescribing inter-agent coordination, as discussed in Section 2.5 and exemplified in Section 5.3

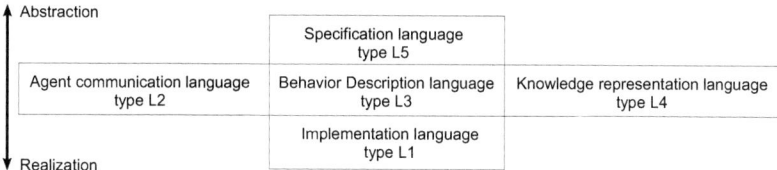

Figure 2.5: Languages for the MAS development, following [Ferber, 1999]

Agent Middleware Platforms

Agent-oriented software systems are typically built on top of specific (middleware) platforms that provide services and infrastructures for recurring aspects of MASs, most prominently the execution, communication, and coordination of agents [Bordini et al., 2006; Braubach et al., 2005b]. Platforms for the execution of agents can be classified as *middleware* or *reasoning-oriented* systems [Braubach et al., 2005b]. Middlewares provide services for agent execution. Examples are message passing and persistence techniques [Braubach et al., 2005b]. Design concerns include the interoperability of agents and the scalability of the execution infrastructure, e.g. [Braubach et al., 2005b]. Reasoning-oriented frameworks deal with the decision making inside agents. For specific agent programming languages (see above), these infrastructures realize the programming semantics [Bordini et al., 2006], e.g. by providing the interpreter-algorithms that control the agent execution. Since the execution of agents is controlled at this level, agent-specific development tools, such as the introspection and the motioning of agents, are provided as parts of the execution platform. Prominent instances of execution-level platforms are reviewed in [Braubach et al., 2006b] and their selection for a specific development project is discussed. The coordination of agents using specific frameworks is discussed in Sections 2.3.1 and 2.5.

Example: The Jadex Agent Platform

The *Jadex*[2] system is an open-source development framework for developing of BDI-style, goal-oriented agents. This system provides a reasoning layer that can be executed on a custom middleware [Pokahr and Braubach, 2007b] or on top of other agent middlewares [Braubach et al., 2005b]. The reasoning mechanisms used to control the agent execution are discussed in [Braubach, 2007]. The Jadex system makes use of a hybrid language model for the agent implementation (L1; see Figure 2.5) that blends communication (L2), agent behavior (L3), and agent knowledge (L4) aspects in a coherent format. This language combines the procedural description of agent activities with the declarative models of the agent structure and the agent-intern data. The declarative

---
[2]http://jadex-agents.informatik.uni-hamburg.de

aspects are prescribed by an XML dialect and the procedural aspects are programmed, using the Java programming language. The language models are described in depth in [Pokahr, 2007].

A canonical view of a Jadex-based MAS is given in Figure 2.6. The major design elements, part of the declarative models of agents, are *beliefs*, *goals*, *plans*, and *events*. Beliefs contain the data available to the agent. Arbitrary programming language objects can be stored and modified. Goals describe the states that agents can commit to bring about. Goal declarations contain conditions and invariants that control the individual commitments. Plans are executable means that are activated to handle agent-intern events. These means intersect both description levels: the content of a plan, which is described procedurally in the programming language, and the plan declarations, which are partitions of the agent declaration and contain references to the plan realizations. Besides the conditions and invariants that guard the execution of plans, declarations of plans also denote the events that can trigger the activation of a plan. Plans can be activated to respond to goals or to handle declared events, such as incoming *messages* and *internal events*. Jadex declarations also contain the messages that can be sent and/or received. Internal events are optional means for agent-intern communication. Within plans these events can be dispatched for the subsequent activation of plans. The agent declarations contain additional, framework-specific partitions, e.g. for prescribing the initialization of agents. These partitions are not described here, but details can be found in [Pokahr and Braubach, 2007b]. The programming of plans is facilitated by a library for accessing and modifying of the agent declarations, e.g. to modify belief contents or to activate goals.

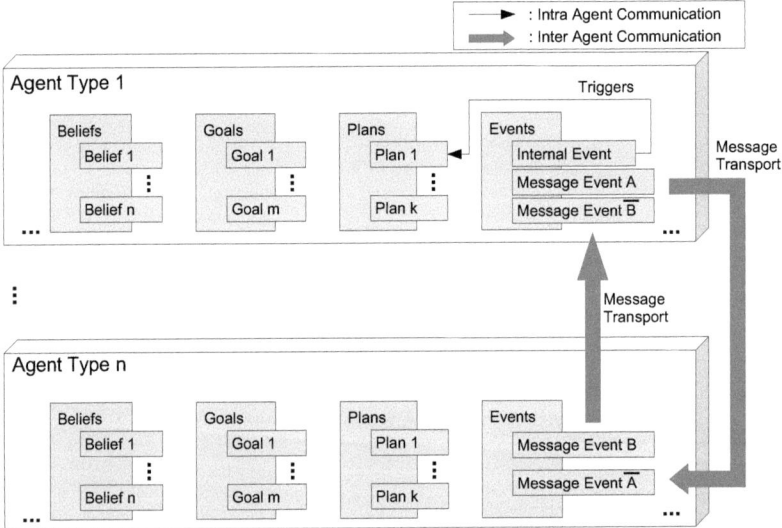

Figure 2.6: A canonical model of a Jadex-based MAS [Sudeikat et al., 2006]

2.3 Environments

Environments are the execution contexts of agents, and typically all non-agent elements within an MAS are understood to be parts of the environment. Considerable work addresses the use of

2.3. ENVIRONMENTS

environments to coordinate the activities of agents. In this section, the engineering of environments and their embedding in the architecture of an MAS is discussed.

The separation of the agent and its environment is an immanent principle of agent-orientation, e.g. see Figure 2.2 [Russell and Norvig, 1995]. A prominent classification of environment properties that abstract from a particular domain is given by [Russell and Norvig, 1995]:

- *Accessible vs. inaccessible*: Environments are accessible when agents are enabled to perceive the entire state of the environment. Alternatively, the *effective* accessibility describes that all information that are relevant for a specific, agent-intern selection of an action can be perceived.

- *Deterministic vs. nondeterministic*: Environments are deterministic when the current state of the environment and the actions of agents determine the following state. Inaccessible environments might seem to be nondeterministic to an individual agent.

- *Episodic vs. nonepisodic*: An episode denotes the agent's perception and action cycle. If these episodes are independent from another, i.e. are not affected by previous episodes, the environment is episodic. This property describes whether agents have to project ahead or not.

- *Static vs. dynamic*: Dynamic environments are subject to ongoing changes that occur parallel to agent deliberations. This means that dynamic environments may change when the agent is deliberating on the next action to take.

- *Discrete vs. continuous*: In discrete environments, only a fixed set of atomic perceptions and actions is possible, e.g. the set of possible moves in a board game. Alternatively, gradations and continuous parameters are found in continuous environments.

In [Weyns et al., 2007], definitions of the environment are reviewed and combined. It is stated that (page 15):

> The environment is a first-class abstraction that provides the surrounding conditions for agents to exist and that mediates both the interaction among agents and the access to resources.

The environment is understood as a separate, stand-alone design element. This element is embedded in an application architecture and carries its own responsibilities. Three essential objectives are highlighted. A major objective is the provision of the logical context for the agent execution. This context is detached from the technical execution of agents but provides a logical surrounding that agents can perceive and modify. Another foundational objective is the enabling of interactions. The environment provides a communication infrastructure based on message transports, the concurrent modification of environment elements, or the observation of the activities of other agents. An aspect of this mediation is that environments may contain their own dynamics, e.g. as information propagates towards agents. This view is commonly emphasized, e.g. in [Parunak, 1997] where the environment is defined as a tuple of two fundamental elements, namely the state of the environment and the process that modifies this state: $Environment = < State_e, Process_e >$.

In [Weyns et al., 2007], these types of objectives are detailed by a list of five basic responsibilities that are commonly attributed to MAS environments. These objectives are design aspects that have to be considered in the conception of an environment. First, environments allow to *structure the MAS*. Agents and non-agent entities are embedded in a shared space. These structures result from the deployment context or are purposefully designed. There are three basic types of structuring: (1) *Physical* structures, that reflect the spatial, distributed topology of the physical deployment context. These environment models reflect the physical layout and properties and make them accessible to the agents. (2) *Communication* structures constrain the transmission of data among agents. Transmissions can be based on the *direct* transfer of information between agents or the *mediated* dissemination of information through the environment. Examples for the direct transfer of information are message-based communications that are incorporated in MAS middleware (cf. Section 2.2.2). Mediating environments provide processes that agents can use to spread information, e.g. based on *stigmergy* [Brueckner and Czap, 2006]. These mechanisms are reviewed and classified in Section 3.2.1. (3) *Social* structures partition the set of agents according to organizational concepts, e.g. *groups* and *roles* [Mao and Yu, 2004].

Environments, as a design concept, can be used to *embed resources and services*. In this respect, resources and services denote non-agent elements. Resources are state-full elements that are accessed and modified by agents. Services are entities that provide functionalities to agents, e.g. operations on data-bases, shard printers or network-based communication.

The environment concept can also be used to *embed dynamics*. Environment models can integrate processes that modify environment concepts [Parunak., 1997]. A typical scenario is the realization of mediated mechanisms of agent interactions, e.g. *stigmergy* [Brueckner and Czap, 2006] or *computational fields* [Mamei and Zambonelli, 2005a]. These mechanisms decouple agents. Interactions are initiated by agents that trigger a perceivable modification in the environment. This modifications are subject to environment processes, e.g. propagation, evaporation, diffusion, and are perceived by agents that interpret their observations. These mechanisms are reviewed and classified in Section 3.2.1.

The local *observability* of the environment defines how agents perceive their surroundings. Observations are typically limited by the spatial, communicational or social context of the agent. The observations define the abstraction level of inputs for agents and thus affect their reasoning abilities. The observability pertains to the perceptions of non-agent as well as agent elements.

Inverse to the observability, the *accessibility* of environments defines the modifications that can be affected by agents. The access of agents to non-agent elements as well as to other agents is constrained by the spatial, communicational or social context of the agents.

The environment can be used to enforce *rules for the MAS*. This is an optional design perspective and allows the embedding of restrictions in order to ensure the consistency of the environment, with respect to the application domain. These rules can be enforced by constraining the previously considered design aspects, e.g. by limiting the observability and accessibility or the communicational abilities of agents.

2.3.1 Infrastructures

The vital importance of the environment for the development of MAS-based software applications justifies research in their engineering. Providing reusable infrastructures for the provision of environments is of scientific and practical importance. Infrastructures provide a context in which to carve out the essential parts of agent environments and serve as tool sets that facilitate practical development efforts. The multi-tier structure of an MAS-based software application, and particularly the logical localization of frameworks for environment support, is discussed in [Viroli et al., 2007], based on [Weyns et al., 2006], where a three-layer model is proposed to describe situated MASs. The three layers are: (1) the *physical* execution context, (2) the execution middleware *platform*, and (3) the agent-based *application* (see Figure 2.7).

The *Physical Support* contains two supplementing tiers. The *physical world* describes physical elements in the MAS that result from the localization of an application in a real-world context. In [Weyns et al., 2006], this level is exemplified by a transportation system, which controls a set of *automatic guided vehicles* (AGVs), and in an information system for museums. These systems are made aware of physical infrastructures, e.g. the loads to transport, a navigation infrastructure, and the artworks present.

The *Execution Platform* contains the *Software Deployment Context* and the *MAS Middleware Layer*. The deployment context is composed of the software environment that is used to host the software system. This environment contains the operating systems and supportive middleware infrastructures [Weyns et al., 2006]. The middleware layer contains the infrastructures, here agent-oriented middleware, that provide services for the realization of distributed applications, e.g. to hide the heterogeneity of system elements and the transparency of the distribution of the system [van Steen and Tanenbaum, 2002]. There are two principal types of middleware. The *Agent Middleware* provides infrastructures for the execution of agents, as discussed in Section 2.2.2. The

2.3. ENVIRONMENTS

Environment Middleware serves as an infrastructure for environment abstractions. Examples are reviewed in [Viroli et al., 2007], e.g. the *TOTA* [Mamei and Zambonelli, 2005c], *TuCSoN* [Ricci et al., 2002] and *AMELI* [Esteva et al., 2004]. An established conception is the *Agents & Artifacts* (A&A) meta model [Omicini et al., 2008], where agents represent active entities and artifacts describe passive, reactive elements in the environment. The artifacts, as MAS design elements, provide means, e.g. services and functionalities, for the collaboration of agents, and can be used to encapsulate interaction techniques (see Section 5.1.2, page 138).

The inter-operation of both types of infrastructures is prepared by an overlap. The infrastructures need to be well-matched to allow agents to interact with environment concepts, i.e. to perform actions in the environment and perceive modifications of the environment. The main strategy for enabling the inter-operation of these infrastructures is to provide agent developers with programming interfaces that allow them to encode the interactions with the provided environment concepts in the agent logic. Examples are the provision of interfaces in the L1-level (see Figure 2.5) programming languages that underly MAS development, e.g. [Ricci et al., 2002], and the extension of L3-level languages, e.g. [Ricci et al., 2008; Piunti et al., 2008], to augment the programming constructs for the description of agent-behaviors with environment-related operations.

The topmost layer (*MAS Application*) contains the software application that is composed of agent models and environment elements. Agents interact with each other and environment elements (solid arrow). Environment elements are able to interact with each other (solid line), to realize the dynamics of the environment (cf. Section 2.3), and are perceived by agents (dashed arrow).

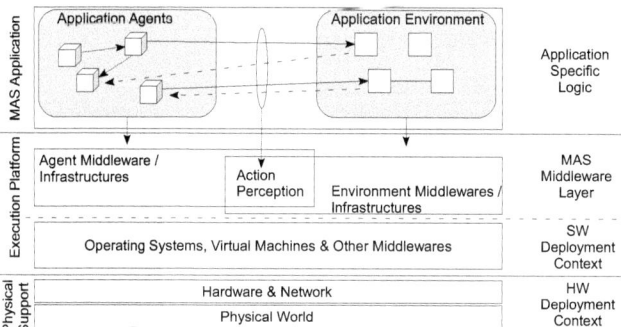

Figure 2.7: Layered MAS architecture, following [Viroli et al., 2007]. Agents are illustrated as cubes and environment elements as squares. Rectangles denote hardware and software tiers.

2.3.2 Multiple Environments

Conventionally, agents are expected to be situated in *one* environment, e.g. as denoted in Figure 2.1. In [Gouaich and Michel, 2005], the conception of MASs with multiple environments is discussed. This separation is relevant for this thesis as it allows that different environmental aspects, such as the inter-agent coordination, are separated into independent design spaces. The conceptual and technological separation of coordination spaces is prepared by the middleware layer for coordination integration that is presented in Chapter 5.

This approach facilitates the modularization of MASs by separating environment models. Different aspects of the application can be encapsulated in a separate environment model. This separation of different environments is approached by conceptualizing a unified view on the relationship between an agent and an environment. Five elements are proposed to characterize an agent-environment relationship. First, the *ontology of the environment* describes the concepts of an environment model. For a spatial environment these concepts contain the notions of position, motion, etc. Secondly, *perception means* is a subset of the concepts of the ontology that describe how agents can perceive the environment. Inversely, *action means* are the concepts that allow agents to affect the environment. Relationships between action means and perception means are described by *interaction functions*. For spatial environments, an additional *localization function* is proposed to localize agents, e.g. infer their position. The description and integration of environments is demonstrated. The set of considered environments comprises an organizational model, following the *Agent/Group/Role* model [Ferber et al., 2004] (see Section 2.6.1, page 27). In this respect, the embedding of the agent in an organizational structure, as discussed in Section 2.6.1, is considered to be an environment abstraction. For the technical realization of the integration of agents in several environments, the use of a specific infrastructure, MIC* [Gouaïch et al., 2005], is proposed. MIC* provides an algebraic model that allows agents to be associated to logical partitions, so-called *interaction-spaces*. In these spaces *interaction objects* are used to represent information transports as well as the actuators and sensors of agents. This infrastructure allows interactions with environments to be mediated.

The technical decoupling of agent and environment realizations is enabled, and the mediation by a dedicated infrastructure structures the application design, e.g. to support the changeability of implementations. On a conceptual level, the agent designs are tightly coupled to the concepts of the utilized environments. The defined ontology serves as an interface and the knowledge about these concepts is built into the agents to enable their internal reasoning.

2.4 A Conceptual Model of Multi-Agent Systems

Agent-oriented development contains a multitude of different development concepts, tools and methodologies. The major uses for conceptual models are the documentation of development methodologies [Bernon et al., 2005b] and the provision of integrative agent languages [Beydoun et al., 2009]. These models contain concepts with detailed semantics. Particularly, development methodologies are based on specific conceptual models of the design and implementation concepts (e.g. as discussed in [Bernon et al., 2005b]). The integration of these models in a unifying model is an academic challenge in and of itself, e.g. the integration of several established models is discussed in [Beydoun et al., 2009].

For the generality of the work in this dissertation, a minimalistic conceptual model serves as the basis. This model does not describe design concepts, e.g. roles or groups, as the diversity of concepts is prohibitive [Beydoun et al., 2009]. Instead, the basic structure of the run-time elements that constitute an agent-based software system is given in Figure 2.8, using the *Unified Modeling Language* (UML)[3] that is a standardized notation for the modeling of software systems from the *Object Management Group* (OMG).[4] This model describes the software systems that are to be supplemented with self-organizing features in Part II of this dissertation.

These systems are *MASs*, which contain *Environments* and agents (*Agent Model*). Agents are composed of *Agent Elements*. These types of elements depend on the specific agent architecture, but can be distinguished into two essential element types. First, *Knowledge Elements* refer to information that is locally available. Secondly, *Behavior Elements* represent the activities and courses of actions that an agent can show. Examples are executable *Plans* or *Tasks*. Besides agent-internal functions, these elements also realize the interactions with the immediate environment (*sense/act*) as well as *communications* with other agents. Agents can also be structured in *Modules* that themselves are containers for agent elements. The execution of agents, e.g. updating knowledge and triggering behaviors, is controlled by a reasoning mechanism that is contained in an *Agent Reasoning Component*. The Reasoning is provided by the execution platform, based on the agent-architecture, and makes use of *Reasoning Events*. These events signify occurrences that

---
[3] http://www.uml.org/
[4] http://www.omg.org/

2.4. A CONCEPTUAL MODEL OF MULTI-AGENT SYSTEMS

are to be handled by the reasoning and describe *external* influences, e.g. the reception of inter-agent messages, as well as *internal* changes of the agent state, e.g. goal activations or knowledge updates. These events reference the agent elements, e.g. the beliefs or plans, that are modified by an event.

This minimalistic model describes a generic structure that neglects details on the agent architecture and the design elements. These details can be fit in by extending model elements, as indicated with the two types of Behavior Elements. For example, BDI agents follow this basic structure, but contain two types of behavioral elements, i.e. goals and plans. Goals can be further refined by the different goal types that are available in a specific development framework (see Section 2.2.1).

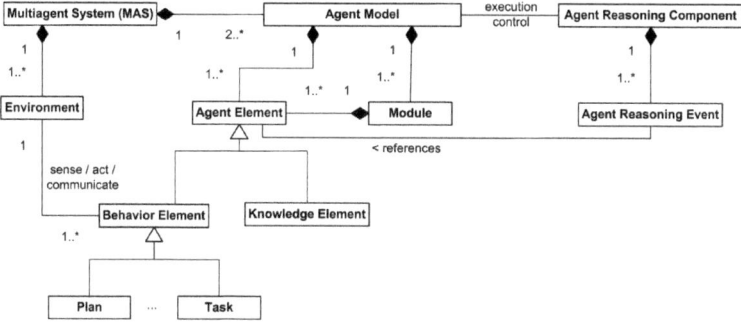

Figure 2.8: Conceptual structure of an MAS

Classification of Agent Behaviors Using the Example of BDI Agents

The distinction between the behaviors that are available to an agent is crucial for the design of individual agents and the analysis of agent coaction. In Section 2.5 behaviors are used to characterize the coordination of agents. Meta models of development frameworks, e.g. reviewed in [Bernon et al., 2005b], describe the concepts that are used to define the activities of individual agents and behaviors refer to specific patterns of the timely exhibition of activities. Some development frameworks directly support behavior concepts, e.g. [Bellifemine et al., 2007], but in general, the identification of behaviors is a modeling effort, based on the design concepts that are available in a specific development environment.

Here, the identification of behaviors is exemplified for an established agent architecture which is based on a conceptual model that does not contain a behavior concept, following [Sudeikat and Renz, 2007a]. The activities of BDI-based agents (see Section 2.2.1) are controlled by the goal deliberation and means-end reasoning of the execution platform, which in turn lead to the activation of the goals and plans of individual agents. Typically, plans provide alternative means for achieving a goal, but the repeated or sequential execution of plans may be necessary as well. The means-end reasoning selects goals and decides for the repeated or sequential activation of plans. The execution of plans optionally effectuates the commitment to (sub-)goals, that subsequently drive the agent execution by causing the activation of subsequent plans. Thus the agent design can be understood as a *Goal-Plan Tree* (GPT) [Padgham and Winikoff, 2004] (chapter 2). Agent design principles or standards may constrain the branching of child nodes, e.g. as assumed in [Padgham and Winikoff, 2004] (page 16). In Figure 2.9, the general case is illustrated where branches in the tree either denote alternative options for the achievement of goals/plans (*OR*) or indicate that the successful execution/achievement of all child elements is required (*AND*). Different embodiments of BDI agent architectures provide different types of goals, e.g. reviewed in [Braubach et al., 2005c]. These do not constrain the structure of the GPT, since goals are used to abstract the context in which plan executions are appropriate. Plans are created by developers at design-time, therefore, the procedural logic can prescribe the selection of alternative subgoals as well as the concurrent or subsequent activation of sets of subgoals.

In [Sudeikat and Renz, 2007a] this tree structure is applied to identify the macroscopic observable behaviors of BDI agents. OR decompositions require the agent reasoning to decide for different courses of actions. Consequently, the tree structure can be processed to identify the different distinct behaviors that denote alternative approaches to achieving goals or to succeed plan executions. This results in a hierarchy of (sub-)behaviors. The level 0 (see Figure 2.9) indicates the *top level* goals and plans and the leaf nodes of the graph are plans that represent the basic activities of an agent.

This processing structures the agent-internal design elements. Based on this partitioning, the behaviors that are relevant for a specific system analysis can be deliberately identified. The relevance is based on the intended level of granularity and the effects that are caused by the traversing of the subtrees. These effects range from the modification of internal data structures to the affecting of the agents' immediate environment.

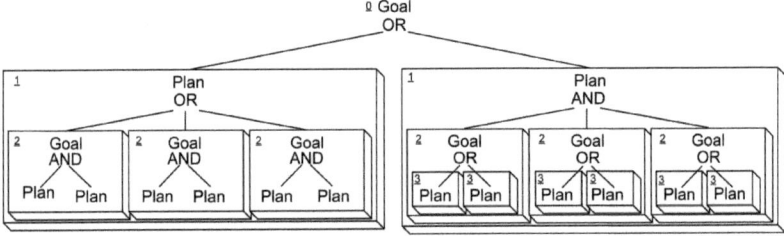

Figure 2.9: A generic goal-plan tree. It is partitioned into distinct subtrees that resemble different courses of action. The notation of the graph follows [Padgham and Winikoff, 2004] (Chapter 2) and the classification of behavior levels follows [Sudeikat and Renz, 2007a].

2.5 The Coordination Concept: A Pragmatic Perspective

The coordination of agents is a crucial concern for the development of MASs. When the software system is understood as an assembly of autonomous actors, their cooperation and collaboration have to be prepared in order to create a functioning system in which agents act in concert. Here, a pragmatic viewpoint on coordination is described, that, in particular with regard to self-organizing dynamics, describes the concerted coaction of agents. The described notion of coordination is adopted throughout the reminder of this dissertation for both a conceptual foundation and a quantitative measurement.

A multitude of mechanisms can be used to make agents work together, including organizational structures, contracting, distributed planning, negotiations, and auctions (e.g. see [Bedrouni et al., 2009], Chapter 5). This diversity makes the coordination itself an interdisciplinary and ill-defined concept, e.g. as discussed in [Bedrouni et al., 2009] (Chapter 1). An abstract, widely accepted definition is given in [Malone and Crowston, 1994] (page 90):

Coordination is managing dependencies between activities

This viewpoint abstracts from the utilized means but stresses that the objective is to constrain the individual degrees of freedom to make the system elements show concerted activities. The diversity of computational techniques for the agent coordination is reviewed elsewhere, e.g. see [Bedrouni et al., 2009].

2.5. THE COORDINATION CONCEPT: A PRAGMATIC PERSPECTIVE

Important aspects, relevant for the work in this dissertation, are the conceptual distinction and the technical separation of computation and coordination [Gelernter and Carriero, 1992]. Computations refer to the stepwise activities that are carried out by computational system entities and the coordination can be understood as an orthogonal aspect that addresses the collaboration of computations. This separation facilitates the reuse of both computational entities and coordination mechanisms/patterns (e.g. see [Bedrouni et al., 2009] pages 4, 5). The realization of this separation is facilitated by software frameworks/languages and coordination can be attributed to the environments of MAS (see Section 2.3). A *coordination model* consists of three essential parts [Papadopoulos and Arbab, 1998; Ciancarini, 1996]: (1) a set of *entities* that are coordinated, a set of *media* that are used for the coordination, and a prescription of the model. In [Papadopoulos and Arbab, 1998] the latter component is characterized as a *semantic framework*, while in [Ciancarini, 1996] this element is understood as a set of *coordination laws*. Coordination languages allow the effectuation of coordination to be prescribed, e.g. by controlling the involved communications and activities [Papadopoulos and Arbab, 1998]. The major architectural elements are the coordination media, which provide communication abstractions and infrastructures, e.g. blackboards or tuple spaces [Denti et al., 1997]. Media overlap with the environment models and infrastructures (see Section 2.3.1). It is argued that the coordination infrastructures are major design abstractions that provide services, here the coordination, for agents [Viroli and Omicini, 2003]. This viewpoint corresponds to the environments as abstractions and providers of functionalities to agents (see Section 2.3). The operation of media can be distinguished between *data-driven* and *control-driven* media [Papadopoulos and Arbab, 1998]. The former media type decouples system entities by means of an infrastructure for the exchange of data. Consequently, the entities are responsible for coordination-related activities which include the invocation of coordination mechanisms and the local processing of the exchanged data. Consequently, the separation of coordination and computation aspects is not enforced. The prevention of the blending of these aspects within the system entities is an additional design concern for the programmer. The control-driven media enforce this separation by providing novel programming languages that interface the coordinated entities via interfaces. The entities serve as black boxes and their coordination is prescribed in externalized language models. A common operation principles is event-based processing, where state changes are monitored and communicated [Papadopoulos and Arbab, 1998].

In this dissertation, self-organization is advocated as a means for the decentralized coordination. This viewpoint is based on a pragmatic notion of coordination. An empiric and thus phenomenological stance towards coordination leads to an informal taxonomy of the interactions of agents [Parunak et al., 2004a]. The most fundamental concept for describing the joint activities of agents is the correlation of their activities. Correlations can be measured for various aspects of agents, particularly the exhibited behaviors, as indicated by the execution of specific patterns or sets of actions. The correlations express that the aspects measured statistically depend on aspects of other agents. A common measurement is the *correlation entropy* or *mutual entropy* (e.g. see [Adami, 1998], page 70). Alternatively, correlations can be extracted by the direct comparison of time series, as demonstrated in Section 4.4.2 and discussed in Section 6.7.3. These measurements are phenomenological, i.e. they are calculated from observations/measurements and detach the observation of relationships from the causative mechanisms, such as centralized controllers or subjective reasoning inside agents.

Based on this notion, three principal, orthogonal types of agent coaction are defined [Parunak et al., 2004a]. (1) *Coordination* is understood as correlations that result from causal processes which involve information flows among agents. Sharing and interpreting information enables agents to align their individual operating sequences. (2) *Cooperation* and *contention* imply that agents have intentions. Cooperation is found among agents with agreeing intentions, e.g. *joint intentions* [Cohen and Levesque, 1991], while contention describes settings in which the individual agents interfere with other agents, resulting in frustrations due to disagreeing intentions. (3) *Congruence* and *Coherence* denote the agreement of the individual objectives of agents with system-level objectives. The latter objectives describe the intended functionality of the ensemble of agents and individual goals may deviate, due to localized reasoning. In this respect coherence is understood as the relation among agents that show congruence.

In the remainder of this thesis the notion of coordination as *purposeful correlation* of agent aspects, e.g. behaviors, activities, tasks, is adopted. This view makes it possible to abstract from the internals of agents and is particularly useful for the study of decentralized, self-organizing effects in MASs that are introduced in Chapter 3. IT is used in both the application design and the analysis of the system dynamics. With respect to the application design, the aim of the application development is to bring about specific patterns of behavior correlations. The correlations signify that the system responds to external or internal variations of system variables. The analysis of a self-organizing mechanism is facilitated by the derivation of a measurement that quantifies the intended behavior of the system (e.g. exemplified in the Sections 6.8.3, 5.4.2). These observables depend on the application domain. An alternative, generic approach is the direct measurement of the dependencies of agent behaviors. Particularly for self-organizing dynamics, this measurement is useful as it can be used to trace the manifestation of distributed feedbacks (see Section 3.1.4). A mathematical measurement of the interdependency of agent activities is their cross-correlation. The numbers of agents that show a specific behavior are measured as integer values. The time series of these values can then be interpreted as signals, x and y. The parameter n is the size of the summation interval and τ is the lag between the signals, that corresponds to an observable delay of responses to influences, and the *correlation function* of these measurements that develops with the time t is given by [Sudeikat and Renz, 2009h] (following e.g. [Van Kampen, 2007]):[5]

$$C_{x,y}(\tau) = \frac{\sum (x(t) - \overline{x})(y(t+\tau) - \overline{y})/n}{\sqrt{(\sum x(t)^2/n - \overline{x}^2)(\sum y(t)^2/n - \overline{y}^2)}} \quad (2.1)$$

This function describes the time lag between the changing signal values. This correlation describes the timely behavior of signals. Signals are mapped onto each other and the agreement of the timely behavior, with respect to the time delay τ, is expressed. A related concept is the auto-correlation where x and y are the same signal. These correlations are used in this dissertation to show the presence of causal interdependencies in MAS implementations (see Sections 4.3.4 and 4.4.2). The measured correlations are manifested by the presence of causal interdependencies, e.g. side effects that make agents in a local sphere of influence adopt a specific behavior. The inversion of this argument is not always acceptable. Observations of correlations do not automatically imply a causal dependence.

2.6 Engineering Agent-based Software Systems

In the following, a subcategory of development support is outlined to characterize the necessary adjustments of software engineering practices to support the *engineering*, here understood as the systematic, disciplined development [IEEE Computer Society, 2004], of MASs. The discussion focuses on the construction of MASs; auxiliary activities, e.g. the operation and maintenance, are not discussed in this dissertation.

In particular, development activities are addressed that can also be used for the construction the self-organizing MAS, as discussed in Chapter 3. First, general design techniques for individual agents and their arrangement in ensembles are characterized (Section section:organizational-modeling). Then the validation of agent-based application in order to show that the ensembles behave as intended is discussed (Section 2.6.2). Finally, two aspects of the systematic application development are discussed. Application development is systematized by development methodologies (Section 2.6.3) and the tailoring of development procedures, with respect to specific development contexts is addressed by the adoption of method engineering techniques (Section 2.6.3).

2.6.1 Designing Agent-Based Applications

The basic building blocks of an agent-based software system, the agents (see Section 2.2) and the environments (see Section 2.3), distinguishes it from traditional software engineering concepts.

---

[5]$\overline{x}$ denotes the (arithmetic) average value of x

2.6. ENGINEERING AGENT-BASED SOFTWARE SYSTEMS

While the realization of these components can be based to a large extent on established, e.g. object-oriented, implementation techniques, the elevated abstraction-levels of these engineering artifacts demands dedicated design tools. Two principal directions for supporting the design of agent-oriented applications are the modification of established modeling tools in order to augment agent-specific semantics, and the conception of new design models from scratch.

An example for the customization of established design techniques is the (re)use of the Unified Modeling Language (UML) [Huget, 2004; Odell et al., 2000]. The widespread use of the UML notation makes it beneficial, and a customization, *Agent UML* (AUML), is proposed in [Odell et al., 2000]. In this work the adoption of the different UML diagram types for describing agents and MASs is discussed, with an emphasis on agent interactions. Sequence diagrams from the UML notation are adopted to describe the sequential exchanges of messages among agents. The use of this notation is exemplified in Section 4.3.4. Lifelines, i.e. vertical bars, describe participants in an interaction and horizontal arrows denote message-based communication. This notation has found widespread adoption in the MAS community. It is an intuitive notation for describing patterns of agent interactions, e.g. interaction protocols [Napoli, 2009].

The conceptual difference between agents, i.e. proactive software components, and classical software elements justifies the conception of tailored design perspectives that take into account the concept of an agent as an actor that is socialized in a complex of other agents. An influential field of research is the adoption of organizational modeling perspectives, as reviewed in [Mao and Yu, 2004]. Organizational concepts are introduced as a means for designing MASs. These concepts describe the behavior of agents and their social context. Widespread examples are *roles* and *groups*, e.g. as adopted in the *Agent/Group/Role* model [Ferber et al., 2004]. The role concept is used to characterize agent behaviors. They abstract a specific course of action and denote functional aspects, e.g. the required qualifications and implied commitments. A sample use is the description of interaction partners in interaction protocols [Ferber et al., 2004]. In this respect, groups are understood as partitions of an organizational structure [Ferber et al., 2004]. This modeling approach describes how the MAS is to be structured and agents are expected to behave in specific contexts.

2.6.2 Validating Agent-Based Applications

The validation that an implemented software system works as intended is an inevitable activity in software development. In [Menzies and Pecheur, 2005], the principal validation techniques for adaptive and/or distributed systems are categorized into five disciplines, according to the amount of expertise that is required to use them. The adoption of these techniques for MAS development is reviewed in [Timm et al., 2006]. First, (1) *Testing* requires the least expertise and can be automated. Output is generated from predefined input sequences and the results obtained are compared to expectations. (2) *Run-time Monitoring* enables further analysis. The execution of the system or a subsystem is observed under given conditions. The (3) *Static Analysis* of source codes allows defects to be found. (4) *Model Checking* examines the space of reachable program states and shows the compliance with formal specifications. Finally, (5) *Theorem Proving* requires the most expertise but correctness can be formally shown.

For the validation of MASs, two additional, MAS-specific aspects require examination. First, high-level, speech act-based communication of agents has to be validated. These examinations ensure that agents agree to predefined communication protocols. Secondly, the validation of the functioning of agents is affected by their inherent autonomy. Agents decide by themselves on the courses of actions to take and developers have to ensure the reasoning of agents affects activities that are appropriate for the current execution contexts.

Validating Agent Communication

Communicativeness is a fundamental property of agents. The exchanged messages are clearly defined artifacts, e.g. in L2-level languages (see Section 2.2.2), and the observed message sequences constitute an abstract view of the MAS operation that neglects the internal processing of the agents. Several approaches for the effective runtime monitoring and (semi-)automated analysis have been devised, e.g. [Padgham et al., 2005; Chesani, 2005]. These tools observe sequences of messages, compare them to protocol definitions, and report disagreements. Visualizations of messages facilitate the identification of irregularities, e.g. agents that consume but fail to send messages. An example is the *Java Sniffer* [Bellifemine et al., 2007] (Section 13.3) for the the visualization of inter-agent messages. The use of data-mining techniques has also been studied to reveal system properties and systematically cluster large amounts of message data, e.g. [Botía et al., 2004].

Alternatively, the static analysis of agent models allows acquaintance relationships between agents to be examined. These are prerequisites for the participation in interaction protocols. These efforts are facilitated by declarative agent models, e.g. the declarations of Jadex-based agents contain definitions of the messages that can be sent and received (see Section 2.2.2). The visualization of the network of acquaintances that result from these definitions is discussed in [Sudeikat et al., 2006]. A set of agent declarations is converted to a graph G, which is defined as a tuple $G = \langle A, M, Ae, Me \rangle$. The sets of the declared agents (A) and the contained messages (M) constitute the nodes of the graph. Ae denotes the set of edges between agents and messages $(Ae \subseteq A \times M)$ and Me denotes a set of edges between the messages that are sent and received by agents $(Me \subseteq M \times M)$. The elements in Ae describe in which agent messages are declared and the edges $(e(m, m'))$ in Me describe the possible message exchanges. The declarations of messages contain implementation details, e.g. performatives that comply to the specification of the *Foundation for Intelligent Physical Agents* (FIPA)[6] or the permissible message content, and these details constrain the message exchange. Messages are received when an incoming message matches the declaration of a receivable message. The edges between messages (Me) describe the possible matches $((m, m') \in Me \Leftrightarrow m, m' \in M)$[7]. Consequently, the identification of these relationships depends on the utilized agent platform. These graphs can be used to validate assumptions, e.g. the expectation that all messages (m) declared in one agent (a) can be sent/received (m') by at least one other agent (a') in the MAS:

$$\forall (a, m) \in Ae. \ \exists (a', m') \in Ae \land (((m, m') \lor (m', m)) \in Me)$$

The static analysis of the message declarations is addressed in [Sudeikat et al., 2006]. Graph representations in a three dimensional space are generated. These allow the possible acquaintances to be studied and search for flaws, e.g. orphaned messages, that are declared to be sent/received by one agent but are not matched by message declarations in other agents.

Validating Agent Reasoning

The principal parts of a comprehensive validation procedure for MASs are illustrated in Figure 2.10, following [Sudeikat et al., 2006]. This procedure moves from the examination of the agent internals to the overall system functionality. First, the basic functional parts of agents are checked (I). The basic functional abilities, e.g. the execution of plans, the achievement of goals, and the valid updates of the internal knowledge have to be checked. Within modular agent designs, these abilities are pooled to functional clusters. In a consecutive validation stage, the composition of these modules, e.g. *capabilities* (see Section 2.2.1), in an agent has to be validated (II). This stage is necessary to ensure that the assembly of an agent, as a container of different functionalities, leads to the intended individual behavior(s). As the functionalities of the clusters have been previously examined, this stage is mainly concerned with ensuring that the internal reasoning triggers the right clusters according to the perceived agent context. Thereafter the interplay of the set of agents is examined to ensure that these sets are able to provide the intended functionality. One aspect is the correct encoding of the functional dependencies. These dependencies describe that the function of an agent depends on the provision of certain functionalities of another agent, e.g.

---

[6]FIPA is a non-profit organization that standardizes agent technology. A historic review is given in [Bellifemine et al., 2007] (Section 2.2); http://www.fipa.org/

[7]Me is the identity relation when messages are declared globally

2.6. ENGINEERING AGENT-BASED SOFTWARE SYSTEMS

by the delegation of sub-goals to other agents. Another important aspect is that the concurrent interactions with the system's environment lead to mediated interactions among agents (see Section 3.2.1). Finally, the embedding of the MAS in the surrounding software infrastructure(s), e.g. the interactions with third-party software systems, is to be examined (IV).

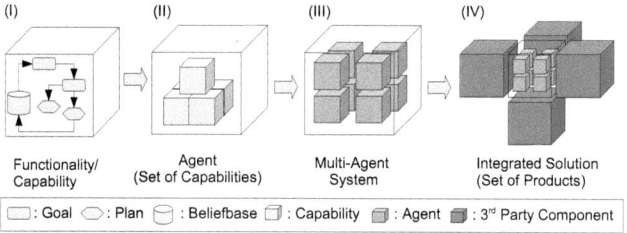

Figure 2.10: Testing stages for MASs [Sudeikat et al., 2006]

An aspect that crosscuts these stages is the consideration of the agent reasoning. Since the contained software elements are autonomous, it has to be ensured that the internal reasoning, which can range from reactive to cognitive mechanisms (see Section 2.2.1), effects the invocation of the activities that are appropriate for the current context of the agent or MAS, respectively. This examination of the agent-internal reasoning demands tool support that is customized for the specific reasoning mechanism. In the following, techniques for the validation of BDI agents are outlined. Three successful strategies are (1) the examination of the compliance of the observed agent execution with design artifacts that result from MAS development methodologies [Padgham et al., 2005], (2) the comparison of the observed agent internal reasoning with models of the expected sequences of reasoning events [Lam and Barber, 2005] and (3) the generation of test cases for BDI-plan executions [Low et al., 1999].

An established methodology for designing BDI-based MASs is the *Prometheus* methodology [Padgham and Winikoff, 2004] and the use of Prometheus-specific design artifacts for validation of communication protocols [Poutakidis et al., 2002; Padgham et al., 2005] and agent communication [Poutakidis et al., 2003]. In addition, tests for the *coverage* and *overlap* of BDI plans are examined. A method and tool support for the study and explanation of BDI-based agent behaviors is proposed in [Lam and Barber, 2005]. The runtime monitoring of message exchanges is extended by observing the agent-internal reasoning activities as well. This makes it possible to trace the execution of agent models, e.g. by expressing that the reception of messages causes the modification of belief values. These approaches focus on relating the microscopic agent behaviors and activities to each another.

The automated generation of test cases for BDI-plans is discussed in [Low et al., 1999], in accordance with coverage criteria. These criteria consider the execution of plans as well as plan statements and are used to ensure that test cases cover relevant execution paths.

In [Sudeikat et al., 2006], the examination of BDI reasoning is discussed. Functional aspects are (1) the consistency of beliefs, (2) the adoption of appropriate goals/plans, and (3) the correct plan execution. These aspects ensure that agents operate correctly when a course of action is decided by the reasoning mechanism. In addition, it is necessary to ensure that this reasoning draws the intended conclusions, i.e. the agent shows the intended responses to external influences and changes in the execution context. The corresponding study of BDI-agents is based on two parts [Sudeikat et al., 2006]. Misconceptions in the agent code are identified by the annotation of *assertion* statements. These statements are trigged by BDI reasoning events to check invariants, as well as expectations of the agent state that permit reasoning activities. Secondly, the *static analysis* of BDI agent models can be used to inspect the consistency of agent specifications.

Assertions are a classical programming tool that allow expectations on the state of programs during their execution to be declared. The assertion concept has found application in program verification [Floyd, 1967] and traces back to the seminal works of Turing [Turing, 1949], that introduce this concept for the specification of *interfaces* between parts of programs. Hoare [Hoare, 2003] defines assertions as (page 14):

> "... Boolean formulas placed in program text at places where their evaluation will always be true. ..."

The evaluation of the formula to false signifies that a program has entered an inconsistent state and completes testing techniques for software systems. The identification of defects requires that observable, incorrect output is generated by testing efforts. This *observability* of software artifacts is given when (1) inputs cause the execution of defective code sections, (2) the program data is consequently corrupted, and (3) this corrupted data is propagated to incorrect output(s) [Voas, 1997]. *Encapsulation* and *information hiding* may mask errors and the value of assertions for the detection of erroneous program parts is acknowledged, e.g. as argued in [Voas, 1997]. Analogously, the event-based processing inside agents, controlled by conditions that are annotated to goal and plan elements, can be detrimental to the observability of error states [Sudeikat et al., 2006].

The ability to document BDI concepts with assertions allows (1) *relations* between these concepts and the state of the agent to be specified and the agent to be documented with (2) *invariant* properties. The conditions of BDI goals and plans enable the automated reasoning, i.e. the goal deliberation and means-end reasoning (see Section 2.2.1). This reasoning should lead to specific agent configurations and behaviors. Assertions provide a means for explicitly annotating the intended context to BDI concepts. The automated notifications of violations of these specifications increases the observability of unintended and/or inconsistent agent states. Unlike programming language assertions, BDI-based assertions are evaluated when the annotated BDI-element is accessed by the reasoning mechanism. Details of the technical realization are discussed in Section 5.2.6. Examples for the use of assertions in BDI agents can be found in [Sudeikat et al., 2006].

The static analysis of agent models, as discussed in [Sudeikat et al., 2006], can be used to check that means for the handling of potential events are available. The approach has been exemplified for the declaration of inter-agent messages, as previously discussed in this section. Besides the message-based communication, the generation of inter-agent graphs may be applicable to visualize other inter-agent properties, such as shared resources or service utilizations [Sudeikat et al., 2006], and compare them to design models.

In addition, the analysis of agent-intern events is exemplified in [Sudeikat et al., 2006]. The Jadex system provides an *internal* event concept that can be used to trigger the execution of plans (see Section 2.2.2, page 18). These events serve as a means for intra-agent communication, and the checking of the event handling, by iterating agent models, is discussed and exemplified in [Sudeikat et al., 2006]. The handling of events may also be implicitly defined within Java code, using the Jadex programming libraries. A specific annotation type, using the Java 5.0 annotation mechanism,[8] is provided. The implementation classes that handle events can be documented with this meta-data facility. Agent models are processed in order to validate that events are handled inside the agent and that the declarations of plans in agent models refer to valid agent-intern events. The realization of this processing and its utilization is exemplified in [Sudeikat et al., 2006].

2.6.3 Development Methodologies

The widespread adoption of agent-orientation as an engineering discipline requires the availability of development methodologies, e.g. as argued in [Luck et al., 2003]. Methodologies pertain to the cost-effective collaborative construction of software systems, based on the division of labor. In [Rumbaugh et al., 1991] (page 144), a *software engineering methodology* is defined as:

> ... a process for the organized production of software, using a collection of predefined techniques and notational conventions. A methodology is usually presented as a series of steps, with techniques and notation associated with each step.

---
[8]http://java.sun.com/j2se/1.5.0/docs/guide/language/annotations.html

2.6. ENGINEERING AGENT-BASED SOFTWARE SYSTEMS

Thus a methodology is composed of three foundational components. A (1) development process, is given by a series of distinct development steps, and the conduct of each step makes use of (2) specific techniques and (3) notations. A detailed view of these building blocks is given in [Sturm and Shehory, 2003] to ground a framework for the comparison and evaluation of agent-oriented development methodologies (see Figure 2.11). The techniques (*Technique Set*) concern the provision of *Metrics*, quality assurances (*QA*), *Standards* and (development) *Tools*. The *Modeling Language* is based on a conceptual model (*MetaModel*) and a *Notation*. Tools, e.g. diagram editors, can be used to express the concepts of the MetaModel using the corresponding notation. Finally, the development process (*Lifecycle Process*) contains the control flow of development steps to prescribe the permitted sequences of development activities that constitute the *Procedure*. *Roles* in this respect describe the different actors that participate in the development. The *Project Management* prescribes how the development is structured and carried out and the outcome of the development steps are *Deliverables*. These contain design documents that utilize the notation to define the operation of the software system.

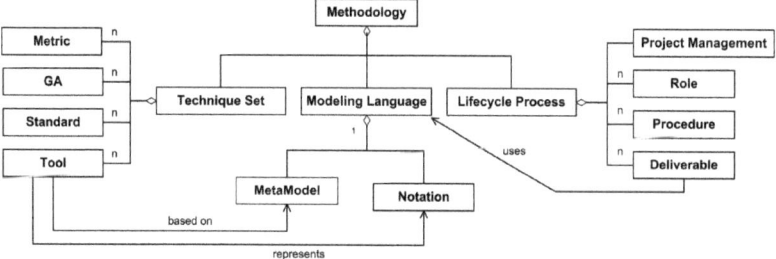

Figure 2.11: Elements of a Development Methodology, following [Sturm and Shehory, 2003]

Development methodologies abstract from problem domains and support cost- and target-oriented development of software systems. A multitude of development methodologies is a available [Tveit, 2001; Iglesias et al., 1999; Henderson-Sellers and Giorgini, 2005; Sturm and Shehory, 2003] and the extent of support for the fundamental components of a methodology varies. This diversity and heterogeneity counteracts the consolidation, and therefore a subsequent standardization, of established development practices. A practical concern is the section of a methodology, according to the context and objectives of a specific project [Cockburn, 2000]. With respect to agent-oriented software systems one important aspect for this selection is the agreement between the utilized design concepts and the target implementation platform [Sudeikat et al., 2004]. A related movement for the structuring of the development practices is the partitioning of methodologies into reusable fragments that can be combined into customized design processes. This approach is followed by the *FIPA Design Process Documentation and Fragmentation Working Group*[9] [Cossentino et al., 2007].

In the following sections, the methodology-related concepts is disused that are relevant for the constructive approach presented in Part II. A prominent methodology that particularly facilitates the design of BDI-based agents is characterized, the evaluation of methodologies with respect to a specific implementation platform is discussed and the adoption of method engineering principles in MAS development is outlined. Methodologies for the development of self-organizing systems are described in Section 3.2.4.

---

[9]http://www.pa.icar.cnr.it/cossentino/fipa-dpdf-wg/

An Example for a BDI-Oriented Development Methodology: TROPOS

Within this dissertation, application development is exemplified with a BDI-based agent architecture. Therefore, goal-oriented development methodologies, tailored toward the design of BDI agents, are most relevant. Two examples are the *Prometheus* [Padgham and Winikoff, 2004] and the *Tropos* [Giorgini et al., 2005; Bresciani et al., 2004] development methodologies. A detailed evaluation of the appropriateness of these methodologies for the Jadex programming platform is given in [Sudeikat et al., 2004]. In this dissertation, the Tropos methodology is used for the initial MAS models. Experience has shown, e.g. see [Sudeikat and Renz, 2011], that the modeling concepts are intuitive and the mapping to Jadex-based implementations is not problematic.

Two distinctive features of the Tropos methodology are the use of BDI-style mentalistic notions throughout the development cycle and the support of an *early requirements* analysis where the application context as-is, prior to the design of the software system, is modeled [Bresciani et al., 2004]. The consequent use of mentalistic notions allows both software and human actors to be described in a coherent framework. The early requirements, based on the i^* framework [Yu, 1997], focus on the context and the justification of the software system. An analysis of the actors and their interdependencies in the application domain facilitates the fitting in of the newly developed software in subsequent development steps. The main development phases are the *Early Requirements*, the *Late Requirements*, the *Architectural Design*, and the *Detailed Design* [Giorgini et al., 2005]. These phases prepare the implementation of the MAS. The implementation is carried out manually or by using code generation techniques [Giorgini et al., 2005]. In the requirements disciplines, the system stakeholders, i.e. actors, and the interdependencies among them are identified. Dependencies express that actors depend on the activities of other actors. Examples are, using mentalistic notions, that actors depend on the achievement of goals or the execution of a plan by another actor. In the Late Requirements, the developed software system is introduced as another actor and the interdependencies with the system actors, which define the context of the system, are denoted. In the Architectural Design, the structure of the software system, as a collection of actors, is conceived. The flow of data and control is also described in terms of dependencies. The identified actors are the later software agents. Their realization is prepared in the Detailed Design that specifies the agent interactions and their individual capabilities.

Tropos makes use of three modeling levels. First, the Actors and their dependencies are denoted in an *actor diagram*. The actors, i.e. system stakeholders and software agents, are represented by circles. Their individual goals can be annotated with the actors. Hard goals (ovals) and soft goals (clouds) are distinguished. The latter type describes non-functional requirements. Dependencies are illustrated by arrows. Agents (*depender*) are connected to the item (*dependum*), e.g. a resource, goal, or plan, on which they depend. This item is then connected to the agent (*dependee*) that provides the dependum.

The internal operation of an actor can be refined in *goal diagrams* [Bresciani et al., 2004]. Three types of relationships can be denoted. Means-end relationships describe the means, e.g. plans, resources and soft goals, that are available to achieve a goal. In addition, contributions can be denoted, which describe if an element contributes positively of negatively to the achievement of a goal. Finally, the AND/OR decompositions are expressed. These describe sub-goal relationships. For the detailed design of agents, i.e. their capabilities and plans, the utilization of UML activity diagrams and AUML interaction diagrams (see Section 2.6.1) is proposed [Bresciani et al., 2004].

The Relation between Methodologies and Architectures

The heterogeneity of the agent development environments has to be taken into account when selecting a methodology [Sudeikat et al., 2004; Braubach et al., 2006b]. Even for specific architectural styles, e.g. the BDI model (see Section 2.2.1), peculiarities can impair the applicability of methodologies. While some methodologies have been revised to be architecture independent, e.g. [Zambonelli et al., 2003], their higher grade of abstraction increases the effort of transferring design models into executable agent models. Tailored methodologies and design techniques provide an enhanced support when applied to a well-matching counterpart.

2.6. ENGINEERING AGENT-BASED SOFTWARE SYSTEMS

This dependence is relevant for this dissertation as is shows the lack of a universal methodical foundation for MAS development. In order to prepare the general applicability of the systematics that are devised in this dissertation, it has to be enabled that the systematic MAS development and the integration of self-organizing features can be combined. It is necessary that both a methodology, suitable for a given development context, and the novel construction approach for self-organizing processes (see Chapter 6), can be used within one development project. This leads to the adoption of method engineering concepts, which are described in the following section.

The evaluation and selection of appropriately matching methodologies and development frameworks is studied in [Sudeikat et al., 2004]. A fist step is the analysis of the problem domain and the software platforms that are available. The application context or the software producing organization may constrain the set of available choices. For example, the developed software may have to fit into a software landscape and the interoperability with third party systems may have to be ensured. After choices have been narrowed down, the match can be examined using criteria catalogs. A detailed review of applicable criteria is given in [Sturm and Shehory, 2003]. Two types of criteria are distinguished (see Figure 2.12). (1) Platform *independent* criteria describe desirable properties of a development methodology, which can be evaluated in a feature analysis. Examples are *pragmatic* aspects, e.g. the available tool support, characteristics of the *design notation*, e.g. the expressiveness and traceability of design models, and properties of the *development process*, e.g. the coverage of a complete development life cycle. In contrast, (2) other criteria are platform *dependent*. The quality of these criteria depends on the match with the agent platform that is used for the application development. These criteria concern the design time support for the implementation concepts of the agent architecture. They are evaluated by examining the degree of conformity. The appropriateness of a methodology is given when concepts are supported on the design level and the implementation level in comparable ways. In this respect, the shared absence of a criteria also indicates a match [Sudeikat et al., 2004]. In addition, criteria can be weighted to indicate the relevance and irrelevance of specific criteria/properties for a given application domain.

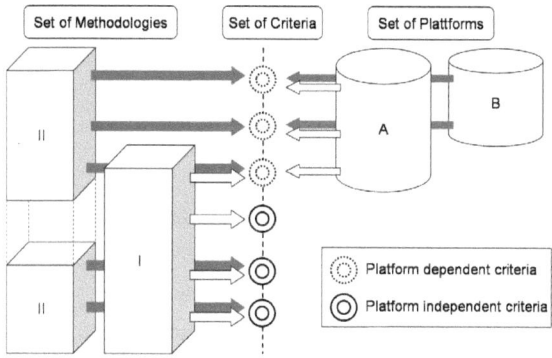

Figure 2.12: The platform-dependent evaluation of methodologies [Sudeikat et al., 2004]

Method Engineering for Agent-Oriented Systems Development

The diversity of agent-oriented development methodologies challenges not only the methodology selection, as discussed in the previous section, but also impairs the elicitation of universal design and development principles for MAS-based software systems. Method instances broadly agree in their coverage for the principal phases and disciplines in software development and commonly support iterative construction of applications. However, they differentiate on the modeling tools/notations used and the techniques applied during development (see Section 2.6.3). The diversity results from inherent foci on specific development tools, modeling techniques, application domains, etc., that are addressed by a specific methodology instance. Therefore, methodologies imply differing advantages and limitations, when applied in a specific development context.

One branch of research on agent-oriented software engineering examines the adoption of the *Method Engineering* (ME) paradigm to facilitate combining the *best practices* of methodology instances to processes that are designed to meet the needs of specific projects and development contexts [Cossentino et al., 2007]. This approach is adopted in Chapter 6. It provides a framework (see Section 6.1.2) for the documentation of the basic activities that constitute the conception and integration of self-organizing dynamics in agent-based applications (see Section 6.3). Using method engineering concepts this documentation can be given in a methodology-independent format and the integration of the described development activities in customized development processes is prepared. ME is defined in [Brinkkemper, 1996] (page 276):

> Method engineering is the engineering discipline to design, construct and adapt methods, techniques and tools for the development of information systems.

Research on ME originates in the customization of development methodologies for the construction of information systems [Brinkkemper, 1996]. Development methodologies are partitioned into coherent, reusable process components, called *Method Fragments*. These fragments are the basic building blocks for customized method instances. Their reuse and selection is facilitated by infrastructures that provide *repositories* for the storage and retrieval of fragments [Brinkkemper, 1996] as well as design environments [Niknafs and Ramsin, 2008] that support the design of fragment combinations. The importance of the context in which the newly created method is to be applied is stressed by the term *Situational Method Engineering* (SME) [Harmsen and Brinkkemper, 1995].

Appropriately prepared fragmentations enable the *ad hoc* assembly of a methodology for a particular development project. The main phases of the process composition are the construction of a *repository* of fragments, the *assembly* of customized processes from the contained fragments, and the deployment of the processes in the development context [Cossentino et al., 2007]. The two basic approaches for the assembly of fragments are *meta-model driven* or *development-process driven* [Cossentino et al., 2007]. The starting point for the meta-model oriented approach is the definition of a conceptual model of the MAS that is appropriate for a specific application context. The selection of fragments is guided by their ability to generate the elements of the MAS. The order of the selected fragments is inferred from the relationships among meta-model elements. In addition, constraints on the order of fragment executions, if they exist, have to be respected. Alternatively, the assembly can begin with the definition of a specific life-cycle model that is appropriate for the application context. Then the principled development phases are filled up with adequate fragments. Between these extremes hybrid composition strategies can be found [Cossentino et al., 2007].

Different fragment description formats are available that are supported by corresponding tool sets. Two prominent frameworks are the OPEN Process Framework (OPF) [Henderson-Sellers, 2003] and the *Software Process Engineering Meta-model* (SPEM)[10] [Object Management Group, 2008], both of which have been extended to support the description of agent-oriented software engineering processes [Seidita et al., 2009; Debenham and Henderson-Sellers, 2002].

In Section 4.3 and throughout Chapter 6, the SPEM description format is used to describe the systematic analysis and integration of decentralized coordination processes in MAS designs. SPEM-based modeling is favored as it is an established standard of the OMG. Most notably, this format has been adopted by the FIPA *Methodology Technical Committee*[11] and its successor the IEEE FIPA *Design Process Documentation and Fragmentation Working Group* (DPDF WG).[12] In addition, tool support that facilitates the development of fragment libraries (e.g compared in

---
[10] http://www.omg.org/technology/documents/formal/spem.htm
[11] http://www.pa.icar.cnr.it/cossentino/FIPAmeth/metamodel.htm
[12] http://www.fipa.org/subgroups/DPDF-WG.html

2.6. ENGINEERING AGENT-BASED SOFTWARE SYSTEMS

[García-Magari et al., 2009]) is freely available.[13] The practicability of SPEM-oriented modeling of agent-oriented design processes is reported by several authors and the use of this generic modeling framework for the description of agent-oriented development is under active investigation. Examples are the fragmentation of established development methodologies to SPEM-based process definitions, as discussed in [Rougemaille et al., 2009b], and the use of this framework, together with appropriate extensions, for the description of agent-oriented development methodologies that is reported in [Seidita et al., 2009]. Thus, SPEM is adopted for the methodology documentation and the fragmentation. Documentations make uses of the standardized notation and fragmentations adopt this modeling framework to divide methodologies into coherent reusable partitions, such as phases and disciplines. The partitioning of the ADELFE methodology demonstrates this approach [Rougemaille et al., 2009b]. The methodology itself is described in Section 3.2.4 (page 66). An example for an independent fragment definition is given in [Pena and Corchuelo, 2004]. This work focuses on the analysis stage in MAS development and a SPEM-based description of an analysis procedure is given that does not reference a particular development methodology.

The SPEM standard defines an MOF-based meta-model [Object Management Group, 2006] and a UML 2.0 profile that reuses the UML 2 Infrastructure library[14] for the definition of software and systems development processes [Object Management Group, 2008]. The modeling concepts are described as stereotypes for elements of the UML 2 Superstructure model, thus the corresponding models can be described in Unified Modeling Language (UML) diagrams. The vocabulary is deliberately narrowed to the basic description concepts. Following the specification [Object Management Group, 2008] (page 9) this conceptual framework addresses the:

> ... modeling, documenting, presenting, managing, interchanging, and enacting development methods and processes.

Details on the internal structuring of the specification can be found in [Object Management Group, 2008]. In the following, the subset of SPEM concepts that are used in this dissertation is introduced. In the SPEM specification, meta model elements and their corresponding UML stereotypes are described. Using these stereotypes, SPEM concepts to be denoted in UML notations. The graphical nation is shown in Section 4.3 and Chapter 6. Development processes are structured in sequences of *Activities*. These represent fundamental units of work that rely on the provision of inputs and produce outputs. The work within an Activity can be structured in *Tasks*, which represent distinguished partitions of work with a specific purpose. The granularity of Tasks ranges from hours to days [Object Management Group, 2008] (page 90) and can be subdivided into *Steps* (page 89). Tasks affect, i.e. consume, produce or modify, a set of *Work Products*. Pre-defined Work Product types are *Artifact*, *Deliverable*, and *Outcome*. Artifacts are generic representations of concrete, i.e. tangible, types of products that may contain other Artifacts [Object Management Group, 2008] (page 166). Deliverables represent packages of Work Products that are passed to distinct parties. Finally, the Outcome refers to informally defined or intangible types of Work Products. With regard to agent-oriented development processes, the specialization of the Artifact concepts is proposed in [Seidita et al., 2006]. In the following sections, the design and development models that are affected by activities are understood as specific types of artifacts.

Using SPEM, the *progression* and also the *contents* of processes can be structured. The control flow among development Activities, Tasks, and Steps shows how the development proceeds. The contents of process are stored for reuse. An example categorization of development tasks are *Disciplines*, e.g. the requirements or analysis stages in software development [Object Management Group, 2008]. *Capability Pattern* are used to aggregate approaches for development problems. They serve as building blocks for larger collections of processes, i.e. higher-level process patterns or development processes. Due to the self-contained aggregation of Activities, these patterns can be used to document best practices for a development discipline. Details on these concepts for the description of development processes can be found in [Object Management Group, 2008], where the physical arrangement of partitions of processes is discussed. These are stored in *Method Libraries* that contain collections of *Method Plug-ins*.

---
[13] E.g. the *Eclipse Process Framework*: http://www.eclipse.org/epf/
[14] www.omg.org/uml

2.7 Effects on the Structure of Software Implementations

The advantages that result from adopting agent-oriented development practices as a software engineering discipline are justified by the enhancements in design concepts for the development of complicated, distributed systems that account for the commonly found context-dependence of functionality providers, e.g. [Jennings, 2001]. Little is known about the effects that development approaches and procedures have on the structure of the resulting implementations of software systems. The quantification of these effects allows for the scientific evaluation of design stances.

Here, an example quantification is discussed. It indicates that the use of agent-oriented design and development techniques affects the implementation-structure of the resulting software systems. Insights in these influences can justify the adoption of agent-orientation. System realizations are understood as a graph of interconnected implementation elements, e.g. programming language classes, and the characteristic properties of these graphs are compared and interpreted. These characteristics also serve as an abstract quality measure, e.g. to indicate the potential propagation of errors among the system elements.

A wide range of agent-oriented development platforms are based on object-oriented programming languages. Developers realize functional parts in these languages and configure the agency of software components, using declarative approaches or platform-provided programming libraries. This common grounding provides a basis for the comparison and evaluation of design stances. The statistical analysis of large-scale modular software systems, which are represented as directed graphs, reveals *small-world* and *scale-free* phenomena [de Moura et al., 2003; Valverde and Sole, 2003; Marchesi et al., 2004], i.e. characteristics that are typically found in complex systems [Newman, 2003]. These results indicate the resulting properties of systems, e.g. their robustness due to the limited propagation of bugs [Challet and Lombardoni, 2003]. In [Baxter et al., 2006], different distributions are observed within a set of systems in the same implementation language. It is an open research question how the characteristics found arise from development efforts [Ichii et al., 2008] and how they are related to the specifics of application domains as well as design approaches [Baxter et al., 2006].

In [Sudeikat and Renz, 2007b], it is argued that the adoption of agent-oriented design and development techniques affect the structure of the resulting software systems. The effects of applying different engineering paradigms are approached by comparing the statistical properties of the resulting software structures. The analysis of graphs that represent agent-oriented software applications are compared to representations of conventionally developed software systems. The structural differences found suggest that the applied design stance, particularly the autonomy of agents, is reflected by the graph-based representations of software system. Particularly, an indication is found that the agent autonomy impedes the propagation of code changes.

Graph-Structures in Software Systems

Natural and engineered systems, e.g. *food webs*, *airline routes* and *coauthorship relations* are intuitively represented as graphs (see [Newman, 2003] for a comprehensive review). Prominent properties of interest for mathematical analyses are *path length distributions*, *degree distributions* and the *network resilience*. The average path length is a measure for the mean *geodesic*, i. e. shortest, distance between vertex pairs, given by of numbers of edges. A prominent characteristic is the *small–world* effect [Watts and Strogatz, 1998], where the mean node distance is small compared to the overall network size. The *degree* of a vertex is the number of connected edges. The degree distributions are typically examined with histograms of the fractions (p_k) of vertices with a certain degree (k). For directed graphs, the degrees of *incoming* and *outgoing* vertexes are distinguished. These distributions in large, real-world networks often follow either *power law* $p_k \sim k^{-\alpha}$ or *exponential* distributions $p_k \sim e^{-k/\kappa}$, where α and κ are constant exponents [Newman, 2003] (page 12). Power Law distributions are *scale-free*, i. e. obey $p(bx) = g(b)p(x)$, where g is independent from x. Consequently, rescaling depends on the ratio b. The resilience of networks relates to degree distributions and describes the stability of graphs when vertices are removed. Assuming that the function of the network relies on the (transitive) connections between nodes,

2.7. EFFECTS ON THE STRUCTURE OF SOFTWARE IMPLEMENTATIONS

the gradual removal of vertices increases the average path length and leads to disconnected vertex pairs. In power law distributed graphs, large numbers of vertices have small degree distributions. These graphs are resistant to the random removal of edges but are vulnerable to the removal of the few highly connected vertices. Details on the stochastic properties of random and power law distributed graphs are discussed in Section 5.4.2 where the impact of this graph topology on information dissemination processes is studied.

Modular software systems can be studied with these analysis techniques [Valverde and Sole, 2003; de Moura et al., 2003; Myers, 2003; Ichii et al., 2008]. Software designs are abstracted to digraphs [Valverde and Sole, 2003]. The mapping of software structures to graphs is exemplified in Figure 2.13 (I). The elements and their directed relations in a software design, e.g. given in UML[15] notation, are abstracted in graph structures. Elements, i. e. *packages*, *classes* and *interfaces*, are abstracted to nodes and the relations between them, e.g. *aggregations*, *dependencies* and *inheritances* are mapped to directed edges. Graph representations vary, according to the interpretation of the code structures found. In the following, directed and possibly cyclic graphs (*digraphs*) composed of one node type are used to represent software systems. High outdegrees of nodes indicate code reuse by the represented artifacts and high indegrees indicate that artifacts provide complex functionalities to other elements (see e. g. [Henderson-Sellers, 1996]). The studied systems include C++ open source applications [Valverde and Sole, 2003; Myers, 2003; de Moura et al., 2003], the *Java Development Kit* (JDK) as well as Java-based applications [Potanin, 2002; Potanin et al., 2005; Wheeldon and Counsell, 2003; Baxter et al., 2006], and Smalltalk systems [Marchesi et al., 2004]. Power laws and small-world properties have been identified in the degree distributions. Particularly power laws are commonly found, but in [Ichii et al., 2008] an asymmetry between in- and outdegrees is reported. The detailed results and parameters vary due to different mappings from source codes to graph abstractions. The presence of these characteristics is explained by optimization [Valverde et al., 2002], i. e. the refactoring [Fowler et al., 1999] of large-scale applications [Myers, 2003].

In [Challet and Lombardoni, 2003; Challet and Du, 2003], this notion of network resilience is transferred to software systems, by discussing the effects of the graph structures on the exhibited *bug dynamics*. The propagation of failures of vertices is anticipated by assuming that connected vertices are negatively effected. In *optimistic* settings, only immediate neighbors are effected and in the *worst case* all connected vertices do not function properly. These examinations suggest that the structural stability of software systems can be inferred from the implementation structure [Challet and Lombardoni, 2003] and is represented by the α and κ values of degree distributions. Low values indicate stability, due the limited propagation of code changes [Challet and Lombardoni, 2003].

Corresponding abstractions can be derived for agent-oriented software systems by tracing how agent models relate to the finally executed artifacts in the implementation language [Sudeikat and Renz, 2007b]. For Jadex-based agents, the abstraction is illustrated in Figure 2.13 (II). Agent declarations reference implementation elements (see Section 2.2.2, page 17), such as the object-oriented realizations of knowledge elements that are contained in the agents' *Beliefbase*) and the executable plans (*Planbase*). The set of the declared agent-internal events (*Eventbase*) describes the possible inter-agent messages and the individual message declaration reference the objects that constitute the message contents. It is assumed that these elements describe ontology elements that are shared in the MAS (*OntologyElement*). The agents and the referenced elements are represented by vertices. The references found are mapped to directed edges.

Analysis Results

The *Structural Analysis for Java*[16] (SAfJ) application was used to retrieve the graph structures that represent software implementations in the Java programming language. SAfJ can be used to visualize the network structure of software artifacts, calculate a set of metrics, and search for undesirable node relationships, called *anti-patterns*. The *extends*, *implements*, and *uses* relations, as specified by method arguments or return values from methods, and *contains* relationships

---
[15] http://www.uml.org/
[16] freely available at http://www.alphaworks.ibm.com/tech/sa4j

38   CHAPTER 2. AGENT-ORIENTED SOFTWARE ENGINEERING

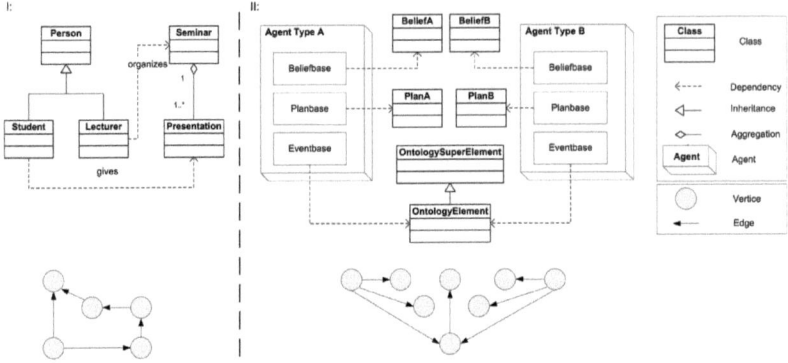

Figure 2.13: Graph-based representation of object- and agent-oriented software systems, following [Sudeikat and Renz, 2007b]

between *classes*, *interfaces*, and *packages* are considered. Four degree distributions in the resulting graphs are examined [Sudeikat and Renz, 2007b]:

- **Incoming edges (dependents)**: # of vertices that depend on a specific vertice.
- **Outgoing edges (dependencies)**: # of dependencies to other vertices.
- **Affected**: # of times a given object is affected when any other object changes.
- **Affects**: # of objects affected when a given object changes.

The first two distributions correspond to the in- and outdegree distributions as explained above. The latter two distributions measure the propagation of code changes through the implementation network. The set of classes is constrained to the application-specific implementation artifacts in order to focus on the realization of the application functionality. Thus references to programming libraries, e.g. provided by the JDK (java.*, javax.*, com.sun.*) or the agent platform (jadex.*) are ignored. The same is true for auxiliary implementation elements, i.e. exceptions, inner classes, and test classes.

The measurements of the software graphs are summarized in Table 2.1. First, the graphs that are present in three conventionally designed Java-based, open source software systems are examined. These are the Jadex system implementation (cf. section 2.2.2), the apache *Ant* framework[17], and the *Tomcat* system.[18] These are compared to MAS implementations that are based on the Jadex agent platform. These are two example applications (*Marsworld*, *Cleanerworld*) that are available with the Jadex distribution (version 0.951 beta),[19] and a student project developed at the *Distributed Systems and Information Systems* of the University of Hamburg.[20]

The first two MASs exemplify the development of Jadex-based applications in simple game settings and the aim of the student project was the development of an agent-oriented, web-based book store inspired by the case study discussed in [Padgham and Winikoff, 2004]. This system was constructed by 40 students collaborating for 14 weeks in 7 teams. The teams were responsible for developing agent type implementations, the required communication ontology and database schema.

---

[17] http://ant.apache.org
[18] http://tomcat.apache.org
[19] see: http://vsis-www.informatik.uni-hamburg.de/projects/jadex/examples.php
[20] http://vsis-www.informatik.uni-hamburg.de/teaching/ss-05/rva

2.7. EFFECTS ON THE STRUCTURE OF SOFTWARE IMPLEMENTATIONS

	Applications		
	Jadex (V 0.951 beta)	Ant (V 1.6.5)	Tomcat (V 6.0.0)
# Elements	1393	1574	1488
# Relationships	13532	12525	15503
Max. Dependencies	113	134	247
Average Dependencies	9.71	7.95	10.41
	Multi–Agent Systems		
MAS	Student Project	Marsworld	Cleanerworld
# Elements	259	34	81
# Relationships	1131	146	419
Max. Dependencies	55	17	25
Average Dependencies	4.37	4.29	5.17

Table 2.1: Summary of the studied implementation networks [Sudeikat and Renz, 2007b]

The in- and outdegree distributions found [Sudeikat and Renz, 2007b] behave comparably to prior measurements of software graphs [Myers, 2003; Baxter et al., 2006]. The exhibition of power law distributions is exemplified in Figure 2.14. These measurements are presented in log-log plots of the commutative distribution function

$$P_k = \sum_{k'=k}^{\infty} p_{k'} \qquad (2.2)$$

to accurately measure the tails of the degree distributions and reduce noise. A discussion of common complications can be found in [Newman, 2003]. The incoming degree distributions (*dependents*) of three systems, including an MAS, are plotted in Figure 2.14 (I) and can be fitted with a power law $\propto x^{-1}$ that is multiplied with a Gaussian $e^{-\frac{x^2}{2r}}$.[21] The introduced Gaussian describes the size-dependent cut-off, where the number of relations, denoted by r, scales with size squared.

Figure 2.13 (II) shows the distribution of *affected* elements, i. e. the number of times an element is affected when one element changes. The observed distributions follow power laws for small degree values. For the MAS implementations, the inferred α values ($\alpha \approx -1.68$) are notably smaller than for the object-oriented implementations (ranging from -1.08 to -1.28). The cut-off of the MAS implementations scales with the square-root of the number of relations, but it is very sharp-edged according to the few statistics available. According to the different exponents for the object-oriented systems the cut-off is shifted. The lower exponents and the sharp-edged cut-offs indicate that the number of classes that cause high sensitivity to code changes, i. e. bugs, is smaller in the MAS implementations.

Discussion/Interpretation

A qualitative difference between the system realizations originating from the design paradigms is observed. The examination of the degree distributions confirms power law observations in software systems, but the examination of the affected distribution (cf. Figure 2.14, II) suggests a structural difference between systems that follow purely object-oriented design principles and those systems that follow agent-oriented design/development techniques. This distribution describes the scaled range of elements that are sensitive to code changes. The exponents that control this range are notably smaller for the MAS implementations examined, and this indicates that the agent-oriented implementations are less sensitive.

In [Sudeikat and Renz, 2007b] it is speculated that the autonomy of agent designs causes the observed difference. Agents are conceived as autonomous actors that are responsible for specific partitions of the system functionality. Thus their implementations are conceptually separated from another and this affects the reuse of implementation artifacts. Typical sources of shared references are platform elements, which were explicitly excluded from the analysis, and the ontology elements that are exchanged via message-based communications. The results obtained suggest that the

---

[21]MAS Project: $1.2x^{-1}e^{-\frac{0.5x^2}{1131}}$, Jadex: $2.5x^{-1}e^{-\frac{0.5x^2}{13500}}$, Tomcat: $2.5x^{-1}e^{-\frac{0.5x^2}{13530}}$

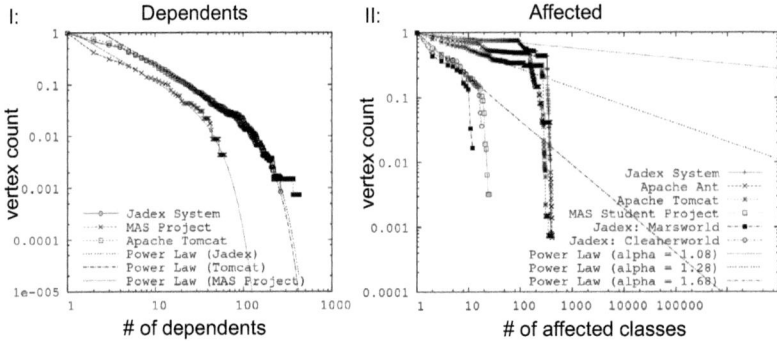

Figure 2.14: The commutative distributions of the degree of incoming edges (dependents, I) and the affected nodes (II) [Sudeikat and Renz, 2007b]

hybrid agent architectures facilitate partitioned implementation structures. The agents reference selected implementation elements and thus the implementation is composed of clusters that are connected by communication ontologies. These ontologies manifest small sets of highly referenced nodes. Due to the limited number of systems and the comparatively small size of the available agent-based system realizations, the results found are only an indication of the manifestation of structural differences by agent-oriented development practices. This relation requires further evaluation.

The analysis results confirm the inherent presence of power law distributions in software systems. It is an open research question how the characteristics of the distributions affect non-functional system properties, e.g. the robustness and maintenance, as well as how these characteristics are affected by development procedures and paradigms. Power law distributed systems are sensitive to the removal of the few highly connected nodes [Newman, 2003]. In modular software systems, it is typically intended that systems be composed of independent and interchangeable components, e.g. the *Lego Hypothesis* in [Baxter et al., 2006]. This enforces the absence of system-wide important and therefore highly connected nodes. The observation of self-similar distributions contradict the presence of atomic building blocks that contain more than one element [Baxter et al., 2006]. The examination of bug propagation in [Challet and Lombardoni, 2003] reveals another important property of power law distributed systems. Their relatively short average path length facilitates the propagation of bugs, and respectively code changes, through the graph. The sharp bend that is observed in the distributions of agent-oriented systems possibly indicates an application- or platform-dependent size of building blocks, i. e. a characteristic size of agents. This indication also needs further evaluation.

The comparison of the affected distributions suggests that an increase in the exhibited distribution exponents and/or the enforcement of cut-offs may be beneficial for the software system, as these characteristics degrade the propagation of changes/failures throughout the system. An increase of this stability is indicated in the affected distribution of agent-based systems, as these systems quickly leave the power law and follow exponential distributions (cf. Figure 2.14, II). It remains to be examined whether this behavior is indeed inherent to MASs and how MAS architectures contribute to the structural properties.

2.8 Application Areas

Originating in academic research, agent-based software systems have found applications in a wide range of areas. In this dissertation, agents are mainly discussed as an enabling technology for self-organizing systems, but the paradigm itself is a promising approach for the construction of modern distributed software systems [Jennings, 2001]. Here, three important design aspects of MAS are singled out to demonstrate the applicability of agent technology. Agent-based applications combine these principal design aspects (see Figure 2.15) in a coherent technological framework. At first MAS provide a conceptual framework and infrastructures for the development of distributed software system (*distribution*, x axis). This distribution addresses not only physically arrangements of remote agents but can also be logical concept, e.g. when agents act in a virtual environment. Both the control of the functioning and the data in the system can be distributed. Secondly, the software elements are enabled to be locally adaptive (*system-entity adaptivity*, y axis). They can reason about and adjust their local configuration based on changes in their environment. This allows software agents to serve as representatives for stakeholders and to manage subsystems in a software application. In the following chapter mechanisms and techniques for the coordination of local adaption is discussed. This is a means for creating system-level adaptiveness (see Section 3.5). Finally, the agents are *autonomous* entities (*system-entity autonomy*, z axis). They function individually as independent building blocks of the software system. This is an intuitive design stance for distributed applications in several application domains.

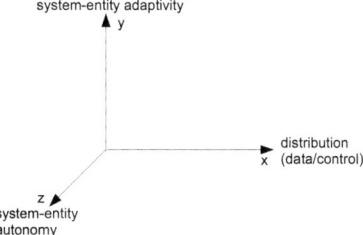

Figure 2.15: Application design aspects for agent-oriented applications; Self-Organizing application designs, discussed in Chapter 3, address system level aspects that are based on and extend these characteristics (see Figure 3.17).

The combination of these aspects is relevant for a large set of application domains. Prominent examples are distributed business-to-business e-commerce systems ([Sterling and Taveter, 2009], Chapter 8), intelligent homes ([Sterling and Taveter, 2009], Chapter 9), manufacturing logistics (e.g. [Jennings and Bussmann, 2003], [Kirn et al., 2006], Part II), and logistics/scheduling in the health-care industry ([Kirn et al., 2006], Part III). Agent technology has also been adopted in interesting niches such as film animations of large crowds[22] and spacecraft control [Truszkowski et al., 2009]. In all application domains the distribution of the system entities is evident. Most systems are physically distributed and the animation of crowds is an example for a logical distribution that structures the application by placing software entities in a *virtual* environment. In addition the software elements are required to be adaptive and autonomous. The adaptivity allows the system entities to manage local resources such as hardware and software subsystems, e.g. home appliances ([Sterling and Taveter, 2009], page 13) or manufacturing lines [Jennings and Bussmann, 2003]. The autonomy is necessary as the system elements have to function when communications are delayed or interrupted.

The integration of self-organizing features extends these aspects (see Section 3.5). Systems are not only distributed but their *decentralized* management is enabled. Also the autonomy and

---
[22] http://www.massivesoftware.com/

adaptiveness of the system elements are elevated. Here, the characteristics describe the individual system elements. The systems that are discussed in the following chapter show autonomy and adaptiveness also on the *system level* and not only on the level of the individual agents (see Figure 3.17). The usage of self-organization can be seen as an extension to current MAS development practices. The integration of self-organizing features into MAS is discussed in Part II.

2.9 Conclusions

In this chapter, the agent-oriented development of distributed software systems is discussed and major development concepts and techniques for the software technological realization of agent-based applications are outlined. Agent-orientation is introduced as a novel development paradigm that distinguishes itself from other development stances, since software systems are assembled as collectives of autonomous and pro-active actors. The inherent autonomy has far-reaching consequences for development practices. Development efforts are based on dedicated middleware infrastructures that provide the execution environment for these activated software components. In addition, modeling and design practices are revised to express the concepts that manifest the agency of software elements. Initial results also indicate that structural properties of the underlying software implementation are affected by the use of this novel development stance.

Agent-orientation provides a versatile development approach for distributed systems that allows a life-like intuitive modeling of applications as collectives of interactive actors. The coordination of the activities of these actors is a crucial development concern.

Chapter 3
Self-Organization: A Software Perspective

Self-organization is a ubiquitous phenomenon in nature [Kauffman, 1996] that describes the decentralized formation and maintenance, when perturbed, of system level structures. These structures arise from the coaction of autonomous system entities. When this phenomenon is applied to software, the system entities, hereafter called software agents, are not required to reason about an explicit blueprint of the overall structure, but rather structures emerge from concurrent, localized operations and interactions. Applications are based on the mapping of structure formations to computational problems. The use of self-organizing dynamics is attractive for the construction of distributed software systems as it is an effective means for the decentralized coordination of system elements.

Due to the inherent autonomy of agents, agent-based software systems are suited to show self-organizing phenomena. These systems provide the basic building blocks, namely autonomous, interactive system components and their embedding in shared environments. Agent-based systems are a technological foundation for the construction of self-organizing applications. However, these phenomena can also result unexpectedly from application designs and can be detrimental for the operation of an application. Thus it is indispensable for MAS development practices to be able to treat these phenomena on a systematic basis, either to enforce them or to prevent their occurrence.

In this chapter the relevance of self-organizing dynamics for the development of distributed, particularly agent-oriented, software systems is discussed. The inherent ability of MASs to show these phenomena is justified and the current practices for the analysis and synthesis are reviewed. This chapter discusses conceptual models for self-organizing, agent-based applications and the building blocks of the inter-agent processes that effectuate self-organizing dynamics. In addition, the necessity for multi-level modeling techniques is argued and further developed to a redesign technique for MASs that guides their purposeful adjustment to fine-tune self-organized system properties.

3.1 Self-Organization in Software

Self-organization is a concept that originates in the study of natural systems [Haken, 2006]. There are a multiplicity of descriptions and and definitions of this term. Here, these concepts are reviewed with respect to computational systems, particularly as a distinct (software) engineering discipline.

3.1.1 Self-Organization

A historic review of the concept can be found in [Shalizi, 2001], where the origins are traced back to Descartes. In several works, e.g. [Prokopenko, 2008a] (page V), the first use of the term *self-organizing* in the scientific literature of the last century is attributed to [Ashby, 1947]. The concept of self-organization became an established notion for the description of collective phenomena in natural, i.e. physical, biological and social, systems. In these phenomena, *organization*, i.e. structure formations, arises from the local interactions of autonomous system elements, e.g. particles, cells, agents, etc., without external intervention (*self*). While the formalization of this concept is a research topic, the phenomenology of self-organizing phenomena is widely agreed upon [Polani, 2008] and is studied in a range of research fields. Examples are found in *biology*, e.g. in social insect colonies [Bonabeau et al., 1999] and pattern formations [Camazine, 2006], in physics, e.g. in lasers, where the interactions of atoms lead to the coherent emission of laser waves [Haken, 2006], and social systems, such as the collaborations of movie actors [Watts and Strogatz, 1998].

Several definitions have been given, as reviewed in [Anderson, 2002]. Following [Prokopenko, 2008b], the basic properties of self-organizing systems are described informally, based on two prominent definitions. First, the concept describes that the systems show the formation of structures by themselves. Thus it is stated in [Haken, 2006] (page 11):

> ... a system is self-organizing if it acquires a spatial, temporal or functional structure without specific interference from the outside.

The *specific interference* refers to any type of external *control* that may be imposed. However, the system is subject to non-specific influences from its context. These influences can effectuate the (re)structuring as systems adjust themselves to their context but do not govern the structuring. Instead the interactions within the system lead to the structure formation. Therefore, the control of the formation is distributed among the interacting elements. It is a (collaborative) *process* among the elements, e.g. as pointed out by in [Camazine et al., 2001] (page 8), against the background of biological self-organizing systems:

> Self-organization is a process in which pattern at the global level of a system emerges solely from numerous interactions among the lower-level components of the system. Moreover, the rules specifying interactions among the system's components are executed using only local information, without reference to the global pattern.

Due to the collaboration, the control is shared among the system elements. In addition, the *information* used for the control is shared as well. These entities interact to *dynamically* establish order, i.e. the system is gradually structured. These structures are manifested at the system level and result solely from the activities of system elements. The arising structures are (1) not imposed by external authorities, (2) not controlled by a subset of system elements, and (3) not directly encoded in the system entities. The absence of external authorities means that the system operates autonomously and exhibits the collaborative process. These processes can respond to external influences, e.g. changes in the environment, but the collaboration of agents steers the structure formation. In addition, all agents participate in the forming process. Due to the shared control, the system is resilient to failures, as dedicated managing entities could be points of failure and bottlenecks. The individual elements possess and exchange only local information, not information about the global configuration of the surrounding system. Finally, agents are not bound to explicit prescriptions of the arising structure, e.g. see [Herrmann et al., 2006]. A consequence of this collaborative structuring is that the rise of formations can only be explained by the coaction of the system elements. Rather it is a *collective phenomenon* and the analysis of the participating agents supports only limited conclusions on the system-wide behavior.

Common properties of systems that show self-organization are discussed in [Prokopenko, 2008b; Herrmann et al., 2006; DeWolf and Holvoet, 2004]. These systems are composed of a *multitude* of *interacting* components. The capabilities of these elements are limited with respect to the global system proprieties that are established. Self-organization makes use of redundancies in the system. The participating agents are typically similar or only a limited number of different types is present. This redundancy allows similar activities to be carried out in parallel and makes the system resilient to individual failures. The responsibility and functions of erroneous entities can be taken over by other entities.

When transferred to software systems, self-organization finds expression in three phenomenological properties. The key characteristics are *system-level adaptivity, structure creation and main-*

3.1. SELF-ORGANIZATION IN SOFTWARE

tenance, and a *decentralized operating principle* [Mühl et al., 2007; Herrmann et al., 2006] (see Figure 3.1). These properties neglect system-internal operating principles and this combination signifies the presence of self-organizing processes. A corresponding procedure for identifying self-organizing software systems is given in [Herrmann et al., 2006]. That a system is self-organizing can be validated by (1) deriving a succinct representation of the fundamental system elements, (2) showing the adaptivity of the collective of elements, (3) showing that the adaptivity results from structural changes, and (4) showing the absence of centralized control.

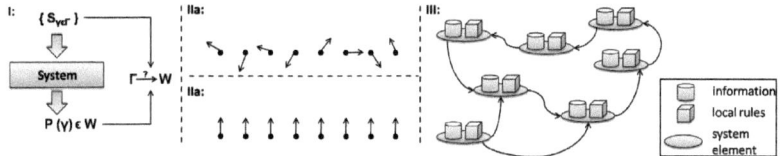

Figure 3.1: The phenomenological properties of self-organizing software systems. I: Adaptivity, adapted from [Herrmann et al., 2006], IIa, IIb: Increase in order, following [Haken, 2004], III: decentralization of information and control.

Self-organization is used to bring about *adaptive* features in software systems. An instructive description of this system property is the definition from [Zadeh, 1963] that follows a black box approach (see Figure 3.1, I). The *system* is exposed to a set of families of time-dependent input functions ($\{S_\gamma\}$). Each family of functions (S_γ) contains a set of functions that represent the (possibly stochastic) system context or the timely changes in this context. The contained functions describe a vector of external inputs, which emulate control inputs as well as environment properties, at any given time point. The performance of the system, faced with one family of input functions, is given by the function $P(\gamma)$. An acceptability criterion is given by $P(\gamma) \in W$, where W is a class of functions that describe acceptable performances. The changes in a concrete system context are given by a relation $\gamma \in \Gamma$. Γ is a set of, possibly statistical distributed, γ values. Based on these definitions the adaptivity is expressed as a mapping of a given Γ to a given W (see [Zadeh, 1963], page 470). This definition stresses that the system responds to changes in its context. Adaptivity is given when the responses match the context changes in expected ways.

Secondly, the system creates *structures* and maintains them. This is pictured in Figure 3.1 (IIa,b), taking the example of ferromagnets (see [Haken, 2004], page 3). These can be understood as a collection of atomic magnets, i.e. *spins*, to explain the temperature-dependence of the shown magnetization. At higher temperatures the collective loses its magnetization because the individual spins point in various (random) directions (IIa). The local magnetizations neutralize each other and no global magnetic field is established. At lower temperatures the spins are aligned and sum up to a coherent field (IIb). Both states are *phases* of the material, and a *critical* temperature (T_c) marks the *phase transition*. A popular approach for describing organization and their changes is to use information-theoretic concepts, i.e. *entropy* [Herrmann et al., 2006; Polani, 2008]. The entropy of a system is a measure of the disorder, e.g. see [Haken, 2004] (page 14). The adoption of this concept and the efforts required to describe self-organization are described in [Polani, 2008; Mnif and Müller-Schloer, 2006]. An alternative approach is to understand a system organization as a network of relationships [Brueckner and Czap, 2006]. Due to the diversity of conceptions, this dissertation describes the rising structures and their dynamics informally at the application level using application domain concepts.

The decentralization of the control of the structure formation (see Figure 3.1, III) is inherent in self-organizing systems [Brueckner and Czap, 2006; Heylighen, 2003; Serugendo et al., 2006]. The control of the structure formation is shared by all system elements. If the responsibility were attributed to a subset of system elements, their (hypothetical) removal would eliminate the system's ability to structure itself. This feature is attractive in engineering contexts, as the decentralization implies resilience to failures of individual agents. When facing failures, the ability to structure and the efficiency of the process degrades gradually.

A closely related concept is the *emergence* of structures. It describes the presence of higher-level constructs, generated and maintained by the coaction of system elements. These constructs are clearly distinguishable artifacts that exist on a higher system level. Like self-organization, emergence is an interdisciplinary research topic. With respect to MASs, the distinction between emergence and self-organization is discussed in [DeWolf and Holvoet, 2004] and a working definition is given (page 98):

> A system exhibits emergence when there are coherent emergents at the macro-level that dynamically arise from the interactions between the parts at the micro-level. Such emergents are novel w.r.t. the individual parts of the system.

This definition points out that emergents are high(er)-level system entities that result from the agent coaction. The novelty refers to the fact that the system elements have no explicit representation of the emergents, but rather that they result from the dynamical coaction.

In this dissertation an engineering-oriented viewpoint from [Parunak and Brueckner, 2004] is adopted. Emergent phenomena are understood as a *subcategory* of self-organizing phenomena (see page 347). This practical notion distinguishes the rising structures by the level of their manifestation. Self-organization is a structuring of agents and the elements in their sphere of influence. Examples are spatial formations of agents or the formation of coalitions. Emergents are structures that find manifestations on a higher abstraction level and can be analyzed separately. These are structures that find an independent existence and show individual properties and dynamics that are independent from the lover-level elements. An example is the formation of traffic jams [Resnik, 1997] (page 140), which result from the slowing down of cars. These move against the driving direction and therefore are discriminable artifacts that show their own dynamics. Section 3.4.2 shows that the individual trans-locations of environment elements by agents lead to coherent aggregations, i.e. clusters, that show individual dynamics, e.g. clusters can converge [Sudeikat and Renz, 2006].

This viewpoint implies that self-organization can be used to construct and maintain emergent properties. While emergent properties can be present independently from self-organization, as is argued in [DeWolf and Holvoet, 2004], self-organization can be used to construct emergent structures and the dynamics of these emergents are then also governed by the collaborative process, i.e. the self-organization, that is responsible for their creation and maintenance [Renz and Sudeikat, 2006] (see Section 3.4.1, page 70).

This dissertation concerns the construction of self-organization. The means for building these systems are the collaborative processes that give rise to and maintain structures. These structures can be used to organize the system level elements or control emergent phenomena. In the remainder of this chapter, these types are not distinguished, but rather the structure formation itself is modeled, designed, and integrated in software systems.

3.1.2 Self-Managing & Self-Adaptive Software Architectures

The imperative necessity to enable run-time adjustments in software systems is addressed by a broad research community. These works offer alternative techniques to self-organization that can be used to build distributed adaptive software systems. Here, these research efforts are not extensively reviewed, but important directions are outlined to indicate the conceptual alternatives for constructing adaptive distributed software systems. Detailed reviews can be found in [Salehie and Tahvildari, 2009; Huebscher and McCann, 2008].

A set of terminologies is used to describe the common vision of software systems being enabled to adjust themselves at run-time. Most prominently, these systems are described as being *self-adaptive* [Salehie and Tahvildari, 2009], *autonomic* [Kephart and Chess, 2003] or *self-managing* [Mühl et al., 2007] (following [Salehie and Tahvildari, 2009]). While these terms refer to a shared objective, the types and ranges of addressed adaptiveness vary. It is pointed out in [Salehie and Tahvildari, 2009] (page 4) that self-adaptivity is mainly concerned with the management of elements in application and middleware layers and the autonomic computing has a broader scope

3.1. SELF-ORGANIZATION IN SOFTWARE

as it also concerns the lower level functionalities of network layers and the underlying operating systems.

Self-adaptive systems embody a control loop [Salehie and Tahvildari, 2009]. The software system is *monitored* and situations are *detected* that require adjustments. Then appropriate exertions of influence are *decided* and (en)*acted*. Control loops are revisited in Section 3.1.4. A common approach is to support the execution of this control loop in a *managing* software artifact. A range of architectural styles and corresponding frameworks for these managers are available. The significance of these models is the support of the reuse of adaptation techniques. One successful strategy is the use of architecture-based self-adaptations [Garlan et al., 2004]. The management is controlled by a separate architectural model of the managed software system that facilitates the computation of valid adjustments.

An influential initiative is the *autonomic computing* [IBM, 2001; Kephart and Chess, 2003]. Driven by IBM, this initiative addresses the enabling of systems self-management. The term autonomic refers to biological systems, e.g. the *autonomic nervous system* that controls vital activities such as the heart rate [Kephart and Chess, 2003]. However, the initiative is not fixed on this source of inspiration but provides a generic set of adaptivity attributes, i.e. self-* properties (see Section 3.1.3) and a general-purpose model for management control. The managed system is composed of *autonomic elements*. These are subsystems or system elements that are managed by one *autonomic manager*. The contained system elements are ordinary software elements except for the preparation that they are monitored and controlled by the manager. A reference model for the management logic inside the managers is the *MAPE-K* model (*Monitor,Analyse, Plan, Execute, Knowledge*) [Huebscher and McCann, 2008] and implementations of this loop are described in [Huebscher and McCann, 2008]. Within this initiative, the applicability of agent technology is recognized [Kephart, 2005] and autonomic elements can be equated to software agents [Tesauro et al., 2004].

In addition, to the integration of specific interfaces, which enable the management by remote system entities, management can also be based on influencing the execution of system elements on the programming language level, e.g. the program execution. In [Baresi et al., 2008], a distributed approach for the supplementation of self-adaptivity is discussed. So-called *probes* are augmented to system elements and use aspect-oriented techniques to sense and influence the execution of the entity-internal business logic. The augmented system components are partitioned in *clusters*, and each cluster is controlled by a special-purpose component, the *Supervisor*, that implements a control loop to governs the adjustments of subordinate entities. Supervisors are informed about the local processing by probes and inform probes about the changes to be made. Changes are enacted synchronously, i.e. the entity operation is interrupted until control information has been given by the corresponding Supervisor, or asynchronously, i.e. the entity operations are interrupted to send information and modifications are made when they arrive. Supervisors themselves are arranged in *federations* that support the information exchange among supervisors. Using this model, cluster-wide and federation-wide adaptations can be enacted, and the governing control loop is configured by a combination of a declarative configuration language and procedural specifications.

A related research initiative is *organic computing* [Branke et al., 2006]. It shares the biological connotation that software systems are equipped with life-like, i.e. organic, properties. A vision of this initiative is that the inclusion of manging entities is a means for enabling *controlled self-organization* [Branke et al., 2006] and *controlled emergence* [Müller-Schloer, 2004]. This ambitious vision contains fundamental challenges, such as the detection of emergent system level features [Mnif and Müller-Schloer, 2006]. The key design element is the *observer/controller* architecture that is responsible for managing a *system under observation and control* (SuOC) [Richter et al., 2006]. These elements observe the operation of the SuOC and deduce when interferences are required. As their name suggests, their internal structuring distinguishes between *observer* and the *control* aspects. Sub-aspects of the observer partition are monitoring, pre-processing, data analysis, prediction and data aggregation. This list indicates the complexity of the reasoning about the system behavior. The controller aspect is mainly addressed by a adaptation module that contains the planning and learning abilities [Branke et al., 2006]. Additional segments are an optional simulation model, the user-specified objectives, the evaluation of the actions based on local histories, and the selection of actions. Architectural strategies are: (1) equipping a system with one controller/observer (*central*), (2) *decentral* arrangements, where each system element is controlled by separate controller/observer, and (3) a *multi-level* structure in which each element is locally managed by a controller/observer and the collective of controller/observers at one abstraction level is itself managed by a superior controller/observer [Branke et al., 2006].

Apart from the architectural and technological concerns, the systematic development of organic systems is a crucial challenge itself. One approach is pattern-based development, as approached by the *Organic Design Pattern* (ODP) [Seebach et al., 2007]. This pattern provides a generic software design and particularly suits one type of distributed system (*resource flow systems*) [Steghöfer et al., 2010]. The system development is supported by a framework [Nafz et al., 2009b] based on the agent middleware that is presented in Section 2.2.2. This pattern and the addressed application domain are detailed in Section 6.8.1.

3.1.3 Manifestations of Self-organization in Software Systems

The use of self-organization is attractive for software engineers as it makes adaptivity, robustness and scalability possible [Prokopenko, 2008b]. With respect to dynamic software landscapes and execution contexts the adaptivity of software systems is a major research concern (see Section 3.1.2). The adaptive system features, i.e. self-* properties, can be structured in a hierarchy (see Figure 3.2) that is composed of three abstraction levels [Salehie and Tahvildari, 2009]. The lowest level (*Primitive Level*) contains enabling mechanisms. Examples are the awareness of (1) the system state(s) (*self-awareness*) and (2) the execution environment (*context-awareness*). Obtaining this information is a prerequisite for realizing the adaptive features that are contained in the super-adjacent *Major Level*. According to [Salehie and Tahvildari, 2009], these features correspond to the four basic self-* features that were defined in the autonomic computing initiative [Kephart and Chess, 2003], namely the ability to show *self-configuring*, *self-healing*, *self-optimizing*, *self-protecting* behaviors. These abilities ground the features of the *General Level*, which fall into two categories. *Self-Adaptiveness* represents the most abstract system properties that enable the autonomous operation of computing systems and infrastructures. Examples are *self-managing*, *self-governing* and *self-maintenance*. The second category are *self-organizing* features. These are based on decentralized system structures and are an alternative approach to the establishment of system-level adaptiveness [Salehie and Tahvildari, 2009].

Self-organization allows adaptive properties to be integrated by the decentralized control of local adjustments of agents. The required computations are evenly distributed among the agents and this distribution implies several attractive features, most notably robustness and scalability [Prokopenko, 2008b]. The absence of managing entities removes possible sources of bottlenecks and single points of failures. Self-organization principles enforce that system elements are prepared to provide different functionalities and select their current provision(s) at run-time. This *redundancy* supports robustness as the effects of individual system elements are minimized. Other system elements are prepared, and decide by themselves, to replace deficient elements, thus systems continue to function. A common feature is that the possibility of disastrous crashes is minimized and replaced by localized failures that imply a gradual loss in performance [Prokopenko, 2008b]. When these systems are extended, the introduction of new components is not necessarily preplanned but these can integrate themselves.

Limitations and Complications

The adoption of self-organization principles in industry implies inevitable limitations and hindrances. The limitations originate from the decentralization of the problem solving strategy. Thus the need for decentralization, imposed by the application domain or a demand for the absence of single points of failures, has to be justified when taking the use of self-organization into consideration. Self-organizing algorithms are typically associated with near-optimum solutions [DeWolf et al., 2004]. The distribution of computations and information among system elements affects the performance of the structuring and centralized solution strategies may outperform decentral-

3.1. SELF-ORGANIZATION IN SOFTWARE

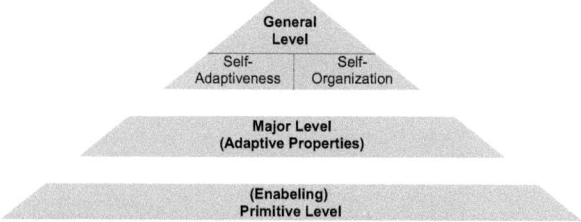

Figure 3.2: A hierarchy of adaptive system properties (self-*), adapted from [Salehie and Tahvildari, 2009]

ized techniques. The decentralization of computations also implies the multitudes of interactions among the distributed agents. This poses an inevitable communication overhead that may by prohibitive, due to limitations of the available communication infrastructures [Prokopenko, 2008b]. Another effect of distribution is the embedding of local background processing inside agents. Besides functional aspects, the coordination-related activities, e.g. when to initiate, participate, and reason about interactions, are also embedded. Thus parts of the control flow within agents are blended with these activities. The sharing of the computational resources with these supplementary activities can be avoided when reconfigurations are externally imposed. The outplacement of the required processing may be an architectonic means for relieving system components (e.g. [Serugendo et al., 2008b]), but also contributes to the communication overhead that is necessary for the distributed observation and control of system elements.

Hindrances to the adoption of self-organization pertain to their use in engineering disciplines. First, levels of control are handed over to the collective effects among system elements and these outputs are inherently non-deterministic. For example in [di Nitto et al., 2009] the stochasticity of nature-inspired problem solving strategies is summarized (page 70, emphasis taken from the original):

> When we use bio-inspired algorithms our question is no longer *when they actually work*, but *what the probability that they work is*.

The ability to explore the configurations' space and autonomously establish patterns is a feature of self-organizing systems but burdens engineering techniques as verifications are impaired [Prokopenko, 2008b] (approaches discussed in Section 4.1.2). The properties of the structuring processes, e.g. time-constraints or performance measurements, can only be given in stochastic terms (e.g. [di Nitto et al., 2009]).

Finally, the self-organization of a system deviates from incremental development approaches that are applied in industry [Prokopenko, 2008b]. The centralization of the problem solving process in managing entities supports engineering practices. That the management algorithm is encoded in a single software artifact or a hierarchy of artifacts facilitates its specification [Nafz et al., 2009a] and integration [Seebach et al., 2007]. For the purely decentralized self-organization, the solution strategy is distributed among all agents. The ability of a system to solve the given problem has to be shown with an appropriate representation of the system components, e.g. via system simulation [Casadei et al., 2007], but can not be inferred from the individual system elements. Approaches to engineering the intended dynamics are discussed in Section 3.2, but it has been argued that the construction of software systems solely on the basis of self-organization is not applicable for industry settings [Prokopenko, 2008b]. The conception of a self-organization process requires to view the problem in its entirety. The partitioning of the self-organizing process is is infeasible — the coaction of the agents is responsible to bring about the overall system dynamics. This contradicts incremental development practices that are applied in industrial settings.

Alternatives are *composite* approaches where traditionally designed systems are supplemented with self-organizing aspects. These demand engineering techniques that allow self-organization in dedicated components to be outsourced, separated, and encapsulated [Prokopenko, 2008b]. The Hypotheses 1.3 and 1.4 reference this complication, i.e. the need for a conceptual separation of the self-organization. The separation of the processes as independent design elements allows to supplement these to existing applications (Hypothesis 1.4, page 5). Consequently, system elements can be engineered in established ways and the inter-agent process is supplemented to the compound system. The self-organization is one part of the application development and used to control specific system aspects or subsystems. An example for this supplementation is given in Section 6.8.2. A conventional software system is supplemented with an orthogonal architecture that manages self-organizing features. A related aspect is the separation of the process configuration from the system implementation (Hypothesis 1.3, page 5). This facilitates incremental development since the process execution by itself can be adjusted and/or modified.

Unintended Phenomena

Observations of unintended, damaging phenomena that result from the coaction of elements in computational systems have been reported, e.g. in [Parunak and VanderBok, 1997; Mogul, 2005]. In [Mogul, 2005], these *emergent misbehaviors* are categorized with respect to distributed software systems:

- **Thrashing** is caused by the competition for resources. When the cost of accessing and/or switching resources is unproportional, the systems operation is handicapped. An increase of resources can intensify the problematic behavior and consequently scale down the systems performance [Mogul, 2005].

- **Unwanted Synchronization** describes settings where time dependent aspects, e.g. elements configurations, states, activities etc., synchronize undesignedly. These synchronisms may overwhelm system infrastructures, e.g. supplies of communication bandwidth or power supply, which are dimensioned for moderate utilizations, e.g. see [Parunak and VanderBok, 1997].

- **Unwanted oscillation or periodicity** describes the continuous, periodical synchronization of time-dependent aspects of the system elements. An example is the periodic activation/deactivation of spot-welding robots that is studied in [Parunak and VanderBok, 1997].

- A **Deadlock** results from circular dependencies of system elements. Each system element, taken by itself, functions correctly but in combination, the (inter-)dependencies among system elements force sets of elements to wait for each other in order to proceed with their individual operating sequences. Thus partitions of the overall system come to a halt [van Steen and Tanenbaum, 2002].

- A **Livelock** describes that increases in the inputs of a system, e.g. the request rates, cause decreases of the throughput, due to resource starvations [Mogul, 2005]. Assuming that a subset of system elements is required to perform the system's function, the resource consumption of high-priority elements starves other elements that, despite their lower priority, are necessary to finish certain activities. Thus sets of underserved elements limit the systems operation.

- **Phase change** denotes sudden, radical changes in the behavior or configuration of a system that is controlled by a specific parameter. When the parameter exceeds a certain threshold, the behavior of the system is radically affected. These phenomena are well studied in physics, e.g. when substances change their aggregate states, and similar observations for these transitions in MASs have been reported, e.g. in [Parunak et al., 2004b] in simulation models for resource allocation problems.

3.1. SELF-ORGANIZATION IN SOFTWARE

- **Chaotic Behavior** refers to an extreme sensitivity of a deterministic system to its initial conditions [Strogatz, 2001]. Minor deviations in the starting conditions lead to drastic changes in the resulting system behavior.

In [Parunak and VanderBok, 1997], concrete strategies for handling these effects in engineered systems are given. Faced with an obstructive system behavior caused by the coaction of system elements, the basic options are to (1) remove causative non-linearities from the system, given that the cause lies with in the design scope of the system and is not an immanent property of the application context. Alternatively (2), a centralized control can be imposed (cf. Section 3.1.2). According to [Parunak and VanderBok, 1997], the economic benefits of decentralized architectures are overwhelming. Another approach is to (3) limit the effects of non-linearities by reducing the system workload. From an engineering perspective this is unsatisfactory as the efficiency is affected. Thus it is concluded that the use of (4) agent-based coordination techniques, as discussed in Section 2.5, is indicated as a means to counteract the identified collective misbehaviors.

3.1.4 The Fundamental Design Element: *Distributed* Feedback

Equipping software systems with adaptive features requires the integration of feedback loops. In software systems, feedback can be present in two distinct forms. Architectures and frameworks for the self-managed systems enact feedbacks as *control loops* and in a self-organizing system the governing feedback(s) are distributed among the system elements [Brun et al., 2009].

Self-management by Control Loops

The architectures (e.g. [Richter et al., 2006]), design patterns (e.g. [Seebach et al., 2007]), and frameworks (e.g. reviewed in [Huebscher and McCann, 2008]) for the development of self-managing systems (see Section 3.1.2) support the insertion of dedicated system entities that are responsible for the management of (sub)sets of system elements. Networked arrangements of managing elements enable distributed system architecture as well as the ability to constitute hierarchies of management (for a survey see [Huebscher and McCann, 2008]). The inevitability of feedbacks for the conception of adaptive systems is well-understood and the necessity to make these feedbacks explicit in development efforts has been argued in [Müller et al., 2008]. The basic activities for the automation of control are illustrated in Figure 3.3 (I)[1] [Dobson et al., 2006]. The *collection* of data prepares the management, as information about (1) the managed system entities, (2) the contexts of the system, e.g. the environment, and (3) the requirements and/or objectives of the system are gathered. The *analysis* of the information leads to a model of the situation toward which the system is moving. Based on this model, *decisions* are computed and consequently enacted. The effects of the adjustments are perceived by the subsequent collecting of information, thus the control loop is closed. This kind of feedback is embedded within the managing entities.

A fundamental challenge is the integration of feedback design techniques into software engineering practices. In [Brun et al., 2009] the means to use feedback for building self-adaptive software systems are reviewed. The discussion focuses on the architectonic means that are available to integrate feedbacks in software systems. It is also argued that the lack of modeling techniques for the explicit documentation of feedbacks in standard software engineering contexts is limiting their systematic use, e.g. the design, analysis, and validation (page 57), in software development. Consequently, the systematic design of feedbacks in software is a research challenge. The transfer of *control theory* concepts to designing software systems is discussed in [Hellerstein et al., 2004]. It is shown how control theory can be used to control computational systems. Form these works it becomes apparent that the construction of the software and the control of the run.-time adaptivity are two separate engineering aspects that are addressed by different tool sets and development practices. This implicit separation is reflected in the Hypotheses 1.3 (page 5) and 1.4 (page 5). The implicit technological separation finds expression in development practices.

---

[1] This is an abridged chart. In [Dobson et al., 2006], the sample actions and activities are annotated to the four generic activities.

Self-Organization by Distributed Feedback

Different authors examine the sources of self-organized and emergent behaviors. Taking the example of manufacturing systems, occurrences of collective system phenomena are attributed to *capacity limits*, (temporal) *delays*, and *feedback loops* in [Parunak and VanderBok, 1997]. The computational system is understood as a coupled set of software components. Non-linearities in the couplings can result from capacity limits as these force system elements to wait. Dependent system elements are consequently effected. Filled/empty buffers that affect the elements which place/draw items serve as an example. Delays in material flows have comparable effects. Feedback loops describe mutual, circular interdependencies among system elements. These are explicitly encoded in the control flow or result from the deployment context of the system.

Swarm Intelligence approaches the use of nature-inspired self-organizing processes [Bonabeau et al., 1999]. The collective behaviors of insect colonies are recreated to solve computational problems. With respect to this field four foundational constituents of a self-organizing mechanism were identified. These are *positive feedback*, *negative feedback*, the *amplification of fluctuations*, and *multiple interactions* [Bonabeau et al., 1999] (Chapter 1). The type of feedback is distinguished by its effect on the system entities.

Positive feedbacks signify amplifications of system aspects and generate structures. The authors describe the recruitment in honey bee societies [Bonabeau et al., 1999] (page 9) as an example. One activity in a bee society is to forage for resources and transport food to the nest. Bees are able to communicate the direction and distance to found sources via *waggle dances*. These advertisements attract other bees to join the exploitation of a resource site. Thus the dances, which cause local adjustments of agent behaviors, are a mechanism for establishing a positive feedback that amplifies the number of recruited bees. Additional mechanisms are required to steer which amplifications are appropriate. In the bee scenario, this is exemplified by a relatively higher probability to communicate the presence of good food sources, thus agents are drawn to exploit restrictively better resources.

Negative feedbacks lead to the stabilizations of structures and counteract positive feedbacks. Examples are saturation and obliteration effects that contain the impact of positive feedbacks. For the bee scenario, the availability of bees and resources in the environment are among the limiting factors.

The enforcement of fluctuations allows the system to explore different configurations. Positive/negative feedbacks steer the establishment of structures, so to speak fixed points in a space of possible system configurations. Since these configurations may be suboptimal, allowing for randomness and perturbations lets the system re-organize to explore novel solutions and structures. In [Bonabeau et al., 1999], fluctuations are compared to *seeds* which initiate the rise of structures.

Finally, agents are to be enabled to participate in different types of interactions. A prominent mechanism is digital pheromones [Parunak and Brueckner, 2004], i.e. imitations of chemical messenger substances, that enable agents to perceive and the activities of other agents to their advantage. In [Bonabeau et al., 1999], this is exemplified by the trail formation in ant colonies. Agents that transport resources mark their way to the home nest with pheromones that diffuse in the environment and attract other ants. Thus agents make use of prior discoveries of others and are guided to nearby resource locations.

The described feedbacks govern the operation of a system of autonomous entities but result from the mutual influences and interactions among system elements that have equal rights. This type of feedback is illustrated in Figure 3.3 (II) in order to compare it to and distinguish it from control loop structures. Multitudes of system elements influence each other and a subset of these influences forms a circular structure. In this subset, changes feed back to the participating system elements as influences propagate through the system. The mechanisms that are available to embed feedbacks are reviewed in Section 3.2.1 [Sudeikat and Renz, 2008a].

3.1. SELF-ORGANIZATION IN SOFTWARE

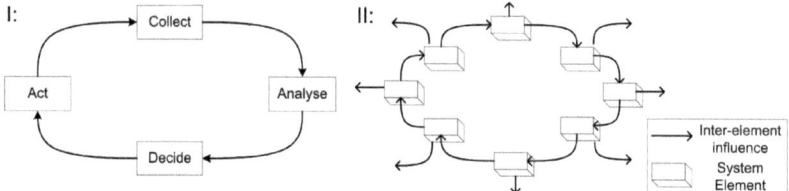

Figure 3.3: Illustrations of a generic autonomic control loop (I), adapted from [Dobson et al., 2006], and a distributed feedback among autonomous system elements (II)

3.1.5 The Relevance of Self-Organization for Multi-Agent Systems

Agent-based modeling is a widespread technique for analyzing of complex systems. Using agents as a modeling abstraction, natural phenomena, which arise from the coaction of autonomous system entities, can be emulated *in vitro*. A serious implication is the potential that these system phenomena occur, intended or not, in agent-based software systems.

Agent-based Modeling and Simulation

Agent-based modeling is a major tool for the study of self-organizing and emergent phenomena (e.g. see [Resnik, 1997; Schut, 2007]). An introduction to agent-based modeling is given in [North and Macal, 2007]. In [Schut, 2007], agent-based simulation techniques for the analysis of collective phenomena, called *Collective Intelligence*, are discussed given and simulation tools/frameworks are summarized. Also in the initial works of this dissertation, agent-based simulations are used to model and analyze self-organizing dynamics. These case studies (see Sections 4.3.4, 4.4.2) use the freely available *NetLogo*[2] simulation framework [Tisue and Wilensky, 2004]. This framework is based on a simple programming model where agents are located in a virtual environment. The framework particularly supports the use of *digital pheromones* [Parunak and Brueckner, 2004] (see Section 3.2.1), i.e. artificial scents that propagate in the environment. The framework can be used to link prescriptions of agents with a graphical user interface that provides a means for to control the execution and observation of simulations. In addition, it provides a modeling component that allows Stock-and-Flow diagrams to be drawn, parameterized and executed.[3] This diagram type is introduced in Section 4.2.1.

The Immanent Potential for Collective Phenomena in MASs

The inherent congruence between agent-based and complex systems has been used to argue the benefits of agent-oriented development practices. In [Jennings, 2001], the canonical structure of an MAS (see Figure 2.1) is compared to the structure of *complex systems*, based on the discussion in [Booch, 1994] (chapter 1), where these systems are characterized as networks of interrelated subsystems, as found in living creatures, the physical structures of matter and social institutions. This congruence justifies the appropriateness of agent-oriented application designs.

The indisputable expressiveness of agent-oriented software architectures is a major feature but also raises serious concerns for engineering these software systems. The rise of complex system behaviors, e.g. self-organized and emergent phenomena, have been observed [Parunak et al., 2004b; Edmonds and Norling, 2006]. These phenomena arise from the interactions of system elements and typically cannot be straightforwardly inferred from the designs of the agents models. While these phenomena have been observed in software systems, agent-based models emulate these

---
[2] http://ccl.northwestern.edu/netlogo/
[3] http://ccl.northwestern.edu/netlogo/docs/systemdynamics.html

systems more accurately and therefore the rise of complex phenomena is enforced. Consequently, application developers are faced with the challenge of handling these phenomena.

In [Henderson-Sellers and Giorgini, 2005] (page 4), the ability to show complex system behaviors such as emergence, is identified and the resulting challenge for systematic development processes is stated:

> ... To alleviate this concern of an uncontrolled and uncontrollable agent system wreaking havoc, clearly emergent behaviour has to be considered and planned for at the systems level using top-down analysis and design techniques. This is still an area that is largely unknown in MAS methodologies. ...

In this context, the rise of system properties is considered a desirable feature of MASs, but the need to control the coaction of system elements is identified. Compared to the considerable amount of research effort that pertains to the engineering of MASs, only a small subset, e.g. [Bernon et al., 2005a], considers the rise of macroscopic system properties. Constructively, agent technology is a conceptual foundation for the development of self-organizing applications. Destructively, the rise of unintended emergent properties is a threat to agent-based applications (see Section 3.1.3) and needs to be addressed systematically to reinforce the recognition of agent technology as an engineering discipline. In the remainder of this chapter, corresponding engineering techniques are discussed.

3.1.6 The Relevance of Self-Organization for Self-Adaptive Systems

Enabling the self-organization of system configurations and controlling system configurations by self-adaptive software architectures are commonly regarded as alternative construction approaches for adaptive distributed systems, e.g. as opposed in [Salehie and Tahvildari, 2009] (pages 5, 23). However, it has also been argued that the self-adaptive management of distributed systems also requires the control of collective behaviors, which can arise from the managed system elements.

Prominent approaches to the development of self-adaptive software systems focus on the architectural aspects and enable developers to localize the observation of (sub-)systems, the planing of adjustments and the enactment of the management decisions in dedicated software components. The capabilities and constraints of these managing entities and/or utilized networking techniques that connect system elements to enable sensing and actuations may force partitionings, where each segment is locally controlled (cf. Figure 3.4). The managers of distinct partitions are arranged in peer-to-peer topologies (1) or hierarchies (2) [Huebscher and McCann, 2008]. These, possibly connected, managers impose control loops, thus adjustments are imposed top-down on the subordinate system elements. When system elements are equipped with degrees of autonomy the unwanted, system-level properties (see Section 3.1.3) or dynamics may arise from bottom-up principles that manifest phenomena in the *Macroscopic System Behavior* (cf. Figure 3.4). These unintended effects may work against the management by superordinate managers. Thus the need to relate the concerted adaptations of system entities to system-level properties has been recognized as a development challenge, e.g. [Kephart, 2005; Huebscher and McCann, 2008]. In [Huebscher and McCann, 2008], the challenges that result from the dynamics of the managed subsystems, particularly the relevance of unwanted emergent phenomena, e.g. *state-flapping*, which corresponds to unwanted oscillations (see Section 3.1.3), are thematized. That systems have the freedom to show collective phenomena and are *also* explicitly managed is described by the notions of *controlled self-organization* [Branke et al., 2006] and *controlled emergence* [Müller-Schloer, 2004]. The managing system elements intervene when phenomena compromise the system functionality.

An integrative perspective does not only relate to per se unwanted phenomena but also promises the ability to exploit the decentralized nature of self-organizing algorithms to increase the robustness and fault tolerance of self-adaptive systems. In the context of autonomic computing it is stated in [Kephart, 2005] (page 20):

> ... more unified and concentrated efforts to understand and exploit emergent behavior in autonomic systems could have a radical and profound influence on their architecture,

and could lead to much more decentralized and robust system structures than have yet been imagined. ...

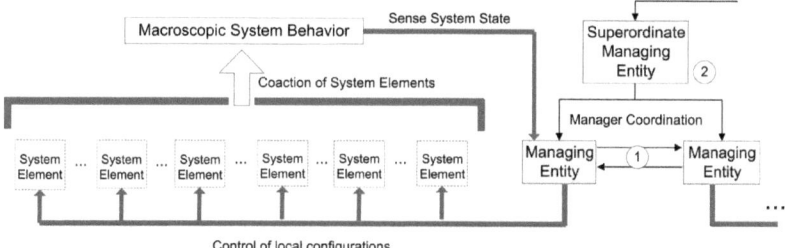

Figure 3.4: Self-organization within a managed, distributed system

3.2 The Construction of Self-Organizing Systems

In [Prokopenko, 2008c], a statement about the lack of engineering approaches to self-organizing phenomena is given (page V):

> If engineers have ignored self-organization, it is not because self-ordering is not pervasive and profound. It is because we engineers have yet to understand how to think about systems governed simultaneously by two sources of order: traditional design and self-organization.

This *ignorance* has been partly relieved as the development of self-organizing applications has become an active research area. However, development approaches are dominated by domain experts that study and understand specific techniques, such as coordination mechanism and architectural styles, that enable software systems to exhibit self-structuring properties.

Another aspect of this ignorance is that the self-organization phenomenon inherently contradicts conventional engineering approaches [Prokopenko, 2008b; Edmonds, 2004]. Development efforts face the challenge of appropriately distributing computations. The collective effects, i.e. the resulting system-wide properties, are designed by revising the local activities of system elements. Engineering techniques deal with the top-down, stepwise planning, design, and realization of foreseeable outcomes while self-organization is based on non-determinism and effects among ensembles of system elements. Planning for these effects implies that system elements are not designed in isolation but need to be revised with respect to the context in which they (inter-)act. This requires comprehension of, or at least intuition about, the behavior of collections of elements in varying contexts. Another major challenge is balancing the degrees of freedom and non-determinism of system elements with the control of the intended system properties (e.g. discussed throughout [Prokopenko, 2008b]). A deliberate balance has to ensure that systems adjustments are not solely imposed by outside influences and remain predictable.

Two fundamental approaches for constructing self-organizing systems are the handmade design of the self-organizing process and the automation of the discovery of a solution process. The former approaches are based on the (software) engineering of systems that show self-organization. Development teams apply software engineering practices and one aspect is the self-structuring of the application. The adaptive processes are *handmade* and customized during the system development (e.g. see [Edmonds, 2004]). Alternatively, the search for and configuration of problem solving strategies can be automated. The difference between the present and the intended system performance is measured and system entities are repeatedly adjusted to tune the system behavior.

The use of evolutionary methods (e.g. see [Prokopenko, 2008b]) is an example, where ensembles of systems are exposed to a selective pressure that evaluates the system performance in different contexts. The former development approaches point out the internal workings of the involved adaptive processes, and the latter approaches mask the internal working of the application. The latter approach is not further discussed in this chapter (details can be found in [Floreano and Mattiussi, 2008]); instead software engineering approaches are discussed.

Distributing Feedback

The presence of distributed feedbacks among multitudes of system elements is the basic characteristic of systems that show self-organizing features (see Section 3.1.4). Consequently, feedback design is an attractive starting point for development approaches. The embedding of these feedbacks is based on two fundamental design elements [Sudeikat and Renz, 2008a]. First, system elements are to be equipped with the ability to adjust local internal aspects, e.g. behaviors, configurations, and states. The adaptiveness of individual system elements can be addressed with *internal* and *external* techniques [Salehie and Tahvildari, 2009]. Internal approaches blend the realizations of the system elements with the logic that controls and enacts adjustments. Alternatively, the adaptation can be separated and encapsulated in external computational elements (see Figure 3.5, I). In principle, these externalized elements maintain a closed feedback loop to intervene and adjust system elements as needed (cf. Section 3.1.4). The realizations of managers can be based on the frameworks and architectures for self-adaptive systems (cf. Section 3.1.2) or agents, as exemplified in Section 6.8.2. A related technique is the *wrapping* of legacy components with agent realizations [Wooldridge, 2002] (page 226). This approach supplements agency properties to software components.

The second design element is the information flow among system elements, which enables individual agents/components to reason about the appropriate adjustments. This spreading of information follows its own dynamical process, which controls the subsequent adjustments of individuals. One dominant principle is the *locality* (see e.g. [Viroli et al., 2009]) of information transfers, as visualized in 3.5 (II). Computational elements perceive the variations in their immediate, logically or spatially defined, context. The perceptions diminish with the relative, corresponding distance. When the perceptions cause adjustments that are noticeable by nearby agents, these changes *propagate* through the system. Consequently, aging information can be attenuated by constraining propagations. The general features of these information flows and mechanisms realizing them are discussed in Section 3.2.1.

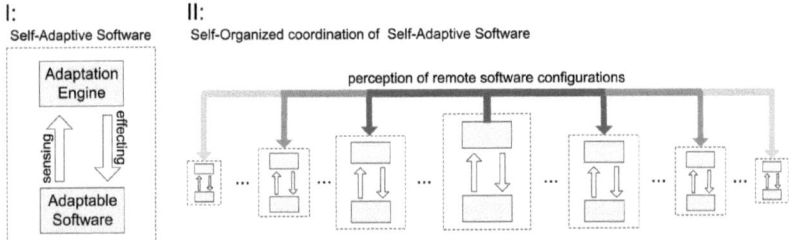

Figure 3.5: The basic elements for the establishment of distributed feedback are *external* self-adaptive software components (I), following [Salehie and Tahvildari, 2009], and the propagation of influences (II).

3.2. THE CONSTRUCTION OF SELF-ORGANIZING SYSTEMS

Reuse: Coordinating Processes and Coordination Patterns

The creation of distributed, self-organizing problem solving algorithms demands considerable expertise. Due to the lack of principled design techniques, pattern-oriented development is a significant construction approach. Collections of *design patterns* and *template system designs* have been identified in physical, biological, and social systems [Sudeikat and Renz, 2008a]. These describe reusable mechanisms for decentralized problem solving and thus facilitate the *bionic* reconstruction of well-known and field-tested system dynamics in vitro. However, no mutual consent has been reached on the structure and abstraction-level of applicable *design patterns* that support self-organization. Categorizations of pattern and template mechanism refer either to the computational techniques used, particularly interaction mechanisms, [DeWolf and Holvoet, 2006, 2007a; Babaoglu et al., 2006; Serugendo et al., 2006; Mamei et al., 2006; Gardelli et al., 2007], their sources of inspiration in nature [Mamei et al., 2006; Hassas et al., 2006; Mano et al., 2006] or their applicability in application domains [DeWolf and Holvoet, 2007b; Mamei et al., 2006].

The following discussion of template proposals is based on [Sudeikat and Renz, 2008a, 2009c]. Based on these classifications and their comparison, the distinction between two abstraction levels, namely the inter-agent process(es) exhibited and the mechanism(s) used for the establishing of these processes, is proposed in [Sudeikat and Renz, 2009c]. The former abstraction level describes archetype application dynamics that serve as design inspirations and describe the dynamics of decentralized coordinated systems. The latter abstractions, describe *coordination mechanisms* and *computational techniques* that support the manifestation of these dynamics. These mechanisms are often derived from natural sources of inspiration but pertain to the realization of a process, e.g. the properties of the information flows.

The relations between these design levels are illustrated in Figure 3.6. The software systems (*Application*) show an observable behavior, i.e. the intended *Adaptation Dynamic* on the system level, that describes the intended adaptivity of the software system. This dynamic is manifested by a *(self-regulatory) Coordinating Process*. This processes describes a self-organization that is continuously structuring, adapting, and regulating aspects of the software system. The governing process is built-in by integrating sets of (decentralized) *Coordination Mechanisms*. These mechanisms are distinguished between techniques for the adjustment of system elements (*Local Entity Adaptation*) and realizations of agent interactions (*Information Propagation*). These mechanisms control the microscopic activities of system entities that collectively lead to the manifestation of the intended Application Dynamic. The integration of the mechanisms is prescribed by process definitions, which structure the participating mechanisms and instruct their operation.

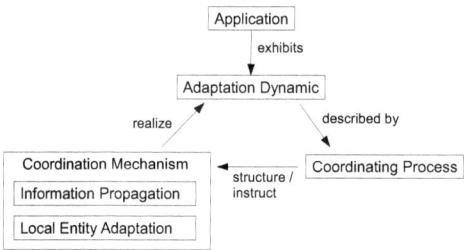

Figure 3.6: The relationships between the software Application, the observable Dynamics, the Coordinating Process and the Coordination Mechanisms, following [Sudeikat and Renz, 2010c]

The following review of engineering techniques and approaches is based on and extends [Sudeikat and Renz, 2008a]. First, coordination mechanisms, which describe reusable techniques for the decentralized coordination of agents, are reviewed (cf. Section 3.2.1). Then reusable inter-agent processes, a higher abstraction level, are outlined (see Section 3.2.2). These are studied as design elements throughout Part II of this dissertation. The consideration of software engineering aspects leads to sets of general design guidelines and principles (see Section 3.2.3) that provide a basis for development methodologies (see Section 3.2.4).

3.2.1 Decentralized Coordination Mechanisms

The identification of generic mechanisms for implementing of self-organizing processes is of practical and academic interest. Development efforts are assisted by frameworks for the comparison and selection of building blocks for the system construction. The identification of these reusable construction elements and the subsequent study of their commonalities and differences provides indications for the generic properties that are able to produce the collective effects. These two aspects of the study of implementation mechanisms are reflected by alternative discussions of mechanisms, according to their functional aspects [Serugendo et al., 2006; Mamei et al., 2006; Sudeikat and Renz, 2008a]. In [Sudeikat and Renz, 2008a,c] a unifying classification, that integrates the criteria from [Serugendo et al., 2006; Mamei et al., 2006] is discussed, and it is used to relate prominent instances (e.g. see [DeWolf and Holvoet, 2007a, 2006; Serugendo et al., 2006; Gardelli et al., 2007]).

In [Serugendo et al., 2006], five pivotal mechanisms are distinguished. A first approach it the localization of agents in an environment and the enabling of *direct interactions* [Serugendo et al., 2006], based on the topology and/or direct communication lines of agents. These mechanisms rely on environment abstractions that allow agents to directly sense the information from other agents/elements in the system. The example of field-based coordination mechanisms (discussed throughout [Mamei and Zambonelli, 2005a]) is given.

A second type of mechanism is *indirect interactions* [Serugendo et al., 2006], particularly the use of *stigmergy*-based techniques, where interactions are mediated by modifications of a shared environment. The most prominent form is the stigmergy principle [Grasse, 1959], which describes that the activities of individuals to modify the environment in a way that consequently stimulates corresponding activities by other agents. Activities leave marks in the environment that signal to other agents. One approach for signaling is the release of digital pheromones in the environment, e.g. discussed as a design technique in [Parunak and Brueckner, 2004].

A third realization mechanism is called *reinforcement of agent behaviors* [Serugendo et al., 2006]. This type of mechanism is embedded within agents and controls behavior selection, e.g. [Weyns et al., 2004]. This selection is based on past experiences and a common variation is the inclusion of probabilities in the selection processes to enable the exploration of the behavior space.

The *cooperation behaviour of individual agents* [Serugendo et al., 2006] is an alternative mechanism. Agents are enabled to detect and enact cooperations, based on their local abilities. When the collective cooperations in an MAS are well-matched, the global system behavior is positively affected. The mechanism are instanced in [Ishida et al., 1992; Gleizes et al., 1999]. In [Ishida et al., 1992], the composition and decomposition of agents models is used to adapt to the environment, e.g. to adjust response times. The AMAS theory proposes the enabling of agents to detect and resolve unwanted *non-cooperative situations* [Gleizes et al., 1999], for example by adjusting interactions. Thus the system can recover and reconfigures to bring about the intended functionality. This approach is discussed below and a corresponding development methodology (ADELFE) is outlined in Section 3.2.4.

The fifth type of mechanisms is the use of a *generic architecture* [Serugendo et al., 2006] that allows agents to change the structure of the MAS at run-time. Two examples are the direct modification of the structure, for example given in holons and holarchies [Koestler, 1967], or the processing and modification of meta-models of the agent organizations [Dowling and Cahill, 2001].

An alternative set of classification criteria is proposed in [Mamei et al., 2006] for the characterization of environment-mediated interactions. Three criteria types are found and are visualized as orthogonal axes that define a space of self-organizing mechanisms and application areas (cf. Table 3.1).

First, two types of vehicles for communications are distinguished — this aspect is coined *what information is communicated*. First, dedicated elements, i.e. *markers*, are used to communi-

3.2. THE CONSTRUCTION OF SELF-ORGANIZING SYSTEMS

cate information (*Marker-based interactions*). These elements emulate the emitting of sounds or pheromones, for the purpose of informing other agents. Alternatively, the information is communicated implicitly. The state of the perceivable environment (*Sematectonic Interaction*) contains the information and it is inferred by agents from their observations. This mechanism is the kind of communication that is exemplified in Section 3.4.2. An orthogonal axis characterizes the propagation of information through the system (*how information flows*). In *serendipitous* modes, information is placed in the environment and the agent models are responsible for actively searching the environment. Alternatively, the environment can contain dynamics for the transport of information items. The movement of information is called *diffusion*. An additional aspect is the modification of information, e.g. its attenuation to emulate the evaporation of chemical messenger substances. This is omitted in [Mamei et al., 2006]. A third axis denotes the processing of perceived information. This perception is characterized as *trigger-based* or *follow-through*. The former characteristic describes scenarios where the perception of information directly triggers specific agent-actions. Alternatively, the actions can be gradually induced by the availability of information, e.g. pheromone gradients that guide directions of movement [Mamei et al., 2006].

An integrative categorization of coordination mechanisms is illustrated in Figure 3.7 [Sudeikat and Renz, 2008a,c]. Mechanisms are classified according to their contribution to the establishment of inter-agent feedback loops, as discussed in Section 3.2. *Information Propagation Level* mechanisms deal with the transport of data items among agents. The content of these communications ranges from simple data items such as numerical values to application-domain concepts, for example commitments to provide services. The *Entity Adaptation Level* mechanisms contain techniques for managing the agents' localized responses to the perceived information. These responses pertain to the local adjustments within agents. In [Sudeikat and Renz, 2009a], the combinability of both mechanism levels is examined and it is concluded that development efforts typically focus on one level in the design of a problem solving strategy. Thus sophisticated interaction models or elaborated agent realizations are utilized with simple counterparts.

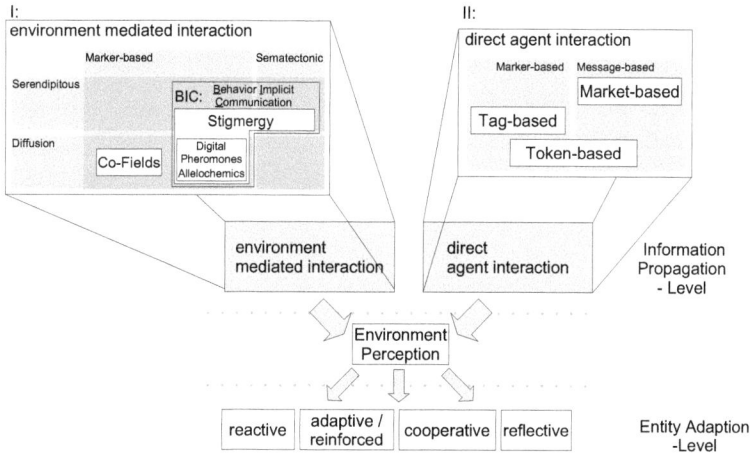

Figure 3.7: Decentralized Coordination Mechanisms as patterns for establishing mutual agent interdependencies, adapted from [Sudeikat and Renz, 2008b,a]

Information Propagation-Level Mechanisms

Specific interaction techniques promote the rise of self-organizing structures. A thorough review of techniques is given in [DeWolf and Holvoet, 2007a] and detailed descriptions of their mechanisms and their applications can be found in [DeWolf and Holvoet, 2006]. The classification presented here is based on [Sudeikat and Renz, 2008a]. The mechanisms are distinguished between *environment mediated interactions* (see Figure 3.7, I) and *direct agent interactions* (II). The former types of mechanisms rely on the positioning of agents in (virtual) environments and these environments transport the communicated information and control the perceptions. The latter mechanisms control the direct exchange of information among agents.

The interaction-related criteria from [Mamei et al., 2006] are used to characterize mediated interactions (see page 58). These are classified in a matrix that distinguishes mechanisms by their use of *marker-based* or *sematectonic* modifications of the environment. An orthogonal aspect is the serendipitous or diffusion-based perception of information. An example is computational fields (*Co-Fields*) [Mamei and Zambonelli, 2005a]. System elements, i.e. agents and environment elements, are equipped with the ability to emit virtual, computational fields. These fields represent spatial or contextual information and their emitting can be regarded as a broadcast to the subset of agents in perception range [Serugendo et al., 2006]. The fields are propagated via the environment and the perception of field gradients enables agents to compute their relative distance and adjust themselves, e.g. their spatial positioning. These mechanisms are suitable for controlling spatial and/or structural aspects of MASs, e.g. see [Mamei and Zambonelli, 2005b; Hagebäck and Johansson, 2009; Mamei and Zambonelli, 2005a].

Another prominent technique is the *stigmergy* principle [Grasse, 1959], which describes that agents communicate via modifications of their environment. The modifications either pertain to elements that are already present, such as elements of the application domain, or dedicated markers that are present in the environment for the purpose of conveying information. A prominent instance are digital *phenomenons* [DeWolf and Holvoet, 2007a; Parunak and Brueckner, 2004] that emulate the dynamics of chemical scents that are used by insects. In [Kasinger et al., 2008], it is pointed out that pheromones refer to chemicals that are used for communications among the members of a species (intra-species) and that chemicals for the communications among members of different species, *allelochemics*, can also serve as coordination mechanisms. A generalization of the stigmergy principles is the *Behavioral Implicit Communication* (BIC) [Omicini et al., 2004b]. It is noted that communications can also be based on the observation of the behaviors of other agents and their local interpretation rather than the communicative modifications of the environment. This generic conceptualization denotes both marker-based and sematectonic coordination mechanisms.

Direct interactions describe that agents establish a direct communication by means of message exchanges, token distributions, and the modification of publicly visible tags. Message exchanges are used in *market-based* mechanisms where virtual marketplaces are established for inter-agent negotiation. Market dynamics are used to balance demand and supply. Another technique is the exchange of *tokens* that contain information or grant permissions. When agents posses tokens they are equipped with this information or permission, e.g. resource usages. Tokens are passed between agents. In addition, *tags* can be used to annotate information, e.g. trust or reputation, to agents. This information can be interpreted by agents to constrain the selection of interaction partners or team formations. Details on these mechanisms and their applications can be found in [DeWolf and Holvoet, 2007a,b].

Engineering practices are supported by providing of reusable infrastructures that support the described types of interactions. In [Viroli et al., 2009], fundamental characteristics of these infrastructures are identified. These enable the realization of appropriate interaction mechanisms. A first property is the support for a *topology* of system elements. Connecting elements to subsets of other elements allows the application to be structured and emulate the layout of system elements in the application domain. The distribution of infrastructures is a non-mandatory aspect. A related feature is the *locality* of interactions. Agents and non-agent elements sense and act in local spheres of influence, which represent partitions of the system. The interactions are

3.2. THE CONSTRUCTION OF SELF-ORGANIZING SYSTEMS

understood as atomic activities in the local sphere and long-range or long-lasting interactions result from the sequencing of interactions. The *on-line character* of the infrastructures describes the ability to provide background processing to control the dynamics of information transports, e.g. to realized the propagation and attenuation of information elements. The *time* property describes the time-dependency of interactions. The on-line dynamics in the infrastructure require a timing that is adjusted to the system elements. Examples are interaction rates, time-delays, and time-based constraints on the workability of interactions. Finally, the support for stochastic interactions (*probability*) is identified as an inherent property. Non-determinism is an inherent feature of a self-organizing application. Besides the non-determinism of the local element decision making, prescribing the stochastics of interactions is identified as a means for enforcing behavioral diversity. Generic coordination and environment infrastructures (cf. Sections 2.3.1, 2.5) can be exploited to provide all or a subset of these features for encoding interaction mechanisms, e.g. [Viroli et al., 2009; Mamei and Zambonelli, 2005c]. These infrastructures can also be ranged in the categorization described here. An example is the utilization of *Tuple Spaces* [Gelernter and Carriero, 1992], as discussed in [Viroli et al., 2009]. Tuples can be used to represent markers and the perceptions of these markers can be adjusted to emulate serendipitous encounters or diffusion (see Appendix B). These infrastructures allow the realizations of interactions to be separated and provide programming constructs (see Section 2.3.1) that agent-developers use to trigger interactions. Thus the control flow of the agents contains the logic for when and how to interact.

Entity Adaptation-Level Mechanisms

These mechanisms control the engagement of agents in and the responses to interactions. Four types of principled mechanisms can be used (see Figure 3.7, bottom). First, *reactive* mechanisms equip agents with predefined responses to certain inputs. One prominent approach is the prioritization of behaviors/activities (e.g. [Brooks, 1986]). Despite their simplicity, these models can be used to show collective effects when the dynamics of interactions are well-matched. The other four categories are adopted from [Serugendo et al., 2006] (see page 58). The category *adaptive/reinforced* contains mechanisms that are based on the reinforcement of agent activities, based on past experiences. Within agents, the outcome of the execution of behaviors and/or activities are inferred. This information is used to enforce courses of action that are positively valued. These models are typically supplemented with stochastic elements to enable the testing of less enforced but potentially effective activities. Examples are outlined in [Serugendo et al., 2006]. Another category is *cooperative* mechanisms [Serugendo et al., 2006]. Agents maintain a model of the cooperations in which they participate and are equipped with procedures for re-establishing cooperations when necessary. Examples are outlined in [Serugendo et al., 2006] and this design approach is adopted in the ADELFE development methodology (see Section 3.2.4). Finally, the *reflective* mechanisms correspond to the generic mechanisms identified in [Serugendo et al., 2006] (see page 58). Here, these mechanisms are named reflective to express the ability of individual agents to trigger reconfigurations of the MAS.

Mechanisms as Design Patterns

For the assistance of development practices it is of interest to provide mechanisms in reusable formats that support their selection and integration by software development teams. The adoption of the *Design Pattern* concept [Gamma et al., 1995] has been proposed, e.g. [Babaoglu et al., 2006; DeWolf and Holvoet, 2007a; Gardelli et al., 2007]. Design Patterns describe generic solutions to recurring problems for the construction of software systems. In [Gamma et al., 1995], the notion of Design Patterns as reusable solutions is adopted from [Alexander et al., 1977] and transferred to software construction. Patterns are a successful approach to sharing constructive knowledge and have also been transferred to the construction of agent-oriented systems (e.g. [Aridor and Lange, 1998],[Deugo et al., 2001]). Patterns are described in varying textual formats and in [Babaoglu et al., 2006; DeWolf and Holvoet, 2007a; Gardelli et al., 2007] this approach is mainly adopted for the description of interaction mechanisms.

3.2.2 Self-Regulatory Coordinating Processes

In addition to the conceptualizations of concrete construction patterns or techniques (see above), mechanisms have also been described on a higher abstraction level to indicate the operating principles of processes that give rise to self-organization. These are templates that generalize from specific solutions and refer to the design metaphor that gave inspiration to a computational process. These descriptions also refer to the interaction and adaptation techniques (cf. Figure 3.6), e.g. the use of stigmergy and reactive reasoning, and indicate their embedding in a system.

Conceptually, these templates are on a higher abstraction level, as they describe the process itself and the interrelations of agents that make a system show self-organization. Implicitly, these descriptions refer to the distributed feedbacks that effectuate the self-organization (see Section 3.1.4). The operating principles can be described by the system elements as well as the interdependencies and influences among them. In order to denote the different quality of these abstractions, they are distinguished from the coordination mechanisms. This differentiation structures design concepts and is a step towards a consistent model of self-organizing systems. These abstractions are called Coordinating Process to denote that they describe distributed processes that govern the collaborative structure formation.

Definition 3.1 *(Coordinating Process) A Coordinating Process is a network of relations, i.e. influences and interdependencies, among the activities of system elements. These relations result from information flows and the ability of receiving system elements to respond by local adaptations.*

This abstract definition is concretized in Chapter 4. A modeling techniques is developed to express these processes in MAS. Typical sources for the derivation of these processes are *natural* self-organizing systems. For example, in [Floreano and Mattiussi, 2008] the use of bio-inspired techniques in computer systems is reviewed and the uses of self-organization for controlling collectives of system elements is distinguished by the types of collective behaviors found in insect colonies (see [Floreano and Mattiussi, 2008], section 7.1), namely *Aggregation, Clustering, Nest Construction, Foraging,* and *Division of Labor.* A comprehensive review of corresponding design inspirations can be found in [Mamei et al., 2006]. Due to the multitude of collective processes that can be used in software, an extensive review of techniques is not attempted in this section. Instead the selection of processes from [Mamei et al., 2006] is adopted and extended with additional patterns that are studied throughout the case studies in this dissertation. In alphabetical order, these template processes are:

- S1: Brood Sorting [Mamei et al., 2006]
- S2: Convention Emergence [Delgado, 2002; Shoham and Tennenholtz, 1997]
- S3: Epidemics [Eugster et al., 2004]
- S4: Flocking [Mamei et al., 2006]
- S5: Foraging, Ant-based [Mamei et al., 2006]
- S6: Foraging, Bee-based [Nakrani and Tovey, 2004]
- S7: Molding and Aggregation [Mamei et al., 2006]
- S8: Morphogenesis [Mamei et al., 2006]
- S9: Nest-Building [Mamei et al., 2006]
- S10: Quorum [Mamei et al., 2006]
- S11: Web Weaving [Mamei et al., 2006]

Explicit models of the distributed feedback structures, which define their operating principles, are given in Section 4.4.1. In the system development, these processes serve as design inspirations and their integration in applications is typically an *ad-hoc* design challenge. The development of Coordinating Processes is addressed in the subsequent chapters of this dissertation. These processes are converted as self-contained design elements that can be integrated in agent-based applications. Their modeling (see Chapter 4), implementation (see Chapter 5) and design (see Chapter 6) are discussed.

In [Mamei et al., 2006], these processes are characterized along three distinct axes, which describe the contents (*what*), the propagation (*how information flows*) and the interpretation of exchanged information among agents (see page 58). In table 3.1, these characteristics are summarized. The values for the processes from [Mamei et al., 2006][4] are taken from that work. The remaining processes are classified accordingly.

		Decentralized Coordination Strategy										
		S1	S2	S3	S4	S5	S6	S7	S8	S9	S10	S11
what is	sematectonic	x		x							x	x
communicated	marker-based		x	x		x	x	x	x			
How info.	trigger-based	x	x	x		x		x	x	x		
is used	follow-through				x	x		x				x
How info.	serendipitous	x	x	x		x	x			x		x
flows	diffusion				x			x	x		x	

Table 3.1: Classification of Coordination Strategies, following the classification criteria from [Mamei et al., 2006]

3.2.3 Development Principles

For the construction of self-organizing applications, the local adjustments and the propagation of information/influences have to be well-matched in order to elicit the intended system behaviors. The identification of generic practices and guidelines are the basis for development methodologies. These are reviewed to indicate the current development practices.

Balancing Top-Down and Bottom-Up Practices

The use of self-organization principles requires planning for the collective effects of system elements. Adjustments of system elements have to be supervised with assessments of the effects on the dynamical system properties. This inherent duality of the top-down design and bottom-up analysis practices is recognized as a fundamental aspect of development processes (e.g. [Sudeikat et al., 2009b; Gardelli et al., 2006]).

This acknowledgment manifests itself by the inclusion of simulation techniques in established development methodologies, e.g. [Bernon et al., 2007], as well as the use of simulations during application design (e.g. [Casadei et al., 2007; Gardelli et al., 2006]; see Section 4.1.2). In this context, the *experimental method* for the development of self-organizing applications is proposed in [Edmonds, 2004]. Two fundamental types of development approaches are distinguished: the *engineering* of systems and the *adaptive*, where an available system is successively tested and modified. It is concluded that the systematic development faces the challenge of developing systems while there is no comprehensive understanding of the internal workings and mechanisms that give rise to system-level properties. The rationale is that in these scenarios, the appropriateness of the system behavior cannot be formally ensured, but that the scientific study of the system, based on the conception of hypothesis and their corroboration/falsification by experiment, is required to systematically show that the system behaves as intended. Consequently, the engineering of systems and their purposeful adjustment are combined to an abstract development model [Edmonds, 2004]. The development is composed of the alternation between engineering phases and experimenting with the priorly engineered system.

Design Guidelines/Paradigms

Stigmergy-based self-organization is a well-studied phenomena and heuristic development guidelines have been revised with regard to distribution of problem solving strategies [Parunak., 1997; Parunak and Brueckner, 2004; Brueckner and Czap, 2006]. Here a revised set of *design principles* is outlined that originate in [Parunak., 1997] and were subsequently expanded and revised

---
[4] these are: S1, S4, S5, S7 to S11

in [Parunak and Brueckner, 2004] and [Brueckner and Czap, 2006]. These heuristics are well-investigated, are general enough to be transferred to other types of self-organization, and thus give an impression about the concerns that development practices have to address.

The principles are segmented in three categories [Brueckner and Czap, 2006]. The first set of principles concerns the design of *agent populations*. The use of a (1) *distributed environment* is the first principle and describes that agents are to be situated in a shared space that enables interactions. Secondly, the mediation of interactions is described by the demand for an (2) *active environment*. This environment embeds processes that control interactions, e.g. the propagation and evaporation of digital pheromones. As described in Section 3.2.1, well-adjusted dynamics of the environment support the system's execution, e.g. by the attenuation of outdated information. The following two principles stress the locality of the actions of agents, as depicted in Figure 3.5. It is advised to (3) *keep agents small* in respect to the system and problem size. The rationale is that small-scale agents contribute to the locality as agents are responsible for smaller partitions of the problem space and system functionality. Finally, it is advised to *map agents to entities* rather than to functionalities. This contributes to the locality of agents as they are used to represent system entities. Refraining from making agents responsible for specific functionalities prepares the rise of functionalities from from their interactions.

The second category of design principles concerns the *agent interactions* [Brueckner and Czap, 2006]. First, it is advised to (1) design *flows rather than transitions*. The conception of closed loops of information flows among agents is identified as a major design effort. In addition, appropriate flows of information are to be ensured. Keeping the information low within the appropriate ranges demands the preparation of constraints as well as reinforcement. Finally, the consideration of the (3) diverseness of agents (*diversify agents*) is recommended as a means of ensuring information flows. It is proposed that the variety of the local aspects of agents be used, e.g. their positioning in the environment or stochastics inside the agent reasoning process, as a means to control and enable a variety of the (inter-)actions of agents.

The last category of principles prepares the rise of the intended system functionality (*emergence of desired functions* [Brueckner and Czap, 2006]). These guidelines pertain to the enabling of the software system to explore the space of individual behaviors while taking into account the global system properties. In agreement with the diverseness of agents each agent is to be prepared to show a set of behaviors (*behavioral diversity*) to enable the exploration of the space of individual agent behaviors. In addition, the provision of a *fitness measure* to agents is proposed. These functions enable agent reasoning about the contribution of their local behaviors to the overall system perspective. The design challenge is to derive a function that gives an appropriate estimate of the global system state, based on the local information that is available to agent instances. This principle is closely related to the provision of a mechanism for *selecting among alternative behaviors*. A fitness measure can be supported by local reasoning mechanisms and heuristics, such as the local comparison of the performance of behaviors.

Fundamental design paradigms for self-organizing systems are given in [Prehofer and Bettstetter, 2005], with respect to the design of protocols for the management of communication networks. The first paradigm is to *Design local behavior rules that achieve global properties* [Prehofer and Bettstetter, 2005] (page 80). This principle refers to the fundamental design challenge. One heuristic is the reduction of the desired global property to the local properties of system entities. In these cases, the intended system-level property can be achieved by enabling the system entities to bring about their individual-level properties. Clarifications of this principle are given in Section 3.2.4. A subset of development methodologies illustrate and guide the use of this principle: for example the ADELFE methodology [Bernon et al., 2005a] guides the design of agents that detect and resolve locally problematic scenarios in order to (re-)establish a globally functioning systems. A second paradigm is to *exploit implicit coordination* (page 81). Instead of explicitly transmitting the information needed to coordinate the networked system elements, elements infer this information from their local execution context by themselves. The third paradigm also addresses the required information and advises to *minimize long-lived state information* (page 82). Information about the state of the network should not be maintained by the network nodes. Instead, the nodes should retrieve this information when needed. An example is the use of discovery mechanisms.

3.2. THE CONSTRUCTION OF SELF-ORGANIZING SYSTEMS

Finally, it is advised to *design protocols that adapt to changes* (page 83). This principle refers to the ability of system elements, here network nodes, to adapt to changes. In the absence of a centralized control, each networked element has to monitor its environment and adapt locally.

These principles provide general design guidelines. How to realize self-organization in a specific application context, while complying to these principles, must be decided case-by-case. An abstract view on a development process that makes use of design paradigms is given in [Prehofer and Bettstetter, 2005]. In the following section, development methodologies are discussed that guide application development.

3.2.4 Development Methodologies

Methodologies structure the development of self-organizing applications, as reviewed and fragmented (see Section 2.6.3) in [Puviani et al., 2009]. The techniques and principles outlined above, guide application development. The extent of this support differs and approaches highlight different foci of the development. Instances can be characterized along three orthogonal aspects (see Figure 3.8). First, the methods differ in their coverage of the fundamental disciplines that constitute the complete software development cycle [Jacobson et al., 1999] (x axis). While *comprehensive* methodologies describe a complete development cycle, from the description of the system requirements to the test of the final product, others refer solely to the design of the algorithms and operating principles of the system elements involved (*partial*). Another aspect is the support for different coordination mechanisms (y axis). Methodologies follow fundamental design principles and guide how to act up to these principles during the system development. These principles may focus on the use of specific mechanisms. Thus the methodologies may apply to a specific type of interaction technique of computational infrastructures, e.g. agent architectures (*single*) Alternatively, sets of mechanism types can be supported (*multiple*). Finally, the integration in existing software engineering contexts varies (z axis). The transition of the structured development of feasibility studies in academic contexts to functional applications in industry would benefit from an integration and reuse of conventional development techniques and processes. The extent of this reuse ranges from ignored (vague) to plausible integrations (well-defined).

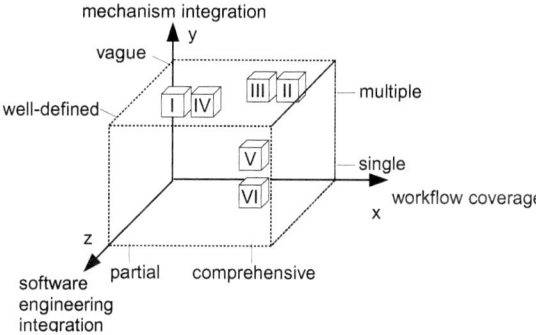

Figure 3.8: Aspects of the methodology support

An example for the structuring of specific development partition is the *simulation-driven approach* from [Gardelli et al., 2008] (I). It focuses on an *early design* phase in MAS development that concerns the conception of self-organizing applications. The constituent steps are the *modeling* of a system abstraction, the *simulation* of this abstraction to infer appropriate parameter ranges, and the final tuning, where parameters are adjusted with respect to the intended system behavior. It also addresses the use of environment-mediated coordination mechanisms. In this respect, the *Agents & Artefacts* meta model (see Section 5.1.2) is adopted. The generic artifact concept allows the integration of different mechanisms types, e.g. direct interactions (see Section 5.1.2). This approach is based on the adoption of stochastic simulation techniques (see Section 4.1.2) to anticipate the application dynamics. This approach focuses on a specific aspect (*partial,vague*) of the application development and supports *multiple* interaction mechanisms.

Another example for the structuring of the conception of a self-organizing application is the *Autonomy Oriented Computing* (AOC) approach [Liu et al., 2005] (II). System development is structured in three phases. In the first phase, an appropriate *analogy*, i.e. a design inspiration, is identified. The second phase pertains to the system construction. It is subdivided in the construction of environment models and the models of the autonomous system entities. The third phase addresses the evaluation of the developed system. Measurements indicate the adjustments in the designed models. The AOC development process structures the iterative model construction and identifies the basic activities in simulation-based design approaches. Due to the abstract nature of these activities, it is generally applicable with respect to different coordination mechanisms. The described processes denotes the principal stages and activities in the development of the self-organizing system (*comprehensive*) and is, due to its abstraction level, not biased toward specific (software) development processes (*vague*) or coordination mechanisms (*multiple*).

The *general methodology* [Gershenson, 2007] (III) is based on the inclusion of *mediators*, i.e. constraints that arbitrate among the individual objectives/activities of autonomous agents (page 41). A set of generic development steps structures the complete system development cycle with emphasis on the conception of system (simulation) models and their analysis. The process is characterized as a *guideline* for the search of self-organizing solutions (page 44). These steps are the *representation* of the system, the *modeling* of the control mechanism, the construction of and experimentation with *simulation* models, the transition to a real system (*application*), and the *evaluation* of the system performance. This approach also focuses on the principal development (*comprehensive, vague*). The use of mediators is a specific design concept but it can be used in combination with different coordination mechanisms (*multiple*).

The *MetaSelf* framework [Serugendo et al., 2008b] (IV) provides a service-oriented run-time environment for the provision of decision-making and adaptation mechanisms (see Section 5.1.2). A set of development activities guides the utilization of this framework [Serugendo et al., 2008b]. In an *analysis phase* functional requirements, e.g. self-* properties, are identified. Subsequently, patterns and mechanisms, e.g. managing entities and stigmergy, are selected and refined in a *design phase*. Then the run-time system is constructed (*implementation phase*). This architecture is conceived as a versatile support of different types of management patterns and coordination mechanisms and the process documents the essential development steps. The principal development stages for making use of this framework (*partial*) are described without bias to a specific development process (vague) or coordination mechanism (*multiple*).

Two approaches deal with the integration in conventional software engineering processes. In [DeWolf, 2007], a *Customized Unified Process* is proposed that extends the *Unified Process* [Jacobson et al., 1999] with considerations about the macroscopic system behavior (V). The requirements analysis is extended with the identification of the system properties that should be maintained at run-time, and related performance measurements. During the application design, the use of design principles, self-adaptive architectures, and coordination mechanisms is referenced. A pattern catalog of coordination mechanisms [DeWolf and Holvoet, 2007a] is provided and the UML-notation is used to visualize the information and control flows [DeWolf and Holvoet, 2007c]. The testing of the application is supported by system simulations that feed back to the design decisions. Particularly the *Equation-Free Macroscopic Analysis* ([DeWolf, 2007], chapter 5) was developed to support the simulation-based systems analysis. This approach refers to (*well-defined*) and extends a *comprehensive* development process. Mechanisms are understood as reusable design patterns (*multiple*).

The *ADELFE* methodology [Bernon et al., 2005a] (VI) is based on the *Adaptive Multi-Agent System* (AMAS) theory. Self-organization is used to maintain the system's functionality. Agents are designed to continuously maintain cooperative interactions when facing perturbations. An important part of the agent's design is preparing them to detect and resolve *Non-Cooperative*

Situations. The sum of the local resolutions of problematic situations leads to system-wide recoveries. A generic structure for these *cooperative* agents (cf. Section 3.2.1) is outlined in [Bernon et al., 2005a] (page 174). The fragmentation of this methodology is reported in [Rougemaille et al., 2009b] and the programming support comprises a model-driven development environment for code generation [Rougemaille et al., 2009a] (see Section 5.1.2). Goal-oriented modeling techniques have also been proposed to describe the problematic situations and the appropriate recoveries Morandini et al. [2009]. While inherently based on a top-down development procedure, the supportive use of system simulations is proposed in [Bernon et al., 2007]. This methodology is a customized version of the *Rational Unified Process* (RUP) [Kruchten, 2003]. In this respect, a complete development cycle is covered and integrated within an established development framework, but the methodology pertains to a specific agent model, i.e. the utilization of *cooperative* mechanisms (limitations outlined in [Bernon et al., 2005a]). The integration in the established RUP processes and the fragmentation of the development activities are worked out in several publications (comprehensive, well-defined). The development focuses on cooperative agents but may also use interaction mechanisms (e.g. see Bernon et al. [2007]; *single/multiple*).

The denoted development aspects describe the properties of a comprehensive support for application development. The coverage of the development work-flow and the engineering integration describe that the embedding of the self-organizing aspects go along with the application development. The mechanism support denotes the inherent focus for specific templates or patterns. In general, two types of methodical supports can be distinguished. First, development procedures focus on the planning of applications and the studied dynamics are subsequently integrated in a functioning software system. Simulation practices are transferred to the software development. These procedures guide the derivation of abstractionist of software systems, in particular simulation models, that allow to anticipate the application behavior. These abstractions serve as a blueprints and in the subsequent application development. In addition, integrations into software engineering practices has been proposed. These methodologies blend established procedures with activities that focus on the the integration of established patterns or mechanisms in the software system.

3.3 Conceptual Model of a Self-Organizing MAS

Figure 3.9 illustrates the conceptual structure of an agent-based application, where self-organizing system properties are established by integrating decentralized coordination techniques (cf. Section 3.2). The presentation distinguishes between *implementation elements*, i.e. components of system realization, and *design elements* that denote the distributed problem solving strategy. The application is realized as an *MAS* and therefore comprises *agent*[5] and *environment* models. Agents sense and act in the available environment(s). The application exhibits a macroscopic observable behavior (*System Behavior Space*). In agreement with mathematical modeling approaches of MASs (e.g. [Lerman and Galstyan, 2001], cf. Section 4.1.2), this behavior space is given by the macroscopic observable MAS configurations and the transitions between them. MAS configurations characterize the macroscopic observable states that the system can exhibit, defined by the sum of the agent configurations. Transitions between these states are manifested when agents collectively and concurrently adjust their local behavior (cf. Section 4.1.2). Consequently, trajectories in this space represent the dynamics of system reconfigurations. This space can be multi-dimensional; it serves as a design abstraction rather then a concrete modeling technique.

The collective adjustment of local agent behaviors is conceived by designing the (inter-) dependencies of agent activities (*Agent Activity Interdependency*). These dependencies describe how agents affect each other, and are established by enabling agents (1) to exchange information (*Information Flow*) and (2) respond to this information by adjusting the local configuration, i.e. observable behavior (*Behavior Adjustment*). These interdependencies correspond to the relations that constitute the distributed feedbacks that cause self-organization (see Section 3.1.4).

---

[5]It is assumed that the number of agents is more than two to justify the term <u>Multi</u>-agent System

68   CHAPTER 3. SELF-ORGANIZATION: A SOFTWARE PERSPECTIVE

The detailed realization of the local adaptivity of an agent model depends on the agent architecture (cf. Section 2.2.1) and adaptation-level mechanisms (see Section 3.2.1) used. Information exchange can be *direct* (*Direct Information Exchange*) or *mediated* (*Decentralized Coordination Mechanism*). Direct information flows are realized between agent components (agent-internal) or by the immediate communication between agent instances (inter-agent). Mediated information flows are established using of information propagation mechanisms such as digital pheromones, computational fields, tags, etc. (cf. Section 3.2.1), that provide interaction models (*Interaction Model*) to augment information flows with dynamic properties, e.g. to perturb communications and/or degrade information that is not reinforced. Interaction models describe how the information flows between agent instances are to be organized and these models are realized by specific infrastructures (*Coordination Infrastructure*, cf. Section 3.2) that utilize interaction techniques (*Interaction Technique*) such as tuple spaces or token exchange algorithms. These infrastructures, i.e. the availability of additional information to the agents, can be conceptually regarded as additional environment(s) [Gouaich and Michel, 2005] that are augmented to the MAS with the sole purpose of enabling agent coordination.

Transitions of MAS configurations such as collective responses to system external perturbations can be steered by controlling how agents mutually influence their local behaviors. Therefore, the interdependencies of agent behaviors can be regarded as the design concepts that allow developers to conceive decentralized coordination. The design of appropriate sets of interdependencies from first principles is feasible, but inherently difficult as it requires the anticipation of the effects of circular interrelations (cf. Section 3.2). Therefore, developers may refer to field-tested structures (*Coordinating Process*) of interdependencies. These structures are patterns of agent interdependencies (cf. 3.2.2) that establish well-known dynamic properties. Strategies are composite elements, as these can be composed of (sub-)strategy definitions.

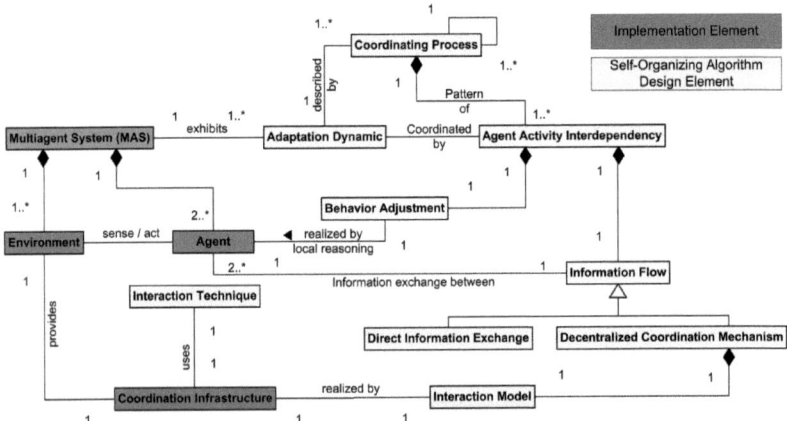

Figure 3.9: The conceptual structure of a self-organizing software application, adapted from [Sudeikat and Renz, 2009c]

Beginning with an agent-based design of a software system, the fundamental design activities which particularly concern the use of self-organizing processes are [Sudeikat and Renz, 2009h]:

1. the selection of an appropriate Coordinating Process and its constituent mechanisms,
2. the refinement of an application design to map the process structure to the application domain and the constituent agent models,

3. the implementation of the design, and

4. the calibration/parameterization of the system elements to induce the intended behavioral regime.

The first two activities are guided by heuristics and the designer's personal competence. Criteria for the selection of processes and mechanisms are discussed in Section 3.2 but the diversity of processes and mechanisms prohibits their generic treatment. The latter two activities pertain to the creation of the executable software system. The integration of coordination processes, for example the required interaction techniques, is facilitated by interaction infrastructures that allow the decoupling of agents. The conception of development methodologies, as reviewed in Section 3.2.4, instructs the system creation and parameterization.

The design tools presented here typically focus on the use of coordination mechanisms and interaction techniques. The intended coaction is not explicitly modeled and, if considered, only serves as an informal design inspiration [Mamei et al., 2006]. On the basis of these works, a modeling approach that concerns the explanation of decentralized coordinated system phenomena is discussed in the following section. The purposeful adjustment of application designs, in order to tune the system behavior, is made possible by the insights gained.

3.4 Intermediate Behavior Classification

The processes discussed in this chapter organize the behaviors of autonomous system entities to establish and alter structures that are manifested in the global system behavior. The conceptual model of self-organizing applications (Figure 3.9) contains both the microscopic and the macroscopic description levels. Implementation-related elements are the *microscopic* realizations of agents and environment elements. The coaction within the MAS generates the *macroscopic* system behavior (*Adaptation Dynamic*). The dependencies between the microscopic and macroscopic system properties are difficult to infer and bridging this gap is a major challenge to the development of decentralized coordination in software systems.

Multi-level modeling techniques allow self-organizing processes to be explained. The key objective is to abstract the activities of system entities according to their contribution to system-level phenomena. The abstraction is conducted in two steps. First, the behaviors that are shown by agents are examined and cataloged. Then these behaviors are classified according to their contributions and effects on the global system properties. System simulations are necessary to detect how agents behave and contribute.

The abstracted agent-behaviors provide an *intermediate* modeling level. In [Sudeikat and Renz, 2008a; Renz and Sudeikat, 2006, 2005b,a], this description approach is called *mesoscopic* to indicate an affinity to modeling techniques that describe phase transitions in physical systems, e.g. [Haken, 2004]. In Figure 3.10, the relations between the modeling levels (left) and their relation to system realizations (right) are illustrated. *Macroscopic* models describe properties of the system's behavior space, i.e. the adaptation dynamics (cf. Section 3.3). These models represent the behavior that systems show or are expected to show. *Microscopic* modeling levels contain details about the realizations of agents and their environment(s). These models *describe* the behaviors and interactions of agents as well as the reasoning within agent models that decides the adoption of courses of actions. Conversely, these models prescribe the implementation of system elements (*build-in*).

The rise of macroscopic system configurations are explained by intermediate system models (*Mesoscopic MAS Model*). These models contain the transitions between abstractions of microscopic agent activities that represent *coarse-grained* agent behaviors. These artifacts are derived (*modeling effort*) by merging sets of microscopic agent activities and replacing them with abstractions of agent-behaviors. These behaviors are not necessarily directly observable in microscopic agent configurations but can also involve *hidden* behaviors that average short time fluctuations among the microscopic activities. The interactions between the groups of agents that show the intermediate behaviors *explain* the establishment and modifications of the macroscopic properties.

70 CHAPTER 3. SELF-ORGANIZATION: A SOFTWARE PERSPECTIVE

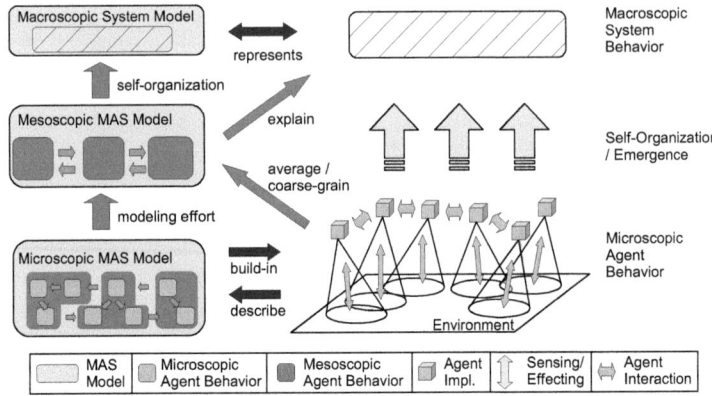

Figure 3.10: Micro-, Meso- and Macroscopic modeling of self-organizing system phenomena, adapted from [Sudeikat and Renz, 2008a]

The intermediate behavior abstractions differentiate from macroscopic models as their interactions contain the mechanics that cause short-time dynamics of a self-organizing process [Renz and Sudeikat, 2006]. The construction of the intermediate models is a considerable modeling effort. The abstraction and classification of agent-behaviors is fitted to explain a specific macroscopic property. Therefore, multiple mesoscopic models can exist for the same application, depending on the phenomena that are to be explained. Formal concretizations of these models, such as rate equations [Sudeikat and Renz, 2007a] or stochastic process algebra (see Appendix A) [Sudeikat and Renz, 2007d; Renz and Sudeikat, 2009], can be used to anticipate the possible system behavior(s).

3.4.1 Redesigning Multi-Agent Systems

Besides explaining self-organizing system phenomena by bottom-up system analyses, intermediate description levels facilitate the *redesign* of applications in order to tune the exhibited system behavior. The starting pint is a system that shows emergent properties. The *redesign* of these systems refers to the reconstruction of these systems with equivalent macroscopic behaviors. The reconstruction allows to control and enhance the system's operation, i.e. to tune the arising structures and emergents. This approach is conceptually interesting as it allows to relate emergent and macroscopic system properties to the self-organization of behaviors at intermediate description levels. It is of practical relevance as it systematizes the adjustment of system-level phenomena.

The generation of the equivalent *Macroscopic System Behavior* is illustrated in Figure 3.11. A *Microscopic Agent Model* gives rise to emergent properties as the macroscopic system level (*emergent*). This model is encoded in the *Microscopic Agent Behaviors(s)* (*built-in*). The microscopic behaviors can be abstracted to a *Mesoscopic Agent Model* (see Figure 3.10). The *self-organization* of the mesoscopic agent behaviors averages out the short-time fluctuations and can be used to bing by the macroscopic system behavior. The mesoscopic models are used to clarify the underlying dynamics that give rise to emergents. The explicit control of these dynamics is enabled by considering the mesoscopic agent states in the agent design in the second and/or fourth development activities in Section 3.3.

Macroscopic system models describe the principally possible space of system configurations. Based on the intentional phenomena, the configuration space can be partitioned in *intended* and

3.4. INTERMEDIATE BEHAVIOR CLASSIFICATION

unintended subareas of configurations. Then the phenomena can be described by the potential transitions between these partitions and consequent design objectives are to encourage intended configurations and suppress unwanted configurations. The intended emergents are described as a consequence of the coaction of mesoscopic agent behaviors. Thus the intermediate models prepare a vocabulary that bridges the gap between micro- and macroscopic system properties. The system's operation can be enhanced by identifying the behaviors that are favorable in specific application contexts. The macroscopic system configurations are indirectly controlled by adjusting microscopic system elements to encourage the exhibition of the subset of behaviors that support the intended configurations, or to suppress unwanted configurations, on the macroscopic system level. By controlling the adoption of these mesoscopic agent behaviors, the expected behavior can be build into the MAS.

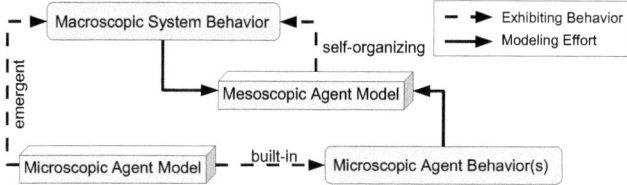

Figure 3.11: Micro-, meso- and macroscopic models [Renz and Sudeikat, 2006]

Two redesign approaches allow for the control of mesoscopic agent behaviors. First, the microscopic models can be *modified* to encourage the exhibition of favorable behaviors. The environment elements, (microscopic) agent behaviors, and the agent-intern reasoning, which controls the activation and execution of behaviors, can be modified by changing parameterizations or adjusting implementation elements. Alternatively, the intermediate behaviors can be directly embedded in agent implementations. This *redevelopment* is a straightforward way to embed additional rules and parameters within agents to control self-organizing phenomena. This approach increases the development efforts, as new agent models are constructed, but enhances the control of the arising phenomenon. The first redesign technique (*by modification*) is exemplified in Section 3.4.2 and the latter approach (*by redevelopment*) is demonstrated in Section 3.4.3.

3.4.2 Example: Collaborative Sorting / Clustering

Bio-inspired coordination strategies, as reviewed in Section 3.2.2, provide field-tested template solutions to distributed coordination problems. One prominent example is the *Brood Sorting* behavior of insect colonies. Items of differing types, such as eggs and larvae, are ordered as individual agents constantly and spontaneously transport them to nearby elements that satisfy a similarity criterion. Without an overall nest architecture the dynamics of the individual transports cluster items, e.g. separate eggs from larvae. These algorithms are well-studied in computational and robotic application domains and have found application in the clustering of large-scale data in open systems where streams of incoming elements are to be structured (cf. Section 3.2.2).

In [Sudeikat and Renz, 2006], the systematic adjustment of realizations of this coordination strategy, following the described redesign approach, is discussed. The system performance is enhanced by abstracting the agent activities and identifying behaviors that have to be influenced. The adoption of positively contributing behaviors is increased and the execution of negatively contributing behaviors is decreased. In this scenario, functional aspects such as the movement velocity, sensor capacity, etc., are not modified and auxiliary functions for example communicative abilities, are not added. System performance is adjusted *by modification* of the agent and environment elements.

Microscopic System Model and Macroscopic Established Structures

The microscopic system model contains a number (N) of reactive agents that are situated in a torus shaped environment. The environment is evenly partitioned in rectangular patches that are identified by Cartesian coordinates (x, y). Initially, a fixed number of items is randomly distributed, i.e. placed on randomly selected coordinates. Items are distinguished by one property, namely their color value. The agents perform a completely random walk (Brownian motion) in the environment, i.e. in every simulation step the heading is set to a random number of degrees and the agent moves one step forward. While moving in the environment, agents show two behaviors. By default, agents are unbound and *search* for items. When an item is encountered, i.e. is placed on the same patch, the agent is bound to it and *transports* the item. Upon the encounter of a similar item, as specified by a similarity criterion, the bound agent searches for a free, nearby location, deposits its item, and subsequently reverts to the unbound, searching behavior. The deposit is inhibited when non-similar items are present within a fixed repulsion range, i.e. a distance that is specified as a number of patches.

In principle, five types of macroscopic structures can arise [Sudeikat and Renz, 2006]: the initial, (1) *unsorted* distribution of items persists, items are arranged in (2) one *large cluster* or (3) a set of *smaller clusters*. The repulsion parameter controls the deposit of items and influences the composition of clusters. The pro principal forms are the establishment of (4) *distinguishable* clusters or (5) one large cluster with *distinguishable regions*.

The agents continue to operate when all items have been arranged in clusters. Therefore, the clusters are emergents that show their own dynamics. It can be observed that larger clusters assimilate smaller clusters, i.e. clusters converge. In addition, the clusters do not persist at the same position but their center moves, based on the stochastic transport of items [Sudeikat and Renz, 2006]. Based on the parameterization of the system, the convergence can lead to distinct clusters (cf. 4), one for each item type. Alternatively, a cluster can emerge that comprises all item types (cf. 2) or exhibits item-specific regions (cf. 5).

Mesoscopic System Model

The purposeful adjustment of the system behavior requires reasoning about the contribution of the individual agents to the arising structures. The observation of agent activities has shown that the Brownian motion of agents influences the formation of clusters in three distinct types. The identification of these contribution types constitutes the intermediate, mesoscopic system model and is illustrated in Figure 3.12 (I, II). First, agents transport items comparatively *fast* when the agent is coincidentally heading toward another cluster. Secondly, a transport is comparatively *slow* when agents, based on their stochastic movement, detour before their arrival at a cluster. Finally, the transports add items to the same cluster, i.e. *pack* them.

The objective of the system (re-)design is to enhance the clustering. This demands that the averaged transportation time be accelerated, i.e. *fast* (1) transportations be enforced. The averred transportation time is related to the environment size, the walking behavior of the agents and the probability of arriving at a cluster.

Redesign of Agent Activities: Stiffening the Random Walk

The first redesign addresses the random walk behavior of agents. The Brownian motion leads to erratic paths of agents where the Euclidean distance between origin and destination positions is comparatively short compared to the number of steps. Consequently, the walking pattern of agents is *stiffened* in a first redesign. Agents measure their current velocity, based on the walked euclidean distance from an item pick-up location. The velocity constrains the deviation of the current agent heading, i.e. when agents accelerate, the deviation of their heading is reduced. The trajectories of the agents stiffen over time and consequently the mean velocity increases.

3.4. INTERMEDIATE BEHAVIOR CLASSIFICATION

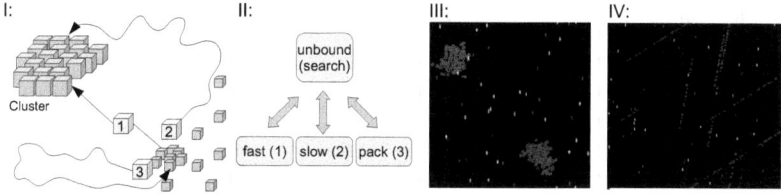

Figure 3.12: Transportation behaviors (I, II; following [Sudeikat and Renz, 2008a]), and simulation screen-shots (III, IV)

Redesign of Environment: Spatial Cluster Layout

An alternative approach to increasing transport velocities is to raise the probability that transporting agents encounter clusters. This probability is raised by increasing the surface of the spatial cluster. In an alternative redesign, agents end their transport behavior by placing transported items on the patch where a subsequent encounter triggers the deposit. Dropped items adopt the heading of the nearby items and move (slide) to next empty patch. Consequently, the clusters are arranged in elongated structures of aligned items with similar colors. The different shapes are illustrated in Figure 3.12.[6] Conventionally established clusters are roughly circular shaped (III) and the proposed redesign establishes elongated structures (IV). Corresponding simulation models contain agents that show the adjusted walking behavior.

Simulation Results

The two redesigns are compared to the original system behavior [Sudeikat and Renz, 2006]. For 10000 time steps, 50 agents cluster 200 items equally divided between two colors. The agent-based simulation models were realized with the Netlogo framework (cf. Section 3.1.5).

In Figure 3.13 (I), the temporal changes of the mean transportation velocity are plotted. This velocity is measured by the squared displacement of items divided by the transportation time [Sudeikat and Renz, 2006]. Brownian moving agents exhibit the slowest, most uniform transportation of items (a). The *stiffened* random-walking agents, which follow the first redesign, show an initially high transportation velocity that subsequently slows down (b). This change results from the randomness of the agent movement. Initially, items are randomly distributed and picked-up items are dropped at comparatively small clusters after relatively short travel times. The convergence of bigger clusters decelerates the individual transports. Transporting agents need longer to approach the fewer clusters of increasing size. The cluster shapes require perturbations of the agent movement. Deterministic straight-walking agents frustrate the establishment of larger clusters as the increasing density affects fractions of continuously transporting agents that do not reach clusters. Following the second redesign, the spatial shape of the clusters constantly affects the release, i.e. evacuation, of items. The transportation speed remains at a comparatively high level during the convergence of larger clusters (c).

The observed transportation velocities correspond roughly to the averaged workloads of the individual agents, which are plotted in Figure 3.13 (II). The workload of the agent population is measured by the sum of time steps in which individuals are transporting over the whole simulation period [Sudeikat and Renz, 2006]. The Brownian-moving agents quickly approach a high average utilization (a). Their utilization decreases as their transportation times decelerate. The agents spend more time searching than transporting. The stiffened walking agents improve the agent utilization in system configurations with scattered items (b). Their long-term behavior approaches

---
[6]Boxes denote items and are colored according to the item type (red/blue). Pictographic characters indicate agents and are colored according to the transported item type (red/blue). Unbound agents are colored white.

a workload that is similar to the Brownian-moving agents. In the second redesign, the increased probability of encountering clusters raises the averaged agent workload (c). The decrease of this workload in the long-time behavior is significantly reduced.

The transport velocities exhibited affect the clustering efficiency, as plotted in Figure 3.13 (III). This efficiency is measured by the fraction of items in the environment that are located in clusters [Sudeikat and Renz, 2006]. This measure expresses the time needed to place items in clusters, i.e. how items are initially located and transported. The convergence times of larger clusters is ignored. Open environments, with a fluctuating inflow of new items, impede the complete convergence of clusters, but the comparison of initial allocations indicate the effectiveness of item search and transport [Sudeikat and Renz, 2006]. Brownian-moving agents exhibit the lowest effectiveness (a). The increased transport speed of the first redesign increases effectiveness (b) and the second redesign leads to the quickest initial arrangement of items (c).

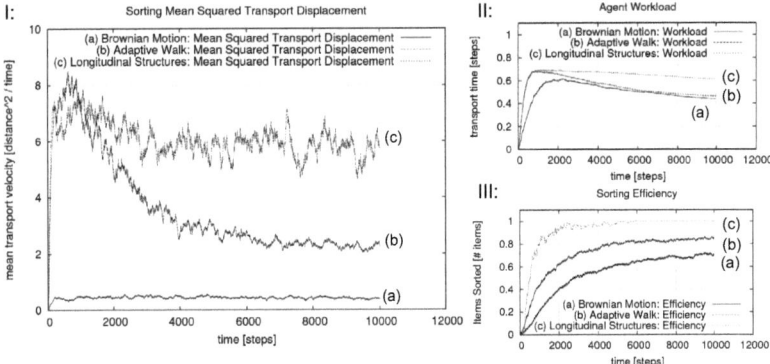

Figure 3.13: Collective clustering simulation results [Sudeikat and Renz, 2006]: the mean squared transportation displacement (I), the mean workload (II), and the effectiveness of the clustering, measured by the number of items that are arranged in clusters (III)

This case study examines how the global system dynamics, i.e. the clustering behavior, can be adjusted by minimal redesigns of the original reactive agent models and their environment. The qualitative difference between the two redesigns is demonstrated and the effects of introduced parameters are not considered [Sudeikat and Renz, 2006]. When the computational resources of the agents/environments are not strictly constrained, redesign efforts may provide agents with enhanced sensors/effectors, communicative abilities, and/or reasoning capabilities.

3.4.3 Example: The Minority Game

The Minority Game (MG) is a well-studied theoretical setting that shows complex behaviors despite simple definitions of the game environment and the actors [Challet et al., 2004]. This section discusses, a novel solution to this game that balances the profit of individual players with the overall gain that is generated by the player community. Having found this solution, the implementation in an MAS is discussed by directly encoding the mesoscopic player strategies in the agent models (cf. Section 3.4.1). The redesign *by redevelopment* is exemplified where the agent-internal reasoning is rebuilt to enforce the intended system behavior. This section summarizes the results that are discussed in [Renz and Sudeikat, 2005b,a, 2006].

In socio-economic settings, it is often not feasible to compute sound solutions to decision problems. Rational agents can be overchallenged, due to (1) their bounded rationality (2) or their

3.4. INTERMEDIATE BEHAVIOR CLASSIFICATION

participation in interactive scenarios where assumptions of the future behavior of other agents are required [Arthur, 1994]. Consequently, agents have to reason inductively, e.g. by revising their internal hypotheses about the effects of their activities. A prominent hypothetical setting for examining the effects of collective inductive reasoning is the *El Farol Bar Problem* (EFBP) [Arthur, 1994]. This scenario is named after a bar in Santa Fe and agents repeatedly have to decide if they are going to *go* to the bar or *stay home*. Agents have to make binary decisions and benefit from choosing the minority side. Visiting this venue is only enjoyable if it is not overcrowded, defined by a fixed threshold of visitors. All agents decide autonomously and their only source of information is the history of visitor-counts from the past evenings. Thus agents can not decide rationally. They can not anticipate the number of agents that will go at the same time. Instead inductive reasoning is required, based on past experiences.

Minority Games are socio-inspired, exact formulations of this type of scenario. An odd number of N players repeatedly and simultaneously makes binary decisions (yes or no, 1, or 0, etc.). For each round, the majority of agents comes away empty-handed, but the agents that are in the minority, i.e. that only agree with $\leq N-1$ agents, are awarded a reward, e.g. a score increment. This hypothetical scenario can be transferred to daily life decisions where it is beneficial to choose the minority side. In an economic-inspired interpretation, agents represent consumers that have the choice between two suppliers.

In the classical model, agents use a set of *strategies* to decide which supplier to take [Challet and Zhang, 1997]. These strategies are tables that map a sequence of past minority values to the consequent decision of the agent. With a memory size of m, there are 2^m possible histories and 2^{2^m} possible strategies. Agents are initialized with a set of randomly generated strategies. The agents are informed about the results of every round and compare the performances that would have resulted from applying each strategy. The most productive strategy[7] is used by the agent.

Numerous modifications of the game that refine the decision making process within agents have been introduced, including evolutionary [Metzler and Horn, 2003] and stochastic approaches [Reents et al., 2001]. The rich behaviors found in this class of simple game settings exemplifies how self-organization arises from simple rule sets [Burgos and Ceva, 2000]. The minimalistic setting is of conceptual interest to understand the basic factors of these behaviors, e.g. as examined in [Parunak et al., 2004b].

The performance in a minority game can be evaluated on the system and the individual level. In one round, the maximal possible reward is generated if the size of the minority is maximal, i.e. $\frac{N-1}{2}$. This behavior can be obtained by synchronizing agents to constant groups of winning and losing agents. The individual success of agents is given by their individual score, which is increased by successful selections of minority values. The overall and individual success can be examined by the resulting score histograms and their statistical properties. In addition, *fairness* is desirable. In this context, fairness is understood as the approximately equal distribution of minority values and agent scores. The selection of minorities and the participation in this group are not biased but all values are selected with equal rights and agents are not excluded from the minority side.

The *Schwarzer Peter* Solution

In an *adaptive stochastic* variant of the MG (SMG) [Renz and Sudeikat, 2005b,a, 2006] adaptive agent behavior are realized by controlling the selections of agents with time evolving probabilities. Self-organized synchronization and behavior rotation can be realized within a small strategy space. The model presented here generalizes simple stochastic MGs [Reents et al., 2001] and evolutionary MGs [Metzler and Horn, 2003] and displays a dynamic adaptation of decision behaviors, such as are discussed in [Xie et al., 2005; Zhong et al., 2004].

Each agent (i) maintains a probability value $p_i(t) \in [0,1]$ that defines the likelihood that the agent changes its selected value in the next round. In the round-based setting the time t corresponds to the indices of rounds. Consequently, the agent i selects the same value that was selected in the previous round with the probability $1 - p_i(t)$. The current selection of the agent i is

---
[7]ties are randomly broken

given by $s_i(t) \in 0, 1$. Initially, selection values ($s_i(0)$) are randomly set and the agent probabilities are uniformly distributed within the interval $[0, 1]$. Agents adjust the probability values after every round as illustrated in Figure 3.14 (I). The agents that are in the minority update their probability value by multiplying their current probability with a fixed parameter $\lambda_+ > 0$ ($p_i(t+1) = \lambda_+ \cdot p_i(t)$). The remaining agents multiply with the parameter λ_- ($p_i(t+1) = \lambda_- \cdot p_i(t)$). When $\lambda_+, \lambda_- > 1$, the maximum probability is 1.

The parameters λ_+, λ_- define how agents react to success and failure. This is the control space of the adaptive behavior that arises among agents. The system can exhibit a mixed space of individual strategies that fluctuates or converges to steady states where the configurations of individuals are balanced. Simulations of this stochastic variation of the Minority Game revealed at least five different regimes of system behaviors [Renz and Sudeikat, 2005b]. In the partition $\lambda_+ > 1, \lambda_- = 1$ of the parameter space a phenomenon occurs that has been called the *Schwarzer Peter* solution [Renz and Sudeikat, 2005b, 2006].[8] The agent population is gradually partitioned to an equal amount of $\frac{N-1}{2}$ agents that are alternating selections with $p_i = 1.0$. One additional agent is left with $p_j \neq 1.0$. These agent-groups counter-rotate their selections continuously. Since these groups are equally sized, the selection of the not synchronized agent (p_j), determines the majority. To put it in other words, the selection of the agent j is always the losing majority, therefore this group pulls the short straw, by coinciding with the additional agent.

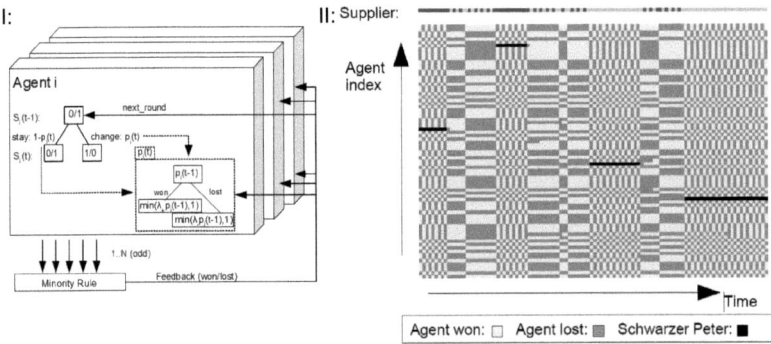

Figure 3.14: The stochastic selection process inside agents (I) and a sample simulation run that exemplifies the rotation of the *Schwarzer Peter* behavior (II). Both figures follow the presentation in [Renz and Sudeikat, 2006].

When λ_- is set slightly below 1, the members of losing groups minimize their probability to alternate. A set of mixed strategies establishes a cooperative behavior. These are potential new p_j agents and the role of determining the minority circulates among the agent population by chance. A sample simulation run is illustrated in Figure 3.14 (II). Each line represents the local behavior of one agent. The presence of a *Schwarzer Peter* agent is accompanied by strict alternation of the two agent groups that are spontaneously formed. These phases are intermitted by unorganized phases where the p_i-values increase until one agent is left to play the distinct agent role for a limited number of subsequent time steps. As the role is only adopted for a limit amount of time, the associated loss is shared among the agent community. This role is not prescribed in the agent reasoning but arises from the interactions of the agents. That an agent plays this role can not be inferred from its local p_i-value, but results from the absence of lower p_is in the agent population. Consequently, this type of role is called an *emergent* role in [Renz and Sudeikat, 2006]. These

---
[8]In german-speaking countries *Schwarzer Peter* is an idiom, which originates from a children's card game and means "to pull the short straw".

3.4. INTERMEDIATE BEHAVIOR CLASSIFICATION

roles result from the agent interplay and are only observable in the macroscopic system behavior.

Reconstruction by Embedding Mesoscopic Agent Strategies

Monitoring the observable agent behaviors and comparing them to the local configuration space of agents allows the fundamental agent behaviors to be classified according to their contribution to the global system behavior. The local configurations of agents are neglected but the principal, coarse-grained effects of agents to the system behavior are accounted for. The strategies identified in the stochastic MG correspond to the averaged, intermediate agent behaviors that are discussed in Section 3.4, which describe the contributions of agents to the global system behavior.

The pivotal strategies of agents are summarized in Table 3.2. For each strategy, the current agent value $s_i(t)$ is related to the consequently selected value $s_i(t+1)$. When the p_i values approach extremes, nearly deterministic *loyal* and *alternating* agent behaviors can be observed. For $p \to 0$ this strategy is called $supplier-loyal$ (L) and $p \to 1$ signifies an *alternating* (A) strategy. Between these extremes agents are *undecided* (U), i.e. the agents select by chance according to their local p_i value.

$s_i(t)$	probability	$s_i(t+1)$
0L		0L
1L		1L
0U	p, 1-p	0U, 1U resp.
1U	p, 1-p	1U, 0U resp.
0A		1A
1A		0A

Table 3.2: The mesoscopic agent strategies: Loyal agents (0L,1L) adhere to their previous selection, alternating agents (0A,1A) change their selection, and undetermined players (0U,1U) rotate their selection with the probability p [Renz and Sudeikat, 2005a].

As discussed in Section 3.4.1, the building of a self-organizing structure can be approached by (re-)designing agent models to directly reflect the mesoscopic behaviors in the implementation. In [Renz and Sudeikat, 2005b,a, 2006], the redesign is approached by replacing the stochastically determined strategies of agents with reversible deterministic transitions between a set of agent states. Each state represents one of the pivotal strategies that agents can adopt, i.e. the *loyal, alternating* and *undecided* behaviors. For each of the strategies, a selection function is provided that determines the next selection, based on the current agent selection or the agent p_i value. Agents keep track of their history. When their individual success and failure exceeds fixed thresholds, they transition into an adjacent strategy. Details on the implementation can be found in [Renz and Sudeikat, 2005b].

In order to track the evolution of strategy adoptions, the correlation of strategies and selection values are modeled, leading to a six-strategy model (cf. Figure 3.15). The quantities $N_{0/1,L/O/U}$ describe the numbers of agents that exhibit a certain strategy. This models abstracts microscopic models of the stochastic Minority Game as the continuous space of the evolving strategy is replaced by a set of averaged strategies. This model is not macroscopic, as it is time-discrete and allows short-time fluctuations. The illustrated states are not directly observable in the macroscopic system behavior, which only denoted the overall supplier choice. However, the individual agent history determines the exhibition of these individual behaviors.

This reimplementation not only structures the behavioral model of agents but also introduces additional parameters, i.e. a set of time-dependent, deterministic transition rates λ, μ, which, in addition to the individual probability p_i, affect the individual changes under the influence of their individual success/failure. These are determined by the individual histories and the winner side $i(t)$. The winning selection value is self-consistently determined by [Renz and Sudeikat, 2006]:

$$N_1 - N_0 = \sum_{j \in \{L,U,A\}} (N_{1j} - N_{0j})$$

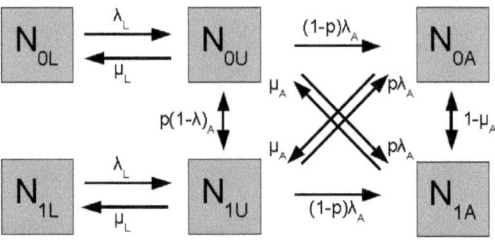

Figure 3.15: The transitions between the implemented agent behaviors [Renz and Sudeikat, 2006]

Formally, the time-discrete evolution of the strategy occupation numbers (cf. Figure 3.15) follows [Renz and Sudeikat, 2006]:

$$\begin{aligned}
N_{0L}(t+1) &= (1-\lambda_L(t))N_{0L}(t) + \mu_L(t)N_{0U}(t) \\
N_{1L}(t+1) &= (1-\lambda_L(t))N_{1L}(t) + \mu_L(t)N_{1U}(t) \\
N_{0U}(t+1) &= \lambda_L(t)N_{0L}(t) \\
&\quad + [(1-\lambda_A(t))(1-p) - \mu_L(t)]\,N_{0U}(t) \\
&\quad + (1-\lambda_A(t))pN_{1U}(t) + \mu_A(t)N_{1A}(t) \\
N_{1U}(t+1) &= \lambda_L(t)N_{1L}(t) + (1-\lambda_A(t))pN_{0U}(t) \\
&\quad + [(1-\lambda_A(t))(1-p) - \mu_L(t)]\,N_{1U}(t) \\
&\quad + \mu_A(t)N_{0A}(t) \\
N_{0A}(t+1) &= \lambda_A(t)(1-p)N_{0U}(t) + \lambda_L(t)pN_{1U}(t) \\
&\quad + (1-\mu_A(t))N_{1A}(t) \\
N_{1A}(t+1) &= \lambda_A(t)pN_{0U}(t) + \lambda_L(t)(1-p)N_{1U}(t) \\
&\quad + (1-\mu_A(t))N_{0A}(t)
\end{aligned}$$

A detailed analysis of the agent behaviors explains the self-organized optimization. Agents are driven to the opposing instances of the alternating strategies. Due to the deterministic transition rules, agents return to the undetermined strategy after a while, thus losing agents are able to change to the winning side. Consequently, all agents are able to rotate through the winner and loser sides, thereby establishing averaged, long-term fairness in the agent population. The same behavior makes the emergent *Schwarzer Peter* role rotate among agents. In the stochastic MG this behavior is emergent, while it is build in the redesigned agent model.

Comparison and Simulation Results

The behavior of the reimplementation of the averaged agent strategies is equivalent to the behavior of the microscopic, stochastic Minority Game with indefinitely many strategies [Renz and Sudeikat, 2006]. The reimplementation also supports the mixing of strategies, as well as the evolution of loyal and alternating strategies as observable in the purely stochastic model. These regimes are defined by the parameters λ's, μ's and p in the sic-strategy model.

The intended behavior is observed in the mixing regime of agent strategies. Both selection values are chosen almost equally often while agents win an average of half of the time steps. This behavior, as observed in the parameter region $\lambda_+ > 1, \lambda_- < 1$ of the microscopic model, is found in the reimplementation for the parameters $\lambda_j > \mu_j$ for $j = L, A$. When the minority group is not maximally sized, the agent population is not generating the maximal available score. Thus

3.4. INTERMEDIATE BEHAVIOR CLASSIFICATION

global performance of a set of agents can be quantified by the difference of the agent selections $s_i(t)$ in one round [Renz and Sudeikat, 2005b]:

$$A(t) = 2 \sum_{i=0}^{N-1} s_i(t) - N \qquad s_i(t) \in \{0, 1\} \tag{3.1}$$

The global loss of scores, due to repeated unbalanced selections, is expressed by the long–time average $\bar{A} = \langle A(t) \rangle_t$. Consequently, the deviation is given by [Renz and Sudeikat, 2005b]:

$$\sigma^2(t) = A^2(t) - \bar{A}^2 \quad \text{and its long–time average} \quad \overline{\sigma^2} = \langle \sigma^2(t) \rangle_t \tag{3.2}$$

In Figure 3.16, simulation results for both implementations[9] are compared. The averaged reimplementation is parameterized with $\lambda_L = 1, \lambda_a = 1/s$ for successful agents and $\mu_L = 1/10, \mu_A = 1/f$ for unsuccessful agents. The probability is $p = 0.95$. The microscopic, stochastic model is examined in the region $\lambda_+ > 1, \lambda_- < 1$, where $1 - \lambda_- << \lambda_+ - 1$.

Within these parameter ranges, equivalent behavior can be observed. In Figure 3.16, the deviation from the global optimum, i.e. the loss of the system, is plotted as function of the scaled number of agents. The scaling is used to place simulation data on a theoretical fit that shows a crossover between the theoretical optimum and the $O(N)$ behavior of the systems. The displayed data collapse results from a scaling with $ln\lambda_-$ for the microscopic model and with $\frac{f}{f+s}$ for the reimplementation. Both models generate the almost individually fair and nearly globally optimal behavior at arbitrary large numbers of agent N limited by $\lambda_- \to 1$ or $f \to \infty$, respectively.

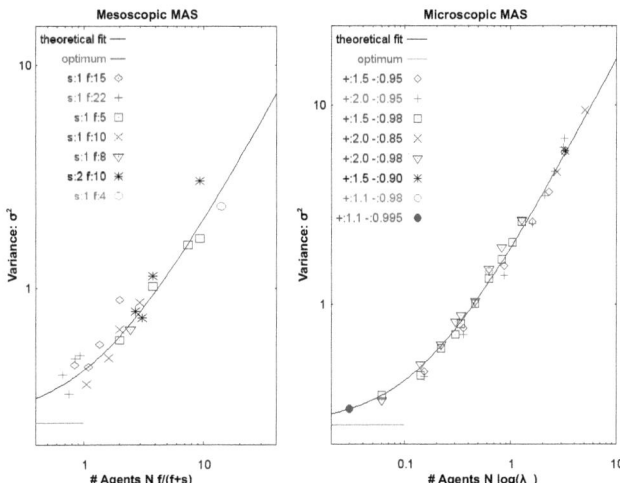

Figure 3.16: The squared global loss of the microscopic and mesoscopic implementations models, plotted as a function of the scaled numbers of agents [Renz and Sudeikat, 2006, 2005a]

Here, it is shown how a self-organizing, microscopic mechanism can be purposefully redesigned. This exemplifies a constructive approach to the implementation of self-organizing dynamics. A set of agent states, here the decision strategies, are derived from the analysis of a self-organizing phenomenon. When the rise of the phenomenon is understood in such detail that the contributions

---
[9]Based on the Jadex System, see Section 2.2.2.

of the pivotal agent states to globally arising structures are known, the direct implementation of the identified states can be used to structure that agent model. Additional parameters are induced that facilitate the tuning of the system behavior as their effects on the global structure can be anticipated. Therefore, similar behaviors can be generated in a controlled and predictive way. A drawback of this approach is the manual modeling effort that is required to appropriately analyze the phenomenon, i.e. the adaptive process that gives rise to the structures of interest.

3.5 Application Areas

Here, prominent application scenarios, which are studied in academics and/or are adopted in industry, are outlined. The list is not intended to be exhaustive, but conveys an impression of the range of application domains that benefit from using self-organizing processes. Additional reviews can be found in [Serugendo et al., 2003; Bernon et al., 2006]. Prominent research areas are *networked* software systems such as in Sensor and Actuator networks (SANETs) [Dressler, 2007], peer-to-peer systems [Milojicic et al., 2003], and routing in communication networks [Ducatelle et al., 2010]. Particularly pertinent, annual conference series, such as *Self-Adaptive and Self-Organizing Systems* (SASO)[10] were searched for case studies and applications. These works are arbitrarily as well as deliberately selected to indicate the spectrum of application areas in this active research community. The classification of application scenarios is related to the *Market and Deployment Analysis* from [Luck et al., 2005] (Section 6). In this work, experts from academics and industry were surveyed for industry sectors where the adoption of agent technology is anticipated. In a subset of these domains, the adoption of self-organizing solutions is reported and/or studied.

The virtue of these solutions is the joint support for three orthogonal application aspects (see Figure 3.17). When an application setting demands *decentralized* coordination (x axis), a high degree of system-wide *adaptivity* (y axis), and a high degree of system-level *autonomy*, the use of self-organization principles is indicated. The decentralization of the application structure is a possible response to inherent application properties, e.g. the number of system elements or their physical distribution. In addition, the decentralization of the control and information of the system coordination adds to the robustness and scalability of applications. The responsibilities pertaining to the coordination of the system are equally shared and thus the addition, removal, and adjustment of system elements has only a local impact (see Section 3.1.1). When facing failures, the systems ability to structure itself is gradually degrading and not instantly disabled. The y axis describes the degree of system level adaptivity that is required in the application domain. The exhibited adaptivity ranges from the management of partitions or (sub-)components to the system level adaptivity of the application itself. When inter-component structures must be managed, self-organization is a viable solution approach. The degrees of the system-level autonomy (z axis) describe the ability and practicability of manual interventions. The utilization of self-organization implies that the control logic is shared among the system elements. Consequently, modifications of the control logic, e.g. the updates of the local rules, constraints, or policies that steer the local coordination-related activities, is associated with additional effort. Self-organization is most appropriate for scenarios where the system is expected to work autonomously with minimal administrative interventions.

The use of *Self-Organization* (see Figure 3.17) is a means to combine all three design aspects. These processes combine an inherent decentralization with the autonomous and adaptive operation of the software system. The use of Self-Management technologies (see Section 3.1.2) also allows the support for the autonomous, adaptive operation of the distributed software system. The decentralization of these approaches is limited since subsystems are explicitly controlled by managing software entities or hierarchies of these managers.

The three aspects extend the design aspects that motivate the adoption of agent technology (see Section 2.8, page 41). The decentralization of the application management is based on the distribution aspect of agent-based systems. The system is not only composed of remote agents

---

[10] http://www.saso-conference.org/

3.5. APPLICATION AREAS

but the information and control of system aspects is shared by the agents. The system level adaptivity is an enhancement of the localized adaptivity of software agents. While agents can manage their local responsibilities self-organization is a means to manage the system-wide properties. The system level autonomy can also be understood as an enhancement of the autonomy of software agents. The system itself is autonomous as it exhibits the structure formation without external interventions. However, the exertion of influences, e.g. via control parameters, to control the formations can be prepared. These influence the arising structures but the causative process is integrated in the software system. The combination of these aspects can be relevant for systems that are based on different technologies that prepare the construction of distributed applications. Examples are *Web Services*, *Peer-to-Peer Computing*, and *Grid Computing*, e.g. reviewed with respect to MAS in [Luck et al., 2005]. These provide concepts and infrastructures for the distribution of software systems and the size and/or the complexity of computational problems, when a approached by a compound of system entities, can justify solutions that combine these design aspects (see Figure 3.17). In the remainder of this section three prominent application domains are outlined.

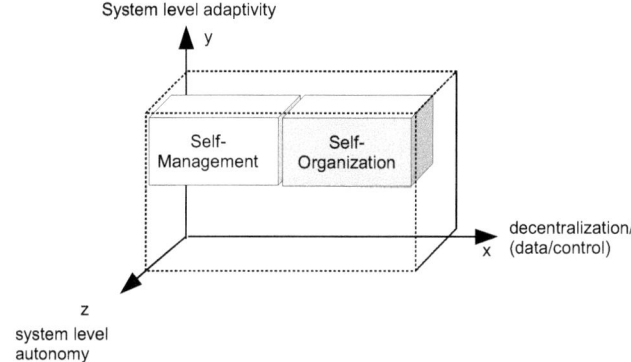

Figure 3.17: Design concerns that motivate the adoption of self-organizing solutions

Infrastructure & Information Management

Sophisticated infrastructures are used to provide today's distributed software systems and the elements in these infrastructures, such as application and data servers, can be themselves complex elements [Garlan et al., 2004; Abdellatif et al., 2007]. The automated maintenance of these infrastructures is an active research field for technology providers. It motivates research on self-managing architectures (see Section 3.1.2) and is of economic interest as it makes the infrastructures adaptive and frees providers from manual maintenance. Example fields are the power management [Jeffrey et al., 2008] and dynamic server migration/consolidation in data centers [Bobroff et al., 2007]. When centers are dimensioned for a low average utilization of the individual servers, the adaptive management is of economic interest. Examples are the reduction of the energy consumption by adaptively powering servers on/off and the dynamic association of virtual machines in order to adapt to demand changes.

Self-organizing approaches can be used to eliminate the need for distinct managing entities such as *resource brokers* in service grids [Schlegel and Kowalczyk, 2008]. In this work services are nomadic, i.e. the decide locally whether to interact remotely with interaction partners or to migrate to the location of interaction partners, in order to interact locally. Another example is the adoption of nature-inspired management processes in [Nakrani and Tovey, 2004] to control the service deployments in server farms. These deployments are balanced with the fluctuating demands for specific service types. This scenario is demonstrated in Section 5.4.1 and an agent-based management of service deployments on open source application servers is demonstrated in Section 6.8.2.

Another concern that falls into this category is the processing of large data sets in information systems and data visualization. The processing of large and possibly ever-growing amounts of data justifies their processing with collectives of decentralized processes. An example is the utilization of swarm techniques for data visualizations [Moere, 2008]. The objective is to generate visual representations of data that convey interrelations such as trends and outliers. Self-organization is used to allow the data sets to order themselves. Data items are associated to agents and the data properties control the visual agent behavior, for example the position and speed. In [Moere, 2008], different organization methods, such as those inspired by flocking or particle movements, and the arising visual pattern are discussed. A related approach is the use of self-organizing process for information retrieval in large sets of documents [Parunak et al., 2005]. The basic activities of this processing are the clustering of relevant data (sort) and the removal of less relevant data (sift). The former is realized in analogy to the brood sorting of ant colonies (e.g. as exemplified in Section 3.4.2) [Parunak et al., 2005] and the latter is based on a the emulation of foraging dynamics (see Section 3.2.2).

Manufacturing Control

The applicability of agent technology for the development of control systems that operate in dynamic environments is demonstrated in [Jennings and Bussmann, 2003], using the example of manufacturing line management [Jennings and Bussmann, 2003]. In these systems, the objective is to process streams of incoming work pieces by sequentially applying distinct production steps. Typically, these lines are arranged in static configurations. Machines, each responsible for a production step, are connected with fixed transport mechanisms such as conveyor belts [Jennings and Bussmann, 2003]. This fixed structure implies rigid run-time management by global schedules. Unexpected events, such as disturbances or machine failures affect the whole production process and force a centralized rescheduling. Thus centralized management approaches are inappropriate [Jennings and Bussmann, 2003] and distributed agent-based systems are proposed. An example is the *Organic Design Pattern* (ODP) [Seebach et al., 2007] that generalizes this application domain and provides an architectural model for the introduction of managing software entities that automatically reconfigure the system to establish valid flows of work pieces. Particularly for small production volumes, it is desirable that systems are able to reconfigure themselves [Frei et al., 2008].

In this application domain, the use of self-organization is studied as well. An industrial application is deployed by DaimlerChrysler [Jennings and Bussmann, 2003; Bussmann and Schild, 2000]. Machines are interconnected with flexible transport mechanisms. This enables an agent-based, continuous management process. Work pieces and production line elements, e.g. machines, are represented by agent. Machines aim to maximize their throughput and the conduct of a production step is auctioned. Besides system simulations, this techniques is deployed in a prototype as a bypass of an industrial manufacturing line [Jennings and Bussmann, 2003]. An alternative approach is the use of insect-inspired mechanisms such as the foraging in ant colonies to plan the routes of work pieces [Hadeli et al., 2004b]. Light-weight agents are sent out to explore the possible routes. The use of these mechanisms can be separated from the agent-based control by allowing agents to delegate the route exploration to supportive agents [Holvoet and Valckenaers, 2007]. The combination of stigmergy-based task allocations with a crystal growth inspired formation of configurations is discussed in [Frei et al., 2008], using the metaself programming framework (see Section 5.1.2). The conception of a novel decentralized reconfiguration strategy, based on conceptual model of the ODP [Seebach et al., 2007], is demonstrated in Section 6.8.1.

Robot/Vehicle Management

In physical robots, which interact with their immediate environment, self-organization principles have been successfully applied to coordinate robot collectives. The use of stigmergy techniques is particularly attractive as it achieves coordination among agents that lack a means for direct communication. Instead agents communicate implicitly via environment modifications, e.g. see [Holland and Melhuish, 1999]. Another aspect is the miniaturization of robots, which is supported when the coordination can be enabled by minimal local reasoning abilities. An example is given in [Halloy et al., 2007], where insect-size robots interact with and manipulate the collective behavior of insect groups. In these scenarios, the limitation of the local reasoning and communication abilities enforce decentralization and the collective behavior is adaptive.

Certain application domains pose extended requirements on the autonomy of robot collectives. A prominent example, where stigmergy-based coordination mechanism are also applied, is the coordination of unmanned air/ground vehicles, such as those used for for surveillance missions and infrastructure protection missions [Sauter et al., 2009]. Placed in military settings, these systems have to adapt to dynamic environments. An industrial setting is the management of *Automatic Guided Vehicles* that automate transports in warehouses and factories [Weyns et al., 2005]. The use of self-organization in this setting is particularly studied in [DeWolf, 2007]. An extreme case is the deployment of small-size, *pico-class* [Truszkowski et al., 2009] (Chapter 10) satellites for the collaborative conduct of space missions. The adoption of agent technology in space missions and the use of swarm techniques is discussed in [Truszkowski et al., 2009].

3.6 Conclusions

Self-organization is introduced as a powerful but intricate means for constructing of distributed software systems. Development practices benefit from an approach to the *decentralized* creation of *system-level adaptivity*, but the analysis and conception of the dynamics are inherently difficult and require expertise. The current best practices (see Section 3.2), i.e. analysis techniques and development processes/frameworks, as well as reusable templates, are characterized in this chapter. The analysis is facilitated by multi-level modeling, where the activities and/or configurations of system entities are iteratively averaged and condensed to explain a global system phenomenon (see Section 3.4). Based on this concept of intermediate, mesoscopic modeling levels, the redesign of agent-based application designs is discussed. Two basic strategies are the enforcing of behavior exhibitions, by modifying the microscopic implementations of system elements and the restructuring of the internals of system elements in order to explicitly represent the inferred element behaviors. The conceptualization of self-organizing applications (see Section 3.3) and the embedded processes (see Figure 3.6, page 57) that cause decentralized adaptivity ground the subsequent elaboration of appropriate engineering practices.

The concepts and tools that were presented in this and the previous chapter are the basis for the constructive approach for distributed self-organizing systems. Agent-orientation is selected as a technological basis as it supports the construction of flexible distributed systems. The notion of agents as autonomous, proactive actors allows self-organizing processes as found in natural self-organizing systems. These processes are governed by distributed feedbacks that result from networks of mutual interdependencies among system elements. The fundamental building blocks for these networks are interaction mechanisms, for the propagation of information, and adaptive software components that adjust themselves at run-time. Agent-orientation provides development frameworks for both aspects. The development of locally adaptive agents is supported. In addition, sophisticated interaction and environment models / frameworks are available for constructing of decoupled, interactive agents.

The relevance of the modeling and designing feedbacks for the development of self-adaptive software systems is well-acknowledged [Brun et al., 2009]. The highlighting of these feedbacks is a tool to plan for the adaptive behavior of a software application. Using traditional development approaches, this feedback is realized by specialized software systems such as managing software entities. For self-organization, the distributed feedback, shared among system elements, is the major design principle.

A systematic development approach for self-organizing systems has to address these feedbacks. Consequently, in the following chapters, *distributed* feedbacks, which constitute the decentralized, adaptive inter-agent process, are elevated to a separate design element. The development of these feedbacks spans the fundamental construction aspects, namely the *modeling*, *programming* and the *development process* (see Figure 1.1).

A key design objective is that the developed concepts and tools conform with the initial hypotheses for the development of self-organizing systems (see Section 1.2). A separate modeling level, orthogonal to conventional agent-oriented modeling techniques (Hypothesis 1.1), is developed (see Chapter 4) that allows for multi-level modeling and incremental refinements (Hypothesis 1.2). The separation of process prescriptions from the coordinated software elements (Hypotheses 1.3, 1.4) is realized by a specific programming model (see Chapter 5). The organized application of the modeling and programming tools is outlined by the development process, which systematizes the conception, prescription, and integration of inter-agent processes (see Chapter 6).

Part II

A Systemic Development Approach

Chapter 4

Systemic Modeling of Collective Phenomena in MASs

In this chapter, a *systemic* modeling approach that describes the dynamics of agent-based software systems is presented. By adopting a holistic view of the agent operation that expresses the interdependencies and side effects of the execution of software agents, developers are able to deduce and plan for collective phenomena in MASs. The description-level advocated here can be used in parallel to established MAS modeling techniques. The latter engineering models focus on the structure, the internal processing, and the interactions of system elements. Systemic modeling supplements these aspects with descriptions of the macroscopic observable behavior of the software system. A key characteristic of systemic models is the singularization of inter-agent feedbacks, thus they can serve as vehicles for describing decentralized inter-agent processes.

The modeling approach is named *systemic* because it serves as a tool for holonic models that express the software system dynamics. System behavior is modeled as a network of interdependencies between system element activities. This approach takes its inspiration from *System Dynamics* (cf. Section 4.2.1) modeling techniques and highlights the circular interdependencies among system elements that effectuate the self-organizing phenomena. This chapter discusses and gives examples for the use of this modeling approach for the analysis and design of decentralized inter-agent coordination. For the analysis, it shows the systematic derivation of systemic models from AOSE design artifacts is shown and demonstrates the anticipation of the effects of the identified interdependencies by deriving of simulation models (see Section 4.3). For the design of inter-agent coordination, a set of the principal self-organizing MAS dynamics (see Section 4.4) are cataloged as application-independent template processes. Phenomenological criteria for the selection of Coordinating Processes are indicated and the combination of templates is demonstrated by assembling the constituent feedback structures.

4.1 Motivation

When designing agent-based software systems, it is not sufficient to merely prescribe the implementation of agent models. A key activity in MAS development is the detailing of MAS-blueprints to prepare for the implementation of agents and environment(s). Therefore, established design techniques typically focus on the depiction of individual agents as well as their arrangement in organizational structures (cf. Section 2.6).

When the degrees of freedom are sufficiently constrained, these designs represent the behavior of the resulting system. For ensembles of software elements, e.g. distributed systems, this representation is not always straightforward. In the natural sciences, it is observed that *more is different* [Anderson, 1972]. The collective behavior of simple system elements that are controlled by simple, deterministic rules, e.g. physical laws, can, when they are arranged in large sets, give rise to complex system behaviors. In addition, the arising phenomena themselves can be nondeterministic, despite their foundation in deterministic laws [Strogatz, 2001]. Similar effects are observed in engineered systems (see Section 3.1.3).

In agent-oriented development practices, traditional development approaches are challenged by the autonomy of the constituent software elements. Agents are software entities that are equipped with additional degrees of freedom, making them autonomous — they are able to reason and act independently. Agent-oriented development provides an intuitive modeling approach for distributed and socio-technical systems (e.g. see Sterling and Taveter [2009]), but has far-reaching implications for design practices. One major challenge is deducing the collective system behavior from the microscopic designs of autonomous actors. Application designers are required to show that the collections of agents are appropriate to achieving the intended system functionality. Agent-oriented software engineering provides tools and concepts for the design of decentralized software applications in particular (cf. Chapter 3). Using decentralized system architectures is attractive for developing distributed systems, but doing so also magnifies the need to purposefully plan the coaction of system elements. Bottom-up design principles are applied to build decentralized architectures, therefore the simulation of systems and the interpretation of the observed system properties are integral parts of development process.

In order to move from these practices to principled design techniques, is it necessary to model the coaction of agents. Descriptions of the effects of individual activities and interactions on the collective behavior of the system entities are a prerequisite to enabling developers to plan for the coactions in agent-based software systems.

4.1.1 Challenges

C 4.1: Modeling the Causes of Collective Inter-Agent Phenomena

The driving force behind decentralized, collective phenomena of inter-agent operation is the presence of feedbacks among system entities (cf. Section 3.1.4). A major requirement of models is that they emphasize the causative structure that underlies agent-based application designs. When sets of agents influence each other by non-linear and/or cyclic interdependencies, the resulting system behavior can be complex and counter-intuitive. Insights into the non-linear relations and cyclic interdependencies, i.e. feedback loops, allow designers to estimate the impact of agent coaction. Consequently, the modeling technique needs to be able to describe how the adoption of agent behaviors impacts both environment properties and the adoption of behaviors by other agents. Distributed feedback loops, i.e. cyclic relations among system elements, need to be highlighted.

C 4.2: Supporting Intermediate Description Levels

In particular the models must support the expressing of intermediate, mesoscopic modeling levels, as discussed in Section 3.4. In order to do so, the notation must be able to describe behavior abstractions, e.g. mesoscopic agent states that are abstracted from the detailed implementation of the system entities and represent averaged agent behaviors. The intermediate modeling levels are subject to iterative and exploitative modeling processes, as developers revise their understanding of the arising phenomena. Therefore both the refinement and abstraction of entity behaviors must be expressible.

C 4.3: Linking Process-Models to AOSE Design Concepts

The applied modeling approach will be used to describe the coaction that arises from application designs that follow established design notations (cf. Section 2.6), e.g. as provided by development methodologies (cf. Section 2.6.3). it is an additional modeling level that addresses the dynamical properties of the application to be. Since the modeling level is a supplement to conventional design efforts, design concepts must be mapped. Concepts that are used during the system conception and detailed design of agent/environment models, have to be mapped to the new modeling notation. Because agent-oriented modeling concepts are so diverse, it is not intended to constrain the design concepts that are used in the MAS development. Therefore the focus must be on the *extensibility* of the modeling approach: users must be able to introduce those concepts that correspond to and describe the behavioral stance of system entities and map these design concepts, used in the agent development, to the descriptions of the MAS dynamics.

4.1.2 Related Work

The view point that software development has to consider dynamical properties is not new. In [Bernstein, 1996], for example, *software statics*, i.e. the static structure of software designs and realizations, are distinguished from the *operational dynamics*, that refer to the dynamic behavior of the software system. The author argues that the principled study of the software statics ignores the nonlinear, non-stationary behaviors of applications. The evaluation of these behaviors and the *dynamic design* of software are identified as research challenges.

The need for modeling techniques that express feedbacks in software systems has been identified (see e.g. Brun et al. [2009]). For the development of self-organizing systems in particular, the modeling of the possibly non-linear application dynamics gains center stage and techniques for expressing and analyzing the *distributed* feedbacks among system elements (see Section 3.1.4) are relevant. One approach is to informally express the interdependencies of agents. An example is given in [DeWolf and Holvoet, 2007c], where the control flow and the flow of information is integrated in UML diagrams to express feedback structures in MAS designs.

Here, formally grounded modeling techniques are reviewed. In addition to the description of feedbacks, these can be used in two distinct practices. First, they facilitate the designing of systems because they allow developers to study the dynamics of the software system prior to its implementation. Secondly, they aid in analyzing existing application design for intended and/or unintended collective processes. In both cases, abstract representations of the software system that can be simulated/iterated are necessary. System simulations are an inevitable part of development methodologies (see Sections 3.2.3, 3.2.4).

For the described practices, mathematical modeling techniques (e.g. as reviewed in [Holzer et al., 2010]) as well as formal methods are applicable (e.g. reviewed in [Rouff et al., 2006] with respect to nature-inspired swarm systems). The system abstractions describe the underlying process that governs system behavior. A common approach is the assumption of Markovian processes, and different description formats are available that match specific analysis techniques. Here, a non-exhaustive list of prominent techniques is categorized into three distinct types that represent distinct modeling approaches and their associated analysis techniques. The transition between these types is fluid since these different modeling techniques can be studied with different analysis approaches.

Modeling techniques are characterized by two orthogonal aspects (see Figure 4.1). The x-axis represents the (system) description levels, which can range from microscopic to macroscopic approaches. Microscopic models describe the behaviors of the system entities. Macroscopic models abstract from the detailed agent behaviors and describe the system dynamics in terms of macroscopic system variables that characterize the system configuration. A continuum of modeling abstractions exists between these extremes, i.e. the operations of agents can be arbitrarily abstracted. In Section 3.4, these modeling levels are distinguished and the advantages of using intermediate modeling levels are discussed. The second, correlated aspect (the y-axis) is the degree of abstraction of the utilized models. Microscopic models are concrete, as they describe the transitions between agent states/configuration. They enable the verification of system properties and the derivation of system implementation parameters. More abstract description levels blur the details of individual agents. Generalizations, e.g. mean-field assumptions, are used to characterize the transitions between agent states. These models show the operating principles of systems and allow the qualitative system behavior to be anticipated. The alignment with concrete system realizations is generally possible, but can require considerable mathematical expertise, e.g. [Axtell et al., 1996; Wilson, 1998]. The indicated correlation (see Figure 4.1) denotes the inherent trade-off between modeling effort and the agreement of the obtained dynamics with the concrete software system.

Examples for formal analysis approaches (I) are adoptions of temporal logics, such as those

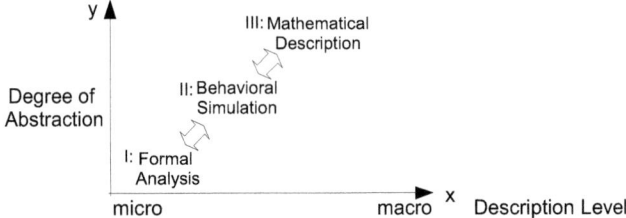

Figure 4.1: Modeling techniques for self-organizing MASs

used for *model checking* [Winfield et al., 2005; Casadei and Viroli, 2009b,a] and *organizational* modeling [Hoogendoorn et al., 2006]. These models describe the operations of agents by their execution states and the valid transitions. Using these techniques, the space of the possible transitions can be iterated to show the validity or probability of system configurations. The state explosion of these models is problematic, thus hybrid approaches, which increase the abstractions level, are recommended (e.g. see [Casadei and Viroli, 2009a]).

Behavioral simulations of the system operation (II) form an intermediate class, in which the agent execution is described by models that describe distinct agent behaviors but abstract from their concrete execution. Examples are process algebraic modeling techniques [Sumpter et al., 2001; Renz and Sudeikat, 2009; Casadei et al., 2007]. The processing states of agents are represented by processes that can interact with each other. This level of abstraction facilitates the study of the dynamical properties, e.g. the dynamics of activity changes [Gardelli et al., 2005]. Using this modeling level to anticipate the dynamics of a self-organizing process is discussed in Section 6.7.3. Commonly, stochastic modeling notions are adopted in type I and II efforts, allowing probabilistic influences that vary due to changing environmental contexts to be accounted for, e.g. see [Gardelli et al., 2005].

The most widespread technique for modeling self-organizing processes is the use of mathematical modeling techniques (III) [Holzer et al., 2010; Lerman and Galstyan, 2004, 2001]. Dynamical system models, i.e. differential and difference equations [Kaplan and Glass, 1995], are used to describe the behavior of self-organizing systems, e.g. [Bonabeau et al., 1999; Haken, 2006]. System states are characterized by macroscopic system variables and their mutual influences on each other. The variables are aggregations of microscopic agent states and their relations between them average the microscopic interactions and influences among agents. These relations are denoted by equations which describe how variable values change over time. Only simple systems can be solved and thus often graphical methods and system iterations are necessary to examine dynamical properties, e.g. the stability of fixed points [Kaplan and Glass, 1995]. Variations on this method are the use of discrete or continuous variables and discrete or continuous time increments (e.g. see [Holzer et al., 2010]). An example process for the abstraction of a homogeneous, reactive agents to differential equations is given in [Lerman and Galstyan, 2004]. First, a reactive model of the operation of the individual agents, i.e. an automaton, is derived. Then the states of this automaton are elevated to the macroscopic variables. These describe the numbers of agents that are in the corresponding execution state at a given time-point. Differential equations are used to denote the averaged changes between these execution states.

4.2 Systemic Modeling Approach

The tools that are typically used to describe self-organizing and emergent phenomena require formal or mathematical expertise (see previous section). While formal treatments of inter-agent processes enable the detailed analysis of system phenomena, the skills required to implement them

4.2. SYSTEMIC MODELING APPROACH

often prohibit their adoption by non-experts. Here, a graphical modeling approach is preferred, which facilitates the description of inter-agent coaction in conventional software engineering practices. The adoption of this modeling approach is motivated by the ability to visualize the distribution of feedbacks among system elements. It allows development teams to communicate insights on the system behavior, the reasons of self-organized phenomena in particular, as non-experts can be provided with informal system abstractions.

Intuitive graphical formalisms for the modeling of complex system behaviors are provided by the *System Dynamics* research community (cf. Section 4.2.1). These techniques highlight the feedback structure that explains system phenomena. This modeling stance and the available tools are presented in the following section. The subsequent Section 4.2.3, discusses the transfer of these modeling concepts to the description of agent-based software systems.

This approach does not address the precise parameter predictions or the prediction of the quantitative estimation of system behaviors. It is in principle possible to reproduce agent-based systems with equation-based models, e.g. as demonstrated in [Axtell et al., 1996; Wilson, 1998], but this requires considerable mathematical expertise. Instead, the modeling stance presented here focuses on qualitative predictions of dynamical modes, e.g. steady states or oscillations, that the application may exhibit under different configurations and parametrizations. It is argued and demonstrated how systemic modeling allows developers to estimate the qualitative system behavior at design-time. These estimations require the mathematical concretization of system models.

4.2.1 System Dynamics

The umbrella term *Systems Science* describes an multidisciplinary research area that examines the principles of *complex systems*. This research field spans a family of disciplines that provide concepts and techniques for modeling timely system behaviors. The disciplines contain formal approaches (e.g. *dynamical systems theory* and *cybernetics* [Ashby, 1956]), engineering related techniques (e.g. *control theory* [Åström and Murray, 2008]) and research directions that focus on the study of social or natural systems (e.g *systems biology*).

One prominent discipline is *System Dynamics* (SD), an interdisciplinary modeling and simulation methodology that addresses the analysis of complex systems [Forrester, 1961] and particularly focuses on management problems. SD addresses the assessment of the dynamic consequences of business processes and management decisions, i.e. interventions in these processes. Consequences are estimated by modeling processes as continuous systems and enabling their simulation.

The pivotal idea of SD is that system behaviors are consequences of the *causal* structure that underlies systems. The proposed methodology guides the elicitation and analysis of system structures to identify these *endogenous* structures that cause the exhibited dynamics of a system. The driving force behind the rise of complex system behaviors are cyclic interdependencies among system elements, not the internal complexity of the involved elements. Therefore, SD focuses particularly on the identification and analysis of the feedback processes that, along with time delays and nonlinearities, determine the exhibited dynamics.

SD particularly addresses management problems. It provides a methodology and modeling tools that enable *Systems Thinking* (ST), e.g. as described in [Senge, 1990]. Particularly in management disciplines, it has been observed that interventions in complex behaving systems do not lead to the intended results but engender unexpected dynamics, such as side effects or unanticipated consequences, a.k.a. *policy resistance* [Sterman, 2000]. These dynamics result not from misconceptions about the behavior of system elements, but from the lack of knowledge about their mutual interdependencies. An insufficient knowledge of system structures is a major source for *unintended consequences* that arise from interventions in system operations. Accordingly, the management of complex behaving systems requires a holistic view to anticipate side effects that may be distant in time and space. This paradigm differs from event-oriented modeling approaches that describe chains of causes and effects, but do not acknowledge the possibility of cyclic interdependencies.

A good example for an unintended consequence — one that is well-known to software engineers — is described by Brooks's Law ([Brooks, 1995], page 25): *Adding manpower to a late software project makes it later*. Increasing the workforce on an software project with the intention of speeding up its development has inevitable (side-)effects, such as additional training and communication overheads that reduce the productivity. An SD-based analysis of this law is given in [Madachy, 2008] (page 16).

SD modeling is based on the theory of non-linear dynamics and control theory. In order to examine the effects of these structures, systems are abstracted to continuous quantities, called *system variables*, that are interconnected. The examined structures typically include *feedbacks*. System elements interdepend in cyclic structures, where changes in system variables propagate over time, by the transitive affection of quantities connected to the original variable. These feedbacks are either *positive*, a.k.a. *self-reinforcing*, or *negative*, a.k.a. *balancing* or *self-correcting*. While the former type amplifies perturbations, the latter ones damp variable fluctuations. The models describe coupled networks of feedback loops that comprise multiple delays, nonlinearities and accumulations. This modeling approach allows the formulation of *dynamic hypotheses* to explain observed behaviors as endogenous consequences of feedback structures [Sterman, 2000] (page 86).

The purpose of SD modeling is to enhance the intuition about the behavior of complex systems. The SD-based modeling methodology does not focus on precise *quantitative* predictions of timely system behaviors but focuses on the *qualitative* anticipation of the dynamical properties that arise from system structures. The construction of meaningful models is a manual modeling effort that has to extract the *relevant* system details while preserving the tractability of the derived representations. Another challenge is the unbiased elaboration of the actual system structure, that may contradict intended theorems or desired system properties. Details on the modeling challenges and the qualitative modeling methodology can be found in [Sterman, 2000] (Chapter 3).

Reasons for common misconceptions about the dynamic behavior that is exhibited by coupled feedback loops are discussed in [Sterman, 2000] (page 29). Estimating the dynamical behavior exhibited by a given feedback structure and, even worse, inferring the effects of the intervention is complicated and counter-intuitive. Technically speaking this would require the intuitive solution of high-order nonlinear differential equations. Therefore the simulation of these structures is an integral part of the SD methodology. Simulations allow hypotheses on the effects of system configuration, parameterizations and modifications of the dynamical system behavior to be tested.

Modeling and Simulation Tools

Two major modeling formalisms are available to express the causal structure of systems. The *Causal Loop Diagram* (CLD) [Sterman, 2000] is an established notation for the representation of coupled feedback loops. The *Stock-and-Flow Diagram* (SFD) facilitates the formalization of the time-dependent changes of system variables in preparation for the model iteration/simulation.

CLDs visualize the structure of the causal influences among system variables as directed graphs (see Figure 4.2). Connections of variables (nodes) represent *causal links* that describe the propagation of variable changes. The *polarity* of links indicates how dependent, i.e. influenced, variables are affected when the values of independent, i.e. originating, variables change. For *positive* (+) links, the effects work in the *same* direction. Thus an increase of the independent variable causes a subsequent increase of dependent variables and the decrease of originating variables effects the decrease of dependent values. *Negative* (-) links denote that changes are transmitted in *opposite* directions. For these links, an increase effects decreases and decreases effect increases. The links describe independent and simultaneous effects on variable values. The sum of these effects determines the increase/decrease of values. There is an inherent lag in the propagation of changes. Sizeable delays, i.e. delays that are significant within the examined timespan and thus affect the system operation, can be annotated to a link (cf. Figure 4.2, III).

Cyclic chains of causal relations form feedback loops and are indicated by a *loop identifier* that denotes the polarity of the loop as either *reinforcing* (+) or *balancing* (-). The former amplify variations of variable values, while the latter loop structures damp fluctuations. These polarities

4.2. SYSTEMIC MODELING APPROACH

are identified by tracing the propagation of an imaginary change through the transitive relations. Formally, this tracing corresponds to the calculation of the sign of the *open loop gain* in control theory [Åström and Murray, 2008], [Sterman, 2000] (page 145). This *gain* describes the strength of a signal that passes through a single cycle of a feedback loop, hence *open loop*. It is calculated by extracting the sequence of variables $(x_1...x_n)$ that makes up a single passage through the loop. This sequence can be constructed by replacing an arbitrary variable (x_1) with two disconnected variables that serve as the input (x_1^I) and output (x_1^O) of the link sequence. A signal that originates in x_1^I has traversed the sequence when it has propagated to x_1^O. The gain of an individual link is given by $\frac{\partial x_i}{\partial x_{i-1}}$. The resulting polarity (p) of such a sequence is given by (cf. [Sterman, 2000], pages 145,146):

$$p = sgn(\frac{\partial x_1^O}{\partial x_1^I}) \tag{4.1}$$

$$p = sgn((\frac{\partial x_1^O}{\partial x_n})(\frac{\partial x_n}{\partial x_{n-1}})(\frac{\partial x_{n-1}}{\partial x_{n-2}})...(\frac{\partial x_2}{\partial x_1^I})) \tag{4.2}$$

$$p = sgn(\frac{\partial x_1^O}{\partial x_n}) \cdot sgn(\frac{\partial x_n}{\partial x_{n-1}}) \cdot sgn(\frac{\partial x_{n-1}}{\partial x_{n-2}}) \cdot ... \cdot sgn(\frac{\partial x_2}{\partial x_1^I}) \tag{4.3}$$

where $sgn()$ is the sign function:

$$sgn(x) = \begin{cases} +1 & \text{if } x > 0 \\ -1 & \text{if } x < 0 \\ 0 & \text{otherwise} \end{cases}$$

The gain of a loop is $\neq 0$. In equation 4.2 the gain is calculated from the chain of the individual links that make up the loop. This can be simplified to equation 4.3 by replacing the sign of the product with the products of the individual signs. According to this equation, an even number of negative links indicates a reinforcing and an odd number of negative links indicates a balancing feedback.

For the interpretation of these networks, it is imperative to distinguish between two variable types, namely *stock* and *flow* variables [Sterman, 2000]. Stocks describe accumulative values that characterize the system state, while flows indicate rates of changes of connected variables, i.e. the incrementing and decrementing effects on stock quantities. While the relations that originate in stocks affect connected values causally, as described above, links that originate in flows produce additive/subtractive influences, depending on their polarity. These types of system variables are shown in Figure 4.2 (I), where the mutual connections of a stock (*System State*) and a flow (*Increase Rate*) form a balancing feedback loop. The link from the stock to the flow value describes a causal relation. The link between the flow and the stock value describes an additive influence. When a rate increases, e.g. the birth rate in an population model, it adds to the increases in connected stocks. However, the decrease in this rate limits only the adding influence but does not subtract elements from the stock value. Notation refinements have been proposed (e.g. discussed in [Richardson, 1986]) to visually distinguish the types of relations.

A virtue of CLD-based models is their simplicity and the inherent highlighting of feedback loops [Sterman, 2000; Richardson, 1986]. The resulting models allow system behaviors to be analyzed manually. Due to the non-linearity of system behaviors and dynamical properties, it is often necessary to simulate system models in order to animate the behavioral dynamics and examine the effects of different parameter configurations and initial conditions. SFDs express causal dependencies in a format that is particularly appropriate for system simulation. As suggested by its name, the SFD explicitly distinguishes between aggregate quantities, stocks, and the rates of variable changes, flows. Using a hydraulic metaphor [Forrester, 1961], the continuous values of stocks is represented by a hypothetical fluid that moves between reservoirs. Rectangles represent stocks and thick arrows, conventionalized pipes equipped with valves, represent the flows through the stock variables. Inflows are denoted by an arrow that points toward the stock and outflows are represented by arrows that originate from stocks. Tool support for the iteration of these models is commercially [Sterman, 2000] and freely[1] available. These tools allow to assign initial values to stocks and equations describing the rate of inflow/outflow in simulation time units to valves. Optionally, sources and sinks outside the system boundary can be represented by cloud icons. Auxiliary variables can be defined as well. Figure 4.18 shows an example of a stock and flow diagram.

SFD models concretize the causal relations among system variables with a precise mathematical representation that prepares system models for iteration. Systems are descried a set of continuous variables that are modified by the instantaneous inflows and outflows, defined as functions of the stock, auxiliary state variables, and parameters. Consequently, networks of stocks and flows can be transferred to equivalent systems of integrals and differential equations [Sterman, 2000]. First, the aggregation of quantities can be described by the *integration* of the inflow(s) and outflow(s) in a given time interval. The dynamics of a single stock element connected with one inflow and one outflow can be represented by [Sterman, 2000] (page 194):

$$Stock(t) = \int_{t_0}^{t} (Inflow(s) - Outflow(s))ds + Stock(t_0)$$

where $Inflow(s)$ and $Outflow(s)$ denote the increase/decrease of the stock value for any time point s ($t_0 < s < t$). Secondly, the net change rate of an aggregate variable at any time point t is given by the derivative that is controlled by the instantaneous inflow and outflow:[2]

$$\dot{Stock} = \frac{d(Stock)}{dt} = Inflow(t) - Outflow(t)$$

Fundamental System Modes and System Archetypes

A minimal set of essential modes of *dynamic* behaviors has been identified (e.g. [Sterman, 2000], Chapter 4). The various dynamics exhibited by interdisciplinary systems can be explained as combinations of these fundamental patterns of behavior. Figure 4.2 illustrates these modes and the feedback structure that leads to their exhibition. First, *exponential growth* (Figure 4.2, I) can be explained by a single reinforcing feedback loop. Aggregative variables in these loops increase indefinitely and exhibit a constant doubling time, i.e. grow exponentially.

In Figure 4.2 (II), *goal-seeking* behaviors originate from balancing feedbacks that let aggregate system variables, here the *System State* variable, approach a desired value. The current value of the system state is compared to the desired state (*Goal*) and according to the measured difference (*Discrepancy*), manipulative activities (*Corrective Action*) are initiated to adjust the system state.

Finally, Figure 4.2 shows that goal-seeking feedback system with significant delays exhibits *oscillations*. The delays cause a lag between the observation of the discrepancy and initiation of corrective actions. Therefore corrections regularly overshoot and undershoot the intended value. The aggregate values oscillate. Particular structures and parameterizations control the strength of enacted effects and the length of delays. These configurations produce different types if oscillations, e.g. *damped oscillations*, which gradually approach the goal value, and *limit cycles*, which repeat the cyclic behavior indefinitely.

Additional commonly observed modes of system behaviors can be explained by combinations of these fundamental structures. Examples are shown in Figure 4.3, from [Sterman, 2000] (Chapter 4). *S-shaped Growth* starts with an exponential growth that gradually slows down to an asymptotic approach to an aggregate goal value. This behavior can be explained by a combination of a reinforcing and a balancing feedback loop. Initially, the reinforcing feedback dominates the system and causes the exponential increase (cf. Figure 4.2, I). Thereafter, the balancing effects of the additional feedback loop grow stronger (cf. 4.2, II) and they limit the growth and forces the system state to approach the goal value. In this setting, the goal value can be compared to a *carrying capacity* [Sterman, 2000] (page 118), as is known in ecological modeling.

---

[1] e.g. in the Netlogo simulation framework: http://ccl.northwestern.edu/netlogo/docs/systemdynamics.html
[2] In the following, the abbreviated notation $\dot{x}$ will be used to denote time derivatives

4.2. SYSTEMIC MODELING APPROACH

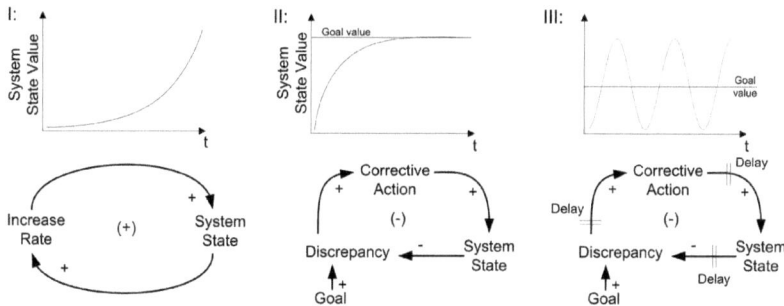

Figure 4.2: Fundamental modes of behaviors: Exponential growth (I), goal-seeking (II), oscillation (III), following [Sterman, 2000]

The presence of delays leads to a different mode, the *S-Shaped Growth with Overshoot*, where the goal value is not reached but is repeatedly over- and undershot. When the reinforcement of an aggregate (cf. Figure 4.2, I) is coupled with the a delayed balancing feedback (cf. Figure 4.2, III) the growth is limited but the aggregate value oscillates around the goal value. The configuration of the balancing sub-structure controls the oscillatory dynamic that can be damped or fluctuate infinitely (see above).

Finally, another common mode of behavior is the *Overshoot and Collapse*, where an aggregate system value approaches a dynamically adjusted, i.e. declining, goal value. This mode can be explained by a coupled network of three feedback loops. The combination of the reinforcing and balancing feedbacks that exhibits S-shaped Growth (see above) is supplemented with an additional balancing feedback loop that adjusts the approached goal value. Assuming that the goal value represents a carrying capacity, the damping of this loop describes the consumption of resources. After the initial phase of exponential increase, the goal-seeking behavior prevails and follows a dynamically adjusted goal value.

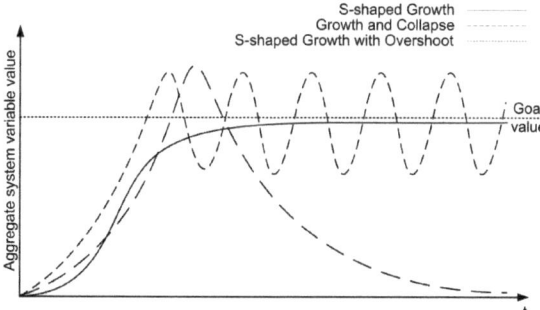

Figure 4.3: Examples of combined behavior modes: S-shaped growth, growth with overshoot and growth with collapse, following [Sterman, 2000]

These structures outlined here are examples of coupled feedbacks that are capable of exhibiting these types of dynamics. The three fundamental loop types cf. Figure 4.2) serve as building blocks.

Each of these building bocks is associated to a significant behavioral mode and the intensification of these modes, by decomposing the observed behavior, indicates arrangements of feedbacks that cause the exhibited system behavior. This connection between system structure and exhibited behavior is a fundamental concept of the SD modeling approach.

In addition, ten generic pattern of feedback structures, *System Archetypes* [Senge, 1990], have been identified (e.g. cataloged in [Braun, 2002]). Archetypes describe generic networks of feedback loops that recur in interdisciplinary modeling domains and serve as templates to classify structures as well as behavioral insights. These generic structures can be applied *diagnostically*, as a means of predicting system behaviors from identified similarities in system structures, or *prospectively*, as a means of anticipating the effects of structural adjustments that introduce archetype structures [Wolstenholme, 2003]. These archetypes describe frequently observed patterns of feedback structures and system behaviors that are detectable in differing application domains. Alternatively, domain-specific archetypes have been identified, e.g. for organizational safety [Marais et al., 2006].

Guidelines for the CLD-Based Feedback Modeling

The CLDs are adopted in this dissertation as a means to model the dynamics of agent-based software systems. This formalism individualizes the feedbacks that are distributed among the system elements and mathematical precise models can be inferred when needed. The modeling of MAS is discussed in the following section (see page 98). This modeling stance is unusual in software contexts. Therefore, guidelines for the CLD-based modeling and the organization of these diagrams are briefly discussed. The guidelines given are stated in [Sterman, 2000] (Section 5.2) and document the use of the modeling technique. These are discussed here to indicate the expressiveness of these models and facilitate the comprehension of CLD-based models that are used in the remainder of this dissertation.

(1) Links are used to represent causal relationships, not correlations (see Section 2.5, page 26) of variables. The Diagram is used to describe the underlying *causal structure* of the system. Changes in the context of the system can lead to changes in the observable dynamics but the underlying structure is not affected. Later in this work, diagrams partly deviate from this guideline since the models are also used to describe the expected causal structure of a system. These models indicate the requirements on the system behavior and indicate the causal structure that is intended to be achieved by the application development.

(2) The link polarities have to be annotated to very link. These polarities should be unambiguous. An indetermination indicates that different causal relations underly the system. These relations should be made explicit.

The link polarities are necessary to infer the types of the feedback loops, as discussed on page 92. (3) The identification of the loops types and (4) the naming of every loop is advised. The systems typically comprise sets of coupled feedback loops so it is necessary to be able to navigate these when studying or discussing CLD-based models. In this work, Greek lower case letters are used to name feedback loops.

(5) Delays affect the system behavior, e.g. give rise to oscillations (see Figure 4.2, III), and thus have to be annotated to links. The decision which delays are relevant for the system model is a modeling effort. Often, interactions and activities imply delays and the delays that are significant for the dynamic behavior have to be identified.

(6) Variables are named with nouns not verbs. The rationale is that CLDs represent the causal structure of the system. The behavior is a consequence of this structure. A related aspect of the variable naming is their direction. Variables represent qualities that increase and decrease in time. Therefore, names should convey these alternative directions. In this dissertation, the variables are used to represent the number of agents that show a specific behavior or are in a specific configuration.

(7) The diagram layout should illustrate the circular structure of feedbacks and crossings of links should be avoided. The use of additional symbols is discouraged, when not provided with a clear meaning.

4.2. SYSTEMIC MODELING APPROACH

(8) The level of aggregation has to be appropriate for the intended audience. Coarse-grained CLDs can be used to represent the principal feedback structure but the lack of detail can also complicate the understanding and the credibility of the models. CLDs are abstractions that should not be as detailed as the equations of the system behavior.

(9) The feedback models should be partitioned. Comprehensive diagrams can be overwhelming and it is advised to model distinct parts of the system dynamics in a single diagram. This is practiced in this dissertation since the models of cases study systems describe a particular segment of the (software) system behavior.

(10) Negative loops have goals, i.e. tend to a target state/configuration. These goals should be made explicit in the graph (see Figure 4.2, II and III).

(11) The perceptions of actors in the system can deviate from the actual system state. These differences can affect the dynamics and should be modeled, when it is significant for the system behavior.

4.2.2 Applications in Software-Engineering

The use of feedback concepts in computer science typically focuses on the adaptation of control theoretic concepts and tools to govern individual software components [Hellerstein et al., 2004]. Closed feedbacks are established in single software elements by integrating control structures that continuously observe and adjust the element configuration. Particularly system architectures that facilitate the distribution of closed feedback loops among sets of system entities have been examined [Seebach et al., 2007; Garlan et al., 2004]. These works provide architectures for realizing of dedicated elements that control the adaptivity of (sub-)systems of system elements. Differing approaches to the specification of adaptation policies and the realization of the control logic are available (cf. Sections 3.1.2, 3.1.4).

However, the present feedbacks are typically not modeled/visualized explicitly but are implicitly present in the software implementations. For example in [Brun et al., 2009], the need for explicit modeling techniques is argued [Brun et al., 2009] (page 57):

> ... , we suspect that the lack of a notation leads to the absence of an explicit task to document the control, which leads in turn in failure to explicitly designing, analyzing, and validating the feedback loops. ...

For the development of self-adaptive, distributed software systems, this design principle has to be extended to distributed settings [Brun et al., 2009] (see Section 3.1.4). SD modeling techniques provides a notation for feedbacks that are distributed among system entities. In software engineering contexts, SD modeling concepts have been used to model management concerns and the dynamics of software applications. This approach is particularly suited to express the dynamics of collectives of autonomous software elements.

Describing the Dynamics of Software Development

One prominent example is the planning of software engineering projects under consideration of the dynamics of software construction processes [Madachy, 2008]. The SD methodology and tool set is used to model development processes and the corresponding simulation models are used to anticipate the *dynamic consequences* of management decisions. The management and maintenance of IT infrastructures has also been addressed, e.g. in [Rosenfeld et al., 2007], and security aspects of the maintenance of an enterprise IT system are modeled with SD concepts. Another example is the modeling of the impact of management decisions on product safety [Marais et al., 2006]. A simulation model is used to examine the effects of different security policies. What-if questions are answered by adjusting simulations, where the simulation parameters support the configuration of differing system properties and system contexts, e.g. the system usage, vulnerabilities, and defense profiles. The dynamics of well-known system archetypes [Braun, 2002] have been identified in this application domain, e.g. [Rosenfeld et al., 2009].

Describing the Dynamics of Software Systems

The adoption of SD-based techniques for the modeling, simulation, and anticipation of the dynamics of software systems is not widespread but has been proposed in isolated works. These are not extensively reviewed but the range of proposals is illustrated by examples. In [Zalewski, 2005, 2003] the association of dynamic properties to software components is discussed. This enables the description of real-time software architectures as continuous dynamical systems. Another approach is the mapping of established modeling tools to continuous models to describe the dynamical behavior of software systems. This is exemplified in [Tignor, 2004], where the mapping of UML language models (e.g. referenced in Section 2.6.1) to System Dynamics modeling tools is discussed. An example for the inverse transformation from system dynamics models to UML representations is given in [Chang and Tu, 2004].

Describing the Dynamics of Agent-Based Software Systems

The graphical notations and simulation tools for System Dynamics cover the formal, mathematical background of this modeling approach. Equation-based models, including SD-based models, and agent-based modeling techniques are traditionally used as contrasting modeling stances. The comparison of these approaches (e.g. in [Parunak et al., 1998; Norling, 2007; Wakeland et al., 2004]) accentuates the different foci of the modeling techniques as a guide for their selection for specific domains, but comparisons also show the fundamental correspondence of both modeling levels, e.g. as studied in [Parunak et al., 1998] (see Figure 4.4). Both modeling techniques allow the description of the coaction of system elements. Agent-based models follow a bottom-up approach that explicitly describes the behaviors and the decision making inside *individual* system elements, which react to each other by showing behaviors. Equation-based models, including SD-based models, abstract the operation of individuals and use equations to characterize the relations of specific system variables, *observables*. Both description levels are linked as observables give a description of the individuals and, vice versa, individual activities have an effect upon observable values.

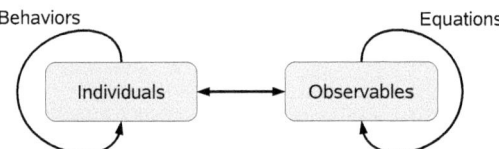

Figure 4.4: A characterization of the relation between *individual* system elements and system *observables*, following [Parunak et al., 1998]

Using aggregate observables to describe sets of reactive agents is a common technique for abstracting individual-based system models. Examples are the correspondence of chemical reaction equations with individual-based models of chemical reactions [Cardelli, 2008], and the mathematical modeling approach from [Lerman and Galstyan, 2001, 2004], where the dynamics of homogeneous, reactive MASs are derived from averaging agent interactions (cf. Section 4.1.2). In [Borshev and Filippov, 2004], this correspondence is examined and exemplified for reactive agents. In agreement with these modeling approaches, it is proposed that the operation of MASs be characterized by defining observables that describe aggregates of agents, i.e. observables that denote the numbers of agents that share a common aspect [Sudeikat and Renz, 2009c, 2008c, 2007c]. Examples for these observables are sets of agents that show corresponding configurations and comparative behaviors.

4.2. SYSTEMIC MODELING APPROACH

The equation-based model describes the stochastic process that underlies the operation of the MAS. In the remainder of this chapter, it is argued and exemplified that modeling the structure of these processes is valuable to the conception of MASs. First and foremost, these structures are used to give a qualitative representations of the system-level behaviors of MASs. These representations allow developers to reason about the distributed feedbacks (cf. Section 3.1.4) that are present in an MAS. The quantitative representation of application dynamics is not addressed in this dissertation but is in principle possible. Equation-based models average interactions and thus abstract the effects of the locality of agents. An example for the resolution of discrepancies is given by the adjustment of equation-based models in [Wilson, 1998] to resemble spatial effects in an agent-based model of population dynamics.

The abstractions are most accurate when used to describe the operation of reactive agents, as the determinism of agent actions facilitates the averaging of interactions. Due to the qualitative nature of the modeling level, this does not limit the principal applicability. Practical architectures for agent-development (cf. Section 2.2.1) provide for degrees of reactivity. Agent actions are typically immediate or mediate consequences of the interplay with the environment and/or other agents and justify Markov assumptions, e.g. as argued in [Sudeikat and Renz, 2007a]. Consequently, it has been shown that hybrid agent models, such as the BDI-based agents can be described by stochastic processes, e.g. Markov Decision Processes (MDP) [Simari and Parsons, 2006]. These results suggest that hybrid agents architectures, e.g. BDI-agents, can be abstracted as reactive systems.

SD-based models describe the structure of inter-agent processes as a network of influences and interdependencies among agent aspects. This structure determines the behavioral modes that can be exhibited, but the system behavior that is actually exhibited depends on additional aspects that control the rates of interactions. These factors are the configurations of the participating system elements and the properties of the information flows among them. Due to varying system configurations, i.e. here of variable values, and interaction rates, that are influenced by system external and/or internal influences, the same process structure can give rise to a multitude of system behaviors. Thus the graph-based process models describe *types* of processes. In Figure 4.5, the relation of systemic models of inter-agent processes (*Systemic Process Model*) are related to the generic structure of the Coordinating Processes that is discussed in Section 3.2. A software system can contain an instantiation of these structures due to the detailed configuration of the participating coordination mechanisms. The intended dynamics of system-level adaptivity are enabled and implicated by the process model. The concrete exhibition of the described dynamics is enabled by the appropriate configuration of the process instance.

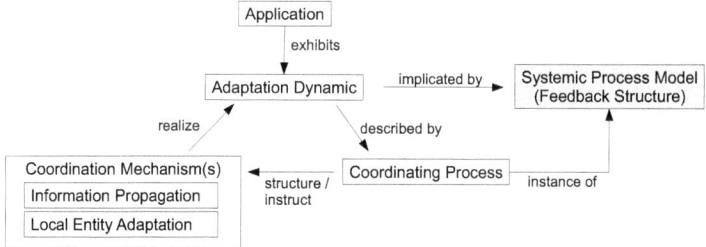

Figure 4.5: Systemic feedback models describe types of Coordinating Processes [Sudeikat and Renz, 2010c]

4.2.3 Agent Causal Behavior Graph

The manifestation of self-organizing phenomena is driven by the mutual interdependencies between system elements. In this respect, the SD modeling approach is particularly attractive to the modeling and design of self-organizing agent-coordination as it highlights the structure of these interdependencies. These structures influence the dynamical properties of systems, i.e. the occurrence of fixed points. Therefore, the qualitative system behavior can be anticipated when the structure of interdependencies is known. This modeling stance does not describe the self-organizing phenomena themselves, but rather it describes the network of interdependencies that causes their manifestation.

In the following, it is shown how the dynamical behavior of a software system can be described using a systemic modeling approach. A systemic model of an MAS, based on the CLD modeling formalism, describes the dynamical behavior of an MAS using a set of system variables and their causal interdependencies. In agreement with mathematical modeling approaches to MASs (e.g. [Lerman and Galstyan, 2001]), the set of system variables characterizes the macroscopic state of an MAS at any given time by representing the aggregate numbers of agents that exhibit specific behaviors. The causal interdependencies between these variables indicate that specific role/group activities mutually influence each other. This viewpoint is based on the assumption that the system elements are locally adaptive, i.e. can adjust their behavior based on a local reasoning. Thus, system elements respond to the influences of other elements, e.g. to the direct request of a particular function or the indirect perception that the state of the MAS or its environment(s) changes and requires an adjustment of the local behavior. In this context, a *behavior* refers to (1) agent activities, e.g. the execution of a workflow or the provision of a specific service, (2) agent states, e.g. local configuration, and (3) transitions between states [Devescovi et al., 2007a].

Figure 4.6 illustrates the abstraction of a software system to a systemic model. *System Implementation* models (Figure 4.6 bottom) specify the microscopic behaviors of the individual system elements, e.g. software components (left) or agent models (right). From these models, developers can infer the degree of freedom of the individual element, i.e. the set of behaviors that each element is able to exhibit. A *Systemic Model* can be constructed by projecting the individual behaviors onto the aggregate system variables that characterize the system state. These relations between state variables can be inferred by examining the detailed designs of agent behaviors and how agents interact, i.e. how agent interactions cause population members to change their allocations to behaviors. The systemic system representation then allows the qualitative *Macroscopic System Behavior* of the MAS under different parameter regimes and initial configurations to be anticipated.

Systemic models can be constructed from agent-oriented application designs and implementation models. A systematic procedure to the processing of design models if given in Section 4.3. It guides construction of aggregate system variables by searching agent designs for individual behaviors and the influences on individual agents that make them adopt or abandon these behaviors. The variable types of systemic models refer to agent-oriented modeling concepts in order to describe the aggregate agent behaviors. Agent-oriented development approaches, as discussed in [Mao and Yu, 2004], commonly refer to *role* and *group* concepts to abstract agent behaviors. Roles describe normative agent behaviors to which individual actors can commit. Groups describe the formation of collaborations among individuals that share mutual characteristics, e.g. common objectives. In the following sections, a modeling formalism is discussed that uses these concepts to describe the aggregate system behavior of MASs. This formalism is used in the remainder of this thesis to describe the decentralized coordination in agent-based systems of varying application contexts. This modeling approach is extensible, as complementary modeling abstractions of individual agent behaviors can be added. However it is necessary that system variables describe the local behavior of individual agents. Agents are not constrained to only exhibit one behavior at any given time-point, i.e. agents can simultaneously contribute to system variables.

Systemic representations of MASs can be given by CLDs, as in SD (e.g. [Sudeikat and Renz, 2008c, 2007c]), but the abstract nature of this modeling formalism can lead to ambiguities, e.g. as discussed in [Richardson, 1986]. The unambiguous modeling of agent-based software systems

4.2. SYSTEMIC MODELING APPROACH

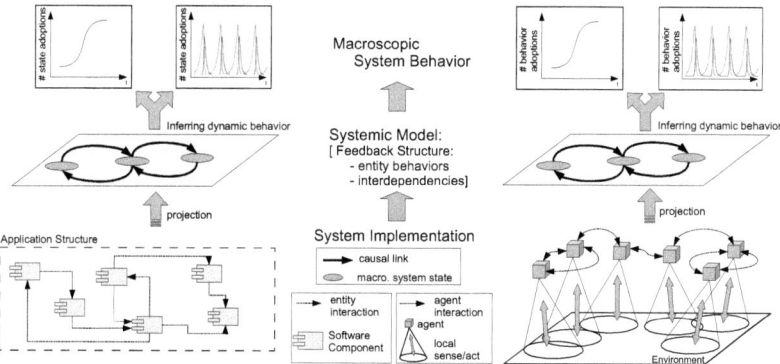

Figure 4.6: Illustration of the projection of software designs to systemic models, adapted from [Sudeikat and Renz, 2009h]. The timely changing properties of system elements, i.e. software components (left) or software agents (right), are abstracted to dynamical system models that are composed of sets of system variables and their mutual interdependencies.

is addressed by a refinement of system variables and the types of causal relations among them.

Graph Structure

Definition 4.1 *(Agent Causal Behavior Graph)* An Agent Causal Behavior Graph *(ACBG)* is given by $ACBG := <V_{acbg}, E_{acbg}>$, where V_{acbg} indicates a set of nodes and E_{acbg} denotes a set of directed edges ($E_{acbg} \subseteq V_{acbg} \times V_{acbg}$).

These nodes represent the system state variables that characterize the macroscopic configuration of an MAS. Each variable indicates the number of agents which exhibit a distinct, observable behavior [Lerman and Galstyan, 2004]. Different node/variable types indicate the number of current *role activations* ($r_{(x)}$), the number of *active groups* ($g_{(x)}$) and the *size* of specific groups ($gs_{(x)}$). At early design stages modelers may not want to define the representation of an agent behavior. Therefore, a neutral *behavior* ($b_{(x)}$) node type is available that provides an abstract representation of observable behaviors without referencing an organizational modeling concept. An additional node type indicates the accumulative values of *environment properties* ($e_{(x)}$).

The interdependencies between nodes, i.e. the represented variables, are indicated by edges (e) that represent *causal* (e^c) or *influencing* (e^i) relations. These relations can be *positive* or *negative* and are either *direct* ($e_{(d+/-)}$), e.g. based on inter-agent communication, or *mediated* ($e_{(m+/-)}$) by coordination media, e.g. shared environments [Gouaich and Michel, 2005]. Causal relations describe causal influences as known from customary CLDs (cf. Section 4.2.1), i.e. an increase in origins of positive causalities force connected variables to increase after a time delay. Vice versa, negative relations describe changes in opposite directions [Sterman, 2000]. The influencing edges describe additive or subtractive relations. These links are present when changes in system variables, e.g. the increase of adoptions of a specific role, enforce only the increases (positive) or decreases (negative) of connected system variables. In these cases the relation does not have a causal impact, but rather variable changes cause only additive/subtractive changes in connected variables. In principle, causal links can be dissolved by replacing them with the flows between system variables that manifest the causal relationship. This enables the representation of CLDs with SFD, e.g. to prepare system simulations [Sterman, 2000].

Influences between system variables are not only 1:1 but can be *contributive*, as variable changes jointly influence each other. An additional node type expresses these composite relations by joining edges to a combined interaction *rate* ($\lambda_{(x)}$). Connections from rate-nodes have only an influencing impact (e.g. [Richardson, 1986]).

Notation

The graphical notation of an ACBG is summarized in Figure 4.7. The different node types are indicated by graphical representations (I). Edge types are distinguished by the different arrow shapes and line types (II). According to the CLD notation, significant delays can be indicated by annotating links with a double bar (cf. Figure 4.2). The icons that are used to indicate the presence of feedback loops, i.e. sets of circular interdependencies , also correspond to the CLD notation (III). The rules for the identification of a feedback loop are the same as for a CLD (cf. Section 4.2.1). Nodes of the same type that participate in a common causality can be *stacked* to abridge models (IV). For such nodes, the set of included variables can be specified (in curly brackets) by listing them explicitly or providing a set definition. Links to stacked nodes affect all included nodes by default. Outgoing links indicate by default that each of the contained nodes can serve as the origin of the interdependency. Alternatively, the sets of influencing and influenced variables can be annotated to links, also as a set definition or a list of elements in curly brackets, to constrain the origins and destinations of links. The language that is used to specify sets of nodes is not constrained. In the remainder of this thesis sets are typically specified by boolean expressions. When links are annotated, the expression *source.x* refers to properties (x) of the software elements, e.g. agents and environment elements, that contribute to the originating node/variable. Respectively, the expression *destination.x* refers to the properties of elements that exhibit the behaviors of the nodes/variables that the links point to.

The behavior node type ($b_{(x)}$) is an abstract representation of a generic agent behavior without reference to agent design concepts. Therefore, the other node types that represent agent behaviors ($r_{(x)}$, $g_{(x)}$, $gs_{(x)}$) are specializations of the behavior node type (V). Comparatively, the ACBG causality (VI) and influence (VII) types are specializations of the unspecified link types (see II). The three abstractions allows for abstract node/relation definitions in ACBGs. These can be used to model the principal dynamics and subsequently refine nodes/links with the abstractions that are appropriate to an application context or system design.

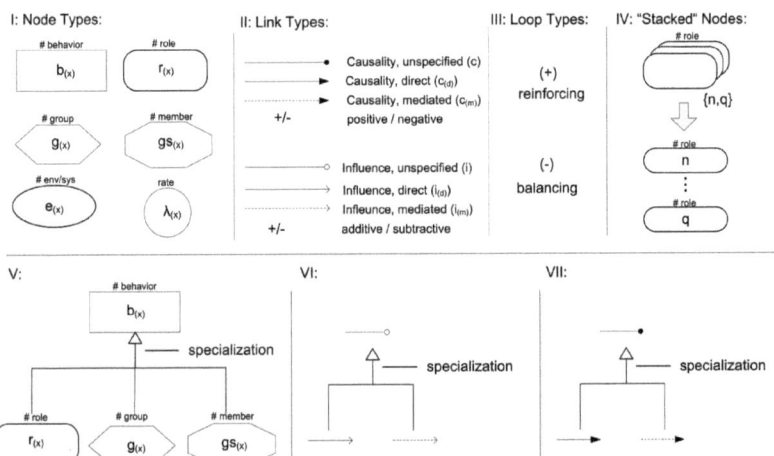

Figure 4.7: ACBG notation, adapted from [Sudeikat and Renz, 2010a, 2008b; Renz and Sudeikat, 2009]

4.2. SYSTEMIC MODELING APPROACH

Figure 4.8 (left) illustrates a hypothetical application setting using the ACBG notation. A set of agents is able to adopt the role *Producer*. Two role types that describe the activity of producing two element types (A, B) are available. Active producers create *product* elements at a constant rate. Therefore, the number of *Products* in the system increases proportionally to the number of active Producers. This is modeled as an additive influence (production). Products are stored in a storage facility and their warehousing reduces the amount of the available *Storage capacity*. This relation is described by a negative causal relation (storage) which indicates that the capacity decreases when the products increase and, vice versa, the capacity increases when the number of products decreases. An additional, positive causal relation (*availability*) describes that the activation of producers is controlled by the current capacity value. When storage space is available, Producers are activated. When the space decreases, the number of activated Producers decreases as well.

This modeling level focuses on the description of the observable dynamical behavior of the MAS. It makes no assumptions about the realization of the described causal relations. For example, the third Causal relation would be realized by letting agents monitor the capacity value, or by a dedicated managing agent type that orders subordinate Producers to activate. Therefore, this modeling level supplements agent-oriented design techniques with the description of the intended system behavior.

The structure of the interdependencies reveals that the system exhibits a balancing (negative) feedback loop. This indicates the qualitative behavior of the system, i.e. balancing feedbacks are known to enforce s-shaped (a.k.a. goal-seeking) behaviors. The exhibited system behavior can be estimated by transferring the identified relations to mathematical models. Figure 4.8 (right) illustrates how this system approaches a steady state.[3]

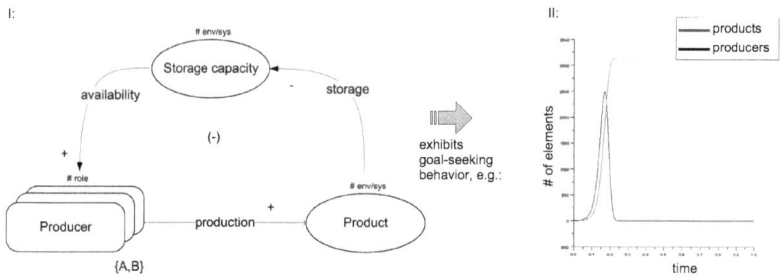

Figure 4.8: ACBG example, following [Sudeikat and Renz, 2009c]

Multi-Level Modeling of Agent Coordination by ACBG Refinement

ACBGs allow the dynamical behavior of MASs at different levels of granularity to be represented, ranging from the abstract representation of an intended system behavior, e.g. as a requirement on the behavior that the application to-be is expected to manifest, to detailed coordination models that describe the collaboration of microscopic agent models.

Transitions between these modeling levels, e.g. in iterative development processes, is facilitated by the refinement and abstraction of ACBGs (cf. Figure 4.9). Models are extended by the *attachment* (I) of additional states and associated interdependencies. Both nodes (II) and edges (III) can be individually refined and abstracted. These graph elements are detailed by replacing them

---

[3] The graph has been derived using a system of differential equations that describes how the storage capacity is filled: $\frac{dx}{dt} = x \cdot z - x$, $\frac{dy}{dt} = +\beta \cdot x$, $\frac{dz}{dt} = -y$, where x represents the number of activated Producer roles, y represents the number of generated products, z represents the available storage capacity and β describes the rate of element production. Initial values are: x =2, y=0, z = 50, β=20

with a subgraph. The coarsening of ACBGs, vice versa, is carried out by replacing subgraphs with graph elements. Additionally, the *traceability* of ACBG refinements is facilitated by visualizing hierarchies of state variables. That a variable value is composed of (sub-)variable values can be expressed by enclosing the subordinate variable representation (IV). This notation is borrowed from the *Statechart* formalism, that supports the description of hierarchies of state machines and state diagrams [Harel, 1987], and indicates that a variables value is composed of the values of the enclosed variables. Interdependencies and influences can link the enclosed (a,b) or superordinate variables (c,d). By default, links that point to a variable equally affect all enclosed variables, and links that originate in a variable transmit changes of any enclosed variable.

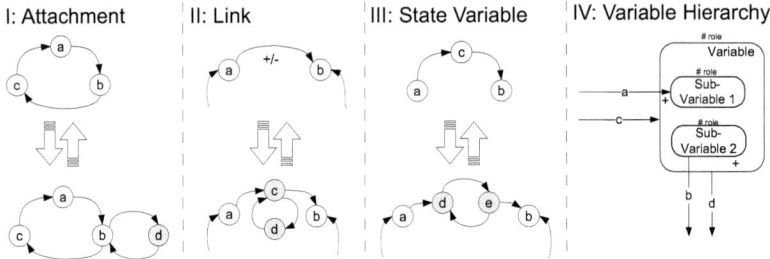

Figure 4.9: ACBG refinement / abstraction operations, adapted from [Sudeikat et al., 2009b]

Section 3.4 discussed how the derivation of intermediate system description levels, based on the classifications of agent-behaviors, facilitates the analysis and redesign of MASs that exhibit self-organizing phenomena. ABCGs particularly support the transition between intermediate (a.k.a. *mesoscopic*) description levels. ACBG nodes can describe concrete design elements, e.g. roles and groups, that are found in agent-oriented design models, but can also denote behavior abstractions, i.e. represent classes of agent behaviors. In this respect, system state variables can be used to indicate the mesoscopic agent states that define how agents contribute to arising structures/phenomena. The illustrated refinement or coarsening of these behavior classifications facilitates the traversal between the different description levels (cf. Figure 4.9). An example for this expressiveness is given in the following sections, where the analysis (cf. Section 4.3) and design (cf. Section 4.4) of collaborative effects in MASs is discussed.

4.3 Systemic Analysis of MAS Behavior

This section discusses and demonstrates how (1) systemic descriptions can be systematically deduced from the designs of agent-oriented software systems and (2) the resulting models enable the examination of the space of potential application dynamics at design-time.

The fundamental structure of this analysis process is illustrated in Figure 4.10 [Sudeikat and Renz, 2009g]. Agent-oriented design models (I) are processed and an ACBG is constructed (II) that represents the embedded causative interdependencies that affect the application behavior. The structure and dynamical properties of the ACBG-based application representation are then analyzed (III). The insights gained may indicate redesigns of the application design (IV).

Primary activities for constructing an ACBG (II) are the extraction of the relevant system variables (*System Variable Identification*) and their interdependencies (*Interdependency Identification*). Variables, i.e. ACBG node elements, are identified by searching design models of agent(s), environment(s) and optional models of the organizational structure(s). *Agent Design* models are searched for the observable behaviors, e.g. indicated by task or role concepts, that are available to the individuals. These are mapped to the behavior ($b_{(x)}$) or role ($r_{(x)}$) nodes of an ACBG. *Environment Design* models are processed to identify the environment properties that are influenced

4.3. SYSTEMIC ANALYSIS OF MAS BEHAVIOR

by the identified agent behaviors. These properties are abstracted to aggregate system variables ($e_{(x)}$). Organizational models of the MAS describe which organizational structures partition the MAS design and provide input to the identification of role ($r_{(x)}$) and group nodes ($g_{(x)}, gs_{(x)}$). Not all systematic development procedures demand organizational modeling, therefore this is optional input. The identified behaviors are subject to classifications that adjust the granularity of the derived system representation [Sudeikat and Renz, 2007a].

The identification of the interdependencies that relate system variables requires design models to be searched for the causes that make agents adopt a behavior and change their behavior allocations. Direct interdependency edges are identified by tracing the direct, i.e. message-based, interactions. Mediated edges are identified by tracing agent-activities that mutually influence environment elements. Some methodologies provide explicit representations of the acquaintance and interactions of agents. Examples are the *Acquaintance Diagram* of the *Gaia* methodology [Zambonelli et al., 2003] and the *System Overview Diagram* of the *Prometheus* methodology [Padgham and Winikoff, 2004], where message-based interactions are denoted as *Protocols*. These models can be traced to identify the agent-internal elements that are influenced by the indicated interactions, i.e. acquaintance relationships. Another common formalism is the *(A)UML Sequence Diagram* [Bauer and Odell, 2005] that expresses the role-changing behavior of agents and relates the changes to the interactions among agents.

The structure of the ACBG allows the dynamical properties of the represented system to be inferred. These structures can be examined manually to estimate the dynamical modes of the represented system. As the behavior of non-linear, coupled and possibly cyclic interdependencies is often counter-intuitive, the manual examination is typically assisted by the simulation of ACBGs. Simulations assist the estimation of dynamical system properties and facilitate the explorations of the space of system behaviors under different initial conditions and parametrizations. The simulation requires the derived graph to be concretized to a mathematically precise model that can be iterated. Two classes of simulation models are examined. First, stochastic simulations are established tools for simulating complex behaving MASs and have been applied to animate systemic MAS models [Renz and Sudeikat, 2009]. Secondly, SD research provides tools and guidelines for translating CLDs to equation-based models, i.e. systems of differential equations or rate equations. These can be iterated to animate the timely behavior of these systems (e.g. cf. Figure 4.8) and can also be treated formally, e.g. via stability analysis [Kaplan and Glass, 1995]. The simulation of ACBGs is detailed in Section 4.3.3.

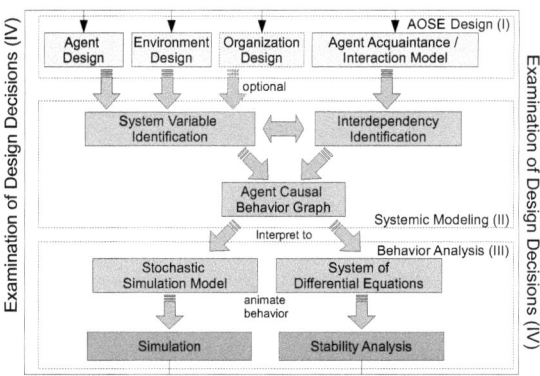

Figure 4.10: Illustration of the qualitative examination of the dynamics of MAS designs [Sudeikat and Renz, 2009g]. Agent-oriented application designs are abstracted by the identification of system variables and their interdependencies.

106   CHAPTER 4. SYSTEMIC MODELING OF COLLECTIVE PHENOMENA IN MASS

In [Sudeikat and Renz, 2011], this conception has been refined to a systematic process that guides the systemic modeling and analysis of MASs. The intended audience is AOSE practitioners, who can use this process to augment the analysis and design phases of their application development with an optional activity. The presentation of this activity (cf. Figure 4.11) follows the *Software Process Engineering Meta-Model* (SPEM) [Object Management Group, 2008]. The adoption of method engineering for agent-based systems development, modeling formalisms and the SPEM modeling concepts are discussed in Sections 2.6.3, 6.1.2. According to SPEM, development processes can be understood as sequences of *Activities*. The definition of Activities comprises *Tasks*, i.e. definitions of work units. Tasks consume, produce, or modify work products, called *Artifacts*.

A reusable analysis activity (*Systemic Agent Coaction Analysis*) is depicted in Figure 4.11 and consists of three phases. Initially, the design models are (pre-)processed (I). The information that is relevant to the construction of an ACBG is extracted and stored in two intermediate data structures (*Agent Acquaintance/Interaction Model, Agent Behavior Change Model*). Based on these Artifacts, a representative ACBG is deduced (II) and analyzed (III). This generic activity can be customized to different AOSE modeling formalisms by adjusting the initial Tasks (*Interaction Extraction, Agent Behavior Extraction*) by providing guidelines for the extraction of the intermediate data structures.

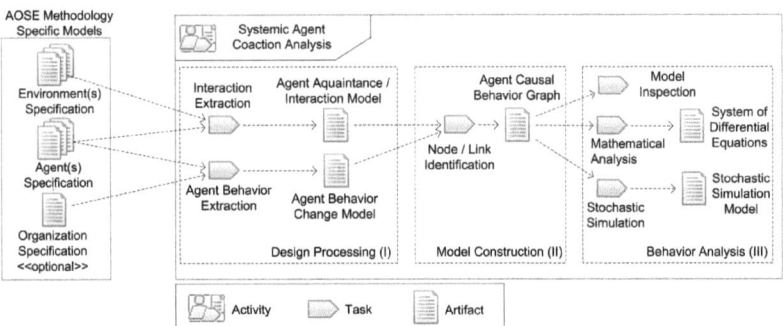

Figure 4.11: The qualitative analysis process [Sudeikat and Renz, 2011]

4.3.1   Processing Agent-Oriented Application Designs

Three types of agent-oriented design models provide information that is relevant to the derivation of an ACBG. The *Agent(s) Specification* models describe the internal working of the agent models. These serve as guidelines for the implementation of agent types and describe (1) the sets of behaviors that are available to the individual agents as well as (2) the contexts in which agents are expected to exhibit them (cf. Section 2.6.3). A prominent example for expressing the context of agent behaviors is the *AUML Sequence Diagram* [Bauer and Odell, 2005] (see Section 2.6), an extension to the UML Sequence Diagram that allows to describe interactions between agents and other software elements as sequences of agent interactions, e.g. message exchanges. This formalism has been used to describe directly the circumstances in which agents change roles [Odell et al., 2003]. Development methodologies typically supplement models of the interactions between system elements with views on behavioral abstractions that are used to express the activities of agents. Examples are the *Agent Descriptors* (in textual format) of the *Prometheus* methodology [Padgham and Winikoff, 2004] and the *Role Description* models of the *Passi* methodology [Cossentino, 2005], or the *Actor/Goal Diagrams* of the *Tropos* methodology [Giorgini et al., 2005]. *Environment(s) Specifications* describe how the environment interacts with the agents and how it responds to

4.3. SYSTEMIC ANALYSIS OF MAS BEHAVIOR

the activities of agents. *Organization Specification* structures agent-based applications in terms of organizational concepts, e.g. roles and groups [Coutinho et al., 2005; Mao and Yu, 2004] (cf. Section 2.6).

The design of an MAS, guided by an arbitrary development process (cf. Section 2.6.3), is given by sets of these design models. The processing of these models abstracts them by identifying the observable behaviors of agents (Task: *Agent Behavior Extraction*), i.e. the future ACBG nodes, and the interactions among agents and environment elements (Task: *Interaction Extraction*), that affect the exhibition of behaviors and manifest ACBG interdependencies.

Figure 4.12 illustrates the resulting data structures. An *Agent Interaction Model* (AI) (left) documents the sum of the interactions that are embedded in the application design. *MAS Element* entities represent the software elements, i.e. *Agent*s or *Environment Elements*. These elements are connected by unique *Element Interaction*s and indicate directed influences. It is a common concern for agent-oriented desing models to express which system elements interact. Therefore, some AOSE methodologies, such as *Gaia* [Zambonelli et al., 2005] and *Prometheus* [Padgham and Winikoff, 2004], provide formalisms for expressing acquaintances among agents. Mutual influences on environment elements indicate mediated agent-interdependencies.

An *Agent Behavior Change* (ABC) model (right) documents the identified *Behaviors* of the specified agent types as well as the causes that make agents adjust their local behavior. The model comprises a set of representations of the identified *Agent* types. These representations contain descriptions of the *Behavior*s that can be exhibited. Interactions cause agents to join or leave a behavior [Odell et al., 2003]. These causes indicate influences within agent models (Agent-Intern Interaction), e.g. when agent modules influence each other by goal adoptions or periodic stimuli, or by influences between system elements (*Element Interaction*). The interactions among elements are identified in AI models. The denoted interactions may not cause exclusively the adjustments of local agent behaviors but have contributive effects in combination with other interactions (*contributives*).

It must be noted that the interdependencies between agents do not only represent reactive responses to perceptions. The interactions, as understood in this section, abstract the influences to which agents are exposed. These influences range from sensor perceptions to high-level negotiation protocols. Interdependencies are established as agents reason on their influences and then adjust their local behavior accordingly. In particular cases, these adjustments depend on microscopic details and fluctuate, but systemic modeling aims at describing the general *trend* of responses to interactions (cf. Section 4.2.3).

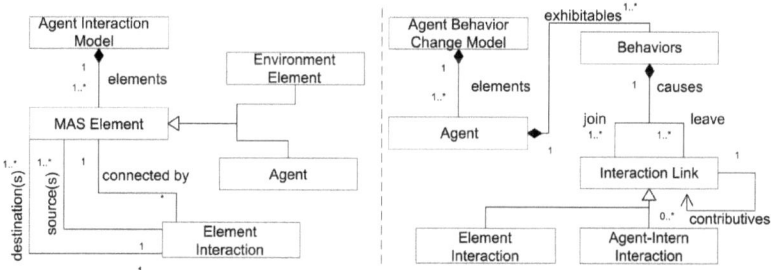

Figure 4.12: Conceptual models of intermediate data structures that prepare for ACBG construction, following [Sudeikat and Renz, 2011]

Interaction Extraction

The major activities in the construction of an AI model are identifying the types of interactive system elements and determining of the interactions that take place between them. The *Interaction Extraction* Task (c.f Figure 4.13) consists of two phases.

First, the application design models are processed to identify the referenced system element types. Active elements, i.e. actor and agent types (*Identify Actors/Agents*), as well as passive software elements (*Identify Environment Elements*) are identified by searching the design models for corresponding design concepts.

Secondly, the interactions are identified. Direct interactions (*Identify Direct Interactions*) are indicated by the message exchange of agent models. Agent-oriented modeling formalisms rely on varying modeling concepts to describe the communication between agent types. Examples are acquaintance diagrams [Zambonelli et al., 2003; Padgham and Winikoff, 2004], dependency relationships [Giorgini et al., 2005] and *Protocol* definitions [Padgham and Winikoff, 2004]. The mediated agent interactions are also identified. The environment models are searched for (1) the interactions of the passive software elements (*Environment/Environment*) and (2) the interactions between agents and passive elements (*Agent/Environment*), i .e. the activities of agents that send and modify the application environment(s). Based on the latter two sets of interactions, the mediated interactions between agents can be inferred by tracing how agent types affect each other by the mutual modification of environment elements. The identification of the influences of environment elements is necessary determine transitive, mediated interactions where effects on environment elements are passed on before they are perceived by agent types.

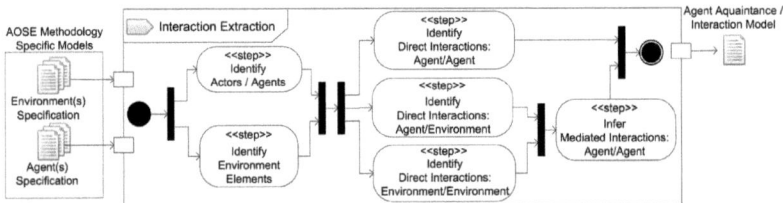

Figure 4.13: The Interaction Extraction, represented by a stereotyped UML Activity Diagram

Agent Behavior Extraction

The construction of ABC models requires the identification of the *behaviors* that are available to the system agents and their relation to the influences that *cause* their exhibition. Behaviors abstract the agent activities by describing observable courses of actions. Agents are considered to reason upon the state of the environment and to identify the behaviors that are appropriate to certain execution contexts. Therefore, the causes do not only describe when agents reactively respond to an interaction with the adoption of a behavior, but also when the interaction causes modifications of the agent state, e.g. by providing stimuli or additional information, that increase the possibility that agents will adjust their behavior in later time steps.

The Task *Agent Behavior Extraction*, as illustrated in Figure 4.14, addresses the construction of ABC models. Agent as well as organizational models are iterated, the behavior spaces of individual system elements are identified and the behaviors are related to the interactions among system elements. Initially, the available behaviors are identified in all agent models (*Identify Behaviors*). This manual modeling effort depends on the agent architecture, or on the modeling formalism that describes the conceived agent realization. The granularity of the analysis is controlled by this categorization of the agent activities. An example is given in [Sudeikat and Renz, 2007a], where distinct courses of actions are identified within the designs of cognitive agents that follow the *Belief-Desire-Intention* architecture [Rao and Georgeff, 1995]. The agent designs comprise trees

4.3. SYSTEMIC ANALYSIS OF MAS BEHAVIOR

of Goal, (sub-)Goal and Plan concepts, and sub-trees describe different practices for achieving goals (cf. Section 2.4). Behaviors are not bound to specific agent types but describe observable activities within the MAS.

Subsequently, the set of identified behaviors is iterated and for each of them, the design models are searched for the influences that actuate agents to adopt or abandon them (*Search Causes*). Each of the causes describes an interaction in the ABC (*Add Interaction*). These are identified by tracing the influences that make agents adjust their local behavior. Examples are (A)UML models of role changing behaviors [Odell et al., 2003] or organizational models [Ferber et al., 2004]. For the added interactions it is checked whether it actuates agents by itself, i.e. is the only influence that makes agents adjust the specific behavior, or whether it conjointly *contributes* to the actuation by other interactions. In the latter case, these interactions are added (*Add Contributive interactions*) and are marked for later processing. An example for contributive interactions can be found in Section 4.3.4, where the activation of an agent type depends on the availability of both (1) inactive individuals and (2) environment elements in varying processing states. The identified interactions and behaviors are uniquely marked to ease the construction of ACBGs in the subsequent Task.

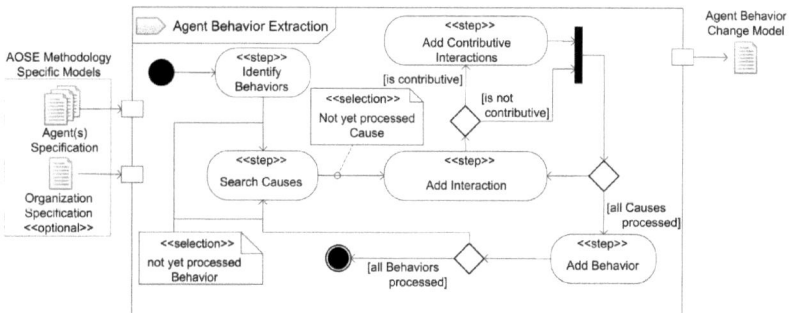

Figure 4.14: The Agent Behavior Extraction, represented by a stereotyped UML Activity Diagram.

4.3.2 Constructing the Systemic Abstraction

The construction of the ACBG-based representation, as illustrated in Figure 4.15 (*ACBG Construction*), is based on the processing of the previously constructed AI and ABC models, i.e. the preprocessed application design. First, both models are searched for references to behaviors of system entities. These references are transformed to system variables, i.e. ACBG nodes (*Add ACBG nodes (ABCM/AIM)*). This transformation primarily concerns the classification of the referenced behaviors as appropriate node/variable types. Behaviors in the ABC model are mapped to behavior abstractions ($r_{(x)}$, $g_{(x)}$, $gs_{(x)}$, etc.). Environment elements, given in the AI model, are mapped to environment variables ($e_{(x)}$). Secondly, the relationships between the variables, i.e. ACBG nodes, are deduced and inserted. The set of identified ACBG-nodes is iterated and for each element the causes for their behavior adoption and abandonment are iterated. These causes are mapped to relations that are added to the ACBG (*Add ACBG Edge*). This mapping is based on the interpretation of the identified interactions. It is determined whether the relation describes a causal interdependency or an additive/subtractive influence. In addition, it is checked if the relation is *contributive*, as indicated by the ABC model. In this case (*Add Contribution + Join Edges*), the contributive relations are added as well and these edges are joined by a rate variable (cf. Section 4.2.3). In the resulting structure, contributive affections are expressed by the joint contribution to a rate that influences element behaviors. Finally, the introduced rate nodes, are connected to the originating and affected behaviors (*Connect Nodes*). The construction Task is finished when all interactions among all behaviors in the AI and ABC models have been processed.

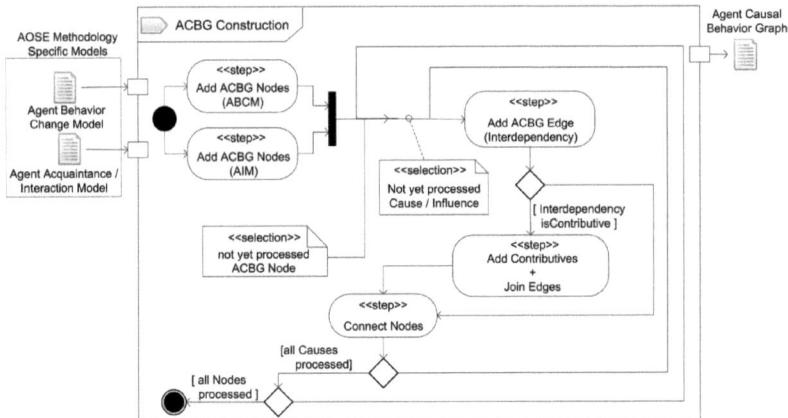

Figure 4.15: ACBG construction, following [Sudeikat and Renz, 2011]

4.3.3 Analyzing the System Behavior

The derived ACBG models highlight the underlying causal structure of an application design that affects the dynamic behavior of accordant applications (cf. Section 4.2). These models can be analyzed by three basic approaches.

First, the manual study of ACBGs (*Model Inspection*, cf. Figure 4.11) allows irregularities and anomalies to be identified. For example, the ACBG construction process (cf. Section 4.3.2) does not include validating whether graph nodes are linked, as orphaned nodes may indicate negligences in the application design. In particular, ACBGs facilitate the identification of cyclic causalities that form feedback loops. The awareness of these structures theoretically allows the qualitative system behavior to be estimated. However, tracing and valuing the effects of causal relationships requires experience as intuitive inferences typically fail, due to the *dynamic complexity* of feedback structures (e.g. discussed in [Sterman, 2000], pp. 21-39). Therefore, these efforts are typically supplemented with two analysis techniques that animate the timely changes of system variables and examine the effects of different parameterizations and initial conditions.

Secondly, *Stochastic Simulation* practices (cf. Figure 4.3.2), allow the dynamics of ACBGs to be examined [Renz and Sudeikat, 2009; Sudeikat and Renz, 2009h]. These approaches are based on previous works that use stochastic simulation techniques to represent MASs and examine their dynamical behavior, e.g. [Gardelli et al., 2005; Casadei et al., 2007; Sudeikat and Renz, 2007d]. MASs are represented by specifications of processes that imitate the activities of individual agents. The simulation of the concurrent execution of these processes is used to estimate the system behavior. The rise of collaborative effects, e.g. self-organizing phenomena, from the interactions of system elements demands the *stochasticity* of system simulations. These simulations allow to examine the synergetic establishment of global system properties under unstable system configurations, parameterizations and external perturbations (cf. Section 4.1.2). The language used to represent processes has implications on the practicability and effectiveness of system simulations (e.g. discussed in [Gardelli et al., 2005]). For focusing on self-organizing effects, *stochastic process algebras* [Clark et al., 2007] are particularly applicable [Gardelli et al., 2005; Casadei et al., 2007; Sudeikat and Renz, 2007d] (cf. Section 4.1.2). In [Renz and Sudeikat,

4.3. SYSTEMIC ANALYSIS OF MAS BEHAVIOR

2009] these algebras were applied to model and simulate the dynamics that are represented by ACBGs. The values of system variables are reproduced by the numbers of active processes, and the activation and deactivation of processes is modeled by exponentially distributed interaction rates between process types. Details of this simulation approach can be found in Section 6.7.3.

Thirdly the *Mathematical Analysis* (cf. Figure 4.3.2) of feedback structures enables a formal analysis of the anticipated system behaviors. Ordinary Differential Equations (ODE) are typically employed to express the rates of changes of system variables. Their iteration in numerical computing environments animates the time-dependent variations of variables and supports formal treatments such as the analytical or graphical stability analysis of fixed points (e.g. [Kaplan and Glass, 1995], Chapter 1). The derivation of ODEs can be guided by the *Stock-and-Flow Diagram* (SFD, cf. Section 4.2.1), in which stocks represent system variables and flows between these variables describe their timely modifications, specified with mathematical expressions. The semantics of the resulting system description are given in ODEs and these models can be iterated directly (cf. Section 4.2.1) or can be used as an intermediate step for their formal system analysis.

The latter two analysis techniques require a manual modeling efforts, in particular mathematical specification of, the system structure, interaction rates between system entities, and realistic model calibrations. These specifications are estimations when realizations of the design are not available to compare simulation results. However the animations can be used to answer *what-if* questions. In the following sections, the mathematical analysis of ACBGs is exemplified. The use of stochastic simulation techniques and their applicability for examining the capabilities of coordination models are discussed in Section 6.7.3.

4.3.4 Example: Marsworld Dynamics

In the following section, the analysis approach presented here is exemplified [Sudeikat and Renz, 2011], to show that non-intuitive, collective effects can be exhibited by comparatively simple applications. The causal structure of an agent-based application design is derived and analyzed. The inferences dynamics are compared to the behavior of an agent-based simulation model to show qualitative agreement.

The *Marsworld* scenario is inspired by a hypothetical application setting from [Ferber, 1999] (pages 43-45, 119 ff.). A set of autonomous robots is sent to a far off planet to mine ore. All robots search the environment for locations where ore is expected. The mining process comprises three distinct activities: (1) *examine* locations to verify the presence of or, (2) the mining (*production*) of the ore, and (3) *transporting* the ore to the home base after it has been retrieved.

An agent-based realization can be based on a *variable structure organization* [Ferber, 1999] (page 124). The robots, controlled by software agents, are specialized to perform one of the constitutive mining activities. *Sentry* agents are equipped with sophisticated sensors, *Producer* agents carry a mining device and *Transporter* agents are able to move fixed loads of ore. The exploration and production have a fixed time delay and all agents move with a fixed velocity. Initially, all agents search the environment. Producer and Transporter agents are equipped with inferior sensors and communicate encountered locations that may contain ore to a randomly selected Sentry agent. The mining process is transacted collectively. When Sentry agents have verified the presence of ore at a location they request the mining of the ore from a Production agent. Similarly, the Production agents request the transport of the mined ore from Transporter agents. The system exhibits no predefined organizational structure; rather teams of agents are formed ad-hoc. In the simulation models, the agents are selected randomly for reasons of simplification. Alternative agent realizations could adjust the allocation of agents to the requested activities, e.g. by allocating the agent with the minimal distance to a reported location. These improvements only affect the fluctuating durations of agent allocations, not the systemic description of the qualitative system behavior.

The designs of the agent types specify two observable behaviors: the default searching of the environment and the achievement of the specialized agent activity. The dependencies of the three agent types and the structure of Sentry agents are illustrated in Figure 4.17 (I) in Tropos notation [Giorgini et al., 2005]. The behaviors of agents are represented by Goals and the hierarchies of

Tasks and (sub-)Goals that enable their achievement [Sudeikat and Renz, 2007a]. For example, the searching behavior of an agent includes the task of randomly exploring the environment (*wander environment*), which references the (sub-)Tasks of stepping to another location (*move to location*). Tropos proposes the modeling of dependencies between system actors. *Dependers* depend on the provision of a *Dependum* by *Dependees*. Sentry agents depend on the communication of potential locations (*examination locations*), where the presence of ore is to be verified. These communications trigger the execution of the specialized Sentry behavior, here modeled as the adoption of a Goal (*sensing*). In addition to the external provision of ore locations, Sentry agents can identify the locations themselves. The default searching behavior (Goal *searching*) provides ore locations (*examination locations*) that are communicated internally. When the presence of ore is affirmed (Task: *examine location*), the mining of the ore is requested (Goal: *request production*).

The designs of the other agents follow a comparable structure. The execution of the specialized agent activities depends on the request from other agent types, i.e. the production by Producer agents is requested by Sentry agents and the transport by Transporter agents is requested by Producer agents. Producer and Transporter agents are also equipped with the searching behavior (Goal: *searching*) but communicate identified locations to Sentry agents.

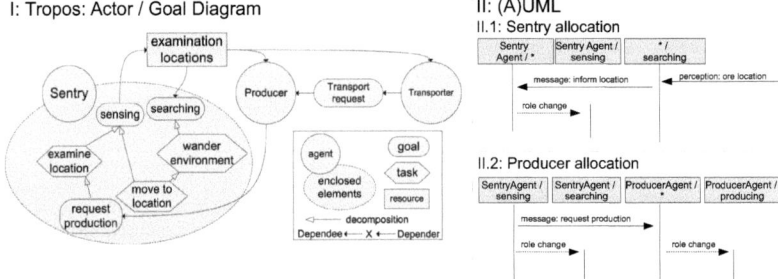

Figure 4.16: Application design, following [Sudeikat and Renz, 2011]. I: Tropos Actor / Goal Diagram, II: (A)UML Sequence Diagrams.

A detailed view of the activation of Sentry and Producer agent types is given in Figure 4.16 (II) by (A)UML Sequence Diagrams [Bauer and Odell, 2005], where the agent behaviors are modeled as roles. All agent types (*) exhibit the *searching* behavior and may perceive ore locations (II.1). The locations are communicated to a Sentry agent (*message: inform location*) and the reception of these messages activates the *sensing* activity. The activation of the *producing* activity (II.2) is initiated by a request from a Sentry agent (*message: request production*). The request reception triggers the behavior adjustment of Producers (*role change*) and ends the *sensing* by Sentry agents, as they adopt the default *searching* behavior, also modeled as a *role change*.

Construction of the ACBG

Figure 4.17 illustrates an ACBG-based representation of the Marsworld design that is derived by the construction process presented in Section 4.3.2. The intermediate AI model records the three agent types and the ore locations in the environment. The locations are classified according to their processing state, i.e. if they are subject to the sensing, production or transportation activity. The ABC model describes that agents change roles when they send/receive communications of environment (ore) locations (cf. Figure 4.16).

Each agent type is mapped onto two role variables that represent the number of activated (*active*) or searching (*passive*) agents. The cumulative number of present ore locations is represented by an environment variable (*Resources*). The number of ore locations that are subjects to

4.3. SYSTEMIC ANALYSIS OF MAS BEHAVIOR

the activities of Sentry, Production and Transporting agents equals the numbers of requests that are issued to communicate these locations and activate agents. These numbers are represented by environment variables (*Examination requests*, *Production requests*, *Transportation requests*) as they describe the environment state. The sum of these variables plus an unknown fraction of not yet discovered locations equals the Resources variable. The hierarchical notation of variables (cf. Section 4.2.3) is not used to abbreviate the model. The amount of the not-discovered locations is factored out in the following discussion; their explicit modeling refines the activation of Sentry agents, but a simplified model is sufficient to describe the exhibited dynamics.

The mining process starts with the activation of Sentry agents (*Sentry (active)*). Their sensing activity adds to the number of communicated ore locations where production can occur (*Production requests*). The handling of these requests requires the availability of searching (*Producer (passive)*) and increases the amount of activated Producer agents (*Producer (active)*). When the mining activity is finished (delay) the amount of requests for the transportation of ore is increased (*Transportation requests*). Their handling effectuates the activation of Transporter agents (*Transporter (active)*). The transportation of ore reduces the amount of *Resources* in the environment. Sentry agents are activated by two possible interactions. First, searching Sentry agents may accidentally encounter potential ore locations and activate themselves, which can be regarded as the internal processing of an *Examination request*. Secondly, searching Producer and Transporter agents may accidentally encounter not-examined locations and communicate them to Searching agents. In both cases, these activations require the exhibition of the searching (passive) agent behaviors as well as the availability of Resources. Both types of influences cause Sentry activation and are therefore modeled as *contributives* that are joined by three distinct activation rates (cf. Section 4.3.1).

The established mining process leads to the transportation of mined ore to the home base (*Transporter (active)*). This behavior reduces the amount of resources in the environment (subtractive influence). Consequently, the MAS establishes a balancing feedback loop as Resources are continuously reduced (α). The activation of the agent types necessarily reduces the number of passive, i.e. searching, agents of the corresponding agent type. Thus, the system exhibits three feedback loops (β, γ, δ) that *balance* agent activations with the available agents. These feedbacks also affect the activation of Sentry agents, since the exhibition of passive behaviors contributes to Sentry activation rates and these activations propagate the activation of Producer (*Producer (active)*) and Transporter (*Transporter (active)*) agent types. These coupled feedbacks are inherent in the application design. Their effects on the global system behavior is examined in the following section.

Behavior Analysis

In this section, two examples for the analysis of the application structure are given. First, an SD simulation model, namely an SFD, is derived from the ACBG. This model is compared to an agent-based simulation of the Marsworld scenario and the congruence of both models is demonstrated as these show a comparable systematic behavior. In addition, the ACBG is used to explain a characteristic initialization behavior and to estimate the effects of different system initializations. Secondly, the initialization behavior is examined in detail by deriving and analyzing a mathematical model, namely a system of rate equations.

The manual examination of the identified feedback structure reveals opposing dependencies among the agent activations. The activation of Sentry agents enforces the consequent activation of the remaining two agent types (cf. Figure 4.17, positive relations from left to right). However, these activations decrease the number of passive, i.e. searching, agents in the system and the availability of these agent types reinforces the activation of Sentry agents ($A2$, $A3$). In parameterizations where the contribution of non-Sentry agent searches to the activation of Sentries can be neglected, e.g. when the number of Sentries is large enough to quickly explore a bounded environment, the identified interdependencies will not affect the global system behavior. However, in other parameterizations the number of active Sentry agents is expected to increase after periods when the majority of agents have been searching. Vice versa, high numbers of Sentry activations are

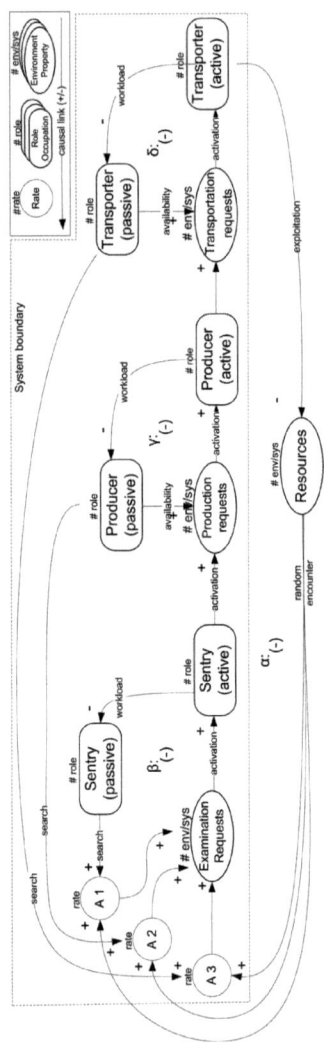

Figure 4.17: ACBG representation of the Marsworld dynamics, following [Sudeikat and Renz, 2011]

4.3. SYSTEMIC ANALYSIS OF MAS BEHAVIOR

expected to force the reduction of the fraction of searching agents in subsequent time steps.

Figure 4.18 illustrates an SFD[4] that resembles the dynamics of the ACBG. Stocks represent the system variables (cf. Figure 4.17) and the connecting flows concretize causal relations with rates of value transfers between variables. The semantics of this notation differ from the ACBG. Stocks represent aggregate quantities. The connecting flows express *fluxes*, i.e. passage rates, of elements that move from originating to connected variables (cf. Section 4.2.1). Stocks represent the number of agents that play a specific behavior. For each Stock, the incoming and outgoing flows denote the changes of values, as agents are influenced to adopt or abandon the represented behaviors. These influences are described as averaged inflows and outflows of agents from other stocks. This continuous modeling approach enforces specific assumptions about the system behavior. The cardinality of agents is expected to be above one and the possible non-determinism of agent activities, e.g. imposed by serialization constraints, is ignored.

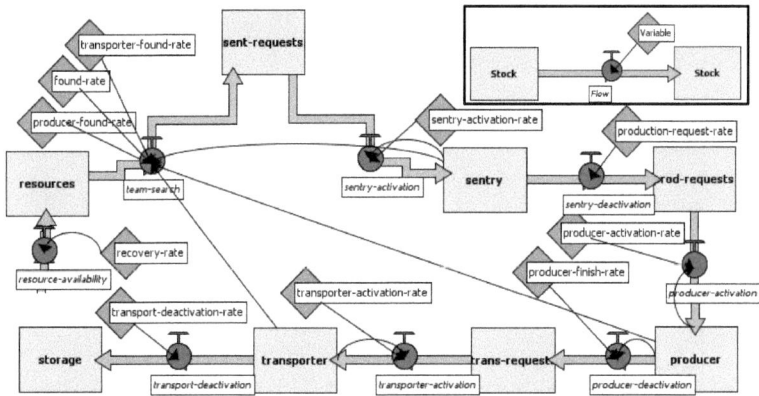

Figure 4.18: Simulation model of the Marsworld ACBG: Stock-and-Flow model

The SFD-based model is used to animate the system dynamics that are indicated by the ACBG. Simulation results are compared to an agent-based simulation[5] of the Marsworld design to validate the congruence of the systemic model with the exhibited MAS dynamics. In addition, a characteristic initialization behavior, exhibited by both models, is examined and the impact of differing fractions of agent types is anticipated.

Figure 4.19 (I) illustrates the system initialization and animates the exhibited mining process for an environment with limited resources. The numbers of agent activations are relatively scaled and show that the encounter of resources leads to the activation of Sentry agents, followed by the activations of Producer and Transporter agents (1). When the number of sentry agents decreases, the remaining agent types are also deactivated. Afterwards the model exhibits a steady but low activation of the agents, due to a low reinforcement of ore locations. The model exhibits a small peak (2), when inactive agents automatically continue their searching behavior and contribute to the activations of Sentry agents.

The agent-based simulation model exhibits a comparable behavior. The limitedness of resources is represented by an initially fixed amount of ore that is reinforced at a low rate. The Sentry and

---

[4]Based on the *System Dynamics* environment of the freely available *Netlogo* system: http://ccl.northwestern.edu/netlogo/

[5]also using the Netlogo environment (see Section 3.1.5), the discussed results were obtained by simulating 100 Sentry, Producer and Transporter agents in a grid of 625 (B) respectively 1225 (C,D) patches.

Producer activities are represented by fixed time delays and the measurement of agent activations includes travel times, i.e. it starts when agents are activated by a request and ends when the communicated assignment is completed. The observed behavior (an example run is shown in Figure 4.19, II) is heavily perturbed. The major source of these perturbations is the spatial distribution of agents and ore locations that enforces varying durations of agent activations. In addition, the unexploited resources are encountered coincidentally, while the systemic representation describes these encounters at steady rates. The agent types are quickly activated (1) and subsequently decrease in sequence when the available resources are depleted. Due to the described stochastics, the peaks are not only observed when the agent activations decrease (2), but also in later time steps as the system cannot settle into a steady rate of activations. These peaks follow the (perturbed) pattern of subsequent Sentry, Producer, and Transporter activations (3).

After this qualitative comparison for a specific type of environment configuration, correlation function techniques (see Section 2.5) are used to examine the basic congruence of the systemic model with the exhibited MAS behavior. In order to observe and quantify the interdependencies between agent activities, a *stationary working regime* is enforced by a fixed input rate of resources. The correlations of the agent behavior show a systematic that indicates the interdependencies of the systemic representation of the MAS design. The cross-correlation of the active Sentry and Producer agents reaches its maximum at a delay time of approximately 60 time units (cf. Figure 4.19, III).[6] Due to the asymmetry of the curve the mean delay time is longer (about 70). The correlation of active Producers and Transporters shows the same delay time. The longer tail of this function is caused by the longer activation of Transporters as they shuttle between ore-sources and the home-base until the ore is depleted. Accordingly, the correlation between the active Sentries and Transporters[7] also exhibits a long tail at a delay time that equals to the sum of the mean delay times of the other two correlations.

The auto-correlations (Figure 4.19, IV) exhibit symmetric decays. The auto-correlation times for Sentry and Producer agents are comparatively short. The longer auto-correlation time of the Transporter agents results from their extended activation times (see above). Moreover, the Sentry agents also exhibit negative auto-correlation values which indicate the interactions with the non-active agent types. The examination shows that in a stationary, but *highly fluctuating*, working regime the characteristic interdependencies of agent activities, as indicated by ACBG-based system representations, can be validated.

Previously, the dynamics of the ACBG-based system representation were analyzed by examining an intermediate, mathematically refined model, namely an SFD-based representation (cf. Figure 4.18). An alternative approach is the explicit specification and parameterization of the underlying stochastic models. These models also describe the numbers of agents that exhibit specific behaviors in continuous, averaged and time-dependent quantities. When the underlying dynamical process can be approximated by a Markovian process, the changes of agent behaviors are described by the averaged transition probabilities per time unit. A formal description technique for these processes is the use of Master Equations that, based on local transition probabilities, enable the derivation of the governing Rate Equations [Van Kampen, 2007]. The resulting model represents an average over ensembles of process realizations with given initial conditions and identical environments. The use of this modeling approach is discussed in Section 4.2.2 [Cardelli, 2008; Lerman and Galstyan, 2001]. As the agent and environment states are identified in the ACBG, the major modeling effort is the mapping of the ACBG relations to the exhibited transition rates. These adjustments of the rates allows different system configurations and parameterizations to be described.

With this stochastic interpretation, the underlying dynamics can be understood as a chain of reactions, similar to chemical processes. The detections of ore locations *generate*, i.e. bring about, the activation of Sentry agents and these activations then actuate the mining process that is executed by the subsequent modifications of ore locations and activations of agent types. The resulting system model is visualized in Figure 4.20 (I) and specified by the following set of Rate

---

[6]imposed by the simulation engine
[7]Figure 4.19 (III) plots the opposite correlation with a negative time lag

4.3. SYSTEMIC ANALYSIS OF MAS BEHAVIOR

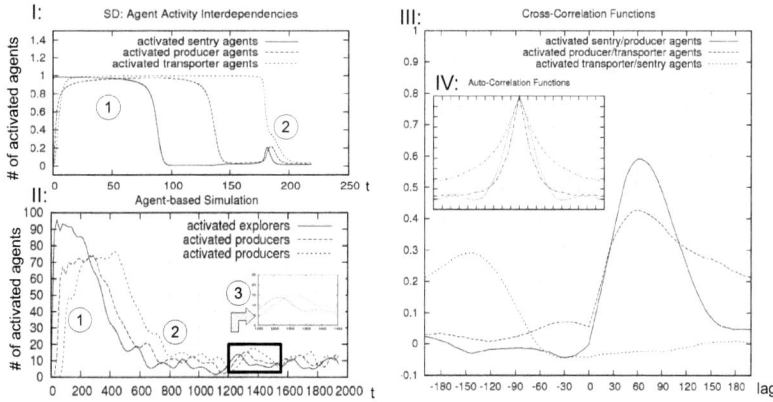

Figure 4.19: Simulation results for the Marsworld dynamics, from [Sudeikat and Renz, 2011]

Equations:

$$\dot{N}_l(t) = -\alpha_{ls}(M_s - N_s)N_l - \alpha_{lp}(M_p - N_p)N_l - \alpha_{lc}(M_c - N_c)N_l$$
$$\dot{N}_s(t) = \alpha_{ls}(M_s - N_o)N_l + \alpha_{lp}(M_\mu - N_p)N_l + \alpha_{lc}(M_c - N_c)N_l - \mu_s N_s$$
$$\dot{N}_a(t) = -\alpha_{ap}(M_p - N_p)N_a + \mu_s N_s$$
$$\dot{N}_p(t) = \alpha_{ap}(M_p - N_p)N_a - \mu_p N_p$$
$$\dot{N}_e(t) = -\alpha_{ec}(M_c - N_c)N_e + \mu_p N_p$$
$$\dot{N}_c(t) = \alpha_{ec}(M_c - N_c)N_e - \mu_c N_c$$
$$\dot{N}_d(t) = \mu_c N_c$$

As in the derived ACBG, the occurrence of requests for the different agent types is reflected by the inclusion of the examined ore *locations* (L) that are communicated by the corresponding requests. The perceived/communicated locations are distinguished according to their processing state, where $N_k, k \in \{l, a, e, d\}$ denotes the numbers of locations that are *loaded, activated, exhausted* and *depleted* respectively. In sequence, these types of locations are processed by the activated Sentry, Producer and Transporter agents. These activities transform location elements to the next state, e.g. the Sentries examine loaded locations and activate them for the later processing by Producer agents. This processing transforms activated locations to exhausted locations, signifying positions where the ore has been mined and is ready for transportation. At depleted locations, the ore has been completely removed. The quantities $N_j, j \in \{s, p, c\}$ represent the numbers of activated Sentry, Producer and Transporter agents respectively. These agents are bound to the specific location elements and execute their corresponding activities. Optionally, the (re-) generation rate of ore can be specified (λ, cf. Figure 4.20).[8] The numbers of agents of each type are fixed $M_j > 0$ ($j \in \{s, p, c\}$) and the number of deactivated, i.e. searching agents is $M_j - N_j \geq 0$.

Non-linear terms describe the activation of agents. The rate coefficients $\alpha_{kj} > 0$ ($k \in \{l, a, e\}, j \in \{s, p, c\}$) describe the averaged, system rate at which specific agent type encounter the appropriate location elements. Linear terms describe the averaged deactivation of agents as these finish their processing of locations after fixed delays. These averaged deactivations are controlled by corresponding release rates $\mu_j > 0$ that denote mean inverse processing times per target.

---
[8]This rate is not specified in the given equations, but is as a tool for establishing the working regime in the SFD-based analysis, as discussed above.

Agents are activated when they encounter an appropriate location element or receive their position via inter-agent communication. Therefore, the averaged processing times include not only the processing itself, but also fluctuating travel times to location elements. For transporter agents, the processing also includes the varying times of a fixed number of round-trips between the location and the home base.

Additional approximations simplify this model. The variables N_a and N_e exhibit quasistationary values without delay. The stochastic encounters of these elements can be neglected as the Sentry and Producer agents immediately communicate requests when they have finished their processing, i.e. when these types of elements have been created. Therefore, the elements are instantaneously assigned to agent instances. Without a significant delay, the these variables can be eliminated by setting their derivative to zero. In this approximated model the effects of the spatial distribution of the environment are not explicitly modeled but averaged.

However, the model exhibits a non-linear behavior that is comparable to the observations in the agent-based realizations. A simplified implementation of the Marsworld scenario is publicly available for the *Jadex* agent system (cf. Section 2.2.2).[9] This framework provides a generic infrastructure for the construction of agent-based software systems, thus macroscopic system simulations are not directly supported.[10] Therefore, the available agent realizations have been equipped with a minimal invasive monitoring technique [Sudeikat and Renz, 2007a], described in Section 5.2.6, is used to observe agent execution and measure the activations of agents (cf. Figure 4.20).

Small systems, composed of up to ten agents and up to ten targets, were simulated. Figure 4.20 shows the averaged[11] time series of the activations of the three agent types in a small team composed of 1 Sentry, 2 Producer and 2 Transporter agents that process 6 targets. As indicated in the previous analysis of a large-scale system realization, the agent types are sequentially activated. The amplitude is small and the agents are quickly deactivated, due to the small system size. All simulations were initialized with random but identical locations of ore, called *frozen-in disorder*. Assuming a given environment, this is a realistic setting but the initial spatial inhomogeneity causes additional delay times. The initial activations of agents are delayed as agents, starting at the home base, travel random but identical path lengths to become activated. As the rate equations given above describe the averaged system behavior, the initial delays were included to fit simulation results. For the Sentry, Producer and Transporter agents these measured delays are 2, 6 and 16 seconds.

The analytical solution of the rate equations is fitted to the observed agent activations (cf. Figure 4.20). The equations do not describe the effects of the spatial distribution and frozen-in disorder, but their agreement with the measured time series show that the derived abstraction describes the underlying dynamics of the system realization. In this configuration, the search efficiency of the MAS $\mu_l := \alpha_{ls}M_s + \alpha_{lc}M_c + \alpha_{lp}M_p$ is $\mu_l = 0.019 s^{-1}$ and leads to an approximately exponential decay of *loaded* ore locations with a mean decay time of 53 seconds. The onset of activations is controlled by the mean time to reach communicated locations and the mean processing time. These are approximated by the deactivation rates $\mu_j, j \in \{s, p, c\}$. The onset of Sentries is fitted with $\mu_s = 0.13 s^{-1}$. The Producer agents follow with the same rate. Due to their repeated shuttling, Transporters are slower and their deactivation is approximated by $\mu_c = 0.07^{-1}$.

4.4 Systemic Design of Decentralized MAS Coordination

Systemic modeling allows the causal structure of an agent-based software system to be described. It gives insights into their structural properties and allows to draw inferences about the exhibited qualitative dynamics of corresponding applications. This section, it is discusses how this modeling approach facilitates the design of application dynamics.

First, systemic modeling is used to describe prominent templates of self-organizing processes.

---

[9]http://jadex.informatik.uni-hamburg.de/bin/view/Usages/Examples
[10]At the present time simulation support is under development within the *SodekoVS* research project [Sudeikat et al., 2009a], but has not been available for these particular simulations.
[11]325 runs to ensure appropriate statistics

4.4. SYSTEMIC DESIGN OF DECENTRALIZED MAS COORDINATION

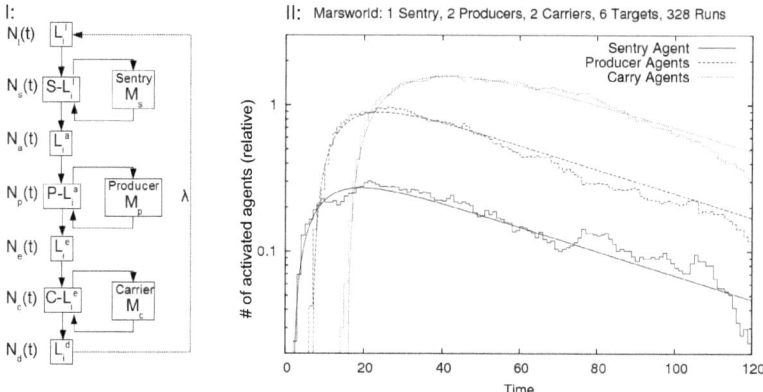

Figure 4.20: A visualization of the stochastic process that governs the initialization of the Marsworld scenario (I), following [Sudeikat and Renz, 2007a], and the averaged activations of the specialized agent behaviors (II) [Sudeikat and Renz, 2007a]

The processes are classified according to their structural properties and the exhibited dynamical properties. Secondly, it is discussed how descriptions of the intended application behavior, i.e. the intended manifestation of feedback loop structures, can be refined to detailed models of coordination strategies that serve as blueprints for system implementations. This design approach complements established AOSE techniques. While AOSE modeling formalisms correspond to the applied realization concepts, e.g. the utilized agent architecture (as discussed in [Sudeikat et al., 2004]), systemic modeling addresses the logical structure of the agent and entity interdependencies. A refinement process helps to conceive the dynamics of the planned system. In addition, the selection of template processes for inclusion in an application design is facilitated by matching the structural properties of these pattern with the structure of the intended dynamics.

4.4.1 Structural Classification of Coordination Strategies

Field-tested coordination pattern and interaction techniques are powerful tools for engineering of self-organizing applications. Their utilization as reusable design elements has been proposed (cf. Section 3.2), but requires guidelines for the systematic selection, combination and integration in applications. The available classifications address the modes of coordination that application designs can follow (cf. Section 3.2.2) as well as the applicable interaction techniques (cf. Section 3.2.1). Selection criteria characterize the operating principles of established adaptation processes and mechanisms (see Section 3.2). Their selection with respect to certain computational problems remains problematic and demands individual expertise.

Here, two additional sets of criteria are proposed that address the description, selection and comparison of process templates: first, the characterization of the structural properties and secondly, the attribution of phenomenological qualities of the structures that arise from the integration of these templates in software systems.

The *Regulation Polarity* (RP) describes the intended regulation of system structure that can be *compensating*, *amplifying* and *selective*. The polarity is a structural property that is determined by the numbers of manifested feedback loops. Amplifying structures contain a majority of reinforcing feedbacks that are bounded by (1) opposing reinforcements or (2) limiting capacities. These strategies enforce system adaptations by reinforcing fluctuations. Compensating strategies prescribe predominant sets of balancing feedbacks that damp fluctuations and drive applications to steady states. Selective strategies comprise even combinations of balancing and reinforcing feedbacks. The system history as well as stochastic factors determine, i.e. *select*, at run-time which system variables are reinforced or balanced.

The second criteria set gives a phenomenological characterization of the acquiring of system structures. As discussed in Section 3.1, the major properties of a self-organizing systems are the establishment and adjustment of *structures*. Two *Types* (T) of self-adaptive structurings are distinguished to discriminate the foci of agent coordination. The manifestation of a self-organizing phenomenon can be used to adjust the *configuration* of system elements. Examples are the enforcement of commonly agreed *conventions*, *coalition formations* or *resource allocation* problems. In addition, self-organization can be utilized to regulate element activities and bring about the exhibition of collaborative *processes*. In these cases, the decentralized coordination controls the chronology of element activities in order to establish collaborations. The established structure is the timely concerting of agent activities.

Another fundamental property of a self-organizing system is its adaptivity. Agent configurations or collaborations (processes) are structured in order to adapt the system (see Section 3.1.1). The exhibited *Adaptivity* (A) is classified according to the influences that cause the (re-) structuring. The adaptivity is *endogenous* when adjustments originate from system-internal processes or events. Examples are system configurations at specific time points, e.g. at system initialization or in response to significant system events or ongoing collaborative processes. *Extrinsic* adaptivity of systems is a response to external events, i.e. externally caused variations of the system context.

The enactment of decentralized coordination addresses the adaptation of different system qualities. The *Subjects* (S) of the structuring process are categorized as the *differentiation* of system entities, the *synchronization* of the entity-activities, and the modification of *external* system properties. Differentiation refers to the establishment of structures by partitioning the system entities, e.g. the segregation of an initially homogeneous MAS into different groups or the specialization of agents to enable division of labor. Synchronization describes the establishment of timely structures, e.g. cyclic agent-activities (oscillations) or coincident activities of agents. Thirdly, the self-organizing process may not manifest itself by structuring the MAS itself but by a modification of the external environment, such as the clustering of environment elements (see Section 3.4.2) or decentralized assembly processes. These properties are not exclusive, e.g. synchronized differentiations are conceivable.

Finally, the structures that are generated and maintained are categorized according to their *Composition* (C). The structures are either *coherent* or *partitioned*. The establishment of coherent structures refers to processes that reduce heterogeneity. These processes approach steady states where the behavior or configurations of agents correspond to each other. The subjects (S) agree with each other, as controlled by the structure-building processes. Partitioned structures describe the establishment of coherent substructures, i.e. when the adaptation segregates the system into different logical partitions that are internally coherent. Examples are the formation of coalitions and the spatial clustering of environment elements.

In the following, the set of process templates that is given in Section 3.2.2 is related to the proposed classification scheme. First, ACBG-based models of each template are given. These models describe the macroscopic system behavior that complies with process behavior. The aim is to signify the underlying causal structures that dominate the system operation. Secondly, the impact of these structures on the dynamic system properties are discussed. Process templates are selected as described in Section 3.2 and cover the structural (RP) and structure-acquiring (T,A,B) categories.

Amplifying Coordination Strategies

One subset of the coordination strategies contains a majority of reinforcing cycles. System adaptations are induced by amplifying changes of system variables. These changes propagate through the interdependency-structures. These processes enable applications to respond to changes in the external system context.

A prominent example is *Ant-based Foraging* (cf. Figure 4.21, S5). As described in Section

4.4. SYSTEMIC DESIGN OF DECENTRALIZED MAS COORDINATION

3.2, this strategy template is inspired by the collective formation of trails in foraging ant colonies. Initially, agents randomly wander the environment as they are *Searching* for resources. Agents that arrive at a resource location pick up a resource element and transport it to their home base. The *Transporting* activity is are enabled when resources are encountered, and it reduces the number of *Available Resources* in the environment. Both relations form a balancing feedback loop (α). Transporting is associated with a delay, caused by the time needed to return to the home base, and leads to the *delivery* of resources. Delivering activities are characterized by a global rate that influences both the amount of successfully *Foraged Resources* and the number of Searching agents, as deliveries make agents return to their default Searching behavior. Homing agents communicate their behavior (*Resource Communication*) via a Coordination Mechanism, e.g. by releasing digital pheromones (cf. Section 3.2.1). The interactions of Searching agents and those disseminating information are characterized by a *binding* rate. Searching agents are bound to emerging trails (*Trailing*) as they follow a pheromone gradient toward resource locations (*resource: 1..n*).

The removal of resource elements is expedited by two reinforcing feedbacks (β,γ) that make agents repeatedly show Searching and Transporting behaviors. These repetitions establish a collaborative *process* in the MAS that is controlled by *extrinsic* factors and addresses the modification of *external* system properties, i.e. the MAS environment. The repeated transports approach a *coherent* configuration of the environment where all resource elements are removed to the home base.

The *Molding and Aggregation* strategy (cf. Figure 4.21, S7) describes the dynamics of protozoic life forms (cf. Section 3.2). An external factor (*Resource Availability*) controls the exhibition of two basic behaviors. At any given time point agents are either acting individually (*Autonomous Behavior*) or they are part of an *Aggregate* that is ≥ 0. The transitions between these agent states are characterized by rates that describe the joining (*Clustering*) or leaving (*Un-Clustering*) of an Aggregate. Reductions of external stimuli, e.g. the density of a resource, make agents *Cluster* as they join an aggregate of individuals. The disposability of this factor affects the *Un-Clustering* of agents as they leave the aggregate and exhibit an *Autonomous Behavior*, i.e. the figurative exploitation of the available resources. The rates of joining and leaving the cluster (*Clustering / Un-Clustering*) affect the number of aggregated individuals (*Aggregation*), and the size of the Aggregate affects the ability of individuals to leave the Aggregate. These relationships form a single reinforcing feedback loop (α) as individuals agents respond to an external stimulus. In this model, the effects of the *Autonomous Behavior* on the *Resource Availability* are neglected. If agents consume resources efficiently, it would negatively influence the availability of resources.

The aggregation and dissolution of the cluster is controlled by the availability of the (external) resource (*Resource Availability*). This strategy exhibits a single reinforcing feedback loop and addresses the coherent *configuration* of agents. These configurations are adjusted according to *extrinsic* factors, i.e. variations in the availability of the resource, and agent activities *synchronize* as the configurations of the MAS alternate between homogeneous, *coherent* settings.

The *Nest-building* of termite colonies (cf. Figure 4.21, S9) provides a template strategy for governing collective, decentralized construction processes (cf. Section 3.2). Constructions are built by the coordinated placement of artifacts in the MAS environment. Agents are capable of producing these artifacts (*Brick Creation*), transporting them (*Roaming*) and approaching indicated sites for depositing artifacts (*Brick Deposit*). Artifacts are able to communicate their location (*Brick Communication*) by means of a Coordination Mechanism and receptions of the communications (*attraction*) make Roaming agents change their behavior from roaming to approaching a specific resource deposit site (*Brick Deposit*). Successful deposits increase the number of deposited elements (*# of Bricks per Site*) as the transported artifacts are added (*Brick Deposit*). In addition, agents are freed. Based on the availability of the resources, needed for the production of the assembled artifacts (*Resource Availability*), and the number of unbound agents, an interaction rate (*brick production*) is established, which characterizes the enforcement of building blocks (*Brick Creation*).

These interactions from two reinforcing feedback loops. The overall production of artifacts is reinforced but controlled by the available resources (α). In addition, the supply of building blocks for each deposit site is reinforced (β). This strategy also addresses the establishment of a collaborative *process*, as agents repeatedly produce, transport, and place building blocks. These activities modify the metaphoric, *extrinsic* environment of the MAS. The collaboration of agents is controlled by *external* factors, i.e. resources. Due to the stochastics of the agent transportation and attraction, the resulting constructions are typically irregular. The adaptive process leads to a diversity of sites that are not uniformly reinforced (*partitioned*). Adjustments are necessary to enable the collaborative construction of regular structures (cf. Section 3.2).

The *Web Weaving* (cf. Figure 4.21, S11) strategy describes the creation of spider webs (cf. Section 3.2). Particular spiders species construct webs by sequentially connecting ground spots with drag-lines. The basic agent activity is the creation of new lines (*Line Creation*). The created lines either connect locations that are already reachable in the network (*Connected Drag-Lines*) or connect locations that are not reachable, i.e. disconnected from the largest graph structure (*Un-Connected Drag-Lines*). A macroscopic interaction rate (*connect*) describes the reinforcement of connections by the introduction of new drag-lines, i.e. novel shortest paths between locations. These new paths increase the number of connected lines (*Connected Drag-Lines*) and reduce the number of disconnected locations and subgraphs (*Un-Connected Drag-Lines*). Initially arbitrary positions are connected, but agents prefer to follow established connections rather than using other movement methods: metaphorically speaking, they avoid walking on the ground. Therefore, the availability of *Connected Drag-Lines* contributes to the agents' *Walking* rate and consequently agents traverse the connected locations more often and reinforce the web by establishing connections between already located positions.

This process strategy exhibits a single, reinforcing feedback that controlsa *process* that condenses an initially loosely connected graph with a highly connected web of interconnections. The constructed graph is an *external* environment element. Here, the continuous creation of drag-lines serves as an *endogenous* input to the construction process that governs the placement of environment modifications, i.e. drag-lines. The process addresses the structuring of a *coherent* network.

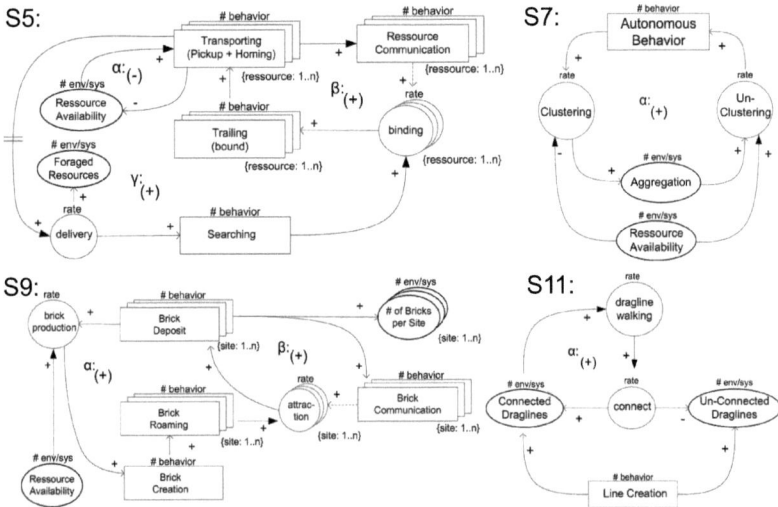

Figure 4.21: Systemic models of the amplifying coordination strategies: Ant-based Foraging (S5), Molding (S7), Nest-Building (S9) and Web-Weaving (S11) [Sudeikat and Renz, 2010c]

4.4. SYSTEMIC DESIGN OF DECENTRALIZED MAS COORDINATION

Compensating Coordination Strategies

A second subset of strategy templates contains a majority of balancing feedback loops. These strategies compensate fluctuations of system variables and maintain variable values. Their integration in applications aids the maintenance of perturbed structures.

Brood Sorting (cf. Figure 4.22, S1) [Mamei et al., 2006] refers to the distributed clustering that can be observed in ant colonies (cf. Section 3.2). The offspring in a nest are sorted according to their developmental stages. Different items, e.g. eggs, larvae, etc., are randomly encountered by individual ants. Misplaced items, judged by their difference to the other items nearby, are picked up and carried until a location containing similar items is encountered. While the ants' paths are random, clusters of similar items emerge from the collective transport of items. Agents randomly search their nest (*Wandering*) for isolated or outnumbered items. The averaged encounters of elements is characterized by a rate (*encounter*). The dispersion of elements in the environment (*Element Dispersion*) as well as the number of searching agents reinforce this rate. The rate of encounters governs the behavior adjustments of agents, as wandering agents are bound to encountered elements and transport (*Transportation*) them to nearby, similar elements. The similarity of elements is evaluated by the agents and successful relocations of elements contribute to the system-wide *deposit* rate.

The collaboration of agents is governed by three feedbacks. The focus of the strategy is the reduction of element dispersion. A balancing feedback steers the repeated relocation of elements (α). The activation of these transports is controlled by two auxiliary feedbacks that reinforce the availability of searching agents (β) and balance the encounters of elements by these agents (γ). The agent interactions establish a collaborative clustering *process*, where the structuring of the *extrinsic* MAS environment is controlled by *external* factors, i.e. the dispersion that may fluctuate as elements are added to the environment (cf. Section 3.2). These processes reduce the disorder, quantifiable by the entropy concept [Haken, 2006], of environment elements. Based on the configuration of the element deposit, *partitioned* or globally *coherent* structures can be established, as discussed in Section 3.4.2.

Flocking (cf. Figure 4.22, S4), a.k.a. schooling or herding, describe the movement pattern of flocks of birds or fish (cf. Section 3.2). It describes an application scenario where agents (1) mutually maintain a set of highly fluctuating properties and (2) concurrently guard invariant properties. For example, individual movements of agents in these swarms are governed by three aspects. Agents avoid collisions, match their speed with neighboring agents, and a tend to move towards the center of the collective. These local rules give rise to complex movement patterns. When any of these aspects arise within the local configuration, a *Disagreement* and agents take countermeasures (*Adjustment*). These measures enforce subsequent, i.e. delayed, agreements between the observed variables but introduce additional *Disagreements* as the adjustments propagate through the population and affect adjustments by other agents. Environment properties, such as changing wind velocities also contribute to the *Disagreements* that are counterbalanced. A side effect of the *Adjustment* is that given invariants may be violated (*Violated Invariant*), e.g. a minimal distance between agents. Detected violations trigger the *Maintenance* of the invariant. Maintenance activities reduce violations but also introduce additional *Disagreements* as these reconfigurations make the agent disagree with the configurations of the surrounding agents.

The dynamics of a flock are steered by n balancing feedback loops. One feedback (α) per adjusted property and two feedbacks (β, γ) per maintained invariant. In the example given here, only typical properties of swarm simulations are denoted, but in principle, other properties, e.g. agent colors, size, etc., may be integrated as well (cf. Section 3.2). The agent collaboration establishes an adaptive process that continuously adjusts the *configuration* of individual agents. Agents mutually influence and *synchronize* their spatial movement and local *configuration* to respond to *extrinsic* system influences. Based on the system parameterization, the system does not necessarily settle to a fixed spatial arrangement of agents but steadily approaches a *coherent* configuration of the participating agents.

In addition to the foraging dynamics in ant colonies (S1), *Bee-based Foraging* (cf. Figure 4.22, S6) has also been adopted in computational systems (cf. Section 3.2). The foraging strategy of honey-bee colonies provides agents with a central communication channel to signal locations of resources. This pattern differs from Ant-based Foraging (S1) in that two types of agents are distinguished. Scouting agents are responsible for exploring the environment. When resources are found (*Scouting*) they are consumed and their locations are communicated (*Resource Communication*). Foraging agents are bound to specific resource locations (*resource:1..n*) and make round-trips to transport resources to the nest (*Foraging*). The communications of resources by *Scouting* agents include information about resource attributes, such as the distance from the nest or the quality of the nectar. Based on this information, foraging agents decide (*Change Resource Assignment*) whether to switch to the communicated discoveries (*self.resource != destination.resource*) or continue their transporting behavior (*self.resource == destination.resource*). The changes of forager assignments (*Change Resource Assignment*) adjusts the number of Foraging agents, depending on their bound resource type.

This coordination strategy governs the consumption of external resource deposits by using two balancing feedback loops. The activities of Foragers (α) and Scouts (β) reduce the resource elements in the environment. In addition, the utilization of foragers is reinforced as resource locations compete for the assignments of Foraging agents (γ). The restructuring of assignments causes preferred resource types, distinguished by their quality criteria, to be consumed with higher priority. The system does not necessarily approach a coherent assignment since individual agents may have differing preferences. The strategy addresses the *configuration* of the MAS as it governs the assignment of agents to specific resources, i.e. their *differentiation*. These dynamical adjustments of assignments respond to *extrinsic* factors, i.e. the gradually discovered resource locations. The assignments affect the MAS organizational structure as well as the MAS environment. Based on the local policies of the Foragers, their configurations converge to a system-wide *coherent* assignment of partitions of assignments (*partitioned*).

The reconstruction of *Morphogenesis* (cf. Figure 4.22, S8) provides an alternative approach to differentiating agent configurations (cf. Section 3.2). This approach is appropriate for homogeneous MAS that is composed of undifferentiated agents. A number of system elements, possibly but not necessarily agents, communicate a morphogen (*Emitting*) and maintain a specific *Density* of these information elements in their local area. This maintenance is based on the Coordination Mechanism used, e.g. diffusing markers requires reinforcement or replicated tokens demand constant distribution. Agents perceive different types of morphogens and adjust their local configuration (*Configuration Adjustment*). According to the distribution of the locally perceived concentrations, the agents specialize (*Specialized Agents*) into different types (*Types:1..n*).

The described process forms a single balancing feedback loop (α). It addresses the *partitioned configuration* of the MASs by the *differentiation* of agents. The enacted adjustments respond to *endogenous* factors, as the placing of morphogen distributors is a design effort.

Selective Coordination Strategies

The third subset of strategy templates contains an equal number of reinforcing and balancing feedback loops. These strategies prescribe adaptive processes, where the system history decides which structures are to be enforced or discriminated.

Convention Emergence (cf. Figure 4.23, S2) [Delgado, 2002; Shoham and Tennenholtz, 1997] describes the collective agreement of a set of agents on a single value, based on local point-to-point interactions (cf. Section 3.2). The system is composed of a set of agents that are positioned in a graph. Each agent is equipped with a local value, e.g. a binary flag, and the initial values are randomly distributed. Agents are able to interact and exchange their local values. The local reasoning inside the agents decides, e.g. based on a majority rule determined by a fixed memory of past communications, when to adjust the local value. When the graph topologies, interactions and local decision rules are well matched, consent on a uniform value is gradually established. External stimuli (*Activity Stimulus*) trigger agent activities (*Activity*). A side effect of these activities is that agents communicate their local configuration value (*inform convention value*) that is to be agreed upon as a system-wide convention. The communications are realized by Coordination Mechanisms that control the receivers and potential communication delays. Receptions trigger

4.4. SYSTEMIC DESIGN OF DECENTRALIZED MAS COORDINATION

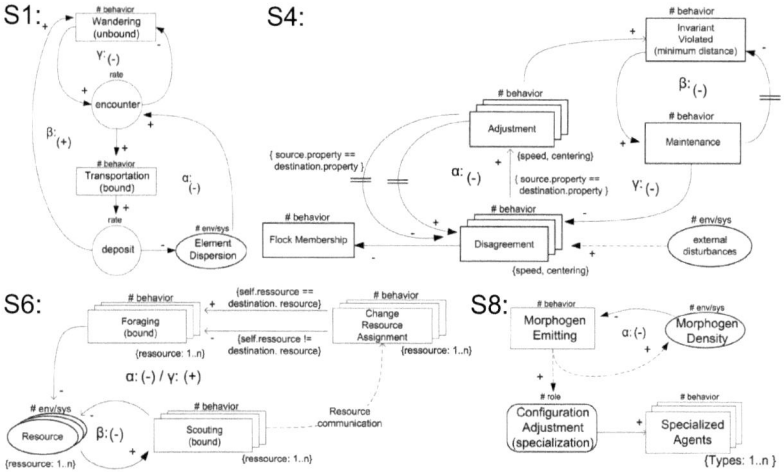

Figure 4.22: Systemic models of the compensating coordination strategies: Brood Sorting (S1), Flocking (S4), Bee-based Foraging (S6) and Morphogenesis (S8) [Sudeikat and Renz, 2010c]

the adaptation of the local agent configuration (*Convention Adjustment*), following a predefined policy. The adjusted value (*Type:2..n*) feeds back to the observable agent activities (*Type:2..n*), e.g. when the local configuration (*source.type*) constrains the activities (*destination.type*) that are available to the agents.

The causal relations form a reinforcing (α) and a balancing (β) feedback loop. The stochastics of the system history determine the value that is reinforced (α). Consequently, alternative values are suppressed (β). The adaptation is caused by *endogenous* factors and the collective *configuration* of agents is adjusted. The established structure is their *coherent differentiation*. This process is examined in Section 5.4.2.

Epidemic dissemination processes (cf. Figure 4.23, S3) are means of ensuring the spread of information in large-scale networks [Eugster et al., 2004] (cf. Section 3.2). These processes correspond to mathematical models of the spreading of disease. Metaphorically, the spreading infection is the information, and it is propagated from infected to uninfected agents. Mathematical formulation and application scenarios are given in [Eugster et al., 2004]. *Susceptible* and *Infectious* agent configurations are distinguished. The interactions of these agent types are described by an *infection* rate. Infections require the availability of both agent configurations, increase the number of Infectious agents, and reduce the number of Susceptible agents.

The Susceptible configurations are gradually removed by a balancing feedback (α), while Infectious configurations are reinforced (β). These coupled feedbacks adjust the *configuration* of agents that are steered by their *endogenous* interactions. The established structure deals with the *differentiation* of agents in a *coherent* setting. The dynamics of infections in a hypothetical MAS are described in Section 6.8.3.

A prominent extension to the epidemic dynamics is the *Susceptible-Infectious-Recovered* (SIR) model [Murray, 2002] (page 320). An additional agent configuration *Recovered* is introduced and Infectious agents recover from infections with a fixed rate (*recovery*). These recoveries exhibit an additional balancing feedback (γ) that subsequently contains infections by eliminating Infectious agents. This adjustment exhibits the same system properties as described above.

Quorum can be observed in biological and physical systems when agent activities stimulate coherent activities of neighboring agents. *Coherent* agent behaviors are driven out of sync by external influences (*perturbation*). Coherence of agent behaviors is (re-)established as agents perceive the activities of neighboring agents and *adjust* their own behavior accordingly.

A reinforcing feedback loop (α) steers the reestablishment of coherence and an opposing balancing feedback reduces Non-Coherent agent configurations (β). The exhibited adaptive process addresses the establishment of coherent agent *configurations*. Adaptation is triggered by *extrinsic* influences that perturb coherence and the resulting structure manifests the system-wide, i.e. *coherent, synchronization* of agent activities.

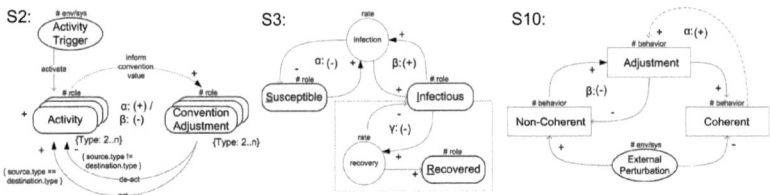

Figure 4.23: Systemic models of the selective coordination strategies: Convention Emergence (S2, [Sudeikat and Renz, 2010a]), Epidemics (S3), Quorum (S10) [Sudeikat and Renz, 2010c])

Discussion

The feedback structures presented here provide field-tested types of template inter-agent processes with well-known dynamic properties. The relation between these templates and the system behavior actually exhibited is illustrated in Figure 4.5. In particular the appropriate parameterization of the mechanisms, used for the realization of processes is an immanent development effort that is required to adjust the processes for a specific (software) application. However, referring to nature-inspired processes templates is a successful strategy for achieving self-organizing dynamics in artificial systems (see Section 3.2.2).

The reuse of this constructive knowledge requires development teams to decide whether the utilization of a template process is appropriate for a given application scenario. Classifications of decentralized coordination patterns, their attribution to specific application domains, and the study of reported utilizations help in making the selection, but do not offer unambiguous choices, as is summarized and discussed in Section 3.2. The set of phenomenological description criteria proposed here supplement previous efforts to describe self-organization in MASs by characterizing the exhibited structure formation. These properties indicate the system-level behavior that can be manifested by template processes and can be used to explain why a process is applicable to a specific application context, as shown in Sections 5.4.1 (page 187) and 5.4.2 (page 187). Table 4.1 summarizes the properties of the amplifying, compensating, and selective strategy templates. The structure of the feedbacks (RP) does not allow conclusions to be drawn about the properties of the generated structures (T,A,S,C). The template instances show a variety of features that cannot be attributed to structural properties without exception, and consequently the process types demonstrate the range of possible dynamic features. However, the structure determines the dynamical modes that are to be exhibited. In amplifying processes, fluctuations in system variables are propagated to actuate the exploration of system configurations. The compensating processes counter-balance fluctuations and maintain system structures. The selective processes conform by producing coherent structures of system configurations, but the Adaptivity and Subjects of these structures vary. The Sections 5.4.1 and 5.4.2 discuss the integration of template processes and their selection is justified by the properties of the intended system structures.

The combination of coordination templates in a single application has been considered in a few works (cf. Section 3.2) and the elicitation and comparison of the structural properties of

4.4. SYSTEMIC DESIGN OF DECENTRALIZED MAS COORDINATION

		Decentralized Coordination Strategy										
		S1	S2	S3	S4	S5	S6	S7	S8	S9	S10	S11
RP (I)	amplifying					$-/+^2$		$+$		$+^2$		$+$
	compensating	$-^2/+$				$-^n$		$-^2/+$		$-$		
	selective		$-/+$	$-^{(2)}/+$							$-/+$	
T	configuration		x	x	x		x	x	x		x	
	process	x				x				x		x
A	endogenous		x	x					x			x
	extrinsic	x			x	x	x	x		x	x	
S	differentiation		x	x			x		x			
	synchronization				x			x		x		
	external	x				x				x		x
C	coherence	x	x	x		x	x	x			x	x
	partitioned	x			x		x		x	x		

Table 4.1: Classification of Coordinating Processes, according to the regulating polarity of loop structures (RP) and the properties of the resulting structures (T,A,S,C) [Sudeikat and Renz, 2010c]

the processes allows for an alternative approach to the selection and combination of coordination templates [Sudeikat and Renz, 2008c]. Beginning with a structure that expresses the intended processes within an agent-based application, templates can be mapped by matching them to this structure. The selection process is broken down to identify the smallest possible coupling of templates that allows the realization of the intended causal structure. After a matching set has been found, developers can look up the details on the agent designs, related interaction techniques and possible parameterizations that instruct the system realization. In the following sections, this approach is discussed and exemplified.

4.4.2 Example: A Simplified Computer Immune System

Natural immune systems exhibit adaptive, self-regulated mechanisms to protect living beings from pathogens, e.g. viruses, bacteria and parasites. These systems are one prominent source of inspiration for nature-inspired computing systems [Liu and Tsui, 2006]. In particular it has been proposed that computing infrastructures be equipped with *Computer Immune Systems* (CIS) [Forrest et al., 1997]. These systems can be regarded as bio-inspired extensions of *Intrusion Detection Systems* (IDS) [Debar et al., 1999]. IDS identify malicious components or processes, i.e. *intruders*, and enable protective, administrative interventions to protect and maintain computational infrastructures. Detections are typically approached by monitoring system elements and comparing the observations to a database of regular behaviors, based on system element specifics, e.g. element architectures, software configurations, and usage patterns [Forrest et al., 1997]. One approach to automating interventions and enabling the *self-protection* of infrastructures is to pattern the design of protective processes on natural immune systems, e.g. as is argued in [Forrest et al., 1997]. The internal workings of these immune systems are complex, but on a highly coarse-grained description level two types of system elements, cell types and proteins, can be distinguished. *Detector* elements, e.g. *T-cells*, and *antibodies* are responsible for identifying foreign pathogens. Identifications are signaled to *scavenger cells* that *remove* pathogens by eating them.

Designing Application Dynamics

Here, the systemic modeling approach is exemplified by the design of an IDS simulation model. An initial model of the intended dynamical process is refined to a detailed coordination model that was realized in an agent-based simulation model. The detailing focuses on the selection and combination of two coordination patterns.

128   CHAPTER 4. SYSTEMIC MODELING OF COLLECTIVE PHENOMENA IN MASS

The guarded system is envisaged as a regular lattice of hosts that can execute arbitrary processes. These nodes are inherently *susceptible* and can be infected by malicious software processes. The detectability of infections is assumed, e.g. by the abnormal utilization of computational resources. Figure 4.24 (I) shows a *Problem Model* that depicts the behavior of an *unsheltered* system in absence of the simulated IDS. The number of infected nodes in the system is represented by a behavioral system variable (*Intruders*). These nodes are behaviorally distinct as they exhibit the malicious behavior. In addition, intruder processes *infect* connected hosts, i.e. these processes multiply and convert connected, susceptible hosts. The number of susceptible hosts in the network is denoted as a system variable (*Susceptible Nodes*) that influences the spread of infections. The spread of infections is controlled by an *infection* rate. Intruders and susceptible hosts must be available for the malicious processes to spread. Therefore, these variables positively contribute to the globally exhibited rate of infections. The infection rate reinforces the number of infected hosts and reduces the number of susceptible hosts. These relations form a reinforcing feedback loop that describes the increasing number of infections. This increase can be assumed to be exponential, as all infected nodes contribute equally to the infection rate. The infection process is only limited by the availability of hosts. Therefore the occurrence of an initial infection of a single host is expected to cause a goal-seeking behavior (cf. Figure 4.2, II) that successively infects all hosts.

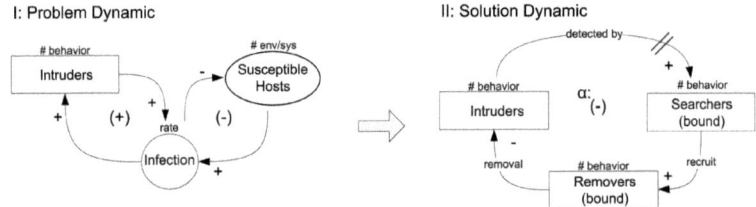

Figure 4.24: ACBG refinement example (1), II adapted from [Sudeikat and Renz, 2008c]

The Problem Dynamic describes an inherent process of the application domain. A corresponding Solution Model provides a complementary set of feedback loops to adjust the system behavior (cf. Figure 4.24, II). In this example, the design challenge is to provide an additional limitation to the growing number of malicious processes. Taking inspiration from the metaphor of a computer immune system, the goal-seeking behavior is opposed by an additional, balancing feedback loop (α). This feedback is established by the introduction of *Searcher* and *Remover* behaviors that correspond to the simplified view of the operation of immune systems. The presence of Intruder processes in the system leads to their *detection* by searching processes (Searchers (bound)). These detections are signaled to *recruit* system entities that are able to enforce the *removal* of Intruder processes (*Remover (bound)*) and consequently limit the number of Intruders in the system. The supplement *bound* denotes that the exhibition of a behavior is associated to a particular instance of an Intruder process. It is assumed that the detection of Intruders (*detected by*), is associated with a significant delay, as detections require roaming the network and examining hosts.

The Solution Model describes the intended dynamics of the problem solving strategy. Subsequent refinements detail the dynamics of the agent activities and their interdependencies, i.e. *detection*, *recruitment*, and *removal*. The enforcement of the intended feedback is denoted in Figure 4.25 (I). Two agent types partition the behaviors that are conceptually related to the detection and removal of intruder processes. *Searcher* agents exhibit two behaviors. First, they exhibit an *unbound* searching behavior and randomly inspect hosts. When an infected host is *encountered*, the presence of an infection is signaled (*Intruder Communication*). *Remover* agents also exhibit a searching behavior (*unbound*). Upon the perception of an infected node, removers adopt a *bound* role while moving to the specific host. Once at the infected host, bound agents disinfect it, i.e. remove Intruder processes (*Intruder Removal*).

4.4. SYSTEMIC DESIGN OF DECENTRALIZED MAS COORDINATION

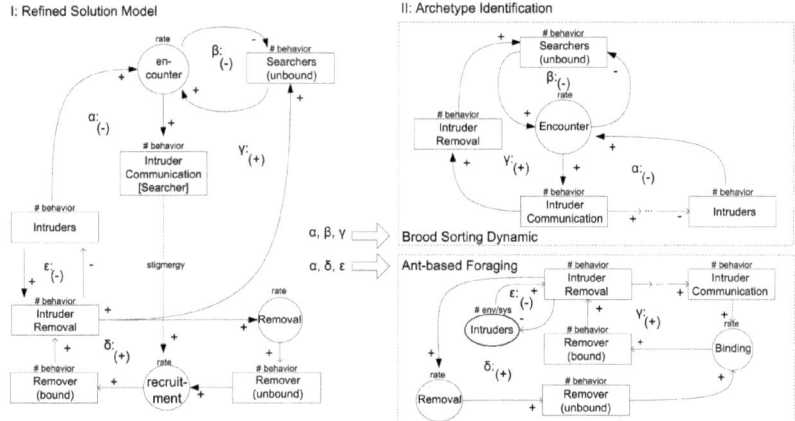

Figure 4.25: ACBG refinement example (2), adapted from [Sudeikat and Renz, 2008c]

For each interdependency in the Solution Dynamic (*detected by, recruit, removal*), a corresponding rate is introduced (*encounter, recruitment, removal*) to express the contributions to the macroscopic, averaged frequencies of interactions. The *encounter* rate characterizes the binding of searching agents (unbound) to instances of Intruder processes. These bindings depend on the availability of searching agents and undetected Intruders. Encounters lead to the subsequent decrease of Intruders, thus these encounters are balanced by the number of Intruders (α) and bound Searchers (β). The communication of detections leads to the subsequent removal of Intruders. The removal frees Searchers to return to the unbound, i.e. searching, behavior (γ). The removal is controlled by two feedback loops. First, the communications of detections and the availability of unbound Removers contribute to the recruitment rate. Recruited removers approach the host, remove the detected Intruder, and are subsequently deactivated, i.e. return to their default behavior. These interdependencies form a reinforcing feedback loop (δ). Finally, the actual removal of an intruder is balanced with the availability of Intruders on the hosts that are visited by Removers (ϵ).

The refinement identifies three balancing and two reinforcing feedback loops that must be established ($-^3+^2$). Referring to the systemic models of template processes (cf. Section 4.4.1), process instances that provide appropriate templates for the realization of sub-structures (cf. Figure 6.7) can be identified. This identification is based on the mapping of strategy-structures onto sub-structures in the Solution Model. These identified strategies guide the implementation by providing template designs of agents and interaction techniques (cf. Section 3.2.2).

For this example, it has been shown that strategy structures can be coupled to describe the intended dynamics [Sudeikat and Renz, 2008c]. The detailed Solution Dynamic can be mapped to the *Brood Sorting* (S1;$-^2/+$) and *ant-based Foraging* (S5;$-/+^2$) processes. These mappings are illustrated in Figure 4.25 (II). Brood Sorting is used to control the detection and communication of Intruders (α, β, γ). The mapping describes that the detection can be metaphorically designed as a process of randomly wandering ants that spread pheromones once they have encountered an infected host. The process is adjusted, since ants do not handle the encountered intruders themselves but reinforce pheromones until the host is disinfected. The dynamics of the triggered removals are controlled by the dynamics of Ant-based Foraging (γ, δ, ϵ). The design follows the metaphoric inspiration that agents resemble ants that follow pheromone gradients to form trails to resources. The design is adjusted as the agents do not forage items but head towards infected hosts. The communication, i.e. release of pheromones, is omitted as this functionality is provided by the previous template.

These models are coupled and arrows that are interrupted by ... indicate that intermediary relations are defined in the complementary strategy mapping. The connecting activity is the communication of Intruders (*Intruder Communication*) that is present in both models and both strategies utilize stigmergy-based communication. The coupled models also share the γ loop that controls that agents return to their default behavior after identified Intruders have been removed.

Simulation Results

Based on this design of the intended MAS dynamics, an agent-based [Sudeikat and Renz, 2007c] simulation model has been developed.[12] Agents move in a quadratic grid of patches and each patch represents a networked host. These hosts contain a *resource* variable that is slowly reinforced. Intruder agents move between hosts randomly and remove resources. When a fixed number of resources has been collected, the Intruder multiplies. Activated Searcher agents distribute a *digital pheromone* (cf. Section 3.2.1) to communicate identifications of infections. These pheromones are disseminated to neighboring patches and evaporate gradually. Initially, the agents are randomly placed in the environment.

In [Sudeikat and Renz, 2007c], it has been validated that an application that follows the conceived design exhibits the intended dynamical properties. Two types of properties are examined. First, system-level properties that refer to intended behavior of the application can be checked. Secondly, the congruence with the Solution Dynamic (cf. Figure 4.24) can be determined under differing system calibrations.

An example for an intended system-level property is the *containment of epidemics*, i.e. the removal of sudden infections by several Intruders multiply quickly. This behavior is indicated by the transition between two types of MAS configurations. Faced with a configuration where a number of undetected Intruders is in the environment and the Searchers and Removers are deactivated, the system is expected to adjust itself to a configuration where all intruders have been removed by the activation of all available Remover agents, as described by the Solution Dynamic. Since this model imposes the presence of a single balancing feedback loop at the macroscopic system level, the removal of intruders is expected to exhibit a *goal-seeking* behavior (cf. Figure 4.2, II), in this case an exponential decay as the number of Intruders approaches zero. Assuming that Intruders multiply slowly, the delay of the detections, caused by the spatial search of patches (hosts) only affects the response of the MAS to the sudden change of its configuration by adding a fluctuating lag to the individual removals.

The congruence of the exhibited system behavior with systemic models of the application dynamic can be examined by monitoring the timely changes of system variables and quantifying the causal relations between these measurements. Causal relations manifest *cross-correlations* of system variables, i.e. the fluctuations of an originating variable are followed by fluctuations of dependent variables. Systematic fluctuations of a variable can be examined by their *auto-correlation*. The causal relation between the occurrence of Intruders and the activation of Removers is examined. According to the built-in Solution Dynamic (cf. Figure 4.24), the number of activated Removers is expected to be *dynamically adjusted* to the number of Intruders in the system. Based on the surveillance of Intruders (*detected by*) and the activation of Removers (*recruit*), the Removers are activated. The absence of detections leads to a relaxation, i.e. the deactivation of agents. In the Solution Dynamic (cf. Figure 4.24), it is assumed that the communication (*recruit*) and *removal* of an Intruder is quicker then their detection (*detected by*). When the system is faced with a steady inflow of Intruders, the delay of detections affects the systems operation. The system is expected to oscillate (cf. Figure 4.2, III) when the repeated activation of Removers is dominated by the delay that is needed to detect Infections. The delay that has been introduced by the stigmergy-based communication of detections (cf. Figure 4.25) adds to this effect.

Simulation results are plotted in Figure 4.26 and show two system calibrations that induce

---

[12]using the *Netlogo* simulation framework (see Section 3.1.5)

the expected dynamics. The environment contains 3600 patches that are randomly wandered by 40 Searcher and 15 Remover agents. Plot I displays the system response to a sudden infection by 60 Intruder agents. The number of Intruders decreases exponentially, due to the activation of Removers. Plot Ia shows a fit of this decay on a logarithmic scale with $f(x) = Ae^{-\frac{x}{x_0}}$.[13] The repeated observation of this dynamic, i.e. the transitive activation of Searchers and the subsequent activation of Removers, ensures the qualitative exhibition of the intended balancing feedback.

The validation of the congruence is achieved by computing the cross-correlation of the number of Intruders and activated Removers. This requires that the system exhibits a *working regime*, where agent activations and deactivations are controlled by the internal dynamics of the system design, not as responses to external factors. These regimes are induced by providing a constant input on the system. Here, the system is put under *stress*, i.e. a constant, high rate of infections by quickly multiplying Intruders. The system shows the anticipated cyclic behavior, as the limiting number of all available Remover activations is repeatedly approached and the activations decay correspondingly to the removal of intruders. The causal relationship between the system variables is indicated by the cross-correlation of the measured time series (cf. Figure 4.26 (II)). The auto-correlations of both time series reveal the underlying oscillation, that is hidden by the stochastics of the spatial environment, particularly of the stigmergy-based communication.

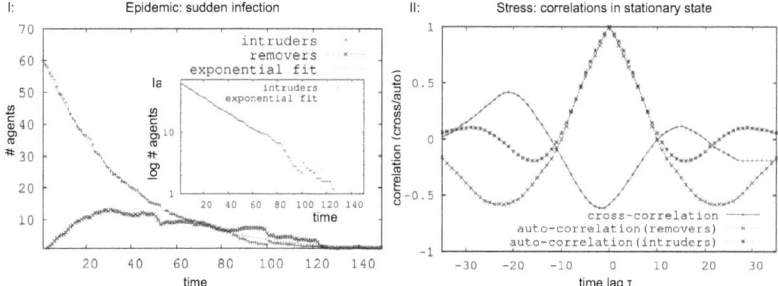

Figure 4.26: Simulation results of the intrusion detection system, following [Sudeikat and Renz, 2007c]. The handling of a sudden epidemic (I). Under a high rate of constant (re-)infections (approx. 200 time steps) the intended causal interdependency between the activations of intruders and removers can be observed by their cross-correlation (III; approx. 400 time steps).

4.5 Conclusions

In this chapter, a novel modeling-level for MASs, which focuses on the characterization of the collective behavior of system elements, is discussed. The *Agent Causal Behavior Graph* (ACBG) refines System Dynamics concepts to express the networks of interdependencies among agent behaviors that are present in MAS designs. This modeling approach is particularly appropriate for highlighting the structure of feedbacks that underlie an MAS design. The analysis of the causative structure of interdependencies and influences allows the possible system behaviors to be anticipated. Detailed analyses are enabled by concretizing the mathematical interpretation of the ACBG graphs. These structures describe the stochastic processes that govern the operation of MASs (see Section 4.2.2) and explain how the coaction of agents affects the global system behavior.

Two principal application modes of this modeling level are discussed and examples are given. First, systemic modeling can be used to analyze the causal structure of conventional designs of agent-based applications. The systematic derivation of ACBGs from agent-oriented designs was

---
[13] The parameters used in Figure Ia are: $A = 62; x_0 = 35.5$

discussed in Section 4.3. The examination of the derived systemic models then allows developers to anticipate the space of qualitative behaviors that applications which correspond to the characterized design can exhibit. When the presence of collective phenomena is intended, systemic modeling can be used to show that the application design is in principle able to show them. When the absence of a collective phenomenon in required, systemic modeling can be used to examine whether unintended cycles of interdependencies are present in the design that cause detrimental effects on the system's performance or functionality.

Secondly, it was discussed and exemplified that the systemic modeling level can also be used to deliberately design Coordinating Processes (c.f. Section 4.4). Developers can describe the structure of a decentralized inter-agent process and use this technique to catalog nature-inspired templates of coordination processes. The catalog illustrates the expressiveness of the proposed formalism and the instances described serve as templates that can be deliberately combined by interlinking their graph-structures. An example for this design is given in Section 4.4.2, where two nature-inspired coordination patterns were combined into one comprehensive process. The refinement of the intended feedback structures and their mapping onto process templates are proposed for selecting these templates. While this design approach provides coordination designers with a principled modeling technique, this modeling effort requires manual modeling and expertise. In Chapter 6, the systematic construction of coordination models is addressed.

Explorations of the space of possible processes is facilitated by mathematical modeling of stochastic system simulations. For analysis activities, it has been advocated that the systemic structures of an application be extracted and analyzed, prior to system simulations. The resulting system representation exposes these effects and facilitates their explanation as a consequence of (possibly cyclic) agent interdependences. The observation of collaborative effects in MASs requires parameter sweeps and the adjustment of system configurations. Insights into the causal structure can guide these efforts, as it is possible to infer the expected effects.

Modeling the Distributed Feedbacks that Cause Collective MAS Phenomena

The key criterion for the modeling approach presented here is the expression of *distributed* feedbacks among system elements (see Challenge 4.1, page 88). This distribution is reflected by the ability to link behavior abstractions of different agent types. This connection results in a characterization of the network of inter-agent relations. The relation between the proposed modeling level of stochastic inter-agent processes and the described MAS-implementations is discussed in Section 4.2.2. The process models illustrate the structure of the exhibited processes and these structures relate to classes of process types. The MASs exhibits, depending on the detailed parameterization of the system elements, a specific process instance that structurally conforms to a process class. Thus systemic models make it possible to reason about the space of processes that system implementations can show.

Supporting Intermediate Description Levels by the Abstraction/Refinement of ACBGs

Intermediate description levels are a prerequisite for the incremental analysis of process models (see Challenge 4.2, page 88). The demand for these *mesoscopic* modeling levels is discussed in Section 3.4. The nodes in the graph-based models represent freely selectable behavior abstractions. Since the abstraction level of these nodes can be selected arbitrarily (see page 103), intermediate modeling levels can be represented. The transformation of models between micro-, meso- and macroscopic modeling levels is supported by refinement and abstraction operations. Refinements can be denoted in the graphical notation to support their traceability. The iterative conception and refinement of systemic models is systematized in Chapter 6.

Enabling the Linkage between Process-Models and AOSE Design Concepts

The use of ACBGs nodes to denote generic behavior abstractions also makes it possible to link these models to conventional MAS design techniques (see Challenge 4.3, page 88). A generic

4.5. CONCLUSIONS

node type (*behavior*) can be extended with specific abstractions that mimic concepts from other modeling disciplines. In this chapter, this linkage is exemplified by node refinements that reference organizational modeling concepts, i.e. roles and groups. The generic role concept is used in the remainder of this thesis, as it is found in widespread modeling approaches for MASs.

Chapter 5

A Systemic Programming Model

In the previous chapter, it was argued and exemplified that systemic modeling provides a supportive description level that facilitates the application-domain independent specification of decentralized coordination strategies. It was demonstrated that a *systemic* modeling supports facilitates the anticipation of the effects of agent coaction in agent-based application designs. Besides the analysis of applications, ACBG models can also be used to express the structure of decentralized coordination strategies (cf. Section 4.4.1).

In this Chapter, the modeling stance is extended to a programming model that allows Coordinating Processes to be adjusted and integrated into agent-based system implementations. It is discussed how systemic coordination models can be integrated into agent-based software systems. Based on a reference architecture for the integration of self-organizing dynamics, a tailored programming model is presented that allows developers to supplement MAS implementations with the enforcement of externalized coordination models. In principle, the architectonic conception presented here provides a means to integrate decentralized processes in distributed systems. Here, the integration in agent-based systems is addressed and hereafter *agents* are a synonym for *systems elements*. The proposed programming model is comprised of two parts: a distributed execution environment which supports the enforcement of decentralized coordination models (see Section 5.2) and a tailored language which allows inter-agent processes to be configured by detailing ACBG models (see Section 5.3).

5.1 Motivation

Systemic modeling supports the description of self-organizing processes. The modeling of template Coordinating Processes and their combination using systemic modeling was discussed and exemplified in the previous chapter. The ad-hoc integration of these processes into agent-based applications is unsatisfactory, as the inclusion of the process requires the conception of dedicated agent models tailored for self-organization. Here, the reuse of these processes models as reusable design elements is further developed. A key issue is the systematic integration of systemic models of inter-agent processes into agent-based software applications.

When developers use systemic modeling to describe the intended self-organization, it is desirable that these models can be directly used to implement the process to a software system. The aim is to enable that the so described processes can be enacted within an MAS. Design concerns are to allow for reusable and exchangeable process models which enable developers to (re)use abstract models of inter-agent processes that resemble ACBGs. This modeling level is converted to an implementation technique by the preparation of the detailing of abstract processes models to specific system realizations. Thus the models are not merely design models that must be manually transformed into agent-realizations, but the prescribed processes can be configured and supplemented to existing applications.

It has been observed, e.g. in [Cheng et al., 2009], that the control/feedback loop structures that govern the dynamics of self-adaptive and self-organizing software architectures are not explicitly described, but are abstracted or internalized. This lack of description makes it even more difficult to include nature-inspired self-organizing applications in engineering efforts. Planing for the system dynamics requires that the couped and decentralized sets of feedbacks (cf. [Cheng et al., 2009], page 16) which govern the system behavior are explicitly modeled (see Section Sections 4.1.2, 4.4.1). It is therefore necessary to treat the control/feedback loops as a first-class modeling, design and implementation entity [Cheng et al., 2009] (pages 17, 22). Whereas the previous chapter discussed the modeling of inter-agent feedback, this chapter presents tool support for the minimally invasive integration of these feedbacks.

5.1.1 Challenges

Two development aspects constitute the construction approach for the integration of self-organizing dynamics. A *reference architecture* prepares the enactment of process specifications. It facilitates the manifestation of self-organizing phenomena by enacting externalized process descriptions. Programming aspects are addressed and the systemic modeling approach is refined to a declarative *configuration language*. This language facilitates the detailed definition of Coordinating Processes and prepares their automated enactment. The realization of these constituents has to meet the following challenges that are the basis for a practical development framework. These challenges result from the task to integrate processes in applications.

C 5.1: Separating Inter-Agent Coordination and Agent Functioning

Supplementing coordination aspects to agents requires a clear separation of the functioning of the system entities from the activities that are conceptually related to the inter-agent coordination, e.g. the initialization of an interaction or the processing of perceptions. Established agent programming frameworks (see Section 2.2.2), encode the control flows in the agent models. These frameworks provide a coherent programming interface that allows developers to prescribe the control of all agent-intern activities to realize agent functionalities, e.g. goal achievement and message-based agent communication. Additional frameworks allow mediated interaction models to be integrated by extending the available programming primitives (cf. Section 2.3.1). This development stance makes the application logic accessible, but inherently blends the coordination and adaptation logic and is justified only when the requirements of the intended system adjustments are known in advance and are approached with a predefined coordination pattern. In scenarios where the applied coordination strategy is subject to variations or additional coordination aspects are to be integrated in later development steps, e.g. as the system requirements are adjusted by stakeholders, the blending of development necessitates elaborate redesigns of agent models, i.e. the embedded control flows within agent models. The challenge is therefore to create a programming model that allows coordination to be integrated into functioning agent models. A clear separation demands that the prescription of the process be externalized from the realization of agents.

C 5.2: Coordinating Autonomous Software Components

The coordination of agent-based application demands that the autonomy of agent models be preserved. Agents must retain full authority over their activities. Imposing external influences that telecontrol adjustments would violate basic agency principles and limit the expressiveness of agent-oriented application designs, since the coordinated system elements would be converted to obedient subordinates.

C 5.3: Separating Interaction and Adaptation

Information exchange and entity adaptation are the constituent elements of Coordinating Processes (see Section 3.2, page 56) and these elements are addressed by implementation mechanisms, as reviewed in Section 3.2.1. The software technological treatment of these processes demands flexible configurations and adjustments of process realizations. Thus at the language level, it should be

5.1. MOTIVATION

possible to combine both concerns freely. On the architectural level, this separation must be enforced by decoupling the coordination infrastructure from the agent models.

C 5.4: Coordination as a Stand-Alone Design Element

The incremental development of Coordinating Processes must be supported. Process configurations must be embedded in self-contained design artifacts that can be shared and reused in software development organizations. One important aspect of this self-containment is the preparation of the mapping of generic process templates to concrete MAS realizations. These templates of self-organizing processes, as identified in the Sections 3.2.2 and 4.4.1, are structures of inter-agent relations that are associated with specific dynamic properties. Their enactment requires that process participants be mapped to concrete agent models. The major aspects of this mapping are the configuration of the interaction mechanisms and the mapping of the abstract behaviors of process participants to the concrete processings inside agent implementations.

5.1.2 Related Work

In this chapter, an alternative programming approach for inter-agent coordination is proposed. Frameworks for the programming of self-organizing applications have three orthogonal characteristics (see Figure 5.1). In Section 3.2.1, the distinction between information-exchange (*interaction*) and *adaption* mechanisms is explained. One characteristic is the extent of support for these types of mechanisms (y axis), a framework may be biased toward a specific mechanism type. A second orthogonal characteristic is the integration of coordination mechanisms. Possible modes are the *internal* embedding of mechanisms inside agents and the *external* influencing of elements by remote software artifacts (x axis). The internal mode refers to approaches that modify the internal structure or control flow of the agents. The integrated mechanisms are integrated in the agent and share the computational resources, e.g. memory and processing time, of the agent. The external mode describes that system elements are influenced by agent-extern elements. A third characteristic is the use of mechanisms in software development practices. This characteristic refers to the way in which an implementation framework is intended to be used (z axis). Most commonly, frameworks are used during agent development to embed specific mechanisms into the agents (*built-in*). Alternatively, the framework can *supplement* mechanisms to already functioning agents. The agents' operating principles are not explicitly dependent on the invocation of the framework(s), but rather mechanisms are integrated as additional run-time aspects that influence the agents' execution. Each of the three characteristics is addressed by a spectrum of development frameworks that can be used to implement inter-agent coordination. Here, the range of these spectra is elucidated by the classification of sample frameworks.

Interaction vs. Adaptation

The distinction between *information propagation* and *adaptation* mechanisms is discussed in Section 3.2.1. This distinction is also reflected by the programming frameworks for the construction of self-organizing systems. An example is the discussion of coordination languages in [Ciancarini, 1996]. In this work, the significance of coordination models for the development of distributed systems is argued and the need for high-level coordination languages is identified. These languages are expected to combine two orthogonal languages: one to express *inter-agent actions* and one to express the *intra-agent actions* [Ciancarini, 1996]. A similar distinction is present in programming frameworks and architectures. Agent-programming environments, as discussed in Section 2.2.2, focus on the development of the agents and their internal control flow. Supplementary coordination infrastructures are proposed, e.g. [Omicini et al., 2004a] (see Section 2.3.1), to provide programming support for the agent interactions. Programming constructs of the agent platform prescribe the local decision making and adaptivity of software agents. The coordination infrastructures provide high-level constructs to program the interactions and information exchange between agents, for example infrastructures that follow the established tuple space approach [Gelernter and

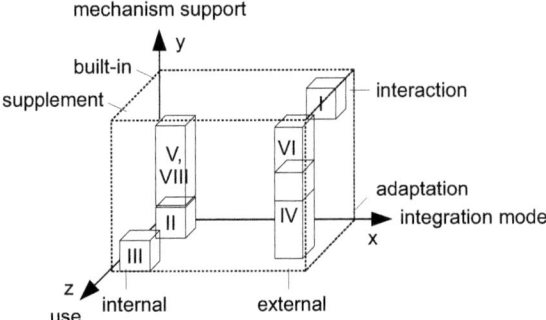

Figure 5.1: Orthogonal aspects of the integration of inter-agent coordination; cut surfaces describe an overlap in the characteristics and the support for a specific aspect is approximately reflected by edge length of cuboids

Carriero, 1992], e.g. the *TuCSoN* system [Viroli et al., 2009]. The ability of these coordination models to reflect the interaction-dynamics, e.g. the locality and stochastics of interactions, that facilitate self-organizing properties is demonstrated in [Viroli et al., 2009]. A unifying conception is the *Agents & Artifacts* (A&A) meta-model [Omicini et al., 2008]. Artifacts serve as abstractions of reactive system entities that offer functionalities to agents. Artifacts can serve as containers for interaction techniques, e.g. interaction protocols [Viroli and Ricci, 2004]. A common approach for the integration of both infrastructure types is the provision of agent programming constructs that allow the invocation of elements in the interaction-infrastructure to be explicitly referenced, e.g. [Piunti et al., 2008; Ricci et al., 2008]. Thus interactions can be integrated in the agent control flow (*built-in*). The generic nature of the artifact concept allows both direct and mediated *interaction* mechanisms to be integrated. However, the invocation of interactions and the processing of the received information and obtained results is left to the agents. The artifacts are provided by a dedicated middleware, and thus are separated from the agents (*external*).

Equipping agent models built in general-purpose programming environments with adaptation mechanisms can be achieved by adjusting the internal structuring of agents. This allows the consistent separation of adaptation aspects from the core agent functionalities. An example for this separation is an extension of the Ingenias agent meta model [Pavon et al., 2005], which is proposed in [Sansores and Pavón, 2008; Sansores and Pavon, 2009] (II). Goal-directed agents are equipped with an internal reinforcement learning mechanism. In the internal model of agents, a *motivation* concept is added. Positive feedback, based on the prior experiences of the agents, influences goal adoption. Agents receive feedback from their interactions in a *social network*. In this approach, the adoption of roles is associated to the pursuit of goals and the behavior of agents is affected by biasing their run-time adoption of goals. The extension addresses the control of the adaptive behavior of individual agents (*adaptation*). This modification structures the agent model and supports the integration of the adaptation (*built-in*) that is embedded in the agent (*internal*).

An alternative approach is the use of parasite-like entities, called *Behaviosites*, that autonomously integrate themselves into agent models and affect their behavior [Shabtay et al., 2007]. The behaviosite and the host agents are closely coupled. The agents, design has to allow for potential influences by behaviosites, and the design of a behaviosite must be tailored to suit the infected agent types. Behaviosites are divided into two categories, based on how thy influence the agent. External behaviosites manipulate the agent's interactions with the envirorent (sense/act). Internal behaviosites manipulate either the internal data structures of the agent or its behavioral elements. The use of these element is exemplified for the *El Farol Bar Problem* [Arthur, 1994] (see

5.1. MOTIVATION

Section 3.4.3, page 75). Thus the mechanisms also provides a means to control the local behavior of agents (*adaptation*). The control is control is *supplemented* to the agents and is realized inside the agents (*internal*), i.e. the behaviosites consume the resources of the agents.

Internal vs. External

The examples given above for the integration of coordination mechanisms also show the internal and external approaches. Adaptation-level mechanisms are integrated into agents by extending their architecture [Sansores and Pavón, 2008; Sansores and Pavon, 2009; Shabtay et al., 2007] or the execution infrastructure that underlies the agent implementations. The latter approach is also followed in [Seiter et al., 2006], where *aspect oriented programming* [Kiczales et al., 1997] is used to influence the execution of agents.

Alternatively, distributed architectures can be used to influence the execution of system entities remotely. In [Serugendo and Fitzgerald, 2009; Serugendo et al., 2008a] (IV), a distributed architecture is proposed that addresses the coordination of autonomous system elements, e.g. agents and robots. System elements are associated with *metadata* and *policies*. The former ones describe functional and non-functional characteristics and the later ones prescribe local adjustments to changes of conditions and metadata. A service-oriented architecture provides a run-time environment [Serugendo et al., 2008b] that coordinates system elements (*external*). The corresponding system architecture contains autonomous software components, metadata repositories, executable policies and reasoning services. Services and individual components access, i.e. store, publish, and update, metadata. Services in the run-time environment are responsible for evaluating metadata and enforcing the adjustments prescribed by policies. Thus the framework allows the explicit control of system elements to be *supplemented*. The enforced policies describe high-level goals (*guiding policy*), e.g. the activation/deactivation of sets of system elements, environmental constraints (*bounding policy*), and reflexive adjustments of system components (*sensing/monitoring policy*). The architecture particularly focuses on assuring self*-properties; the realization of policy is not constrained, so as to enable the integration of differing coordination techniques (*interaction,adaptation*) that realize self-organizing (cf. Section 3.2.1) or self-adaptive techniques (cf. Section 3.1.2). Applications include the simulation of an evolvable assembly system, where manufacturing robots coordinate tasks and configure their layout, as well as a Web-service Mediator framework that maintains dependability metadata that allow the enforcement fault-tolerance polices [Serugendo et al., 2008b].

Another distributed service architecture for self-organizing systems is developed in the *SELF-MAN* project [Roy et al., 2008] (V). The objective of the project is to combine a specific interaction infrastructure, i.e. structured overlay networks, with tailored component models. This approach particularly addresses the programming of inter-element feedbacks. The network infrastructure is designed to provide basic services, i.e. reliable communication, quick re-routing when facing failures, and transactions. The significance of enhanced component models of the reconfigurability of systems is argued in [Roy, 2007]. The individual reconfiguration of system entities has to be prepared for, as it is of vital importance in a self-organizing system that the structure of system elements, e.g. components, can be adapted. Therefore, the framework also addresses supporting for both adaptive and interactive mechanisms, whereby interactions are particularly constrained to overlay networks. The specific component model is a means to integrate (*built-in, internal*) the participation in the decentralized coordination into system elements.

Built-in vs. Supplement

Another practical aspect is the extent of agent-model modifications that are assumed by the programming framework. One extreme is to tailor that the agent models specifically for the framework. An example is the use of model-driven development techniques [Rougemaille et al., 2009a; Dong et al., 2009]. Executable agents are generated from specifications that are given in domain-specific languages.

An intermediate approach is the supplementation of mechanisms to agents, whereby the minimization of the exerted influences and the preservation of the agent autonomy presents a challenge. One example for this approach is the coordination (service) middleware that is proposed in [Singh, 1998] (VI). Agents and the middleware are separated by an abstract interface, based on a finite state automaton. Events, which signify state transitions, describe the activities of agents and are the means of influencing the agent execution. The middleware is notified about agent events, and it then controls agent execution by permitting or triggering the events (*external*). Interaction-level mechanisms, e.g. interaction protocols, can be supplemented to agents, as demonstrated in [Singh, 1998].

Finally, extensions can be based on standard component models. This approach prepares the reuse and integration of generic component realizations. The *Selflet* system [Devescovi et al., 2007b,a] (VIII), for example, is a design-time approach to the integration (*built-in*) of decentralized coordination in distributed applications. The authors aim at combining bio-inspired coordination with autonomic system development. A specific component architecture guides the realization of an autonomic system element, i.e. a *Selflet*. These elements contain a local knowledge base and are connected by a communication infrastructure that enables negotiations. Components' activities are given as sets of *Behaviors*. These executable means are defined as state machines and their execution may involve invocating services that are defined as *Abilities*. These are encapsulated and provided as *OSGi* components[1] and an embedded execution environment enables the run-time management, e.g. adding and removal. The self-management of these components is carried out by an internalized component, the *Autonomy Manager*, that triggers adjustments and is configured using a rule-based interface (*internal*). In [Devescovi et al., 2007a], the realization of clustering algorithms in the *Selflet* framework is discussed. The framework focuses on the prescription of the local adaptations and adjustments in the components and a communication infrastructure is provided as well (*adaptation,interaction*).

A comprehensive programming approach to self-organizing dynamics requires the integration of both *interaction and adaptation* mechanisms in a coherent framework. Using externalized framework architectures, both mechanism types can be outsourced and encapsulated (cf. Hypothesis 1.3, page 5). From an engineering perspective, the *supplementation* of mechanisms to software systems is beneficial. This approach minimizes the interactions with the engineering of the software system, e.g. development tools and practices can be used unaltered. More invasive approaches, such as the model-driven generation of agents, imply that application development aspects other than the coordination, are addressed as well, either by integrating them, e.g. allowing the generation of fully functional agents, or preparing the integration with conventionally developed implementations and models. However, this supplement poses the challenge of interfacing the framework functionality with the execution of the actual MAS (see Hypothesis 1.4, page 5). Finally, the *internal* integration mode allows makes use of the computational abilities of the involved system elements. This approach prevents the inclusion of additional, i.e. agent-extern, system components that explicitly control the coordination in the system. Instead, the self-organization is embedded as an additional aspect of the agent execution. A programming approach that combines these aspects is proposed in this Chapter.

5.2 Architecture: Decentralized Coordination Enactment

The reference architecture describes a conceptual framework for the integration of diverse coordination strategies into agent-based application designs. In this architecture, agents are understood as autonomous, pro-active providers of application-dependent functionalities. A key concern for this construction approach to integrating decentralized Coordinating Processes is a structured approach to design the interplay of agent functionalities and their coordination.

This concern is addressed by the strict separation of coordination and application logic (see Challenge 5.1, page 136). Definitions of the coordination strategies, i.e. the ACBG-based models of self-organizing processes, are provided as externalized design models that are enacted in MASs.

---

[1] http://www.osgi.org

5.2. ARCHITECTURE: DECENTRALIZED COORDINATION ENACTMENT

In this context, *enactment* means bringing about the influences that constitute the Coordinating Process by *observing* and *modifying* agent executions at run-time.

A key design criterion is that the coordination architecture provides a framework that can be adjusted to coordinate the activities of agents in different agent architectures. The coordination architecture is not based on the modification of a specific agent model or the generation of executable agent models (cf. Section 5.1.2), but rather is conceived as an extension that realizes a coordination middleware layer. The agent architectures used are not constrained, as the architecture can be adapted to specific agent models and execution platforms. The rationale for adopting of the enactment approach, based on the interpreting of externalized coordination models and the run-time modification of agent execution, is the support it offers for the integration of different agent platforms and agent architectures. Their integration demands the realization of a specific agent module that enacts coordination by controlling local modifications and access to the middleware layer. The assumptions about the assimilable agent platforms/architectures are minimized by an event-based interface between the prescriptions of agent modifications and the agent logic. The use of this interface is also a means for preserving the autonomy of agents (see Challenge 5.2, page 136).

The two foundational activities, necessary for the establishment of self-organizing processes are (1) the realization of information flows between system elements and (2) the local adaptation of system elements resulting from the obtained information. These are conceptually separated in distinct design elements (see Challenge 5.3, page 136). Agents intern components are used to contain adaptations and these containers are interconnected via infrastructures for the propagation of information. In the architecture discussed here, the basic activities are not only encapsulated but also automated. Encapsulation is achieved by separating these activities from agent models. Therefore, the coordination is not built into the agent model, but rather agents are equipped with coordination models at later development stages. The automation of coordination related activities supports the declarative definition of coordination strategies. Developers configure the self-organizing process to enable the enactment. The configuration of processes by an external artifact supports the interdependent design of the configured inter-agent processes (see Challenge 5.4, page 137). The mapping of generic templates to implementations is prepared.

5.2.1 Reference Architecture for Embedding Self-Organization

The corresponding reference architecture is based on a layered approach and the three fundamental abstraction layers are illustrated in Figure 5.2. This architecture can be realized on top of arbitrary middleware platforms. An indispensable requirement is that the coordinated system be composed of locally adaptive software elements [Salehie and Tahvildari, 2009]. In the following, agent-oriented infrastructures are used.

The top layer contains the software elements that provide the application functionalities. As the application is realized by an MAS, it is composed of sets of agents as well as passive software components. The agents involved serve as autonomous, pro-active providers of application functionality (*application dependent functionality*). The local agent reasoning governs the provision of functional elements such as the satisfaction of inter-agent service requests. Agents are able to communicate (*generic agent interaction*) and coordinate their activities with conventional techniques (cf. Section 2.5).

The subjacent *coordination layer* realizes the Coordinating Process. It consists of partitions of agents and a virtual sub-layer that contains *Coordination Media*. These media encapsulate specific interaction techniques, i.e. instances of Coordination Mechanisms (cf. Section 3.2.1). The media provide, interfaced by a generic publish/subscribe interface, the interaction techniques that facilitate the realization of self-organizing dynamics. These media are accessed by *Coordination Endpoints*. The agents that participate in a Coordinating Process are equipped with these modules.

Coordination Endpoints encapsulate and automate the activities that are conceptually related to the coordination of agents. First, they interlink the surrounding host agent with the Coordination Media. The use of these media is hidden from the agent logic. Secondly, these modules

142   CHAPTER 5. A SYSTEMIC PROGRAMMING MODEL

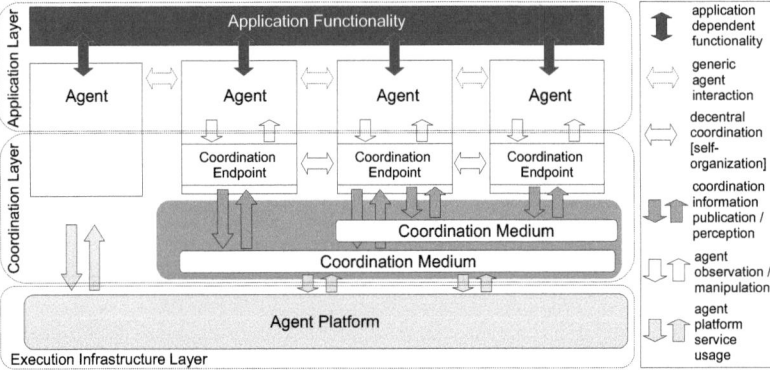

Figure 5.2: The layered structure of the coordination enactment architecture, following [Sudeikat et al., 2009a]

interpret declarations of Coordinating Processes and infer the coordination logic that controls (1) when to publish coordination-related information via Coordination Media and (2) how to respond to this information. Coordination Endpoints enact the coordination logic by observing and modifying the execution state of agents (*agent observation/manipulation*) as well as by sending and receiving information via coordination Media (*coordination information publication/perception*). The interplay of the local reasoning within Coordination Endpoints and the interactions between these agent modules, that are routed by Coordination Media, establish the intended, coordination process (*decentral coordination*).

The realization of these layers is based on an *Execution Infrastructure Layer* that provides a middleware for the construction of distributed systems. This layer provides fundamental services for the coordination and application layer (*agent platform service usage*), e.g. an execution infrastructure and element management.

This architecture supports the enactment of externalized models of coordination strategies that configure three principal aspects. First, internal data of the software element, here agent, which are relevant for the coordination are exchanged. Secondly, the dynamics of the information flows are configured by the parameterization of Coordination Media. Finally, process definitions describe how agents respond to perceptions of coordination information.

The fundamental operating principle of the proposed architecture is summarized in Figure 5.3. Agents are executed on a specific platform that provides the run-time environment. In particular, this platform provides the reasoning mechanisms that govern the internal reasoning of individual agents (cf. Section 2.4). According to the enacted process, Coordination Endpoints register with the underlying execution environment for the observation of the agent execution. When a relevant observation has been made, the Endpoint initiates a corresponding communication, i.e. publication, via an associated coordination Medium. The Medium realizes the dynamics of publication dissemination, following specific Decentralized Coordination Mechanisms that control the propagation of information (cf. Section 3.2.1, page 60). Endpoints subscribe at Media instances to be informed about publications. Upon reception, the relevance is checked and, if appropriate, the agent execution is modified. The distinction of Endpoints end media realizes the separation of the local adaptations and the information exchanges (see Challenge 5.3, page 136). The exertion of influence by Endpoints can be designed to preserve the autonomy of the agents (see Challenge 5.2, page 136). The specification of the enacted inter-agent process determines the relevance of the observations, the potential modifications of the agent execution, and the associated Coordination Media. The publication format, i.e. the inclusion of agent-internal data, and the interpretation of

5.2. ARCHITECTURE: DECENTRALIZED COORDINATION ENACTMENT

this format at the receiving Endpoint can be also configured (cf. Section 5.3).

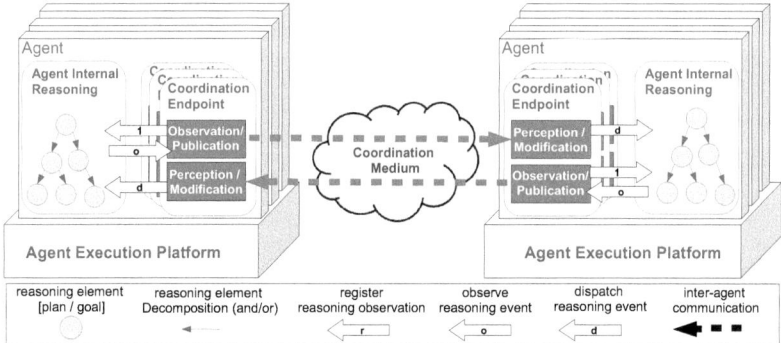

Figure 5.3: The operating principle of the coordination enactment, adapted from [Sudeikat and Renz, 2008b]

The proposed architecture provides a middleware layer that connects agents via a *Distributed Event-Based System* (DES), as defined in [Mühl et al., 2006]. Event-based Systems equip applications with *event-notification services* or *publish/subscribe middlewares*. Connections among system components are established by these infrastructure as they allow the occurrence of *events*, i.e. specific incidences of interest [Mühl et al., 2006] (page 3) in components, to be disseminated among sets of interested system elements. *Producers* (*publishers*), make *notifications* of event occurrences known to the middleware which then forwards them to *consumers* (*subscribers*).

These systems have been identified as a distinct *architectural style* [Carzaniga et al., 1998] for the design of software systems. In this respect, an architectural style refers to reusable software system structures [Abowd et al., 1993],[Shaw and Garlan, 1996]. Despite a generally accepted definition of the term, the common understanding of the term is summarized in [Qin et al., 2008] (page 34) as:

> ... a certain style or a class of styles are abstracted from the successful software system's organization structure, and can be used in different software development fields.

Early event-based styles, known as *implicit invocation* or *reactive broadcast* [Shaw and Garlan, 1996] (page 23), proposed the publication of events in order to enable loose couplings and avoid the explicit invocation of procedures. Instead, components register themselves for publications and invoke associated procedures when they are notified of events. DES prepared the decoupling of distributed system components by providing sophisticated infrastructures for the dissemination of notifications to remote components. The outstanding property of this system design approach is the *decoupling* of system elements as well as the separation of *communication* and *computation* [Mühl et al., 2006]. Producer and consumer elements are designed towards the processing of the exchanged information within notifications, and are unaware of the locations and times of publications. This inherent separation of elements supports the integration of heterogeneous components.

In [Mühl et al., 2006] the principal interaction models are characterized by two attributes (see Table 5.1): the initiation of the interaction (*Initiator*) and the addressing of recipients (*Addressee*). The producer or the consumer can initiate interactions and the recipient of an interaction may by directly or indirectly addressed. These models are independent of the utilized communication techniques but characterize the principal inner structure of interacting components. Based on this characterization four essential interaction models can be distinguished (see Table 5.1). In the

Request/Reply model interactions are initiated by a consumer that is aware of the addressee. Examples are client/server-based interactions. The components are tightly coupled and publications are typically answered with reply messages. In *Anonymous Request/Reply* models, the addressees of requests are not specified by the initiator, i.e. the consumer. Requests are are delivered to an arbitrary selection of providers and the selection may be made dynamically, e.g. to identify appropriate providers or realize load-balancing. Anonymous providers enhance the flexibility of interactions but components depend on the provision of data/functionality [Mühl et al., 2006]. In the *Callback* model the consumers register at providers to be notified about event occurrences. The provider is responsible for maintaining the list of registered components that are to be informed. A prominent example is the *Observer* design pattern [Gamma et al., 1995]. The awareness of registered consumers enables the customization of notifications, e.g. the account for application-dependent requirements, but building in this domain-knowledge blends the component logic with integration concerns. Finally, *Event-based* interactions are initiated by the providers and their notifications are directed to unknown selections of consumers. The fundamental characteristic of these interactions is the anonymity of the consumers, which enforces the *self-containment* of component designs. Components are equipped with the logic to publish and/or process notifications, based solely on the communicated data. In this model, the control of interactions that steer system functionality lies not within the components but arises from the concurrent processing within the participating components.

		Initiator	
		Consumer	Producer
Addressee	Direct	Request/Reply	Callback
	Indirect	Anonymous Request/Reply	Event-Based

Table 5.1: The principal interaction models [Mühl et al., 2006]

The architecture discussed here uses the event-based interaction model to provide a middleware layer that automates the coordination of system entities. The operation of this layer is separated by the Endpoint modules that are equipped with the coordination logic, i.e. the information about how and when to publish notifications and how to respond to the receipt of notifications. Thus, these modules act as consumers or producers, depending on the configuration of their ambient system element, which they are able to observe and modify. The definition of the significant events that are to be published and perceived is based on the systemic modeling approach (cf. Chapter 4), thus endpoints inform each other about the adjustments of behaviors within components, here agents. The effects of perceptions are also expressed in terms of agent behavior, i.e. endpoints are enabled to suggest behavior adoptions to their host agent.

A fundamental motivation for the event-based realization is that this interaction mode minimizes the dependence between system components. Participating components are not aware of the anonymous consumers and producers of notifications and recipients of a publications are unknown. In this model the consumers are anonymous as well. Agents are inherently autonomous, i.e. locally control their behavior, so imposing a strict external control over the local behavior of system components would violate the autonomy of the participants, i.e. agents. The internals of the coordination medium inherently preserve autonomy, since endpoint modules are not aware of consumers or recipients. Heterogeneous applications require the availability of endpoint modules which are tailored for a specific agent execution platform or component execution environment. The architectural model allows autonomy to be preserved but, when misused, the embedding of interferences at the inter-agent and agent level is possible. The operations inside Endpoints should be designed as self-contained activities that process the provided information. dependencies to specific external elements, e.g. reposes by another endpoint instance, have to be avoided. In addition, he event-based interface between Endpoints and agents (see Section 5.2.7) can be exploited to impose control on the agent model, when the agent and the Endpoint are prepared for this purpose. In this respect, it is a design effort to use the architecture for the correlation of autonomous entities.

5.2. ARCHITECTURE: DECENTRALIZED COORDINATION ENACTMENT

The integration of non-agent elements is not impaired. These elements do not have the authority to object to suggestions for behavior adjustments, but the event-based interface between endpoints and their ambient component can be supplemented with procedural knowledge that enables them to fine-tune the context in which suggestions are made (cf. Section 5.2.7). These supplemented logic always accept the adoption of behaviors that are suggested by contained endpoints.

A positive side-effect of decoupling endpoints and preserving agent autonomy is that the independence of individual components is not affected. Reliability of component designs would be compromised if the provision if its functionality is affected by failures within dependent components. The application design may contain such dependencies, e.g. the relying on the achievement of goals by allied agents, but supplementing the proposed coordination layer cannot introduce additional dependences, due to the strict and anonymous separation of endpoints that is present in DES (cf. [Mühl et al., 2006], page 17).

5.2.2 Conceptual Model

The conceptual structure of the basic architectural constituents is illustrated in Figure 5.4. Four different element types are indicated by their shading. *Agent Implementation* elements are artifacts that are given by the utilized agent platform or are realized in the agent-specific programming technique. *Coordination Enactment* elements provide realizations of Coordination Endpoints. *Interaction Model Implementation* elements of the utilized coordination mechanism realize inter-agent interaction techniques. Finally, elements of the declarative specification of the Coordinating Process (*Coordinating Process Definition*) control the enactment. The elements of the enactment provide the run-time framework and the elements of the process definitions describes the configuration and intermediate data structures that control the participation in the process. The essential parts of the run-time environment are identified and their major functional constituents are identified. Each of these components is responsible for a specific functionality. The capabilities of these elements and their realization are discussed separately in subsequent sections.

The enactment influences the execution of the agent implementations (*Agent Model*). They contain a local *Agent Reasoning Component* that controls agent execution by processing *Agent Reasoning Events*. These events indicate distinct steps in the agent execution, e.g. the adoption of a goal or the update of a knowledge element. The events can originate from event-based execution cycles, e.g. as present in BDI agents (cf. Section 2.2.1), or from the observation of the execution of agents. In this context, event occurrences are interpreted and signify changes of agent behaviors or configurations that are relevant for the participation in a Coordinating Process.

A *Coordination Endpoint* (CE) is an agent module (*coordinated by*) that encapsulates the local enforcement of a Coordinating Process inside the surrounding host agent. These modules encapsulate a contributive process that automates the activities which are causally related to the coordination of agent activities. Agent models are not prepared to include coordination, but these activities are scheduled and executed inside CE modules. As these modules observe and modify the agent execution, the coordination enactment is provided as a *transparent* background process. The automated activities deal with (1) the establishment of information flows between system actors and (2) the local modification of agent behaviors.

The Endpoints inform each other, decoupled by Coordination Media, about adjustments within host agents. The processing inside agents is observed by an *Agent State Interpreter* component. The observation is based on an event-based interface (*Observation*) that informs the interpreter about the agent-internal reasoning. When the perceived events indicate adjustments of the agent behavior that are relevant to the inter-agent coordination, the publication of this adjustment via an associated *Coordination Medium* is triggered.

These media provide *virtual* communication channels that are accessible by a generic publish/subscribe interface. Specific components provide the ability to publish and perceive adjustments within connected agents that are relevant for the enactment (*Coordination Event Publication/Perception*). The communicated data elements follow a specific Interface (*Coordination Information*).

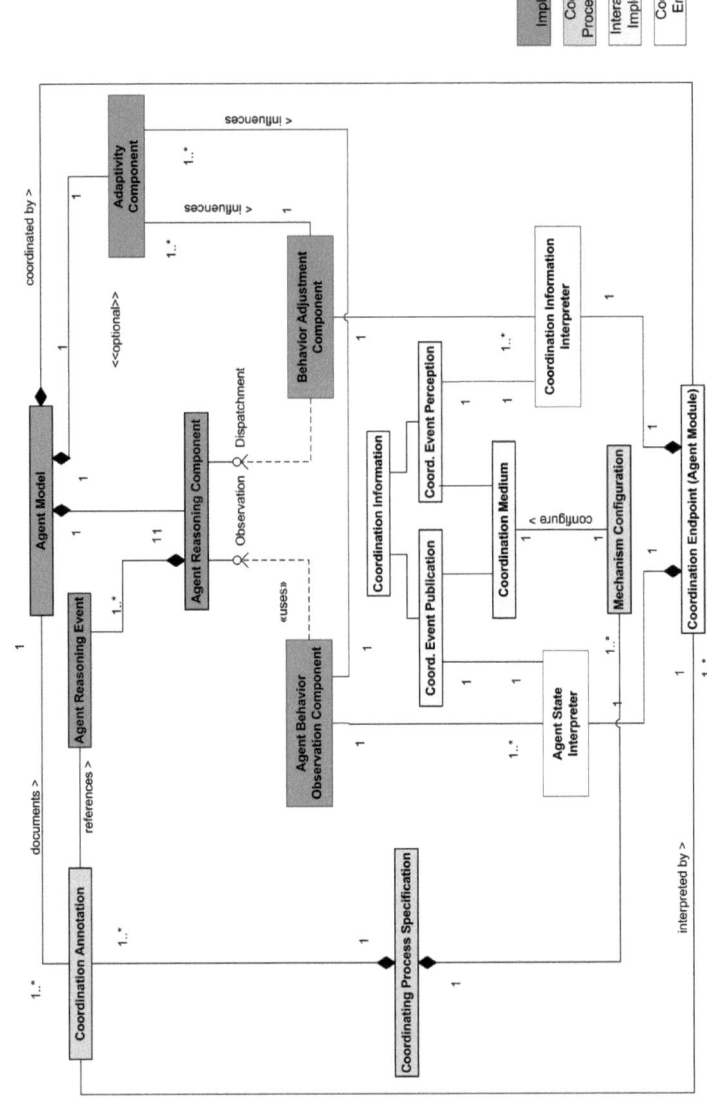

Figure 5.4: Conceptual model of the realization of the reference architecture, following [Sudeikat and Renz, 2009b]

5.2. ARCHITECTURE: DECENTRALIZED COORDINATION ENACTMENT

Inside the subscribed CEs, the *Coordination Information Interpreter* processes the transmitted information. When indicated by the process definition, the behavior of the surrounding agent is modified by dispatching agent reasoning events. The dispatching is based in an interface (*Dispatchment*) that is offered by the agent platform and allows events in the reasoning cycle to be added that control agent execution (cf. Section 2.4, example in Section 2.2.1).

The segmentation of Endpoints facilitates the reuse of the contained components. Interpreter components process incoming information (whether agent-reasoning events or the publications that are spread through a Medium), examine the agent state, and, if appropriate, actuate coordination-related activities, i.e. publications or adjustment within the agents. The interpreters need to be adjusted to meet agent architectures, while the publication/perception components are tailored to access certain Medium realizations.

The operation of Coordination Endpoints is configured by the *Coordinating Process Specification*. These specifications define the relevant observations and appropriate modifications of the agent execution. These are defined as lists of agent events that signify the relevant adjustments. The specification associates them with specific Coordination Media and contain their configuration (*Mechanism Configuration*). The configuration language is discussed in Section 5.3. For a given host agent, only a subset of the specification is relevant. The enactment is prepared by extracting sets of *Coordination Annotations* that describe the relevant observations, modifications and utilizations of Coordination Media. These *document* the coordination of a specific agent type and are stored within each agent model, e.g. as a specific belief value or agent property. The Coordination Endpoints access these annotations and interpret them at run-time (*interpreted by*) to control the enforcement operations. Modifications of the local annotations at run-time support the on-line adjustment of coordination enactment.

Using the configuration language, the observation (*Agent Behavior Observation*) and modification (*Agent Behavior Adjustment*) of the agent execution can be constrained declaratively by a logical formula. In addition, supplementary procedural realizations can be provided in optional *Adaptivity Components*. These contain definitions of agent-behavior classifications and behavior adjustments, which are defined in the programming concepts of the utilized agent platform.

5.2.3 Coordination Endpoints

Coordination Endpoints (see Figure 5.4, page 146) separate the agent-internal reasoning from the coordination-related activities, namely the establishment of information flows and the local entity adaptation, based on the received perceptions. The two principal functional aspects of this architecture element are the observation and, if appropriate, manipulation of the agent execution as well as the publication and reception of coordination-related information.

Definition 5.1 *(Coordination Endpoint) A Coordination Endpoint (see Figure 5.4, page 146) is a component that separates the agent-internal reasoning from the accessing of Coordination Media (cf. Definition 5.4). Each endpoint is associated to one agent (1:1) and interacts with other endpoints via one Medium (1:1). Agents are associated to a set of endpoints (1:n). Endpoints utilize an event-based interface to observe/modify the associated agent.*

Endpoint realizations can follow three basic design alternatives. First, the Endpoints can be integrated directly into the agent execution environment, i.e. agent platform. The execution environment is responsible for loading an endpoint for each agent that participates in a Coordination Process. This approach allows for efficient implementations, since the observation/modifications can be directly integrated into the agent reasoning cycle. However, the resulting realization is highly customized for a specific agent model or platform realization.

Secondly, agents can be equipped with an interface that allows agent-extern system elements to access the internal processing. This design stance supports the separation of concerns since Endpoints are provided in an additional execution context, e.g. as service-based realizations. However, the disclosure of agent-internals contradicts the autonomy-property of agents (see Section 2.2). In addition, the Endpoints have to connect to agents via communication infrastructure and an additional communication overhead is implied by the externalized management.

Finally, Endpoints can be conceived as agent modules that are embedded within the agent that participates in a Coordinating Process. This approach is a compromise between the two previous alternatives. The separation of agent coordination and agent functionality is satisfied due to the modularization that encapsulates the coordination logic embedded in the module. Modules are specific to an agent model but their non-invasive realization, i.e. the realization without modifications of the utilized agent platform, guides the realization of Endpoints for other agent models. On a conceptual level the integration of the coordination logic supports the self-containment of agent models. The configured agent executable contains all functionality to function as desired, i.e. provide coordinated functionalities, without relying on components other than the communication infrastructures, i.e. Coordination Media. This self-containment requires that the reasoning about the coordination logic consumes the computational resources of host agents.

In the remainder of this chapter, the integration of the coordination architecture in an agent platform, using the third realization approach is discussed. This approach is selected as it provides the ability to separate the coordination logic and minimizes the platform specific adjustments within implementation elements. This approach implies that Endpoint realizations are customized towards the architecture of their host agent/component. The endpoint conception is discussed generically; details on the concrete realization can be found in Section 5.3.5.

5.2.4 Activated Agent Modules

The realization of Endpoints as agent-intern modules is based on an *activation* technique that enables modules to observe and influence surrounding agents. Conventional agent module concepts, e.g. capabilities in BDI agents (see Section 2.2.1), are based on the pooling of functionalities and the preparation of their reuse. Agent elements, required for the provision of a specific function, are contained and encapsulated in modules to structure individual agents (see Section 2.2.1). In this respect, agent-modules agree with their counterpart in conventional software development disciplines [Parnas, 1972] as information hiding and functionality reuse are supported. Further developments refine the use of these principles in agents to fine-tune the control of module activations (see Section 2.2.1).

The explicit invocations of modules, e.g. via programming language constructs, are problematic when recurring functionalities are frequently referenced in different partitions of a software artifact. These functionalities *crosscut* the software as the contained functionalities are repeatedly invoked in different execution contexts [Kiczales et al., 1997] and this practice leads to scattered references that complicate the internal structure of agents. Primary examples are *logging, monitoring, synchronization*, and *failure recovery* [Kiczales et al., 1997; Seiter et al., 2006]. One technique for encapsulating and integrating these issues in software systems is *Aspect-Oriented Programming* [Kiczales et al., 1997]. Particularly for software agents, *mobility, learning*, and *collaboration* have been identified as recurring crosscutting concerns and their treatment with AOP techniques has been studied (e.g. [Garcia et al., 2006]).

The automation of the coordination-related activities, as proposed by the conceptual model of the process enactment (see Figure 5.4), is another example for a crosscutting concern. The prescription of a Coordinating Process specifies interferences in the agent execution. These are to be encapsulated and separated from the agent model. Explicitly referencing the module functionality, i.e. the interpreter elements, would enforce the modifications of the agent models when endpoint internals are modified.

An enhancement of agent modules, their *activation*, was proposed as an alternative means to embedding crosscutting concerns activation [Sudeikat et al., 2006; Sudeikat and Renz, 2007a]. This enhancement exploits the event-based reasoning mechanism of BDI-based agent platforms. The referencing of module-internal elements is automated by enabling modules to observe the agent execution and autonomously determine the modifications in the surrounding agents. Consequently, modules are transfered to active entities that autonomously influence their execution context, i.e. the configuration of their host agent. These modifications are configured by defining mappings between agent reasoning events. Observed events are mapped to events that are imposed in the agent execution cycle in order to cause appropriate modifications. These modules were coined

5.2. ARCHITECTURE: DECENTRALIZED COORDINATION ENACTMENT

co-efficient, as they register for a contributive processing. The realization of Endpoints using this mechanism is discussed in [Sudeikat and Renz, 2010b].

Module Structure and Operating Principle

The activation of modules is a consequent step in accounting for the pro-activeness of agent-based software components. Not only the agent but also the contained modules themselves are understood as active context-aware elements. Agents can be structured as sets of active modules, each encapsulating and providing the handling of a specific execution concern. These modules control when the functionality contained is used. The conceptual structure of these modules is illustrated in Figure 5.5. This model extends the minimal, generic structure of MASs that is discussed in Section 2.4.

Agents can contain conventional *Modules* that are containers for agent model elements. A specialization is the *Co-Efficient Module* that features two additional elements. The first element, an *Observation/Adjustment Component*, enables the monitoring and modification of the local reasoning. The agent development platform is required to offer two interfaces that enable the *Observation* and *Inducement* of reasoning events. The types of events and their available interfaces depend on the agent execution platform used. The second element, the *Event Mapping*, specifies which observations cause the introduction of additional events in the agent reasoning. In early conceptions [Sudeikat et al., 2006; Sudeikat and Renz, 2007a], these mappings were procedurally preprogrammed, and the Endpoint realization illustrates their declarative specification in an externalized language model [Sudeikat and Renz, 2010b].

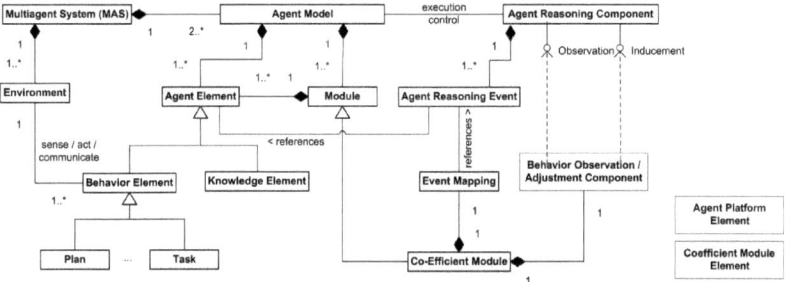

Figure 5.5: Conceptual Structure of coefficient capabilities [Sudeikat and Renz, 2010b]

The run-time operating principle of an activated module is illustrated in Figure 5.6. The initialization of the agents implies the initialization of the contained modules and co-efficient modules initially registering for the observation of agent events that are denoted as significant observations in their internal Event Mapping (1). The agent execution is controlled by the Reasoning Mechanism and the registered modules are informed, e.g. via an event-listening mechanism [Sudeikat et al., 2006; Sudeikat and Renz, 2007a], about the occurrences of observed reasoning events (2). These notifications are processed by the Observation/Adjustment Component and mapping events are induced in the reasoning of the surrounding agent. The processing contains the evaluation of optional constraints on the agent state that guard inducements. The induced events reference behavior elements inside (3) or outside (4) the module. In the former case, internal processings inside the module are triggered while the latter cases describes the modification of elements inside the surrounding agents including other modules.

The event-based reasoning mechanisms in agents can be exploited to control the provision of functionalities that crosscut agent models. An example is the separation and control of message-based communications. Two approaches are the use of an *interaction aspect* [Garcia et al., 2004]

150 CHAPTER 5. A SYSTEMIC PROGRAMMING MODEL

and the use of the capability concept in BDI agents to contain the roles of participants in interaction protocols [Busetta et al., 2000] (see Section 2.2.1). However, even in these flexible agent models references can become scattered when the contained elements, e.g. goals, require explicit referencing. In general, when the functionality within a module is frequently referenced and the applicability of the functionality is decided by the local execution context, a coefficient realization, that modules with the ability to autonomously decide the provision of their internal activities should be considered. Examples are given in Section 5.2.6. In these scenarios, it is beneficial to contain the logic when events should be imposed as responses to prior reasoning events in a single place. The reasoning mechanism of agents is not affected by these modules, but the *contributive* introduction of *additional* events, e.g. goal activations, is automated. The local reasoning controls the handling of events, thus the authority of the agent is not violated. The proposed automation of references is a reactive approach to embedding crosscutting concerns that agrees with the demand for reactivity of software agents (see Section 2.2.1). The described mechanism is a powerful means for equipping agents with auxiliary functionalities and background processing but must be applied carefully. Recursive activations of events are possible and the preprocessing inside co-efficient modules should make deliberate use of the computational resources of the host agent.

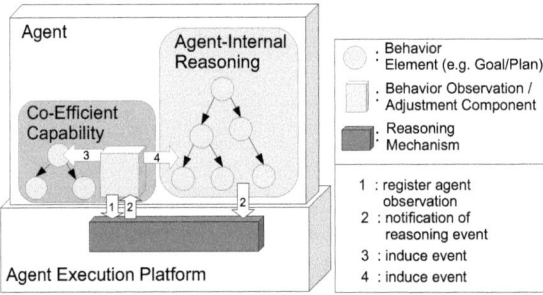

Figure 5.6: Operating principle of activated modules, following [Sudeikat and Renz, 2010b]

5.2.5 Formalization of Activated Agent Modules within BDI Agents

After the informal description of the operating principle of activated agent modules (see page 149), the formal definition of the functioning of these modules is summarized in this section, following [Sudeikat and Renz, 2010b]. This formalization unambiguously specifies the method of operation that is used to activate agent modules and illustrates how they affect the surrounding agent. The sample implementation of the activated modules [Sudeikat et al., 2006; Sudeikat and Renz, 2007a] and the Coordination Endpoints [Sudeikat and Renz, 2010b] is based on the BDI agent architecture. Therefore, a formalization framework is used that addresses this specific agent architecture.

In [Rao and Georgeff, 1995] the BDI architecture is defined by an abstract agent interpreter and the *AgentSpeak(L)* language [Rao, 1996] is a corresponding programming language. An Agentspeak-based implementation frameworks is freely available[2] [Bordini et al., 2007]. The semantics of this programming language are formally described in [Vieira et al., 2007], using the *Operational Semantics* formalism [Plotkin, 2004]. This formalization describes the fundamental activities of BDI-based reasoning and formally defines the operation of Agentspeak interpreters [Bordini et al., 2007]. In the absence of a generally established theory of BDI agents, we adopt this formalization to express the operating principle of activated, co-efficient capabilities.

---
[2]The *Jason* system: http://jason.sourceforge.net

5.2. ARCHITECTURE: DECENTRALIZED COORDINATION ENACTMENT

The (Operational) Semantics of BDI Agents

Operational Semantics is an established formalism for describing the semantics of programming languages [Plotkin, 2004; Fokkink, 2000]. The functioning of a program is described by a transition relation between program configurations [Plotkin, 2004]. This relation is given by *transition rules*, which define the valid transitions. In [Vieira et al., 2007], based on prior formalizations in [Moreira and Bordini, 2002; Moreira et al., 2004], this technique is adopted to describe the operation of the Agentspeak interpreter. This work focuses on a specific interpreter but identifies principal reasoning steps and illustrates the execution of BDI agents. This work is selected as a basis for the formal description of the semantics of co-efficient modules, as it is based on an established formalism. In addition, the partitioning of the agent reasoning in distinct transition rules prepares for the following specification of co-efficiency. It can be expressed as a refinement of a single transition rule.

The basic steps in the reasoning cycle and the potential transitions are illustrated in Figure 5.7. The initial point is the processing of inter-agent messages (*ProcMsg*). Thereafter, an agent-intern event is selected (*SelEv*) for subsequent processing. Relevant plans (*RelPl*) are declared to handle the selected event. A subset of these plans are applicable (*ApplPl*), i.e. can be executed in the current execution state of the agent. This state is guarded by conditions that are annotated to plans (see Section 2.2.1). One of the applicable plans is then selected for execution (*SelAppl*) and this plan is added as an intention (*AddIM*). In this context, an *intention* is a *stack of partially instantiated plans* [Vieira et al., 2007] (page 231). The execution of a plan can cause events that cause the execution of other plans, e.g. when a plan involves the achievement of a subgoal by another plan. The intention keeps track of these causation of plan instantiations and denotes a course of action. Agents concurrently pursue a set of intentions and one instance is selected (*SelInt*), thereafter executed (*ExecInt*), and removed when finished (*ClrInt*). This cycle is shortcut when no events are to be handled or no plans are applicable for a selected event (arrows from SelEv to SelInt and from ApplPl to SelInt, respectively). The execution is directly transferred to the selection of an intention.

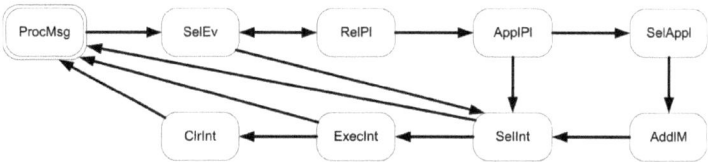

Figure 5.7: The reasoning cycle of Agentspeak-based BDI agents, following [Vieira et al., 2007]

This overview of the reasoning cycle is detailed in [Vieira et al., 2007]. In the following section, a subset of the contained formalization, concerning the selection of events (SelEv) is summarized. The operating principle of co-efficient modules is described as a refinement of this step in the following section. Transition rules control the execution of an agent by modifying its *configuration*. It is given be the tuple $< ag, C, M, T, s >$.

The first element is the *agent program* (ag). It contains the beliefs bs and plans ps that are available to the individual agent.

The element C denotes the execution context, *Circumstance*, of the agent. It is a tuple $< I, E, A >$. The element I is the current set of *intentions* $\{i, i', \ldots\}$ that the agent is pursuing (see above). The element E denotes the set of events $\{(te, i), (te, i'), \ldots\}$ that are processed and handled by the reasoning. Events are given as pairs (te, i) of the actual event (te) that triggers (further) processing and an associated intention (i). When events result from prior processing *inside* the agent, they are associated to the corresponding intention. Otherwise, events are related to the empty intention $\top$. Finally, the element A contains the available actions that enable an agent to modify the environment.

The communication of an agent is characterized by the element M of the configuration. It contains information about the reception and sending of messages, as well as the suspension of intentions to await the reception of messages. The ability to communicate and the processing of messages are not affected by co-efficiency, thus the management of communications is neglected here. Details are given in [Vieira et al., 2007].

The tuple T is used to store the volatile information that is made available to the reasoning mechanism. The information is stored in the elements $< R, Ap, \iota, \rho, \epsilon >$. The first two elements store the sets of plans that are relevant and applicable for the currently handled event (R and Ap, respectively). The latter three elements describe the focus of a reasoning cycle. They refer to the current intention (ι), the currently handled event (ρ), and the currently selected applicable plan (ϵ).

The final element s denotes the current reasoning step. It refers to one of the steps that are illustrated in Figure 5.7 [Vieira et al., 2007].

Co-efficiency deals with the apposition of events in addition to the handling of events by the agent reasoning. Deliberately adding events, causes contributive activities within an individual agent as an additional response to events. The *Event Selection* step (*SelEv*, see Figure 5.7) describes that the reasoner picks out an event for further processing. This selection initiates a reasoning cycle and is described by two transition rules [Vieira et al., 2007].

The rule *SelEv1* applies to configurations where the set E is non-empty. This set contains the possible events and a *selection function* S_E is used to select an event for further processing. The notation X_y is used to denote the element y of the superior element X, e.g. C_E refers to the event set E in the Circumstance C. The rule states that the selected event (te,i) is removed from the set of events (C_E) and is stored as the currently handled event (T_ρ). The reasoning continues with the selection of relevant plans (*RelPl*). Otherwise, no event is waiting to be dealt with and the rule *SelEv2* applies, which triggers the following step, i.e. the selection of an intention (*SelInt*) for further processing [Vieira et al., 2007]:

$$\textbf{SelEv1} \quad \frac{S_E(C_E) = \langle te, i \rangle}{\langle ag, C, M, T, SelEv \rangle \longrightarrow \langle ag, C', M, T', RelPl \rangle} \quad (5.1)$$

$$where: C'_E = C_E \backslash \{\langle te, i \rangle\}$$

$$T'_e = \langle te, i \rangle$$

$$\textbf{SelEv2} \quad \frac{(C_E) = \{\}}{\langle ag, C, M, T, SelEv \rangle \longrightarrow \langle ag, C, M, T, SelInt \rangle} \quad (5.2)$$

The Operational Semantics for Co–Efficient Capabilities

Co-efficient modules register themselves for the observation of reasoning events. When one of these events is noticed, it is processed and additional reasoning events are added for future processing by the surrounding agent (see page 149). This operating principle can be described by a refinement of the *SelEv* reasoning step. An additional transition rule is introduced (see Equation 5.3) Sudeikat and Renz [2010b] that describes the processing of observed events. It is an extension and the original transition rules are not affected.

Modules are configured by a set of event mappings K. Each mapping specifies (1) the events that are to be observed and induced as well as (2) the execution context that permits the addition of the event(s). These mappings are contained in tuples $\langle te_s, te_d, \lambda, \kappa \rangle$:

- The element te_s is a triggering event that is marked for observation. The set of observed events is denoted by S ($te_s \in S$), which is a subset of the platform-specific reasoning events ($S \in E$).

- The element te_d is the corresponding event that is induced when te_s is observed. The set of actuated events (D) is also a subset of the reasoning events ($te_d \in D, D \in E$).

5.2. ARCHITECTURE: DECENTRALIZED COORDINATION ENACTMENT

- The element λ describes the destination intention of event additions. Events (te_d) are placed in the active intention (i) or in a new intention ($\top; \lambda \in \{i, \top\}$).

- The optional element κ contains a boolean condition, which defines when the event te_d is to be added. The condition is given by a logical expression that refers to the current agent state (ag, C, M, T) and indicates when the introduction of the event (te_d) is permitted.

In addition, three functions for the accessing of the mapping information are used. These simplify the semantics of agent state modifications. The *mapping function* $m(x)$ returns the event that maps a triggering event ($m : S \longrightarrow D$). This function searches the configurations in K and returns the event(s) that are to be induced in response ($m(te_s) = te_d$). The *intention-selection* function $l : S, D \longrightarrow \lambda$ returns the target intention (λ) for an event mapping (S, D). λ indicates either the current intention (λ_c) or the new intention (λ_n). The inclusion in a new intention starts a new course of actions that is concurrently followed by the agent. The inclusion in the same intention indicates that the additional, i.e. coefficient, events are processed as a (new) part of the current intention. Additional events are included in set of events in the agents' circumstance (see page 151), therefore the exact sequence of event processing is not controlled explicitly. The platform-specific function $eval(te_s, te_d)$ evaluates condition statements (κ) with respect to the current execution context of the relevant agent. A boolean is returned ($eval : S, D \longrightarrow \{true, false\}$).

The additional rule (see Equation 5.3) describes the operating principle of activated modules [Bordini, 2010]. Implementations of these modules interpret the provided mapping configuration and induce the indicated events in the surrounding agent. Afterwards the agent reasoning continues and is not affected. This is expressed by extending the specification of the event selection step *SelEv* with a rule (see Equation 5.3) that defines the processing of events that are in the set of observed events S. If $te \notin S$, the original selection rules (SelEv1,2) are applicable (see Equations 5.1 and 5.2). The original event (te) is selected for processing ($S_E(C_E) = \langle te, i\rangle$) and is stored in the temporal structure (T'_ϵ) for subsequent processing. The insertion of events ($te_d \in D$), which correspond to observed events $m(te)$, is guarded by the conditions (κ). The insertion is carried out when the condition of the current mapping evaluates to true ($eval(te, m(te))$). Otherwise, the event is not inserted and the reasoning continues. The function $l(te_s, te_d)$ determines the intention in which events are inserted. The reasoning cycle of BDI agents is only minimally extended, thus the events te_d are not immediately processed. Instead these events are queued in C'_E for subsequent processing by the original reasoning cycle.

$$\textbf{SelEvCM} \quad \frac{S_E(C_E) = \langle te, i\rangle \quad (te \in S)}{\langle ag, C, M, T, SelEv\rangle \longrightarrow \langle ag, C', M, T', RelPl\rangle} \quad (5.3)$$

where:

$$C'_E = \begin{cases} C_E \cup \{\langle m(te), l(te, m(te))\rangle\} \setminus \{\langle te, i\rangle\} & if\ eval(te, m(te)) = true \\ C_E \setminus \{\langle te, i\rangle\} & otherwise \end{cases} \qquad T'_\epsilon = \langle te, i\rangle$$

5.2.6 Application Examples of Activated Modules

Besides the realization of Coordination Endpoints (cf. Definition 5.1) [Sudeikat and Renz, 2010b], the described extension to the capability concept has been applied to supplement the distributed monitoring of agent executions [Sudeikat and Renz, 2007a] and to integrate run-time execution checks [Sudeikat et al., 2006].

The activation of agent modules was field-tested as an extension of Jadex-based *capabilities* [Braubach et al., 2006a] (cf. Section 2.2.1). The observation of events is realized with a platform-level event-listening mechanism. Within this particular agent programming framework, conventional program objects can be registered for the observation of reasoning events, which are defined in the package jadex.runtime.Systemevent. Observations are enabled by the implementation of a specific interface (jadex.runtime.ISystemEventListener) and consequently, the registered objects are are notified about the occurrence of events. Platform-level observation tools, i.e. the *Jadex*

Introspector and *Tracer* [Pokahr and Braubach, 2007a], use this mechanism to visualize the agent reasoning. The induction of reasoning events can be triggered with the *application programming interface* (API) that is provided by the agent framework. it enables the procedural prescription of modifications of the surrounding agent from within a capability [Pokahr and Braubach, 2007b].

Monitoring Agent Execution

The monitoring of the agent execution is a basic requirement for the simulation-based analysis of agent-based applications that is indispensable for the construction of self-organizing systems (cf. Section 6.7). When the utilized development frameworks do not support the observation of agent execution, development teams have to realize this functionality by themselves. The encapsulation of the monitoring of agents in coefficient agent modules is discussed in [Sudeikat and Renz, 2007a].

The operating principle of the observation is illustrated in Figure 5.8. Agents are prepared for observation by including a specific, activated capability module (*Co-Efficient Capability*). This module is configured to observe the execution within the host agent (*Observed Agent*). In [Sudeikat and Renz, 2007a], the monitored agents follow the BDI architecture, thus the observable behaviors are defined as sub-graphs of their contained goal/plan tree-structure, cf. Section 2.4. The reasoning inside the module detects the agent's adoption of a different behavior, makes the required time measurement, and communicates observations to one or more agent(s) (*Observing Agent*). The reactive handling of the incoming messages and the processing of the contained observations are encapsulated in a conventional *Capability* [Busetta et al., 2000; Braubach et al., 2006a]. The measurements are stored in the agent's knowledge base and are subsequently available for processing inside the observing agent. The observations of the Marsworld example (cf. Figure 4.20) were obtained with this mechanism.

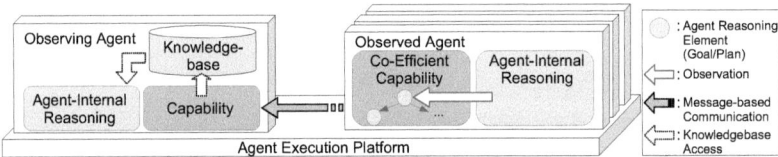

Figure 5.8: Monitoring of agent execution, following [Sudeikat and Renz, 2007a]

Embedding Agent Assertions

The use of assertion statements inside BDI-agents to document agent models and increase the observability of erroneous agent states is described in Section 2.6.2. The encapsulation of the evaluation of assertion statements in activated agent modules is demonstrated in [Sudeikat et al., 2006] for the Jadex agent system (cf. Section 2.2.2). The evaluation of assertions is enabled by including a specific capability (*jadex.assertion.Assert*). Otherwise assertions are ignored. On agent startup this capability registers for the events that originate from belief accesses and the adoption of goals or plans. Upon notification of these events, the assertion, which is annotated to the modified agent element, is extracted, evaluated, and violations are reported with detailed warnings [Sudeikat et al., 2006].

Assertions can be given by arbitrary Java programming language statements, which correspond to the Jadex-specific expression language [Pokahr and Braubach, 2007b]. These can be annotated to belief, beliefset, goal, and plan elements in the declarations of Jadex agents. Listing 5.1 is an example of the annotation of an assertion to a beliefset, i.e. a set of agent knowledge values. The code fragment is an excerpt from the *Sentry* agents of the Marsworld example,[3] (cf. Section 4.3.4). The set of target-locations, which are to be examined for the presence of ore, are stored in the

---

[3]http://jadex-agents.informatik.uni-hamburg.de/xwiki/bin/view/Usages/Examples

5.2. ARCHITECTURE: DECENTRALIZED COORDINATION ENACTMENT

set *my_targets*. The annotated assertion checks that the sum of locally stored locations does not exceed the absolute number of available targets in the simulation environment.

```
...
<!-- The seen targets. -->
<beliefset name="my_targets" class="Target">
  <assertion>
    $agent.getBeliefbase().getBeliefSet("my_targets").getFacts().length
    &lt;=
    ((Environment) $agent.getBeliefBase().getBelief("environment").getFacts())
    .getTargets().length
  </assertion>
</beliefset>
...
```

Listing 5.1: An assertion statement, which is annotated to a *beliefset* declaration, checks the maximum amount of contained elements [Sudeikat et al., 2006]. The entity < escapes the < character.

Coordination Endpoints: Separating Process-Participation from Agent-Functionality

The realization of Coordination Endpoints as agent-internal elements allows the communication overhead that results from externalized approaches to influencing/configuring agents (see Section 5.1.2) to be avoided. Instead endpoints only communicate via the associated Coordination Media. Extending the module concept is an approach to integrate the required functionality in general-purpose agent architectures without explicit preparation of coordination concerns by modifications of the agent architectures. Instead localized modifications of the module realizations are required.

The generic structure of an Endpoint contains three major concerns [Sudeikat and Renz, 2010b] (see Figure 5.4). The publication and perception of events are two facets of the Medium-based interactions that can be encapsulated in a single *communication* component. The *Coordination Information Interpreter* processes the perceived information, interprets the local process configuration, and determines how the surrounding agents are affected. This functionality is realized as a conventional agent module, except for the utilization of the Inducement interface to inject contributive reasoning events into the agent [Sudeikat and Renz, 2010b]. The *Agent State Interpreter* is realized as a co-efficient module. It registers for the observation of behavior adjustments, encapsulates the processing of these observations inside the module and affects, according to the circumstances, the initiation of interactions via Media.

5.2.7 Event-based Configuration Interface

The operation in Endpoints requires to observe and influence the execution of the host agent. The design objective is to provide an abstraction level that can be used to define the interface between Endpoints and agents. The behaviors that agents can show are described and the integration of different agent architectures is enabled by a generic conception. Using this abstraction, developers define an interface that is sued by Endpoints to get notified about changes in the agent execution and to propose the adoption of behaviors. Here, the interface definition is described on a conceptual level. Its use is part of the configuration language that is discussed in Section 5.3.

Agent-based programming languages and execution environments typically rely on event-based execution cycles (cf. Section 2.4, example in Section 2.2.1). Events denote changes in the state of the agent execution, e.g. the reception of a message or the change of an agent-intern data element. The observable events can be classified in four principal categories. Their actual embodiment depends on the agent architecture and agent platform used. *State Events* signify modifications of agent-internal data structures, e.g. belief updates. *Activity Events* indicate that agents start the exhibition of specific activities, e.g. the activation of tasks or plans. *Model Events* denote run-time changes of the underlying agent model, e.g. the loading of agent modules or registration of new belief values. Finally, *Communication Events* mark communicative activities, e.g. the sending and receiving of inter-agent messages.

Systemic descriptions of coordination processes rely on the classifications of agents according to the behavioral stance that agents currently adopt. These classifications serve as an abstraction of the agent execution configurations and are used to describe the subsets of agents that causally influence each other. The events that result from the event-based reasoning within agent-oriented execution environments provide a convenient interface to the classification of agent activities into distinct behavior types. The identification of events, which are significant for the coordination, within general purpose software components typically requires preparations of the executables. One prominent means for integrating perceptions of events is *Aspect-Oriented Programming* (AOP) [Kiczales et al., 1997] or the use of Architectural Styles and Design Pattern, e.g. *implicit invocation* [Shaw and Garlan, 1996] or *observer* pattern [Gamma et al., 1995].

Here, events are used to categorize the execution states of agent types. Subsets of reasoning events are associated to *behaviors*. The set of behaviors (B) corresponds to the behavior-oriented nodes in an ACBG-graph and associated events signify when the agent adopted the described behavioral stance. This categorization of events corresponds to the classification of intermediate, *mesoscopic* agent behaviors (cf. Section 3.4), as it is defined when the agent changed the behavioral stance within the application domain. These identified behaviors do not necessarily find a 1:1 correspondence in the programming constructs, but may also signify the congregation of different activities that change the observable behavior of the agent. Examples are changes in the agent knowledge-base or the adoption of goals. An agent model of a hypothetical robot design, may comprise an internal representation of the battery charge the supplies the hardware. Within certain value ranges of the available charge, the agent may behave differently as the lack of energy renders it not fully operational. It may have to reduce speed, carry less cargo or search for recharge stations. Differing nuances of the operational state of an agent are modeled as behaviors that are signified by the ranges of charge values. Events that modify the charge into a different value range or lead to deviations within a certain time frame would be associated to these behaviors. In addition, actuated agent elements, e.g. the activation of a goal, can be used to signify a behavioral stance. Even when goals are currently suspended [Braubach et al., 2005c], the activation of a goal indicates that the agent is committed to achieving a certain condition. Groups of these commitments can be classified as distinct behavioral stances on a macroscopic observation-level.

These behaviors of agents are associated to sets of events which signify that the agent adopted a specific behavioral stance. These events are denoted by modifications of agent model elements. The set of reasoning events that are executed by the agent reasoning mechanism vary, based on the agent platform used. Agent-oriented programming languages conceal these events from the developers of agents as the events concern the detailed realization of the agent-reasoning mechanism. However, the agent model elements are programming constructs that are exposed to agent developers. Therefore, the introduced indirection allows the designer of Coordinating Processes to map process-behaviors to elements of the agent-design. Otherwise the mapping would reference platform specific events that are internal to the platform realization.

Providers of the endpoint realizations are responsible for defining the semantics of references to agent elements for the underlying agent platform. Agent elements are defined as either *continual* or *volatile*. Continual elements are always present in the agent model. These refer to static properties of agent configuration, such as the availability of belief properties or capabilities. Volatile elements describe design elements that change over time. These elements *persist* for a certain time or are *instantaneous*. Examples for persisting elements are goal and plan elements. These are activated and deactivated by the agent reasoning. Correspondingly, design elements that are immediately handled, i.e. removed, are instantaneous, e.g. the reception of a message. Agent-knowledge elements themselves are continuous but are treated as volatile elements as the content objects may be changed, i.e. are not persistent. The modifications of the specified element are observed and actuations are realized as modifications of these elements.

A language model that expresses these mappings is discussed in Section 5.3. This language describes Coordinating Processes as structures of relations among agents and allows the definitions of behaviors with references to reasoning events within agent models to be concretized. The operation of endpoints is prepared by including the required endpoint modules within agent types and providing them with specifications of the agent elements that have to be observed or actuated

5.2. ARCHITECTURE: DECENTRALIZED COORDINATION ENACTMENT

by endpoints. This can be done manually and the automation of the filtering and the loading of endpoint modules is discussed in Section 5.3.4.

The identified subsets of relevant events are *annotated* to the agent instances. These annotations are meta information that document the events that are relevant for the coordination. Using annotations, it is declared that an agent-reasoning event signifies the adoption of an agent-behavior. Besides the documenting, the associating of this information to agents allows Endpoint realizations to be decoupled from the coordination models. At run-time, the endpoints do not process the complete coordination model but only the relevant annotations. A side effect of this decoupling is that annotations can be modified at run-time to manipulate the coordination-related activities of individual agents. The run-time adjustment of Coordinating Processes is not addressed in this dissertation but is, in principle, prepared by the architectonic conception. Upon startup of the endpoint, it searches the local annotations and configures itself accordingly. Annotations are compacted and contain only relevant information for the operation of Endpoints in order to minimize their memory overhead. Therefore, the associations to behaviors are neglected, but only the effects of event observations and perceptions about coordination media are provided. Consequently, only the necessary information about the prescribed process are made available to the Endpoints.

Definition 5.2 *(Coordination Annotation)* A *Coordination Annotation (CA)* is a data-structure that documents an agent model (see Figure 5.4, page 146). It is a tuple of the form $ca = <e_i, e_t, r_i, r_d, r_t, m_i, c, I, M_p, M_d>$. The elements are: an identifier (e_i) and the type (e_t) of an agent element; the identifier (r_i), the direction (r_d), and the type (r_t) of a systemic relation; the identifier m_i of the affected module; a condition (c); a set of inhibiting agent elements (I); a set of mappings of element parameters (M_p) and a set of mappings of agent data elements (M_d).

The two initial elements uniquely identify agent model elements by an agent-intern *identifier* (e_i) and the *type* (e_t) of the element. The set of valid event types $(E_t, e_t \in E_t)$ depends on the utilized agent platform. For BDI-style agents examples of this set are given in Section 5.3.2. The following element r_i is a unique *identifier* of the relation that the annotated event is associated to. The element r_d denotes the *direction* of the event processing. Two values are valid for r_d to indicate that event observations are *published* (d_{pub}) or that the denoted event is to be dispatched upon the *perception* of influences (d_{per}). The element r_t denotes the *type* of influence that is enacted at the receiving endpoints. The influences are either positive or negative (+/-). The element m_i is an *identifier* of the medium-specific endpoint module that is used for enactment. Endpoint realizations are provided in libraries of uniquely identifiable components. The processing of events is guarded by the following two elements.

The element c contains a *condition* statement that guards the communication and affection of events. Providers of endpoint realizations are responsible for equipping a function $eval(c)$ that interprets the condition statement on the current agent state and returns a boolean value. When the condition is not valid, the corresponding event is ignored. The subsequent element I is a set of *inhibiting* agent elements. When these elements are active the corresponding event, as identified by the combination of e_i, e_t, is ignored.

The last two elements define data that are communicated within publications of behavior adjustments. These elements configure a mapping mechanism that is detailed in Section 5.3.2. Publishing endpoints extract data values from the agent state and integrate these in the communications of observed adjustments. These values can be referenced by a key that is used at the receiving Endpoints to control where the contained values are stored. Two sets define the mapping of element *parameters* M_p, respectively of agent *data* elements M_d, e.g. parts of the agent-knowledge. When the agent programming language supports the parameterization of agent elements, e.g. the goals in BDI agents, the mappings $m_p \in M_p$ describe that parameters of the annotated element (e_i, e_t) are communicated. A single mapping (m_p) is a tuple $< p_i, r >$ that contains the *identifier* of the parameter (p_i) and a *reference* (r). When events (e_i, e_t) are published, the given parameter (p_i) is extracted and integrated in the communication under the corresponding reference identifier (r). Vice versa, perceiving endpoints extract communicated values by the reference (r) and store the value in the identified parameter (p_i) of the event (e_i, e_t). In addition, agent data elements can be communicated. These mapping declarations ($m_d \in M_d$) consist of a tuple $< d_i, r, e_{td}, m >$. In addition to the identifier of the data element (d_i) and the referencing identifier (r), the type of the data element (e_{td}) and the mode (m) of extraction or insertion, of the data is specified. The set of element types ($e_{td} \in E_{td}$) is a subset of the agent model elements that are provided by the agent platform ($E_{td} \subset E_t$). Single valued data elements are communicated and overwritten by these mappings and the mode element allows the extraction and insertion of other data types, e.g. vectors of values, to be configured. For BDI-style agents, the configuration of mappings in concretized in Section 5.3.2.

These annotations are specific for each agent type, in order to enable the declaration of joint influences on different agent types. The differing internal structures of the agent models are considered by providing separated declarations of the extraction and storing of information for each agent type. The filtering of specifications of Coordinating Processes, which prepares the influence enactment (cf. Section 5.3.4), is responsible for equipping each endpoint with the annotations that are tailored to its internal structure.

This information is annotated to agent instances at run-time. The techniques that are used for associating annotation models to agents depend on the agent-execution environment. Some languages provide means for associating meta-information to programming language constructs, e.g. in the Java programming language (see Section 2.6.2, page 30) or the Jason agent platform [Bordini et al., 2007]. Alternatively, annotations can be integrated as specialized data-structures inside the agent knowledge.

5.2.8 Extending Agent-Interfaces by Adaptivity Components

The practicability of the Endpoint-based integration of coordination logic is enhanced by providing the ability to procedurally define the observations and modifications that are available to Endpoints. The original events within the agent reasoning cycle provide a fine-grained interface to the execution of agents and the classification of behaviors and developers need tool support to tune their classification, i.e. the decision whether an event signifies the adoption of a significant event.

Definition 5.3 *(Adaptivity Component) An Adaptivity Component (AC) is an agent module that provides an optional interface between the agent and contained Endpoints (see Figure 5.4, page 146). The AC provides a set of events (S), stimuli, that are to be triggered or observed by Endpoints.*

The events that are offered by ACs extend the set of reasoning events that are available to Endpoints for observation and actuation. The additional events that concern the observation of agents allow developers to procedurally define the observation of agent-behavior adjustments. In this respect, the AC contains the agent-reasoning logic that decides when an adjustment has taken place. The logic raises the event in order to signal the happening to observing Endpoints. Alternatively, modifications can be encapsulated within ACs to enable fine-grained control of modifications of the surrounding agent. Besides the constrains that are available in the annotation format (see above), the invocation of the domain knowledge when their activation is appropriate can be procedurally encoded. This allows the prescription of activities that are required for the coordination and can are not available in the functionality of the agent implementations. Examples are considerations whether the current behavior should be adjusted or complex updates of the agent knowledge, and the scheduling of elaborate modifications. In these cases, it is purposive procedurally encode the adjustments/activities.

Figure 5.9 illustrates the mediation of ACs between the application logic, which is encoded in the agents, and enclosed Endpoints. This illustration magnifies the internal structure of the agents that participate in a coordination process, as shown in Figure 5.2, and introduces ACs as agent-intern elements that interface between Endpoint and application logic. ACs do not encapsulate the agent logic but extend the set of available specialized reasoning events. These events do not

5.2. ARCHITECTURE: DECENTRALIZED COORDINATION ENACTMENT

result from the agent internal-logic design but are introduced as coordination-related markers. Prescriptions of the rise or processing of these events realizes partitions of the coordination logic. The observation and actuation of these events is enabled by the same technical facilities that facilitate the accessing of the agent-intern application logic.

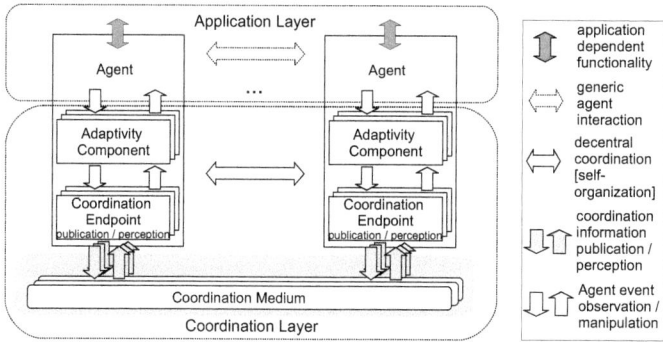

Figure 5.9: Adaptivity components are an optional means for defining events for the observation/manipulation of agents

Providers of ACs have to ensure that their internal processing does not interfere with the processing of agents. Observation-related events are assumed to be devoid of side-effects and the events that trigger associated agent modifications are to suggest the adoption of a behavior. Programming constructs may enable the enforcement of behavior adoptions, but it is imperative that AC-designs ensure the autonomy of host agents. Substantial processing in the classification/modification of agents must be balanced against the frequency of their invocation, as the procedural instructions are executed whenever the observations or modifications are considered.

The ACs define clusters of agent observations and/or modifications and the Endpoint access is not restricted, so that they may be shared concurrently by several endpoints. ACs are realized in the agent-programming framework that is used to built the host agent. A drawback of this approach is that the programming of ACs is not supported by a coherent language model. Instead the internal operation of the AC is realized with the programming abstractions that are provided by the development environment. This approach is used since the reuse of platform-concepts idioms that may be specific to a certain agent-oriented programming language to be reused. Developers that integrate the coordination are assumed to be familiar with the programming models that were used to realize the agent and application logic.

Endpoints realize coordination-related activities, i.e. the monitoring and publication of agent-behavior adjustments, as well as the processing of these publications and subsequent adjustments of agents. The presented interfacing between these activities and the agent-internal reasoning enforces a separation of the prescriptions of agent-activities and their interdependencies. Using event-based reasoning for this purpose allows for a novel, non-invasive separation technique. Related approaches (cf. Section 5.1.2) to the integration of coordination rely on blending the coordination logic into agent models. Examples are the provision of specific API elements that facilitate the prescription of coordination-related activities in the agent programming language [Piunti et al., 2008; Ricci et al., 2008] or the modification of agent models to influence the agent execution, e.g. suspending of activities until permission is granted by external services [Singh, 1998]. The presented interface allows the inclusion of coordination-related activities without modifying the agent models themselves. In addition, agent execution is not constrained but rather the modifications rely on supplementing the agent with additional, coordination-related activities that are introduced to the agent execution when appropriate. The additional activities use the computational resources of the host agent, e.g. CPU cycled memory consumption, etc., but do not affect the operation of the agent models. Therefore, the approach allows for *transparent* coordination, as agent models are not modified to prepare coordination. Instead agent execution is modified by supplemented activities that are automatically integrated in the agent execution.

5.2.9 Agent-State Interpreter

The *Agent-State Interpreter* (ASI) is a reusable component that observes agent execution to identify the modifications of agent elements that signify the publishable adjustments within agents. These observations and their publications via the Coordination Medium (cf. Section 5.2.10) are configured by CAs (cf. Definition 5.2).

The initialization of these components processes the set of annotations that are present in an agent model and configures the utilized conservation mechanism. The initialization relies on inferring the agent-reasoning events that are to be processed from the set of elements that are given in the annotation models. This mapping is prescribed by a function $trans : E_t \to Ev_t$, which translates the type of an agent model element ($e_t \in E_t$, cf. Section 5.2.7) to a set of reasoning events that modify it. In general, the sets of model elements correspond to the applied agent architecture, except for platform-specific extensions. Examples are the different goal types that are supported by BDI-oriented agent platforms [Braubach et al., 2005c]. The projected set of reasoning events is specific to the processing inside the agent-platform.

At the initialization of the interpreter the function $trans$ is evaluated for all annotations to infer the set of relevant agent events. The interpreter then registers itself for the observation of the host agent, as described in Section 5.2.4. Subsequently, the interpreter is notified when an event of interest occurs during agent execution and the Algorithm 5.1 describes the processing of these events. These data elements within Annotations are described in Section 5.2.7. The reasoning events are platform-specific. It is assumed that these events allow the agent models element that is accessed or modified to be identified.

The function $appl : Ca, Ev \to Ca$ returns the set of Annotations ($ca \in Ca$) that are *applicable* for the run-time event that has occurred ($ev \in Ev$). Only those annotations in which the direction element r_d is set to *publish* are applicable. This function checks whether the event modified the agent elements that are identified by the elements e_i, e_t within a given ca. For each Annotation in this subset, it is checked if the agent state permits the publication (line 3). The function $eval$ (cf. Section 5.2.7) checks if the corresponding condition statement ($ca.c$) evaluates to true and the function $chck$ checks if one element in a specified set of agent elements ($ca.I$) is currently active. Taking the example of foraging ants (see Section 4.4.1, page 120), the transport of resources to the nest could be indicated by the activation of a goal *transporting*. Additional constraints could indicate that this behavior is only relevant for publication when the quality or amount of the transported goods exceeds certain thresholds and there is no other behavior, e.g. *flee_from_predator* is not active at the same time (inhibition). Only the enabled annotations are processed. Declared mappings of element parameters (lines 5 to 7) and agent-intern data (lines 8 to 10) are extracted and added to the data structure D that contains key-value records ($d =< k_i, V_i >$). This data structure corresponds to the map of attributes that are contained in the *Coordination Information* (cf. Section 5.2.10) that is communicated by Coordination Media. The function $extr_p$ extracts parameter values from the processed event. The parameterized model element is identified by the element identifier and the type of the element ($ca.e_i, ca.e_t$). The declaration of the mapping denotes the identifiers of the parameter value ($m_p.p_i$) and the key ($m_p.r$) under which the value is stored in the data structure D. The extraction of agent data elements is denoted by the function $extr_d$. The information that is needed to identify and store an agent-intern data element is given in the mapping declaration m_d (cf. Section 5.2.7). With respect to the ant example, communications, e.g. via a digital pheromones in a virtual environment, could contain quality attributes of the transporter resources or the distance of the resource location from the nest. These could be extracted from the parameters of the currently active element, e.g. the transport goal, or from the agent knowledge.

After these preparations, the publication of the event observation is triggered. The method

$pupl()$ creates a *Coordination Information* element and actuates its dispatch by the *Publication* component (cf. Section 5.2.2), which encapsulates the accessing of the associated Medium. The publication contains the identifier of the enacted relation (r_i) and the extracted data. The details of the processed event are omitted. This anonymizes publishing agents and enforces the decoupling of Endpoint components.

Algorithm 5.1: Agent observation

input: Agent-reasoning event (ev)
1 initialization: CA_a = the set of annotations in the agent model;
2 **foreach** $ca \in appl(CA_a, ev)$ **do**
3   **if** $eval(ca.c) = true \land \neg chck(ca.I)$ **then**
4         $D = \{\}$;
5   **foreach** $m_p \in ca.M_p$ **do**
6             $D \leftarrow extr_p(ca.e_i, ca.e_t, m_p)$;
7   **end**
8   **foreach** $m_d \in ca.M_d$ **do**
9             $D \leftarrow extr_d(m_d)$;
10   **end**
11         $publ(r_i, D)$;
12   **end**
13 **end**

5.2.10 Coordination Media

Coordination Media provide a shared coordination space that allows Coordination Endpoints to inform each other about the locally exhibited adjustments of system elements. Located in a logical middleware layer, distinct Media coexist and realize separated coordination spaces. It has been noted that MAS designs can make use of different environment models [Gouaich and Michel, 2005] (see Section 2.3.2, page 21). In this respect, Media are solely responsible for the transfer of coordination-related information and are separated from the agent logic. With respect to the architectural model proposed here, the generic concept of a coordination medium (see Section 2.5, page 25) is concretized. In this context, Media do not only provide environmental abstractions but are conceived as encapsulations of distinct dynamics of information flows between agents. The media provide realizations of Decentralized Coordination Mechanisms (cf. Section 3.2.1) [Sudeikat and Renz, 2008b] to provide additional environments that control the dynamics of information exchanges. These realizations of mechanisms make use of specific interaction models (cf. Figure 3.9), as provided by coordination infrastructures (cf. Section 5.1.2). Optionally, implementations of CM may provide synchronization facilities, e,g, round-based interactions, e.g. to facilitate system simulations.

Definition 5.4 *(Coordination Medium) A Coordination Medium (CM) is a design abstraction that describes the encapsulation of an interaction technique (see Figure 5.4, page 146). Media encapsulate Decentralized Coordination Mechanisms (cf. Section 3.2.1) that can be accessed by a publish/subscribe interface. The Media serve as communication-infrastructures that decouple Coordination Endpoints (cf. Definition 5.1).*

The media provide realizations of coordination mechanisms, i.e. the interaction techniques that allow for decentralized inter-agent coordination (cf. Section 3.2.1). The basic functionality of these Media realizations is the *filtering* and *routing* of the published information [Mühl et al., 2006] to control the dynamics of information dissemination.

There are two principal design approaches for realizing CMs. First, a Medium can be provided by a dedicated networked entity. This approach is particularly appropriate if it is crucial for the Mechanism functionality that a consistent model of the agents and their interactions is maintained. This is particularly the case for environment-mediated mechanisms [Weyns et al., 2008] that localize agents in a virtual environment. These infrastructure elements are conceptionally centralized and contradict the MAS philosophy, as the system becomes dependent on a single component. However on a technical level, distributed computing techniques, e.g. clustering and replication mechanism, allow the infrastructures to be distributed in order to support increasing scaling to meet increasing system sizes. These design approaches are named *infrastructure-based*, since they rely on a networked data-structure that maintains the consistency of the published information and controls the access by system elements.

Secondly, Media can exist as design abstractions that do not map to particular computational elements but result from the message exchange between Endpoints. Different messaging infrastructures are applicable for realizing this kind of media. This Media are named *routing*-based, since the dynamics of information dissemination are controlled by the collective forwarding of messages. In agent-based systems the messaging infrastructure of the platforms can be used to implement these Media. Interoperability is enabled by standard messaging formats, e.g. the FIPA Agent Communication specifications [Foundation for Intelligent Physical Agents, 2003]. Alternatives are dedicated messaging infrastructures for distributed systems, e.g. the *Java Messaging Service* (JMS) [Sun Microsystems, 2002] and the *Corba Notification Service* [, OMG]. These infrastructures particularly support the integration of heterogeneous system elements. An example is the arrangement of Endpoints in overlay networks that constrain the forwarding of publications to connected system elements (cf. Appendix B.1.2).

In [Sudeikat and Renz, 2008b], the principal design alternatives for the realization of Coordination Media are discussed (cf. Figure 5.10). Fully *decentralized* realizations (I) emulate a shared coordination space by the mutual exchange of inter-agent messages. The participation in these Media can be implemented by communicating agents or can be separated by using networked communication frameworks. These frameworks are infrastructures for the environments and/or the coordination of agents and are discussed in the Sections 2.3.1, 2.5, and 5.1.2).

Alternatively, *centralized* provisions of coordination spaces (II) can be used. These shared spaces can be established and maintained by dedicated agents (IIa) or on dedicated coordination infrastructures (IIb) that are deployed on networked servers. The providing elements are responsible for managing the concurrent access of spaces and to ensuring consistency. These approaches are called *centralized* [Sudeikat and Renz, 2008b], because the space is provided by dedicated infrastructures, i.e. agents or middlewares, as publicly accessible components. Specific infrastructure realizations may enable distribution, e.g. multiple servers, by supporting the required administrative functions, e.g. duplications, replications and load-balancing. Prominent examples of coordination infrastructures are Linda-style *tuple spaces* [Gelernter and Carriero, 1992]. In addition, specific infrastructures particularly address the provision of environment abstractions in agent-based applications at run-time and support their accessing by agent implementations [Viroli et al., 2007] (cf. Section 2.3.1).

Thirdly, the coordination activities can be *delegated* to another (situated) MAS (III). The agents in the supplementing MAS function as proxies for agents in the original MAS and interact autonomously in the coordination space to provide coordination-related information to their individual orderer agent. This design principle is successful in application settings, where spatial environment interactions can be decoupled from the problem-solving agent models, e.g. in manicuring control [Hadeli et al., 2004b; Holvoet and Valckenaers, 2007]. System elements *send out* mobile agents to distribute and/or collect information in a shared environment. Implementation patterns for delegation are reviewed in [Holvoet et al., 2009].

Here, Coordination Media are described on a high abstraction level that focuses on the requirements of Medium implementations, rather than on their detailed realization. The internally utilized interaction technique is encapsulated and hidden from the Coordination Endpoint, thus direct interactions, e.g. interaction protocols [Viroli and Ricci, 2004] and environment-mediated techniques, e.g. digital pheromones [Parunak and Brueckner, 2004], can be interchangeably integrated in applications. A collection of coordination media was realized in the DeCoMAS prototype realization. These include decentralized (I), agent-based (II) and middleware-based (II) implementations. The configuration of Media is outlined in Appendix 5.3.2 and Media realizations are exemplified in Appendix B.

5.2. ARCHITECTURE: DECENTRALIZED COORDINATION ENACTMENT

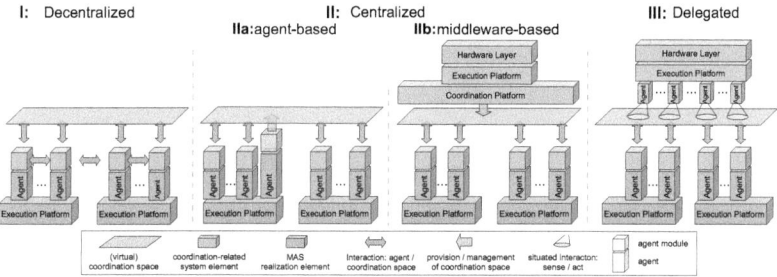

Figure 5.10: Alternatives for the realization of Coordination Media [Sudeikat and Renz, 2008b]

Notification Content Format

The notifications that are spread by Coordination Media must comply with a *record*-oriented datamodel [Mühl et al., 2006] (Chapter 3). The data-model specifies the content of event-notifications that are communicated to inform Endpoints about the occurrence of events. These elements are propagated by the the Media and contain the information about the events and optional data about the state of agent agent that published the happening.

Definition 5.5 *(Coordination Information) A Coordination Information (CI) is a data element that is communicated through Coordination Media. These elements are tuples $ci = <r_i, D>$, where D is a record model, i.e. a map, that stores data entries $d = <k_i, V_i>$ as key/value pairs. The key elements k_i are unique and map to a single value element d_v.*

The CI elements are equipped with the identifier of the relevant influence that lead to the publication of the event occurrence. The records contained are *structured* since the key values are unique [Mühl et al., 2006] (page 36). In addition, the records are *flat*, i.e. not hierarchically structured [Mühl et al., 2006]. The key elements are specified as Strings and the data values contain arbitrary programming language objects (details on a concrete realization can be found in Section 5.3.5). Each key maps to one data element and different key can be mapped to the same value.

Record-based content models enable the transport of optional data entries in event notifications, as receivers only extract the values of known keys. This model is more flexible than the detailed prescription of the contained data, e.g. as in tuple-based infrastructures [Mühl et al., 2006] (page 35) where an ordered set of attributes is predefined.

The ability to provide optional data values is required to enable the conjoint participation of different agent types in the enactment of a joint influence. The internal differences of multiple types of event publishers are taken into account by providing distinct mappings for each publishing and receiving agent type. This allows the affected elements within distinct agent models to be specified. Data values that are not processable by a receiving agent model are ignored by the endpoint. The data that can be extracted from endpoints in differing agent models is likely to vary, therefore receiving endpoints need to be adjusted to handle missing values. If necessary the extraction and processing of the communicated data can be procedurally defined in *Adaptivity Components* (cf. Section 5.2.8).

Event Publication/Perception

The internal structure of an Endpoint realization separates the logic of how to observe and influence the agent execution from the communicative behavior of endpoints (cf. Section 5.2.2). The interpreter modules (cf. Sections 5.2.9, 5.2.11) realize the observation and modification of the agent operation. Two components encapsulate the publication and perception of event observations via an associated Coordination Medium. This separation support the reuse of the internals of the Endpoint realizations. Interpreter elements only depend on the agent architecture. Once these components have been realized for an execution environment, they can be reused within Endpoint realizations that support interactions via different Media types. The interface between these components is not specified so as not to constrain the realization of these elements in different agent architectures. Details on an example realization can be found in Section 5.3.5.

The internal processing to realize publications and perceptions via Media depends greatly on the accessed medium. The perception components deal with the reception of messages via the utilized communication infrastructure, the extraction of the communicated CI-element, and the forwarding of the element to the corresponding interpreter (cf. Section 5.2.11).

Publication components encapsulate the accessing of communication infrastructures. *Agent State Interpreters* (cf. Section 5.2.9) trigger publications and provide the CI-elements that are to be sent. Publication components connect to the utilized communication-infrastructure and send the CI-element. Optionally, these elements may implement conversions of the data that are contained in CI-elements to support heterogeneous agent architectures and communication-infrastructures.

The operation of these modules can be adjusted by the configuration (language) model that is discussed in Section 5.3. These configurations are tuples of the form $mc = < m_i, P, M_{mp} >$ The element m_i refers to the identifier of the medium. The set P contains key/value pairs ($p \in P, p = < k_i, V_i >$) of statically set parameters of the interaction technique. The range of specifiable parameters is specific for each medium instance. In addition, a set of dynamically evaluated mappings (M_{mp}) can be specified. The elements m_{mp} contained in the set M_{mp} are tuples $m_{mp} = < a_i, e_i, e_t, k_i >$. The element k_i refers to the identifier of a parameter. The value of this parameter is set to a value that is extracted from the agent state at the time-point of publication. The element is identified by the identifier of the element (e_i) and the type of the element (e_t). Medium configurations can be shared among different agent types, thus the type of agent that contains the referenced element is also given (a_i). When a publication is sent, the publication component is responsible for looking up these specified mappings, extracting the agent value and storing it in the configuration. This configuration format allows parameters to be set to values to of the content of agent data elements, as described in [Sudeikat and Renz, 2008b]. The detailed configuration of the extraction of element parameters and different agent knowledge types is discussed in the Sections 5.2.7 and 5.3.2. The dynamic parameters are updated before every publication and the set of static and dynamic parameters is considered when CI-elements are communicated. Examples for the possible configurations are given in Appendix B, where examples for medium realizations are given.

5.2.11 Coordination Information Interpreter

The Coordination Information Interpreter reacts to the receipt of CI elements. The *Perception* component in an Endpoint retrieves these elements from the Medium and forwards them to the interpreter, which then processes the CI-elements and maps them against the annotations within the host agent. The annotations found indicate the required modifications of the agent instance.

The Algorithm 5.2 illustrates the processing of incoming notifications (ci, cf. Definition 5.5), i.e. CI elements. The only additional input is the set of agent annotations (CA_a) that are applicable for perceptions, i.e. the r_d element is set to *perceive*.

Only that subset of annotations is considered (line 2) in which the identifiers of the relation within the perceived element ($ci.r_i$) match the corresponding identifier in an annotation ($ca.r_i$). For each of these annotations it is checked whether the current state of the agent allows it to be influenced. The condition statement ($ca.c$) and the absence of inhibiting agent elements is checked as described Section 5.2.9. The processing of events is determined by the type of the relation ($ca.r_t$). Negative relations are handled by deactivating the agent elements. The function $deact()$ contains the platform-specific functionality for deactivating agent elements, e.g. goals (line 5). Positive relations (line 7) are handled by activating an agent-behavior,i.e. the significant agent element given in the annotation (ca, cf. Section 5.2.7). The function $evnt()$ creates the reasoning event, stored in e, that activates the agent model element indicated by the agent element identifier and the element type ($ca.e_i, ca.e_t$). The function realizes a platform-specific mapping of agent model elements to the activating reasoning event. Subsequently, the communicated parameter values are set for the event. The declared mappings ($m_p \in ca.M_p$) are iterated. For each mapping, the parameter of an event e, identified by $m_p.pi$, is fetched by the function $parm()$. This parameter is set to the value that is stored under the referencing key $m_p.r$ in the communicated ci-element. The value is extracted by the function $val()$.

Data elements are updated before the agent elements, since the functioning of the actuated agent-behavior may rely on the availability of the communicated information. The annotated mappings of communicated values to agent knowledge elements ($ca.M_d$) are iterated (line 12) and for each mapping the modified agent knowledge element is identified by the function $know()$, which is parameterized by the identifier ($m_d.d_i$) and the type ($m_d.e_{td}$) of the agent element (line 13). The value, identified by the referencing key $m_d.r$, is extracted from the communicated ci-element by the function $val()$. The update of the data element by the function $updt()$ is controlled by the parameter $m_d.m$ that identifies the mode of modifications for data structures that support different types of operations (cf. Section 5.3.2). Finally, the identified and parameterized event is dispatched in the surrounding agent model.

Algorithm 5.2: The processing of received Coordination Information

input: A received Coordination Information element (ci)
1 initialization: CA_a = the set of annotations in the agent model;
2 **foreach** $ca.r_i == ci.r_i$ **do**
3   **if** $eval(ca.c) = true \land chck(ca.I)$ **then**
4   **if** $ca.r_t = -$ **then**
5             $deact(ca.e_i, ca.e_t)$;
6   **end**
7   **else if** $ca.r_t = +$ **then**
8             $e \leftarrow evnt(ca.e_i, ca.e_t)$;
9   **foreach** $m_p \in ca.M_p$ **do**
10                 $parm(e, m_p.p_i) \leftarrow val(ci, m_p.r)$;
11   **end**
12   **foreach** $m_d \in ca.M_d$ **do**
13                 $ke \leftarrow know(m_d.d_i, m_d.e_{td})$;
14                 $d \leftarrow val(ci, m_d.r)$;
15                 $updt(ke, d, m_d.m)$;
16   **end**
17             $disp(e, D)$;
18   **end**
19   **end**
20 **end**

5.3 MASDynamics: Coordination Configuration

The previous sections discussed the architecture and prototype realization of a coordination architecture for the enactment of externalized, systemic coordination models. This architecture is complemented by a coordination language model that allows systemic coordination models to be detailed in order to prepare this enactment, i.e. the automation of inter-agent influences and interactions.

The language provides an format that is used to prescribe the participation of agents in inter-agent process. These processes, regarded as independent elements of the application design, are supported by a specific notation. Using this notation, the processes can be treated as software development artifacts that can be shared and reused. Design criteria are based on the intended use in software development. The conceptual model of a inter-agent process is given by the ACBG-based modeling of the agent coaction. Therefore, the language should allow to express the ACBGs in as abstract templates. Subsequently, these abstract representations of process will be refined and mapped to an actual software system. This mapping has to be supported in generic ways to support the mapping onto application designs that use different agent architectures. The extensibility of the language is prepared to enable that architecture specific design concepts can be integrated when needed.

The language supports two modeling levels. First, coordination strategies scan be defined in an application-independent form. These definitions consist solely of generic variable (node) and interdependency (edge) definitions. This level facilitates the reuse of coordination models since field-tested structures of interdependencies can be defined and shared in a generic description format (cf. Section 5.3.2). Secondly, an application-dependent modeling level allows both modeling elements to be detailed. System variables can be mapped to specific agent implementations by referencing the elements of agent models. These references declare in which run-time states agent instances are considered to contribute to the accumulative value of a variable, i.e. when agents exhibit the behavior that is represented by the variable. The interdependencies between these variables can be detailed by configuring which agent internal-information is to be communicated and parameterizing the interaction mechanism that realizes the actual communicative activities (cf. Section 5.3.2).

5.3.1 Language Structure

The principal structure of the MASDynamics language [Sudeikat and Renz, 2009c] is depicted in figure 5.11. The language allows a *Decentralized Coordinating Processes* among agents to be described as an *Agent Causal Behavior Graph* (ACBG, cf. Section 4.2.3). The automated enactment of this model is prepared by the detailed prescription of the design elements that constitute the self-organizing process. The generic structure of Coordinating Processes is described and the design elements, i.e. Coordination Mechanisms, are specified and configured. The process is then associated to the participating system elements. The system variables, i.e. the ACBG nodes, are mapped onto agent-based applications by referencing agent *Implementations Concepts*.

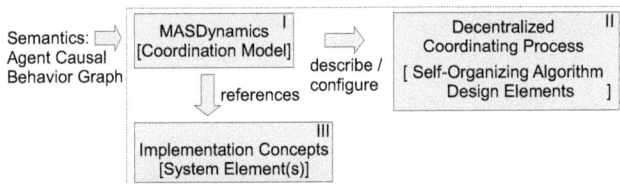

Figure 5.11: An overview of the systemic coordination language

This generic structure is detailed in Figure 5.12. ACBG graph elements (top left) are related to the conceptual model of the *Self-organizing Algorithm Design Elements* (top right) that is discussed in Section 3.3 and to the abstract structure *MAS Implementation* (bottom) that is depicted in Section 2.1.

A *MASDynamics* model describes the Coordinating Process (*Self-Regulatory Coordinating Process*) that is to be integrated in an application that is realized as a *MAS Implementation*. The model describes an ACBG, since it contains a set of *System Variables* that are connected by causal relations (*Causal Link*). Links describe the effects of *Agent Activity Interrelations* that originate from causalities and influences (cf. Section 5.3.3) among system variables. *Direct* and *Mediated* declarations of influences are explicitly distinguished. Both of them describe information flows between agents. Direct links model the direct informations flows that are emended in the application design. These links primarily describe the interrelations that are inherently present in the

5.3. MASDYNAMICS: COORDINATION CONFIGURATION

agent designs, but their enactment can be configured as well (cf. Section 5.3.2). The utilization of Decentralized Coordination Mechanisms is modeled by mediated links. The configuration of the automated enactment of interdependencies is discussed in Section 5.3.2.

The System Variables provide abstractions of the agent behaviors and the environment state. The mapping of the Coordinating Process on a concrete MAS realization is done by associating these abstractions, i.e. the ACBG nodes, to implementation elements. Declarations of behavior-related nodes $((r_{(x)}, g_{(x)}, gs_{(x)})$, cf. Section 4.2.3) indicate the agent-internal processing that signifies the activation of a relevant behavior. Environment-related nodes describe qualities of environment models.

5.3.2 Coordination Language Model

Specifications of a decentralized process are composed of three basic building blocks (cf. Figure 5.13, I). A *MASDynamics Model* can be named (*name*) and includes containers for sets of *Definitions*, *System Variables* and the *Relations* that connect variables.

Definitions: Referencing Implementation Elements

The *Definitions* section contains sets of declarations of agent types (AgentModel) and declarations of Coordination Media Endpoint realizations (*MechanismModel*). The specification of these elements is optional, as the relevant information can also be specified inline in the agent model. The redundant declaration documents the implementation elements that are referred to by the mapping of the Coordinating Process to an MAS implementation. AgentModels denote the agent implementations that participate in the described process. MechanismModels denote the endpoint models that are configured to automate enactments. Both elements allow to define an identifier (*id*) that refers to an implementation element, i.e. the path to the agent implementation (*agentModel*) or the endpoint implementation (*endpointModel*), to be defined. This available prototype implementation supports only the Jadex agent architecture (AgentModelType). For future extensibility, AgentModels contain the type of the agent implementation (*type*).

System Variables: Definition of Behavior Abstractions

The *System Variables* section contains the declarations of system variables, i.e. ACBG graph nodes, and details which agents exhibit specific behaviors. In the illustration of the model structure in Figure 5.14 the elements are distinguished by their description level. Elements either describe the macroscopic process or address the referencing of implementation elements. The former elements reflect the generic graph structure of a Coordinating Process while the latter elements define the semantics of variables, i.e. ACBG nodes, by referencing the agents that are able to exhibit the represented behaviors.

Variables are named (*name*) and it can be indicated that variables represent groups of nodes (*multiple*) and correspond to the stacked notation of graph nodes (cf. Section 4.2.3). This information allows nodes to be matched with their graphical representation. The given model denotes the variable types that were discussed in Sections 4.2.3 and 4.2.3 namely *RoleOccupation* ($r_{(x)}$), *Group* ($g_{(x)}$), *GroupMembership* ($gs_{(x)}$), and *EnvironmentProperty* ($e_{(x)}$). The behavior-describing variables extend the generic *BehaviorVariableModel* and refer to sets of agents that are able to exhibit the described course of action (*agents*). The description formalism is extensible, since additional environment elements and behavior abstractions can be integrated as specializations of the SystemVariable and the BehaviorVariableModel elements.

The referencing of implementation elements (gray-colored elements in Figure 5.14) is optional. Behavior-describing nodes reference agent models (*AgentReference*), which are identified by a unique name of the agent type (*agentId*). The stereotype <<*references*>> indicates that this identifier refers to the name of the agent type in the implementation model. The notation assumes that agent instances are realizations of an agent type, i.e. a class of agent realizations. An example is the XML-based specification of the structure of agents in the Jadex system (see Section

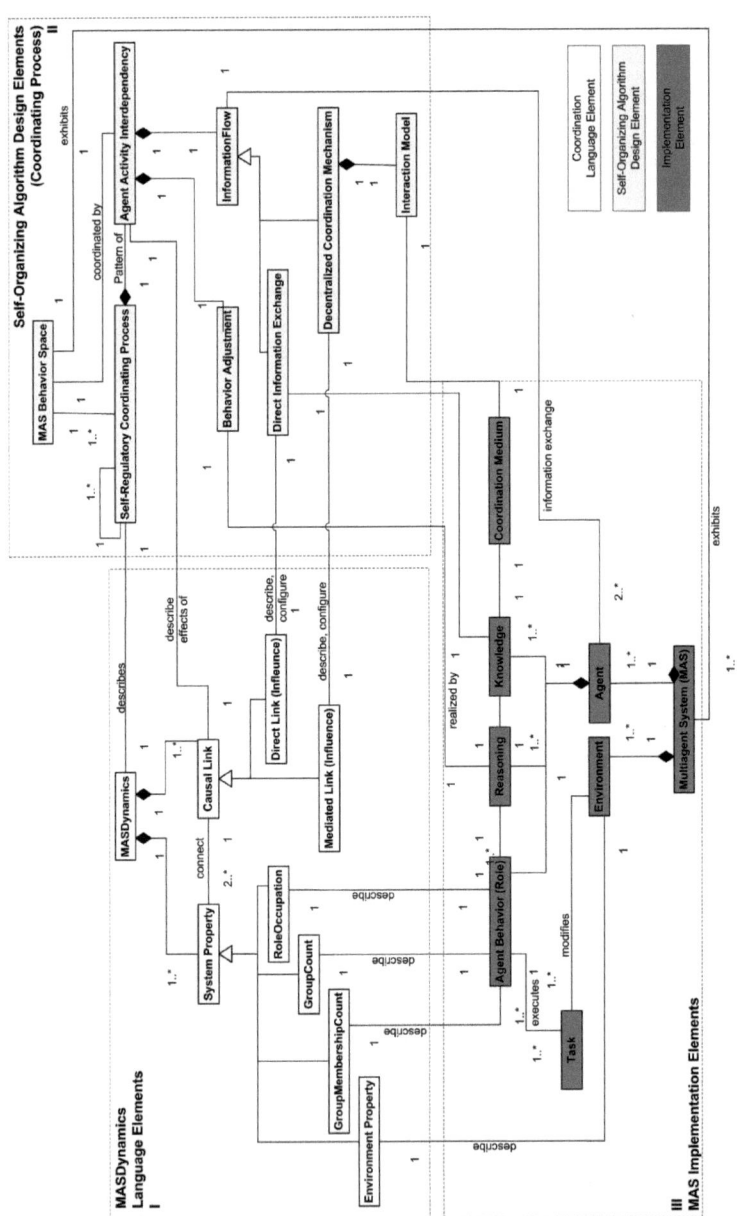

Figure 5.12: The detailed structure of the systemic coordination language, adapted from [Sudeikat and Renz, 2009c]; The layout relates to the three principal partitions of the language model (I,II,III; see Figure 5.11)

5.3. MASDYNAMICS: COORDINATION CONFIGURATION

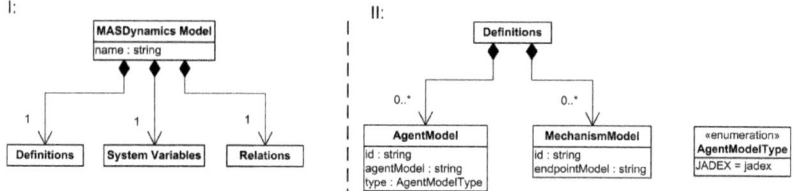

Figure 5.13: The structure of the specification of a decentralized inter-agent process (I) and the *Definitions* section (II)

2.2.2). These specifications are templates for the run-time instances of agents. References can be annotated with information that describes when the agent instances exhibit the denoted behavior. A set of references to agent-internal implementation elements can be given and the activation and/or modification of these elements indicates the events that signify the adoptions of behaviors (cf. Section 5.2.7).

An element is uniquely identified by the combination of its name (*elementId*) and its type (*elementType*). The agent elements that can be annotated are either *volatile* or *continual*. Volatile elements refer to abstractions of agent activities, e.g. tasks, goals and plans. The static structure of the agent model defines which activities are available to agent instances, and at a certain time point a subset of these is active in an individual agent. The referencing of these events indicates that a behavior is exhibited when the referenced element is activated. Continual elements are always present in the agent model. These refer to static properties of agent configuration, e.g. the presence of certain belief data structures or agent capabilities. These properties are static in the way that they define the configuration of the agent. The values change at run time but the structure of the agent remains the same. When continual elements are referenced, their modifications signify agent adjustments.

Element types are specific for the target agent platform(s) and their availability is an extension point for the conceptual model. The language is adjusted by providing tailored tests of element types. Figure 5.14 gives an example of a BDI-specific extension (*BDIAgentElementTypes*). The available types are prescribed in an *enumeration*. Using the Jadex-specific BDI architecture (see Section 2.2.2), *belief*, *beliefset*, *goal*, and *plan* elements can be referenced. The concept of an *internal event* is not specific to the BDI architecture, but these are also available in Jadex agents. The first two element types are examples for continual elements. The knowledge base of the agent is defined on agent start-up and value changes can express significant adjustments of the agent configuration. The other elements are volatile, as they are started during the agent execution. Their initialization, i.e. the adoption of a goal, the execution of a plan or the occurrence of an internal event, can signify that the agent adjusts the exhibited behavior.

The references can be annotated with a filter *Constraints* that defines when the modifications of the referenced agent elements are significant. Filters can be defined by a boolean *Condition*. A boolean condition statement (*expression*), identified by a *name*, is given to express the circumstance in which the event indicates the adoption of the behavior. This condition is to be evaluated in the agent's context at the time point when the event occurs. Alternatively or in addition, a list of inhibiting elements (*inhibitions*) can be specified. These are also references to agent elements (*AgentReference*) of the same agent and when one of these elements is concurrently active in the same agent instance the observation of the event is not significant, i.e. the adjustment is inhibited.

170   CHAPTER 5. A SYSTEMIC PROGRAMMING MODEL

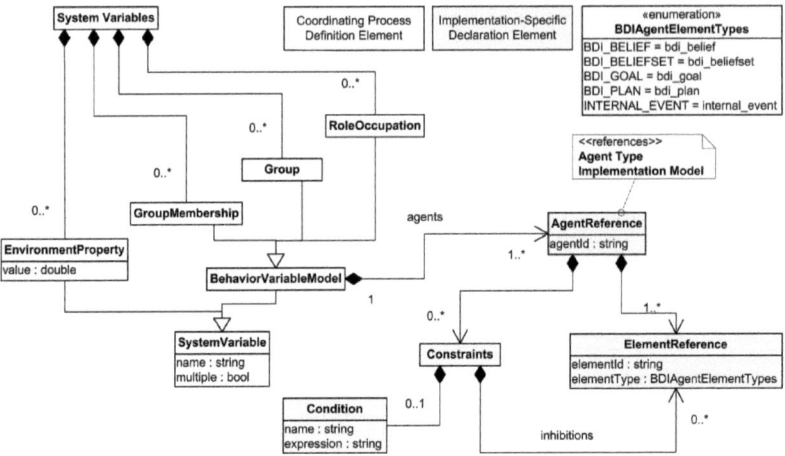

Figure 5.14: The structure of the specification of system variables

Relations: Preparing Influence Enactment

The *Relations* section of an MASDynamics model defines the causal connections between system variables that set up the collaborative process which establishes coordination. The conceptual structure of this partition is illustrated in Figure 5.15. Elements of the process definition (*Coordinating Process Definition Element*) are distinguished from elements that reference concepts of the agent implementations (*Agent-Specific Declaration Element*) or Medium realizations (*Medium-Specific Declaration Element*).

This section contains two sets of declarations of inter-variable relations. Direct (*DirectRelation*) and mediated (*MediatedRelation*) relations are distinguished. These describe the causal interdependencies and influences (cf. Section 4.2.3) that result from direct or mediated interactions among system elements. Relations can be purely descriptive, e.g. to show the relationships that are present in an implementation or the intended nexuses of a planned application. Alternatively, relations can be used as implementation elements. Their automated enactment is enabled by detailed configurations and two corresponding sets contain the corresponding models of realizations of relations (*DirectInfluenceRealization*, *DeirectInfluenceRealization*).

The configurations are separated from the relation declarations to facilitate incremental development and prototyping. Models may contain gradually expanded and revised libraries of relation configurations. Relations reference, as indicated by the annotated UML stereotype (<< *references*>>), the configuration that controls the enactment. Not-referenced configuration models are ignored, thus different medium configurations and parameterizations can be kept for later reuse and/or comparison. The detailed configurations are highly dependent on the coordinated MAS as well as on the described process. Therefore, these are contained in one data structure. Incremental development and prototyping are facilitated, as the change of a configuration only requires the adjustment of a link attribute (*realization*) that identifies the realization model currently under consideration. Links without such a reference are descriptive and therefore ignored by the enactment architecture.

The declarations of relations (*Causal Relation*) are named (*name*), and a *type* attribute describes the effects of relations. Corresponding to the connection in ACBGs (cf. Section 4.2.3) these relations are either positive or negative (*InfluenceType*). An optional *rate* attribute specifies the expected or measured averaged rate of interactions that are described by the connection.

5.3. MASDYNAMICS: COORDINATION CONFIGURATION

This is only used to document relations. The *realization* attribute refers to a realization model (see above). Finally, the links reference the connected variables (*SystemVariable*). Two possibly overlapping sets distinguish the publishing (*Publisher*) and the subscribed (*Subscriber*) variables.

The distributed coordination architecture (cf. Section 5.2) enables the automated enactment of influences among system variables. The enactment of a relation is configured providing declarations of *realization* sections (*MediatedInfluenceRealization, DirectInfluenceRealization*). Realizations contain two fundamental declaration areas.

First, the declarations of agent behaviors are concretized by mapping the adoption of behaviors to agent-intern events. These concretizations are described in a generic structure *RealizationModel* that is shared by both configuration types. Realizations contain a unique identifier (*id*) that is used to reference a concrete realization within declarations of relations. The enactment architecture automates the influences among behavior-abstracting variables (*BehaviorVariableModel*, cf. Figure 5.14) that are referenced in link declarations. Corresponding to the description of behavior-related system variables (cf. Figure 5.14), significant events are indicated by *referencing* (<< *references*>>) agent-intern implementation elements that are modified or initialized (cf. Section 5.2.7) at run-time. Two types of references are distinguished. First, the *observation* of agent elements is declared. These events signify behavioral changes in the agent execution. Secondly, a set of elements can be declared that allow to cause behavior changes (*inducement*). These elements are induced or modified, depending on the agent architecture, to influence the agent execution and propose the adoption of specific behavioral stances. Referenced elements (*AgentElement*) are uniquely identified by the identifier of the containing agents (*agentId*), the element identifier (*elementId*), and the type of the element (*elementType*). The set of valid implementation element types is specific for the applied agent architecture, e.g. for the Jadex-specific BDI dialect (see Section 2.2.2); the valid set is given by the *BDIAgentElementTypes* (cf. Figure 5.14).

Part of these references are optional specifications of transmissions of agent-internal data elements that are to be communicated within publications. Transmissions are denoted by sets of *mappings* (*Mapping*) that are declared for published and subscribed agent-elements and the communicated values are uniquely identified (*referenceId*). Mappings that are annotated to published elements define the data that are to be extracted from the agent run-time instance and communicated. These declarations are complemented with corresponding mappings within the declarations of subscribed elements that define where the transmitted data are stored upon reception. Communicated data are accessed via the referencing identifier (*referenceId*). The mappings of both sides of the communication are unconstrained, thus the mapping concept allows the definition of communications that occur between pairs of agent-event types (1:1), between a single subscribed event type and multiple published events types (n:1), vice versa between multiple subscribed events and one published event type (1:n) and among sets of published and subscribed event types (n:m).

Two types of mappings describe the possible data sources and destinations. First, agent knowledge can be extracted or modified (*DataMapping*). Agent knowledge elements are identified by their name (*elementName*) and type (*elementType*). Type definitions allow different knowledge representation concepts to be distinguished, e.g. the Jadex system allows to store local agent-knowledge to be stored in a *Belief* or a *Beliefset* (see Section 2.2.2). These types are a subset of the agent element types (e.g. *BDIAgentElementTypes*, cf. Figure 5.14). The *mode* element configures the extraction/modifications of data according to the specifics of the applied agent platform. The prototype implementation (cf. Section 5.3.5) supports four mode types. Belief Elements hold a single data object and the default mode identifier *content* indicates that this data element is to be extracted upon publication and replaces the belief value at the subscriber(s). Beliefsets hold a vector of data elements and the mode identifier *content* indicates that all contained values are to be transmitted. In addition, a numerical index and the keywords *first*, *last*, which control where elements are extracted or inserted, can be specified. The respective elements are fetched from the data structure and communicated elements are inserted in the vector at these positions.

The second fundamental partition of a realization (*RealizationModel*) is the configuration of Coordination Media implementations (cf. Section 5.2.10). Two media types are distinguished, both of which address the enactment of direct (*DirectInfluenceRealization*) and mediated (*MediatedInfluenceRealization*) influences. These types share the above described configuration of published and subscribed events and are distinguished to clearly separate these kinds of link declarations in the language. The contained elements apply to declarations that configure Medium realizations. The realization models contain differing kinds of configuration models (*InfluenceConfiguration*) which prescribe and parameterize the media that are used for enactment. Configurations of a mediated influence (MediumConfiguration) reference (*mediumId*) medium-implementation concepts, i.e. the Coordination-Endpoint components (cf. Figure 5.4) that control the enactment and accesses the specific Medium. In the prototype realization, this reference contains the path to the executable agent module that is to be loaded at run-time (cf. Section 5.3.5). Endpoint realizations are specific for a certain agent type, which is also specified (*agentType*), and refer to the list of supported agent platforms (*AgentModelType*, cf. Figure 5.13). The direct influences are typically purely descriptive, i.e. they describe relations that are present in the agent design (cf. Section 4.2.3). However, for completeness and convenience these influences can also be enacted when they are equipped with a reference to a realization model (*DirectInfluenceRealization*). The prototype implementation provides a default medium realization that uses FIPA compliant ACL message-based communication [Foundation for Intelligent Physical Agents, 2003] to inform subscribers about publications (cf. Appendix B). Therefore, the contained configuration (*DirectInfluenceConfiguration*) omits annotation of agent types and media types.

Configurations of Coordination Media share a generic mechanism to parameterize instances of Media and Endpoint implementations by specifying configuration properties as *key-value* pairs (*InfluenceConfiguration*). Values can be specified statically (*Property*) or dynamically (*MediumParameterMapping*). In the former case the parameters are given as literals while in the latter case the dynamic assignment of property values is controlled by the Endpoint components that extract the identified data element from the agent state at the time point of a publication of a corresponding events and assign the value. The property key is declared (*property*) and the corresponding values to be extracted are identified by the identifier of the agent type (*agentId*), the type of the agent-element (*elementType*) and the identifier of the data value (*elementId*). The prototype implementation supports the extraction of agent knowledge elements, i.e. beliefs and the latest elements from beliefsets, as well as agent execution elements, i.e. goal and plan parameters.

Coordinating Process Definition

The language model supports the clear distinction between the definition of Coordinating Processes and the configuration of their enactment. Elements of process definitions are indicated in the Figures 5.14 and 5.15. These elements refer to the generic structure of an ACBG and allow the graph-based process structure that is discussed in Section 4.2.3 to be expressed. These process definitions are apriori independent of system implementations but refer only to generic behavior and environment abstractions. Optionally, agent types and logical constraints can be annotated to variable types to clarify the semantics of agent-behavior abstractions (cf. Figure 5.14).

Coordination Enactment Configuration

The preparation of the automated enactment requires the process definition to be mapped to the concrete models of agents and Coordination Media. These mappings are given as sets of configurations of the influences that are to be automated. These configurations are specified as sets of *RealizationModels*. These models describes a declaration of a relation. As shown in Figure 5.15, a *RealizationModel* interrelates elements of the agent implementation with realizations of Coordination Media. References to agent-implementation elements indicate the significant events. These are published or issued by the Endpoint models and define the interface between the Endpoint and the agents. The references to Medium implementations define how information is transmitted by the parameterization of Media. In addition, Endpoints look up and evaluate the optional constraints (*Constraints*, cf. Figure 5.14) that are annotated to agent behaviors (cf. Figure 5.14).

The mappings are specified at the agent and event type-level. They describe the types of events in the types of agent models that correspond to agent-behavior abstractions. The dynamics of the

5.3. MASDYNAMICS: COORDINATION CONFIGURATION

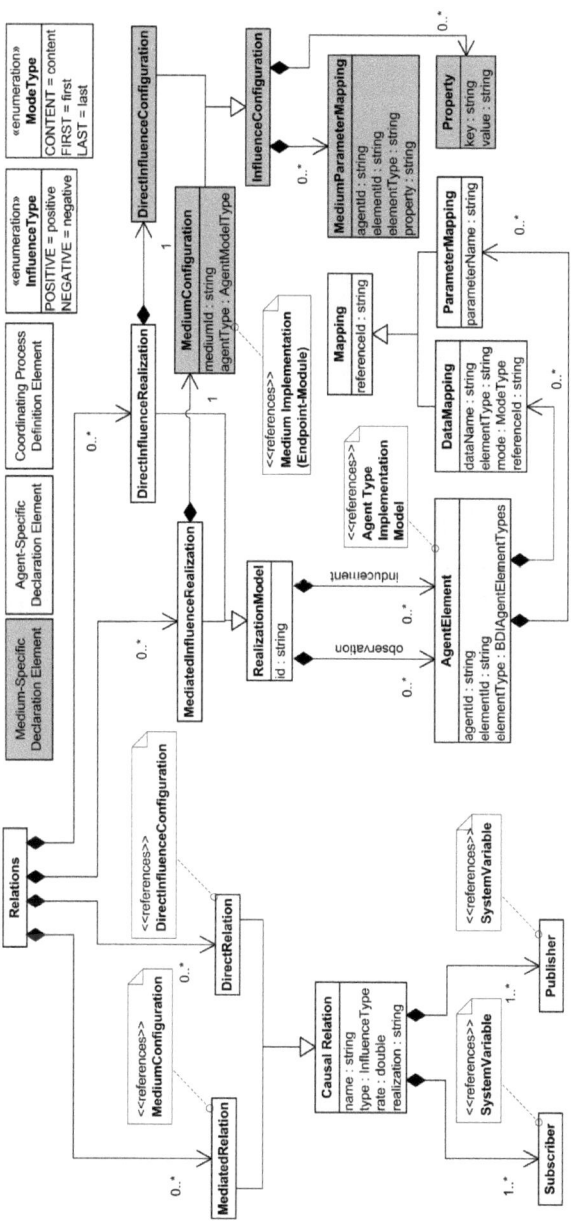

Figure 5.15: The structure of the specification of system relations

medium-specific dissemination determines the number and delay of publication receptions.

Only the declarations of realizations that are referenced by the declarations of influences are enacted at run-time. This allows descriptions of generic coordination pattern and sets of application-specific mappings to be maintained in a single file.

Extensibility of the Language Model

The described structure of the configuration language defines the principled elements of the description and configuration of ACBG-based coordination models. It is concretized towards the configuration of the prototype enactment architecture (see Section 5.3.5) that addresses the coordination of Jadex-based agent systems (see Section 2.2.2). A design criterion is the extensibility of the language model to facilitate future support of additional types of system elements. Here the possible *extension points* are outlined. The language structure prescribes Coordinating Processes and is not affected by extensions. Instead the references to differing implementation concepts can be extended to support differing agent models.

Language extensions tailor the configuration of Endpoint modules and apply to the run-time observation and modification of agents. First, support for different system entities, e.g. component types and agent architectures, can be supplemented. Preparing additional sets of event references, to be observed within differing types of system elements, allows the observations and modifications within other types of software artifacts to be prescribed. References to agent models are typed, therefore extending the set of support types of agent models (*AgentModelType*, cf. Figure 5.13) allows model elements to be distinguished. An inherent assumption for the references to agent model elements is that they can be identified by a unique combination of element types and element names. In declarative and procedural agent-oriented programming languages agents as well as agent elements are typically named. Therefore, a consequence of supporting differing system entities is the need to support corresponding sets of element types. The provision of BDI-oriented types is exemplified in the *BDIAgentElementTypes* structure (cf. Figure 5.14) and alternative sets or extensions can be included as well. According to the use of types in the *AgentReferences* (cf. Figure 5.14) and the connecting *RealizationModel* (cf. Figure 5.15), the language prepares the prescription of the behaviors of and influences among differing types of agent/component architectures.

The configuration of the agent-internal data to be transmitted is agent architecture specific. These declarations assume that data elements are typed and named to allow their unambiguous identification. The mode element within *DataMapping* (cf. Figure 5.15) elements allows different modes to be supported in order to access agent-intern data structures. Alternative modes could be integrated, e.g. the sum of numerical data or set operations on collection-based elements. Similar extensions allow the differing data structures that agent languages may provide to be supported. A special case is the ability to parameterize agent execution elements. This feature is included to support Jadex-style agents but may be not available in other agent programming languages.

Another implementation-specific aspect is the specification of the Conditions that can be annotated to the variables to constrain and refine the represented agent-behaviors (see Figure 5.14). These conditions are evaluated, within Endpoints, with respect to the current agent execution state. It is practical to use agent implementation concepts for the specification of these constraints. These specifications describe sets of valid agent states and these states are most naturally represented with the concepts that are used in agent development. Besides, agent developers are accustomed to these notations, thus the specification format is familiar to development teams. An alternative is the introduction of constraint languages that allow abstract from the concrete agent model. These language could be used to provide a generic specification format, e.g. via inference techniques (e.g. see [Russell and Norvig, 1995]). However, this approach implies an additional language level. Developers need to become accustomed to this additional level. In addition, it raises the issue of linking specifications to the executable agent realizations. In the prototype implementation (see Section 5.3.5), the evaluation of condition statements is delegated to the agent platform. Therefore, the expression format of the execution platform is reused. The underlying agent platform provides a specific expression language [Pokahr and Braubach, 2007b].

5.3. MASDYNAMICS: COORDINATION CONFIGURATION

The delegation of the expressions is an extension point for the use of other platform-specific or generic specification formats.

The configuration of Medium instances, based on key-value pairs, lacks expressiveness but has been carefully selected to make no assumptions about the internal structure or the operating principle of medium realizations. A natural extension point is to provide refined language (sub-)models for specific types of Mechanisms, respectively Media. A proposal for a conceptual model for the configuration of environment-mediated coordination mechanisms is given in [Vilenica et al., 2010]. This model is more expressive, as it provides a structured view on the internals and working principles of this class of interaction mechanism. Specifications declare three fundamental aspects. First, the agents are referenced that are enabled to use the interaction technique. Secondly, the environment and the situated environment elements are configured. The declaration of the elements allows distinct types of elements to be defined. They distinguish themselves from others by their ability to diffuse, replicate, propagate, and evaporate in the environment. In addition, the modes of perception can be configured. The configuration of the environment deals with the referencing of environment realizations and (background) processes that modify the environment, e.g. altering environment elements. The derivation of conceptual models of other types of coordination mechanisms, e.g. based on direct interactions (cf. Section 3.2.1), remains for future work. Details on the outlined configuration proposal for mediated mechanisms, which is developed in the SodekoVS research project (see Section 7.2.1), can be found in [Vilenica et al., 2010].

5.3.3 Notation(s)

Two notations allow the prescription of coordination models in the MASDynamics language. These provide markup languages for instantiating the discussed conceptual structure of a decentralized Coordinating Process (cf. Figure 5.11). The specifications prescribe and configure the design elements that constitute the decentralized process and allow implementation concepts of the system elements that participate in the prescribed process to be referenced. The referencing follows the BDI-specific concretization of the language model (cf. Section 5.3.2).

First, A *Extensible Markup Language* (XML) [World Wide Web Consortium (W3C), 2008] dialect is defined that describes coordination models in an established syntax. Secondly, a tailored *Domain Specific Language* (DSL) abridged notation is conceived [Sudeikat and Renz, 2009c] specifies coordination models in a concise notation. The former markup format integrates into established development environments as XML-based data formats are widespread in software engineering contexts. The latter declaration language uses a concise but unusual format and editing support is constrained to language specific realizations. Whether the benefits of the concise description format outweigh the benefits of the use of an established, but lengthy, markup format is to be evaluated by the user acceptance. Examples of both notations are given in Section 5.4.

Both formats follow the conceptual model described in Section 5.3.2 and process models, in one language format, can be projected onto the alternative. Transformations are possible because the contained data fields and values match. The mapping is realized in the processing of processes models in the DSL notation. The prototype realization of the middleware layer (see Section 5.3.5) internally uses the XML-format. Therefore, models in the DSL notation are automatically converted in the editing environment to compliant XML documents that can be processed by the middleware realization. The opposite transformation of process models is not implemented but could make use of the inverse transformation rules.

Using the Extensible Markup Language

The XML [World Wide Web Consortium (W3C), 2008] is a markup language format that provides an established syntax for describing semi-structured data in human readable form. Due to the widespread use of this language format, sophisticated processing and editing tools are available. Languages are available, namely the *Document Type Definition* (DTD) [World Wide Web Consortium (W3C), 2008] and *XML-Schema* [World Wide Web Consortium (W3C), 2004], to prescribe the structure of XML documents in order to define XML dialects. An XML-based dialect has been defined by using a XML data binding framework.[4] The object-oriented structure of the language model is realized in the Java programming language and is equipped with annotations that define the corresponding XML syntax. Based on these annotations syntax definitions in XML-Schema format can be generated and the annotated object structure can be used to write (*marshal*) and read (*unmarshal*) XML documents.

The complete description of the language syntax is not discussed as the syntactic details follow the XML standard. The language model is hierarchically structured and corresponds to the structure of the UML-based models that were discussed in Section 5.3.2. XML-tags are used to represent language elements while XML-attributes, annotated to these tags, are used to represent the attributes of the corresponding language elements. The basic structure of the XML-based representation is shown in Listing 5.2. The top-level tag $MASDynamics$ contains the language model and is attributed with a *name*. The $<definitions>$, $<system\_variables>$, and $<relations>$ tags contain the three basic language partitions, as illustrated in Figure 5.13. The relations partition is subdivided, as shown in Figure 5.15, into four distinct partitions that contain the declarations of direct ($<direct\_relations>$) and mediated ($<mediated\_relations>$) relations as well as the corresponding configurations of their realization ($<mediated\_influence\_realizations>$,$<direct\_influence\_realizations>$). Examples for the specification of Coordinating Processes, using this notation, are given in the Sections 5.4.2 and 6.8.3.

```
<MASDynamic name="model_name">                                                      1
   <definitions> ... </definitions>
   <system_variables> ... </system_variables>                                        3
   <relations>
     <direct_relations> ... </direct_relations>                                      5
     <mediated_relations> ... </mediated_relations>
     <mediated_influence_realizations> ... <mediated_influence_realizations>         7
     <direct_influence_realizations> ... </direct_influence_realizations>
   </relations>                                                                     9
</MASDynamic>
```

Listing 5.2: The basic structure of XML-based MASDynamics models

Using a Customized Notation

A *Domain Specific Language* (DSL) provides a tailored notation to describe application domain concepts. These languages are less expressive then general-purpose programming languages but facilitate the description of domain specific data models in concise, precise notations. The focus on a specific domain facilitates their use by domain experts, rather then IT personal, to describe domain knowledge. These resulting language models are typically designed to be processed by dedicated tools.

The definition of XML dialects provides language models but the lengthy notation and strict format is not necessarily convenient for non-computer scientist users. That providing DSLs is gaining currency in general-purpose software development is witnessed by the widespread use of specific DSL-frameworks. Besides the existence of specialized language definition frameworks, mainstream software development environments have recently been augmented with language definition tool sets. Examples are the embeddings of language modeling frameworks in the *Eclipse*[5] and the *Microsoft Visual Studio*[6] development environments. These environments support the definition of specialized syntax and language models. DSLs can rely on textual and/or graphical languages. Textual languages rely on specifically formatted text files, while graphical languages provide dedicated drawing tools that express domain concepts in diagrams. Frameworks Diagram elements are annotated with the textual information that is needed to configure domain concepts and consequently allow the generation of tailored data structures or executables.

---

[4]using the *Java Architecture for XML Binding* (JAXB) https://jaxb.dev.java.net/
[5]e.g. Textual Modeling Framework (TMF) http://www.eclipse.org/modeling/tmf/
[6]e.g. Microsoft DSL Tools: http://msdn.microsoft.com/de-de/library/bb126235.aspx, Microsoft OSLO http://msdn.microsoft.com/de-de/data/default%28en-us%29.aspx

5.3. MASDYNAMICS: COORDINATION CONFIGURATION

Recurring concerns for designers of DSLs are the provision of tools for deriving editing support for end-users and for checking the correctness of models, and the ability to generate deliverables that can be integrated in run-time infrastructures. Frameworks address these concerns with differing tool sets. Examples are tools to generate editing applications from language models or languages that allow constraints and correctness rules to be described. The integration of user-provided domain models into applications can be approached by interpretation or code generation. Interpreters traverse the language model instances and induce side effects. Code generation frameworks realize model transformations that result in equivalent models in a differing language, which are to be interpreted or compiled.

In the following, a DSL for MASDynamics models is described. The language provides an alternative, terse notation for the specification of ACBGs and the configuration of influence enactments. Examples can be found in the Sections 5.4.1 and 6.8.2. The *Extended Backus-Naur Form* EBNF is an established and standardized metalanguage for the definition of language syntaxes. The language structure is partitioned and the possible embodiments of the syntactic parts, named *non-terminal* symbols, are defined by production rules. Rule definitions contain *terminal* symbols that provide the atomic, i.e. indivisible, language elements. An *International Organization for Standardization*[7] (ISO) standard [International Organization for Standardization (ISO), 1996] describes the EBNF that is based on the original Backus-Naur Form and contains widely accepted extensions. BNF-based language definitions indicate the syntactic parts of a language, the syntactic structure of language sentences, and define the set of valid sequences of symbols [International Organization for Standardization (ISO), 1996].

The non-terminal symbol *model* denotes the entire language model. Optional inputs name the model (*name:*), specify a file name to store generated output (*output:*), and comment the model (*description:*). In the following, the tokens *ID*, *STRING*, and *INT* are utilized. These are provided by a DSL framework [Efftinge et al., 2008] that is used to realize editing support and model transmigration (see below). ID refers to character sequences of the form $'a - zA - Z\_'('a - zA - Z\_0 - 9)*$ ([Efftinge et al., 2008], page 111), STRING refers to multi-line string literals that are delimited by double or single quotes, and the token INT refers to integer literals. This comment is preserved in the generation process. The remainder of the model refers to lists of four types of language elements. These elements can be specified arbitrarily often or not at all.

The symbol *predefinition* corresponds to the *Definitions* partition of the MASDynamics language (cf. Figure 5.13). Two types of declarations are available that allow developers to reference agent implementations (*agent-model*) as well as the realizations of Endpoints for Coordination Media (*medium:*). These declarations contain the name the agent type (*agent:*) or endpoint type (*medium:*) and implementations are referenced by specifying the file name of the implementation model (*model*) and the type of the utilized agent architecture (*type*). Predefinition elements are optional the references to the agent/endpoint implementation models can be specified in the configurations of influence enactments (*configuration*, see below). Their main purpose is to document mappings of process definitions to applications.

Variable elements prescribe the declaration of system variables. The available rules (*role-occupation*, *group-membership*, *group-count*, and *environment-property*) correspond to the variable types of the MASDynamics meta-model (cf. Figure 5.14). These declarations begin with the variable type followed by a colon and an Identifier (ID) of the variable name (*variable_type_name* : variable_name). Variable declarations contain optional references to agent models (*agent* : agent_name). Variable types that describe agent behaviors contain optional lists of references to agent-intern elements (*agent-reference*). These references name the agent type that is able to exhibit the behavior (*agent:* agent_type_name). Optional refinements of the context of the behavior exhibitions are enclosed in squared brackets. First, the relevant events are denoted by referencing agent implementation elements (*agent-element*). These references contain the unique combinations of element names (*element:* element_name) and the type of element (*type* element_type_name). These references denote that an agent-behavior is active when one of the contained agent elements is activated or modified (cf. Section 5.3.2). The available element types, exemplified for

---
[7]http://www.iso.org/iso/home.htm

the Jadex-style BDI agents, are specified by the non-terminal *agent-element-type*. In addition, the *Constraints* (cf. Figure 5.14) can be defined to specify the agent-context in which element creations or modifications signify the exhibition of the denoted behavior. A *condition* (*condition: "..."*) and a list of references to inhibiting agent elements (*inhibited by:*) can be specified. The references to inhibiting agent elements also follow the rule *agent-element*. The condition must evaluate to *true* and inhibiting elements must not be active (cf. Section 5.3.2). The keyword *multiple* indicates that the variable represents a *stacked* node in the graphical notation of ACBGs (cf. Section 4.2.3).

```
model                    = ["output:" STRING] ["description:" STRING] ["name:" STRING]
                           {predefinition} {variable} {relation} {configuration} ;         2
predefinition            = agent−model | medium−model ;
agent−model              = "agent:" ID   impl−reference ;                                  4
medium−model             = "medium:" ID   impl−reference ;
impl−reference           = "model" STRING  "type" STRING ;                                 6

(* Declaration of variables: *)                                                            8
variable                 = role−occupation | group−membership | group−count
                         | environment−property ;                                         10
environment−property     = "env_property:"   ID  ["multiple"] ;
role−occupation          = "role_occupation:"  ID  ["multiple"]  "["  {agent−reference} "]"  ; 12
group−membership         = "group_membership:" ID  ["multiple"]  "["  {agent−reference} "]"  ;
group−count              = "group−count:"      ID  ["multiple"]  "["  (agent−reference} "]"  ; 14
agent−reference          = "agent:" ID  [ "["
                             ["condition:" STRING] ["inhibited by:" agent−element]        16
                             {agent−element}
                           "]" ] ;                                                        18
agent−element            = "element:" STRING  "type" agent−element−type ;
                                                                                          20
(* Declaration of relations: *)
relation                 = direct−relation | mediated−relation ;                          22
direct−relation          = "−>direct−>(" ID ")["
                           relation−model ["configuration" ID]  "]" ;                     24
mediated−relation        = "=>mediated=>(" ID ")["
                           relation−model ["configuration" ID]  "]" ;                     26
relation−model           = "type" pos−neg "<− {" {ID} "} "−> {" {ID} "}"
                                                                                          28
(* Configuration of enactment: *)
configuration            = config−mediation | config−direct                               30
config−mediation         = "medium_configuration:(" ID "):"
                           publish−perceive medium ;                                      32
medium                   = "by_medium:" STRING  "agenttype" STRING  "["
                           parameterization "]" ;                                         34
config−direct            = "influence_configuration:(" ID "):"
                           publish−perceive direct−influence ;                            36
direct−influence         = "by−influence:" ["delay:" STRING ] "["
                           parameterization "]" ;                                         38
publish−perceive         = "<− {" {publication} "} "−> {" {perception} "}" ;
parameterization         = {mechanism−property} {mechanism−mapping} ;                     40
mechanism−property       = "with: property" STRING  "value" STRING ;
mechanism−mapping        = "while: mapping" STRING  "with element:" STRING                42
                           "from agent:" STRING ;
publication              = "<−:" "agent" STRING  "event" STRING  "type" agent−element−type 44
                           ["while communicating data: {" {data−mapping} "}" ]
                           ["while communicating parameter: {" {parameter−mapping} "}" ] ; 46
perception               = "−>:" "agent" STRING  "event" STRING  "type" agent−element−type
                           ["while storing: {" {data−mapping} "}" ]                       48
                           ["while receiving: {" {parameter−mapping} "}" ] ;
data−mapping             = "value:" STRING  "as:" STRING  "of type:" type=agent−knowledge 50
                           ["using:" mode=data−mode−type | "position:" position=INT] ;
parameter−mapping        = "value:" STRING  "as:" STRING ;                                52

(* Symbol definitions: *)                                                                 54
agent−element−type       = "BDI_BELIEF" | "BDI_BELIEFSET" | "BDI_GOAL" | "BDI_PLAN"
                         | "INTERNAL_EVENT" ;                                             56
agent−knowledge          = "BDI_BELIEF" | "BDI_BELIEFSET" ;
data−mode−type           = "content" | "first" | "last" ;                                 58
pos−neg                  = "+"|"−";
```

Listing 5.3: The DSL notation structure in EBNF

Two kinds of *relation* elements describe the direct (*direct-relation*) and mediated (*mediated-relation*) connections between variables. Declarations of these are prefaced by differentiating keywords (->direct->(,->mediated->() that are followed by an identifier that is enclosed in brackets. The *relation-model* rule prescribes the definition of relations. The annotation of the link

5.3. MASDYNAMICS: COORDINATION CONFIGURATION

type (+/-) is mandatory. Relation models contain lists of publishing (<-{...}) and subscribed (->{...}) variables. These lists are sequences of variable identifiers. Optionally, the declarations of relations can conclude with a reference to a detailed configuration of their enactment (*configuration:* ...). The specification of an identifier of a link configuration indicates that the link is an influence that is to be enacted (cf. Figure 5.15).

The listing of these *configuration* elements is the last principal element of the language model. These models describe the configuration of Coordination Media and Endpoint modules to control the enactment of influences (cf Section 5.2). Rules for the configuration of mediated (*config-mediation*) and direct (*config-direct*) influences are distinguished. These configuration rules have in common that configurations are named with a unique identifier, that is enclosed in brackets. Squared brackets surround the specification of the event-based interface (*publish-perceive*) that is used to observe/modify the agent models as well as to parameterize a Coordination Medium.

The *publish-perceive* rule prescribes declarations of the published (<- {..}) and subscribed (-> {..}) agent events. Specifications of the published (*publication*) and induced (*perception*) agent events are initiated by keywords (<-:,->:) and contain the name of the agent type (*agent*), the name of the relevant event (*event*), and the type of the event (*type*). The set of available events is given by the rule *agent-element-type*. Configurations of communications of agent-internal data are given in squared brackets. The communication of agent-knowledge information or data that is associated to the raised/induced agent events can be specified. These specifications are initiated by specific keywords and follow the mapping mechanism that is outlined in Section 5.3.2. The communications of event parameters (*parameter-mapping*) are described as a mapping of a parameter name (*value:* parameter_name) to an arbitrary reference identifier (*as:* identifier_name). Publishing endpoints (*while communicating data:*, *while communicating parameter:*) are responsible for extracting this value from the observed event and storing it under the reference identifier within the published data structure. Vice versa, perceiving endpoints (*while storing:*, *while receiving:*) interpret the declaration and copy referenced values into the denoted parameter value. The mappings of agent knowledge elements (*data-mapping*) contain the additional specification of the knowledge element type (*of type:*) and the mode of the value extraction or insertion. This additional information accounts for the two kinds of data storage types of the Jadex system. These are denoted by the rule *agent-knowledge* and constrain the selectable element types. While single valued data can be copied directly, interfacing of array-based data structures requires different access modes to be denoted. Optionally, a mode identifier (*data-mode-type*) can be specified (*using:* ...) or an integer position of the target data element can be specified (*position:* ...). As described in Section 5.3.2, the declarations can be crossed, e.g. the value of an agent knowledge element can serve as a parameter for an agent-internal event. Not referenced data values are ignored by receivers.

The configuration rules differ in the initial keywords (*"medium_configuration:()*, *influence_configuration:()*) and the contained parameterization models (*medium*, *direct-influence*) that control the selection and settings of media instances. These rules correspond directly to elements in the conceptual language model (see Figure 5.15, page 173). The configurations correspond to the realization models (*MediatedInfluenceRealization*, *DirectInfluenceRealization*). The parameterizations correspond to the configuration models (*MediumConfiguration*, *DirectInfleuenceConfiguration*). The direct correspondence to the rules to the conceptual language elements supports the ability to map process models in different notations onto each other (see Section 5.3.3, page 175). Direct influences are enacted by a default medium implementation (see Appendix B), therefore an abridged notation is available. The optional delay parameter (*delay:*) controls the deferring of communications. Coordination Media realizations are parameterized by assigning key-value pairs (*parameterization*). The available parameters depend on the medium realization and can be assigned statically (*mechanism-property*), i.e. to non-changing values, or to dynamic data elements within agents (*mechanism-mapping*). Static parameters are set by explicitly stating the value of a property element (*with property:* parameter_name *value* value_literal). Dynamically assigned medium parameters refer to the mapped agent data that are extracted by publishing endpoints. Parameters (*while: mapping* parameter_name) in a specific agent type (*from agent:* agent_name) are set to the mapped value (*with element:* reference_identifier) that was set by publishing endpoints.

180   CHAPTER 5. A SYSTEMIC PROGRAMMING MODEL

The described language has been realized with the *Xtext*[8] framework for the development of textual DSLs [Efftinge et al., 2008]. This framework provides an EBNF-oriented notation to specify the grammar of a DSL dialect and a corresponding tool set that allows to generate a language parser, the language metamodel, and an *Eclipse*-based[9] text editor from these grammar specifications.. The symbols ID , STRING, and INT are predefined by this framework. The notation allows references between identifiers of elements (ID elements) to be configured. These details are omitted in the EBNF model of the language (cf. Listing 5.3), as these are framework-specific extensions. In the realized editor, this referencing is used to enhance the code completion feature. In the rules *agent-model*, *variable*, *config-mediation*, *config-direct* of the language identifiers are specified. The code completion suggests the identifiers that are appropriate in a specific contexts. An example is illustrated in Figure 5.16. A mediated relation is described and the identifier of a medium configuration of a medium has to be specified. The editor suggests the identifiers of the medium configurations that are declared elsewhere in the file (*by_* ...). The *Xpand*[10] template language is used to describe the model transformation that generates XML-based notation models that configure the coordination architecture (see Section 5.3.3, page 175). Details on this language can be found in [Efftinge et al., 2008].

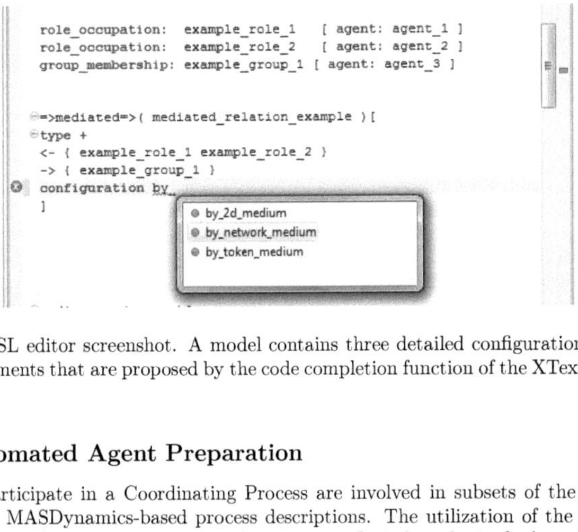

Figure 5.16: DSL editor screenshot. A model contains three detailed configurations of mediated influence enactments that are proposed by the code completion function of the XText-based editor.

5.3.4 Automated Agent Preparation

Agents that participate in a Coordinating Process are involved in subsets of the relations that are declared in MASDynamics-based process descriptions. The utilization of the enactment architecture requires the proper annotation of agents to reflect the subset of relevant relations and the set-up of the necessary Endpoint modules. Here, the automated configuration of agents is discussed (cf. Figure 5.17). A procedure is embedded within agents that filters an MASDynamics model for the influences in which the agent is expected to be involved. For each of these influences, the corresponding configuration is looked up and the appropriate annotation to the agent is made. In addition, the referenced Endpoint modules are loaded at run-time to enable the automated enactment of influences.

Initially, the MASDynamics-based specification of a Coordinating Process is read in (*Read-in coordination process definition*). Thereafter, the host agent is examined to infer the agent type, i.e. the identifier of the agent designing model that corresponds to the agent instance (*Inspect surrounding agent model*). Then a data-structure is initialized that records the configurations of influences (*Initialize local configuration*). The process specification is searched for the influences

---

[8] http://www.eclipse.org/Xtext/
[9] *Eclipse* is a widespread Integrated Development Environment (IDE) that is freely available at: www.eclipse.org/
[10] http://wiki.eclipse.org/Xpand

5.3. MASDYNAMICS: COORDINATION CONFIGURATION

that involves the found agent model, indicated by the <<selection>> stereotype. For this subset, each influence is processed in random sequence. For each influence, its configuration is created (*Extract influence configuration*). These configurations are stored in an intermediate data structure that combines the references to the agent model elements that are observed/actuated (cf. Figure 5.14) with the realization models of the influences (cf. Figure 5.15). These configurations are then processed to annotate the agent and load the required Endpoint (*Load and Configure Medium Access Endpoint*). In this activity, the mechanism configuration is extracted from the realization model of an influence and stored in the agent (*Extract mechanism configuration*). Subsequently, the annotations that control the operation of the Endpoint modules are extracted and annotated to the agent (*Annotate agent*) before the modules are loaded into the agent run-time instance (*Load and configure module*). A side-effect of this Activity is that the configuration and parameterization of the Endpoint are made available to the agent model. When modules are initialized, they look up the configuration to set up their communicative behavior, as described in Section 5.2.10. These activities are repeated for every selected influence and afterwards the optional manual annotations to the agent model are processed and stored in the complete configuration model. The latter activity ensures backward compatibility with early versions of the coordination infrastructure [Sudeikat and Renz, 2008b], where annotations to the agent models and inclusion of Endpoint modules were manual activities. This annotation format is processed, converted and added in the complete model of the agent configuration that is finally stored (*Store complete configuration model*). This models is used to log the Endpoints, the involved influences, and the agent elements that are to be observed or actuated to assist the debugging of applications.

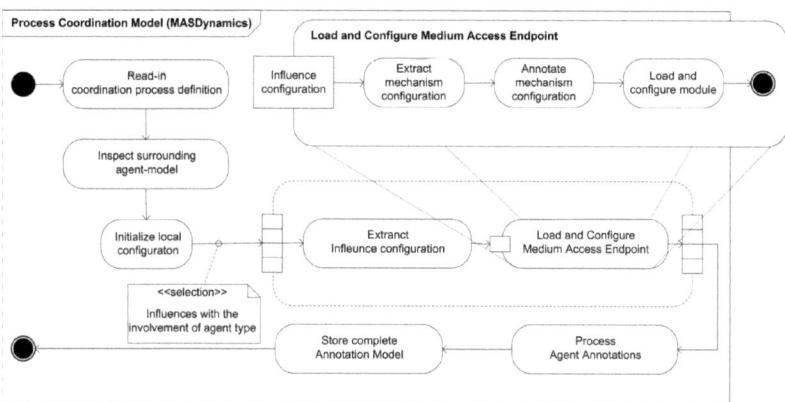

Figure 5.17: The processing of an MASDynamics-based model to configure agent instances, represented by a UML Activity Diagram

The mechanism described automates the detailed preparation of agents to participate in the prescribed coordination process. The usability of the architecture is thus enhanced, as developers do not have to manually prepare agents for coordination. Instead development teams revise the original agent implementations and induce their configuration during the initialization of the application. The mechanism may also be used to store the prepared agent models. This approach delays the MAS startup but allows developers to revise a single set of agents and ensures that these agents participate in the currently prescribed process. Developers maintain a single set of agents and one process configuration that can contain several process realizations. The currently active realizations are determined by the referencing mechanism (see page 172).

5.3.5 Prototype Realization: DeCoMAS on Jadex

A prototype implementation of this architecture blueprint, *Decentralized Coordination for Multi-agent Systems* (DeCoMAS) [Sudeikat and Renz, 2009b], is available as an extension to the *Jadex* agent platform. As described in Section 2.2.2, this system provides an execution environment for BDI-style agents on top of arbitrary distributed systems middleware [Braubach et al., 2005b]. This realization is non-invasive, i.e. the agent platform itself is not modified, but rather an additional middleware layer is embedded among the agents.

The language model (cf. Section 5.3.2) and consequently the extracted agent annotations (cf. Section 5.2.7) allow conditions that ensure that event occurrences indeed signify relevant adjustments of the agent behavior to be specified. These conditions can be given in a Jadex-specific expression language [Pokahr and Braubach, 2007b]. The benefit of this approach is that developers can use a familiar language that supports the modeling elements and idioms of the target agent platform.

The realizations of the Endpoints is based on *coefficient* agent modules that were implemented on top of the Jadex agent platform (cf. Section 5.2.4). The initial preparation of agents to participate in a prescribed Coordinating Process is discussed in Section 5.3.4. This procedure analyses the process specification and loads the required endpoint modules to enable the participation of agents in the process. In the prototype, a realization of the procedure is contained in an agent module to show the feasibility of the automated agent preparation. The inclusion of this module in an agent model triggers the procedure when the agent is initialized. Alternatively, the preparation could also be integrated in the execution platform to modify agent models before the agents are started.

Listing 5.4 illustrates the modification of the agent model that triggers the automated preparation of agents (see Section 5.3.4). First, a specific agent module, which contains the procedural realization of the initialization logic, is included in the agent model. This is done by referencing the model of the corresponding capability [Braubach et al., 2006a], i.e. the realization of the module (Line 5). Secondly, the specification of the Coordinating Process is given (Lines 8 to 12). A dedicated belief inside the referenced capability can be overwritten to reference the process definition that is to be enacted. The declaration of this definition refers to the relative path of the XML file that describes the process (cf. Section 5.3). If no specification is given, a default specification name is used.[11]

```
<agent ...>                                                          1
...
  <capabilities>                                                     3
    <!-- The coordination capability. -->
    <capability name="deco4mas" file="deco4mas.coordinate.Coordinate"/>   5
  </capabilities>
                                                                     7
  <beliefs>
    <belief class="String" name="dynamics_configuration">            9
      <assignto ref="deco4mas.dynamics_configuration"/>
      <fact>process_model_name.masdynamics.xml"</fact>              11
    </belief>
    ...                                                             13
  </beliefs>
  ...                                                               15
</agent>
```

Listing 5.4: Preparation of a Jadex agent

On agent startup, the capability processes the process description and manual annotations to the agent model to load and initialize the Endpoint modules that are required to automate the participation in the process. This processing, as discussed in Section 5.3.4, filters the specification of a decentralized Coordinating Process to identify the subset of in which the agent is involved. For this subset of relations, the corresponding annotations are inferred and integrated in the agent-runtime model. In the prototype, annotations are stored in specific beliefs that are automatically

---
[11] *default.masdynmics.xml*, available in the top-level folder of the MAS realization.

integrated into the agent run-time instance. Endpoint realizations are provided as modules, i.e. capabilities [Braubach et al., 2006a], that are also integrated at run-time. After inclusion, each of these modules configures itself as described in Sections 5.2.9 and 5.2.11.

The concrete realization of the record-oriented content model of event notifications is realized in an object-oriented interface definition. The interoperability of heterogeneous systems is facilitated by the communication of generic Java programming language objects in the content of records. For the integration of agent models that are based on other programming languages, the endpoints must be able to convert record keys and contained entry objects.

The inter-operation between the interpreter elements (cf. Section 5.2.11, 5.2.9) and the components that encapsulate the accessing of Coordination Media (cf. Section 5.2.10) is realized by a goal-oriented interface. The components, here realized as Jadex-capabilities, offer goals that can be parameterized to transmit the required information. Components dispatch these goals to trigger the activities inside the other components of the Endpoint.

5.4 Case Studies

The expedience and practicability of the systemic programming model is shown by two case studies that exemplify the supplementing of conservatively developed MASs with dynamic adaptation processes. Their discussion follows [Sudeikat and Renz, 2008b],[Sudeikat and Renz, 2009c],[Sudeikat and Renz, 2010a]. The agents that constitute the MAS are conceived as providers of abilities that function autonomously. The systems are employable but lack system-wide adaptiveness. Self-regulating, adaptive processes are defined by mapping nature-inspired coordination strategies (cf. Section 3.2.2) onto agent-based application designs. The processes are described in the MASDynamics language (cf. Section 5.3) and their enactment is automated by the DeCoMAS realization (cf. Section 5.3.5) of the layered coordination architecture (cf. Section 5.2).

5.4.1 Case Study I: Bee-Inspired Adaptive Server Allocation

In [Nakrani and Tovey, 2004], a dynamic allocation strategy inspired by the foraging behavior in honey bee societies is proposed for the adaptive management of (web) server allocations. This strategy is applicable to servers that are capable of hosting an application and serving the corresponding HTTP requests. Assuming that the demand of services, e.g. website requests, vary considerably, the adjustment of server allocations is automated by enabling servers to adjust their allocations at run-time. The effort to enable the adaptive allocation of servers can be motivated by economic concerns, e.g. when hosting providers offer their computational resources on a *pay-per-use* Service Level Agreement [Nakrani and Tovey, 2004]. Content providers reward the number of served requests, thus the providers of server capacities are able to maximize the total of served requests by sharing resources, i.e. server capacities. The decentralized coordination of server adjustments is preferable as it fulfills scalability and robustness requirements.

This application scenario is adopted in [Sudeikat and Renz, 2008b, 2009c] to illustrate the use of the systemic programming model. The *Bee-based Foraging* process template (S6, cf. Section 3.2.2,4.4.1) is supplemented to a simulation model of a server cluster. This Coordinating Process describes how two classes of bees collaborate to forage resources. *Scouts* roam through the environment and return to the nest to report encounters of resources via *waggle dances*. Foraging bees are responsible for collecting resources. Upon perception of a dance, they decide autonomously whether to exploit the communicated resource or to remain with their prior assignment. The classification criteria of coordination strategies (cf. Section 4.4.1) explains the appropriateness of this process template. The objective is the adaptive structuring of the *configuration* and *differentiation* as agents adapt their local allocations. Adjustments respond to an *extrinsic* factor, namely the varying request demands, and globally *coherent* as well as *partitioned* allocations have to be enabled to support differing arrangements.

Initially, a simulation model [Sudeikat and Renz, 2008b, 2009c] is realized as a Jadex-based MAS. Servers are represented by agents that are capable of (1) handling requests and (2) changing allocations. The architecture-specific agent design implements serving activities by plans that are triggered by incoming ACL messages. This message content mimics the different request types. Agents register their availability as a recipient for a specific request type at the yellow pages service (Domain Facilitator, DF) of the agent platform. The ability to change an allocation is modeled as an agent-internal goal. The achievement of this goal modifies the agent registration. The MAS-design is operational, as agents can be started and stopped manually to set up static configurations of a server cluster, but does not exhibit adaptive coordination.

Coordinating Process

The intended dynamic behavior of the coordinated server cluster is illustrated in Figure 5.18 (I). Two types (N,M) of external *Requesters* increase the number of inquiries for two request types (*Job*, N,M). The number of requests is reduced as these are handled by *Servers*, which are modeled as agents that are associated (*bound*) to a specific service type (N,M) or are *unbound*, i.e. not associated. The macroscopic configuration of the MAS is characterized by the numbers of agents that play these roles and the number of requests in the system. The requests are reinforced at varying rates and Servers are enabled to change their association to a service type. The intended coordination is governed by a macroscopic, balancing feedback among requests and allocated servers (α). The allocation of servers is expected to follow the changing numbers of requests in the system. When demands for a service type are increasing, the system responds with an increase of the allocations of servers. In [Sudeikat and Renz, 2008b, 2009c], the influence of unbound, i.e. not allocated servers, is also modeled. Being not bound can be understood as an additional type of server configuration and is therefore neglected in the given model.

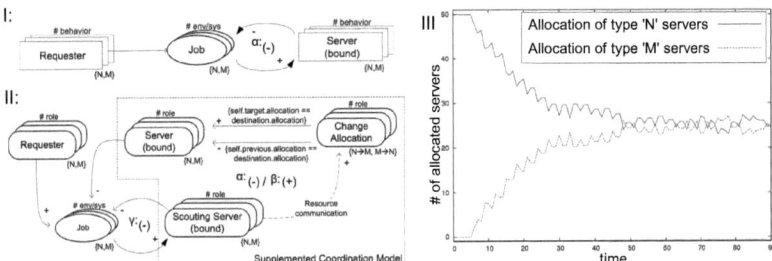

Figure 5.18: Honey-Bee inspired (web) server management: Intended behavior (I), Coordinating Process (II), and a sample simulation run (III), following [Sudeikat and Renz, 2009c]

Prescribed Coordination Model

Realizing the manifestation of the intended macroscopic feedback is a design challenge. The advantages of adopting the bee-inspired foraging process template (S6, cf. Section 3.2.2,4.4.1) are given above. Figure 5.18 (II) illustrates the mapping of this template onto the agent-based simulation model. The external influence of Requesters on the number of requests (Job) is unaltered. According to the embedded process, the bound Servers are categorized as either *Scouting* servers, which search for resources, or ordinary *Servers*. Scouting servers are an agent type that imitates the scouting behavior of bees. These agents are registered to all request types and publish demanded request types, together with an associated quality attribute, which are then advertised via a Coordination Medium (*Resource communication*). Ordinary Servers imitate the foraging entities and have two roles. Their bound behavior (*Server (bound)*) describes that Servers are associated to service type. The perception of resource advertisements triggers an additional role

5.4. CASE STUDIES

(*Change Allocation*). It denotes the agent's reasoning about adjusting their server allocation or not. The available service types and the direction of adjustments are not constrained by the enacted coordination model. The modifications of allocations influence the number of bound servers (*Server*) as the amount of servers of the same type are increased (*self.target.allocation == destination.allocation*) and the number of previous assignments is reduced (*self.previous.allocation == destination.allocation*).[12] The bound servers reduce the number of corresponding requests.

The mapped template exhibits three feedback loops (cf. Section 4.4.1, S6). First, the allocation of servers is balanced with the fluctuating demands (α). This feedback results from the activation of Scouting Servers (positive link) by requests that propagates to the reduction of requests by the bound servers. At the same time the allocations of servers are reinforced, as increases in demands amplify the allocation of corresponding servers (β). Finally, the scouting servers are activated by requests. The handling of requests by these servers completes a third feedback loop (γ) that has a minor contribution to the overall serving of requests. The main purpose of the Scouting servers is to enforce the allocation of bound servers that provide the main work performance.

The definition of the coordination model that automates the enactment is indicated in Figure 5.18 (II). The declaration of this process addresses two constituents. First, the relevant agent behavior, here roles, is defined. Secondly, the automated communication between agents is configured. The participating agent roles are defined by referencing the agent models that are capable to exhibit the roles. Link declarations reference role declarations to denote the relevant relations. Decentralized links indicate the automated utilization of a Coordination Medium. In this example a simple token-based mechanism implementation is configured to randomly distribute advertisements among the agent population. The automation of this communication is prescribed by referencing the agent-internal events that indicate the adoption of a participating role and configuring the agent-internal data that is to be transmitted.

Listing 5.19 shows excerpts of the Coordinating Process declaration, in abridged notation (cf. Section 5.3.3), that controls the enactment of coordination. First (I), the relevant system variables, i.e. the role occupations (*Scout, Server*, and *Requester*) and the environment property (*Jobs*), are declared be denoting which agents are able to play certain roles. Here, the server role can be played by two agent types (*Server1, Server2*). In early development phases, these references refer to agent designs and as the development of the MAS proceeds, these references are updated to the concrete implementation types.

Secondly, the relations among the behavior abstractions are indicated (cf. Figure 5.19, II). The direct influence (*generate*) describes the producing of new requests by the agents that play the Requester role. This relation describes the given system operation as Requester agents generate messages and their output adds to the overall amount of requests in the system. The second exemplified relation (*wiggle*) denotes the realization of the positive influence between Scout and Server agents. This link corresponds to the *Resource communication* by scouts (cf. Figure 5.18), and is a reference to the metaphoric waggle dances of bees. The relation describes that the activities of scout agents leads to the recruitment, i.e. activation, of Servers. Since this relation is not present in the MAS as is, the enactment is indicated by the referencing of a *configuration*. The communications are (randomly) propagated by a Coordination Medium (see Appendix B.1.1). The automated utilization of this medium is controlled by a parameterization and the configuration of the operation of endpoint modules (DCM).

The referenced configuration (*wiggle_by_token*) expresses the application-dependent description level, since the relevant events, which are to be observed and automatically induced by Endpoint modules, and the configuration of Medium implementations are specified (cf. Figure 5.19, III). The first section (<-{...}), declares the published events. Activations of the plan *advertise* in agents of the type *Coordinated(Scout)* are published. Publications contain the value of the plan parameter *service_type* that can be referenced with a mechanism-internal identifier (*type*). The second section (->{...}), configures the affected agent events of subscribed agents. Two agent types (*Server1,Server2*) are subscribed and Coordination Endpoints are free to suggest the pursuit

---
[12]Here, *self* refers to the current node and *destination* refers to the set of nodes that the relation points to. *target* and *previous* refer to the intended and the original allocation of the agent that exhibits the *Change Allocation* role, i.e. that is migrating from one allocation to another.

of the internal goal *change_allocation*. Upon the dispatching of this goal type, the agent-intern goal parameter *service type* is set to the value of the communicated parameter value (type). Finally, the utilized Endpoint module is referenced and specific parameters are set. Here, a simplified distribution mechanism [Sudeikat and Renz, 2008b] is configured by the static setting of a single parameter value, i.e. the *distribution_type* is set to randomly distribute tokens among subscribed agents.

```
I:  ...
    /* System Variables: */

    env_property: Jobs multiple

    role_occupation: Scout
            [ agent: ScoutingServer ]

    role_occupation: Server multiple [
            agent: Server1
            agent: Server2
    ]

    role_occupation: Requester multiple [
            agent: Requester1
            agent: Requester2
    ]
    ...

II: /* Causal Relations: */

    ->direct->( generate )[
    type +
    <- { Requester }
    -> { Jobs }
    ]

    =>mediated=>( serviceAttraction )[
    type +
    <- { Scout }
    -> { Server }
    configuration wiggle_by_token
    ]
    ...
```

```
III: /* Detailed configuration of coordination medium: */
     medium_configuration( wiggle_by_token ):
     <- { /* Published agent events */
         <-: agent Coordinated(Scout)
             event "advertise" type BDI_PLAN
             while communicating parameter: {
                 value: "service_type" as: "type" }
     }
     -> { /* Subscribed agent events */
         ->: agent Server
             event "change_allocation" type BDI_GOAL
             while receiving: {
                 value: "type" as: "service_type" }
         ->: agent Server2
             event "change_allocation" type BDI_GOAL
             while receiving: {
                 value: "type" as: "service_type" }
     by_medium: "deco4mas.mechanism.token.generic.Token" [
         with: property "distribution_type" value "RANDOM"
     ]
```

Figure 5.19: Excerpts from the process definition in abridged notation, adapted from [Sudeikat and Renz, 2009c]

A sample simulation of 50 server agents and 10 scouting agents is shown in Figure 5.18 (III). Initially, the servers are completely allocated as the system is put under a steady demand of requests of the type N (initial 10 time steps). The system responds to the sudden addition of another steady demand of another request type M with a balanced allocation of servers (after 5 seconds) [Sudeikat and Renz, 2009c].

The encapsulation and automated utilization of Coordination Media is shown in this simulation model. Simulations are carried out with an MAS that is build using a general-purpose agent framework (see Section 2.2.2, page 17), thus the practicability in software development is shown. Agents follow their local reasoning and are not aware of implied communicative acts that are carried out in the background to steer the correlation of agent activities. This is a first step to automate the participation of agents in a Coordinating Process, however, the design of the MAS is affected by the implied design metaphor. For example novel agent types have to be introduced to realize the differing agent roles. Therefore, the early architecture blueprint was extended with the Adaptivity Component concept, which allows the procedural adaptation logic to be encapsulated in a format that is accessible to Endpoint modules. Fully transparent supplementation of a coordination process without modification of the agent/MAS design is illustrated in the following case study.

5.4.2 Case Study II: Integration of Convention Emergence

Convention emergence (S2, cf. Sections 3.2.2, 4.4.1) is a decentralized approach to addressing agreement problems in MASs. When MASs are designed to follow social rules it is crucial that the society agrees on the guidelines that individuals are expected to follow [Shoham and Tennenholtz, 1997]. The dynamics of propagation processes are commonly studied by simplifying simulation models [Shoham and Tennenholtz, 1997] that allow the effects of the topological arrangements of agents on the exhibited convergence of commonly agreed values to be studied [Lakkaraju and Gasser, 2009].

The corresponding simulation models abstract agents as reactive entities that are equipped with a local variable, e.g. a color. Initially, the variable values are randomly distributed within a fixed value range. Assuming that agents interact randomly, a commonly agreed *convention* value can emerge when (1) individuals mutually inform other agents about their local configuration and (2) consequently adjust their configuration value. In consideration of the number of agents and the the communication overhead, the broadcast of configurations is permitted. Agents are structured in an (overlay) network and only communicate to connected neighbors. The *suggestibility* of agents, i.e. the likelihood that the reception of non-conforming configurations cause local modifications, is modeled by local policies that prescribe the local reasoning. Prominent examples are combinations of majority rules and bounded memories of past communications (e.g. [Shoham and Tennenholtz, 1997; Lakkaraju and Gasser, 2009]). When both constituent modeling elements are well-matched the space of configurations converges.

Coordinating Process

The causal structure of the convergence process is given in Figure 5.20 (I) as an ACBG [Sudeikat and Renz, 2010a]. The annotations to nodes indicate that the set of possible configurations is constrained to two values (A,B). Consequently, reconfigurations alternate between these values $(A \rightarrow B, B \rightarrow A)$. For this case the explicit ACBG graph is shown in Figure 5.20 (II). External influences (*Activity Trigger*) actuate arbitrary agent activities (*Activity*). The execution of these activities also causes the communication of the local configuration (*inform convention value*) that triggers individual (re-)configuration of agents (*Convention Adjustment*). The policy controls locally whether configurations are adjusted and decides which values are adopted. It is assumed that the agent configuration affects the activities (*Activity*), e.g. by controlling how activities proceed or by constraining the availability of activities.

These causal relationships constitute a reinforcing (+) and a balancing (-) feedback. The process is *selective* as the system history determines which values are to be suppressed. The integration of this process in an MAS is appropriate for addressing distributed agreement problems, as it describes the *endogenous* establishment of a *coherent* structure that controls the *differentiation* of agents (cf. Section 3.2.2). The process does not respond to extrinsic factors and only acts on the adjustment of agent internal data structures. Thus it provides a means to integrating the alignment of agent configurations. This process is separated from the agent functioning.

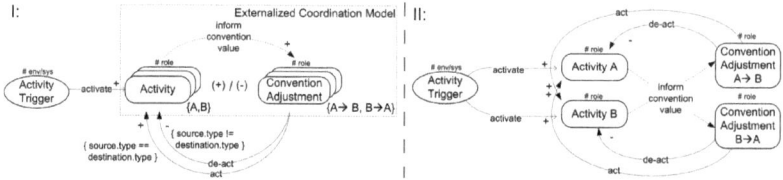

Figure 5.20: Convention Emergence process model: The systemic model of the MAS dynamics in abridged (I, following [Sudeikat and Renz, 2010a]) and explicit notation (II)

Prescribed Coordination Model

The automated coordination model is indicated in Figure 5.20 (I). This model prescribes that the communication of the local configuration (*inform convention value*) is a side-effect of the activation of one element within a set of generic agent activities (*Activity*). The relevant activities are declared, using the event-based interface (cf. Section 5.3.2). The local adaptation logic is encapsulated in an *Adaptivity Component*. Here, the component contains a fixed memory. The latest nine communications are considered and the value of the surrounding agent is adjusted to agree with the majority of the perceived values. Communications are routed through a Coordination Medium that arranges Coordination Endpoints in an overlay network topology (cf. Section 5.2.10).

The declaration of the Coordination Model is given in listing 5.5. This model describes the supplement that realizes the intended side-effect, i.e. the exchange and processing of coordination information. First, the participating agent roles are defined (lines 3-12). As the simulation model is based on a homogeneous MAS, the declarations of *publisher* and *subscriber* roles refer to the same agent type (*SenderReceiver*). The identifiers of the roles are unambiguous but can be arbitrarily selected. The identifier of the agent type refers to the unique name that identifies implementation agent types.

Secondly, the causal influence (*inform_convention_value*) between these behaviors is declared (lines 14-25) by describing a connection between the originating (*publisher*) and the destination (*subscriber*) variables. The specification of a detailed medium configuration (*by_network*) indicates that the relation is to be enacted as an influence, which is *mediated* (*mediated_relation*) by a Coordination Medium. The *type* of the influence controls the direction of the automated enactment. In this case (*POSITIVE*), the activities in the Endpoint component are triggered to decide for and carry out the local *adjustment* of the (host) agent.

```
<MASDynamic name="convention_emergence">                              2
  ...
  <system_variables>
    <role_occupations>                                                4
      <role_occupation name="activity">
        <agent id="SenderReceiver" />                                 6
      </role_occupation>
      <role_occupation name="adjustment">                             8
        <agent id="SenderReceiver" />
      </role_occupation>                                              10
    </role_occupations>
  </system_variables>                                                 12

  <relations>                                                         14
    <mediated_relations>
      <mediated_relation realization="by-network"                     16
                         type="POSITIVE"
                         name="inform_convention_value">              18
        <publishers>
          <publisher>activity</publisher>                             20
        </publishers>
        <subscribers>                                                 22
          <subscriber>adjustment</subscriber>
        </subscribers>                                                24
      </mediated_relation>
    </mediated_relations>                                             26
    ...
  </relations>                                                        28
</MASDynamic>
```

Listing 5.5: Convention Emergence: The enacted Coordination Model

The declaration describes the single missing link that is needed to complete the intended feedback loop among the agents (cf. Figure 5.20). The declaration is in principle independent of the target MAS realization, but variable declarations allow references to implementation-specific agent models. The automated enactment of an influence is controlled by the referenced configuration

5.4. CASE STUDIES

of the Medium (*realization*, line 16). This configuration (*by_network*) is given in Listing 5.6 to illustrate the fine-grained specification of (1) the relevant agent-events and (2) the parameterization of Media. These specifications refer to the actual MAS implementation and describe the mapping of the conceived process, or rather the supplement for realizing this process, onto the agent realizations.

The declarations of the relevant events contain the events themselves, which are observed and actuated by the Endpoint component, as well as the transmitted data. Events are identified by the unique combination of the event name (*element*), the agent type that contains these events (*agent_id*), and the type of event (*type*). Here, the observation of adoptions of the goal *observed_activity* is specified (lines 6-9). The adoption of an agent-internal goal signifies the engagement of the agent in a specific activity [Sudeikat and Renz, 2007a]. These publications contain the current configuration of the actuated agent (lines 9-12). The agents store this value in an agent belief (*color*) and the declaration controls that, upon the occurrence of the observed event, the value of this belief is extracted and included in the communicated data structure. The reception of this information actuates an agent-internal event (*stimulus*) that triggers the local reasoning to decide whether to adjust the local configuration or not. This reasoning and the triggering event is encapsulated in an Adaptivity Component. However, this encapsulation is transparent to the process declaration as it relies solely on the event-based agent interface (cf. Section 5.2.7). The communicated configuration is mapped onto a parameter of the induced internal event (lines 19-21). The declaration of the mapping in the event observation (line 11) assigns the transmitted value to an identifier (*ref*). Upon reception, this identifier is used to reference the communicated data and assign it to a parameter (*color*) of the actuated event (line 20).

The dissemination of information is controlled by a Coordination Medium. In this case study, the Medium constrains the possible communications by arranging Coordination Endpoints in an overlay network (see Appendix B.1.2). On agent start-up Endpoints register themselves at the medium and the medium responds to a registration with a list of virtually connected agents with which the endpoint is allowed to communicate. The medium and the communicative behavior of the agents is configured by specifying a set of parameters (lines 22-37). The specification of the medium-specific Endpoint realization enables the automated loading of this module on agent initialization. The loading is transparent to the agent and the agent realizations are only required to contain the generic bootstrap mechanism (cf. Section 5.3.5) that processes MASDynamics models. Parameters are specified as key/value pairs. In Listing 5.6, two parameters are specified. First, the communicativeness of endpoints is declared (lines 29,30). The endpoints are set to inform 90% of their neighboring agent/endpoints. Other possible values are the keywords *Broadcast* that corresponds to a 100% setting and *Random* that makes Endpoints inform a randomly selected neighbor. The second parameter controls the network topology. Here, the overlay network is laid out as a random graph. The configuration of the differing topologies is based on additional parameters that have been omitted (cf. Section B.1.2).

```
<MASDynamic name="convention_emergence">                                    1
...
 <mediated_influence_realizations>                                          3
  <realization id="by-network">
   <observing>                                                              5
    <agent_element element="observed_activity"
                   agent_id="SenderReceiver"                                7
                   type="BDI_GOAL">
     <agent_data_mappings>                                                  9
      <mapping name="color" data="content"
               ref="convention_value" type="BDI_BELIEF" />                  11
     </agent_data_mappings>
    </agent_element>                                                        13
   </observing>
   <inducing>                                                               15
    <agent_element element="stimulus"
                   agent_id="SenderReceiver"                                17
                   type="INTERNAL_EVENT">
     <parameter_mappings>                                                   19
```

190   CHAPTER 5. A SYSTEMIC PROGRAMMING MODEL

```
            <mapping ref="convention_value" name="color"/>
          </parameter_mappings>                                              21
        </agent_element>
      </inducing>                                                            23
      <medium_configuration
          agent_type="JADEX"                                                 25
          mechanism_id="deco4mas.mechanism.network.Network">
        <properties>                                                         27
          <entry>
            <key>distribution_type</key>
            <value>0.9</value>                                               29
          </entry>
            <key>graph_type</key>                                            31
            <value>Random</value>
          </entry>                                                           33
          ...                                                                35
        </properties>
      </medium_configuration>                                                37
    </realization>
</mediated_influence_realizations>                                           39
...
```

Listing 5.6: The enacted Coordination Model

Simulation Results

A sample simulation[13] run is illustrated in Figure 5.21 (I). Two phases can be distinguished. In the first phase the agents are started and randomly initialized.[14] The agents start and are registered in sequence; the exponential increase of agent values is an artifact that results from a single observing element that processes the registrations of agents in sequence. In the second phase the local activities are randomly triggered and the coordination model kicks in and gives rise to a convention value as the opposing value is gradually removed. Which value is enforced is decided by chance.

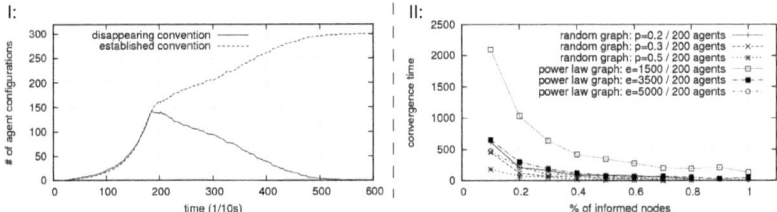

Figure 5.21: Convention Emergence simulation results [Sudeikat and Renz, 2010a]. I: A sample (averaged over 10 runs). 300 agents, which are arranged in a random graph (p = 0.2), reach agreement [Sudeikat and Renz, 2010a]. II: Convergence times on varying agent counts, graph topologies and communication fractions.

The convergence time depends on several parameters. Here, the impact of the constraining network *topology* and the local *communicativeness* of the agents is examined for the given simulation scenario, following [Sudeikat and Renz, 2010a]. The system simulations make use of medium realization that allows to arrange Coordination Endpoints in different network topologies (see Appendix B.1.2). The properties of randomly generated, complex graph topologies are

---
[13]of 300 agents, averaged over 10 runs
[14]normally distributed

5.4. CASE STUDIES

well-investigated, e.g. see [Albert and Barabasi, 2002]. Primary subjects of study are purely random and *power law* distributed graphs, and the effects of these topologies are examined for the given simulation setting [Sudeikat and Renz, 2010a]. The generation of random graphs follows the *Erdős-Rényi* binomial model (cf. [Albert and Barabasi, 2002], p. 8), i.e. pairs of N nodes are connected with a fixed probability p and the expected number of edges is $E(N) = p\frac{N(N-1)}{2}$. The generation of power law distributed graphs follows [Eppstein and Wang, 2002].[14] In these graphs, the distribution of the *node degree*, i.e. the number of edges to which nodes are connected, follows a power law. Therefore, the probability that a node has k edges follows $P(k) \sim k^{-\gamma}$. The *communicativeness* of agents is given by the percentage of connected nodes that are informed when an Endpoint publishes a configuration value. This parameter is specified in the configuration of the Coordination Medium.

The effects of these parameters are displayed in Figure 5.21 (II).[15] The y-axis denotes the exhibited convergence time. The establishment of a convergence is assumed when 95% of the agents agree. The x-axis shows the communicativeness of the Endpoints. The generation of graph topologies is controlled by two distinct parameters. Random graphs are initialized with different p-values (0.2,0.3, and 0.5; cf. Table 5.2) and power law distributed graphs are configured by limiting the numbers of edges between the agents.[16]

Both topology types exhibit a comparative decay of convergence times as the communicativeness is increased. Convergence is reached quickly for mid-level communicativeness values, and increasing the fraction of informed agents to more than 70% has only a minor impact. A comparison of the number of edges (cf. Table 5.2) reveals that power law distributed topologies disseminate information more effectively. These graphs are set to include fewer edges (between 3500 and 5000, cf. figure 5.21). Consequently, the number of sent messages is reduced while similar convergence times are retained.

Graph Type	# of Edges
Random (p=0.2 / 200 nodes)	approx. 3992.7 [5]
Random (p=0.3 / 200 nodes)	approx. 5975.9 [5]
Random (p=0.5 / 200 nodes)	approx. 9949.5 [5]
Power Law (200 nodes)	set to fixed values

Table 5.2: The numbers of edges in the simulated graph topologies [Sudeikat and Renz, 2010a]

In the described MAS, used for simulating convention emergence, the adaptive process that controls the mutual agreement on the convention value is distributed among the agents. This simple scenario is selected to show the practicability of the framework proposed here. It allows to separate activities that are related to coordination from the internals of the agent implementations. The endpoints monitor the agent execution to infer when to communicate the locally contained value. The propagation of these communications is separated as it is carried out by a medium infrastructure. Incoming communications are processed within Endpoints and adjustments of the agent models are determined and carried out. These activities constitute a process that manages an agent belief value. Using the programming approach is supplemented and enacted by the background processing inside the Endpoints. The embedded process manifest the system behavior that corresponds to the dynamics indicated by the ACBG-based process model (see Figure 5.20, I). The expected convergence of agent values is brought about by the integrated background processing. This case study demonstrates, by reference to a simple process, that the programming model proposed here allows to embed inter-agent processes. These processes are conceptually and technologically separated from the agent realizations.

---

[15]For simulations of 200 agents, averaged over 10 simulation runs. The constant initialization delay is removed.
[16]set to: 1500, 3500, and 5000
[5]averaged over 100 generated graphs

5.5 Conclusions

In this chapter, a comprehensive programming approach is presented that allows decentralized Coordinating Processes to be executed as a supplement to MASs. The basic parts of the programming model are the process execution and the process specification. A distributed run-time environment prepares the participation in processes as auxiliary aspects of agent execution (see Section 5.2). The process execution is configured by a corresponding language that is based on the augmentation of systemic process models with configuration details (see Section 5.3).

The parts of the programming model are summarized in Figure 5.22. The initial point for development efforts is the identification of a *Coordinating Process* that is integrated in an agent-based application. Examples for these processes are given in Sections 3.2.2 (page 62) and 5.4 (page 183). The *systemic* modeling approach, as presented in Chapter 4, allows the working principles of decentralized processes which rise from the mutual interactions of autonomous system entities to be described. The *Agent Causal Behavior Graph* (ACBG) (cf. Section 4.2.3) is the major means of describing Coordinating Processes among agents, and this modeling stance is illustrated in Section 4.4.1. In this chapter, the *MASDynamics* language is introduced (cf. Section 5.3), which allows ACBGs to be expressed. The systemic modeling stance is supplemented with the ability to prescribe the enactment of processes. The configured processes are carried out by the coordination architecture that is introduced in Section 5.2. The fundamental building blocks are the *Coordination Media* (cf. Section 5.2.10) and the *Endpoint* modules (cf. Section 5.2.3) that control the access of media and the effects of information exchanges. The MASDynamics language provides a vehicle for externalizing and managing process definitions, as is allows the functioning of these modules to be configured. Coarse-grained process descriptions can be stored and incrementally refined with the information necessary to integrate these processes into *MAS Implementations*.

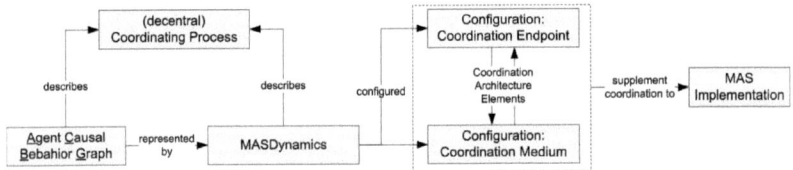

Figure 5.22: The relations between the concepts and tools introduced in this chapter

The focus of the work presented here is the overall architecture of the coordination middleware and the strict encapsulation of the participation in Coordinating Processes. This separation is mainly carried out within Endpoint modules. Besides a detailed discussion of their principled structure, their operating principle is discussed and formalized with respect to a specific agent architecture (see Section 5.2.4). The Endpoints make use of Media which serve as communication infrastructures. The principled implementation alternatives and their embedding in the middleware layer are discussed, but the realization of Media is not explicitly prescribed. Instead these are understood as an extension concept that allows different interaction mechanisms/techniques to be integrated. The media realizations that were utilized in the case studies are discussed in Appendix B.

Two case studies exemplify the utilization of the described tool set (see Section 5.4). The specification of externalized process models, their mapping to an MAS implementation, and the execution of the process are demonstrated. Prominent types of self-organizing processes are adopted and described in systemic models. These models are detailed to configure the enactment of the sections of the process that are not present in the dynamics of the MAS. In the *bee-based server management* (see Section 5.4.1), this concerns the supplementation of a missing influence that completes a nature-inspired process. In the second example (see Section 5.4.2), a generic MAS

5.5. CONCLUSIONS

is supplemented with a process that causes the *emergence of convention* values. It defines a background processing inside an agent population that controls the concurrent updating of agent knowledge bases to cause consent.

The enactment architecture discussed in this chapter is based on the integration of a Distributed Event-based System (DES) that provides a middleware layer for coordination enactments. In software architecture design, DES are powerful tools for conceiving decoupled distributed applications. However, the flexibility of interactions and the decoupling of components models that are imposed by this architectural style complicate the coordination of system elements. The conception of applications demands the proper orchestration of event-based systems, in order to enforce the resulting system functionality, as identified by [Mühl et al., 2006] (page 17). The systemic programming model that supplements the coordination infrastructures presented here is an example of such a design support. This modeling approach allows developers to deduce the macroscopic effects that result from the integration of (event-based) dependencies among types of system elements. While the design stance advocated here (cf. Chapter 4) addresses the circular dependencies that are inherently present in self-organizing systems, it can be speculated that the scheme of classifying component behaviors and modeling their dependencies may be elaborated to an more general approach to the orchestration of event-based systems.

Event-based systems are an active research area in and of itself and ongoing work spans several areas that were not addressed in the presented definition of the coordination architecture (e.g. cf. [Mühl et al., 2006]). *Security*, *fault tolerance*, *congestion* control, and *mobility* are just a few areas that can be mentioned. These issues are relevant for preparing the operation of self-organizing applications in industrial settings and form extension points for future revisions of the architecture.

Enforcement of the Separation of Coordination and Entity Function

The proposed coordination architecture encapsulates the enactment of inter-agent coordination in an additional middleware layer. This layer enforces the architectonic separation of the process execution from the internal logic of agents (see Challenge 5.1, page 136). Different agent architectures can be integrated by realizing architecture-specific Coordination Endpoints, particularly tailored realizations of Agent State and Coordination Information Interpreters (cf. Section 5.2.2). In principle, the architecture supports the integration of heterogeneous MASs. The communicated data follow a generic interface definition and the embedding of the local adaptivity is based on agent architecture-specific events. However, the architecture and interface definitions assume that agent implementations are based on coherent data representations. The transfer of data types between different encodings, e.g. imposed by differing programming languages, requires the preparation of appropriate data conversions.

Preparing the Coordination of Autonomous Software Components

For the design of endpoint modules, minimally invasive integration is a crucial concern (see Challenge 5.2, page 136). The autonomy of the agents is retained by exploiting the event-based execution cycle of agents. In the deliberative language model, reasoning events are declared that are either relevant for the observation of the agent execution or actuate modifications of the agent configuration. The set of events defines the interface between the Endpoints and the agent realization. Endpoints monitor agent execution by observing the events of the agent-internal reasoning. The process logic inside the Endpoint, defined by the declarative configuration language and optional procedural knowledge, controls when the Endpoint engages in activities that are conceptually related to the coordination, e.g. the initiation or the participation in interactions. The outcomes of these activities are implications for the execution of the host agents associated to Endpoints. These implications are injected into the reasoning cycle by dispatching additional reasoning events, as a result of the reasoning inside Endpoints. The dispatched events reference agent elements and can be guarded by logical conditions. These conditions guard the adjustments that Endpoints can affect, thus the agent reasoning retains the authority of adjustments and these can be neglected when the agent context prohibits the proposed modifications. More complicated conditioning of the execution of modifications can be realized in Adaptivity Components. Developers can integrate arbitrary agent-programming code to decide the extent and conditions of modifications. These tools allow both the strict enforcement of the indicated adjustments as well as the deliberate reasoning about the applicability of suggested modifications to be realized.

Realization of the Separation of Interaction and Adaptation

The interactions and the local control of the adaptations, which cause the initiation of and/or result from interactions, are the two fundamental building blocks of a Coordinating Process (see Challenge C 5.3, page 136). The structure of the Coordination middleware separates these aspects and supports combinability. Endpoints and Media are loosely coupled by a generic usage interface. The details of the conduct of interactions are hidden from Endpoints and the Media are used as reusable infrastructure elements. An implication of this approach is the anonymity of interaction partners. This causes a decoupling of agents, and in self-organizing systems the identity of interaction partners is often irrelevant. The examples in this thesis only contain one scenario where the identity is relevant, i.e. as a part of a request for assistance (see Section 6.8.1). In these cases the required data can be explicitly integrated in the data content that is transmitted within an interaction.

Describing Coordinating Processes in Standalone Design Elements

The outsourcing of the configuration of the process enactment, based on the declarative configuration language (see Section 5.3), prepares the design of inter-agent processes as stand-alone design artifacts (see Challenge 5.4, page 137). These artifacts are mapped to MASs by the interface between the Endpoints and their associated agents (see previous section). Besides these connections, the ACBG-based description of a Coordinating Process is independent from specific applications and can be reused in different contexts. This reuse is supported by the different abstraction levels that are integrated in the language model. A generic process structure can be described and this structure is complemented by sets of detailed configurations of processes partitions. The case studies illustrate the mapping of the generic process structures to specific applications.

Chapter 6

Systematic Integration of Decentralized Coordination

The previously described set of techniques (see Chapter 5) facilitates the integration of decentralized, inter-agent Coordinating Processes in conventionally developed software systems, here MASs. The presented programming model allows for the externalization, and consequently the conceptual separation, of the prescriptions of these processes. The automated enactment of these prescriptions within functioning applications is enabled by an execution middleware architecture. In this respect *functioning* means that the application components themselves are operative and provide self-managed functionalities. Due to the enforced separation, the embedding of coordination is transferred to a self-contained design concern that addresses the effective system-wide operation of an application. The Coordinating Processes, which are added to applications to enhance their macroscopic system behavior, becomes an independent design artifact that can be shared, versioned, reused, etc., in a software producing organization.

Making use of this programming model, which gives full control of process definitions and configurations, demands individual expertise and elevates one aspect of the application development, namely the inter-agent coordination. The adoption of this programming approach requires the integration into systematic development practices. In this chapter, the systematic construction of process prescriptions, including requirements, design and validation activities, are addressed. A structured design procedure and its integration in established development practices is discussed. In order to prepare the general applicability of the procedure, it is conceptualized as a complement to development processes. Development teams make use of established development methodologies and *also* supplement self-organizing features to their application, when necessary. The presented procedure highlights the fundamental design activities for the conception of inter-agent coordination and exemplifies these activities using the example of systemic programming.

6.1 Motivation

The ability to treat Coordinating Processes as design artifacts is a prerequisite for their systematic conception and structured supplementation into software systems. The design of these processes has to be aligned with conventional engineering procedures that guide the development of the functional components. The iterative, systematic construction of Coordinating Processes should be instructed by tailored development procedures. These procedures can not dissolve the *creative act* that is constituted by the conception of a decentralized problem solution. However, the principal steps, which are necessary to derive such a solution and to integrate the resulting processes into a software application, are highlighted. The structured documentation of these steps does not only guide system implementations but clarifies the abilities and limitations of the programming model used and allows it to be compared to alternative development techniques.

Agent-oriented development methodologies systematize the development of MAS (see Section

2.6.3). They describe field-tested practices for the development of MAS and the use of this practices is also attractive for the development of self-organizing applications. These applications are MAS that are equipped with adaptive features. This assumption is corroborated by the observation of the relation between development methodologies and the implementation platform used (see Section 2.6.3). The match between design-level and implementation-level concepts affects the effectiveness of the development support. In order to minimize constraints on the used implementation platforms the interchangeable use of development methodologies should be supported. Therefore, it is of practical interest how to combine the MAS development with the development of Coordinating Processes. The programming model allows for the technical separation of the coordination-related activities from the agent models. It is of conceptual interest to continue this separation on the design level, as it prepares the exchangeability of development practices. The development procedure presented in this chapter does not interfere with other aspects of the application development to enable that the procedure can be used in combination with different methodology instances. The use of method engineering concepts (see Section 2.6.3) allows to enforce the needed conceptual separation of the different development aspects.

The use of the described programming model can follow two principal development stances. First, developers decide right from the start of the application development to externalize Coordinating Processes. This approach is justified when the development of the application implies frequent changes of the applied processes, the contained coordination mechanisms, and configuration parameters, e.g. as found when *prototyping* a self-organizing application in bottom-up development. Alternatively, development teams can aim at the integration of a Coordinating Process during or after the construction of the system elements involved. Detrimental effects on the overall system behavior are resolved by supplementing inter-agent coordination as an enhancement of the dynamic system behavior.

In both scenarios, the application development can make use of the available development methodologies for agent-based systems (see Section 2.6.3). The integration of inter-agent processes is a means to adjust the system behavior as it is, i.e. as it results from the behavior of the system elements. The constructed agents do not function in isolation, but inherently interact with other agents to achieve their designated functionality. Thus the application shows a macroscopic observable behavior. The analysis of these behaviors was discussed in Section 4.3 and exemplified given in Section 4.3.4. Using the systemic programming model, the behavior of conventionally developed applications is tuned by supplementing additional interdependencies that constitute inter-agent processes.

6.1.1 Challenges

C 6.1: Conception of Application Dynamic

A fundamental challenge is the conception of an *appropriate* Coordinating Process. The appropriateness is judged by the ability of the supplemented inter-agent process to affect the dynamic system properties as it is intended. This conception requires the developer to span the fundamental development disciplines of an engineering endeavor. Developers need to infer the intended dynamics (requirements), conceive a process structure (analysis), refine it to a prescription that can be enacted (design), and show that the intended effects are manifested (validation). A key challenge is to prepare the revision of a process structure that is capable of introducing the intended effects. This *design* of a self-organizing process is intrinsically difficult, e.g. in [Sudeikat and Renz, 2006] this *Complex Systems Engineering Paradox* is given by the challenge of (page 82):

> how to revise implementations in a way that the rise of macroscopic artefacts is ensured

Reasoning about the structure of the processes that govern the systems operation sequences provides an approach to this challenge. While the intuition and insights into decentralized Coordinating Processes are required, systemic modeling provides a data structure that facilitates design efforts, as discussed in Section 6.2.1.

C 6.2: Integrating Top-Down and Bottom-up Development

Approaching this engineering challenge requires the ability to systematically refine the structure of a Coordinating Process as well as to estimate the effects that result from this process when it is embedded in the target application. The integration of this top-down design and bottom-up analysis is a common theme for development processes, as discussed in Section 3.2.4, and the development of the Coordinating Process must also be founded on this dichotomy.

C 6.3: Supplementation of Application Dynamics

The conception of a Coordinating Process is followed by its integration into an MAS. The previously described programming framework allows the automated enactment of process configurations. Once an intended process structure is found, the mapping of this process to a specific application should be delineated by a repeatable procedure that is independent from the agent platform used.

C 6.4: Methodology Integration

The development of agent-based applications is supported by a set of sophisticated development methodologies, as discussed in 2.6.3. The fact that developers follow an established development procedure should be taken into account, thus the conception of the inter-agent coordination must anticipate the concurrent or subsequent development of the functional application elements, i.e. the agents and their environments. The assumptions about the sequence of development activities should be minimized so as not to constrain the set of compatible development methodologies.

6.1.2 Related Work

The subset of methodologies which specifically address the construction of self-organizing agent-based applications is discussed in Section 3.2.4. The need to prepare for the possible integration of the development approach presented here into established development methodologies is argued in the motivation of this chapter. The set of available agent-oriented software engineering methodologies is extensive (e.g. see [Henderson-Sellers and Giorgini, 2005; Bergenti et al., 2004]) and their attributes are discussed in Section 2.6.3. The set of methodologies that can coexist with the development approach discussed here shall be constrained as less as possible. Therefore the integration is not discussed with a specific set or type of methodologies in mind, but rather a method engineering framework is used (see the following section). The ad hoc creation of tailored development processes using method engineering concepts and tools is discussed in Section 2.6.3. Fragments are not only extracts from complete design methodologies, but can also provide self-contained contributions to development processes. In [Cossentino et al., 2007], the work in [Pena and Corchuelo, 2004] is given as an instance which provides an analysis procedure for MAS development. Thus specific aspects of the MAS development can be systematized and reused in MAS development, without necessarily embedding them in a comprehensive development approach. This ability is attractive, as it allows the description of the use of a specific tool set for a self-contained activity in the development of MASs. Another SPEM-based description of a self-contained MAS-analysis practice is given in Section 4.3. In the remainder of this chapter, this modeling approach is followed to describe the integration of Coordinating Processes in MASs. The presented segment of MAS development is contained in a Process Pattern, as it describes the incremental and iterative conception and integration of Coordinating Processes. The contained Activities described span different development disciplines.

The following presentation of novel partitions of MAS development, which concern the conception and integration of Coordinating Processes, do not follow a rigorous fragment description format. Appropriate formats for agent-oriented development processes are under active study, see e.g. [Rougemaille et al., 2009b; Seidita et al., 2009; Cossentino et al., 2007]. In [Cossentino et al., 2007], the basic elements of a fragment definition are outlined. These are not all mandatory, but are applied when appropriate:

- The specific *portion* of the development process. The order of activities by stakeholders are indicated, using the SPEM notation.

- The *deliverables*, i.e. Work Products, that are accessed, modified, generated, etc., within development Activities.

- The *preconditions* that constrain the applicability of the Activities that are contained in a fragment. Their informal specification is proposed in [Cossentino et al., 2007].

- The *components of the MAS meta model* that are generated or modified by the process elements.

- The *application guidelines* that outline the use of the fragment.

- A *glossary* to unambiguously identify referenced concepts.

- *Composition guidelines* that guide the selection of fragments by highlighting the problem that is addressed by the fragment.

- A textual description of specific *aspects*, e.g. tool sets used or the contexts where the fragment is applicable.

- An indication of the *dependency relationships* among fragments. These particularly support the description of fragments that vary in their extent and groups of conceptually related fragments.

In the following, the partitions for the embedding of Coordinating Processes are structured in a set of conceptually related development *Activities*, using the SPEM notation [Object Management Group, 2008] (see Section 2.6.3). Each Activity is discussed as a self-contained segment of a development process and indicates the Work Products that are accessed and/or generated. The obtained deliverables are discussed for each Activity. Necessary preconditions for each Activity, as well as the dependencies among them, are given by the availability of the required Work Products. These artifacts represent mandatory or optional input/output and thus define how Activities relate. The resulting control flow is discussed in Section 6.3.1, but the Activities are, in principle, independent work units that can be performed in isolation, e.g. examinations of the required system level adaptivity (cf. Section 6.4) or validations of the effects of agent-coordination (cf. Section 6.7) can contribute to generic development efforts, independent of the revision and embedding of a Coordinating Process, which are concerned with collective effects, e.g. application *redesigns* as discussed in Section 3.4.1. However, the set of Activities describes a coherent development processes for externalized coordination models. The underlying MAS meta-model is discussed in Section 3.3. Several Work Products and artifacts refer to design concepts and notations that are introduced in Chapters 4 and 5. In the corresponding sections and definitions, the relations to the conceptual model of a self-organizing MAS can be found. The discussions of the Activities contain separated instructions for their use, references to the concepts and techniques used and additional aspects as well as indications for the addressed objectives and their applicability in a development context.

6.2 Designing Decentralized Self-Organization

The systemic modeling approach (cf. Chapter 4) and the corresponding programming model (cf. Chapter 5) that are discussed in the previous chapters lay the foundation for a novel design approach to the conception of self-organizing dynamics in software.

6.2.1 Partial Resolution of the Contradiction

The design of self-organized coordination is a fundamental engineering challenge, since developers are forced to revise the microscopic system entities to affect the manifestation of macroscopic system properties. The fundamental development problematic is the bridging of the micro-macro-link in MAS development (e.g. see Section 3.2.3). The macroscopic properties that arise from the coaction of interdependent agents can not be straightforwardly anticipated. Thus the modifications of agents, i.e. their redesign, requires adjusted modeling approaches (see Section 3.4) and the conception of self-organizing processes on the drawing board is inherently problematic [Prokopenko, 2008b; Sudeikat and Renz, 2006]. Instead practitioners have turned to successive cycles of application prototyping, system simulation, and detailed modification to bring about self-organizing applications (see Section 3.2).

The key to the circumvention of this dilemma is the explicit modeling of the feedbacks that cause self-organizing phenomena. The distributed interdependencies and influences among system elements are the substantial causes for these system level effects (see Section 3.1.4). Their description expresses the dynamics that cause a self-organizing phenomenon, not the phenomenon itself. In this dissertation, this orthogonal abstraction-level is introduced that facilitates reasoning about the causes of system-level properties. This development conception is conceptually based on the intermediate modeling level that is discussed in Section 3.4. The microscopic agent models are abstracted and the behavior of agents is classified with respect to their contribution to the phenomenon of interest. The influences and side-effects of these distinct behaviors are then modeled. The resulting model highlights the structure of causal influences that underlies in MAS. Consequently, the decentralized process, understood as a structure of mutual and possibly cyclic agent interdependencies, is exposed as a discrete element in the application design and construction.

However, the purposeful conception of a process refinement, in order to achieve an intended system behavior, remains problematic. In general, coupled feedback loops can show complicated, even counter-intuitive, behaviors (see Section 4.2.1). A simple heuristic that has proven to be useful in this context is the extension of models with supplementary influences and feedbacks, to enhance the system behavior. The behavior of an MAS is modeled *as-is* and is searched for the cause of problematic, unintended dynamics. Then additional influences are supplemented to bring about additional feedbacks that oppose the unintended system property. This strategy localizes the adjustments that are made and thus simplifies the task of tracing the consequences that result from the planned adjustments. It is appropriate for the development of self-adaptive systems, as the supplements are the partitions of the governing feedback structure that cause adjustments.

6.2.2 Principled Development Strategies

Three principal development strategies for the integration of Coordinating Processes in MASs are identified and demonstrated in this dissertation. First, the Coordinating Process is blended with the application logic (*Non-Externalized Coordination*). This is the conventional development approach were the conceptual separation of the agent functionality and the inter-agent coordination is neglected. The case studies in Section 3.4 follow this approach. The programming model that is presented in the previous chapter enables two novel design stances that are conceptually based on the integration of inter-agent processes. The coordination can also be completely separated from the agent models (*Externalized Coordination*). This allows for the highest flexibility as the process is completely configured in declarative process models. In addition, there is a hybrid approach which adjusts the dynamic behavior shown by an application by supplementing an externalized coordination model (*Partially Externalized Coordination*). The supplement does not describe a complete Coordinating Process, e.g. a refinement of a process template (cf. Section 4.4.1), but is specifically designed to adjust the dynamics of a specific application.

Non-Externalized Coordination

This development approach is based on an early conception of the dynamic properties that an application is expected to show. When the dynamics of the application domain and the required dynamics of the developed software system are well-understood development teams can directly begin to embed coordination into the designs of the system entities. In the resulting agent models, the activities that concern the inter-agent coordination and the activities that concern the agent functionality are blended.

Conventional development approaches to self-organizing systems, as reviewed in Section 3.2, follow this approach. The fundamental design steps for this development stance are discussed in Section 3.3. The development of a software system is extended with activities that guide the conception and implementation of the self-organized coordination. The coordination, particularly the use of interaction techniques and the local adjustments of agents, are directly implemented in the agent models. Simulations of system abstractions and the software system are used to understand the required dynamics and guide the fitting of agent models. These adjustments concern the parameterization and/or their *redesign* (see Section 3.4.1). The identified interaction pattern (see Section 3.2.1) and template processes (see Section 3.2.2) serve as design inspirations that are to be embedded in MASs. The interaction techniques are integrated by blending the control flow inside agents with the initialization and participation in interactions. Interaction techniques decouple agent models, but the agent designs are dependent on the semantics of these techniques. The template processes are integrated by specifically designing the agents for compliance.

Multi-level modeling techniques (see Section 3.4) which are supported by the systemic modeling approach that is devised in this theses (cf. Chapter 4) assist this development approach. Their use is exemplified in the Sections 3.4.2, 3.4.3, and 4.4.2. This design stance directly leads to the system implementation. When development teams can ensure that the intended dynamics are brought about by specific process templates and/or interaction techniques, their immediate integration is appropriate. This is particularly true when development teams possess expertise in specific coordination mechanisms and are thus able to anticipate the resulting system dynamics. The generated system realizations are tightly coupled with the embedded coordination logic and infrastructures. The exchange of interaction mechanisms or the switching to other coordination templates, as is often necessary in explorative prototyping of applications, implies vital adaptations of the implementation of the application elements.

Externalized Coordination

Alternatively, the construction of a decentralized, adaptive application can be approached by explicitly separating agent function and agent coordination [Sudeikat and Renz, 2009b]. The executable agent models and the model of the governing Coordinating Process are developed in parallel. The agents serve mainly as a provider of functionalities that autonomously control the provision of activities and pro-actively pursue their local objectives. The communication and interaction that are conceptually related to the provision of functionalities are realized with middleware services, e.g. agent communication. The coordination of the provision of activities is explicitly defined in an externalized model, e.g. following Section 5.3.

This approach enforces a clear separation of concerns. In a volatile execution environment, it is appropriate to model service providers as agents. The maintenance of their functionality can require local reasoning and pro-activity that are expressible in agent-oriented designs of software elements. Externalizing the coordination facilitates the analysis, and incremental revision of coordination processes and mechanisms.

The analysis and validation of application dynamics is facilitated by this approach, as descriptions of the expected, qualitative behavior can be directly inferred from the process description. This guides the derivation of simulation models of the application dynamics as well as the preparation of system simulations. System validation using externalized coordination models with the assistance of externalized coordination models is presented in Section 6.7. The externalized coordination model, which uses a declarative approach, facilitates the adjustment of the enacted processes. These adjustments range from the parameterization to the exchange of interaction techniques [Sudeikat and Renz, 2008b]. These adjustments require only the adjustment of the process declaration.

This design stance implies additional overhead for the software producing organization. Two types of models, the functional implementation and the process description, have to be maintained, versioned, etc. The executable software system relies on an additional middleware layer that is discussed in Section 5.2.1. The computational and management overhead that is implied facilitates adjustments of the coordination. This flexibility is valuable for the explorative prototyping of applications. It can be applied when the requirements on the software systems are initially not well defined or are expected to be subject to change, e.g. due to complex application domains where the effects of the newly introduced software system are difficult to predict. Also in well defined application settings application designers benefit from the ability to study the effects of different versions of a Coordinating Process. The language model from Section 5.3 prepares for the exploration of different configurations of process models by its ability to store different sets of link realizations in one file. This development approach is exemplified in the Sections 5.4.1 and 5.4.2, where simulation models were specifically built to demonstrate the minimal invasive embedding of coordination processes.

Partially Externalized Coordination

Finally, hybrid development approaches are enforced when developers do not at first intend to construct a self-organizing solution but the demand for decentralized self-adaptivity is encountered during the application development. Following the conventional development of a distributed application, the revision of requirements or the elicitation of the dynamics of the software system created thus far may show that distributed adaptivity is required. Consequently, developers are faced with the challenge of including system level adaptivity with minimal affect on the system components that have already been developed and tested.

One basic design approach is the inclusion of dedicated managing entities. Corresponding system architectures are provided by the research community of self-managing software architectures (cf. Section 3.1.2). These provide architectures and frameworks for the realization of the managing entities that are introduced to manage the configuration of the system or subsystem. When decentralized adaptivity is required, the architectural model for the enactment of Coordinating Processes can be followed (cf. Section 5.2.1). The Endpoint concept separates the agent function from the coordination logic as discussed in Section 5.2.3. A design challenge is the conception of the overall processes, which, when distributed among the system elements, affects the intended system dynamics.

The first step is the analysis of the as-is dynamics of the application. Developers have already prepared a functional system that includes the coordination of agents, using AOSE techniques (see Sections 2.5 and 2.6). Thus the application as developed thus far already exhibits dynamic properties that need to be mapped to a systemic system description. This process is discussed in Section 4.3. Consequently, the required adaptivity can be conceived by supplementing additional relations among system behavior abstractions to introduce additional feedbacks that constitute the intended Coordinating Process. This development stance is exemplified in the Sections 6.8.1 and 6.8.3. The dynamics of a functional system are analyzed the intended behavior is supplemented.

6.3 Process-Integration: Coordination Development

In the following, a subset of development activities is discussed that outlines the conception and iterative adjustment of decentralized Coordinating Processes as well as the integration of these processes in agent-based applications. These activities supplement the construction of agent-oriented development processes. The assumptions about the agent construction process are minimized to render the supplement as independent as possible from the specifics of agent construction that may be supported by certain methodology instances. Therefore, the conventional processes are understood as a black box that iteratively provides models of the system agents and their environment, as well as executable agent models.

These activities are intended to be interleaved with the development of the MAS, i.e. when the design of the agent-based system changes, as to reflect adjusted requirements of system stakeholders, the coordination models may have to be adjusted as well. The mandatory modifications of Work Products by the activities defined here concern the design elements that are only related to the coordination of agents. Optionally, the development of agents may consider redesigns of agents to facilitate Coordinating Processes.

The process definition is a software artifacts in its own right. It is not just component to be embedded but affects the overall behavior of the software system. A direct consequence is that the development of the process spans the principal development stages of a software system. The abstract structure of the proposed development process is given in Figure 6.1. The centered, circular arrows denote the iterative development of a Coordinating Process that is composed of five fundamental problems to be addressed during coordination development (1 to 5). These problems are related to the fundamental disciplines of iterative software development, namely the *Requirements*, *Analysis and Design*, and *Test* development disciplines, as defined by the *Unified Software Development Process* [Jacobson et al., 1999]. This process also contains an *Implementation* discipline. This is not extended as it describes the provision of executables that correspond to the design models. Instead the design of the coordination models addresses the detailing and integrating of a conceived Coordinating Process into an application implementation.

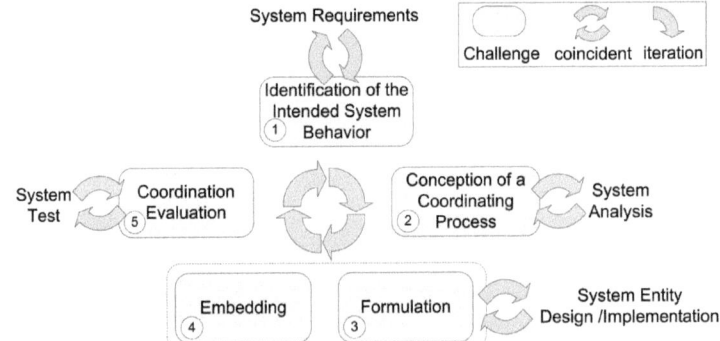

Figure 6.1: Coordination Development: The iterative development of entity coordination is separated but aligned with the application development.

The first design challenge (cf. Figure 6.1, 1) is the *Identification of the Intended Behavior* that stakeholders wish to be exhibited by the future software application. The expectations of the macroscopic exhibited system behavior are formulated to define the purpose of the coordination, i.e. the dynamic modes that the software system is expected to exhibit. This expectation is an additional, functional requirement on the system-wide behavior. In general, the objective of the requirements discipline is to record the requirements for the future software system (e.g. see [Jacobson et al., 1999], Chapter 6). A consensual agreement on the expected system functionality among the system stakeholders is the foundation for the successive development and validation of the constructed software. In this respect, the expected adaptivity and their dynamics are understood as a supplementary set of expectations, i.e. requirements [Sudeikat and Renz, 2007c]. These are recorded in parallel with the other requirements and describe the expected dynamics of adjustments.

The *Conception of a Coordinating Process* (cf. Figure 6.1, 2) concerns the coarse-grained conception of decentralized processes that enables an application to show the intended behavior. Based on models of the intended macroscopic system behavior, i.e. the requirements, these activities concern the inference of the necessary structure of feedbacks among system elements [Sudeikat and Renz, 2010a]. This objective corresponds to the analysis discipline in software development (e.g. see [Jacobson et al., 1999], chapter 8). The purpose of the system analysis is to prepare

6.3. PROCESS-INTEGRATION: COORDINATION DEVELOPMENT

the structuring of the software system and the subsequent application design by processing the requirements and transferring them to technology-oriented models. In this respect, the proposed refinement of the feedback structures is also an (intermediate) analysis activity. The detailed configuration of processes is prepared by the conception of the principal process structure, which is capable of manifesting the intended dynamic behavior. This conception demands the ability to anticipate, e.g. via model simulations, the system-level effects that result from the planned circular interdependencies [Renz and Sudeikat, 2009].

The appropriate feedback structures are expressed as ACBGs (cf. Section 4.2.3) that are the input for the actual integration of the process into an application (cf. Figure 6.1, 3 and 4). The integration is addressed by mapping the process description to the system element implementation (*Formulation*, 3) and the *Embedding* (4) of the prescribed Coordinating Process into the application realization. The mappings (3) can be expressed by the configuration language that is discussed in Section 5.3, and the annotated configurations prepare for the enactment of the conceived process by the coordination execution environment that is discussed in section 5.2. The use of the execution architecture reduces the embedding (4) effort to the triggering of the endpoint initialization (see Section 5.3.4) when agents are started. Alternatively, the participation in the conceived feedbacks has to be prepared manually. This detailing is an instantiation of the process structure with respect to a specific application and therefore corresponds to the design discipline in software development. This discipline produces a *blueprint* (e.g. see [Jacobson et al., 1999], page 216) of the actual implementation of the software. Correspondingly, the preparation of ACBGs concern the derivation of a blueprint for the execution of the inter-agent process. This preparation is sufficient for the supplementation of inter-agent coordination since the execution of process models can be automated (see Chapter 5).

Part of the process development is testing whether embedded processes manifest the intended effects on the observable behavior of the application (*Coordination Evaluation*, 5). This activity extends conventional tests of the system operation, i.e. the operation of the system elements, as addressed in test disciplines (e.g. see [Jacobson et al., 1999], Chapter 11). Besides the validation of the system elements, quantitative system simulations are required that show that the system meets the prior defined requirements, i.e. meets the expectations of the stakeholders. As applied to self-organizing applications, these validations are concerned with the dynamic properties of structure-establishment and the adaptivity of structures, i.e. whether the structures are appropriately modified with respect to external influences (see page 43).

These challenges coincide with the development disciplines, and are sequentially addressed during the iterative development of Coordinating Processes. New iteration cycles can be enforced by modifying MAS-models in the Requirements, Analysis and Design disciplines. Changes in the requirements of the application, the analysis models of the application, or in the element designs can impose modifications in the expected dynamics (1), the process model (2), or the process formulation (3), respectively. Finally, the results of system simulations (5) may indicate adjustments of the process definitions and/or formulations. The essential elements of a development methodology are discussed in Section 2.6. These are a modeling language, a life cycle process, and a a set of supportive techniques. The concepts and tools that are described in the previous chapters 4 and 5 mainly concerned the modeling language and its semantics. The use is supported by selected techniques, including an execution middleware. In this chapter, the development life cycle constituent is addressed.

Following the SPEM terminology, the outlined supplement to application development processes is pooled in a Capability Pattern. These pattern are used to aggregate the method elements to address specific development problems (see Section 2.6.3, page 35). In this context, the pattern *Coordination-Integration* (see Figure 6.2) contains the Activities that relate to the integration of Coordinating Processes.

The *Adaptivity Requirements* Activity supplements requirements engineering disciplines with a procedure to identify the requirements on the adaptivity of an agent-based application [Sudeikat and Renz, 2007c,e]. The main purpose of embedding decentralized Coordinating Processes is to integrate structure formations that realize system level adaptations. These processes enable the application to be adaptive, i.e. to respond to changes in the application context. The derived models complement conventional requirement models with descriptions of system level adjustments.

The *Coordinating Process Definition* Activity provides a set of Tasks to derive and revise a systemic coordination model that enables an MAS to meet the previously defined adaptivity requirements [Sudeikat and Renz, 2010a]. These Tasks guide the refinement of Coordinating Process descriptions and complement the Analysis discipline of iterative software development with the conception of a decentralized process that enables an application to exhibit the previously defined adaptations. Optionally, process templates (cf Section 4.4.1) are integrated. This activity results in an abstract process model that omits application-dependent details but describes the intended coordination process within the application.

The preparation of this process template, in order to prescribe the coordination within a specific realization of the application design, is addressed in the *Coordinating Process Integration* Activity. This Activity extends design disciplines of software projects with the detailed configuration of coordination models. The results of this Activity are executable agent models that are prepared to participate in a Coordinating Process [Sudeikat and Renz, 2009e].

Two Activities concern the validation of Coordinating Processes. Before the revised models are integrated into the software system, the *Coordination Validation (Qualitative)* Activity guides the examination of the revised coordination model in order to check whether it allows MASs to exhibit the intended dynamic, adaptive behavior. Validations are carried out by simulating coordination models and reusing Tasks of the systemic analysis procedure discussed in Section 4.3. Iterative development of coordination models makes use of this Activity to anticipate the impact of revisions of Coordinating Processes.

Finally, testing disciplines are supplemented with procedures to validate that the processes actually manifest the intended dynamic properties *Coordination Validation (Quantitative)* [Sudeikat and Renz, 2009h]. After the integration of the process, this Activity guides the checking of whether the supplemented process has the intended effects on the application behavior.

The primary vehicle to communicate abstract process models is the ACBG graph (cf. Section 4.2.3). In Section 4.3 the derivation of these graphs from agent-oriented application deigns is discussed. The presented Activity is an auxiliary functionality that facilitates the extraction of the causal structure from application designs. Using this Activity, ACBG graphs can be derived from early designs of the applications. These describe the dynamics that the application will exhibit without embedding a Coordinating Process.

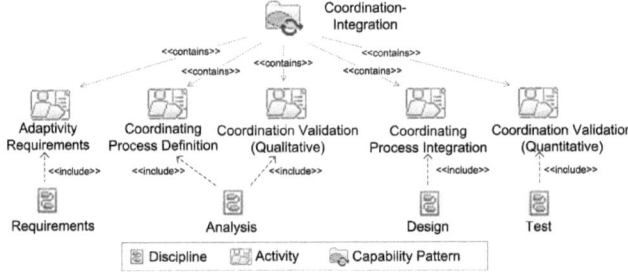

Figure 6.2: Self-contained Activities supplement development disciplines, adapted from [Sudeikat and Renz, 2009e].

6.3.1 Process Life-Cycle and Modified Work Products Overview

The control flow of the outlined development activities is illustrated in figure 6.3. In addition, the Work Products accessed, modified or created are indicated. These Activities and Work Products

6.3. PROCESS-INTEGRATION: COORDINATION DEVELOPMENT

are detailed in the corresponding sections following the outline. Here, the processing of the Activities inside the proposed Capability Pattern is summarized. The individual Activities can also be applied in isolation. Each Activity describes a well-delimited modification of Work Products.

The Adaptivity Requirements Activity precedes the definition of a Coordinating Process. This Activity examines the context of the application in order to identify the intended levels of adaptivity that a software system should show at run-time. The identification of these adjustments is facilitated by the optional creation of a model that describes the dynamics in the application domain (*Systemic Application Domain Dynamics Model*). The identified adjustments concern macroscopic system properties, independent of the individual adjustments within system entities. The application context is given by an informal *Domain Description*. If available, initial models of the basic application structure, i.e. the *Organizational MAS Model* and the *Environment Model* are processed. The activity produces a description of the set of intended system-level adjustments [Sudeikat and Renz, 2007e,c]. The space of adjustments can be given informally or, if the application context is sufficiently elaborated, by ACBG-subgraphs (cf. Section 4.2.3) that describe the responses of the system to changes in the execution context.

Subsequently, the defined requirements for the system adaptivity are considered when defining an appropriate Coordinating Process (*Coordinating Process Definition*). The basis for this top-down definition of the process is the modeling of feedbacks within agent-based applications. A supplement to the dynamical behavior that is per se present in the application is defined and iteratively refined in subsequent cycles of this Activity. The result is an abstract process description (*Coord. Process (MASDynamics Model)*) that excludes implementation-specific details of the agent models but prescribes a set of fundamental interdependencies that constitute the decentralized process among system elements. Optional inputs that support refinements are descriptions of the application design, i.e. *MAS Organization Model*, the *Environment Model* and the *Agent Model(s)*. In addition, refinements may integrate generic sets of interdependencies that are provided by *Process Templates*, as discussed in Section 4.4.1.

Before supplementing the process, the process descriptions may optionally be validated to show their potential ability to meet the identified requirements (*Coord. Process Validation (Qualitative)*). The main tool for this endeavor are stochastic simulation techniques, but formal modeling may also be used as discussed and compared in [Sudeikat et al., 2009b]. The input to this Activity is the derived process model (*Coord. Process (MASDynamics Model)*). This model is transformed into a formalism that allows the simulation, iteration or formal analysis of the process. Since the process model omits details that depend on the actual implementation of the system elements, the applied formalism needs to make justified assumptions about the behavior of the system components. These assumptions are necessary to concretize the derived models to a level that is required for their examination. Therefore, these analyses can only provide estimations of the *qualitative* system behavior.

When it is found that the conceived process is in principle capable of meeting the system requirements, the process is integrated into a concrete system realization that corresponds to the previously processed design models. The Activity *Coord. Process Integration* addresses the joining of implementation-specific details to the process specification to prepare the enactment of the process. The output of this Activity is a group of agent models that are prepared to participate in the process that is controlled by the architecture presented in Section 5.2.

Finally, the resulting application must be validated (*Coord. Process Validation (Quantitative)*). System simulations are required to check that the supplemented process has the intended effects on the system behavior. In addition, the specific parameterizations of elements of the conventionally developed application and the coordination architecture, e.g. the Media used and the processing inside Adaptivity Components, must be tuned, based on system results. This activity follows the same generic outline as the quantitative validation of processes (*Coord. Process Validation (Qualitative)*), but differs insofar as the derivation of the simulation model is fundamentally different in the two Activities.

The Work Products that are marked with arrows ($\rightarrow$ / $\leftarrow$) form the interface between the conventional development of the software application and the supplement of development Activities discussed here. When elements of the application design change ($\rightarrow$), due to the iterative

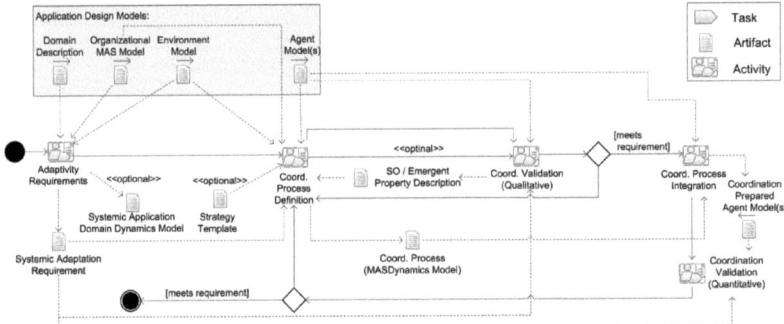

Figure 6.3: Systematic integration of coordination, adapted from [Sudeikat and Renz, 2009e]

development of the application elements, iterations of the Activities described here are indicated, so that it can be reviewed whether the changes induce modifications of the process. These Work Products are used read-only, except for the *Coordination Prepared Agent Model(s)*. These are modified to prepare for the use of the coordination architecture by extending agents with Annotations, Endpoints and Adaptivity Components. The designers of the coordination are responsible for ensuring that these modifications do not have side effects on the behavior of the agents. This effort is facilitated by the non-intrusive design of the coordination architecture, but development teams make certain that the ability to propose agent adjustments is used deliberately to minimize the coordination-related computations inside agent modules and that these computations only affect the agent-internal adoption of behaviors.

6.4 Adaptivity Requirements

Requirements engineering, as a software engineering discipline, concerns the specification of projected system functionality, e.g. [Bray, 2002; Jacobson et al., 1999]. Differing description formats have been proposed, and a format that applies well to designing cognitive agents are *goal-oriented* requirements [van Lamsweerde and Letier, 2004] that uses the goal concept to express the functionality of planned systems. A generally applicable description format are *use cases*, which describe how users interact with the future systems. Graphical notations of these cases, e.g. given in the UML 2.0 format, are supplemented with informal descriptions and models of the sequences of message exchanges, e.g. as UML sequence diagrams, to denote the planned preprocessing inside the system. An additional aspect of this discipline is the prioritization of requirements to focus the subsequent development efforts.

The aim of decentralized Coordinating Processes is the establishment of system adaptivity, i.e. to manifest structures that are continuous adjusted to changes in the application context or influences on the application. The basic properties of the structure-establishing processes are reviewed in Section 4.4.1 and describe the modes and subjects of system adjustments that can be generated by decentralized coordination. When a black-box view on the system adaptivity is adopted (see Section 3.1.1), requirements describe the adjustments that are induced by the inter-agent coordination. The potential system configurations are sized up and the intended reconfigurations, i.e. transitions between macroscopic system configurations are described.

These models supplement established requirements formats with sets of intended system-level reconfigurations that portray the intended macroscopic system dynamics. These descriptions follow a system-theoretic interpretation, where system configurations are understood as points in configuration space. The requirements describe intended trajectories between system configura-

6.4. ADAPTIVITY REQUIREMENTS

tions (cf. Section 3.3). Each requirement describes a class of system configurations that is expected to trigger adjustments. The classifications account for the stochastics of system configurations that are inherent to self-organizing phenomena. In this respect, these models can be seen as use cases for self-organizing systems that denote classes of scenarios where self-imposed adjustments of the system are foreseen. Any details about how adjustments may be enabled are omitted. That an application meets the requirements is validated by inferring simulation calibrations and showing that systems respond as expected.

The basic Tasks of the Requirements specification are illustrated in Figure 6.4. Initially, the context of the planned software system is analyzed to identify the pivotal software elements, their interdependencies, and the processes that are present in the execution context (*Domain Analysis*). Subsequently, the intended system-level adjustments are formulated (*Adaptivity Description*). Optimally, both activities are supported by animating the system adjustments (*System Animation*).

The input to the domain analysis Task is an informal desiccation of the application domain. Optionally, models of the MAS organizational structure (*Organizational MAS Model*) and the system's environment (*Environment Model*) are consulted. Particularity in incremental development, refinements of these models can affect the formulation requirements. A description of the dynamics within the application domain (*Systemic Application Domain Dynamics Model*), i.e. in absence of the planned software system, may be generated by the Domain Analysis Task. The creation/revision of a set of requirements is mandatory (*Systemic Adaptation Requirement*).

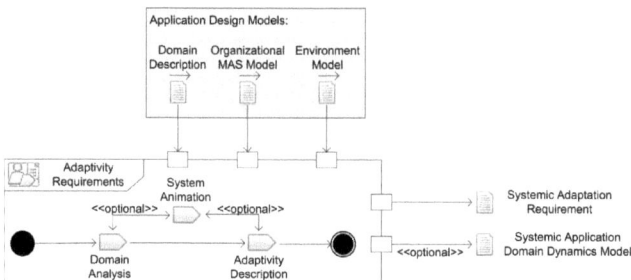

Figure 6.4: Task: Adaptivity Requirements

6.4.1 Domain Analysis

The aim of this Task is to model the dynamics of the context of the planned application and its effects within the application domain. Thus the *actors*, *entities* and their interdependencies are identified. These descriptions must map to AOSE-oriented models of the application and focus on behavioral aspects as to not obstruct their transfer to simulation models and MASDynamics-based Coordinating Process specifications. AOSE practices provide numerous models to define structures of actors and particularly role-based modeling is appropriate, as this concept (cf. Section 2.6.1) provides a common denominator to describe agent activities that can be expressed in simulation models as well as a wide range of design methodology specific notations.

When the purpose of the system is the modification of its context, the system is modeled as a single actor. The requirements describe the effects of this actor on environment elements, e.g. the clustering of environment objects (cf. Section 3.4.2). The need to understand the application domain is found in requirements modeling (e.g. [Yu, 1997]) and has been transferred to the Tropos methodology (cf. Section 2.6.3). During iterative development, details on the system design can be integrated to reflect the expected interactions among the components of the developed application.

6.4.2 Adaptivity Description

In this Task, a set of Adaptivity Requirements are specified. An *Adaptivity Requirement* contains a set of classes of system configurations (*Configuration*) and an *Adaptation Dynamic* that describes how transitions are carried out (cf. Figure 6.5). The configurations are denoted by static organizational structures of the actors that constitute the application context and the application. In principle, diverse agent-oriented modeling notions of organizational structures (see cf. Section 2.6.1), can be used to describe these configurations. As far as decentralized, self-organizing applications are concerned, systems are typically composed of a few agent types with numerous instances. Therefore, the modeling of system configurations by the occupation numbers of specific behavior types, e.g. role adoptions or group memberships, is appropriate [Sudeikat and Renz, 2007c]. Averaged occupation numbers represent macroscopic system continuations, i.e. points in the configuration space. This approach is in accordance with the systemic modeling approach discussed in Chapter 4, and classes of configurations can be defined in absolute value ranges or relative to the system size (%).

The Adaptation dynamics denote how the system gradually changes its configuration, i.e. the set of possible trajectories between points in the configuration space. These transitions can be mathematically formulated, but in order to check the consistency of modeling approaches, CLD diagrams (cf. Section 4.2.1) or the MAS-specific ACBGs can be used. These allow the description of the influences and interdependencies that steer macroscopic changes of the system configurations.

The abstract requirement notion is exemplified for two case studies. For a hypothetical computer immune system, as discussed in Section 4.4.2, the macroscopic requirement is the quick removal of epidemics. An epidemic-configuration is characterized by a sudden high amount of infected agents, e.g. exceeding a percentual threshold. The intended configuration is the absence of infections, i.e. the number of infected agents (i) approaches zero ($i \to 0$). The associated dynamic is controlled by a balancing feedback (IIa) that describes how the amount of intruders is causally related to the effort that that system shows to *disinfect* agents. Thus the removal should be governed by an exponential decay, from the epidemic to the disinfected system configuration (IIb). That the system simulation meets this requirements is shown in Figure 4.26 (I).

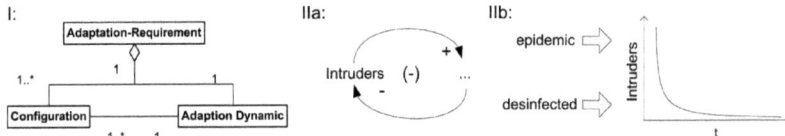

Figure 6.5: The conceptual model of Adaptation Requirements (I) [Sudeikat and Renz, 2007c] and example (IIa,IIb)

6.4.3 System Animation

An optional objective, which assists the conceptualization of the interactions of the actors and elements in the application context and the planned system, is the animation of the expected dynamics. This is done by simulating or iterating the models of the application domain and/or the dynamic that is described by the inferred requirement. Differential equations as well as stochastic simulation models are appropriate for generating these animations [Sudeikat and Renz, 2007c], in that both visualize time series of affected system properties. These visualizations do not only facilitate the formulation of appropriate expectations but are also expected to support the communication with system stakeholders [Sudeikat and Renz, 2007c].

6.5 Coordinating Process Definition

When the required types of adaptivity are conceived, the design of the application coordination is approached to achieve the intended behavior. This refinement is a key challenge for systematic approaches to designing decentralized, self-organizing software systems.

The design of the system behavior is approached by comparing the *as is* system structure and the structure of the idealized system behavior. The difference between both models is factored out, and the identified intersection constitutes the process model that is to be supplemented to the application in the later development Activities.

The supplemented process partitions are introduced to tune the application behavior. Thus the incremental refinement of the application's feedback structure is approached by searching the models for problematic partitions that counteract the desired system behavior. Conceiving a subset of influences among agents that counterbalance these problematic dynamics in the application is a manual modeling effort.

The essential processing within this development Activity is outlined in Figure 6.6. The first Task (*Map Feedback-Structure to Application Model*) concerns the agreement of the requirements with a systemic model of the application dynamics. In this Task the mapping is done and, if necessary, an MASDynamics desiccation of the system dynamics is updated. This updated mode is the basis for refinement operations that are carried out in the Task (*Systemic Coordination Refinement*). The declarative model of a process is refined and supplemented with additional influences to counterbalance feedbacks that cause problematic system properties. Finally, the interaction models that control the spreading of influences among the agents are identified.

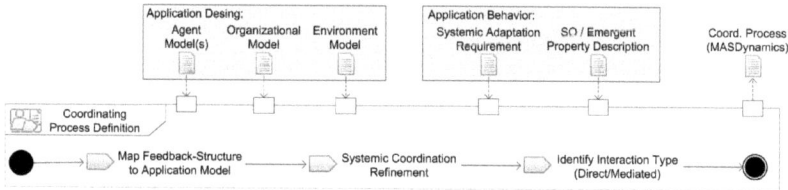

Figure 6.6: Activity: Coordinating Process Definition, adapted from [Sudeikat et al., 2009b]

6.5.1 Map Feedback-Structure to Application-Model

The initial Task provides the basis for the feedback refinements by mapping the intended adaptations, given by the *Systemic Adaptation Requirement*, to ACBG-based design models of the dynamics within an agent-based application (*Coordinating Process Definition*). If a model of the application dynamics is not present, it is created from the available set of agent-oriented design models. Modifications of the application design, brought about by incremental revisions, enforce updates of the process model. The derivation of ACBG-based application models from agent-oriented application designs is discussed in Section 4.3. The Tasks described there are omitted in Figure 6.6 to clarify the basic structure of the design process.

The mapping is carried out by comparing the elements of the adaptation requirements to the elements within the model of the application dynamics. The semantic mapping of system quantities is a manual modeling effort. The involvement of domain experts is required in early iterations to ensure that it is understood how application elements are supposed to modify quantities in the application context. This Task results in an updated model of the application dynamics (*Coord. Process*). Initially, this model describes the dynamics that are present in an application as well as in the application context.

6.5.2 Systemic Coordination Refinement

In this section, the systematic refinement of ACBG models is discussed as an approach to the design of decentralized agent coordination. The modification of the interdependency-network among system elements allows the conception of *intended* structures that, when enacted, enable software systems to meet application requirements. The originating structure results from (1) the analysis of detailed system designs and implementations (cf. Section 4.3) or (2) the abstract conception of an application scenario that is examined prior to the realization of the system elements. Beginning with the identification of problematic dynamics, the obtained causal structure is modified by the inclusion of additional behaviors and interdependencies to adjust the application behavior. For example, the supplementation of additional feedback loops can be used to stabilize unstable systems and enhance the responsiveness to external influences.

The refinement process allows the derivation of an ACBG that describes the intended application structure. This model can serve as a blueprint for the system realization, following two fundamental approaches. First, the application elements can be *built* from scratch or *redesigned*, to realize the conceived interdependencies. Examples of this approach are given in the following section. Secondly, the difference between the actual and the intended element-interdependencies can be factored out into externalized coordination models that can be enacted by a specialized coordination architecture. The latter approach is addressed in the remaining chapters, where the required programming model (Chapter 5) and its systematic use (Chapter 6) are discussed.

The corresponding refinement process is outlined in Figure 6.7 as an SPEM-based development Task. An input is a dynamic model of the application behavior. This input (*Systemic Application Description*) prepares the incremental revision of ACBGs. Alternatively, a CLD can be used to describe the behavior of the application domain. In addition, sets of ACBGs that describe field-tested process templates (*Process Template*), as discussed in Section 4.4.1, can be provided. These serve as a library of reusable structures.

Initially, the original, i.e. un-coordinated, structure of the application dynamic is examined to identify a *problematic* sub-structure (*Problem Dynamic*) that is responsible for unintended dynamic properties. The derived model describes the processes in the systems environment or within the MAS design. The problematic structure is then processed (*Propose Solution Dynamic*) to derive a *Solution Dynamic*, i.e. a systemic model where the problematic structures are supplemented with a network of additional interdependencies and/or feedback loops to adjust the dynamic system properties. This ACBG provides a blueprint of the intended system structure. In the subsequent steps, the proposed solution dynamic is refined to prepare its realization in an agent-based application. This refinement comprises the detailing of variables (*Refine System Variable*) and interdependencies (*Refine Variable Interdependency*). These steps correspond to the refinement operations in ACBGs (cf. Section 4.2.3).

The refinement of the solution dynamic raises the question of how to realize the supplemented structures. When following the externalized implementation approach (see above), tool sets for the realization of agent interdependencies can be used. When the system realization is based in the (re-)design of agent models, it is preferable to base agent designs on established coordination patterns. The integration of these patterns (cf. Section 4.4.1) is denoted as an optional design step (*Integrate Template*). In this step, sets of patterns are selected by their ability to match the refined Solution Dynamic, as proposed in [Sudeikat and Renz, 2008c]. These refinement operations are iterated until a sufficient level of detail has been reached, i.e. the structural elements in the ACBG-based model comprise the conceived set system components and their individual behaviors / configurations. The final output of this Task is a detailed *Coordinating Process*. This model describes a network of agent interdependencies, such as an ACBG, that is tailored to a specific application and its problematic behavior.

6.5.3 Identify Interaction Type

The *Identify Interaction Task* concerns the determination of the interaction mechanisms that are applicable for the realization of specific influences in the Coordinating Process. Their detailed

6.6. COORDINATING PROCESS INTEGRATION

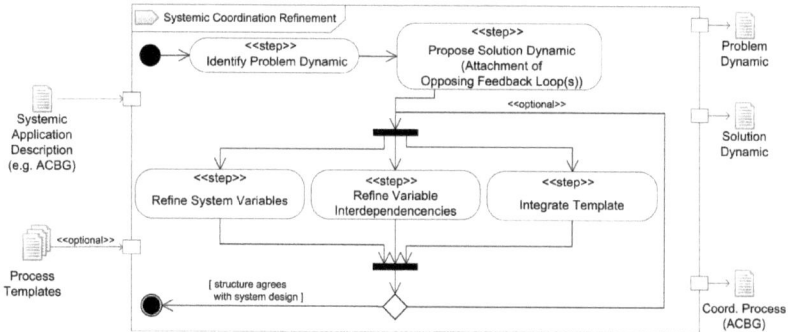

Figure 6.7: The Coordination Refinement

configuration of the interaction techniques, or the media that realize them, is a design effort that is addressed in the Activity *Coordinating Process Integration*, but the decision about the essential aspects of agent inter-actions is an analysis effort that affects the optional validation of the conceived process (Task: *Coord. Process Validation (Qualitative)*) and prepares for the detailed process designs.

This selection mainly concerns the necessary dynamics of the propagation of influences in the system and the possible constraints of interactions. These are determined by the application context, as specific contexts may permit and/or prohibit certain types of media. Also, technical aspects may constrain the applicability of media, e.g. when the future application is to be embedded in a specific computational infrastructure. This may may enforce or forbid the use of centralized /decentralized communication infrastructures. Alternatively, the creation of customized media to meet domain constraints can be indicated (e.g. see the case study in Section 6.8.1).

The elementary design decision is whether influences are to be enacted as *direct* or *mediated* interactions among agents. Direct influences ensure the quick spreading of publications. In mediated mechanisms, the spreading of information, and consequently influences, can be fine-tuned by the explicit control of the dynamics of the (virtual) environment and the contained environment elements. Both approaches are associated with additional computational overhead that need to be considered. This overhead results from the transport and processing of information, i.e. the publication content. For mediated mechanisms, an additional overhead may be implied by provision of the environment model and the maintenance of its consistency. The dynamic properties of the information dissemination that are associated with specific media are an important input to the qualitative validation that the conceived process is capable of achieving the intended dynamics.

The selection is based on the set of media instances that are available in a software-producing organization. If required, the development of a novel medium type may be necessary to meet specific application demands. The fundamental design alternatives for media are discussed in Section 5.2.10. Examples can be found in Appendix B.

6.6 Coordinating Process Integration

The objectives of the *Coordinating Process Integration* Activity are (1) the alignment of a generic process model to a concrete application design and (2) the preparation of agent models to participate in a configured process instance. These configurations are given by the realizations of influence enactments in the *MediatedInfluenceRealization* and *DirectInfluenceRealization* elements (cf. Figure 5.15) of the configuration language (cf. Section 5.3.2). In this Activity the information in these elements is prescribed in the configuration language to prepare for the execution of

212 CHAPTER 6. SYSTEMATIC INTEGRATION OF DECENTRALIZED COORDINATION

Coordinating Processes.
The sequential execution of the Tasks that are contained in this Activity is illustrated in Figure 6.8. The Task *Coordination Alignment* addresses the mapping of process variables to agent-intern elements, and to the events that modify these elements. Inter-variable influences are identified and their enactment is configured in the subsequent Task *Interaction Configuration*. This Task is iterated for all influences in the process model. Finally, the subset of agent models which participate in the process is identified and these agent models are made ready to be coordinated by the coordination architecture (cf. Section 5.2).

The detailed processing inside these Tasks is illustrated by a stereotyped UML Activity Diagram. All Tasks reference the agent models (*Agent Models (executable)*) to look up concrete model elements and modify abstract models of coordination processes (*Coordinating Process*). The modified process description is denoted as a new Work Product that specializes the abstract model of a process, as it contains implementation-specific information and is therefore tailored for an application realization. In addition, the Task (*Agent Model Preparation*) modifies agent models for coordination (*Coordination-Prepared Agent Model (executable)*).

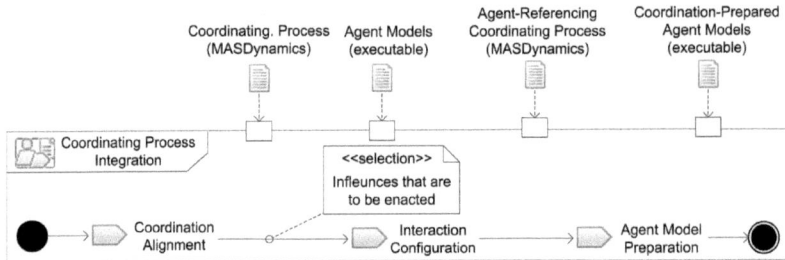

Figure 6.8: Activity: Coordinating Process Integration

6.6.1 Coordination Alignment

The alignment of coordination processes is illustrated in Figure 6.9 (I). Initially, process variables are mapped to elements of agent realizations (*Map Process Variables to Agent Model Elements*). This is done by specifying elements in the agent models elements. Modifications of these elements signify the adoption of coordination-relevant behaviors of agents. In the coordination language, these elements are specified in the *AgentElement* elements of *RealizationModel* (cf. Figure 5.15).

The refined application model (*Coordinating Process*) contains new system variables. These describe additional behaviors, which are related to the inter-agent coordination and must be supplemented to the executable agents in the subsequent development Activity. The Task *Provide Adaptivity Components* is carried out to check whether these behaviors need to be procedurally defined within Adaptivity Components (cf. Section 5.2.7).

The subset of additional behaviors, introduced to supplement adaptivity is processed to compare their semantics with the functionalities that are encoded in the detailed agent designs (*Agent Model(s)*). It is decided whether the denoted behaviors can be declared or have to be procedurally defined. Both approaches to observing/affecting the agent operation are discussed in detail in Section 5.2.7. Declarations configure which agent-internal events signify denoted behaviors. These are specified by the *AgentReference* and *AgentElement* elements of the configuration language (cf. Section 5.3). Particularly, the declaration of *Constraints* to *AgentReferences* allows the configuration of the context in which element modifications signify behavior adjustments.

Complex classifications of agent behaviors can be procedurally encoded in Adaptivity Components. The provided logic defines the inspection of the agent state, is the case of behavior observations, or modifications of the agent state, in the case of affected behavior adjustments.

6.6. COORDINATING PROCESS INTEGRATION

The result of this step is that the behavior declarations are updated and annotated with the required constraints. When the expressiveness of the condition and inhibition elements is not sufficient, behaviors are procedurally defined and these Adaptivity Components are provided as a supplement to *Agent Model(s)*. Due to practical considerations, the procedural logic is defined in the agent programming language that is used to realize specific agent models (cf. Section 5.2.7). Despite the fact that the logic is specified as executable code, this Task concerns the isolated specification of agent configurations. Thus this exercise is not regarded as an implementation- but a design-oriented Task.

In the subsequent steps, the influences among the system elements are identified (*Identify Inter-Agent Influences*). Realization models in the coordination language model are initialized and linked to influence declarations by appropriately updating the *realization* attribute of *CausalRelation* elements (cf. Figure 5.15).

Finally, the medium realization is selected for the management of the interactions among agents (*Identify Inter-Agent Influences*). The set of realizations for the Medium instances (*MediumConfiguration*) that are to be used to disseminate the interactions in the MAS are declared.

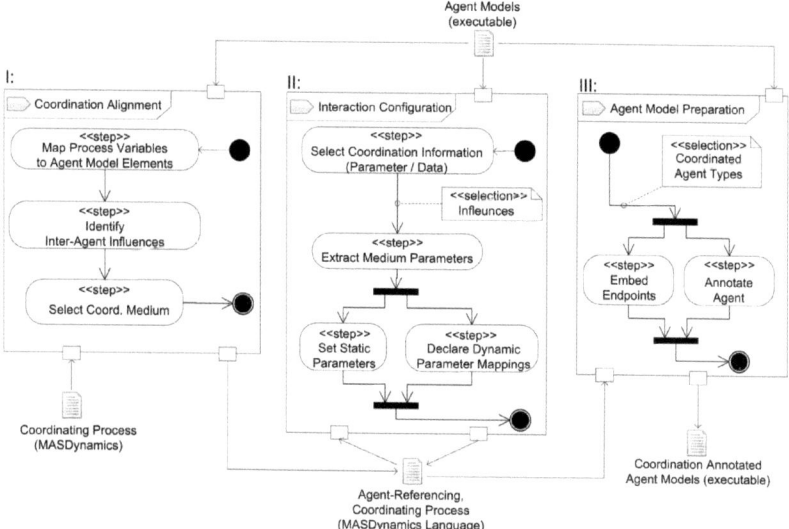

Figure 6.9: The Tasks within the *Coordinating Process Integration* Activity, adapted from [Sudeikat and Renz, 2009e]

6.6.2 Interaction Configuration

The first step of the *Interaction Configuration* is the selection of the information that is to be transmitted in the Endpoint publications (*Select Coordination Information*). Based on the data elements that are available in the agent and the parameters that are annotated to agent elements, the mappings of parameter values for the publishing and subscribed agents is configured (*DataMapping/ParameterMapping*, cf. Figure 5.15).

In the subsequent step for each medium instance, the parameters that can be adjusted (*Extract*

Medium Parameters) are retrieved. These parameters depend on the medium realization, thus developers have to refer to the medium documentation to see how the dissemination of publications can be adjusted. Subsequently, these parameters can be set to static values (*Set Static Parameters*) or mappings to agent-internal data can be declared to dynamically set values at runtime (*Declare Dynamic Parameter Mappings*, as described in Section 5.3.2).

6.6.3 Agent Model Preparation

The preparation of the agent models concerns the embedding of Endpoint modules in agents models and the annotating of agents with the configuration of the Endpoints. When done manually, developers modify the agents accordingly, i.e. agent models are extended. Alternatively, this step can be automated as described in Section 5.3.4. In this case this step concerns the initialization of the described procedure.

6.7 Coordination Validation

The validation Task extends the testing disciplines with checks that the conception of the inter-agent coordination manifests the intended behavior on the system-level. Since the behavior results from the interactions of agents, bottom-up analysis, e.g. via system simulations, is inevitable. Due to the inherent need, considerable work is available which details the methodical simulation of system implementations to examine self-organizing properties. These works are discussed in Section 4.1.2.

Here, a specialization of simulation efforts that supplements methodical MAS development with the validation of the expected system behavior is discussed. System simulations are laborious activities that demand individual expertise. The explicit formulation of expectations of the system behavior (cf. Section 6.4) and Coordinating Processes (cf. Section 6.5) allows a shortcut of these activities. Thus the objectives discussed here are a subset of the generic activities that constitute simulation studies, e.g. as discussed in [Banks et al., 2005; Schut, 2007]. These studies concern the successive experimenting to validate or falsify hypotheses. Therefore, the formulation of research questions, the derivation of falsifiable hypotheses and the verification of the examined simulation models are fundamental activities. It has been argued that this experimental stance is inherently needed to approach the development of self-organizing software systems [Edmonds, 2004].

These activities differ from testing disciplines where development teams routinely have to check application behaviors. In this section, the embedding of bottom-up analysis, most prominently system simulations, in testing disciplines is discussed to guide their routine execution during MAS development. While the formulation of simulation models and their calibration are inherently non-trivial objectives, the auxiliary duties that guide experiments can be simplified when the purpose of a simulation-based validation is the examination of the agreement between a systemic model of the application dynamic, as generated in the requirements (cf. Section 6.4) and design disciplines (cf. Section 6.5.2).

6.7.1 The distinction between Qualitative and Quantitative Validations

It is practical to distinguish between *non-parametric, qualitative* and *non-parametric, quantitative* validations of the inter-agent coordination (cf. Figure 6.10). Qualitative approaches address the simulation of application abstractions [Sudeikat and Renz, 2007c]. These abstractions describe the coordination process that is to be integrated in an application and contain descriptions of fundamental application properties that are relevant in assessing the adequacy of the planned coordination of agents. The derivation of these simulation models requires that assumptions be made about the properties of the software elements to be realized, here agents and elements in the system environment, as well as the realization of the decentralized coordination, i.e. the information dissemination and the local adaptation logic. Therefore, these simulations are appropriate for anticipating the effects of coordination in early development stages. Descriptions of the conceived

6.7. COORDINATION VALIDATION

processes can be animated to validate that process conceptions are, in principle, capable of meeting the system requirements. This particularly allows system stakeholders to agree on the types of dynamics that are to be expected from the later-realized system implementation. Since the integration of Coordinating Processes particularly concerns dynamic properties, it is mandatory that these expectations are also described in dynamics models (cf. Section 6.4).

However, these models are abstractions, and deriving formal simulation models that show a macroscopic system behavior that completely agrees with the dynamics actually exhibited by a system realization requires considerable expertise in formulating appropriate modeling abstractions and tuning the parameters of simulation models, e.g. as discussed in [Axtell et al., 1996; Wilson, 1998]. The complete alignments that allow the prediction of system parameters are mainly of scientific interest and the effort required to create correct predictive models is often prohibitive in engineering projects, except for extreme cases where the required level of confidence in the systems operation demands the complete formalization and analysis. An example are space missions [Rouff et al., 2005]. The implied remoteness enforces the formal assurances that the collectives of system elements act as expected.

The term qualitative is used to describe the animations of the system behavior that show the fundamental modes of system behaviors. These animations are used to anticipate that a process induces appropriate responses to changes in the system context and that these changes follow the intended dynamic models, i.e. these correspond to the requirements in the system adaptivity (cf. Section 6.4).

Quantitative validations also concern the correspondence of the system behavior with the specified requirements. However, the actual system is simulated and these activities allow the details of adjustments to be examined. Most prominently, the exact timely behavior of system responses can only by estimated, but may be crucial for system stakeholders. For example, in the case study discussed in Section 4.4.2 the removal of hypothetical epidemics follows an exponential decay. This assumption results from the intended macroscopic feedback to be manifested in the system behavior. However, the detailed rate of decay is highly implementation-dependent, thus system simulations are inevitable to validate that realizations comply with macroscopic parameter ranges.

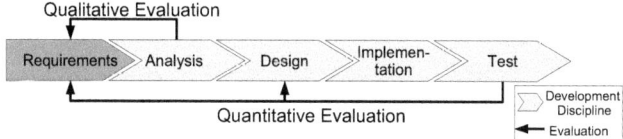

Figure 6.10: The distinction between qualitative and quantitative validations [Sudeikat and Renz, 2007c]

The qualitative and quantitative modes of the validation demand different realizations of this generic structure. These are discussed in the Sections 6.7.2 and 6.7.3. The distinction between these approaches is already indicated by the current approaches to designing self-organizing systems, as summarized in Section 3.2. Most approaches refer to system simulations (see Section 3.2.4), while the simulation of system abstractions has been seen as a supplement to these activities (see Section 4.1.2).

6.7.2 Fundamental Structure

The generic, three-step structure of validations of Coordinating Processes, based on the bottom-up analysis of application realizations as well as application abstractions, is illustrated in Figure 6.11. This structure describes a recommendation for the embedding of established simulation and analysis techniques into software engineering procedures. Initially, the analysis is prepared (*Analysis Conception*) by examining which analysis technique is applicable for the process that

216 CHAPTER 6. SYSTEMATIC INTEGRATION OF DECENTRALIZED COORDINATION

is to be studied. The Task *Simulation/Iteration* contains the preparation and completion of bottom-up analyses. According to the differing analysis methods that are available to study non-linear behaviors in MASs, different specializations of this Task refer to how these methods are used. Finally, the observed or inferred dynamical properties of the system behavior are analyzed (*Interpretation*) and conclusions are drawn that affect the iteration of the design activities. If necessary, e.g. due to inconclusive simulation results, the *Simulation/Iteration* Task is repeated.

Qualitative validations are used to show that the prescribed Coordinating Process (*Coord. Process*) is in principle capable of meeting the application requirements (*Systemic Adaptation Requirement*). Quantitative validations show that the behavior of the implemented system, mainly constituted by the agent realizations (*Coordination Prepared Agent Models*) corresponds to the enacted process prescription (*Coord. Process*) and/or macroscopic requirements (*Systemic Adaptation Requirement*). The Task results in an assessment of the extent to which the process design or the system realization, meets the expectations. Two optional outputs can be generated. The embedding of the Coordinating Process (cf. Section 6.6) is affected by the derivation of parameters for the configuration of interaction mechanisms or system elements (*Parameterization*). The possible parameterizations depend on the Coordination Media and agent models used. The insights gained in the exhibited dynamics can affect the design of a Coordinating Process (cf. Section 6.5), as intended or unintended behavioral properties may be found (*SO/Emergent Property Description*). These are closely related to the inter-agent process that is examined. Due to the specific nature of both Work Products, their formalization has not been examined, instead these are assumed to be specified informally as text documents to allow for generality. The qualitative and quantitative validation Activities, as illustrated in Figure 6.3, are specializations of this generic model that contain specific realizations of the constituent Task. They optionally create intermediate data structures that are exchanged among these Tasks, and access/create subsets of the Work Products that are denoted in Figure 6.11.

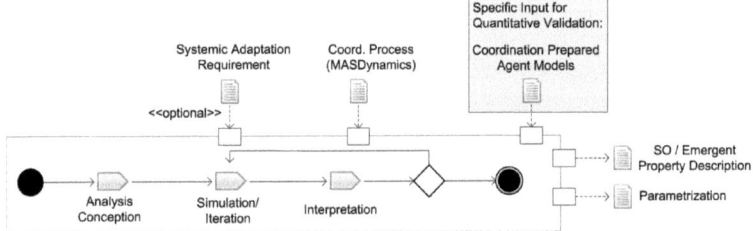

Figure 6.11: The generic structure of simulation-based validations of Coordinating Processes

Quantitative validations, following this generic structure, prepare and interpret simulations of the actual software system to show that the intended behavior, i.e. structure-establishment and structure-adaptation, is present in the system. The simulation of agent-based applications, particularly with respect to self-organizing properties, is the major means of showing that applications meet requirements. This is a well-studied exercise in self-organizing MAS development. Corresponding development methodologies (see Section 3.2.3) make use of simulations. In this dissertation, the simulation of both agent-based models of self-organizing processes as well as agent-oriented software Systems are demonstrated. A readable review of simulation-based studies of collective phenomena can be found in [Schut, 2007]. This work is based on simulation frameworks, but discusses generic concerns and practices. Simulations are inherently a manual development activity. The automation of simulations for the examination of self-organizing properties, is discussed in [DeWolf, 2007], and it is found that the effort to prepare automations, which is implied in the approach, is in general prohibitive, except for certain types of phenomena.

A range of literature is available on the simulation-based study of complex and self-organizing MASs, e.g. see [Schut, 2007]. Here, only the adjustments that are necessary to fit generic simulation practices in the development process presented here are indicated. When used in the context of the development work flow presented here, the system simulations are preceded by the conception of the dynamic that is to be studied. This mainly concerns the calibration of the system to provoke the behavioral model that is to be examined, and the definition of the observables, appropriate to measure the relevant system properties.

After these preparations simulations are carried out. The major difference to the qualitative validation (see Section 6.7.3) is that the system to be simulated is already present. Since this system is realized with software engineering tools, the simulation of the system must be prepared. While simulation frameworks provide facilities for the observation of agents and environments, the simulation of agent-based software systems typically demands the preparation of these measurements on the application level. Within this dissertation, the minimally-invasive integration of these facilities into conventionally developed agent models is discussed in Section 5.2.6, according to [Sudeikat and Renz, 2007a]. Also the control of the system *initialization*, the system *calibration*, and the repeated system *execution* with varying configurations/parameterizations is a simulation-specific concern. These are either prepared on the application level or by the use of external frameworks, e.g. for the configuration of agent deployments [Braubach et al., 2005a] and the configuration/observation of environments [Jander et al., 2010].

The subsequent interpretation of the simulation results (*Interpretation*) concerns the analysis of measurements. The intended system behavior is verified or falsified and application-dependent parameters are adapted. If necessary, subsequent simulations with differing configurations are repeated (see Section 6.7.3).

6.7.3 Coordination Validation (Qualitative)

The bottom-up analysis of the effects of agent coaction was previously discussed in Section 4.3. Two analysis strategies, namely the *Stochastic Simulation* and the *Mathematical Analysis* (cf. Figure 4.11), are distinguished (cf. Section 4.3.3). The mathematical treatment of systemic system models is exemplified in Section 4.3.4, where a structure of agent behavior interdependencies is concretized. Stock-and-Flow diagrams as well as rate equations are derived and the prescription of realistic model parameters, which control the state transitions in these models, enables the iteration of these models to animate the resulting system behavior. These modeling techniques describe the stochastic system behavior by averaging out the stochastic interactions of entities. Instead these are expressed by averaged transitions rates.

In [Sudeikat et al., 2009b], the two principal alternatives to the *stochastic* analysis of self-organizing processes are compared. In this joint work, the formal analysis approach from [Randles et al., 2007] and the animation of system behavior by the simulation of MAS abstractions [Sudeikat and Renz, 2007c; Renz and Sudeikat, 2009] are discussed as mutually supplementing means for the qualitative system analysis. In Figure 6.12, these modeling techniques are denoted as alternative Tasks that can be carried out in parallel. Both validations commence with the definition of the stochastic process that governs the system operation (*Derive Stochastic System Description*). Having knowledge of this process(es) allows the developer to decide which analysis technique is appropriate and therefore subsequently applied. The *Behavioral Analysis* Task concerns the derivation of stochastic simulation models [Sudeikat and Renz, 2007c; Renz and Sudeikat, 2009] for the subsequent examination of the different behavioral regimes of applications (*Examine SO/Emergent Properties*). The alternative *Algebraic Analysis* [Randles et al., 2007], describes the formal definition of the underlying processes. Examples are the averaging mathematical models (cf. Section 4.3.4) and *Markov Decision Processes* (MDP). The formal solution of these processes allow the developer to identify macroscopic system properties (*Examine SO/Emergent Properties*) as well as optimize parameters (*Optimize Model Parameters*). The mapping of these parameters to the microscopic element realization can be used to configure system implementations.

An example of the technique for algebraic analysis is the *stochastic situation calculus*, as applied in [Randles et al., 2006]. It can be used as a bottom-up modeling technique [Sudeikat et al., 2009b], based on [Reiter, 2001]. The system is described in terms of *situations* that correspond to sequences of agent actions. This representation originates in an initial situation and situations are altered

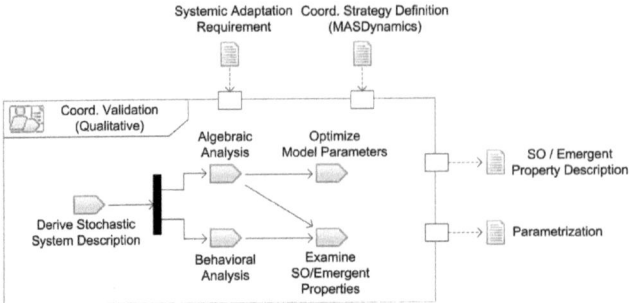

Figure 6.12: Activity: Coordination Validation (Qualitative), adapted from [Sudeikat et al., 2009b]

by the actions that are available to agents. These actions are selected by agents. Besides, actions are stochastic, i.e. their outcome is uncertain. This calculus allows a compact representation of MDPs as process states are pooled. A complete characterization of this modeling approach can be found in [Randles et al., 2006] and the solving of the underlying MDPs for the analyses self-organizing systems is exemplified in [Randles et al., 2006; Sudeikat et al., 2009b]. In the following, the behavioral analysis of agent-based systems is detailed, based on [Sudeikat and Renz, 2009h; Renz and Sudeikat, 2009]. This analysis approach requires less expertise and is exemplified in Sections 6.8.1 and 6.8.3. The essential activities of the analysis process are (1) the formulation of the *hypotheses* that are to be validated/falsified, (2) the conception of a *simulation model*, (3) the *initialization* and *execution* of the simulations, and (4) the *analysis* of the collected simulation data.

The hypotheses describe the expected dynamic behavior of an application. In this context, the aim of the analysis is the demonstration of the expected influences among system variables, i.e. forms of behavioral properties. A corresponding description format is illustrated in Figure 6.13 (I) [Sudeikat and Renz, 2009h]. The expected influence and the system context under which the manifestation of this influence is expected are described. A set of *Hypotheses* contains the qualitative expectations (*Hypothesis*). The *Dynamic* part of each hypothesis contains a set of *Observables* that reference process variables that are expected to be causally related. *Parameter Space* parts contain specific fixed values (*Parameter*) as well as value ranges (*Range*) of parameters of the simulation model.

The concretization of underlying processes to enable system simulations is discussed in [Renz and Sudeikat, 2009]. An abstract understanding of the processes that govern the operation of the software system are concretized to an executable model of the system operation. The models that are used for the animation of the system behavior describe the activities of individuals. Thus, the generation of simulation models requires the *detangling* of the averaged influences that are given by systemic system models to the processes inside the individual system elements [Renz and Sudeikat, 2009]. The semantics of the abstracted behaviors and their averaged influences are examined to infer the individual agent types and their individual stochastic behavior that resembles the internal reasoning and reactive responses. On a conceptual level, this detangling is an inverse operation to the abstraction of MASs, as discussed in Section 4.3.2. The systemic models generated there describe structures that can give rise to sets of adaptive processes, due to the different configurations and parameterizations. Here, these abstraction are converted to an executable that animates a process instance that conforms to the abstract structure. The executables are concretizations but still average the agent operation. The generation of these models and the assurance that the concretization conforms to the process structure is a manual modeling effort that requires competence in the utilized simulation technique.

The detangling is carried out by identifying the agent types and prescribing for each type

6.7. COORDINATION VALIDATION

(1) the individual activities or states that it can operate and (2) the corresponding transition rates. Several executable description formats are available. System Dynamics research established stock-and-flow diagrams that are composed of aggregate states and allow an explicit definition of the in- and out-flow of of these states by individuals. Their use to express the dynamics of ACBG-based models is discussed in Section 4.3.3 and exemplified in Section 4.3.4. The correct mapping of these models is a mathematical modeling effort and their mapping to event-based and agent-based simulation techniques is discussed in [Borshev and Filippov, 2004]. Alternatively, averaged state transitions can be directly expressed by differential equations. These describe self-organizing processes, and their use for the modeling of MASs has been proposed as well [Lerman and Galstyan, 2001] (see Section 4.1.2). The stochastics of the operation of an agent-based software system result from the non-determinism of the individual reasoning and the environmental dynamics. Therefore, it is inherently difficult to show an exact equivalence of of mathematical models and the MAS implementations [Axtell et al., 1996; Wilson, 1998]. Simulation models, that are grounded in computer science can be applied as well. In the following, the use of stochastic analysis/simulation techniques is considered. Following these approaches, the detangled agents are understood as *Continuous Time Markov Chains* (CTMC). The Markovian processes can be expressed in stochastic process algebra, e.g. the stochastic π calculus (Sπ) [Priami, 1995] (cf. Section 4.1.2). Process algebras are an established formalism for the analysis of concurrent systems [Milner et al., 1992]. The system is modeled as a transition system, which is composed of independent, communicating *processes*. Communications take place via *channels*. The analysis of self-organizing systems benefits from stochastic models, thus a stochastic extension (Sπ) of the original π calculus has been used in [Renz and Sudeikat, 2009; Sudeikat et al., 2009b; Sudeikat and Renz, 2009h]. Stochastic properties are added to the algebra by the annotation of stochastic *delays* to process actions and *activity rates* to channels. These define the probability of transitions, inside a processes, by an exponential distribution. Consequently, the probability for a transition increases with time and the underlying transition system is Markovian. A subset of the Sπ language, which is used in Sections 6.8.1 and 6.8.3 is described in Appendix A. The detangling of a systemic model to a simulation model in Sπ is carried out in a two-step process (see e.g. [Renz and Sudeikat, 2009]). First, the nodes in an ACBG are represented by individual process terms. Then the relations between ACBG-nodes are interpreted. Process terms are appended with the influences that make agents adopt a behavior, i.e. increase a node value, or drop a behavior, i.e. decrease the node value. These added terms involve interactions via channels, where channels can be used to resemble mediated as well as direct interactions. The delay in process terms is used to express the averaged durations of agent activities, and the activity rates of channels characterize the dynamics of agent interactions. When the model is derived in this way, realistic parameters have to be inferred/estimated.

The collection of simulation data is commenced by the calibration of simulation models, in order to provoke the processes, which are assumed to be present in the application design, into manifesting observable adjustments. Appropriate initializations engender scenarios in which the expected, collective behavior-adjustments of agents are affected. Two principal types of behavioral regimes can be distinguished for the observation of decentralized system-adaptivity [Sudeikat and Renz, 2007c]. First, the impact of coordination processes is observed when systems *respond* spontaneously to environmental changes or unfavorable system configurations. In these *responsive regimes*, system adaptations respond to external factors. Secondly, systems operate in *working regimes* when the adjustments are continuously executed, due to repeated adjustments of individual system components. These regimes are observed in situations where the system continuously intervenes to work against constant or repeating perturbations of external or internal properties. Responsive regimes are produced by calibrating a system configuration that demands an immediate adjustment, e.g. by initializing simulations in unfavorable role allocations of agents [Sudeikat and Renz, 2007c] (cf. Figure 6.13 (II)). The induction of working regimes demands that the simulation is put under a constant or repeated influence that enforces adjustments (cf. Figure 6.13 (II)), e.g. by the periodic reinforcement of environment elements.

The analysis of the collected simulation data requires the identification of measurements that quantify the expected system behavior. Expressive quantifications depend on the application

220 CHAPTER 6. SYSTEMATIC INTEGRATION OF DECENTRALIZED COORDINATION

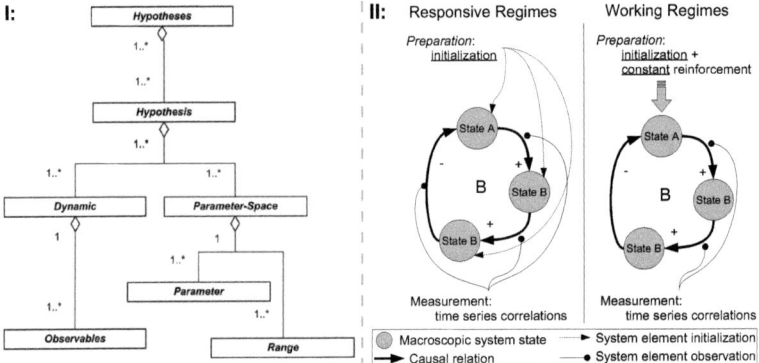

Figure 6.13: Conceptual model of hypotheses specifications (I) and the schematic illustration of simulation preparations (II) [Sudeikat and Renz, 2009h]

domain and therefore need to be specifically devised for the development project. Examples are the measurement of *transport displacements* (cf. Section 3.4.2) or the regime identification by measuring ratios of agent activities (cf. Section 6.8.3). One generally applicable approach is to quantify the manifestation of the expected causal relations. These are indicated by the observation of *correlations* between the time-dependent behavior of system variables (see Section 2.5), i.e. the observables in Hypotheses. Positive relations are mathematically interpreted by equally directed (delayed) changes in connected variables. Vice versa, negative relations indicate changes in opposite directions, i.e. negative correlations. Calculating the cross-correlation of pairs of observables validates the presence of relations. The inversion of the argument is not possible, i.e. the presence of a correlation does not prove a causal relation, but observable correlations can be used to show that expected relations manifest themselves at run-time. This approach is exemplified in the Sections 4.3.4 and 4.4.2.

The manifestation of relations that are indicated in systemic models can be shown in simulation results [Sudeikat and Renz, 2009h]. Here, this approach is demonstrated using the example of the intrusion detection case study in Section 4.4.2. The systemic model of the intended Solution Dynamic in Figure 4.24 (II, page 128) denotes a balancing feedback loop that controls the amount of intruders. One relation in this loop describes that active Intruders are *detected by* Searcher agents. Detections are expected to lead to a positive interdependency of the number of Intruders and the number of activated Searchers. In [Sudeikat and Renz, 2009h], a stochastic, algebraic simulation model (see Appendix A), which resembles the dynamics of the case study system, is used to demonstrate the examination of this relation. For the measurement of the correlation (see Figure 6.14), the simulation[1] is exposed to a steady reinforcement of intruders that makes the system reach equilibrated agent densities that depend on the detection rate. These densities also show stationary correlations, given by the Formula 2.1 (page 26).

The observed correlation maxima indicate a causal dependence. This interdependency is associated with a time delay that depends on the detection rates. The cross-correlation functions for different interaction rates (ranging from 0.4 to 40) are shown. The correlation maxima are normalized to one by shifting time and amplitude (master plot). The time shifts are described by

---

[1] composed of 100 Intruders, 50 Searchers, and 25 Removers

6.7. COORDINATION VALIDATION

a logarithmic fit (II)[2] and the shifts of the amplitudes (III) are described by an algebraic fit.[3]

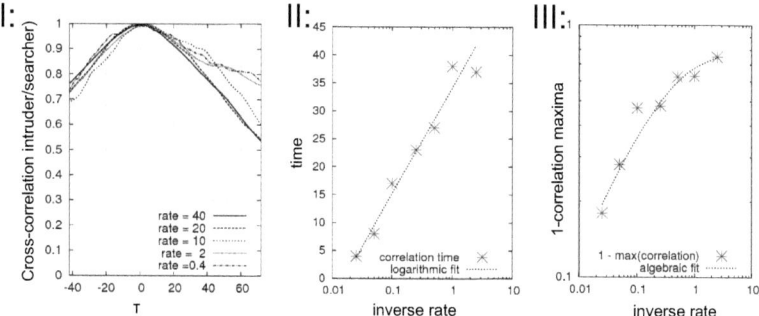

Figure 6.14: A sample correlation measurement: (I) The cross-correlation between intruder and searcher activations shows rate-dependent maxima. Plot I is based on rate-dependent shifts of the time (II) and amplitude (III) of correlation maxima [Sudeikat and Renz, 2009h].

6.7.4 Prototype: Automating Coordination Validations

The integration of simulation-based validations in testing disciplines implies the routine conducting of simulations by development teams. The execution and mathematical treatment of simulations are activities that can be automated and examples of corresponding frameworks are given in [DeWolf et al., 2005; Brueckner and Parunak, 2003; Vilenica and Lamersdorf, 2010]. Based on the conception discussed here of the qualitative validation of inter-agent coordination, experiments with a prototype simulation execution framework are discussed in [Sudeikat and Renz, 2009h]. This framework provides an agent-based,[4] distributed environment for the automation of the required simulation runs and the preprocessing of the obtained data. The simulation models are prepared to provide the time series of behavior adoptions and these data are processed to calculate their correlations. Distinct agent types are responsible for managing user interactions, triggering simulations, to validate hypotheses, and executing simulations.

The conceptual architecture is illustrated in Figure 6.15. *Users* provide a simulation model and infer the questioned *Hypothesis(es)*, as previously discussed. These are described in a machine-readable format, i.e. by defining a XML dialect.[5] These hypotheses are then processed to trigger the required simulation runs and the measurements obtained are preprocessed by automating the calculation of correlations. A *User Agent* interacts with a user and delegates the validation of hypotheses to an *Analysis Agent*. These agents are enabled to use a *Numerical Computing Environment*.[6] The required computations are delegated for the sake of efficiency, and reconfigurability is supported since calculations are prescribed in a scripting language. This language is provided by the numerical environment and can be used to prescribe the mathematical treatment of measurements. The hypotheses contains parameter ranges that are to be swept. Analysis Agents fetch the required data from a *Networked Data Storage*[7] that is used to store measurements. The contained measurements, i.e. time series, can be retrieved by the combination of parameter values. If a specific combination of parameter values is not available, the execution of the corresponding

---

[2] $19 \cdot (\log_{10} x + 1.8)$
[3] $\frac{0.8 \cdot x^{0.5}}{(0.4+x)^{0.5}}$
[4] realized with the Jadex agent framework, cf. Section 2.2.2
[5] The XML language is introduced in Section 5.3.3.
[6] e.g. the *Scilab* system (http://www.scilab.org), using the *javasci* interface for Java-based programs.
[7] using *Java DB* (http://developers.sun.com/javadb/)

222 CHAPTER 6. SYSTEMATIC INTEGRATION OF DECENTRALIZED COORDINATION

simulation run is delegated to a *Simulation Agent*. This agent type encapsulates the capabilities and computational resources that are required to execute simulation models in a *Simulation Environment*. These agents provide the means to *initialize* and *configure* simulation models as well as to retrieve the generated *measurements*. The simulation data obtained, i.e. the observed time series, are stored for later reuse. Based on the data generated, the computed correlations are presented to the user.

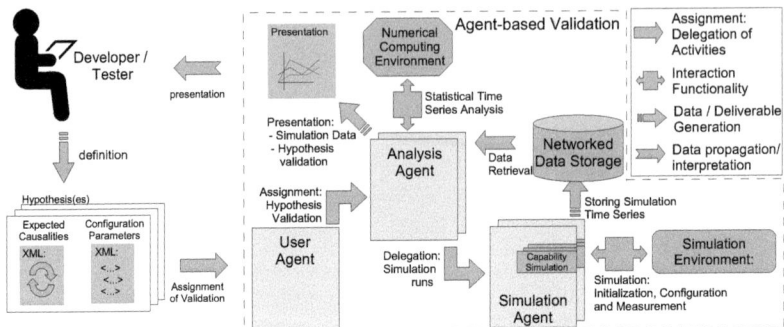

Figure 6.15: Conceptual Testbed architecture, adapted from [Sudeikat and Renz, 2009h]

This system facilitates qualitative validations by automating the execution of simulation models, here the stochastic algebra processes. The automation of MAS simulations to facilitate quantitative validations (cf. the previous section) requires a tool set that integrates with a specific agent platform to support the initialization and observation of agent execution. The development of an environment for the automated simulation of agent-based systems is approached in the research project SodekoVS (cf. Section 7.2.1), which continues the research that is described in this thesis.

6.8 Case Studies

The conception and integration of self-organizing processes is exemplified in three case studies. In the first example (see Section 6.8.1) a decentralized process controls the failure recovery in *resource-flow systems*, e.g. manufacturing lines. This application scenario was devised in cooperation with the Department of Software Engineering and Programming Languages of the University Augsburg [Sudeikat et al., 2010b]. The use of self-organization in an *agent-based control system* [Jennings and Bussmann, 2003] is exemplified and the process is integrated in a conceptual model for the self-management of software systems [Seebach et al., 2007]. In the second case study, demonstrated in Section 6.8.2, decentralized processes are used to manage the deployment of (web) services on application servers. Domain elements, i.e. servers and service providers, are associated with managing agents, and inter-agent processes steer the manipulation of service deployments. This case study demonstrates the integration of self-organizing properties in conventional software systems. Finally, a hypothetical scenario is studied in Section 6.8.3, where the dynamics of combined decentralized processes are examined. The presented system contains a problematic, self-organizing phenomenon and the conception of a self-organizing solution that counterbalances the unintended behavior is demonstrated.

These case studies demonstrate the *partially externalized coordination* approach (see Section 6.2.2). Initially, the systems show a nonadaptive behavior and the intended adaptivity is brought about by the integration of an appropriate supplement. The supplements are designed to complete causal structures with the required feedbacks.

6.8.1 Decentralized Reconfiguration of Resource-Flow Systems

Within the framework of the *Organic Computing* initiative (see Section 3.1.2) one research direction is the autonomous control of *Resource-Flow Systems* (RFS) [Steghöfer et al., 2010]. This class of system types characterizes distributed applications in which system components collaborate by exchanging resource elements. Each component is capable of applying a specific function to a resource and the correct sequencing the individual function effects the intended system functionality. For RFS, this functionality is the correct modification of resource elements.

Prominent instances are *production automation* systems [Seebach et al., 2007; Sudeikat et al., 2010b]. Conventional designs of production lines are based on static configurations that connect machines in series. Machines are prepared to carry out a specific modification of a workpiece and the transport of workpieces is realized by inflexible transport mechanisms, e.g. conveyor belts, and the change of the system configuration requires a considerable effort. A major drawback of these static configurations is that the complete production process is blocked when one machine fails to operate correctly. A prerequisite for the autonomic operation of these systems is the system's ability to reconfigure itself at run-time. Here, it is assumed that the machine configurations are locally managed by software agents. Another aspect of this type of system is the flexible transport of items between machines. An example is the modularization of production lines that has been deployed in a DaimlerChrysler production line [Bussmann and Schild, 2000; Jennings and Bussmann, 2003]. Modules contain machines and a flexible transport mechanism that allows workpieces to move forward, move backward, and enter machines. An alternative approach is the delegation of the transport of parts to robotic agents [Seebach et al., 2007], e.g. *Automatic Guided Vehicles* [Weyns et al., 2005]. A flexible production line is illustrated in Figure 6.16.

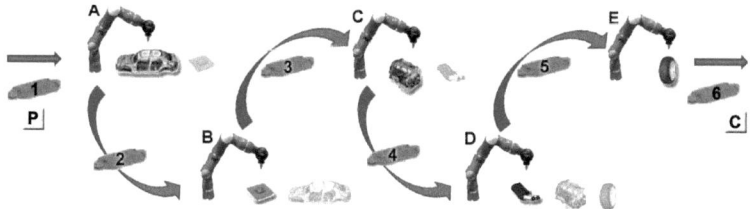

Figure 6.16: A flexible production line [Sudeikat et al., 2010a]

The *Robots* (A to E) are configured to execute a production step, i.e. to apply a specific capability. *Robots* can be (re-)tooled to apply other capabilities. The available options are depicted on the right hand side of each robot and the non-active capabilities are grayed out. *Carts* (1 to 6), i.e. robotic transport vehicles, displace workpieces. The introduction of raw workpieces is denoted by their *production* (P) and the removal of completed workpieces from the system is indicated by their *consumption* (c).

The *Organic Design Pattern* (ODP) is an architectural blueprint that describes the structure of flexible RFS and instructs the integration of self-x properties [Seebach et al., 2007]. The conceptual structure of this pattern is illustrated in Figure 6.17. The active system elements, i.e. the Robots and Carts, are *Agents*. These have specific abilities, which are represented by *capabilities*. Capabilities describe the processing of *resources*, e.g. data or workpiece elements. The three foundational abilities of agents are the introduction of workpieces (*Produce*), the removal of finished workpieces (*Consume*), and execution of intermediate work steps (*Process*). The work steps contain resource-specific activities, e.g. tightening a certain screw type, as well as the *transportation* of workpieces by Carts (see Figure 6.16, 2 to 5). The correct processing of resource element types is prescribed by a *Task* that contains the correct sequence(s) of capability completions. The configuration of an agent is given by a set of currently active *roles*. A role element controls the execution of capabilities by an agent. Roles contain *pre-* and *postconditions* as well as a set of capabilities that an agent applies to a workpiece. *Conditions* control the reception and forwarding of workpieces and contains three elements. First, the *port* refers to the originators (precondition) or the recipients (postcondition) of resource elements. Secondly, the *state* of the condition describes the sequence of capabilities that have been completed. Finally, it contains the *task* (see above) that describes the complete sequence of capability completions that are required to finish a resource element.

These conceptual elements structure the RFS-based applications to prepare the autonomous reconfiguration of the system. A prominent example, studied throughout [Seebach et al., 2007; Nafz et al., 2009a] is the reconfiguration of the agents when one agent fails to bring about a designated capability, e.g. when a drill breaks. Since agents have a set of capabilities, a new configuration is calculated that assigns all agents with roles that contain the capabilities that are individually available. The reconfiguration algorithm is contained in the *Observer/Controller* element. This is a conceptual component that can be directly represented in a software artifact, or can be realized by the interplay of agents or agent components. The *centralized* provision of a reconfiguration algorithm is discussed in [Seebach et al., 2007; Nafz et al., 2009a]. A constraint resolver is integrated in a dedicated software artifact that is informed about individual failures, calculates valid system configurations, and distributes the novel agent configurations.

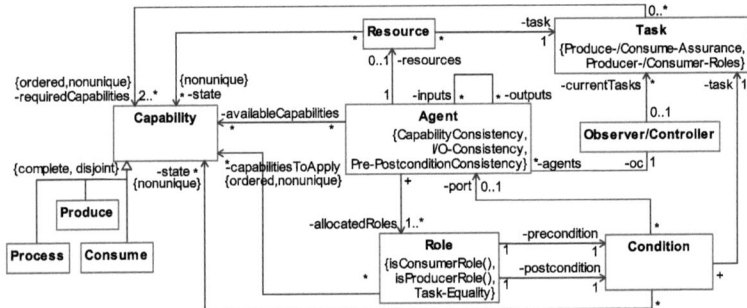

Figure 6.17: The static structure of the Organic Design Pattern, following [Sudeikat et al., 2010a]

In the following, the conception and design of a *decentralized* reconfiguration process is outlined. The advantage of centralized approaches, using designated managing entities, which control the reconfiguration of subordinate agents, is the ability to encode the reconfiguration algorithms in a single entity. This simplifies the development and testing, as well as their formal treatment [Nafz et al., 2009a]. Besides the academic challenge, the decentralization of the reconfiguration is of practical interest. Following the agent-oriented ODP, the overall manufacturing process is decentralized itself, as agents locally manage the execution of robots. In the general case, without the breakdowns of agents, the centralized, managing entity is idle. When error events are not the rule, this resource is only held available for emergencies. Its computational abilities control the calculation of new configurations. Thus managers are to be balanced with the size of their subordinate subsystem and are possibly federated to individually managed reasonably sized subgraphs. Consequently, the managing entities need to be coordinated as well, e.g. to enable the swap of roles across federations. Since the robots themselves are already equipped with considerable computational means, the ability to distribute the failure recovery among them, as another locally handled management aspect, is attractive. Another virtue is the implied localization of the reconfiguration. Since the exchange of roles requires the rerouting of the carts that transport work pieces from/to machines, specific manufacturing layouts may benefit from reconfigurations that are based on the swapping of roles between near-by agents. Based on the assumption that the initial layout of the production line minimizes transport routes, the localization of reconfigura-

6.8. CASE STUDIES

tions, as logically near-by agents swap roles, can serve as a heuristic to limit transport overheads. In addition, the localization allows the production to continue in remote parts of the system.

The development of the decentralized reconfiguration process follows the procedure that is given in Section 6.3.1 (page 6.3.1). Here, the progression of the development is discussed based on the generated artifacts. The requirements for the reconfiguration process were described in the previous paragraph. Subsequently, the Coordinating Process is defined (*Coordinating Process Definition*, see Section 6.5). In this development activity, the Problem and Solution Dynamics are identified and the Solution Dynamic is refined to a concrete process prescription. Before the integration the dynamic properties of the process are qualitatively validated (Coordination Validation (Qualitative)). Then the process is integrated (*Coordinating Process Integration*, see Section 6.6) and the the behavior of the system implementation is examined (*Coordination Validation (Quantitative)*, see Section 6.7) to show that the requirements are met.

Process Definition: Problem and Solution Dynamic

Applications are enriched with the ODP in order to equip the ability for autonomous, adaptive reconfigurations. The intended system dynamic is illustrated in Figure 6.18. The individual agents operate in three distinct behaviors. *Running* agents are appropriately configured and process incoming resource elements. Failures inside an agent make one or more roles inoperable as the required capabilities are not usable. These agents are *Waiting for Reconfiguration*. When a new configuration for the agent is available the corresponding adjustments are carried out (*Reconfigure*). The system-level behavior is characterized by the numbers of agents that exhibit these behaviors.

The Problematic Dynamic of the ODP is that Running agents are inoperable in the event of an internal *Error*. The occurrence of these events is an external influence that interrupts resource flows in the system. The fluctuating rate of interrupts is denoted by a rate node (*RF interrupt*). These interrupts convert agents to the *Waiting for Reconfiguration* behavior. Thus the number of Running agents is decreased and the number of Waiting agents is increased. The value of the conversion rate depends on the occurrence of errors and the availability of running agents. Therefore, the problematic conversion is governed by a negative feedback loop (α) and without intervention the system heads toward the absence of Running agents.

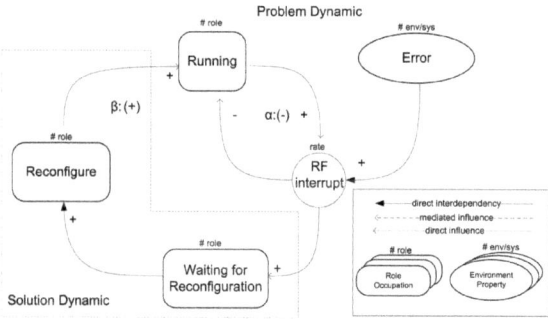

Figure 6.18: The Problem and Solution Dynamic of the ODP [Sudeikat et al., 2010a]

Interventions by the reconfiguration algorithm bring about the Solution Dynamic (see Figure 6.18, bottom left). Waiting agents are informed of their new configuration and reconfigure accordingly. This relation is a causal interdependency. Waiting agents cause reconfigurations, but in the absence of waiting agents no reconfigurations are indicated. The completion of the reconfigurations converts agents to the Running behavior, thus this activity contributes to the number

226 CHAPTER 6. SYSTEMATIC INTEGRATION OF DECENTRALIZED COORDINATION

of operational agents (*Running*). The repeated reconfigurations form a positive feedback loop (β) that counterbalances the problematic decrease (α) of Running agents.

Process Definition: Solution Dynamic Refinement

Despite the centralized calculation of appropriate reconfigurations [Seebach et al., 2007; Nafz et al., 2009a], the central theme of a decentralized reconfiguration approach is to enable agents to search by themselves for agents that can take over their inoperable role. The Waiting agents do not passively stall the operation of the RFS but actively search for agents that are able to switch roles to render the system operable. In the ideal case a direct swap of roles restores the system functionality, but transitive switches are also prepared. These are intermediate swaps that do not directly restore the correct system configuration but enable the subsequent correction. A system configuration that requires intermediate swaps is illustrated in Figure 6.22. This decentralized approach has been coined *wave-like* [Sudeikat et al., 2010b], as reconfigurations move through the system and induce localized adjustments.

The operating principle is illustrated in Figure 6.19 as a refinement of the Solution Dynamic. The Waiting behavior is divided into two sub-behaviors. Inoperative agents are both *Deficient* and *Non-Active*. The *deficiency* of an agent is its inability to execute a previously allocated role and the local agent management attempts to resolve this insufficiency. The distinguishing characteristic of the deficiency is the reason that it has occurred. It can result from internal errors (*By Break*) or from the swapping (*By Change*). Non-Activity denotes the capacity to play additional roles. When agents are configured to play several roles at the same time, the Running and Non-Active behaviors do not exclude each other. The malfunction of one role means that the agent is has the capacity to undertake an additional role on behalf of another agent. The remaining roles of the Non-Active agent are unaffected.

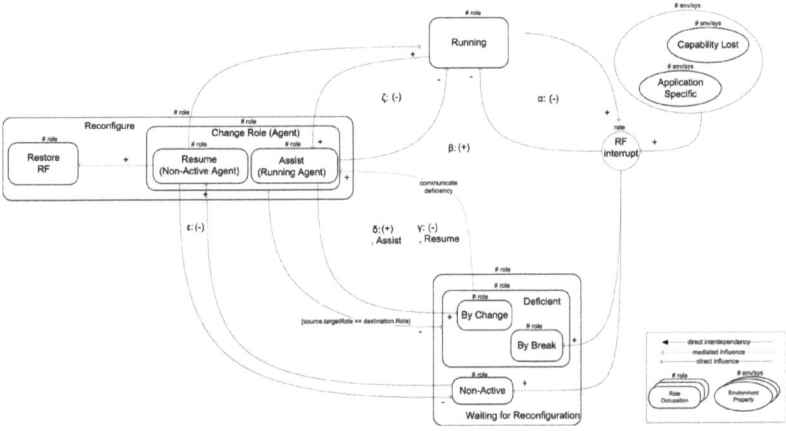

Figure 6.19: The ACBG of the wave-like, decentralized reconfiguration algorithm, following [Sudeikat et al., 2010a]

Agents are equipped with the ability to autonomously reconfigure themselves (*Change Role*). This behavior is differentiated according to the behaviors of the agents that are driven to reconfigure. Non-Active agents *Resume* the role execution, and the reconfigurations of Running agents *Assist* a deficient agent that is requesting a swap of roles. A side effect of role adjustments is that the roles of connected agents are adjusted as well (*Restore RF*). The correct flow of resources is

6.8. CASE STUDIES

restored by changing the ports of the agents that bring resources to it or take them from it after the processing.

Deficient agents, regardless of their source of deficiency, communicate their need for a swap of roles (*communicate deficiency*). The agents that respond to these requests and reconfigure are consequently reducing the communicated deficiency (negative influence). The annotation *source.targetRole == destination.Role* denotes that only the deficient roles (destination), i.e those that are being adopted by the changing agent (source), are removed. This removal manifests a negative feedback (γ) that reduces the number of deficiencies. The Assist behavior is carried out by running agents that need to abandon one role in order to adopt a new one. In this case, a new deficiency (*By Change*) is introduced. This side effect establishes an additional feedback (δ) that cancels out the effects of the role change. The net number of deficiencies remains the same. Finally, the ability to show resuming and assisting role changes depends on the availability of Non-Active (ϵ) and/or Running agents (ζ).

Coordination Validation (Qualitative)

Prior to the integration, the behavior of the reconfiguration algorithm is estimated. The detailed ACBG is transferred to a stochastic process algebra model that allows the dynamics of the reconfiguration in hypothetical system configurations to be examined (see Section 6.7.3). The simulation model used for this examination is depicted in Figure 6.20. Details about the simulation language and the graphical representation can be found in [Phillips, 2010] and appendix A. The derived simulation models abstracts from the operation of agents but expresses the dynamics of behavior changes. Each behavior is represented by a stochastic process term that characterizes the influences that make agents change their behavior. The duration of stay and the durations of interactions, as an influence for behavior adjustments, are normally distributed. The stochastic approach averages the microscopic interactions and activities of agents.

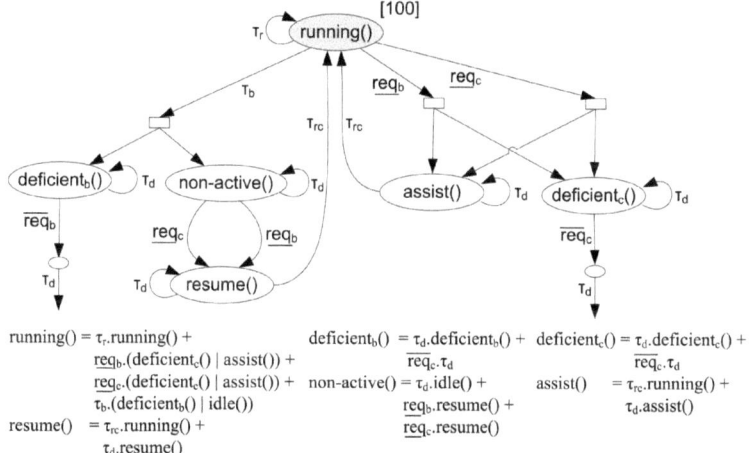

Figure 6.20: Simulation Model of the Solution Dynamic in Stochastic π-Calculus [Sudeikat et al., 2010a]

The agent behaviors in the MAS execution (see Figure 6.19) are represented by the number of active processes. The operative agents are denoted by the process *running()*. Initially a fixed number of agents is started in this configuration.[8] The rate of internal errors is controlled by the delay τ_b. Malfunctioning agents enter the *Waiting for Reconfiguration* behavior, expressed by the concurrent processes $deficient_b()$ and $non\text{-}active()$. The $deficient_b()$ processes request the swap of roles via the channel req_b. After a successful communication, which entails a successful role change, the process terminates after a fixed time delay (τ_d). The $non\text{-}active()$ processes enter the *Resume* behavior ($resume()$) when they receive a request via the req_b or req_c channels. The req_b channel is used by $deficient_b()$ processes and the req_c channel is used by $deficient_c()$ processes, which resemble the *Deficient By Change* behavior. The Resume behavior mimics reconfigurations by a fixed time delay (τ_{rc}). Consequently, the processes behave like the $running()$ process. Running processes can also respond to the requests by both types of deficient processes (req_b, req_c). In these cases, the agents assist and their subsequent reconfiguration is given by the two concurrent processes that result from the assisting role change ($assist()$) and the implied deficiency of a previous role ($deficient_c()$). The assisting adjustment is completed after a fixed time delay ($\tau_r c$). The novel deficiency is communicated via the dedicated channel (req_c). Successful communication also results in a subsequent role swap and the processes terminates after a fixed delay (τ_d). The details of the rerouting of the resource transport, an implication of the reconfiguration of agents is neglected in this model. It is assumed that the required adjustments are always possible and are not significant for the duration of a role change.

The time series of a sample simulation run are illustrated in Figure 6.21.[9] Running agents (I) are continuously disturbed with a relatively a high rate of errors. Due to the reconfigurations (V, VI), the malfunctioning agents (III) quickly return to the Running behavior. Due to the high abstraction level, this model is not used to predict the behavior of algorithm implementations, but ensures that the conceived process is in principle capable of showing the intended Solution Dynamic.

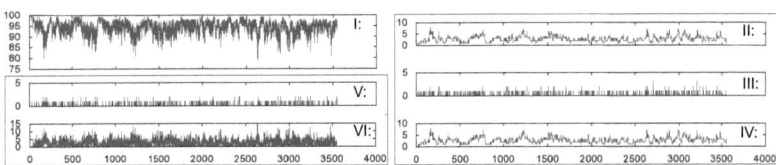

Figure 6.21: Simulation time series. The system continuously counterbalances a high rate of agent-failures (I: $running()$, II: $non\text{-}active()$, III: $deficient_b()$, IV: $deficient_c()$, V: $resume()$, VI: $assist()$).

Process Integration

The process is realized with the systemic programming model discussed in Chapter 5. A Jadex-based MAS (see Section 2.2.2) is used to emulate the functioning of a hypothetical RFS. Software agents are used to represent Carts and Robots and the workpieces are denoted by ordinary programming language objects that are exchanged via inter-agent communication.

The participation in the decentralized reconfiguration process is encapsulated in Endpoint modules (see Section 5.2.3). These interact via an RFS-specific realization of a Coordination Medium (see Appendix B.1.3). This medium controls that information propagate along the inputs and outputs of agents. Endpoints observe the operation of their host agent and send a request for a role swap when a role in the host agent is inoperable. These messages are propagated through the Medium and the receiving Endpoint decides whether it can perform the indicated swap of roles. This decision depends on the capabilities that are available to the agent. When

---
[8] e.g. 100 in Figure 6.20
[9] the configuration used is: $\tau_r, \tau_d, \tau_b = 0.001, \tau_{rc} = 1.0; req_b, req_c = 0.01$

6.8. CASE STUDIES

the indicated swap is not possible, the request is forwarded along the Medium. Otherwise, the Endpoint induces the localized adjustment of an agent role and communicates a response message that informs the immediately connected agents, the incapacitated agent, and the agents that are immediately connected to the incapacitated agent. Upon reception of this information, the associated Endpoints arrange the resulting adjustments of roles to ensure the correct flow of resources. Incoming messages are queued and processed in sequence. The Medium is used to propagate request messages along the flow of resources. The answers to these requests are routed in the opposite direction, and to the immediately connected agents of the originator. Conceptually, the medium is circularly closed to ensure that messages can reach all agents that participate in a resource flow, regardless of the logical location of the communicating agents.

The modus operandi of the decentralized reconfiguration is illustrated in Figure 6.22. In this hypothetical scenario, the disagreement of the agent capabilities requires a transient swap that prepares the subsequent reestablishment of the correct sequence of work steps. Three Robots are connected in series and the locally available capabilities are listed. For reasons of simplification, it is assumed that agents have only one active role and the topmost capability is required to complete it. The correct processing of the workpieces involves the sequential utilization of the capabilities 1, 2, and 3 (see Figure 6.22, 1).

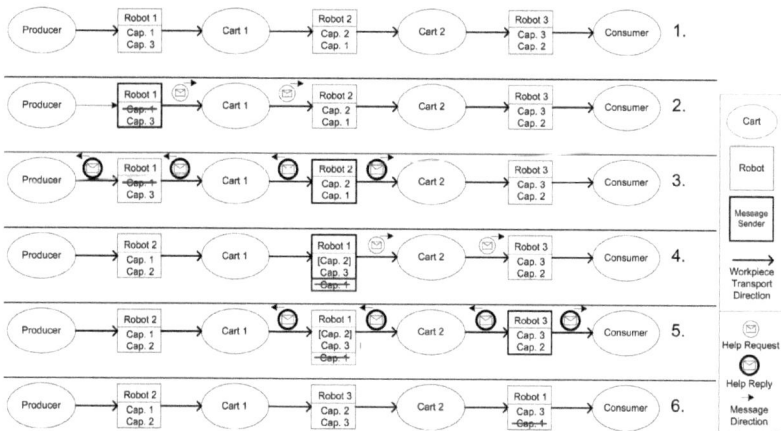

Figure 6.22: Exemplification of the decentralized reconfiguration, following [Sudeikat et al., 2010a]

A reconfiguration is required when the *Cap. 1* in *Robot 1* can no longer be applied (2). Consequently, the Endpoint of *Robot 1* publishes a request for assistance that is propagated along the flow of resources. The request is propagated until it reaches an agent that can replace the incapacitated role. In this scenario, *Robot 2* replies to the request (3). The reply is routed backward and is processed by the Endpoints of the originating Robot, here *Robot 1*, and the connected Carts (*Producer*, *Cart 1*, and *Cart 2*). Subsequently, the Robots and Carts reconfigure asynchronously (4). The Endpoints update the roles of Robots and modify the ports in the pre- and postconditions within the roles of the affected Carts. These modifications realize the swap of roles and reestablish the flow of workpieces. At best, a single swap is sufficient, however in the depicted scenario, the incapacitated Robot (*Robot 1*) cannot replace the assisting agent (*Robot 2*). It lacks a capability (*Cap. 2*) and thus requests additional assistance. This request is forwarded until it reaches another agent that is able to supply the necessary capability. Consequently, a second swap is carried out (5) and the system reaches a valid configuration (6). In this setting the correct sequence of capabilities is reestablished by a logical shift of Robots. In real systems, the spatial

230 CHAPTER 6. SYSTEMATIC INTEGRATION OF DECENTRALIZED COORDINATION

positioning of Robots is fixed and the robotic transport vehicles (Carts), which transport resources [Seebach et al., 2007], are rerouted. The Medium is a logical transport layer that abstracts from the physical layout of the production line but manages the propagation of messages along the logical flow of resources.

Coordination Validation (Quantitative)

A set of simulations for the three-Robot RFS layout (see Figure 6.22) is summarized in Figure 6.23. The processing times of workpieces are stochastically distributed and the changeover time of agents is fixed. The displayed time series are averaged over ten simulations runs and in each plot the time unit corresponds to 1/10 of a second. In each run one randomly selected robot is incapacitated. In Figure 6.23 (I), the numbers of role activations are shown. The subtypes of deficiency are measured and indicate the transitive role swaps. The initial incapacities of agents (By Break) are resolved by subsequent deficiencies (By Change) that are caused by the mismatch of the capability within assisting and originating agents. The number of non-deficient agents includes the Cart agents. A second set of measurements visualizes the changes in the workload of the system. The time series of the number of agents that are actually processing a workpiece are shown in Figure 6.23 (II). After system initialization (< ca. 130 time units), the system processes a constant input of raw resource elements. During reconfiguration, as indicated by the number of Waiting agents (bottom time series), the amount of currently processed resources decreases. This decrease results from the number of reconfigurations and the interruption of supply for the subsequent agents. The workload is reestablished after the reconfiguration.

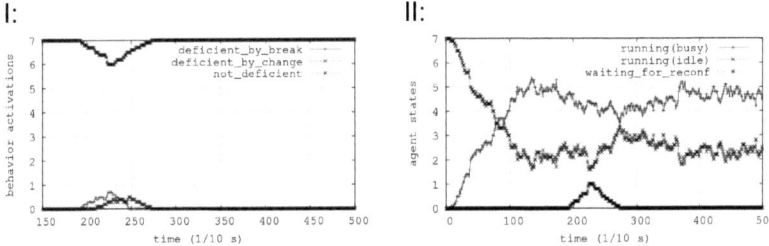

Figure 6.23: Measurements of a single reconfiguration. The duration of deficient agent roles (I) and the workload of the producing agents (II).

The quality of the reconfigurations, e.g. the implied delay and computational cost, depends on the time that is needed to find an appropriate partner for the requested swap. In randomly generated RFS layouts, the probability of a nearby partner is influenced by the redundancy of the capabilities in the system. In Figure 6.24 two complementary measurements are plotted over a control parameter that reflects this redundancy. 10 RFS of homogeneous Robots, i.e. Robots with an equal number of randomly assigned capabilities, are generated. The assignment of capabilities is normally distributed and a system is composed of 10 Robots that utilize a set of 10 capabilities. These systems process a fixed number of workpieces and a randomly selected agent is incapacitated at two fixed time points. The redundancy is expressed by the ratio C_i / C, where C_i is the number of capabilities within individual agents and C is the absolute number of capabilities in the system.

The first measurement is the number of messages that were exchanged via the Medium to realize both reconfigurations (see Figure 6.24, I). This number increases quickly as the redundancy decreases. The second measurement is the number of hops that the requests for swaps which initiate reconfigurations travel before a swapping agent is reached (see Figure 6.24, II). This measurement reflects the logical distance between the swap partners and exhibits a comparable dependence on the redundancy of capabilities. The measurements are fitted with $(c_1 * (1-x))^2 + c_2$

6.8. CASE STUDIES

[Sudeikat et al., 2010b], where c_1, c_2 are application dependent constants.[10] These observations indicate that the decentralized reconfiguration approach is particularly appropriate in applications with high redundancy, i.e. where possible reconfiguration parters are nearby.

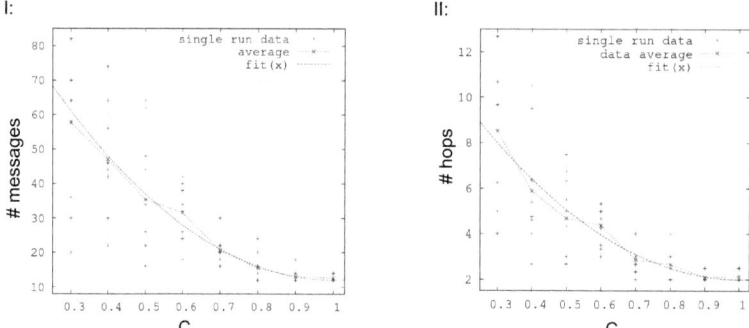

Figure 6.24: Simulation results: The averaged number of messages (I) [Sudeikat et al., 2010a] and the averaged number of hops per request for assistance (II) are plotted over the redundancy of capabilities

Discussion

The feasibility study presented here shows that reconfigurations in RFS can be based on decentralized operating principles. The conception and integration of the concrete inter-agent process follows the development process presented here. The development is initiated by analyzing the intended dynamic and refining it to a detailed model of the intended dynamic. This dynamic is then realized using the systemic programming model, i.e. the process structure is concretized by realizing and configuring the process enactment. The presented process demonstrates the systematic design of self-organized adaptivity. The initial process presented leaves room for further analysis and extensions that will be part of future work. As to the performance analysis of the decentralized approach, only one significant control parameter and one set of performance indicators are examined. Other influences, such as the reconfiguration time and cost measurements, remain to be studied. One important aspect for the further development of the process is the identification of the appropriate swapping partners. Currently the first agent that is able to perform a swap will do so. This approach minimizes the travel times of swap requests but does not consider the system configuration. Thus unnecessary swaps may be implied by unnecessary transitive swaps (assist) that take place before requests reach agents that are able to correct the system in one swap (resume). Approaches to resolve these solutions imply longer travel times but can reduce the number of swaps until the system is reconfigured. The trade-off between these aspects remains to be examined.

In addition, the comparisons of reconfiguration approaches in RFS are planned as a future collaboration of the authors of [Sudeikat et al., 2010b,a]. Here, the developed solution is qualitatively characterized to distinguish the use of decentralized self-organization from alternative techniques. Ants are a prominent source of inspiration for the decentralized management of manufacturing systems. (1) The interactions of ants and pheromones are resembled to explore the space of possible system configurations. Uses range from the *Ant Colony Optimization* for the calculation of schedules [Gagné et al., 2006] and the run-time control of [Cicirello and Smith, 2001] to the

---
[10]In I: $c_1 = 10$, $c_2 = 12$; in II: $c_1 = 3.5$, $c_2 = 2$.

use of stigmergy mechanisms in agent-oriented control systems (e.g. [Hadeli et al., 2004a]). An architectonic conception for the integration of these mechanisms is the *delegation* model [Holvoet and Valckenaers, 2007]. Agent-based representatives of artifacts in the application domain are enabled to send out delegate agents of different types in their environment to explore the possible pathways in a manufacturing system and create processing schedules. (2) An alternative prominent technique for the agent-based management are negotiations, as reviewed in [Cicirello and Smith, 2001]), such as the use of negotiation protocols (e.g. [Parunak, 1987; Bussmann and Schild, 2000]). This approach also found applications in industry settings (see Section 3.5). In the ODP the correct configuration is defined by the constraints and (3) the use of centralized constraint solving is given in [Nafz et al., 2009a]. (4) The use of distributed constraint solving techniques [Yokoo et al., 1998] is studied in [Clair et al., 2008].

In the solution described here the swaps of roles allows to restore the invariants that define a correct configuration. In this respect, the process works as an *optimistic* and *minimalistic* replacement of a constraint resolver. The minimalism is given by the reduction of the required messages and shared information. The process is optimistic as role changes are immediately realized before the complete solution is computed. The characteristics are summarized in table 6.1. As set of criteria for evaluating adaptive systems is given in [Kaddoum et al., 2009] and a subset of these criteria is adapted/extended for comparing run-time aspects of the solution described here with alternative design approaches. One characteristic is the *communication* overhead that is implied by the reconfiguration process. The *number of messages* that is needed for the reconfiguration depends on the availability of redundant capabilities in the system, given by the redundancy measure C. This dependency is shown in Figure 6.24. When nearby agents can take over the roles of deficient agents only a role swap is necessary and communications are minimal. In the worst case, all agents are affected by transient role exchanges (assist). The *communication contents* are minimal, only role configuration of single agents are communicated and the information about the state of the system or of other agents is not required. In the alternative management approaches information about the system state, i.e. the possible production path, are collected. Therefore, more information has to be transported. The *computational resource usage* refers to the overhead of the local reasoning that is implied by reconfigurations. The *entity computations* are minimal, as the processing of the incoming messages requires to decide whether an agent is capable to play a required role or the message contains the answer of an past request. However, these lookups are done for all agents in the message path till a swap parter is found. The effort to change roles of the swap parters the immediately connected agents is a constant effort for all reconfiguration approaches. The *entity information* is minimized since no information about the globals state of the system or the agents neighborhood need to be kept. This distinguishes this work from constraint satisfaction techniques. The centralized resolution of constraints (3) is based on the full knowledge about the system state and distributed resolvers (4) process require the collection of information about the neighborhood(s).

The following set of characteristics describes the generated solution, i.e. the new configuration of the MAS that is found by the collective process. In this case study reconfigurations are based on structure formation and the maintained structure is the correct sequence of agents and is perturbed by the incapacitation of agents. The *quality* of the solution varies. Reconfigurations follows the heuristic that swaps between nearby agents are favorable. These effects of swaps are localized. If this is indeed favorable depends on the layout of the machines. The *progress* describes the establishment of the new configuration. In the best case one swap is sufficient. Otherwise a sequence of swaps gradually resolves the deficiency. The *mode* of the adaptation denotes that the reconfiguration is established in parallel to the system operation (concurrent). The unaffected parts of the production line continue to operate. Work pieces are jammed when the next processing step is not available. Alternatively, it can be necessary to halt the system or subsystems. The explicit consideration of the constraints that describe the correct solutions (3,4) allows, in principle, also to optimize the generated solution(s), but it may be necessary to halt the system [Nafz et al., 2009a] or partitions of the system.

6.8. CASE STUDIES

Execution Aspect	Characteristic	Quality
Communication	# of messages	depends on C (see Figure 6.24)
	communication contents	minimized, only local data
Computational resource usage	entity computations	minimal: only local reasoning
	entity information	minimal: only local information
Solution characteristics	solution quality	heuristic, dependent on the layout
	progress to solution	1 swap, gradually otherwise
	adaptation mode	concurrent

Table 6.1: The qualitative characteristics of the wave-like reconfiguration process

6.8.2 Shoaling Glassfishes: Decentralized (Web) Service Management

An inherent concerns for modern distributed software systems is the continuous maintenance of the required infrastructures. An example are *Service Oriented Architectures* (e.g. [Singh and Huhns, 2005]). The required (application) servers, seen individually, are themselves complicated software systems [Abdellatif et al., 2007] and their proper configuration is imperative. When the applications are exposed to dynamic environments, such as the fluctuation of the request load and resource availability, the autonomic adjustment of the infrastructure is desirable (as argued in Section 5.4.1). The self-management of these infrastructures is a pivotal motivation for the autonomic computing initiative (see Section 3.1.2) and this research topic has also been adopted in agent-oriented research [Jeffrey et al., 2008]. Due to the size and complicatedness of the existing middleware elements, it is necessary to augment adaptive mechanisms. This can be approached by reengineering infrastructure elements (e.g. [Abdellatif et al., 2007; Abdellatif and Danes, 2006]) or the supplementary frameworks (e.g. [Garlan et al., 2004]). One design aspect is the separation of the computational overheads introduced by the control mechanisms in order to minimize effects on system performance and resource usage.

In this section, the supplementation of conventional, i.e. non-agent-based, software systems with self-organizing features is demonstrated. A preparatory step is the conception of an agent-based management architecture that is able to control the relevant properties of the non-agent system. The decentralized coordination is then integrated among the agents, thus the agent-based system serves as an intermediate abstraction layer that interlinks the elements of the managed software with the self-organizing process. An intuitive strategy is a one-by-one mapping of system elements to managing software agents. This approach conforms to the *external* techniques for controlling the adaptiveness of software elements [Salehie and Tahvildari, 2009] (see Section 3.2). Subsequently, the integration of self-organized adaptiveness can follow the development process presented in this chapter (see Section 6.3.1). Here, the execution of this process is not described, it is demonstrated in the previous case study, but the identified and integrated process partitions are discussed and the resulting system behavior is shown by system simulations.

For service-oriented applications, the relevant elements of the required infrastructure are the *Application Servers* used and the *Services* deployed. Using conventional techniques, these elements are manually deployed and configured. The intermediate management MAS associates each of these elements with a software agent. This association requires a management technique that allows element-internal properties to be observed and influence to be exerted on the local configurations (cf. sensing/effecting in Figure 3.5). In the system presented here, agents make use of the *SUN Appserver Management EXtensions*[11] (AMX). This is a generic programming interface that allows the configurations of *Java Platform, Enterprise Edition* (Java EE)[12] application servers to be inspected and manipulated. For example, services can be deployed and undeployed at run-time. The prototype system is realized with the Jadex agent platform (see Section 2.2.2) and manages installations of the freely available *GlassFish*[13] application servers.

---
[11] Version 2 (ur2-b04), https://glassfish.dev.java.net/javaee5/amx/
[12] http://www.oracle.com/technetwork/java/javaee/overview/index.html
[13] https://glassfish.dev.java.net/

Two agent types realize the functions that are required for automated management. *Application Servers* are adapted by an agent type of the same name. The individual service deployments are managed by *Service Endpoint* agents. The agents only implement the activities that are necessary for the management but lack inter-agent coordination. For example, Service Managers have the ability to change their current server offer. This activity also includes failure recovery when the deployment of the new service fails. In this case, the agent recovers by reverting the offer to the original service. The Coordinating process controls when adjustments are attempted. Two auxiliary agent types complete the management architecture. The main objective of management is to adjust the number and server-based positioning of the services. Thus the deployments of services are volatile and the service users, i.e. clients, require a repository mechanism that potential service requesters can use to look up the actual service addresses. This mechanisms is realized by Broker agents. They maintain a registry of service deployments per service type. Inter-agent communication is used to retrieve the actual deployment address that is to be used by clients to invoke a service. Brokers therefore hide the dynamics of service movements. In addition, they realize a simple load-balancing among the registered service providers. In addition, default service configurations can be fetched remotely from repositories.

Two alternative views on this architecture are illustrated in Figure 6.25. Conceptually, the management architecture encapsulates the application layers that constitute a service-oriented application (I) [Sudeikat and Renz, 2009f]. In a layered view, adopted from [Thanheiser et al., 2007], these are the *Service Layer*, where services are made available, and the *Application + Infrastructure Layer*, which contains the required infrastructure elements, i.e. the application servers. The agent-based management can be regarded as an extension to the infrastructure that manages the infrastructure. *Service Consumers* invoke processes as parts of their individual processes and work flows (*Process Layer*). Due to the dynamics of the service repositioning and reconfiguration, these invocations are mediated by Broker agents.

A functional view on the system elements is given in (see Figure 5.2, II [Sudeikat and Renz, 2010b]). The management support is displayed as an orthogonal supplement (right) that manages the functional system (left). *Clients* represent the consumers of services and invoke services with differing request rates. Invocations are initiated with a look-up at the corresponding *Service Broker*, which then returns the physical address that is to be used by the client to interact with the service provider. Each application server (*App. Server*) and deployed *Service* is managed by a *Server Manager* agent or *Service Endpoint Manager*. Servers are dimensioned for a preferential number of services, here 3, and services can be moved between servers.

In both illustrations, the use of the coordination middleware (cf. Figure 5.2) is illustrated. The Endpoint modules are neglected but the Coordination Media, encapsulated in the middleware, are indicated. Particularly, Broker agents feed in their local observations on the service utilization, which are then used by the management agents to conclude the necessary adjustments. In addition, Servers can use media to communicate their local configuration. System simulations make use of the random propagation of publications (see Appendix B.1.1).

The following section discusses the integration of two adaptation dynamics in the managing MAS. First, the Deployments of services are balanced with the fluctuating demand for services. This application scenario is a variation from the system simulation in Section 5.4.1. Secondly, the utilization of application servers is controlled. Servers are enabled to publish their locally available capacities and services reallocate themselves to balance the workload on servers in a server farm.

Balancing Service Deployments

In the first scenario, the deployments of services are balanced with the external demand, based on fluctuating request rates by service clients. The basic building blocks for this kind of decentralized service management are the measurement of the current demand and the ability of servers to change the locally provided service (as discussed in section 5.4.1). The earlier discussion of this scenario is based on the adoption of a nature-inspired template process. Here, the decentralized management is adjusted. The required activities are prescribed in a simplified process model that suits the generic management architecture (see Section 6.8.2).

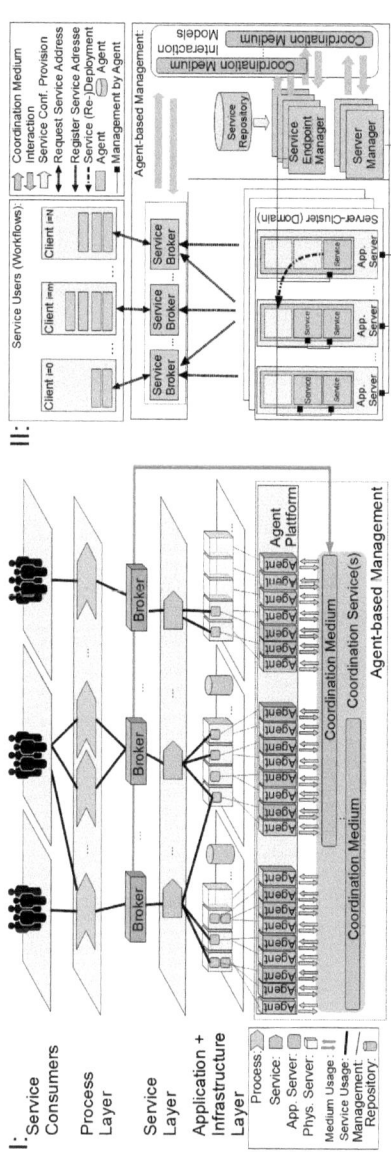

Figure 6.25: Decentralized, agent-based service management architecture: A layered view (I [Sudeikat and Renz, 2009f]) and the detailed view on the operating principle (II, following [Sudeikat and Renz, 2010b])

236 CHAPTER 6. SYSTEMATIC INTEGRATION OF DECENTRALIZED COORDINATION

In the prescribed process, Broker agents are supplemented with the responsibility of publishing significant changes in the request rate for a specific service type. The taking and processing of measurements is encapsulated inside the associated Endpoints and these observations are propagated via a message-based Coordination Medium (see Appendix B.1.1). The incoming measurements are processed by the Endpoints in Server Manager agents, which determine the local adjustment of the offered service. These activities are embedded within Adaptivity Components in the Coordination Endpoint.

The structure of the decentralized process is shown in Figure 6.26 (I). The number of consumers actively invoking services is represented by the variable *Requesters*. They dictate the amount of *Service Requests* that are to be worked off by the system. This amount is causally related to the measured *Service Demand*. Requests are processed by the deployed services, represented by the *Allocated* variable. These agents are configured to offer a particular service type. These variables are typed for the specific kinds of services that are offered by the whole system. These variables and relations describe the behavior of the application domain, i.e. the dynamics of the unmanaged system. The addition of a single influence extends these dynamics and completes their structure to form a balancing feedback loop that controls the (re-)deployments. Service Brokers are equipped with the previously described perception (*Service Reinforcement*) and publication (α) of demand changes. The variable *Changing Service Allocation* represents the set of perceiving Endpoints within Service Endpoint agents, which consider the change their service offer.

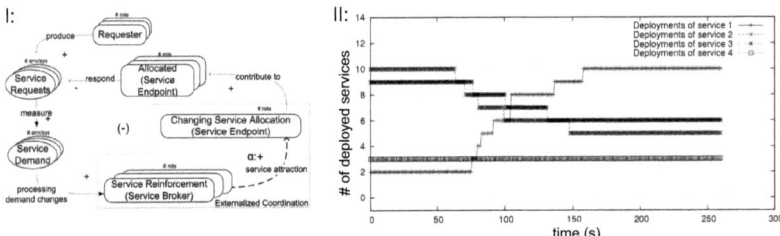

Figure 6.26: Balancing service deployments [Sudeikat and Renz, 2010b]: The management process (I, [Sudeikat and Renz, 2009e, 2010b]) and a sample simulation run (II, [Sudeikat and Renz, 2010b])

Figure 6.26 (I) illustrates a responsive behavior regime affected by the process described above. On one physical machine 10 GlassFish application server instances (domains) are initialized. Each server can offer up to 5 services and on each server only one instance of each service type can be deployed. The system is initialized with an arbitrary distribution of services. After a short time delay, the system responds to a sudden increase in the demand for the service type 1. Services change their deployments and consequently this service type is present on every application server.

In the preceding analysis, a single influence has been identified that, when enacted, completes the existing relationships to a balancing feedback. This link effectuates that demand measurements have an effect upon the selection of service offerings. The process prescription addresses the configuration of this missing influence to prepare the automation. An excerpt from the MASDynamics model, in the customized notation (cf. Section 5.3.3), is given in Figure 6.27 to demonstrate the configuration of mediated influences [Sudeikat and Renz, 2009e]. It contains the parts of the process definition that define the connected variables and configure the mediating medium. The specification of the relation consists of two parts. First, elements of the abstract process model are defined (I). These describe the process structure (see Section 5.3.1). The nodes in the ACBG are denoted and represent the two agent behaviors that are affected (I.a). Optionally, the agent types that are able to show the denoted behaviors, here roles, are annotated. The declaration of the relation between these behaviors indicates the *mediation* by a medium (I.b). The declara-

6.8. CASE STUDIES

tion indicates the type of the relation as well as the publishing and subscribed behaviors. These describe the process structure. Finally, the application-specific configuration is referenced (*configuration*). This section of the declaration contains the details that are relevant for the process enactment, but are specific for the implementations of agents end media (II). In this section, the agent behaviors are refined by references to the Jadex-specific events that signify the adoption of the relevant roles. For each behavior, the agent type (*agent*), the name (*event*), and the type of the event (*type*) are denoted. In addition, the data that are to be communicated are denoted. For publishing behaviors (*while communicating*), it is prescribed that two parameters are communicated. These are the identifier of the relevant service (*serviceID*) and the current workload (*workload(ratio)*). The local names of these parameters (*value*) are masked and the data values are identified by unique identifiers (*as*). These identifiers are then referenced in the declaration of subscribed behaviors (*while receiving*) to map the communicated values (*as*) with the agent-intern locations that are used to store the communicated data (*value*). Finally, the medium realization is referenced (*by_medium*) and a static property is set. This excerpt only illustrates a part of the configuration language, details can be found in Section 5.3.2.

```
...                                                        ...
        Process Definition                                         Enactment Configuration
/* Nodes: */                              I.a     /* Link Configuration: */                                II
role_occupation: ServiceReinforcement             medium_configuration( attractionByToken ):
        [ agent: ServiceBroker ]                  <- {
role_occupation: ChangingServiceAllocation              <-: agent "ServiceBroker"
        [ agent: ServiceEndpoint ]                          event "service_demand_changed"
...                                                         type INTERNAL_EVENT
                                          I.b               while communicating parameter: {
/* Links: */                                                  value: "service_name" as: "serviceID"
=>mediated=>( serviceAttraction )[                            value: "workload_ratio" as:"workload(ratio)"}}
type +                                            -> {
<- { ServiceReinforcement}                              ->: agent "ServiceEndpoint"
-> { ChangingServiceAllocation }                            event "change_service_allocation"
configuration attractionByToken                             type INTERNAL_EVENT
]                                                           while receiving: [
...                                                           value: "serviceName" as: "serviceID"
                                                              value: "workloadRatio" as: "workload(ratio)" }}

                                                  by_medium: "deco4mas.mechanism.token.Token"
                                                        [ with: property "distribution_type" value "RANDOM"]
                                                  ...
```

Figure 6.27: The configuration of the service deployment process, following [Sudeikat and Renz, 2009e]

Server Utilization Management

In this scenario, it is assumed that application servers are dimensioned to host a specific number of services. This preferential utilization is based on the computational resources that are available, e.g. CPU usage and memory consumption. When servers work below this capacity, resources are not used appropriately. Economically, it is more efficient to run and maintain a few properly utilized servers then a multitude of serves that are underutilized. An example is given in [Jeffrey et al., 2008], where energy is saved by powering down underutilized servers.

The process model for the management of server capacity utilization is illustrated in Figure 6.28. This model supplements a balancing feedback that distributes services until a stable configuration is reached at which the server capacities are well utilized. Underutilized servers are freed from service deployments. The variable *Underloaded* denotes a subset of Server Manager agents that are associated to servers where the current service deployment is currently below their preferential utilization. The Endpoints within Service Managers are notified when the deployments on the associated server change. Then Endpoints determine, by a logical condition defined on the knowledge-base of the associated agent, whether the server is underloaded or not. When an underloaded configuration is encountered, the Endpoint triggers the publication of the locally available capacity (β) via a Coordination Medium (see Appendix B.1.1). The Endpoints within Service Endpoint Manager agents are then informed, and the role *Moveable* signifies the local reasoning, within an Adaptivity Component, as to whether the deployment of the associated service should be moved. The determined transfers of deployments manifests the system-wide rate of movements (*Server Change*). This rate corresponds to the movements of services (*Server Deployment Change*) that are actually carried out. Other external influences may also lead to the (re-)deployment of services, and thus influence the transfer rate (*External Influence(s)*). The presented mode is abbreviated and the change of deployments may have additional side effects that are not considered in this context. The dynamics of the process are caused by the perception of available resources. When these are sensed, the circular interdependencies are enacted. The local decision-making about the movement results in services being repelled from nearly empty servers in order to enable their shut-down, and attracted to servers that are near their preferential utilization.

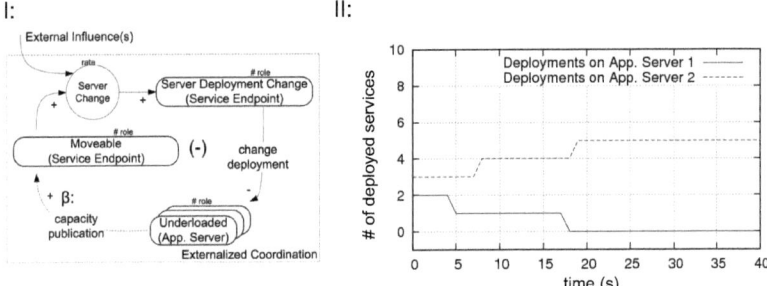

Figure 6.28: Server utilization management [Sudeikat and Renz, 2010b]: The management process structure (I) and an execution snapshot (II). The snapshot shows the service deployments per server (II.a) as well as the service registrations (II.b).

Simulation results for a responsive behavior regime are given in Figure 6.28 (II). In this simulation setting, servers are configured to host 5 services and initially two application servers are utilized by fewer services. The availability of the capacities on both servers is gradually propagated through the medium and the services from the less-utilized server are attracted to the server that hosts more, but less than preferred, services. The time series show the actual deployments on the application servers. A transfer is carried out by the undeployment on the original server and the successive (re-)deployment on the destination server. In the registry of the available services, these movements are observed as the temporally unavailability of services [Sudeikat and Renz, 2010b].

Discussion

In this case study, the integration of a decentralized adaptation process in a realistic software environment is demonstrated. A generic management MAS encapsulates the managed software systems, here third-party application servers and service implementations. This MAS is designed to show only minimal dynamics that concern the detailed management of the individual components, e.g. failure recovery when the deployment of a service fails. These functionalities were realized with a publicly available management interface. That the management system itself shows only minimal dynamics simplifies the attachment of desirable dynamics. In this simple case the supplementation of simple links was sufficient to complete the already existing relations in the application dynamics to balancing feedbacks that counteract fluctuations in the managed system.

6.8.3 Patching Dynamics in Agent Societies

Epidemic algorithms provide stochastic dissemination processes that are attractive to large-scale systems [Eugster et al., 2004]. These describe generic template processes (see Section 3.2.2) that enable the effective spreading of information within distributed systems. Information can be dropped in an arbitrarily selected part of the distributed system and will be transmitted among system entities. The dynamics of the imitated epidemics are exemplified in previous case studies. In Section 4.4.2, the design of an artificial immune system is discussed. Hypothetical epidemics in distributed systems are balanced by combining coordination strategies. The integration of epidemics, using the systemic programming model, is demonstrated in Section 5.4.2.

In this section, the systematic development approach is exemplified in the conception of a responsive dissemination process that counter balances unwanted epidemics. In a hypothetical setting, a network of hosts, which are modeled as autonomous agents, is subject to random *infections*. Infected hosts are captured by malicious processes that randomly infect other hosts. This spreading of infections is a self-organizing property and the design objective is the containment of epidemics. Thus the intended adaptivity of the system is the transition from an infected system, where a multitude of agents is infected, to a system free of infections.

That the unintended behavior is an adaptive process in and of itself poses a novel challenge for the conception and validation of the counteracting process. The aim of this process is not the intended correlation of agent activities, but the limitation of the problematic process. The development of the supportive process follows the generic development procedure that is given in Section 6.3.1. First, the factors that influence the problematic behavior are identified in a systemic representation of the system dynamics. Then the possible exertions of influences on these factors are conceived and a supplementary process is planned and configured that controls these exertions. Here, the generated artifacts and simulation models are discussed in sequence to indicate the relation to the generic development procedure exemplified in Section 6.8.1.

Process Definition: Problem Dynamic

First, the *Problem Dynamic* is identified. A systemic description of the problematic system behavior is the starting point for the alleviation of unintended system properties. Figure 6.29 illustrates an ACBG that describes the spreading of infections. Agents can be classified into two behavioral categories. Non-infected nodes are *Susceptible* and infections make agents *Infectious*. In the ACBG these categories are described as roles that agents exhibit. The sum of the local interactions between susceptible and infectious agents can be described by a fluctuating *infection* rate. The rate characterizes the reduction of the number of Susceptible agents (negative influence: *infection*) and increase of Infectious agents (positive influence: *infected*). The macroscopic observable rate of infections depends on, i.e. is causally related to, the availability of Susceptible (positive interdependency: *susceptible*) and Infectious (positive interdependency: *infecting*) agents. Increases in variable values support increases of the infection rate and reductions of either of these variables cause a decline in the rate of infections. These relations form a pair of counteractive feedbacks. A reinforcing feedback (α) continuously increases the fraction of Infectious agents in the system. This reinforcement is countered by the a balancing feedback (β) that reduces the fraction of Susceptible agents.

The interactions within an artificial system are modeled, therefore infected agents do not recover by themselves but are recaptured by external interventions. In addition, incubation times, i.e. the time that it takes a malicious process to capture a host are neglected. The given systemic description conforms to classical *SI* models from mathematical biology (e.g. see [Murray, 2002], Chapter 10). In these models populations are divided to classes that categorize the condition of individuals. In a simple scenario, agents either might catch a disease (susceptible) or are infectious,

240 CHAPTER 6. SYSTEMATIC INTEGRATION OF DECENTRALIZED COORDINATION

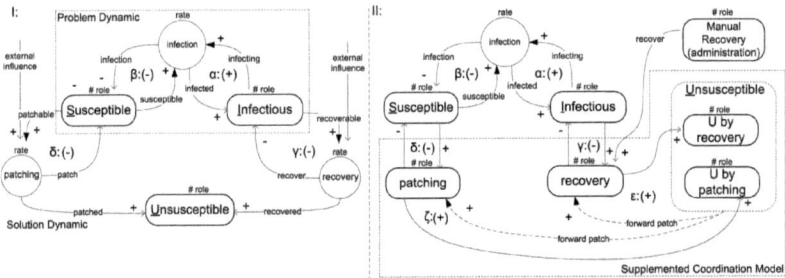

Figure 6.29: Patching dynamics: Problem Dynamic (I), Solution Dynamic(I) and the embedded Coordinating Process (II), following [Sudeikat and Renz, 2010a]

i.e. are infected and capable of transmitting their infection:

$$\frac{dS}{dt} = -rIS \qquad (6.1)$$

$$\frac{dI}{dt} = rIS \qquad (6.2)$$

where $S(t)$ represents the number of healthy, i.e. susceptible, individuals and $I(t)$ represents the number of infected and therefore infectious individuals. The number of individuals $N = S + I$ is constant. The ACBG (cf. Figure 6.29) shows that the infection of susceptible agents is proportional to the number of infectious and susceptible individuals. This is represented by the term rIS, where $r > 0$ is the rate of infection. Extensions of the SI model add additional classes of individuals, e.g. to describe the ability of individuals to recover from infections (*SIR* model) and/or carry latent infections (*SEIR* model) [Murray, 2002].

Without interventions the system approaches a steady state where all agents are Infected. In this simple scenario, the mathematical representation can be simply iterated to anticipate the system dynamics. As argued in Section 6.7.3, a complementary approach is the derivation of stochastic simulation models from coarse-grained, behavioral agent models. A Sπ-calculus model of Susceptible and Infectious agents is illustrated in Figure 6.30 (I). The susceptible agents, represented by the process $s()$, and infectious agents, represented by the process $i()$, interact via a channel *infect*. Upon reception of data via this channel (*infect*), susceptible agents behave like infectious processes. Otherwise, these processes, after a delay (τ_1), continue to behave as susceptible agents. Infectious processes are either passive (τ_2) or cause an infection ($\overline{infect}$). The number of initially active processes is annotated in square brackets next to the yellow shaded nodes.

Simulation results are shown in Figure 6.30 (II).[14] Starting from an initially small fraction of Infectious agents, the velocity of propagation increases and afterwards declines as the number of infected agents approaches the number of agents, i.e. processes.

Process Definition: Solution Dynamic

After the problematic behavior is examined, the design objective is to conceive an opposing dynamic that contains epidemics. The containment of epidemics requires the reduction of Susceptible and Infectious agents. If one or both variable values are reduced, the infection rate is reduced. A *Solution Dynamic* (cf. Figure 6.29) describes the supplementation of an additional agent role *Unsusceptible* which denotes agents that are immune to infections. Two balancing feedback loops

---
[14]The configuration used is: $\tau_1, \tau_2, infect = 0.001$

6.8. CASE STUDIES

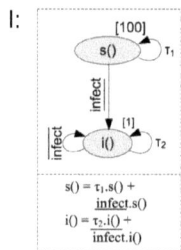 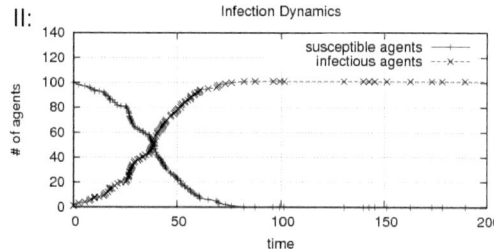

Figure 6.30: Patching dynamics: Animation of the Problem Dynamic. The figure illustrates the structure of the algebraic simulation model (I) and shows a sample simulation run (II).

enforce the conversion of agents to this behavior. First, a *recovery* rate characterizes the doctoring of Infectious agents. The resulting feedback loop (γ) steers the transfer of Infectious agents to the immune configuration. The rate is enforced by the number of agents that can be recovered (positive interdependency: *recoverable*). The effects of recoveries are the reduction of Infectious agents (negative influence: *recover*) and an increase of Unsusceptible agents (positive influence: *recovered*). Susceptible agents are analogously converted by patching them prior to an infection (δ). A *patching* rate describes immunization of Susceptible agents. This rate causally depends on the availability of Susceptible agents (positive interdependency: *patchable*) and immunizations reduce the number of Suscepbtible agents (negative influence: *patch*) and increase the number of Unsusceptible agents (positive influence: *patched*).

This Solution Dynamic is a conception of the intended dynamics that alleviate the problematic system behavior. The dynamics of when and how immunizations take place are not defined but are added by *external influences*. The model serves as a requirement for the design of an appropriate Coordinating Process that prescribes the actual relations and agent behaviors that are used to realize the additional feedbacks. In this hypothetical scenario, the additional balancing feedbacks (γ,δ) are realized by a counteracting dissemination process that spreads patches among the agent population.

The ACBG of the enacted process is illustrated in Figure 6.29 (II). The process details the intended feedback structure in preparation of its enactment. The agent-intern *patching* of Susceptible agents and *recovery* of Infectious agents are denoted as agent roles. Upon reception of a patch (mediated, positive influence: *forward patch*) agents exhibit a behavior that includes the activities necessary to immunize the agent. These abilities are provided by an Adaptivity Component, as these activities only concern the coordination and can be separated from the agent logic. The modification of the agent models, as agents are patched, lend themselves to be realized as procedural logic in the agent programming language. The unsusceptible agent role is refined into two roles that are distinguished by the method of the immunization by the original agent behavior. Agents become unsusceptible as they are recovered (*U by recovery*) or patched (*U by patching*). Both types of Unsusceptible agent roles share the behavior of distributing the processed patch among the agent population (*forward patch*). This distribution of updates is mediated by a Coordination Medium. Agents are equipped with Endpoints and the detection of an Unsusceptible behavior leads to the publication of the update. Endpoints within Susceptible as well as Infectious agents subscribe to the medium to be notified of forwarded patches. The manual treatment of an infected agent (*Manual Recovery (administration)*) initializes the containment process. An administrative intervention triggers the *recovery* of a randomly selected Infectious agent. The agent is converted to exhibit the corresponding unsusceptible role (*U by recovery*). The Endpoint in this agent then transmits the update and triggers subsequent communications of converted agents. The transformations of agents to the Unsusceptible agent behavior, caused by communications of patches, form two reinforcing feedback loops (η,ζ) that enforce the modifications of the agents that balance the unintended agent states (γ,δ). Consequently the infection process is counteracted by two processes ($\gamma + \eta$, $\delta + \zeta$) that reinforce unsusceptability.

Coordination Validation (Qualitative)

Prior to the implementation the effects of this dynamic are anticipated. The inclusion of the unsusceptible agent state corresponds to the *SIR* model from mathematical biology [Murray, 2002]. These models contain a third agent class that is recovered or dead (R) and the rate of removal of infectious individuals is proportional to the number of infected agents. The distinction between the two described methods of becoming unsusceptible leads to:

$$\frac{dS}{dt} = -rIS - pSU_p \qquad (6.3)$$

$$\frac{dI}{dt} = rIS - qIU_r \qquad (6.4)$$

$$\frac{dU_p}{dt} = pIU_p \qquad (6.5)$$

$$\frac{dU_r}{dt} = qIU_r \qquad (6.6)$$

where the additional states U_p and U_r denote the number of agents that are *Unsusceptible by patching*, respectively *Unsusceptible by recovery*. The terms $p > 0$ and $q > 0$ are the rates of healing infected agents. In classical SIR models the recovery is modeled as an internal process, but as stated above it is not assumed that agents recover by themselves but that recoveries depend on the use of a communicated patch (*forward patch*). Therefore, the recoveries are also proportional to the numbers of infectious and communicating, i.e. Unsusceptible, agents (pIU_p, cIU_r).

A stochastic simulation model of this scenario is given in Figure 6.31 (I). According to Figure 6.30, the processes $s()$ and $i()$ represent the susceptible and infectious agents. Additional processes represent the agents that are converted to be unsusceptible by recovering Infectious agents (u_r) or by patching susceptible agents (u_p). The channel p allows the communication of patches by insusceptible agents ($u_{\{p,r\}}$). Receptions on this channel (p) trigger the conversion of agents ($i() \to u_r$, $s() \to u_p$). Each conversion takes a fixed time delay and the recovery of an infected agent (τ_5) is assumed to take longer then the patching of a healthy host (τ_4, $\tau_5 > \tau_4$). Patches are sent ($\overline{p}$) by the unsusceptible agents ($u_{\{p,r\}}$) and after a fixed time delay (τ_8) they return to their original behavior.

The parametrization of the agent activities and the communication Medium control which feedback process dominates, i.e. if the majority of agents is recovered or patched. Simulations show two competing dynamics. The epidemic and the conversion to unsusceptability are propagated within the agent population. The behavior of the containment process ranges between two extreme behavioral regimes. At one extreme, communication delays and the time needed to convert agents can force the patching process to lag behind the epidemic. This process is dominated by the recovery activity, since the majority of recipients of patches are already infected. This behavior is named a *subsequent regime* , since patchings tend to follow infections. An example for this regime is given in Figure 6.31 (II, III).[15] After a large fraction of agents has been infected, the resolving process follows. At the other extreme, when the counteractive process is enacted quickly enough, epidemics are counteracted before the population is infected. The containment is dominated by the patching of susceptible agents. This regime is named *competitive* since both processes compete for resources, i.e. the susceptible agents. It is illustrated in Figure 6.31 (IV,V).[16] The maximum fraction of infected agents is limited as the susceptible agents are quickly converted by both processes. Afterwards the conversion of infected agents continues. The relevant factors for the exhibition of these regimes is the ratio of the system size and the propagation velocities of infections and patches.

---

[15]The configuration used is: $\tau_1 = 0.00001; \tau_2, \tau_3 = 0.001; \tau_4 = 0.01; \tau_6, \tau_7, \tau_8 = 0.1; p = 0.01; infect = 0.001$
[16]The configuration used is: $\tau_1, \tau_2 = 0.001; \tau_3, \tau_5, \tau_6 = 0.1; \tau_4, \tau_7 = 0.1; \tau_8 = \emptyset; p = 0.01; infect = 0.001$

6.8. CASE STUDIES

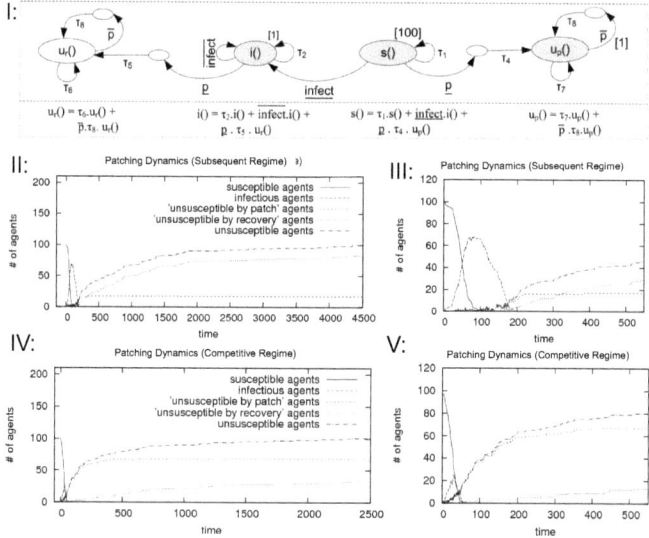

Figure 6.31: Patching dynamics: Animation of the Solution Dynamic(s). The figure illustrates the structure of the algebraic simulation model (I) and shows sample simulation runs (II-V).

Process Integration

The discussed and analysed Coordinating Process was enacted with the systemic coordination architecture (cf. Section 5.3.5). In these simulations all agents are initially susceptible, except for one randomly selected agent that is infected at start-up. After a short time delay, this infected agent randomly infects a fixed number of other agents. As recipients of infections are automatically converted after a fixed time delay, small numbers of forwarded infections are sufficient for a quick spread of the disease.

After a fixed time delay, the first agent is recovered to mimic a manual intervention. This triggers the conversion process and consequently unsusceptible agents spread the patch. To illustrate the enactment of the patch distribution as a transparent background process among agents the declaration of the *recovery* role is exemplified in Listing 6.1. It is declared which agent type (*SenderReceiver*) is capable of exhibiting the role under the precondition that the local configuration of the agent, i.e. the *color* element of the local agent knowledge, indicates that the agent is infected.

```
...
  <role_occupation name="recovery" multiple="false">
    <agent id="SenderReceiver">
      <constraints>
        <condition name="condition">
          $beliefbase.color.equalsIgnoreCase("infectious")
        </condition>
      </constraints>
    </agent>
  </role_occupation>
...
```

Listing 6.1: The enacted Coordination Model

244 CHAPTER 6. SYSTEMATIC INTEGRATION OF DECENTRALIZED COORDINATION

Coordination Validation (Quantitative)

Patches are distributed by a networked Coordination Medium that spans an overlay network among the Coordination Endpoints (see Appendix B.1.2). The configuration of this type of medium is shown in Listing 5.5. The medium is configured to show a power-law distributed topology. The effectiveness of the information dissemination within power-law distributed graph topologies is shown in Section 5.4.2, where the dissemination time is compared to random distributed topologies.

The plot in Figure 6.32 illustrates a simulation run. After initialization a single agent in a population of 200 agents is infected. The infection rate is fixed as infectious agents transmit their infection to two randomly chosen agents after 1 second. This comparatively slow rate allows the infection to spread quickly within the MAS. The recovery of an agent is set to take 4 seconds, twice as long as the patching of a susceptible agent (2 seconds). Delays are scheduled by the Jadex system as these are realized by explicitly making agent modules wait during execution (calling the method waitFor(long ...)).

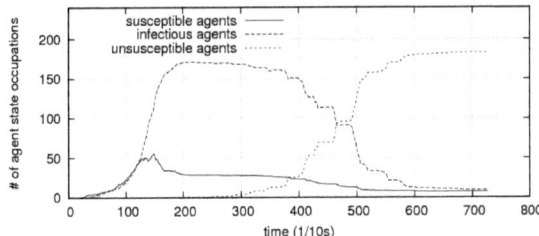

Figure 6.32: Patching dynamics: Sample simulation run. 200 agents (averaged over 10 runs) are patched by a power-law distributed graph (5000 edges, r = 10000) [Sudeikat and Renz, 2010a].

The plots in Figure 6.33 summarize the simulation results. The effectiveness of the supplemented counterbalancing process is measured by the amplitude of infections (cf. Figure 6.33, I).[17] These amplitudes are plotted over the *communicativeness* of Coordination Endpoints. Corresponding to the simulations in Section 5.4.2, this parameter controls the percentage of neighboring agents, according to the imposed overlay network topology, that are informed by publications.[18] The measurements show that the maximum number of infected agents decreases when the communicativeness of agents is increased. This is an expected behavior, as the communicativeness increases the absolute number of messages, i.e. patches, that are distributed in the system.

Simulations of the process abstraction indicate that the supplemented process can be executed in either a *subsequent* or *competitive* regime. The competitive regime is favorable, since it makes the embedded processes compete for susceptible agents. The exhibition of these regimes is indicated by the ratio of agents that are rendered unsusceptible by (1) receiving a patch, i.e. that were previously susceptible, and (2) that are recovered, i.e. that were previously infected. This ratio (ρ) can be quantified by

$$\rho = \frac{max_p - max_r}{|U|} \qquad (6.7)$$

where max_p and max_r are measurements of the maximum number of patched and recovered agents, $|U|$ is the cardinality of the set of agents that were rendered unsusceptible. In this setting, patching and recovery are the only means for converting agents, therefore $max_p + max_r = |U|$) and measurements can range from -1 to $+1$. Negative values indicate subsequent regimes, since

---
[17]averaged over 10 simulation runs per configuration
[18]e.g. 1.0 indicated that all known agents receive publications, i.e. patches

6.9. CONCLUSIONS

the number of recovered agents exceeds the number of patched agents. Vice versa, positive values indicate competitive regimes as more agents were converted (patched) *before* they could be infected than agents were recovered, i.e. treated after an infection. Measurements of this quantity are plotted in Figure 6.33 (II). For small communicativeness values, the process is subsequent but quickly becomes competitive due to the effectiveness of the spreading of patches.

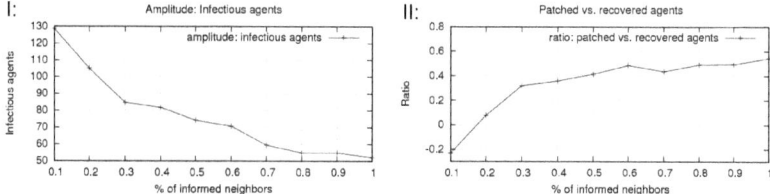

Figure 6.33: Patching dynamics: Simulation results [Sudeikat and Renz, 2010a]

Discussion

The case study concerns a hypothetical scenario, but demonstrates the treatment of problematic self-organizing dynamics. The unintended behavior and the solution dynamic are described and simulated in detail, prior to the process integration. In this example, the Problem and the Solution Dynamic manifest two system-level processes that interact, i.e. compete for resources. Therefore, the analysis revealed two essential types of behavioral regimes. The two processes either consume resources one after another or compete. An application-specific measurement is derived to characterize the proportion of competition in simulation runs. The application development follows the generic development process structure and the systematic conception of the inter-agent process, as a response to an initial inter-agent process, is demonstrated.

6.9 Conclusions

In this chapter, the systematic development of self-organizing software systems is discussed. The development approach presented is based on the separation of the configuration of self-organizing process from the construction of MASs that is enabled by the systemic modeling approach (see Chapter 4) and the corresponding programming model (see Chapter 5). The methodical software development, using this tool set, is prepared by conceptualizing the design of self-organizing software systems (see Section 6.2). The apparent paradox of revising low-level properties of system elements to obtain and adjust high-level system properties is circumvented by the systemic modeling of the causes of self-organization, i.e. the distributed feedbacks among system elements. These are the means of expression for the structure-establishment that is to be integrated in a software application (see Section 6.2.1). Based on this development stance, the essential development strategies have been derived, i.e. the partial or full externalization of process realizations (see Section 6.2.2).

The alternation between the development of the self-organizing process structure and the software system is discussed in Section 6.3. The essential stages of the iterative conception and adjustment of process models are addressed and their integration in software development practices is outlined. This discussion focuses on the embedding of the process development into software development procedures. This integration allows to reuse support for the design of software systems, e.g. a particular type of MAS, while preparing self-adaptive features in decentralized ways. A standard notation is used to describe the execution of the process development. The basic development activities are detailed in the subsequent Sections 6.4 to 6.7. In each section, the control flow within a development activity and the modified work pieces are described.

Three case studies demonstrate the systematic development (see Section 6.8). In each study the dynamics of a software system, as is, are modeled and the requirements are described by an intended dynamic that development aims to bring about. The intended adaptive properties are informally described and the intended dynamic is successively refined to a detailed process description that enables an MAS to show the expected system behavior. The coordination-relevant dynamics of a functioning system, based on their design, are analyzed and modeled as an ACBG. Then these intended dynamics are modeled in an extended ACBG and the delta that is to be supplemented in order to complete the application is identified. This delta is then configured and integrated using the systemic programming model. In the *production line* case study (see Section 6.8.1) a system is built from scratch that follows a generic application architecture for a specific class of agent-based software systems. This system is then equipped with a decentralized reconfiguration process that is completely separated from the application dynamic. In the *service management* case study (see Section 6.8.2 the equipping of non-agent software elements with decentralized self-orgnaization is demonstrated. An agent-based maangement system serves as mediating abstraction. The constituent agents manage software entities via standard interfaces and the coordination of the agent behaviors leads to the coordination of the overall software system. The *pathing* case study (see Section 6.8.3) is different because the inetgrated supplementation concerns a self-organizing process that counteracts an unintended, problematic self-organizing process. Thus a self-organizing process is designed to counteract a problematic, self-orgnizing phenomenon.

Enabling the Design of Application Dynamics

Designing decentralized coordination and self-organization requires the ability to plan for the macro-level effects that stem from the sum of the agent-interactions. This gap challenges traditional software engineering practices (see Section 3.2) and is of major concerns for the development procedure presented here (see Challenge 6.1, page 196). Here, this challenge is approached by the identification of the missing delta needed to convert the original dynamic, i.e. the dynamic of a software system that is not supplemented with a Coordinating Process, to a dynamic that is acceptable and shows the intended level of adaptivity. Both dynamics are expressed as ACBGs and the original dynamic is coined *Problem Dynamic* to indicate that the supplementation addresses a problematic aspect of the application behavior. This can be the absence of an adaptiveness or an unintended behavioral mode. The corresponding *Solution Dynamic* extends the Problem Dynamic with additional influences that constitute or complete feedbacks to adjust the system behavior. The difference between both dynamics are supplemented to MASs, using the systemic programming techniques (see Chapter 5).

Bridging Top-Down and Bottom-Up Development Activities

Bridging the gap between microscopic agent models and the resulting macroscopic system behavior is also a crucial challenge to the systematic development of self-organizing applications (see Challenge 6.2, page 196). The alternation between top-down design of software artifacts and bottom-up analysis of their collective behavior is a fundamental aspect in engineering procedures and the development life-cycle presented here presupposes this alternation.

The design of system elements, mainly agent realizations with their appertaining software artifacts, e.g. environment elements, follows conventional development practices. The analysis of the application dynamics is systematized in Section 4.3. The defined procedure instructs the bottom-up analysis to estimate the potential behavior modes that are implied in the application design. The analysis of the application dynamics is indicated as a precaution or when the simulation/execution of the software system indicates the presence of dynamic phenomena.

When the presence of unwanted, macroscopic system dynamics is revealed the development process guides the adjustment of the system behavior by conceiving and supplementing Coordinating Processes. The incremental design of these processes prescribes the alternation of top-down process refinements and the bottom-up analysis of the resulting system behavior. The operation

6.9. CONCLUSIONS

of this process can be described on micro-, meso-, and macroscopic modeling levels, as discussed in Section 3.4. In Figure 6.34, the modeling levels are related to the development processes. This illustration shows how the development procedure desribed realizes transitions between the modeling levels.

On a conceptual level, the elicitation of requirements (*Adaptivity Requirements*) addresses the description of the intended, macroscopic system behavior. Specifications of Coordinating Process are successively detailed (*Coord. Process Definition*). The resulting process descriptions correspond to intermediate system models that are top-down refined. The analysis of the resulting behavior (*Coord. Strategy Validation (Qualitative/Quantitative)*), affected by the establishment of the conceived processes, corresponds to the bottom-up analysis efforts. The *Process Integration* systematizes the building-in of the abstract process models into microscopic agent models. The process descriptions correspond to the intermediate, mesoscopic models of the system operation. Using the previously described enactment architecture and language support (cf. Chapter 5), these processes are directly enacted. This process corresponds to the second redesign strategy that is presented in Section 3.4.1 and exemplified in Section 3.4.3. The abstracted, behaviors and interactions, that constitute an intermediate system description are directly integrated in the microscopic agent models. The architecture separates the original agent realizations from the coordination logic that describes the semantics of this process model. Thus the necessary modifications of the microscopic agents are minimized, while the described system behavior is affected.

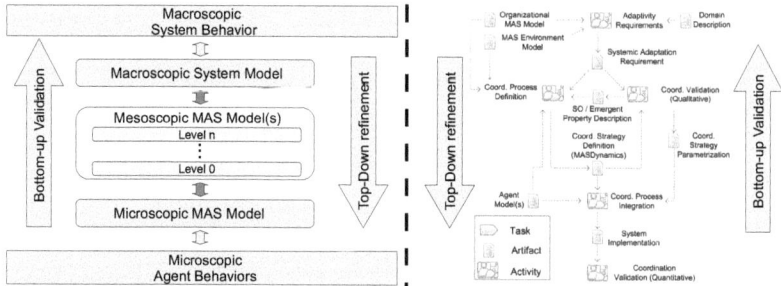

Figure 6.34: Combining top-down and bottom-up development practices. The figure illustrates the modeling levels (left) [Sudeikat et al., 2009b] and the structure of the development activities (right), following [Sudeikat and Renz, 2010a].

Instructing the Supplementation of Inter-Agent Processes

The ability to equip applications with self-organizing features is a novel design stance (see Challenge 6.3, page 196). It is adopted to prepare the integration of self-organization principles in mainstream software engineering. The development procedure systematizes the analysis of applications and the conception of a supplement that adjusts the application behavior. The conception of a self-organizing process is a non-trivial design challenge and must be carried out by experts. The software system engineering is separated from the coordination. Thus the system construction can reuse the best practices and the self-organization is added in later development steps. The key aspect is that developers are able at any development stage to describe the dynamic as is and identify the necessary supplement. The accomplishment of this identification and the consequent supplementation is systematized in this chapter.

Enableing the Integration in Development Methodologies

The procedure descirbed in this chapter descirbes a generic development approach that can be integrated in other development processes. The develpment of the inter-agent coordination is understood as an additional aspect in the application development and the use of self-orgnaization, as an alternative to other cooridnation approaches, is systamtized by the given development process.

Agent-oriented development methodologies guide the development of agent-based software systems. Reuse of this constructive knowledge is preferable to defining yet another specific design methodology (see Challenge 6.4, page 197). The engineering of self-organization addressed here is described as an additional development concern that can be integrated in established development contexts. The multitude of methodology proposals (see Section 2.6.3), where the instances are appropriate for specific development contexts or implementation environments, is a major cause for the absence of a generally accepted reference model. Therefore, the adoption of method engineering concepts (see Section 6.1.2) is attractive. In this chapter, standard notation for the modeling of development processes and fragments is used to describe the lifecycle of the development of Coordinating Processes, using the tool set and modeling concepts that are presented in this dissertation. The provision of fragments standards is an active research area [Cossentino et al., 2007]. The presentation given here contains the key concepts of fragments but does not follow a specific description format. The implicit assumptions about the complementary MAS development procedure(s) used to construct the MAS that will be subsequently equipped with decentralized coordination are minimized. The coordination-related development activities interface MAS development via generic types of design artifacts. These artifacts describe abstractions of methodology-specific design models and agent realizations. This prepares for interactions with development processes, as method designers can refine the specific artifact types that result from the conducting of a specific methodology and integrate model conversions when necessary.

Part III

Conclusions and Appendixes

Chapter 7

Conclusions

7.1 Summary

The motivation for this dissertation is given in Chapter 1. The necessity for the decentralized management of distributed applications is argued and self-organization is introduced as an attractive but also challenging means of equipping applications with decentralized coordination. The focus of the thesis, the use of self-organizing processes in software development, and the contributions, discussed throughout the remaining chapters, are outlined. Finally, the structure of the thesis is delineated.

In Chapter 2, Agent-Oriented Software Engineering is introduced and the discussion focuses on practical development concepts and tools. Distributed applications are designed as collectives of autonomous actors, i.e. *Multi-Agent Systems*, and the major constituents of these systems, namely *Agents* and *Environments*, are introduced as design and implementation artifacts. Agent technology provides a conceptual framework and practical middleware support for the realization of these distributed collectives. A basic conceptual model of MASs is developed that summarizes the generic structure of an agent-based software system. This model serves as a reference and is further developed in the following chapter. Then a foundational development concern, the coordination of agent activities, is discussed and is, since coordination per se is an ill-defined concept, associated to the correlation of activities. This behavioral view point on coordination is adopted as it is applicable in a wide range of scenarios due to its generality. Engineering techniques for MASs are then introduced. The instances discussed span design concepts, validation techniques, and development methodologies. The methodical development of MAS-based software systems is addressed in particular and it is observed that development methodologies are inherently related to the target implementation platform that is used for the system realization. This bias limits the applicability of methodologies and complicates their selection for a specific development context. Thus, the use of method engineering as a technique for customizing development procedures is outlined. This approach is relevant for the customization and integration of coordination-related development activities (see Chapter 6). In addition, the measurement of the effects of the use of agent-oriented development practices on the structure of the resulting system implementation is discussed. Initial results indicate that software structures are positively affected by the adoption of agent-oriented practices. Finally, application areas are outlined and the adoption of agent-orientation in application on development is motivated by a discussion of basic design aspects.

In the third chapter, the self-organization concept is introduced and the relevance of this type of system phenomenon for the development of distributed systems is presented. Self-organization is distinguished from related concepts, namely emergence and self-management. The manifestation of self-organization in software systems, which includes beneficial as well as problematic phenomena, is characterized. The study of these phenomena, which result from the collective coaction of system entities, is particularly related to the development of self-adaptive software systems. Self-organization is not only understood as an alternative approach to enabling systems to manage themselves, but also as an immanent development concern for agent-based applications, as collectives of autonomous system elements have the potential to exhibit these collective phenomena. Thereafter, a comprehensive review of engineering approaches to self-organizing systems is given. These approaches range from reusable coordination mechanisms and template processes to development guidelines and methodologies. The former tool set identifies application-independent mechanisms that can be reused in application design and implementation. The latter aspects concern the adoption of self-organization principles in systematic application development. Based on this review, a novel conceptualization of self-organizing applications is developed. It describes the fundamental structure of self-organizing applications that extends the conceptual model of an MAS (see Chapter 2), and the building blocks of the causative processes that lead to self-organizing effects. In addition, implementation mechanisms are related to each other in a unifying classification. Finally, the demand for intermediate modeling levels in the design of these applications is then argued and examples are given. These modeling levels support the redesign of applications to adjust and fine-tune the manifestation of self-organizing properties.

In Chapter 4, a novel, *systemic* modeling approach is developed and demonstrated. The motivation for such an approach is that the conception of a self-organizing application demands a modeling technique that allows to describe and plan for the application dynamics. An appropriate modeling approach is developed by adopting and extending and established modeling technique. This modeling stance is then used to extend current MAS development practices. First, the analysis of the potential dynamics of MASs is systematized and demonstrated. The derivation of systemic models from application designs is presented as a generic development activity, which allows the space of potential application dynamics to be estimated. Secondly, the use of systemic models for the conception of self-organizing processes is discussed. Systemic modeling is used to describe nature-inspired template processes. Besides the structural classification, based on the underlying feedback structure that causes the collective behavior, a set of classification criteria is derived that characterizes the dynamic formation of structures. The combination of these template processes in the application development is discussed and demonstrated.

In the Chapter 5, a programming technique is developed that allows decentralized inter-agent processes to be specified and integrated into MASs. This *systemic* programming approach is a consequent progression of the systemic modeling approach as it enables the integration of processed in MAS. First, the architecture of a tailored execution environment is presented. This architecture provides a middleware layer for the separation of the process execution from the functioning of the individual system elements. The two fundamental constituents of this layer are interaction infrastructures, called *Coordination Media*, and agent modules, called *Endpoints*, that control the coordination-related activities. Using this middleware, the participation of software agents in self-organizing processes can be encapsulated. During the design and implementation of an MAS, the control of coordination-related activities is separated from the control flow of agents. The structure of the constituents, their operating principle, the exchanged data, and the algorithms for essential execution aspects are presented. Secondly, a configuration language is developed that allows for the prescription of the enactment of processes. This language allows systemic process models to be described and details that are relevant for automated enactment to be annotated. These details configure the execution of Media and Endpoints. Finally, examples for the use of the programming framework are given in two case studies. Agent-based system realizations are equipped with decentralized processes to show the practicability of the conceptual and technical separation of the processes execution from the agent functioning.

In Chapter 6, the systematic use of the programming framework is discussed. The need for a systematic development procedure is motivated. The design of self-organization is often understood as a contradiction and the partial resolution of this dilemma, as exercised in this thesis, is reported. Three principal development strategies are identified and a procedure for the development of self-organizing processes, as a supplement to established development practices and methodologies, is presented. In the subsequent sections, the individual development activities of this procedure, ranging from requirement analysis to system validation, are discussed. Finally, examples for the use of the proposed development approach are given in three cases studies. First, the development of a decentralized reconfiguration process within hypothetical production lines is shown. This case study is an example of the top-down refinement of a Coordinating Process, from the initial requirement to the final reconfiguration procedure. The second case study is an example of the integration of Coordinating Processes in real-world software systems, as the decentralized management of Java EE application servers is enabled. The final example shows the counterbalancing of self-organizing dynamics. An application shows an unintended self-organizing behavior and this behavior is then adjusted by the conception and integration of an appropriately counteracting process.

Finally, Chapter 7 concludes the dissertation. The chapters are summarized, the presented contributions are discussed, and future work is outlined.

7.2 Discussion of Contributions and Outlook

In this dissertation, an integrated development approach for self-organizing processes in MASs is discussed. The acquired set of techniques can be used to equip agent-based applications with adaptive features that result from self-organization principles. It is possible to plan for and integrate self-organizing features in agent-based software systems. The systematic conception of the decentralized processes that cause self-organization and their supplementation to agent-based software systems is systematized as an optional, supportive development aspect.

The transfer of these processes to interdependent elements of the application design and implementation enables the reasoning about agent coaction as an additional development concern. The treatment and planning for self-organizing properties is conceptually and technically separated from the other concerns that have to be addressed during application development. This separation is the superordinate contribution of the dissertation. The fundamental aspects of the process-development are illustrated in Figure 7.1 (inner circle). Primary concerns are the *Modeling* and the *Programming* of Coordinating Processes. These activities are supported by a systematic *Development Process*. These three aspects require individual contributions that, in their combination, enable the envisioned separation (see Figure 7.1, outer circle). The modeling aspect is addressed by a systemic approach (*Systemic Modeling*, see Chapter 4), the configuration and embedding of processes is realized by a specific programming model (*Process Integration*, see Chapter 5), and the development of inter-agent processes, using the elaborated tool set, is structured by a tailored development procedure (*Process Development*, see Chapter 6). The two major development activities are the conception of appropriate processes (*Process Conception*) and their detailed configuration (*Process Prescription*) to prepare their realization. The conception is enabled by the modeling approach and guided by the development procedure. The prescriptions of processes are also based on the modeling technique. Application-independent process models follow this modeling technique and a corresponding configuration language, which allows process templates to be annotated with implementation details, is part of the programming model. The aim of the development is a *Self-Organizing MAS*.

Conceptualization of Self-Organizing Software Systems

The starting point for the elaboration of the presented development approach is a review of engineering techniques for self-organizing systems (see Section 3.2, page 55) and initial experiments with self-organizing simulation models (see Section 3.4, page 69). The techniques considered pertain to software engineering methods, design approaches and development tools. These enable the incremental construction and revision of software components to yield a functioning software system that shows self-organizing features. Related bio-inspired approaches, e.g. the utilization of *neural* or *evolutionary* systems [Floreano and Mattiussi, 2008] are omitted. The conceptual structure of self-organizing applications, taking the example of self-organizing MAS, is derived. This leads to a unifying classification of Coordination Mechanisms (see section 3.2), a conceptual model of self-organizing software systems (see Section 3.3), and the essential concept of Coordinating Processes (see Definition 3.1, page 62) that are the mainspring of self-organizing dynamics. Implementation mechanisms and patterns, introduced by practitioners, are often grounded on

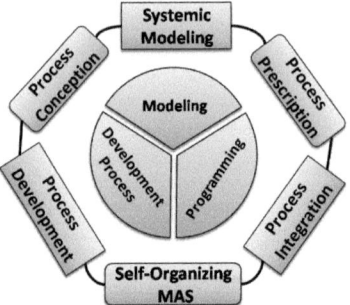

Figure 7.1: An integrated development approach for self-organization processes

conceptually different abstraction levels. The elaborated classification unifies previous works and integrates different description criteria. The conceptual model deals with the abstract application structure. It serves as a foundation for the study of self-organizing applications and grounds the work in this dissertation. The concept of a *Coordinating Process* is introduced (see Figure 3.6, page 57) and is subsequently elevated to an independent design (see Figure 4.4) and implementation element (see Figure 5.11). An additional contribution is the principled study of intermediate, mesoscopic modeling techniques (see Section 3.4), which is advanced to a *re*-design approach for self-organizing MASs. This approach structures the adjustment of applications to tune their behavior, e.g. enhance the performance of the structure formation shown (see Section 3.4.1). This approach is based on the classification of agent behaviors with respect to their contributions to the structuring. Agent models are then modified to reinforce the appropriate contributions. This approach systematizes the adjustment of self-organizing properties, but is limited to applications that already showed such a phenomenon in the first place.

A Systemic Modeling Technique

A *Systemic Modeling* technique (see Figure 6.34, top), as discussed throughout Chapter 4, is proposed to address the description of decentralized, inter-agent processes in MASs. The presented modeling stance provides an orthogonal description level for MAS applications that focuses on the system level dynamics. This modeling stance is based on the transfer of System Dynamics modeling techniques and is used to describe the *distributed feedbacks* that govern the dynamics of a self-organizing process. The abilities and complications to describe collectives of individuals with macroscopic, equation-based models have been previously studied (see Sections 4.1.2 and 4.2.2). This description level is extended and revised to prepare a specific modeling methodology. Consequently, the timely dynamics of behavior activations can be expressed in a graphical notation that can be transferred to mathematical as well as simulation models. A number of detailed adjustments were made and the resulting structure is called an *Agent Causal Behavior Graph*. This graph extends system dynamics notations to provide unambiguous descriptions of MASs and include MAS specific details. In addition, practical concerns, such as the linking of graphs to established MAS design concepts, are addressed and demonstrated by allowing the extending of node types. The refinement of ACBGs via graph operations and the introduction of a state-chart-like notation for tracing refinements, prepares for multi-level modeling as well as an incremental refinement of process descriptions (cf. Hypothesis 1.2, page 4). Two supplementary contributions instruct the use of this modeling approach. First, the analysis of agent-based application in order to estimate potential dynamics is systematized (see Section 4.3). The discussed procedure guides the extraction of ACBGs from MAS designs. The analysis of these models allows the

7.2. DISCUSSION OF CONTRIBUTIONS AND OUTLOOK

space of dynamics that are theoretically possible to be examined. In this respect, application designs can be searched for potential unintended consequences that may result from the agent co-action. Secondly, the modeling stance is used to catalog prominent instances of self-organizing Coordinating Processes (see Section 4.4.1). This catalog extends prior descriptions of template processes with a dynamic perspective that explains how the intended structure formation takes place. Based on these models, which express the dynamics of the inter-agent process, a novel set of description criteria is derived, which characterizes the structuring of software systems. These are phenomenological properties of the structuring itself that facilitate the assessment of the appropriateness of a template processes in given application contexts, as demonstrated in Sections 5.4.1 and 5.4.2. It is shown and demonstrated that the modeling of distributed feedback structures is an appropriate abstraction level for the planning of the dynamics of collectives of system elements (cf. Hypothesis 1.1, page 4).

A Systemic Programming Model

The integration of decentralized processes in MASs (*Process Integration*, see Figure 7.1) is discussed in Chapter 5. The programming model enforces the maximum possible separation between the application logic, i.e. the control flow within agents, and the activities that are relevant for the coordination. This separation minimizes the coupling of the two development issues and the conceptual value of this separation is described by the Hypotheses 1.3 and 1.4 (see page 4). Consequently applications can be equipped with processes and these processes can be revised independently with minimal impact on the agent models. This approach opposes conventional techniques that require mechanisms to be embedded in the agent control-flow. The fundamental elements of the programming model are a middleware layer for the enactment of processes and a language for the configuration of process instances. Conceptually, the middleware layer is a reference model for the integration of decentralized processes, as it structures the integration of the relevant mechanism types, i.e. interaction and adaptation mechanisms, in a coherent architectural framework. The use of a declarative configuration language allows processes to be externalized. These processes can be revised independently from the target MAS. This is attractive in development contexts where process configurations frequently change, such as the prototyping of applications. The realization of the middleware layer on top of general-purpose agent architectures makes use of an extension to conventional agent modules. Modules are equipped with the ability to perceive and influence their immediate execution context, i.e. the surrounding agents. This is a consequent step towards the modularization of software agents, since agents, as active software elements, can be structured as collectives of active elements, i.e. activated modules (see Section 5.2.4, page 148). In the context of the coordination middleware, this extension allows the automation of coordination-relevant activities to be contained inside modules. These observe the agent execution, participate in interactions, and modify the agent configuration as needed. The operation principle of these modules is formalized for a specific agent platform, and other uses of the enhanced module concept are also demonstrated.

Systematic Supplementation of Decentralized Coordination

The systematic development of Coordinating Processes (*Process Development*, see Figure 7.1) is guided by a set of development activities that are discussed throughout Chapter 6. The individual activities extend the principal software engineering disciplines, thus the development of the inter-agent process is composed of requirements, analysis, designs, implementation, and testing stages. The process presented is a direct consequence of the conceptualization of Coordinating Processes as independent construction elements. The conceptualization raises the question how the development of the processes integrates in the application development. This is answered by the elaboration of a development procedure that operates in parallel to the construction of the software system, e.g. the agents and environments. This structuring and alignment approach is selected to facilitate the reuse of existing best practices for agent-development. The major development strategies for equipping MASs with decentralized coordination are also identified (see

Section 6.2.2). These strategies are generally applicable and indicate the different options that developers can follow when constructing self-organizing MASs. The dissertation gives examples for their use.

The major contribution of the development approach proposed here is process refinement. The fundamental obstacle in the design of a self-organizing system is the conceptual gap between the microscopic element refinement and the intended macroscopic system behavior (see Section 3.2 and Challenge 6.1 on page 196). In this dissertation, the resolution of this dilemma is approached using a fundamentally different concept. The gap is circumvented by the systematic refinement of feedback models. Distributed feedbacks cause self-organizing phenomena (see Section 3.1.4) and the elevation of these feedbacks to design concepts allows developers to plan for collaborative effects that result from the agent coaction. The feedback design practiced here is unusual in software engineering contexts and a conception strategy is needed to guide the derivation of structures that manifest the intended system dynamics. A novel strategy the design of the appropriate coaction, practiced in this dissertation, is the identification of the intended feedback structure by analyzing both the problematic and the solution dynamics. The starting point is the identification of unintended dynamic properties. Comparing these with the intended dynamical proprieties allows to derive an additional set of interdependencies that can resolve the unintended behavior. This set is a supplement that is subsequently detailed to a process partition which can be integrated, using the programming techniques presented here.

Characterization of the Development Approach

In the dissertation, principal characteristics of development frameworks and methodologies for self-organizing applications are identified. These are used in Section 5.1.2 to relate development frameworks to each other and to illustrate basic aspects of development methodologies in Section 3.2.4. The corresponding characteristics of the development framework presented in this dissertation are illustrated in Figure 7.2.

Th programming model proposed (see Section 7.2, I) features the support for both interaction and adaptation mechanisms (x axis). The reference architecture proposed here provides a coherent conceptual model for integrating both aspects. This model allows to supplement Coordinating Processes (y axis). The processes is prescribed by using the configuration language and are consequently separated from the agent programming. This separation facilitates the application development. Processes can be revised in parallel to the application development. Nevertheless, it is shown that this separation is not necessarily reflected by the technological integration of processes (z axis). Using the architecture proposed here, the configured processes can be integrated into applications. The participation in the prescribed process is an additional run-time aspect that is carried out in addition to the agent functionality. In this respect, the programming model combines attractive features. The support for both mechanism types is indispensable. The supplementation enforces the separation of the process design and the agent development. The control flow of agent models is not blended with details of the inter-agent coordination. The internal integration mode allows that the computational resources of the participating agents are used for the processes execution. Therefore, the need for additional infrastructures is minimized.

The characteristics of the supplementary development procedure are illustrated in Figure 7.2 (II). It covers the principal development disciplines (x axis). In agreement with the middleware layer used, the integration of multiple coordination mechanisms is supported (y axis). A distinctive feature the process proposed is its design as an extension to agent-oriented development practices. While the process execution is understood as an additional run-time aspect in agents, the integration of these processes is also an additional aspect of the application development. The principal construction phases are identified and their integration into development practices can be adjusted, according to the needs of a software producing organization (z axis). The development activities are defined self-contained work units. This facilitates their integration in development process and methodologies. The process description, using a standardized notation, can also be used as a guideline in ad-hoc development efforts.

7.2. DISCUSSION OF CONTRIBUTIONS AND OUTLOOK

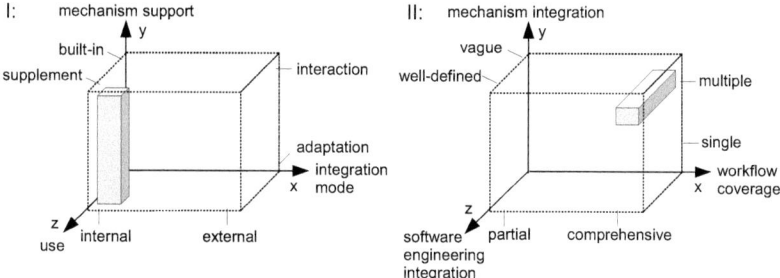

Figure 7.2: Characterization of the programming model (I) and development procedure (II)

7.2.1 Outlook

The modeling approach advocated here is appropriate for expressing the coaction of agents, but the holistic modeling stance requires expertise in the modeling of feedback structures. The revised configuration language allows full control of the process enactment. Therefore, both tools will be most valuable to domain experts who are experienced in the conception of decentralized applications. The derived tools demonstrate the feasibility of embedding decentralized dynamics, but the widespread use of this development approach requires further elaboration. First, the configuration of processes could be simplified by increasing the usability of process configurations. A first step is the use of a customized notation (see Section 5.3.3). Processes can be expressed in a concise notation, and a software framework for domains-specific languages allow editing support to be fine-tuned. Since the process models reference agent and medium implementations, one approach to increasing usability is to provide an integrated environment where agent models, medium implementation and process descriptions can be edited in parallel. Such an environment allows the support of the required references, e.g. by providing the ability to navigate links and check consistency. A potential approach for integrating the language in software engineering tools is its definition in a UML profile. Doing so would also reflect that the process model is an alternative, systemic perspective to software design. The medium implementations are configured by parameter sets, and the semantics for each medium type and its impact on the exhibited propagation dynamics differ. The structuring of media configurations, as approached in [Vilenica et al., 2010] (see Section 7.2.1), is a means to increases the expressiveness of process configurations. Configuration elements are directly integrated into partitions of the language to indicates the relevant configuration options and their relations. In addition, template processes could be associated with default configurations or layered configuration views that initially show coarse-grained configurations and can unfold into more detailed perspectives. A related aspect is the selection of process instances. The criteria set elaborated characterizes the phenomenological system behavior. For a principled and unambiguous selection of processes these classifications have to be elaborated, and process templates could be related to typical application domains or application contexts, as is approached in [DeWolf and Holvoet, 2007b].

The proposed reference middleware layer offers the opportunity for future work on the Endpoint and the Medium prototypes. Endpoints monitor the events of the agent execution to decide when coordination-related activities are indicated. The adoption of a specific agent behavior is signified by the combination of a reasoning event and the annotated conditions and invariants. Alternatively, complicated classifications can be procedurally defined by embedding Adaptivity Components. A straightforward enhancement is the preparation of the processing of composite events, e.g. specific event histories. Correspondingly, the media only transport single events and the endpoints are responsible for processing them locally. An enhancement is the outsourcing of parts of this processing to the media, e.g. to support the subscription for *composite events* (see

[Mühl et al., 2006], Chapter 7). In this work, the assumptions on media models are reduced to an absolute minimum in order to not constrain the types of infrastructures that can be integrated. The elaboration of generic media types is a complement to the reference architecture, and is not detailed in this dissertation.

The proposed development process is a generic systematization for conceiving and creating decentralized processes. As it relates to the principal elements of development methodologies (see Section 2.6.3), this conception spans modeling techniques and the development life cycle. Further study is needed to complete these development aspects with the techniques set proposed here. Example enhancements are acknowledged template processes, quality measures, and implementation standards. The life cycle and artifacts are informally described using the SPEM formalism. A standard for the documentation and fragmentation of agent-oriented development processes is currently being revised (see Section 2.6.3, page 33). The future adoption of a standardized description format is a step towards facilitating the integration of the decentralized design in AOSE contexts. In this dissertation, the MASs, which are equipped with self-organizing features, are developed using standard design techniques, e.g. the Tropos modeling concepts (see Section 2.6.3). The discussion focuses on the unique contributions, i.e. the aspects of the coordination development, and the utilization of the established techniques is only marginally discussed. The illustration of the integration using a well-known methodology is a supplement to the fragment specification that is to be addressed in future works.

Continuation: The SodekoVS-Project

The research project *Selbstorganisation durch Dezentrale Koordination in Verteilten Systemen*,[1] which is funded by the *Deutsche Forschungsgemeinschaft* (DFG),[2] studies the application of nature-inspired self-organizing processes to MASs [Sudeikat et al., 2009a]. The guiding principle of this project is to bring together standard software engineering practices and nature-inspired coordination paradigms. The research challenges presented by this endeavour are discussed in [Sudeikat et al., 2009a]. With respect to this project, the work in this dissertation serves as a feasibility study. It has been shown that self-organizing dynamics can be purposefully conceived and systematically integrated in MASs. Research in this direction is continued by the further development of the modeling techniques and tool support.

In the SodekoVS project, as well as in this dissertation, the technological means of equipping agent-based software systems with decentralized inter-agent coordination and the utilization of these means in systematic development efforts are considered as intertwined aspects that demand a coherent framework [Sudeikat et al., 2009a]. Thus the research challenges address both the software architecture for the integration of nature-inspired self-organization and the development methodology that guides corresponding integrations.

The demand for a distributed integration architecture which allows coordination mechanisms [Sudeikat and Renz, 2008b] to be encapsulated, and the layered reference model, which enforces a clear separation of coordination and functional concerns, is outlined in [Sudeikat et al., 2009a]. In this dissertation, the realization of this architectural support, complemented by a (configuration) language model, is discussed as a platform-independent conception and its integration is concretized for a specific platform, the Jadex system (see Section 2.2.2). The closer coupling of the coordination middleware with the agent platform is one approach to increasing usability. A pluggable architecture for the definition of Jadex-based MASs, coined *Application*, is proposed in [Pokahr and Braubach, 2010]. Part of these definitions is the inclusion of environment models, so-called *Spaces*. This mechanism is used in [Vilenica et al., 2010] to integrate environment-mediated Coordination Media. The functionality of the middleware layer is integrated directly into the agent platform and the declarative configurations of these media are integrated into the Jadex-specific declarations of applications. The configuration of these medium types is enhanced by a specific configuration model that medium-internal details, e.g. the configuration of environment-markers and the control of their perception by agents, to be explicitly declared.

---

[1]Self-Organisation by Decentralized Coordination in Distributed Systems
[2]http://www.dfg.de

7.2. DISCUSSION OF CONTRIBUTIONS AND OUTLOOK

System simulations are an inevitable part of MAS development [Pokahr et al., 2008]. The routine execution of simulation runs, e.g. the configuration simulations and the recording of measurements, are typically not supported by general-purpose agent platforms. Consequently, these activities have to be dealt with ad hoc on the application level. In this dissertation, the monitoring of agents [Sudeikat and Renz, 2007a] as well as a distributed simulation architecture [Sudeikat and Renz, 2009h] were developed. Recently, support for the simulations of spatial agents has been added to the Jadex system [Jander et al., 2010] and a distributed architecture for the simulation of Jadex-based systems is proposed in [Vilenica and Lamersdorf, 2010].

A vision for the development of nature-inspired self-organizing systems has been formulated in [Sudeikat et al., 2009a]. It describes the systematic embedding of template processes in agent-based software systems. This vision corresponds to the development methodology that is developed in this dissertation, as the extension of software development disciplines with specific activities, which concern the integration of nature-inspired patterns of inter-agent coordination. The elicitation of requirements also deals with the definition of the system behavior. The system analysis integrates the selection and combination of appropriate metaphors, i.e. template processes, that effectuate the intended behavior. Subsequently, the mechanisms contained in the selected template processes are configured during the system design and the execution architecture and mechanism libraries are used during the system implementation to realize the MAS. Finally, testing activities also include the system simulation, in order to validate the macroscopic system behavior.

This dissertation lays the foundation for this development process. The development procedure and tools presented here are generic, as they concern not only the configuration and integration of template processes but also the design of Coordinating Processes. The systemic modeling approach, examined in Section 4, is a vehicle for communicating the requirements for the macroscopic behavior of an agent-based software system. A collection of template processes were cataloged in Section 4.4 and criteria for their selection were derived from the phenomenological properties of the shown structure-establishment. The selection and combination of template processes has been demonstrated (see Section 4.4.2), but is not further systematized. The later stages, i.e. the configuration, implementation and testing, are covered by the development activities that constitute the systemic development (see Chapter 6). The configuration of processes is prepared using a declarative language model, thus configurations are per se static. One topic of further development is the automated adjustment of process configurations. This concerns extending the enactment architecture with means for observing the MAS execution and reconfiguring media and/or adjusting the process structure at run-time. The space of possible adjustments and their control are then configured by a complementing configuration model.

Transfer to Development Frameworks and Informatics Disciplines

The assessment of dynamic properties is complicated when the autonomy of the software elements contained in the system increases. Thus the observation of the dynamics of agent-based software systems and how they are influenced is studied throughout this dissertation. One crucial aspect for the introduction of widespread agent-oriented applications is the availability of principled approaches to plan for the system-wide dynamics. A key design criterion for the modeling technique, the configuration language, and the execution architecture is their extensibility. The importance of dynamic aspects justifies further development of the tool support proposed here and the transfer of these tools to other development platform and agent architectures.

A salient characteristic of this dissertation is the management of the dynamics in distributed software systems. The creation of complex dynamics, as found in self-organizing systems, demands the adoption of a holistic perspective on the system components and their interdependencies. Such a perspective is realized in this dissertation using the example of Agent-Oriented Software Engineering. It can be speculated that comparable holistic perspectives are also relevant for other software engineering disciplines. When the modeling of computational systems deals with large numbers of system elements, their dynamic properties, which result from element coaction, are also of interest. An example is the management of the *dynamic complexity* in enterprise architecture (EA) management, as thematized in [Buckl et al., 2008]. The management of enterprise-wide IT-infrastructures commonly concerns the structural properties, e.g. their *cartography* [Buckl et al., 2007]. In [Buckl et al., 2008] it is speculated that enabling the estimation of dynamical properties of infrastructures, e.g. performance measurements, is valuable for their management. An example is the anticipation of the impact of architectural decisions. These estimations require the derivation of simulation models from architectural models. The transfer of the systemic modeling approach (see Chapter 4) and the generic analysis procedure, discussed in Section 4.3, to other engineering disciplines is an interesting direction for future work.

Appendices

Appendix A

The Stochastic π-Calculus

One part of the development process, as described in Chapter 6, is the anticipation of the dynamic behavior of an agent-based software system. The dynamics of the system *as is* and the *intended effects* on this behavior, by means of the supplementation of Coordinating Processes, are visualized (see Section 6.7.3). The applicability of stochastic simulation models for this anticipation in shown in Section 6.8. The adoption of stochastic process algebras for simulating self-organizing agent systems is motived by the ability to represent concurrency among interactive entities and the compositionality as well as modularity of the algebraic models [Gardelli et al., 2006]. The use of these simulation techniques is discussed and exemplified in several works, e.g. [Gardelli et al., 2005, 2006; Casadei et al., 2007].

The simulations in Section 5.4 are carried out with a variant of the *Stochastic π-calculus* (Sπ) [Priami, 1995], namely the *Stochastic Pi Machine* (SPIM). [1] It provides simulation tools and a graphical notation for models in this stochastic process algebra. Here, a subset of the capabilities of this framework is outlined, based on [Phillips, 2010; Blossey et al., 2006], which is used in Section 6.8.

Process algebras, such as the π-calculus [Milner et al., 1992], are established tools to model concurrent communicating systems. A system is described as a set of independently executing *processes* that interact via *channels* and the semantics of the language are given by a transition system [Milner et al., 1992]. The Sπ calculus [Priami, 1995] is a stochastic extension of the original π-calculus. Processes contain actions (π) such as the sending via a channel x ($\overline{x}$), the receiving from a channel x ($\underline{x}$) and a stochastic delay at rate r (τ_r). These notation $\pi.P$ describes that a process executes the action π and then behaves as the process P. A *choice* is given in the form $\pi_1.P_1 + \cdots + \pi_N P_N$ and describes a competition of the preceding actions ($\pi_1, \ldots, \pi N$). One action is executed and the process continues with the subsequent process. The *parallel* execution of two processes (P,Q) is denoted by $P|Q$. Processes interact by complimentary input and output actions on a channel. Optionally, information can be transmitted. The language is more powerful, but these constructs are sufficient to model the processes that are discussed in this dissertation. A detailed discussion of the abilities, e.g. the communication of data, the run-time creation of channels, and the parameterization of processes can be found in [Phillips, 2010; Blossey et al., 2006]. A graphical notation for these processes is illustrated in Figure A.1. Two simple systems, taken from [Blossey et al., 2006], illustrate Sπ-based modeling. Processes and choices are represented by elliptical nodes. Edges between nodes denote an execution path and the executed action is annotated. The parallel execution of processes is indicated by a rectangular node. Edges from these nodes indicate the parallel execution of processes. Highlighted nodes (shaded) represent the currently active process instances [Phillips et al., 2006]. In Figure A.1, this notation is used to indicate the initial configuration and the initial number of processes annotated in square brackets. Also only a subset of the graphical notation for Sπ models is used.

Simulations are carried out with the SPIM tools. Besides the stochastic simulation of process

---

[1] http://research.microsoft.com/en-us/projects/spim/

models, these also allow the generation of the graphical representation. The simulations are based on the *Gillespie* algorithm [Gillespie, 1977], which allows for the exact simulation of coupled reactions. Thus interaction rates are realistically computed and these rates control the probability of the happening of an action/interaction within time t, following an exponential distribution $F(t) = 1 - e^{-r \cdot t}$ and the average duration is consequently given by the mean $1/r$ [Phillips, 2010].

Two example systems, following [Blossey et al., 2006], are illustrated in Figure A.1 to demonstrate this modeling approach. An *radioactive decay* (I) is represented by the process term $x() = \tau_c.z()$. This term describes that each process $x()$ performs a delay action τ_c. The duration of the delay is exponentially distributed and after the delay the process evolves to the process $z()$. In the graphical representation, the process $z()$ is omitted (I) as it is not involved in further interactions [Blossey et al., 2006]. The decline in the number of processes is displayed in Figure A.1 (II) for three simulation runs. Each time 1000 processes were started and the interaction rate c controls the conversion of processes.[2] This example shows that the delays, as well as the interactions are controlled by exponential distributions.

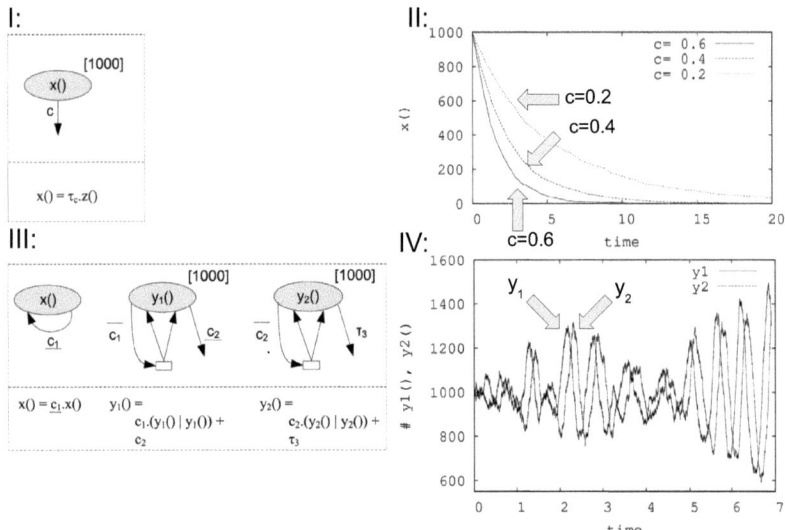

Figure A.1: Example π-calculus models, adapted from [Blossey et al., 2006]

A second example is the *Lotka-Volterra* model of population dynamics, adopted from [Blossey et al., 2006]. This model is a simple representation of predator-prey systems and describes the timely development of population sizes (III). An inexhaustible food source is represented by the process $x()$. An input action on the channel c_1 indicates that an instance of another species consumes the food. The food it not reduced and therefore the process continues to behave as process $x()$. Members of the prey species are presented by $y_1()$ processes. The consumption of food is emulated by a successful output action on the channel c_1 and the subsequent reproduction of prey is indicated by the parallel execution of two y_1 processes. The members of a predator species are denoted by y_2 processes. These interact with prey via the c_2 channel. Output by this channel terminate a y_1 process and an input via this channel makes an y_2 process to reproduce (parallel execution). This interaction represents the consumption of prey and the reproduction of

---
[2] set to: 0.2, 0.4, and 0.6

predators. Alternatively, the y_2 processes terminate after a delay (τ_3). Simulations results (IV)[3] show a characteristic oscillation of the numbers of processes. The number of y_2 processes follows the increase and decline of the y_1 processes. When the number of prey increases, the predators find more chances to reproduce and their net amount increases as well. However, increased levels of predators minimize the numbers of prey, and consequently, the chances for reproduction are reduced. The lifespan of predators leads to a decline in the population of predators that allows the population of prey to increase. This case study shows how mutual interactions among agents can be represented with the Sπ calculus.

The generation of basic Sπ models from agent implementations is discussed in [Sudeikat and Renz, 2007d]. The structure of agent implementations is interpreted and transformed to an abstract representation in Sπ. The generated models serve as templates for system simulations. The fundamental structure of the agents is represented but it is left the user to: configure the system size, i.e. the numbers of agents, provide realistic interaction rates, and include delays in order to characterize the operation of agents. The automated transformation is enabled by the documentation of agent realizations in the Java programming language. A programming language annotation mechanism[4] is used to indicate (1) the initial agent states, (2) the participation in interactions, i.e. the sending / receiving on (virtual) channels, and (3) the decomposition of behaviors. Annotations of initial states indicates processes that are to be started initially in the simulation model. In addition, it can be annotated that a Java classes, e.g. BDI agent plans, realizes a participation in an interaction. These are represented by channels that are included in the generated stimulation model. Finally, the *or* decomposition of behaviors, as found in goal hierarchies (see Section 2.4, page 23), can be indicated. This approach requires that user are aware of the semantics of the Sπ calculus and the transformation that generates skeleton simulation models. Agent realizations are documented by the annotations and this approach is a first step to connect the system abstraction, i.e. the simulation model, with the system realization.

---

[3]The configuration used is: $c_1, \tau_1 = 10.0; c_2 = 0.01$
[4]http://java.sun.com/j2se/1.5.0/docs/guide/language/annotations.html

Appendix B

Coordination Medium Implementations

The system simulations that are discussed in this dissertation make use of a set of *Coordination Media* (cf. Definition 5.4, page 161). These are infrastructures for the dissemination of information that fit in the proposed architectural model for integrating decentralized inter-agent processes. These necessary prerequisites can be derived from the literature on appropriate interaction mechanisms for self-organizing systems (cf. Section 3.2.1) and software frameworks for the MAS coordination (see Section 2.5) or MAS environment (see Sections 2.3.1). The generic medium model (see Section 5.2.10) allows different mechanism types to be integrated.

Medium realizations are configured by sets of parameters that are specified as key/value pairs. The keys and the valid value ranges are specific for each medium. These values are either statically set or are dynamically assigned (see Section 5.3.2, page 172). Static values are given as literals in the Java programming language format and dynamic values are determined by the current state of run-time objects. The configuration of the media controls the dynamics of the information propagation i.e. the distribution of *Coordination Information* elements (see Section 5.2.10). The medium realizations, as parts of the architecture prototype realization (see Section 5.3.5), are provided with a documentation of the available properties.

Here, a subset of media is discussed that were used to obtain the simulation results discussed in this thesis. These are *routing-based* media that propagate information by the exchange of inter-agent messages (see Section B.1). An alternative type of media, which was not used in the discussed simulations, is *infrastructure-based* media. These media are based on a networked software component, such as servers that maintain and mange environment models. The media types are distinguished in Section 5.2.10. Prototype realizations of infrastructure-based media make use of the freely available *TSpaces*[1] tuple space server developed at IBM. This server provides a shared space of *Tuples* that are ordered sequences of *Fields*. Fields are a triple of an object *type*, an actual value, and an optional *field name*.[2] A programming library enables programs to place (write) and extract (take) tuples. One use is the provision of *blackbard* mechanisms, e.g. see [Wooldridge, 2002] (Chapter 8.4), where agents interact via a public space of data items. Parameters configure the interactions of Endpoints with this public space and the behavior of tuples. Examples are the *polling* for tuples at a fixed rate (long value), the notification of Endpoints about the availability of tuples (*event-based*, boolean), and the condition that the first read also removes the tuple (*consuming*, boolean). This blackboard medium was extended to provide a simple two-dimensional interaction space. Specialized tuples contain Cartesian coordinates (x, y) that locate information items and control the visibility to agents. The initial positioning is determined by the position of the publishing agent and the propagation of tuples is prepared, for example to emulate the diffusion of pheromones. The positioning of agents is controlled by the

---
[1] http://www.almaden.ibm.com/cs/TSpaces/
[2] The documentation can be found at: http://www.almaden.ibm.com/cs/TSpaces/html/ProgrGuide.html

current agent state and user-specified code can be provided, using the mechanism that is described in Section B.1.3.

B.1 Routing-based Media

Only routing-based mechanisms were used in the case studies. Conceptually, these media facilitate the decentralized nature of the coordination framework as the application does not depend on specific infrastructure elements. The media types make use of the communication infrastructure that is contained in the agent platform. The prototype realizations used in this work are based on the Jadex agent platform and the platform-level messaging infrastructure is used (see Section 2.2.2).

B.1.1 Random Routing

Initial case studies are based on the random distribution of information. The corresponding media make use of a *yellow pages service*, as defined by the *FIPA Agent Management Specification* [Foundation for Intelligent Physical Agents, 2004], to infer the possible communication partners. This service is provided by the agent platform, i.e. the Jadex system (see Section 2.2.2). The distribution of information elements is configured by the parameter *distribution_type* and the possible values are the *broadcast* of the information and the *random* selection of a recipient (see Figure B.1, I). The value *broadcast* indicates that publications are forwarded to allow known, i.e. connected, agents and the value *random* indicates that publications are forwarded to one randomly selected instance of the connected endpoints. A variation of this medium type is used to realize direct influences. Direct influences serve as a concept for the modeling of the application dynamics as is, i.e. in absence of the coordination enactment that is proposed in Chapter 5, but the automation of these influences is supported for the sake of completeness. In this case, all connected agents are informed.

B.1.2 Network Routing

The study of the effects of the network topology on the information dissemination were carried out with a medium that spans overlay networks among a set of agents (see Figure B.1, II). The topology of the network is controlled by a *Supervisor* agent that maintains a registry of the inter-connected Endpoints. When Endpoints are initialized, these register themselves at the Supervisors(s). Inside these agents, the graph topology is generated using the *Java Universal Network/Graph* Framework (JUNG)[3] open-source library. The agents maintain a mapping of registered endpoints to nodes of the generated network topology. When the generation of the graph and the mapping are completed, Endpoints are informed about the (sub)set of connected Endpoints. Endpoints only communicate with these neighbors, according to their logical positioning in the topology.

The generated topology is controlled by a parameter *graph_type* and experiments were carried out with arrangements of Endpoints in regular lattices (*Lattice2D*), random graphs (*Random*), and power law distributed graphs (*PowerLaw*). For each of these graph types a corresponding set of parameters an be specified. These are forwarded to the integrated algorithms of the JUNG framework that control the graph generation. The lattice is a regular arrangement of nodes. Optionally, the number of rows (*row_count*) and the number of columns (*colum_count*) can be specified as integer values. It can also be state whether the lattice is *toroidal* (boolean). The properties of the latter two graph types are discussed in the context of the *convention emergence* example is Section 5.4.2 (page 190). The random graphs follow the *Erdős-Rényi* binomial model (cf. [Albert and Barabasi, 2002], p. 8). Each node is connected with a *probability* value (double value). Power law graphs are generated according to [Eppstein and Wang, 2002]. The number of edges (*num_edges*) and the iterations of the algorithm can be specified (*iteration_count*) in integer values. The *distribution_type* parameter is extended (see Section B.1.1). In addition, the fraction

---

[3] http://jung.sourceforge.net/

B.1. ROUTING-BASED MEDIA

of informed agents can be specified by a double value ($0 \leq x \leq 1.0$). This value specifies the fraction of connected agents that are randomly selected and informed.

B.1.3 Input/Output-Graph-based Routing

The *production line* case study (see Section 6.8.1) required a medium type that extracts the possible communication parters from the present state of the agent model (see Figure B.1, III). In this example, agents represent machines and transporters in manufacturing line and the communication is constrained by the logical layout of these agents. The agents follow the conceptual model in Figure 6.17 and their configuration is given by the set of allocated *roles*. In these roles the possible exchanges of work pieces are indicated (*port*). The *wave-like* reconfigurations require that messages flow along the input/output ports of agents. The publication modules within Endpoints inspect the local role configuration to infer the possible communication parters, i.e. connected agents. This information is volatile, therefore inspections are carried out immediately before publications.

The inspection must be tailored for the actual agent implementations that are managed by Endpoints. Therefore, developers can provide customized realizations of the inspection, programmed in a Java class. These classes have to implement an inspection-specific interface (*decomas.medium.iog.InputOutputExtractor*) that specifies two function (*getInputs()*, *getOutputs()*) which return lists of known agents. *Inputs* are those from which the agent receives work pieces and *outputs* are the agents that receive workpieces from the agent. The specification of such an implementation is illustrated in Listing B.1.

```
...
<entry>
  <key>extractor</key>
  <value>decomas.medium.iog.CircleInputOutputExtractor</value>
</entry>
...
```

Listing B.1: Specification of a customized extractor; The class *CircleInputOutputExtractor* is provided by the developer.

Requests for a role swap are propagated along the resource flow and the reply messages are routed to all affected agents. These are the requesting agent and the inputs/outputs of the two agents that are swapping roles. In order that the publications can reach all agents, the medium is cyclically closed and the messages can circulate. When messages reach the consumer of a resource flow, these are forwarded to the consumer and travel along the flow of resources. Request message that reach the originating agent indicate that no possible swap parter was found. In addition, the *distribution_type* parameter can be used to control if messages are send to all inputs/outputs (*broadcast*), to a randomly selected one (*random*), or to a *fraction* (double value).

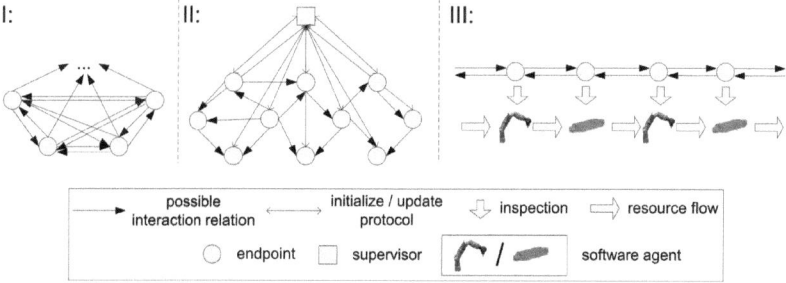

Figure B.1: Illustrations of routing-based Coordination Media

Appendix C

Publications

Journal Articles
(Including Journal-based Conference/Workshop Proceedings)

1. Sudeikat, J. and Renz, W. (2010b). Separating agent-logic and inter-agent coordination by activated modules: The decomas architecture. *Electronic Proceedings in Theoretical Computer Science*, 27:17–31. (Proceedings of the Workshop "Decentralized Coordination of Distributed Processes" — DCDP 2010)

2. Sudeikat, J., Steghöfer, J.-P., Seebach, H., Reif, W., Renz, W., Preisler, T., and Salchow, P. (2010b). A wave-like decentralized reconfiguration strategy for self-organizing resource flow systems (short paper). *Electronic Proceedings in Theoretical Computer Science*, 27:32–33. (Proceedings of the Workshop "Decentralized Coordination of Distributed Processes" — DCDP 2010)

3. Sudeikat, J. and Renz, W. (2010c). Systemic modeling of agent coaction: A catalog of decentralized coordinating processes. *Electronic Communications of the EASST*, 27. (ISSN 1863-2122)

4. Balthasar, G., Sudeikat, J., and Renz, W. (2010). On the decentralized coordination of herding activities: a jadex-based solution. *Annals of Mathematics and Artificial Intelligence*. (http://www.springerlink.de/content/4r36284151738p6x/)

5. Sudeikat, J. and Renz, W. (2009d). On expressing and validating requirements for the adaptivity of self-organizing multi-agent systems (reprint). *International Transactions on Systems Science and Applications*, 5(3):264–274. (Special Issue on Self-organized Networked Systems)

6. Sudeikat, J. and Renz, W. (2009e). Programming adaptivity by complementing agent function with agent coordination: A systemic programming model and development methodology integration. *Communications of SIWN*, 7:91–102. (ISSN 1757-4439)

7. Sudeikat, J., Randles, M., Renz, W., and Taleb-Bendiab, A. (2009b). A hybrid modeling approach for self-organizing systems development. *Communications of SIWN*, 7:127–134. (ISSN: 1757-4439)

8. Sudeikat, J., Braubach, L., Pokahr, A., Renz, W., and Lamersdorf, W. (2009a). Systematically engineering self-organizing systems: The sodekovs approach. *Electronic Communications of the EASST*, 17. (http://journal.ub.tu-berlin.de/index.php/eceasst/article/view/194)

9. Sudeikat, J. and Renz, W. (2008b). On the encapsulation and reuse of decentralized coordination mechanisms: A layered architecture and design implications. *Communications of SIWN*, 4:140–146

10. Sudeikat, J. and Renz, W. (2007c). On expressing and validating requirements for the adaptivity of self–organizing multi–agent systems. *System and Information Sciences Notes*, 2(1):14–19

11. Renz, W. and Sudeikat, J. (2007). Emergence in software. *KI – Künstliche Intelligenz*, 02/07:48–49. (Aktuelles Schlagwort)

12. Sudeikat, J. and Renz, W. (2006). On the redesign of self–organizing multi–agent systems. *International Transactions on Systems Science and Applications*, 2(1):81–89

13. Renz, W. and Sudeikat, J. (2006). Emergent roles in multi agent systems - a case study in minority games. *KI - Zeitschrift fuer Kuenstliche Intelligenz*, 01/06:26–32. (ISSN 0933-1875)

Contributions to Conferences and Workshops Proceedings

1. Sudeikat, J., Steghöfer, J.-P., Seebach, H., Reif, W., Renz, W., Preisler, T., and Salchow, P. (2010a). Design and simulation of a wave-like self-organization strategy for resource-flow systems. In Boissier, O., Seghrouchni, A. E. F., Hassas, S., and Maudet, N., editors, *Proceedings of The Multi-Agent Logics, Languages, and Organisations Federated Workshops (MALLOW 2010)*, volume 627. (http://ftp.informatik.rwth-aachen.de/Publications/CEUR-WS/Vol-627/)

2. Sudeikat, J. and Renz, W. (2010a). On the modeling, refinement and integration of decentralized agent coordination – a case study on dissemination processes in networks. In *Self-Organizing Architectures*, volume 6090/2010 of *LNCS*, pages 251–274. Springer Berlin / Heidelberg

3. Balthasar, G., Sudeikat, J., and Renz, W. (2009b). On the decentralized coordination of artificial cowboys: A jadex-based realization. *Proceedings of the 10th International Workshop on Computational Logic in Multi-Agent Systems 2009*, pages 188–192. (lfl Technical Report Series lfl-09-08)

4. Sudeikat, J. and Renz, W. (2009b). Decomas: An architecture for supplementing mas with systemic models of decentralized agent coordination. In *WI-IAT '09: Proceedings of the 2009 IEEE/WIC/ACM International Joint Conference on Web Intelligence and Intelligent Agent Technology*, pages 104–107, Washington, DC, USA. IEEE Computer Society

5. Vilenica, A., Sudeikat, J., Lamersdorf, W., Renz, W., Braubach, L., and Pokahr, A. (2010). Coordination in multi-agent systems: A declarative approach using coordination spaces. In *In Proceedings of International Workshop From Agent Theory to Agent Implementation (AT2AI-7)*, pages 441–446. Austrian Society for Cybernetic Studies

6. Sudeikat, J. and Renz, W. (2009f). Shoaling glassfishes: Enabling decentralized web service management (short paper). In *3rd International Conference in Self-Adaptive and Self-Organizing Systems*, pages 291–292, Los Alamitos, CA, USA. IEEE

7. Vilenica, A., Renz, W., Sudeikat, J., and Lamersdorf, W. (2009). Multi-agent-architecture for simulating traffic management - a case study on highway networks. In Kyamakya, K., editor, *Second International Workshop on Nonlinear Dynamics and Synchronization*, Smart System Technologies, pages 121–127. Shaker Verlag & IEEE Explore Digital Library

8. Sudeikat, J. and Renz, W. (2011). Qualitative modeling of mas dynamics - using systemic modeling to examine the intended and unintended consequences of agent coaction. In *Agent Oriented Software Engineering X: State-of-the-Art Survey*, volume 6038 of *LNCS*, pages 80–93. Springer Berlin Heidelberg. (to be published)

9. Sudeikat, J. and Renz, W. (2009g). Supporting agent-oriented designs with models of macroscopic system behavior (extended abstract). In Decker, Sichman, Sierra, and Castelfranchi, editors, *AAMAS '09: Proceedings of The 8th International Conference on Autonomous Agents and Multiagent Systems*, pages 1355–1356, Richland, SC. International Foundation for Autonomous Agents and Multiagent Systems

10. Sudeikat, J. and Renz, W. (2009c). MASDynamics: Toward systemic modeling of decentralized agent coordination. In David, K. and Geihs, K., editors, *Kommunikation in Verteilten Systemen*, Informatik aktuell, pages 79–90

11. Pokahr, A., Braubach, L., Sudeikat, J., Renz, W., and Lamersdorf, W. (2008). Simulation and implementation of logistics systems based on agent technology. In *Hamburg International Conference on Logistics 2008: Logistics Networks and Nodes*, pages 291–308. Erich Schmidt Verlag

12. Buckl, S., Matthes, F., Renz, W., Schweda, C. M., and Sudeikat, J. (2008). Towards simulation-supported enterprise architecture management. In *Modellierung betrieblicher Informationssysteme - Modellierung zwischen SOA und Compliance Management - 27.-28. November 2008 Saarbrücken, Germany*, volume 141 of *LNI*, pages 131–145. GI

13. Balthasar, G., Sudeikat, J., and Renz, W. (2009a). On herding artificial cows: Using jadex to coordinate cowboy agents. In v. Hindriks, Pokahr, A., and Sardina, S., editors, *Programming Multi-Agent Systems, 6th International Workshop, ProMAS 2008, Estoril, Portugal, May 13, 2008. Revised Invited and Selected Papers*, number 5442 in LNAI, pages 233–237. Springer

14. Renz, W. and Sudeikat, J. (2009). Modeling feedback within mas: A systemic approach to organizational dynamics. In *Organised Adaptation in Multi-Agent Systems, First International Workshop, OAMAS 2008, Estoril Portugal, May 2008 Revised and Invited Papers*, volume 5368 of *LNCS*, pages 72–89

15. Sudeikat, J. and Renz, W. (2009h). A systemic approach to the validation of self–organizing dynamics within mas. In Luck, M. and Gomez-Sanz, J. J., editors, *Agent-Oriented Software Engineering IX: 9th International Workshop, AOSE 2008 Estoril, Portugal, May 12-13, 2008 Revised Selected Papers*, volume 5386/2009 of *LNCS*, pages 31–45. Springer

16. Sudeikat, J. and Renz, W. (2008c). Toward systemic mas development: Enforcing decentralized self-organization by composition and refinement of archetype dynamics. In *Engineering Environment-Mediated Multiagent Systems*, volume 5049 of *LNAI*, pages 39–57. Springer

17. Sudeikat, J. and Renz, W. (2007b). On complex networks in software: How agent-orientation effects software structures. In Burkhard, H.-D., Lindemann, G., Verbrugge, R., and Varga, L. Z., editors, *Multi-Agent Systems and Applications V, 5th International Central and Eastern European Conference on Multi-Agent Systems, CEEMAS 2007*, volume 4696 of *Lecture Notes in Computer Science*, pages 215–224. Springer

18. Sudeikat, J. and Renz, W. (2007e). Toward requirements engineering for self–organizing multi-agent systems. In *Proceedings of the First IEEE Internaltional Conference on Self–Adaptive and Self–Organizing Systems (SASO 2007)*, pages 299–302

19. Sudeikat, J. (2007). Toward the design if self–organizing dynamics. In Bleck, W.-G., Schwentner, H., and Züllighoven, H., editors, *Software Engineering 2007 – Beiträge zu den Workshops*, pages 361–364. Gesellshaft für Informatik e. V. (GI)

20. Sudeikat, J. and Renz, W. (2007d). On simulations in mas development. In Braun, T., Carle, G., and Stiller, B., editors, *KIVS 2007 Kommunikation in Verteilten Systemen – Industriebeiträge, Kurzbeiträge und Workshops*, pages 279–290. VDE–Verlag

21. Sudeikat, J., Braubach, L., Pokahr, A., Lamersdorf, W., and Renz, W. (2006). Validation of bdi agents. In *Programming Multi-Agent Systems – 4th International Workshop, ProMAS 2006, Revised and Invited Papers*, number 4411 in LNAI, pages 185–200

22. Sudeikat, J. and Renz, W. (2007a). Monitoring group behavior in goal–directed agents using co–efficient plan observation. In *Agent-Oriented Software Engineering VII, 7th International Workshop, AOSE 2006, Hakodate, Japan, May 8, 2006, Revised and Invited Papers*, volume 4405/2007, pages 174–189. Springer Berlin / Heidelberg

23. Renz, W. and Sudeikat, J. (2005a). Mesoscopic modeling of emergent behavior - a self-organizing deliberative minority game. In *Engineering Self-Organising Systems*, pages 167–181

24. Renz, W. and Sudeikat, J. (2005b). Modeling minority games with bdi agents - a case study. In T. Eymann, F. Klügl, W. L. M. K. M. H., editor, *Third German conference on Multi-Agent System TEchnologieS (MATES-2005)*, volume LNAI 3550, pages 71–81. Springer

25. Sudeikat, J., Braubach, L., Pokahr, A., and Lamersdorf, W. (2004). Evaluation of agent–oriented software methodologies - examination of the gap between modeling and platform. In *Agent-Oriented Software Engineering V, Fifth International Workshop AOSE 2004*, pages 126–141

Book Chapters

1. Sudeikat, J. and Renz, W. (2009a). Building complex adaptive systems: On engineering self-organizing multi-agent systems (reprint). In Hunter, M. G., editor, *Strategic Information Systems: Concepts, Methodologies, Tools, and Applications*, pages 767–787. IGI Publishing

2. Sudeikat, J. and Renz, W. (2008a). *Applications of Complex Adaptive Systems*, chapter Building Complex Adaptive Systems: On Engineering Self–Organizing Multi–Agent Systems, pages 229–256. IGI Global

Bibliography

Åström, K. J. and Murray, R. M. (2008). *Feedback Systems: An Introduction for Scientists and Engineers*. Princeton University Press. (http://press.princeton.edu/titles/8701.html).

Abdellatif, T. and Danes, A. (2006). Jmx-based autonomic management of j2ee servers. *International Transactions on Systems Science and Applications (ITSSA)*, 2(3):289–295.

Abdellatif, T., Kornas, J., and Stefani, J.-B. (2007). Reengineering j2ee servers for automated management in distributed environments. *IEEE Distributed Systems Online*, 8(11):1–1.

Abowd, G., Allen, R., and Garlan, D. (1993). Using style to understand descriptions of software architecture. In *SIGSOFT '93: Proceedings of the 1st ACM SIGSOFT symposium on Foundations of software engineering*, pages 9–20, New York, NY, USA. ACM.

Adami, C. (1998). *Introduction to Artificial Life*. Springer.

Albert, R. and Barabasi, A. L. (2002). Statistical mechanics of complex networks. *Reviews of Modern Physics*, 74:47–97.

Alexander, C., Ishikawa, S., Silverstein, M., Jacobson, M., Fiksdahl-King, I., and Angel, S. (1977). *A Pattern Language*. Oxford University Press, NewYork.

Anderson, C. (2002). Self-organization in relation to several similar concepts: Are the boundaries to self-organization indistinct? *Biol. Bull.*, 202:247–255.

Anderson, P. (1972). More is different. *Science*, 177:393–396.

Aridor, Y. and Lange, D. B. (1998). Agent design patterns: elements of agent application design. In *AGENTS '98: Proceedings of the second international conference on Autonomous agents*, pages 108–115, New York, NY, USA. ACM.

Arthur, W. B. (1994). Inductive reasoning and bounded rationality. *American Economic Review*, 84(2):406–11. (http://ideas.repec.org/a/aea/aecrev/v84y1994i2p406-11.html).

Ashby, W. R. (1947). Principles of the self-organizing dynamic system. *Journal of General Psychology*, 37:125–128.

Ashby, W. R. (1956). *An Introduction to cybernetics*. Chapman & Hall.

Axtell, R., Axelrod, R., Epstein, J. M., and Cohen, M. D. (1996). Aligning simulation models: A case study and results. *Computational & Mathematical Organization Theory*, 1(2):123–141.

Babaoglu, O., Canright, G., Deutsch, A., Caro, G. A. D., Ducatelle, F., Gambardella, L. M., Ganguly, N., Jelasity, M., Montemanni, R., Montresor, A., and Urnes, T. (2006). Design patterns from biology for distributed computing. *ACM Trans. Auton. Adapt. Syst.*, 1(1):26–66.

Balthasar, G., Sudeikat, J., and Renz, W. (2009a). On herding artificial cows: Using jadex to coordinate cowboy agents. In v. Hindriks, Pokahr, A., and Sardina, S., editors, *Programming Multi-Agent Systems, 6th International Workshop, ProMAS 2008, Estoril, Portugal, May 13, 2008. Revised Invited and Selected Papers*, number 5442 in LNAI, pages 233–237. Springer.

Balthasar, G., Sudeikat, J., and Renz, W. (2009b). On the decentralized coordination of artificial cowboys: A jadex-based realization. *Proceedings of the 10th International Workshop on Computational Logic in Multi-Agent Systems 2009*, pages 188–192. (lfl Technical Report Series lfl-09-08).

Balthasar, G., Sudeikat, J., and Renz, W. (2010). On the decentralized coordination of herding activities: a jadex-based solution. *Annals of Mathematics and Artificial Intelligence*. (http://www.springerlink.de/content/4r36284151738p6x/).

Banks, J., nad Barry L. Nelson, J. C., and Nicol, D. (2005). *Discrete-Event System Simulation*. Prentice Hall.

Baresi, L., Guinea, S., and Tamburrelli, G. (2008). Towards decentralized self-adaptive component-based systems. In *SEAMS '08: Proceedings of the 2008 international workshop on Software engineering for adaptive and self-managing systems*, pages 57–64, New York, NY, USA. ACM.

Bauer, B. and Odell, J. (2005). Uml 2.0 and agents: how to build agent-based systems with the new uml standard. *Engineering Applications of Artificial Intelligence*, 18(2):141–157.

Baxter, G., Frean, M., Noble, J., Rickerby, M., Smith, H., Visser, M., Melton, H., and Tempero, E. (2006). Understanding the shape of java software. In *OOPSLA '06: Proceedings of the 21st annual ACM SIGPLAN conference on Object-oriented programming languages, systems, and applications*, pages 397–412, New York, NY, USA. ACM Press.

Bedrouni, A., Mittu, R., Boukhtouta, A., and Berger, J. (2009). *Distributed Intelligent Systems: A Coordination Perspective*. Springer.

Bellifemine, F., Caire, G., and Greenwood, D. (2007). *Developing Multi-Agent Systems with JADE*. Wiley.

Bergenti, F., Gleizes, M.-P., and Zambonelli, F., editors (2004). *Methodologies and Software Engineering for Agent Systems The Agent-Oriented Software Engineering Handbook*, volume 11 of *Multiagent Systems, Artificial Societies, and Simulated Organizations*. Springer. ISBN: 978-1-4020-8057-9.

Bernon, C., Camps, V., Gleizes, M.-P., and Picard, G. (2005a). Engineering Adaptive Multi-Agent Systems: The ADELFE Methodology . In Henderson-Sellers, B. and Giorgini, P., editors, *Agent-Oriented Methodologies* , pages 172–202. Idea Group.

Bernon, C., Chevrier, V., Hilaire, V., and Marrow, P. (2006). Applications of self-organising multi-agent systems: An initial framework for comparison. *Informatica (Slovenia)*, 30(1):73–82.

Bernon, C., Cossentino, M., Zambonelli, F., Gleizes, M.-P., Turci, P., and Zambonelli, F. (2005b). A study of some multi-agent meta-models. In *Agent-Oriented Software Engineering V*, volume 3382/2005 of *LNCS*, pages 62–77.

Bernon, C., Gleizes, M.-P., and Picard, G. (2007). Enhancing self-organising emergent systems design with simulation. In *ESAW'06: Proceedings of the 7th international conference on Engineering societies in the agents world VII*, pages 284–299, Berlin, Heidelberg. Springer.

Bernstein, L. (1996). Better software through operational dynamics. *IEEE Softw.*, 13(2):107–109.

Beydoun, G., Low, G., Henderson-Sellers, B., Mouratidis, H., Gomez-Sanz, J. J., Pavon, J., and Gonzalez-Perez, C. (2009). Faml: A generic metamodel for mas development. *IEEE Trans. Softw. Eng.*, 35(6):841–863.

Blossey, R., Cardelli, L., and Phillips, A. (2006). A compositional approach to the stochastic dynamics of gene networks - supplementary material. online available: http://research.microsoft.com/pubs/65225/TCSB06.supplement.pdf.

Bobroff, N., Kochut, A., and Beaty, K. (2007). Dynamic placement of virtual machines for managing sla violations. *Integrated Network Management, 2007. IM '07. 10th IFIP/IEEE International Symposium on*, pages 119–128.

Bonabeau, E., Dorigo, M., and Theraulaz, G. (1999). *Swarm Intelligence: From Natural to Artificial Systems*. Santa Fe Institute Studies on the Sciences of Complexity. Oxford University Press.

Booch, G. (1994). *Object-oriented analysis and design with applications (2nd ed.)*. Benjamin-Cummings Publishing Co., Inc.

Bordini, R., Braubach, L., Dastani, M., Seghrouchni, A. E. F., Gomez-Sanz, J., Leite, J., O'Hare, G., Pokahr, A., and Ricci, A. (2006). A survey of programming languages and platforms for multi-agent systems. In *Informatica 30*, pages 33–44.

Bordini, R. H. (2010). private communication.

Bordini, R. H., Fisher, M., Visser, W., and Wooldridge, M. (2004). Model checking rational agents. In *IEEE Intelligent Systems 19(5)*, pages 46–52.

Bordini, R. H., Hübner, J. F., and Wooldridge, M. (2007). *Programming Multi-Agent Systems in Agentspeak Using Jason: A Practical Introduction with Jason*. Wiley Series in Agent Technology. Wiley & Sons.

Borshev, A. and Filippov, A. (2004). From system dynamics and discrete event to practical agent based modeling: Reasoning, techniques, tools. In *Proceedings of the 22nd International Conference of the System Dnymics Society*. (http://www.xjtek.com/anylogic/articles/33/).

Botía, J. A., López-Acosta, A., and Gómez-Skarmeta, A. F. (2004). ACLAnalyser: A tool for debugging multi-agent systems. In *ECAI'04: Proc. 16th European Conference on Artificial Intelligence*, pages 967–968.

Branke, J., Mnif, M., Müller-Schloer, C., Prothmann, H., Richter, U., Rochner, F., and Schmeck, H. (2006). Organic computing - addressing complexity by controlled self-organization. In *ISOLA '06: Proceedings of the Second International Symposium on Leveraging Applications of Formal Methods, Verification and Validation*, pages 185–191, Washington, DC, USA. IEEE Computer Society.

Bratman, M. (1987). *Intentions, Plans, and Practical Reason*. Harvard Univ. Press.

Braubach, L. (2007). *Architekturen und Methoden zur Entwicklung verteilter agentenorientierter Softwaresysteme*. PhD thesis, Universität Hamburg, Fachbereich Informatik, Verteilte Systeme und Informationssysteme.

Braubach, L., Pokahr, A., Bade, D., Krempels, K.-H., and Lamersdorf, W. (2005a). Deployment of distributed multi-agent systems. In *Engineering Societies in the Agents World V, 5th InternationalWorkshop, ESAW 2004, Toulouse, France, October 20-22, 2004, Revised Selected and Invited Papers*, volume 3451 of *Lecture Notes in Computer Science*, pages 261–276. Springer.

Braubach, L., Pokahr, A., and Lamersdorf, W. (2005b). Jadex: A bdi agent system combining middleware and reasoning. In *Software Agent-Based Applications, Platforms and Development Kits*, Whitestein Series in Software Agent Technologies and Autonomic Computing, pages 143–168. Birkhäuser Basel.

Braubach, L., Pokahr, A., and Lamersdorf, W. (2006a). Extending the capability concept for flexible BDI agent modularization. In *Programming Multi-Agent Systems*, volume 3862 of *Lecture Notes in Computer Science*, pages 139–155. Springer Berlin / Heidelberg.

Braubach, L., Pokahr, A., and Lamersdorf, W. (2006b). Tools and standards. In *Multiagent Engineering - Theory and Applications in Enterprises*, Springer Series: International Handbooks on Information Systems, pages 503–530.

Braubach, L., Pokahr, A., Moldt, D., and Lamersdorf, W. (2005c). Goal representation for BDI agent systems. In *Programming Multi-Agent Systems*, volume 3346 of *Lecture Notes in Computer Science*, pages 44–65. Springer Berlin / Heidelberg.

Braun, W. (2002). The system archetypes. In *The Systems Modeling Workbook*.

Bray, I. K. (2002). *An Introduction to Requirements Engineering*. Addison Wesley.

Bresciani, P., Giorgini, P., Giunchiglia, F., Mylopoulos, J., and Perini, A. (2004). Tropos: An agent-oriented software development methodology. *Journal of Autonomous Agents and Multi-Agent Systems*, 8:203–236. Kluwer Academic Publishers.

Brinkkemper, S. (1996). Method engineering: engineering of information systems development methods and tools. *Information and Software Technology*, 38:275–280.

Brooks, F. P. (1995). *The Mythical Man-Month*. Addison-Wesley. reprinted and updated edition.

Brooks, R. (1986). A robust layered control system for a mobile robot. *IEEE Journal of Robotics and Automation*, 2(1):14–32.

Brueckner, S. and Czap, H. (2006). Organization, self-organization, autonomy and emergence: Status and challenges. *International Transactions on Systems Science and Applications*, 2(1):1–9.

Brueckner, S. A. and Parunak, H. V. D. (2003). Resource-aware exploration of the emergent dynamics of simulated systems. In *AAMAS '03: Proceedings of the second international joint conference on Autonomous agents and multiagent systems*, pages 781–788, New York, NY, USA. ACM Press.

Brun, Y., Serugendo, G. M., Gacek, C., Giese, H., Kienle, H., Litoiu, M., Müller, H., Pezzè, M., and Shaw, M. (2009). *Software Engineering for Self-Adaptive Systems*, chapter Engineering Self-Adaptive Systems through Feedback Loops, pages 48–70. Springer-Verlag, Berlin, Heidelberg.

Buckl, S., Ernst, A. M., Lankes, J., Matthes, F., Schweda, C. M., and Wittenburg, A. (2007). Generating visualizations of enterprise architectures using model transformation. *Enterprise Modelling and Information Systems Architectures - An International Journal*, 2(2):03–13.

Buckl, S., Matthes, F., Renz, W., Schweda, C. M., and Sudeikat, J. (2008). Towards simulation-supported enterprise architecture management. In *Modellierung betrieblicher Informationssysteme - Modellierung zwischen SOA und Compliance Management - 27.-28. November 2008 Saarbrücken, Germany*, volume 141 of *LNI*, pages 131–145. GI.

Burgos, E. and Ceva, H. (2000). Self organization in a minority game: the role of memory and a probabilistic approach. *Physica A: Statistical Mechanics and its Applications*, 284(1-4):489–495.

Busetta, P., Howden, N., Rönnquist, R., and Hodgson, A. (2000). Structuring BDI agents in functional clusters. In *Intelligent Agents VI. Agent Theories Architectures, and Languages*, volume 1757 of *Lecture Notes in Computer Science*, pages 277–289. Springer Berlin / Heidelberg.

Bussmann, S. and Schild, K. (2000). Self-organizing manufacturing control: An industrial application of agent technology. In *Fourth International Conference on Multi-Agent Systems (IC-MAS'00)*, pages 87–94. IEEE Computer Society.

Camazine, S. (2006). Self-organizing systems. In *Encyclopedia of Cognitive Science*, pages 1–4, N.Y. Wiley and Sons.

Camazine, S., Deneubourg, J.-L., Franks, N. R., Sneyd, J., Theraulaz, G., and Bonabeau, E. (2001). *Self-Organization in Biological Systems*. Princeton University Press, Princeton, NJ, USA.

Cardelli, L. (2008). On process rate semantics. *Theor. Comput. Sci.*, 391(3):190–215. (http://lucacardelli.name/Papers/On Process Rate Semantics.pdf).

Carzaniga, A., Di Nitto, E., Rosenblum, D. S., and Wolf, A. L. (1998). Issues in supporting event-based architectural styles. In *ISAW '98: Proceedings of the third international workshop on Software architecture*, pages 17–20, New York, NY, USA. ACM.

Casadei, M., Gardelli, L., and Viroli, M. (2007). Simulating emergent properties of coordination in maude: the collective sort case. *Electron. Notes Theor. Comput. Sci.*, 175(2):59–80.

Casadei, M. and Viroli, M. (2009a). An experience on probabilistic model checking and stochastic simulation to design self-organizing systems. In *CEC'09: Proceedings of the Eleventh conference on Congress on Evolutionary Computation*, pages 1538–1545, Piscataway, NJ, USA. IEEE Press.

Casadei, M. and Viroli, M. (2009b). Using probabilistic model checking and simulation for designing self-organizing systems. In *SAC '09: Proceedings of the 2009 ACM symposium on Applied Computing*, pages 2103–2104, New York, NY, USA. ACM.

Challet, D. and Du, Y. L. (2003). Closed source versus open source in a model of software bug dynamics. *CoRR*, cond-mat/0306511.

Challet, D. and Lombardoni, A. (2003). Bug propagation and debugging in asymmetric software structures. *CoRR*, cond-mat/0306509.

Challet, D., Marsili, M., and Zhang, Y.-C. (2004). *Minority Games - Interacting agents in financial markets*. Series: Oxford Finance Series. Oxford University Press.

Challet, D. and Zhang, Y.-C. (1997). Emergence of cooperation and organization in an evolutionary game. *Physica A: Statistical and Theoretical Physics*, 246(3-4):407–418.

Chang, L. C. and Tu, Y. M. (2004). Attempt to integrate system dynamics and uml in business process modeling. In *Proceedings of 21th International Conference of System Dynamics Society*.

Cheng, B. H., Lemos, R., Giese, H., Inverardi, P., Magee, J., Andersson, J., Becker, B., Bencomo, N., Brun, Y., Cukic, B., Marzo Serugendo, G., Dustdar, S., Finkelstein, A., Gacek, C., Geihs, K., Grassi, V., Karsai, G., Kienle, H. M., Kramer, J., Litoiu, M., Malek, S., Mirandola, R., Müller, H. A., Park, S., Shaw, M., Tichy, M., Tivoli, M., Weyns, D., and Whittle, J. (2009). *Software Engineering for Self-Adaptive Systems*, chapter Software Engineering for Self-Adaptive Systems: A Research Roadmap, pages 1–26. Springer-Verlag, Berlin, Heidelberg.

Cheng, S.-W., Garlan, D., and Schmerl, B. R. (2005). Making self-adaptation an engineering reality. In Özalp Babaoglu, Jelasity, M., Montresor, A., Fetzer, C., Leonardi, S., van Moorsel, A. P. A., and van Steen, M., editors, *Self-star Properties in Complex Information Systems*, volume 3460 of *Lecture Notes in Computer Science*, pages 158–173. Springer.

Chesani, F. (2005). Formalization and verification of interaction protocols. In *Logic Programming, 21st International Conference, ICLP 2005, Sitges, Spain, October 2-5, 2005, Proceedings*, volume 3668 of *Lecture Notes in Computer Science*, pages 437–438. Springer.

Ciancarini, P. (1996). Coordination models and languages as software integrators. *ACM Comput. Surv.*, 28(2):300–302.

Cicirello, V. A. and Smith, S. F. (2001). Ant colony control for autonomous decentralized shop floor routing. *Fifth International Symposium on Autonomous Decentralized Systems*, pages 383–390.

Clair, G., Kaddoum, E., Gleizes, M.-P., and Picard, G. (2008). Self-regulation in self-organising multi-agent systems for adaptive and intelligent manufacturing control. In *SASO '08: Proceedings of the 2008 Second IEEE International Conference on Self-Adaptive and Self-Organizing Systems*, pages 107–116, Washington, DC, USA. IEEE Computer Society.

Clark, A., Gilmore, S., Hillston, J., and Tribastone, M. (2007). Stochastic process algebras. In *Formal Methods for Performance Evaluation*, volume 4486 of *LNCS*, pages 132–179. Springer Berlin / Heidelberg.

Cockburn, A. (2000). Selecting a project's methodology. *IEEE Softw.*, 17(4):64–71.

Cohen, P. R. and Levesque, H. J. (1991). Teamwork. Technical Report 504, Menlo Park, CA.

Cossentino, M. (2005). *Agent-Oriented Methodologies*, chapter From Requirements to Code with the PASSI Methodology, pages 79–106. Idea Group Inc.

Cossentino, M., Gaglio, S., Garro, A., and Seidita, V. (2007). Method fragments for agent design methodologies: from standardisation to research. *Int. J. Agent-Oriented Software Engineering*, 1(1):91–121.

Coutinho, L. R., Sichman, J. S., and Boissier, O. (2005). Modeling organization in mas: a comparison of models. In *Proc. of the 1st. Workshop on Software Engineering for Agent-Oriented Systems (SEAS'05)*.

Dastani, M. and Steunebrink, B. (2009). Modularity in bdi-based multi-agent programming languages. In *WI-IAT '09: Proceedings of the 2009 IEEE/WIC/ACM International Joint Conference on Web Intelligence and Intelligent Agent Technology*, pages 581–584, Washington, DC, USA. IEEE Computer Society.

de Moura, A. P. S., Lai, Y.-C., and Motter, A. E. (2003). Signatures of small-world and scale-free properties in large computer programs. *Physical Review E*, 68.

Debar, H., Dacier, M., and Wespi, A. (1999). Towards a taxonomy of intrusion-detection systems. *Comput. Netw.*, 31(9):805–822.

Debenham, J. and Henderson-Sellers, B. (2002). Full lifecycle methodologies for agent-oriented systems the extended open process framework. In *AgentOriented Information Systems (AOIS-2002)*.

Delgado, J. (2002). Emergence of social conventions in complex networks. *Artif. Intell.*, 141(1):171–185.

Deneubourg, J. L., Goss, S., Franks, N., Sendova-Franks, A., Detrain, C., and Chrétien, L. (1990). The dynamics of collective sorting robot-like ants and ant-like robots. In *Proceedings of the first international conference on simulation of adaptive behavior on From animals to animats*, pages 356–363, Cambridge, MA, USA. MIT Press.

Denti, E., Natali, A., and Omicini, A. (1997). Programmable coordination media. In *COORDINATION '97: Proceedings of the Second International Conference on Coordination Languages and Models*, pages 274–288, London, UK. Springer-Verlag.

Deugo, D., Weiss, M., and Kendall, E. (2001). Reusable patterns for agent coordination. pages 347–368, London, UK. Springer-Verlag.

Devescovi, D., Di Nitto, E., Dubois, D., and Mirandola, R. (2007a). Self-organization algorithms for autonomic systems in the selflet approach. In *Autonomics '07: Proceedings of the 1st international conference on Autonomic computing and communication systems*, pages 1–10, ICST, Brussels, Belgium, Belgium. ICST (Institute for Computer Sciences, Social-Informatics and Telecommunications Engineering).

Devescovi, D., Di Nitto, E., and Mirandola, R. (2007b). An infrastructure for autonomic system development: the selflet approach. In *ASE '07: Proceedings of the twenty-second IEEE/ACM international conference on Automated software engineering*, pages 449–452, New York, NY, USA. ACM.

DeWolf, T. (2007). *Analysing and Engineering Self–Organizing Emergent Applications*. PhD thesis, Katholieke Universiteit Leuven.

DeWolf, T. and Holvoet, T. (2004). Emergence and self-organisation: a statement of similarities and differences. In *Proceedings of the International Workshop on Engineering Self-Organising Applications 2004*, pages 96–110.

DeWolf, T. and Holvoet, T. (2006). A catalogue of decentralised coordination mechanisms for designing self-organising emergent applications. Technical Report Report CW 458, Department of Computer Science, K.U. Leuven. (http://www.cs.kuleuven.be/publicaties/rapporten/cw/CW458.pdf).

DeWolf, T. and Holvoet, T. (2007a). Decentralised coordination mechanisms as design patterns for self-organising emergent systems. In *Engineering Self-Organising Systems*, volume 4335/2007, pages 28–49.

DeWolf, T. and Holvoet, T. (2007b). A taxonomy for self-* properties in decentralised autonomic computing. In *Autonomic Computing: Concepts, Infrastructure, and Applications*, pages 101–120. CRC Press, Taylor and Francis Group.

DeWolf, T. and Holvoet, T. (2007c). Using UML 2 activity diagrams to design information flows and feedback-loops in self-organising emergent systems. In De Wolf, T., Saffre, F., and Anthony, R., editors, *Proceedings of the 2nd International Workshop on Engineering Emergence in Decentralised Autonomic Systems,*, pages 52–61.

DeWolf, T., Holvoet, T., and Berbers, Y. (2004). Emergence as a paradigm to engineer distributed autonomic software. In *Report CW 380*, Leuven, Belgium. Department of Computer Science, K.U.Leuven. (http://www.cs.kuleuven.be/publicaties/rapporten/cw/CW380.pdf).

DeWolf, T., Holvoet, T., and Samaey, G. (2005). Engineering self-organising emergent systems with simulation-based scientific analysis. In *Proceedings of the Third International Workshop on Engineering Self-Organising Applications*, pages 146–160.

di Nitto, E., Dubois, D. J., and Mirandola, R. (2009). On exploiting decentralized bio-inspired self-organization algorithms to develop real systems. *Software Engineering for Adaptive and Self-Managing Systems, International Workshop on*, pages 68–75.

Dobson, S., Denazis, S., Fernández, A., Gaïti, D., Gelenbe, E., Massacci, F., Nixon, P., Saffre, F., Schmidt, N., and Zambonelli, F. (2006). A survey of autonomic communications. *ACM Trans. Auton. Adapt. Syst.*, 1(2):223–259.

Dong, M., Mao, X., Yin, J., Chang, Z., and Qi, Z. (2009). Sade: A development environment for adaptive multi-agent systems. In *PRIMA '09: Proceedings of the 12th International Conference on Principles of Practice in Multi-Agent Systems*, pages 516–524, Berlin, Heidelberg. Springer-Verlag.

Dowling, J. and Cahill, V. (2001). The k-component architecture meta-model for self-adaptive software. In *REFLECTION '01: Proceedings of the Third International Conference on Metalevel Architectures and Separation of Crosscutting Concerns*, pages 81–88. Springer.

Dressler, F. (2007). *Self-organization in sensor and actor networks*. Wiley.

Ducatelle, F., Caro, G. A. D., and Gambardella, L. M. (2010). Principles and applications of swarm intelligence for adaptive routing in telecommunications networks. *Swarm Intelligence*. (http://www.springerlink.com/content/n06gj40984t71583/).

Edmonds, B. (2004). Using the experimental method to produce reliable self-organised systems. In *Engineering Self Organising Sytems: Methodologies and Applications*, number 3464 in LNAI, pages 84–99.

Edmonds, B. and Norling, E. (2006). Emergence in and engineering of complex mas. Technical Report CPM Report No.: CPM-06-160, Manchester Metropolitan University. (http://cfpm.org/cpmrep160.html).

Efftinge, S., Friese, P., Haase, A., Hübner, D., Kadura, C., Kolb, B., Köhnlein, J., Moroff, D., Thoms, K., Völter, M., Schönbach, P., and Eysholdt, M. (2008). openarchitectureware user guide version 4.3. http://www.openarchitectureware.org/pub/documentation/4.3/openArchitectureWare-4.3-Reference.pdf. Chapter 6. Ttext Reference.

Eppstein, D. and Wang, J. (2002). A steady state model for graph power laws. *CoRR*, cs.DM/0204001.

Esteva, M., Rosell, B., Rodriguez-Aguilar, J. A., and Arcos, J. L. (2004). Ameli: An agent-based middleware for electronic institutions. In *AAMAS '04: Proceedings of the Third International Joint Conference on Autonomous Agents and Multiagent Systems*, pages 236–243, Washington, DC, USA. IEEE Computer Society.

Eugster, P. T., Guerraoui, R., Kermarrec, A.-M., and Massoulieacute;, L. (2004). Epidemic information dissemination in distributed systems. *Computer*, 37(5):60–67.

Ferber, J. (1999). *Multi-Agent Systems - An Introduction to Distributed Artificial Intelligence*. Addison Wesley.

Ferber, J., Gutknecht, O., and Michel, F. (2004). From agents to organizations: An organizational view of multi-agent systems. In *Agent-Oriented Software Engineering IV*, volume 2935, pages 214–230.

Floreano, D. and Mattiussi, C. (2008). *Bio-Inspired Artificial Intelligence Theories, Methods, and Technologies*, chapter Collective Systems, pages 515–584. MIT Press.

Floyd, R. (1967). Assigning meaning to programs. *Mathematical Aspects of Computer Science*, XIX American Mathematical Society:19–32.

Fokkink, W. (2000). *Introduction to Process Algebra*. Texts in Theoretical Computer Science. An EATCS Series. Springer. ISBN: 3-540-66579-X.

Forrest, S., Hofmeyr, S. A., and Somayaji, A. (1997). Computer immunology. *Commun. ACM*, 40(10):88–96.

Forrester, J. W. (1961). *Industrial Dynamics*. The MIT Press.

Foundation for Intelligent Physical Agents (2003). Fipa acl message structure specification. http://www.fipa.org/repository/aclspecs.html.

Foundation for Intelligent Physical Agents (2004). Fipa agent management specification. http://www.fipa.org/specs/fipa00023/index.html. Document number: SC00023K.

Fowler, M., Beck, K., Brant, J., Opdyke, W., and Roberts, D. (1999). *Refactoring: Improving the Design of Existing Code*. Addison-Wesley Professional.

Franklin, S. and Graesser, A. (1997). Is it an agent, or just a program?: A taxonomy for autonomous agents. In *ECAI '96: Proceedings of the Workshop on Intelligent Agents III, Agent Theories, Architectures, and Languages*, pages 21–35. Springer.

Frei, R., Serugendo, G. D. M., and Barata, J. (2008). Designing self-organization for evolvable assembly systems. In *Second IEEE International Conference on Self-Adaptive and Self-Organizing Systems*, pages 97–106, Isola di San Servolo (Venice), Italy.

Gagné, C., Gravel, M., and Price, W. L. (2006). Solving real car sequencing problems with ant colony optimization. *European Journal of Operational Research*, 174(3):1427–1448.

Gamma, E., Helm, R., Johnson, R., and Vlissides, J. (1995). *Design Patterns. Elements of Reusable Object-Oriented Software*. Addison Wesley. ISBN 0-201-63361-2.

Garcia, A., Kulesza, U., Sant'Anna, C., Chavez, C., and de Lucena, C. (2006). Aspects in agent-oriented software engineering: Lessons learned. In *Agent-Oriented Software Engineering VI*, volume 3950 of *Lecture Notes in Computer Science*, pages 231–247. Springer Berlin / Heidelberg.

Garcia, A. F., de Lucena, C. J. P., and Cowan, D. D. (2004). Agents in object-oriented software engineering. *Softw. Pract. Exper.*, 34(5):489–521.

García-Magari no, I., Gómez-Rodríguez, A., and González-Moreno, J. C. (2009). Definition of process models for agent-based development. In *Agent-Oriented Software Engineering IX: 9th International Workshop, AOSE 2008 Estoril, Portugal, May 12-13, 2008 Revised Selected Papers*, pages 60–73. Springer.

Gardelli, L., Viroli, M., Casadei, M., and Omicini, A. (2008). Designing self-organising environments with agents and artefacts: a simulation-driven approach. *Int. J. Agent-Oriented Softw. Eng.*, 2(2):171–195.

Gardelli, L., Viroli, M., and Omicini, A. (2005). On the role of simulation in the engineering of self-organising systems: Detecting abnormal behaviour in MAS. In Corradini, F., Paoli, F. D., Merelli, E., and Omicini, A., editors, *WOA 2005: Dagli Oggetti agli Agenti. 6th AI*IA/TABOO Joint Workshop "From Objects to Agents": Simulation and Formal Analysis of Complex Systems*, pages 85–90. ISBN 88-371-1590-3.

Gardelli, L., Viroli, M., and Omicini, A. (2006). On the role of simulations in engineering self-organising mas: The case of an intrusion detection system in tucson. In *Engineering Self-Organising Systems*, volume 3910 of *LNAI*, pages 153–166. Springer.

Gardelli, L., Viroli, M., and Omicini, A. (2007). Design patterns for self–organizing systems. In *Multi-Agent Systems and Applications V, 5th International Central and Eastern European Conference on Multi-Agent Systems, CEEMAS 2007*, number 4696 in LNAI, pages 123–132.

Garlan, D., Cheng, S.-W., Huang, A.-C., Schmerl, B., and Steenkiste, P. (2004). Rainbow: architecture-based self-adaptation with reusable infrastructure. *Computer*, 37(10):46–54.

Gelernter, D. and Carriero, N. (1992). Coordination languages and their significance. *Commun. ACM*, 35(2):97–107.

Georgeff, M. P. and Lansky, A. L. (1987). Reactive reasoning and planning. In *AAAI*, pages 677–682.

Gershenson, C. (2007). *Design and Control of Self-Organizing Systems*. PhD thesis, Vrije Universiteit Brussel.

Gillespie, D. T. (1977). Exact stochastic simulation of coupled chemical reactions. *The Journal of Physical Chemistry*, 81(25):2340–2361.

Giorgini, P., Kolp, M., and Castro, J. M. J. (2005). *Agent-Oriented Methodologies*, chapter Tropos: A Requirements-Driven Methodology for Agent-Oriented Software, pages 20–45. IDEA Group Publishing.

Gleizes, M.-P., Camps, V., and Glize, P. (1999). A theory of emergent computation based on cooperative self-organization for adaptive artificial systems. In *Fourth European Congress of Systems Science*.

Gouaïch, A., Michel, F., and Guiraud, Y. (2005). Mic: A deployment environment for autonomous agents. In *Environments for Multi-Agent Systems*, pages 109–126.

Gouaich, A. and Michel, F. (2005). Towards a unified view of the environment(s) within multi-agent systems. *Informatica (Slovenia)*, 29(4):423–432.

Grasse, P. (1959). La reconstruction du nid et les coordinations inter-individuelles chez bellicostitermes natalensis et cubitermes . sp. la theorie de la stigmergie: essai d'interpretation du comportement des termites constructeurs. *Insectes Sociaux*, 6:41–83.

Hadeli, K., Valckenaers, P., Kollingbaum, M., and Brussel, H. V. (2004a). Multi-agent coordination and control using stigmergy. *Computers in Industry*, 53(1):75–96.

Hadeli, K., Valckenaers, P., Zamfirescu, C., Brussel, H. V., Germain, B. S., Hoelvoet, T., and Steegmans, E. (2004b). Self–organising in multi–agent coordination and control using stigmergy. In *Engineering Self-Organising Systems*, LNCS, pages 105–123. Springer Berlin / Heidelberg.

Hagelbäck, J. and Johansson, S. J. (2009). A multiagent potential field-based bot for real-time strategy games. *Int. J. Comput. Games Technol.*, 2009:1–10.

Haken, H. (2004). *SYNERGETICS. Introduction and Advanced Topics*. Springer.

Haken, H. (2006). *Information and Self-Organization: A Macroscopic Approach to Complex Systems (Springer Series in Synergetics)*. Springer-Verlag New York, Inc., Secaucus, NJ, USA. Third Enlarged Edition.

Halloy, J., Sempo, G., Caprari, G., Rivault, C., Asadpour, M., Tâche, F., Saïd, I., Durier, V., Canonge, S., Amé, J.-M., Detrain, C., Correll, N., Martinoli, A., Mondada, F., Siegwart, R., and Deneubourg, J.-L. (2007). Social integration of robots into groups of cockroaches to control self-organized choices. *Science*, 318:1155–1158.

Harel, D. (1987). Statecharts: A visual formalism for complex systems. *Science of Computer Programming*, 8(3):231–274.

Harmsen, F. and Brinkkemper, S. (1995). Design and implementation of a method base management system for a situational case environment. In *APSEC '95: Proceedings of the Second Asia Pacific Software Engineering Conference*, pages 430–438, Washington, DC, USA. IEEE Computer Society.

Hassas, S., Marzo-Serugendo, G. D., Karageorgos, A., and Castelfranchi, C. (2006). On self–organized mechanisms from social, business and economic domains. In *Informatica*, volume 30, pages 62–71.

Hellerstein, J. L., Diao, Y., Parekh, S., and Tilbury, D. M. (2004). *Feedback Control of Computing Systems*. Wiley-Interscience.

Henderson-Sellers, B. (1996). *Object–Oriented Metrics: Measures of Complexity*. Prentice Hall.

Henderson-Sellers, B. (2003). Method engineering for oo systems development. *Commun. ACM*, 46(10):73–78.

Henderson-Sellers, B. and Giorgini, P., editors (2005). *Agent-oriented Methodologies*. Idea Group Publishing. ISBN: 1591405815.

Herrmann, K., Werner, M., and Mühl, G. (2006). A methodology for classifying self–organizing software systems. *International Transactions on Systems Science and Applications*, 2(1):41–50.

Heylighen, F. (2003). The science of self-organization and adaptivity. In *Knowledge Management, Organizational Intelligence, Learning, and Complexity, in: The Encyclopedia of Life Support Systems*, pages 253–280. EOLSS Publishers Co. Ltd.

Hindriks, K. (2008). Modules as policy-based intentions: Modular agent programming in goal. In *ProMAS'07: Proceedings of the 5th international conference on Programming multi-agent systems*, pages 156–171. Springer Berlin / Heidelberg. (http://journal.ub.tu-berlin.de/index.php/eceasst/article/view/385/359).

Hoare, C. (2003). Assertions: A personal perspective. *IEEE Annals of the History of Computing*, 25:14–25.

Holland, O. and Melhuish, C. (1999). Stigmergy, self-organization, and sorting in collective robotics. *Artif. Life*, 5(2):173–202.

Holvoet, T. and Valckenaers, P. (2007). Exploiting the environment for coordinating agent intentions. In *E4MAS'06: Proceedings of the 3rd international conference on Environments for multi-agent systems III*, volume 4389 of *LNAI*, pages 51–66, Berlin, Heidelberg. Springer-Verlag.

Holvoet, T., Weyns, D., and Valckenaers, P. (2009). Patterns of delegate mas. In *SASO '09: Proceedings of the 2009 Third IEEE International Conference on Self-Adaptive and Self-Organizing Systems*, pages 1–9, Washington, DC, USA. IEEE Computer Society.

Holzer, R., Wüchner, P., and de Meer, H. (2010). Modeling of self-organizing systems: An overview. *Electronic Communications of the EASST*, 27.

Hoogendoorn, M., Schut, M. C., and Treur, J. (2006). Modeling decentralized organizational change in honeybee societies. In *Proceedings of the Sixth International Conference on Complex Systems*. NECSI.

Huebscher, M. C. and McCann, J. A. (2008). A survey of autonomic computing—degrees, models, and applications. *ACM Comput. Surv.*, 40(3):1–28.

Huget, M.-P. (2004). Agent uml notation for multiagent system design. *IEEE Internet Computing*, 8(4):63–71.

IBM (2001). autonomic computing: Ibm's perspective on the state of information technology. http://www.research.ibm.com/autonomic/manifesto/autonomic_computing.pdf.

Ichii, M., Matsushita, M., and Inoue, K. (2008). An exploration of power-law in use-relation of java software systems. In *ASWEC '08: Proceedings of the 19th Australian Conference on Software Engineering*, pages 422–431, Washington, DC, USA. IEEE Computer Society.

IEEE Computer Society (2004). *Software Engineering Body of Knowledge (SWEBOK)*. (http://www.computer.org/portal/web/swebok).

Iglesias, C., Garrijo, M., and Gonzalez, J. (1999). A survey of agent-oriented methodologies. In *Proceedings of the 5th International Workshop on Intelligent Agents V : Agent Theories, Architectures, and Languages (ATAL-98)*, volume 1555, pages 317–330.

International Organization for Standardization (ISO) (1996). Iso/iec 14977. http://standards.iso.org/ittf/PubliclyAvailableStandards/s026153_ISO_IEC_14977_1996(E).zip.

Ishida, T., Gasser, L., and Yokoo, M. (1992). Organization self-design of distributed production systems. *IEEE Transactions on Knowledge and Data Engineering*, 4(2):123–134.

Jacobson, I., Booch, G., and Rumbaugh, J. (1999). *The unified software development process*. Object Technology Series. Addison Wesley. 5th Printing September 2001.

Jander, K., Braubach, L., and Pokahr, A. (2010). Envsupport: A framework for developing virtual environments. In *Proceedings of International Workshop From Agent Theory to Agent Implementation (AT2AI-7)*.

Jeffrey, R. D., Kephart, O., Lefurgy, C., Tesauro, G., Levine, D. W., and Chan, H. (2008). Autonomic multi–agent management of power and performance in data centers. In *Proc. of the 7th Int. Conf. on Autonomous Agents and Multiagent Systems (AAMAS 2008) – Industry and Applications Track*, pages 107–114.

Jennings, N. R. (2001). An agent-based approach for building complex software systems. *Comms. ACM*, 44(4):35–41.

Jennings, N. R. and Bussmann, S. (2003). Agent-based control systems. *IEEE Control Systems*, 23(3):61–74.

Jennings, N. R., Sycara, K., and Wooldridge, M. (1998). A roadmap of agent research and development. *Autonomous Agents and Multi-Agent Systems*, 1(1):7–38.

Kaddoum, E., Gleizes, M.-P., Georgé, J.-P., and Picard, G. (2009). Characterizing and evaluating problem solving self-* systems. In *COMPUTATIONWORLD '09: Proc. of the 2009 Computation World*, pages 137–145.

Kaplan, D. and Glass, L. (1995). *Understanding Nonlinear Dynamics*. Springer.

Kasinger, H., jörg Denziger, and Bauer, B. (2008). Digital semiochemical coordination. *Communications of SIWN*, 4:133–139.

Kauffman, S. (1996). *At Home in the Universe: The Search for the Laws of Self-Organization and Complexity*. Oxford University Press.

Kephart, J. O. (2005). Research challenges of autonomic computing. In *ICSE '05: Proceedings of the 27th international conference on Software engineering*, pages 15–22, New York, NY, USA. ACM Press.

Kephart, J. O. and Chess, D. M. (2003). The vision of autonomic computing. *Computer*, 36(1):41–50.

Kiczales, G., Lamping, J., Menhdhekar, A., Maeda, C., Lopes, C., Loingtier, J.-M., and Irwin, J. (1997). Aspect-oriented programming. In *ECOOP'97 Object-Oriented Programming*, pages 220–242. Springer.

Kirn, S., Herzog, O., Lockemann, P., and Spaniol, O., editors (2006). *Multiagent Engineering - Theory and Applications in Enterprises*. International Handbooks on Information Systems. Springer.

Koestler (1967). *The Gost in the Machine*. Arkana.

Kruchten, P. (2003). *The Rational Unified Process: An Introduction*. The Addison-Wesley Object Technology Series. Addison Wesley Professional.

Lakkaraju, K. and Gasser, L. (2009). Improving performance in multi-agent agreement problems with scale-free networks. In *Proceedings of 3rd International Workshop on Emergent Intelligence on Networked Agents (WEIN'09)*.

Lam, D. N. and Barber, K. S. (2005). Comprehending agent software. In *Proceedings of the fourth international joint conference on Autonomous agents and multiagent systems*, pages 586–593. ACM Press.

Langton, C. G. (1989). Artificial life. In Langton, C. G., editor, *Artificial Life, Santa Fe Institute Studies in the Sciences of Complexity*, pages 1–44, Redwood City.

Lerman, K. and Galstyan, A. (2001). A general methodology for mathematical analysis of multi-agent systems. Technical Report ISI-TR-529, USC Information Sciences Institute, Marina del Rey, CA.

Lerman, K. and Galstyan, A. (2004). Automatically modeling group behavior of simple agents. In *Modeling Other Agents from Observations (MOO 2004)*, New York, NY. (http://u.cs.biu.ac.il/ galk/moo2004/proceedings/07.pdf).

Liu, J., Jin, X., and Tsui, K. C. (2005). *Autonomy Oriented Computing - From Problem Solving to Complex System Modeling*. Kluwer Academic Publishers.

Liu, J. and Tsui, K. (2006). Toward nature-inspired computing. *Commun. ACM*, 49(10):59–64.

Low, C. K., Chen, T. Y., and Rönnquist, R. (1999). Automated test case generation for bdi agents. *Autonomous Agents and Multi-Agent Systems*, 2(4):311–332.

Luck, M., McBurney, P., and Preist, C. (2003). *Agent Technology: Enabling Next Generation Computing*. Number ISBN 0854 327886. Agentlink II.

Luck, M., McBurney, P., Shehory, O., and Willmott, S., editors (2005). *Agent Technology Roadmap*. Number ISBN: 0854328459. Agentlink. http://www.agentlink.org/roadmap/.

Madachy, R. J. (2008). *Software Process Dynamics*. Wiley-VCH.

Malone, T. W. and Crowston, K. (1994). The interdisciplinary study of coordination. *ACM Comput. Surv.*, 26(1):87–119.

Mamei, M., Menezes, R., Tolksdorf, R., and Zambonelli, F. (2006). Case studies for self-organization in computer science. *J. Syst. Archit.*, 52(8):443–460.

Mamei, M. and Zambonelli, F. (2005a). *Field-Based Coordination for Pervasive Multiagent Systems (Springer Series on Agent Technology)*. Springer-Verlag New York, Inc., Secaucus, NJ, USA.

Mamei, M. and Zambonelli, F. (2005b). Motion coordination in the quake 3 arena environment: A field-based approach. In *Environments for Multi-Agent Systems*, volume 3374/2005, pages 264–278. Springer Berlin / Heidelberg.

Mamei, M. and Zambonelli, F. (2005c). Programming stigmergic coordination with the tota middleware. In *AAMAS '05: Proceedings of the fourth international joint conference on Autonomous agents and multiagent systems*, pages 415–422, New York, NY, USA. ACM.

Mano, J.-P., Bourjot, C., Lopardo, G., and Glize, P. (2006). Bio–inspired mechanisms for artificial self–organized systems. In *Informatica*, volume 30, pages 55–62.

Mao, X. and Yu, E. (2004). Organizational and social concepts in agent oriented software engineering. In *Agent-Oriented Software Engineering V*, volume 3382 of *LNCS*, pages 1–15. Springer.

Marais, K., Saleh, J. H., and Leveson, N. G. (2006). Archetypes for organizational safety. *Safety Science*, 44(7):565 – 582.

Marchesi, M., Pinna, S., Serra, N., and Tuveri, S. (2004). Power laws in smalltalk. In *Proceedings of the 12th European Smalltalk User Group Joint Event*.

Menzies, T. and Pecheur, C. (2005). Verification and validation and artificial intelligence. In Zelkowitz, M., editor, *Advances in Computers*, volume 65, pages 153–201. Elsevier.

Metzler, R. and Horn, C. (2003). Evolutionary minority games: the benefits of imitation. In *Physica A329*, pages 484–498.

Milner, R., Parrow, J., and Walker, D. (1992). A calculus of mobile processes (i and ii). *Information and Computation*, 100:1–77.

Milojicic, D. S., Kalogeraki, V., Lukose, R., Nagaraja, K., Pruyne, J., Richard, B., Rollins, S., and Xu, Z. (2003). Peer-to-peer computing. Technical report, HP Laboratories Palo Alto. HPL-2002-57 (R.1).

Mnif, M. and Müller-Schloer, C. (2006). Quantitative emergence. In *Proceedings fo the IEEE Mountain Workshop on Adaptive and Learning Systems (SMCals/06)*, pages 78–84. Logan.

Moere, A. V. (2008). *Advances in Applied Self-organizing Systems*, chapter A Model for Self-Organizing Data Visualization Using Decentralized Multiagent Systems, pages 291–324. Springer London.

Mogul, J. C. (2005). Emergent (mis)behavior vs. complex software systems. Technical Report HPL-2006-2, HP Laboratories Palo Alto.

Morandini, M., Migeon, F., Gleizes, M.-P., Maurel, C., Penserini, L., and Perini, A. (2009). A goal-oriented approach for modelling self-organising mas. In *ESAW '09: Proceedings of the 10th International Workshop on Engineering Societies in the Agents World X*, pages 33–48, Berlin, Heidelberg. Springer-Verlag.

Moreira, A. F. and Bordini, R. H. (2002). An operational semantics for a bdi agent-oriented programming language. In *Proceedings of Workshop on Logics for Agent-Based Systems (LABS-02), held in with the Eighth International Conference on Principles of Knowledge Representation and Reasoning (KR2002)*, pages 45–59.

Moreira, A. F., Vieira, R., and Bordini, R. H. (2004). Extending the operational semantics of a bdi agent-oriented programming language for introducing speech-act based communication. In *Declarative Agent Languages and Technologies, Proceedings of the First International Workshop (DALT-03)*, volume 2990 of *LNAI*, pages 135–154. Springer.

Mühl, G., Fiege, L., and Pietzuch, P. (2006). *Distributed Event-Based Systems*. Springer, 1 edition.

Mühl, G., Werner, M., Jaeger, M. A., Herrmann, K., and Parzyjegla, H. (2007). On the definitions of self-managing and self-organizing systems. In Braun, T., Carle, G., and Stiller, B., editors, *KIVS 2007 Kommunikation in Verteilten Systemen - Industriebeiträge, Kurzbeiträge und Workshops*, pages 291–301. VDE-Verlag.

Müller, H., Pezzè, M., and Shaw, M. (2008). Visibility of control in adaptive systems. In *ULSSIS '08: Proceedings of the 2nd international workshop on Ultra-large-scale software-intensive systems*, pages 23–26, New York, NY, USA. ACM.

Müller, J. P. (1999). The right agent (architecture) to do the right thing. In *ATAL '98: Proceedings of the 5th International Workshop on Intelligent Agents V, Agent Theories, Architectures, and Languages*, pages 211–225. Springer-Verlag.

Müller-Schloer, C. (2004). Organic computing: on the feasibility of controlled emergence. In *CODES+ISSS '04: Proceedings of the 2nd IEEE/ACM/IFIP international conference on Hardware/software codesign and system synthesis*, pages 2–5, New York, NY, USA. ACM Press.

Murray, J. D. (2002). *Mathematical Biology I.. An Introduction*, volume 17 of *Interdisciplinary Applied Mathematics*. Springer. Third Edition.

Myers, C. R. (2003). Software systems as complex networks: structure, function, and evolvability of software collaboration graphs. *Phys. Rev. E*, 68:046116.

Nafz, F., Ortmeier, F., Seebach, H., Steghöfer, J.-P., and Reif, W. (2009a). A universal self-organization mechanism for role-based organic computing systems. In *Autonomic and Trusted Computing*, volume 5586/2009 of *LNCS*, pages 17–31.

Nafz, F., Ortmeier, F., Seebach, H., Steghofer, J.-P., and Reif, W. (2009b). A generic software framework for role-based organic computing systems. *Software Engineering for Adaptive and Self-Managing Systems, International Workshop on*, pages 96–105.

Nakrani, S. and Tovey, C. (2004). On honey bees and dynamic server allocation in internet hosting centers. *Adaptive Behavior*, 12(3-4):223–240.

Napoli, C. D. (2009). *Knowledge Processing and Decision Making in Agent-Based Systems*, volume 170/2009, chapter Software Agents to Enable Service Composition through Negotiation, pages 275 – 296. Springer Berlin / Heidelberg.

Newman, M. (2003). The structure and function of complex networks. M. E. J. Newman. The structure and function of complex networks. SIAM Review, 45(2):167– 256.

Niknafs, A. and Ramsin, R. (2008). Computer-aided method engineering: An analysis of existing environments. In *CAiSE '08: Proceedings of the 20th international conference on Advanced Information Systems Engineering*, pages 525–540, Berlin, Heidelberg. Springer-Verlag.

Norling, E. (2007). Contrasting a system dynamics model and an agent-based model of food web evolution. In *Multi-Agent-Based Simulation VII*, volume 4442 of *LNCS*, pages 57–68.

North, M. J. and Macal, C. M. (2007). *Managing Business Complexity: Discovering Strategic Solutions with Agent-Based Modeling and Simulation*. Oxford University Press, Inc., New York, NY, USA.

Object Management Group (2006). Meta object facility (mof) core specification version 2.0. (http://www.omg.org/spec/MOF/2.0/).

Object Management Group (2008). Software & systems process engineering meta-model specification version 2.0. (http://www.omg.org/spec/SPEM/2.0/PDF). formal/2008-04-01.

Odell, J., Parunak, H. V. D., and Bauer, B. (2000). Extending uml for agents. In Wagner, G., Lesperance, Y., and Yu, E., editors, *Proceedings of the Agent-Oriented Information Systems Workshop at the 17th National conference on Artificial Intelligence*, pages 3–17.

Odell, J., v. D. Parunak, H., Brueckner, S., and Sauter, J. (2003). Changing roles: Dynamic role assignment. *Jounal of Object Technology*, 2(5):77–86.

(OMG), O. M. G. (2004). Notification service, version 1.1. http://www.omg.org/technology/documents/formal/notification_service.htm. formal/04-10-11.

Omicini, A., Ossowski, S., and Ricci, A. (2004a). *Methodologies and Software Engineering for Agent Systems*, chapter Coordination infrastructures in the engineering of multiagent systems, pages 273–296. Kluwer Academic Publishers.

Omicini, A., Ricci, A., and Viroli, M. (2008). Artifacts in the a&a meta-model for multi-agent systems. *Autonomous Agents and Multi-Agent Systems*, 17(3):432–456.

Omicini, A., Ricci, A., Viroli, M., Castelfranchi, C., and Tummolini, L. (2004b). A conceptual framework for self-organising mas. In *WOA 2004: Dagli Oggetti agli Agenti. 5th AI*IA/TABOO Joint Workshop "From Objects to Agents:" Complex Systems and Rational Agents, 30 November - 1 December 2004*, pages 100–109.

Padgham, L. and Winikoff, M. (2004). *Developing Intelligent Agent Systems: A Practical Guide.* Number ISBN 0-470-86120-7. John Wiley and Sons.

Padgham, L., Winikoff, M., and Poutakidis, D. (2005). Adding debugging support to the prometheus methodology. *Engin. Applications of Art. Intel.*, 18(2):173–190.

Papadopoulos, G. A. and Arbab, F. (1998). Coordination models and languages. Technical Report SEN-R9834, CWI (Centre for Mathematics and Computer Science), Amsterdam, The Netherlands, The Netherlands.

Parnas, D. L. (1972). On the criteria to be used in decomposing systems into modules. *Commun. ACM*, 15(12):1053–1058.

Parunak, H. and VanderBok, R. (1997). Managing emergent behavior in distributed control systems. In *Proc. of ISA Tech '97*. Instrument Society of America.

Parunak, H. V. D. (1987). *Distributed Artificial Intelligence*, chapter Manufacturing Experience with the Contract Net, pages 285–310.

Parunak., H. V. D. (1997). 'go to the ant': Engineering principles from natural agent systems. *Annals of Operations Research*, 75:69–101.

Parunak, H. V. D. and Brueckner, S. (2004). Engineering swarming systems. In *Methodologies and Software Engineering for Agent Systems*, pages 341–376. Kluwer.

Parunak, H. V. D., Brueckner, S., Fleischer, M., and Odell, J. (2004a). A design taxonomy of multi–agent interactions. In *Agent Oriented Software Engineering IV*, volume 2935/2003 of *LNCS*, pages 123–137. Springer.

Parunak, H. V. D., Brueckner, S., and Savit, R. (2004b). Universality in multi-agent systems. In *AAMAS '04: Proceedings of the Third International Joint Conference on Autonomous Agents and Multiagent Systems*, pages 930–937. IEEE Computer Society.

Parunak, H. V. D., Savit, R., and Riolo, R. L. (1998). Agent-based modeling vs. equation-based modeling: A case study and users' guide. In *Proceedings of the First International Workshop on Multi-Agent Systems and Agent-Based Simulation*, pages 10–25. Springer.

Parunak, H. V. D., Weinstein, P., Chiusano, P., and Brueckner, S. (2005). Sift and sort: Climbing the semantic pyramid. In *Engineering Self-Organising Systems*, pages 212–221.

Pavon, J., Gomez-Sanz, J. J., and Fuentes, R. (2005). *Agent-Oriented methodologies*, chapter The INGENIAS Methodology and Tools, pages 236–276. IDEA Group Publishing.

Pena, J. and Corchuelo, R. (2004). Macmas/uml: A methodology fragment for the analysis stage of complex/complicated multi-agent systems working document v.2.1. (http://www.pa.icar.cnr.it/cossentino/FIPAmeth/metamodel.htm).

Phillips, A. (2010). *Symbolic Systems Biology: Theory and Methods*, chapter A Visual Process Calculus for Biology. Jones and Bartlett Publishers. (http://research.microsoft.com/apps/pubs/default.aspx?id=79914).

Phillips, A., Cardelli, L., and Castagna, G. (2006). A graphical representation for biological processes in the stochastic pi-calculus. In *Transactions on Computational Systems Biology VII*, volume 4230 of *LNCS*, pages 123–152. Springer Berlin / Heidelberg.

Piunti, M., Ricci, A., Braubach, L., and Pokahr, A. (2008). Goal-directed interactions in artifact-based mas: Jadex agents playing in cartago environments. *Web Intelligence and Intelligent Agent Technology, 2008. WI-IAT '08. IEEE/WIC/ACM International Conference on*, 2:207–213.

Plotkin, G. D. (2004). The origins of structural operational semantics. *Journal of Logic and Algebraic Programming*, 60-61:3–15.

Pokahr, A. (2007). *Programmiersprachen und Werkzeuge zur Entwicklung verteilter agentenorientierter Softwaresysteme*. PhD thesis, Universität Hamburg, Fachbereich Informatik, Verteilte Systeme und Informationssysteme.

Pokahr, A. and Braubach, L. (2007a). *Jadex Tool Guide - Release 0.96*. Distributed Systems Group, University of Hamburg, Germany. (http://heanet.dl.sourceforge.net/project/jadex/jadex/0.96/toolguide-0.96.pdf).

Pokahr, A. and Braubach, L. (2007b). *Jadex User Guide*. Distributed Systems Group University Hamburg, 0.96 edition. http://puzzle.dl.sourceforge.net/project/jadex/jadex/0.96/userguide-0.96.pdf.

Pokahr, A. and Braubach, L. (2010). The notions of application, spaces and agents - new concepts for constructing agent applications. In *Multikonferenz Wirtschaftsinformatik (MKWI): Multi-agent Systems: Decentral approaches for designing, organizing, and operating information systems*.

Pokahr, A., Braubach, L., and Lamersdorf, W. (2005a). A bdi architecture for goal deliberation. In *AAMAS '05: Proceedings of the fourth international joint conference on Autonomous agents and multiagent systems*, pages 1295–296. ACM.

Pokahr, A., Braubach, L., and Lamersdorf, W. (2005b). A flexible BDI architecture supporting extensibility. In *2005 IEEE/WIC/ACM International Conference on Intelligent Agent Technology (IAT-2005)*, pages 379–385. IEEE Computer Society.

Pokahr, A., Braubach, L., Sudeikat, J., Renz, W., and Lamersdorf, W. (2008). Simulation and implementation of logistics systems based on agent technology. In *Hamburg International Conference on Logistics 2008: Logistics Networks and Nodes*, pages 291–308. Erich Schmidt Verlag.

Polani, D. (2008). *Advances in Applied Self-organizing Systems*, chapter Foundations and Formalizations of Self-organization, pages 19–37. Advanced Information and Knowledge Processing. Springer London.

Potanin, A. (2002). The fox – a tool for java object graph analysis. Technical report, School of Mathematical and Computing Sciences, Victoria University. (http://www.mcs.vuw.ac.nz/comp/Publications/CS-TR-02-28.abs.html).

Potanin, A., Noble, J., Frean, M., and Biddle, R. (2005). Scale-free geometry in oo programs. *Commun. ACM*, 48(5):99–103.

Poutakidis, D., Padgham, L., and Winikoff, M. (2002). Debugging multi-agent systems using design artifacts: the case of interaction protocols. In *AAMAS '02: Proceedings of the first international joint conference on Autonomous agents and multiagent systems*, pages 960–967. ACM.

Poutakidis, D., Padgham, L., and Winikoff, M. (2003). An exploration of bugs and debugging in multi-agent systems. In *Foundations of Intelligent Systems*, volume 2871 of *Lecture Notes in Computer Science*, pages 628–632. Springer Berlin / Heidelberg.

Prehofer, C. and Bettstetter, C. (2005). Self-organization in communication networks: principles and design paradigms. *Communications Magazine*, 43(7):78–85.

Priami, C. (1995). Stochastic π–calculus. *Computer Journal*, 6:578–589.

Prokopenko, M., editor (2008a). *Advances in Applied Self-organizing Systems*. Springer-Verlag New York, Inc., Secaucus, NJ, USA.

Prokopenko, M. (2008b). *Advances in Applied Self-organizing Systems*, chapter Design vs. Self-organization, pages 3–17. Springer London.

Prokopenko, M. (2008c). *Advances in Applied Self-organizing Systems*, chapter Preface, pages V–VI. Springer London.

Puviani, M., Serugendo, G. D. M., Frei, R., and Cabri, G. (2009). Methodologies for self-organising systems: A spem approach. In *WI-IAT '09: Proceedings of the 2009 IEEE/WIC/ACM International Joint Conference on Web Intelligence and Intelligent Agent Technology*, pages 66–69. IEEE Computer Society.

Qin, Z., Xing, J.-K., and Zheng, X. (2008). *Software Architecture (Advanced Topics in Science and Technology in China)*. Springer Publishing Company, Incorporated.

Randles, M., Taleb-Bendiab, A., and Miseldine, P. (2006). Harnessing complexity: A logical approach to engineering and controlling self-organizing systems. *ITSSA*, 2(1):11–20.

Randles, M., Zhu, H., and Taleb-Bendiab, A. (2007). A formal approach to the engineering of emergence and its recurrence. In *Proceedings of the Second International Workshop on Engineering Emergence in Decentralised Autonomic Systems (EEDAS 2007)*. CMS Press.

Rao, A. S. (1996). Agentspeak(l): Bdi agents speak out in a logical computable language. In *MAAMAW '96: Proceedings of the 7th European workshop on Modelling autonomous agents in a multi-agent world*, pages 42–55.

Rao, A. S. and Georgeff, M. P. (1995). BDI-agents: from theory to practice. In *Proceedings of the First Intl. Conference on Multiagent Systems*.

Reents, G., Metzler, R., and Kinzel, W. (2001). A stochastic strategy for the minority game. In *Physica A 299*, pages 253–261.

Reiter, R. (2001). *Knowledge in Action: Logical Foundations for Specifying and Implementing Dynamical Systems*. MIT Press.

Renz, W. and Sudeikat, J. (2005a). Mesoscopic modeling of emergent behavior - a self-organizing deliberative minority game. In *Engineering Self-Organising Systems*, pages 167–181.

Renz, W. and Sudeikat, J. (2005b). Modeling minority games with bdi agents - a case study. In T. Eymann, F. Klügl, W. L. M. K. M. H., editor, *Third German conference on Multi-Agent System TEchnologieS (MATES-2005)*, volume LNAI 3550, pages 71–81. Springer.

Renz, W. and Sudeikat, J. (2006). Emergent roles in multi agent systems - a case study in minority games. *KI - Zeitschrift fuer Kuenstliche Intelligenz*, 01/06:26–32. (ISSN 0933-1875).

Renz, W. and Sudeikat, J. (2007). Emergence in software. *KI – Künstliche Intelligenz*, 02/07:48–49. (Aktuelles Schlagwort).

Renz, W. and Sudeikat, J. (2009). Modeling feedback within mas: A systemic approach to organizational dynamics. In *Organised Adaptation in Multi-Agent Systems, First International Workshop, OAMAS 2008, Estoril Portugal, May 2008 Revised and Invited Papers*, volume 5368 of *LNCS*, pages 72–89.

Resnik, M. (1997). *Turtles, Termites, and Traffic Jams Explorations of Massively Parallel Microworlds*. The MIT Press.

Ricci, A., Omicini, A., and Denti, E. (2002). Virtual enterprises and workflow management as agent coordination issues. *International Journal of Cooperative Information Systems*, 11:355–379.

Ricci, A., Piunti, M., Acay, L. D., Bordini, R. H., Hübner, J. F., and Dastani, M. (2008). Integrating heterogeneous agent programming platforms within artifact-based environments. In *AAMAS '08: Proceedings of the 7th international joint conference on Autonomous agents and multiagent systems*, pages 225–232.

Richardson, G. P. (1986). Problems with causal-loop diagrams. *System Dynamics Review*, 2:158–170.

Richter, U., Mnif, M., Branke, J., Müller-Schloer, C., and Schmeck, H. (2006). Towards a generic observer/controller architecture for organic computing. In *INFORMATIK 2006 – Informatik für Menschen*, volume P-93 of *GI-Edition – Lecture Notes in Informatics*, pages 112–119. Köllen Verlag.

Rosenfeld, S. N., Rus, I., and Cukier, M. (2007). Archetypal behavior in computer security. *J. Syst. Softw.*, 80(10):1594–1606.

Rosenfeld, S. N., Rus, I., and Cukier, M. (2009). Modeling the "tragedy of the commons" archetype in enterprise computer security. *Journal of Information Assurance and Security*, 4:10–20.

Rouff, C. A., Hinchey, M. G., Rash, J. L., and Truszkowski, W. F. (2005). Towards a hybrid formal method for swarm-based exploration missions. In *SEW '05: Proceedings of the 29th Annual IEEE/NASA on Software Engineering Workshop*, pages 253–264, Washington, DC, USA. IEEE Computer Society.

Rouff, C. A., Hinchey, M. G., Truszkowski, W. F., and Rash, J. L. (2006). Experiences applying formal approaches in the development of swarm-based space exploration systems. *Int. J. Softw. Tools Technol. Transf.*, 8(6):587–603.

Rougemaille, S., Arcangeli, J.-P., Gleizes, M.-P., and Migeon, F. (2009a). ADELFE Design, AMAS-ML in Action. In *Engineering Societies in the Agents World IX*, volume 5485 of *Lecture Notes in Computer Science*, pages 105–120. Springer Berlin / Heidelberg.

Rougemaille, S., Migeon, F., Millan, T., and Gleizes, M.-P. (2009b). Methodology fragments definition in spem for designing adaptive methodology: A first step. In *Agent-Oriented Software Engineering IX*, LNCS, pages 74–85.

Roy, P. V. (2007). Self management and the future of software design. *Electron. Notes Theor. Comput. Sci.*, 182:201–217.

Roy, P. V., Haridi, S., Reinefeld, A., Stefani, J.-B., Yap, R., and Coupaye, T. (2008). Self management for large-scale distributed systems: An overview of the selfman project. In *Formal Methods for Components and Objects*, volume 5382/2008 of *LNCS*, pages 153–178.

Rumbaugh, J., Blaha, M., Premerlani, W., Eddy, F., and Lorensen, W. (1991). *Object-oriented modeling and design*. Prentice–Hall.

Russell, S. J. and Norvig, P. (1995). *Artificial Intelligence: A Modern Approach*. Number 0-13-103805-2 in Series in Articial Intelligence. Prentice Hall.

Salehie, M. and Tahvildari, L. (2009). Self-adaptive software: Landscape and research challenges. *ACM Trans. Auton. Adapt. Syst.*, 4(2):1–42.

Sansores, C. and Pavón, J. (2008). An adaptive agent model for self-organizing mas (short paper). In *AAMAS '08: Proceedings of the 7th international joint conference on Autonomous agents and multiagent systems*, pages 1639–1642.

Sansores, C. and Pavon, J. (2009). A motivation-based self-organization approach. In *International Symposium on Distributed Computing and Artificial Intelligence 2008 (DCAI 2008)*, Advances in Soft Computing, pages 259–268.

Sauter, J. A., Mathews, R. S., Neuharth, K., Robinson, J. S., Moody, J., and Riddle, S. (2009). Demonstration of swarming control of unmanned ground and air systems in surveillance and infrastructure protection. In *Technologies for Homeland Security, 2009. HST '09. IEEE Conference on*, pages 51–58.

Schlegel, T. and Kowalczyk, R. (2008). *Advances in Applied Self-organizing Systems*, chapter Self-organizing Nomadic Services in Grids, pages 217–246. Advanced Information and Knowledge Processing. Springer London.

Schut, M. C. (2007). *Scientific Handbook for Simulation of Collective Intelligence*. Published under Creative Commons licence. http://www.sci-sci.org/.

Seebach, H., Ortmeier, F., and Reif, W. (2007). Design and construction of organic computing systems. *Evolutionary Computation, 2007. CEC 2007. IEEE Congress on*, pages 4215–4221.

Seidita, V., Cossentino, M., and Gaglio, S. (2006). A repository of fragments for agent systems design. In *Proceedings of the Workshop on Objects and Agents (WOA06)*, pages 130–137.

Seidita, V., Cossentino, M., and Gaglio, S. (2009). Using and extending the spem specifications to represent agent oriented methodologies. In *Agent-Oriented Software Engineering IX*, LNCS, pages 46–59.

Seiter, L. M., Palmer, D. W., and Kirschenbaum, M. (2006). An aspect-oriented approach for modeling self-organizing emergent structures. In *SELMAS '06: Proceedings of the 2006 international workshop on Software engineering for large-scale multi-agent systems*, pages 59–66, New York, NY, USA. ACM Press.

Senge, P. M. (1990). *The Fifth Discipline*. Doubleday.

Serugendo, G. D. M. and Fitzgerald, J. (2009). Designing and controlling trustworthy self-organising systems. *Perada Magazine*, (10.2417/2200903.1534). (http://www.perada-magazine.eu/pdf/1534/1534.pdf).

Serugendo, G. D. M., Fitzgerald, J., Romanovsky, A., and Guelfi, N. (2008a). A generic framework for the engineering of self-adaptive and self-organising systems. In *Organic Computing - Controlled Self-organization*, number 08141 in Dagstuhl Seminar Proceedings, Dagstuhl, Germany. Schloss Dagstuhl - Leibniz-Zentrum fuer Informatik, Germany.

Serugendo, G. D. M., Fitzgerald, J., Romanovsky, A., and Guelfi, N. (2008b). Metaself - a framework for designing and controlling self-adaptive and self-organising systems. Technical Report BBKCS-08-08, School of Computer Science and Information Systems, Birkbeck College, London, UK. (http://www.dcs.bbk.ac.uk/ dimarzo/papers/MetaSelf-TR.pdf).

Serugendo, G. D. M., Foukia, N., Hassas, S., Karageorgos, A., Mostéfaoui, S. K., Rana, O. F., Ulieru, M., Valckenaers, P., and van Aart, C. (2003). Self-organisation: Paradigms and applications. In *Engineering Self-Organising Systems*, pages 1–19.

Serugendo, G. D. M., Gleizes, M. P., and Karageorgos, A. (2006). Self-organisation and emergence in mas: An overview. In *Informatica*, volume 30, pages 45–54.

Shabtay, A., Rabinovich, Z., and Rosenschein, J. S. (2007). Behaviosites: A novel paradigm for affecting distributed behavior. In *Engineering Self-Organising Systems*, volume 4335 of *Lecture Notes in Computer Science*, pages 82–98. Springer Berlin / Heidelberg.

Shalizi, C. R. (2001). *Causal Architecture, Complexity, and Self-Organization in Time Series and Cellular Automata*. Ph.d. dissertation, Physics Department, University of Wisconsin-Madison.

Shaw, M. and Garlan, D. (1996). *Software Architecture: Perspectives on an Emerging Discipline*. Prentice Hall. Prentice Hall Ordering Information.

Shoham, Y. and Tennenholtz, M. (1997). On the emergence of social conventions: modeling, analysis, and simulations. *Artif. Intell.*, 94(1-2):139–166.

Simari, G. I. and Parsons, S. (2006). On the relationship between mdps and the bdi architecture. In *AAMAS '06: Proceedings of the fifth international joint conference on Autonomous agents and multiagent systems*, pages 1041–1048. ACM.

Singh, M. P. (1998). A customizable coordination service for autonomous agents. In *ATAL '97: Proceedings of the 4th International Workshop on Intelligent Agents IV, Agent Theories, Architectures, and Languages*, pages 93–106, London, UK. Springer-Verlag.

Singh, M. P. and Huhns, M. N. (2005). *Service-Oriented Computing: Semantics, Processes, Agents.* John Wiley & Sons Ltd.

Steghöfer, J.-P., Mandrekar, P., Nafz, F., Seebach, H., and Reif, W. (2010). On deadlocks and fairness in self-organizing resource-flow systems. In *Architecture of Computing Systems - ARCS 2010*, volume 5974/2010, pages 87–100. Springer Berlin / Heidelberg.

Sterling, L. and Taveter, K. (2009). *The Art of Agent-Oriented Modeling.* The MIT Press.

Sterman, J. D. (2000). *Business Dynamics - Systems Thinking and Modeling for a Complex World.* McGraw–Hill.

Strogatz, S. H. (2001). *Nonlinear Dynamics And Chaos: With Applications To Physics, Biology, Chemistry, and Engineering.* Studies in Nonlinearity. Westview Press.

Sturm, A. and Shehory, O. (2003). A framework for evaluating agent-oriented methodologies. In *Agent-Oriented Information Systems*, volume 3030 of *Lecture Notes in Computer Science*, pages 94–109. Springer Berlin / Heidelberg.

Sudeikat, J. (2007). Toward the design if self–organizing dynamics. In Bleck, W.-G., Schwentner, H., and Züllighoven, H., editors, *Software Engineering 2007 – Beiträge zu den Workshops*, pages 361–364. Gesellschft für Informatik e. V. (GI).

Sudeikat, J., Braubach, L., Pokahr, A., and Lamersdorf, W. (2004). Evaluation of agent–oriented software methodologies - examination of the gap between modeling and platform. In *Agent-Oriented Software Engineering V, Fifth International Workshop AOSE 2004*, pages 126–141.

Sudeikat, J., Braubach, L., Pokahr, A., Lamersdorf, W., and Renz, W. (2006). Validation of bdi agents. In *Programming Multi-Agent Systems – 4th International Workshop, ProMAS 2006, Revised and Invited Papers*, number 4411 in LNAI, pages 185–200.

Sudeikat, J., Braubach, L., Pokahr, A., Renz, W., and Lamersdorf, W. (2009a). Systematically engineering self-organizing systems: The sodekovs approach. *Electronic Communications of the EASST*, 17. (http://journal.ub.tu-berlin.de/index.php/eceasst/ article/view/194).

Sudeikat, J., Randles, M., Renz, W., and Taleb-Bendiab, A. (2009b). A hybrid modeling approach for self-organizing systems development. *Communications of SIWN*, 7:127–134. (ISSN: 1757-4439).

Sudeikat, J. and Renz, W. (2006). On the redesign of self–organizing multi–agent systems. *International Transactions on Systems Science and Applications*, 2(1):81–89.

Sudeikat, J. and Renz, W. (2007a). Monitoring group behavior in goal–directed agents using co–efficient plan observation. In *Agent-Oriented Software Engineering VII, 7th International Workshop, AOSE 2006, Hakodate, Japan, May 8, 2006, Revised and Invited Papers*, volume 4405/2007, pages 174–189. Springer Berlin / Heidelberg.

Sudeikat, J. and Renz, W. (2007b). On complex networks in software: How agent-orientation effects software structures. In Burkhard, H.-D., Lindemann, G., Verbrugge, R., and Varga, L. Z., editors, *Multi-Agent Systems and Applications V, 5th International Central and Eastern European Conference on Multi-Agent Systems, CEEMAS 2007*, volume 4696 of *Lecture Notes in Computer Science*, pages 215–224. Springer.

Sudeikat, J. and Renz, W. (2007c). On expressing and validating requirements for the adaptivity of self–organizing multi–agent systems. *System and Information Sciences Notes*, 2(1):14–19.

Sudeikat, J. and Renz, W. (2007d). On simulations in mas development. In Braun, T., Carle, G., and Stiller, B., editors, *KIVS 2007 Kommunikation in Verteilten Systemen – Industriebeiträge, Kurzbeiträge und Workshops*, pages 279–290. VDE–Verlag.

Sudeikat, J. and Renz, W. (2007e). Toward requirements engineering for self–organizing multi–agent systems. In *Proceedings of the First IEEE Internaltional Conference on Self–Adaptive and Self–Organizing Systems (SASO 2007)*, pages 299–302.

Sudeikat, J. and Renz, W. (2008a). *Applications of Complex Adaptive Systems*, chapter Building Complex Adaptive Systems: On Engineering Self–Organizing Multi–Agent Systems, pages 229–256. IGI Global.

Sudeikat, J. and Renz, W. (2008b). On the encapsulation and reuse of decentralized coordination mechanisms: A layered architecture and design implications. *Communications of SIWN*, 4:140–146.

Sudeikat, J. and Renz, W. (2008c). Toward systemic mas development: Enforcing decentralized self-organization by composition and refinement of archetype dynamics. In *Engineering Environment-Mediated Multiagent Systems*, volume 5049 of *LNAI*, pages 39–57. Springer.

Sudeikat, J. and Renz, W. (2009a). Building complex adaptive systems: On engineering self-organizing multi-agent systems (reprint). In Hunter, M. G., editor, *Strategic Information Systems: Concepts, Methodologies, Tools, and Applications*, pages 767–787. IGI Publishing.

Sudeikat, J. and Renz, W. (2009b). Decomas: An architecture for supplementing mas with systemic models of decentralized agent coordination. In *WI-IAT '09: Proceedings of the 2009 IEEE/WIC/ACM International Joint Conference on Web Intelligence and Intelligent Agent Technology*, pages 104–107, Washington, DC, USA. IEEE Computer Society.

Sudeikat, J. and Renz, W. (2009c). MASDynamics: Toward systemic modeling of decentralized agent coordination. In David, K. and Geihs, K., editors, *Kommunikation in Verteilten Systemen*, Informatik aktuell, pages 79–90.

Sudeikat, J. and Renz, W. (2009d). On expressing and validating requirements for the adaptivity of self-organizing multi-agent systems (reprint). *International Transactions on Systems Science and Applications*, 5(3):264–274. (Special Issue on Self-organized Networked Systems).

Sudeikat, J. and Renz, W. (2009e). Programming adaptivity by complementing agent function with agent coordination: A systemic programming model and development methodology integration. *Communications of SIWN*, 7:91–102. (ISSN 1757-4439).

Sudeikat, J. and Renz, W. (2009f). Shoaling glassfishes: Enabling decentralized web service management (short paper). In *3rd International Conference in Self-Adaptive and Self-Organizing Systems*, pages 291–292, Los Alamitos, CA, USA. IEEE.

Sudeikat, J. and Renz, W. (2009g). Supporting agent-oriented designs with models of macroscopic system behavior (extended abstract). In Decker, Sichman, Sierra, and Castelfranchi, editors, *AAMAS '09: Proceedings of The 8th International Conference on Autonomous Agents and Multiagent Systems*, pages 1355–1356, Richland, SC. International Foundation for Autonomous Agents and Multiagent Systems.

BIBLIOGRAPHY

Sudeikat, J. and Renz, W. (2009h). A systemic approach to the validation of self–organizing dynamics within mas. In Luck, M. and Gomez-Sanz, J. J., editors, *Agent-Oriented Software Engineering IX: 9th International Workshop, AOSE 2008 Estoril, Portugal, May 12-13, 2008 Revised Selected Papers*, volume 5386/2009 of *LNCS*, pages 31–45. Springer.

Sudeikat, J. and Renz, W. (2010a). On the modeling, refinement and integration of decentralized agent coordination – a case study on dissemination processes in networks. In *Self-Organizing Architectures*, volume 6090/2010 of *LNCS*, pages 251–274. Springer Berlin / Heidelberg.

Sudeikat, J. and Renz, W. (2010b). Separating agent-logic and inter-agent coordination by activated modules: The decomas architecture. *Electronic Proceedings in Theoretical Computer Science*, 27:17–31. (Proceedings of the Workshop "Decentralized Coordination of Distributed Processes" — DCDP 2010).

Sudeikat, J. and Renz, W. (2010c). Systemic modeling of agent coaction: A catalog of decentralized coordinating processes. *Electronic Communications of the EASST*, 27. (ISSN 1863-2122).

Sudeikat, J. and Renz, W. (2011). Qualitative modeling of mas dynamics - using systemic modeling to examine the intended and unintended consequences of agent coaction. In *Agent Oriented Software Engineering X: State-of-the-Art Survey*, volume 6038 of *LNCS*, pages 80–93. Springer Berlin Heidelberg. (to be published).

Sudeikat, J., Steghöfer, J.-P., Seebach, H., Reif, W., Renz, W., Preisler, T., and Salchow, P. (2010a). Design and simulation of a wave-like self-organization strategy for resource-flow systems. In Boissier, O., Seghrouchni, A. E. F., Hassas, S., and Maudet, N., editors, *Proceedings of The Multi-Agent Logics, Languages, and Organisations Federated Workshops (MALLOW 2010)*, volume 627. (http://ftp.informatik.rwth-aachen.de/Publications/CEUR-WS/Vol-627/).

Sudeikat, J., Steghöfer, J.-P., Seebach, H., Reif, W., Renz, W., Preisler, T., and Salchow, P. (2010b). A wave-like decentralized reconfiguration strategy for self-organizing resource-flow systems (short paper). *Electronic Proceedings in Theoretical Computer Science*, 27:32–33. (Proceedings of the Workshop "Decentralized Coordination of Distributed Processes" — DCDP 2010).

Sumpter, D., Blanchard, G. B., and Broomhead, D. (2001). Ants and agents: a process algebra approach to modelling ant colony. *Bulletin of Mathematical Biology*, 63(5):951–980.

Sun Microsystems, I. (2002). Java message service specification - version 1.1. http://java.sun.com/products/jms/docs.html.

Tesauro, G., Chess, D. M., Walsh, W. E., Das, R., Segal, A., Whalley, I., Kephart, J. O., and White, S. R. (2004). A multi-agent systems approach to autonomic computing. In *AAMAS '04: Proceedings of the Third International Joint Conference on Autonomous Agents and Multiagent Systems*, pages 464–471, Washington, DC, USA. IEEE Computer Society.

Thanheiser, S., Liu, L., and Schmeck, H. (2007). Towards collaborative coping with it complexity by combining service–oriented architectures and organic computing. *System and Information Science Notes*, 2(1):82–87.

Tignor, W. (2004). System engineering and system dynamics models. In *Proceedings of 22nd International Conference of the System Dynamics Society*. System Dynamics Society.

Timm, I. J., Scholz, T., and Fürstenau, H. (2006). *Multiagent Engineering Theory and Applications in Enterprises*, chapter From Testing to Theorem Proving, pages 351–354. Springer.

Tisue, S. and Wilensky, U. (2004). Netlogo: A simple environment for modeling complexity. In *International Conference on Complex Systems*.

Truszkowski, W., Hallock, H., Rouff, C., Karlin, J., Rash, J., Hinchey, M., and Sterritt, R. (2009). *Autonomous and Autonomic Systems: With Applications to NASA Intelligent Spacecraft Operations and Exploration Systems*. Springer.

Truszkowski, W., Hinchey, M., Rash, J., and Rouff, C. (2004). Nasa's swarm missions:the challenge of building autonomous software. *IT Professional*, 06(5):47–52.

Turing, A. M. (1949). Checking a large routine. In *Report on a Conference on High Speed Automatic Calculating Machines*. Cambridge University Mathematical Lab.

Tveit, A. (2001). A survey of agent-oriented software engineering. NTNU Computer Science Graduate Student Conference, Nrowegian University of Science and Technology.

Valverde, S., Cancho, R. F., and Solï¿½, R. V. (2002). Scale-free networks from optimal design. *Europhys. Lett.*, 60(4):512–517.

Valverde, S. and Sole, R. V. (2003). Hierarchical Small Worlds in Software Architecture. *ArXiv Condensed Matter e-prints*, (arXiv:cond-mat/0307278). (http://arxiv.org/abs/cond-mat/0307278).

Van Kampen, N. G. (2007). *Stochastic Processes in Physics and Chemistry*. Elsevier. Third edition.

van Lamsweerde, A. and Letier, E. (2004). From object orientation to goal orientation: A paradigm shift for requirements engineering. In Wirswing, M., editor, *Radical Innovations of Software and Systems Engineering in the Future*, number LNCS 2941, pages 325–340. Springer-Verlag.

van Steen, M. and Tanenbaum, A. S. (2002). *Distributed Systems - Principles and Paradigms*. Prentice Hall.

Vieira, R., Moreira, A., Wooldridge, M., and Bordini, R. H. (2007). On the formal semantics of speech-act based communication in an agent-oriented programming language. *J. Artif. Int. Res.*, 29(1):221–267.

Vilenica, A. and Lamersdorf, W. (2010). Towards automated simulation of multi agent based systems. In *12th International Conference on Enterprise Information Systems (ICEIS)*, pages 38–46. SciTePress.

Vilenica, A., Renz, W., Sudeikat, J., and Lamersdorf, W. (2009). Multi-agent-architecture for simulating traffic management - a case study on highway networks. In Kyamakya, K., editor, *Second International Workshop on Nonlinear Dynamics and Synchronization*, Smart System Technologies, pages 121–127. Shaker Verlag & IEEE Explore Digital Library.

Vilenica, A., Sudeikat, J., Lamersdorf, W., Renz, W., Braubach, L., and Pokahr, A. (2010). Coordination in multi-agent systems: A declarative approach using coordination spaces. In *In Proceedings of International Workshop From Agent Theory to Agent Implementation (AT2AI-7)*, pages 441–446. Austrian Society for Cybernetic Studies.

Viroli, M., Casadei, M., and Omicini, A. (2009). A framework for modelling and implementing self-organising coordination. In *SAC '09: Proceedings of the 2009 ACM symposium on Applied Computing*, pages 1353–1360, New York, NY, USA. ACM.

Viroli, M., Holvoet, T., Ricci, A., Schelfthout, K., and Zambonelli, F. (2007). Infrastructures for the environment of multiagent systems. *Autonomous Agents and Multi-Agent Systems*, 14(1):49–60.

Viroli, M. and Omicini, A. (2003). Coordination as a service: Ontological and formal foundation. *Electronic Notes in Theoretical Computer Science*, 68:457–482.

BIBLIOGRAPHY

Viroli, M. and Ricci, A. (2004). Instructions-based semantics of agent mediated interaction. In *3rd International Joint Conference on Autonomous Agents and Multiagent Systems (AAMAS 2004), 19-23 August 2004, New York, NY, USA*, pages 102–109. IEEE Computer Society.

Voas, J. (1997). How assertions can increase test effectiveness. *IEEE Software*, 14(2):118–122.

Wakeland, W. W., Gallaher, E. J., Macovsky, L. M., and Aktipis, C. A. (2004). A comparison of system dynamics and agent-based simulation applied to the study of cellular receptor dynamics. In *HICSS '04: Proceedings of the Proceedings of the 37th Annual Hawaii International Conference on System Sciences (HICSS'04) - Track 3*, Washington, DC, USA. IEEE Computer Society.

Watts, D. J. and Strogatz, S. H. (1998). Collective dynamics of small-world networks. *Nature*, 393:440–442.

Weyns, D., Brueckner, S. A., and Demazeau, Y., editors (2008). *Engineering Environment-Mediated Multi-Agent Systems: International Workshop, EEMMAS 2007, Dresden, Germany, October 5, 2007. Selected Revised and Invited Papers*. Springer-Verlag, Berlin, Heidelberg.

Weyns, D., Omicini, A., and Odell, J. (2007). Environment as a first class abstraction in multiagent systems. *Autonomous Agents and Multi-Agent Systems*, 14(1):5–30.

Weyns, D., Schelfthout, K., Holvoet, T., and Glorieux, O. (2004). A role based model for adaptive agents. In *Proceedings of the AISB 2004, Fourth Symposium on Adaptive Agents and Multi-Agent Systems*, pages 75–86.

Weyns, D., Schelfthout, K., Holvoet, T., and Lefever, T. (2005). Decentralized control of e'gv transportation systems. In *AAMAS '05: Proceedings of the fourth international joint conference on Autonomous agents and multiagent systems*, pages 67–74, New York, NY, USA. ACM.

Weyns, D., Vizzari, G., and Holvoet, T. (2006). Environments for situated multi-agent systems: Beyond infrastructure. In *Environments for Multi-Agent Systems II*, volume 3830/2006 of *LNCS*, pages 1–17, Berlin / Heidelberg. Springer.

Wheeldon, R. and Counsell, S. (2003). Power law distributions in class relationships. *Third IEEE International Workshop on Source Code Analysis and Manipulation, 2003. Proceedings*, pages 45–54.

Wilson, W. (1998). Resolving discrepancies between deterministic population models and individual–based simulations. *The American Naturalist*, 151:116–134.

Winfield, F. T., Sa, J., Fernandez-Gago, M.-C., Dixon, C., and Fisher, M. (2005). On formal specification of emergent behaviours in swarm robotic systems. *International Journal of Advanced Robotic Systems*, 2(4):363–370.

Wolstenholme, E. F. (2003). Towards the definition and use of a core set of archetypal structures in system dynamics. *System Dynamics Review*, 19(1):7–26.

Wooldridge, M. (2002). *An Introduction to Multi Agent Systems*. Wiley.

World Wide Web Consortium (W3C) (2004). Xml schema part 0: Primer second edition. http://www.w3.org/TR/xmlschema-0/.

World Wide Web Consortium (W3C) (2008). Extensible markup language (xml) 1.0 (fifth edition). http://www.w3.org/TR/2008/REC-xml-20081126/.

Xie, Y. B., Wang, B. H., Hu, C. K., and Zhou, T. (2005). Global Optimization of Minority Game by Smart Agents. *Eur. Phys. J. B 47*, pages 587–593. (http://arxiv.org/abs/cond-mat/0406326).

Yokoo, M., Durfee, E., Ishida, T., and Kuwabara, K. (1998). The distributed constraint satisfaction problem: Formalization and algorithms. *IEEE Transactions on Knowledge and Data Engineering*, 10(5):673–685.

Yu, E. S. K. (1997). Towards modeling and reasoning support for early-phase requirements engineering. In *RE '97: Proceedings of the 3rd IEEE International Symposium on Requirements Engineering*, pages 226–235.

Zadeh, L. A. (1963). On the definition of adaptivity. *Proceedings of the IEEE*, 51(3):469 – 470.

Zalewski, J. (2003). Software dynamics: a new measure of performance for real-time software. *Software Engineering Workshop, 2003. Proceedings. 28th Annual NASA Goddard*, pages 120–126.

Zalewski, J. (2005). From software sensitivity to software dynamics: performance metrics for real-time software architectures. *SIGBED Rev.*, 2(3):20–24.

Zambonelli, F., Jennings, N., and Wooldridge, M. (2003). Developing multiagent systems: the gaia methodology. *ACM Trans on Software Engineering and Methodology*, 12(3):317–370.

Zambonelli, F., Jennings, N. R., and Wooldridge, M. (2005). *Agent-Oriented Methodologies*, chapter Multiagent systems as computational organisations: the Gaia methodology, pages 136–171. Idea Group Publishers.

Zhong, L.-X., Zheng, D.-F., Zheng, B., and Hui, P. (2004). Effects of contrarians in the minority game. In *cond-mat/0412524*.

I want morebooks!

Buy your books fast and straightforward online - at one of world's fastest growing online book stores! Environmentally sound due to Print-on-Demand technologies.

Buy your books online at
www.morebooks.shop

Kaufen Sie Ihre Bücher schnell und unkompliziert online – auf einer der am schnellsten wachsenden Buchhandelsplattformen weltweit! Dank Print-On-Demand umwelt- und ressourcenschonend produziert.

Bücher schneller online kaufen
www.morebooks.shop

KS OmniScriptum Publishing
Brivibas gatve 197
LV-1039 Riga, Latvia
Telefax: +371 686 204 55

info@omniscriptum.com
www.omniscriptum.com

Printed by Books on Demand GmbH, Norderstedt / Germany